On Point

The United States Army in Operation Iraqi Freedom

Col. Gregory Fontenot, U.S. Army (Ret.)

Lt. Col. E. J. Degen, USA

Lt. Col. David Tohn, USA

An Association of the U.S. Army Book

NAVAL INSTITUTE PRESS
Annapolis, Maryland

With respect and admiration this book is dedicated to the American Soldier.

On Point for the nation since 14 June 1775.

Library of Congress Cataloging-in-Publication Data
Fontenot, Gregory, 1949–
  On point : US Army in Operation Iraqi Freedom / Gregory Fontenot, E.J. Degen, David Tohn ; [foreword by Tommy R. Franks].
      p. cm.
  Includes bibliographical references and index.
  ISBN 1-59114-279-2 (alk. paper)
  1. Iraq War, 2003—Campaigns. 2. Iraq War, 2003—Personal narratives, American. 3. United States. Army—History—21st century. I. Title: US Army in Operation Iraqi Freedom. II. Degen, E. J., 1961– III. Tohn, David, 1965– IV. United States. Army. Operation Iraqi Freedom Study Group. V. Title.

DS79.764.U6F66 2005
956.7044'3—dc22

                                                                    2005049143

Printed in the United States of America on acid-free paper ∞
12 11 10 09 08 07 06   9 8 7 6 5 4 3

Foreword

During a 38-year career as a soldier that included duty as an artillery forward observer in Vietnam and ended as commander of US Central Command during Operation IRAQI FREEDOM (OIF), I came to appreciate the value of the lessons learned concept to both commissioned officers and NCOs. Studying the successes and failures of recent campaigns is essential to leaders' professional development as they strive toward greater technical and tactical proficiency.

The obvious hard work and dedication that went into *On Point* reinforce that conviction. But this book is far more than a standard campaign history; like the operation it analyzes in admirable detail, the study is unique.

Although Army Chief of Staff General Eric K. Shinseki commissioned the work, the book transcends the Army perspective. OIF was America's first truly joint combat operation, with the services successfully integrated in the battlespace to a degree of mutual support and cooperation that would have been impossible five years ago. The book details the major elements in that evolution in joint warfare as they played out in the deserts, mountains, cities, and skies of Iraq.

The human dimension of war, especially the quality of the men and women in uniform who fought the campaign and won the historic victory, is a major element of the book.

Using hundreds of interviews of the troops and scores of detailed maps and illustrations, *On Point* provides a "user-friendly" guide to shape future force structure and training and help refine America's warfighting doctrine.

The authors worked rapidly and diligently to capture the essential lessons of the campaign; as a result, the study is available today to help leaders at every level.

As I read *On Point*, I was reminded once again of the great honor it was to serve with America's, courageous soldiers, sailors, marines, and airmen.

General Tommy R. Franks
US Army, Retired

Preface

On Point is a study of Operation IRAQI FREEDOM (OIF) as soon after the fact as feasible. The Army leadership chartered this effort in a message to the major commands on 30 April 2003. In his guidance, Army Chief of Staff General Eric K. Shinseki directed "a quick, thorough review that looks at the US Army's performance, assesses the role it played in the joint and coalition team, and captures the strategic, operational, and tactical lessons that should be disseminated and applied in future fights."

For those of us in the Operation IRAQI FREEDOM Study Group (OIF-SG), this translated into three separate products. A "quick look" lessons-learned briefing produced in July, less than 30 days after returning from the theater. *On Point*—this work — is the second product and was largely completed by January 2004. Finally, the most significant product is the archive of 119,000 documents, some 2,300 interviews and 69,000 photos archived with the support and assistance of the Combined Arms Research Library at Fort Leavenworth, Kansas.

We had straightforward guidance and a short time horizon. Simply put, *On Point* tells the Army's story in the only context possible—a combined-arms ground force operating in a joint environment. There is no other way for the Army to tell its story—the Army cannot get to a theater of war, let alone fight, in any context but that of a joint operation. Accordingly, the OIF-SG relied heavily on the cooperation and support of units in the field and from our colleagues on the other services' collection teams. We also drew on the more deliberate efforts of the Center of Military History and unit historians. We encountered only helpful attitudes, with the exception of one or two Iraqi combatants who fired on or threw grenades at members of the team. The joint lessons learned team from the Joint Forces Command (JFCOM) assigned a liaison officer to the OIF-SG who proved helpful in working with our joint counterparts. The Combined Forces Land Component Command (CFLCC) historian, the V Corps historian, the Army Materiel Command historian, and various branch historians all were abundantly helpful.

Like the soldiers bound for the theater, we trained at two different replacement centers, and most of us deployed via military or Civilian Reserve Air Fleet aircraft. Once in theater, we traveled freely throughout area of operations. Members of the team visited Europe, Turkey, and nearly a dozen sites in the US, ranging from Dover Air Force Base, Delaware to Fort Bliss, Texas. To do this in the time allowed, we depended on others for help. We found eager and enthusiastic support at every stop.

Interpreting history is difficult; interpreting ongoing events is even more difficult. *On Point* is not the seminal history of the OIF or even of the Army in OIF. We understand the risks of a rapidly produced history and believe they are worth taking to glean initial insights, or what General Frederick M. Franks, Jr. described after DESERT STORM as "glimmerings" of change.

We wrote *On Point* with a readership of soldiers and those familiar with armies in battle in mind—discussing not only the fighting, but also describing the hard work "behind the scenes" that made the combat victories so successful. *On Point* is an operational history that derives some provisional insights that soldiers, our colleagues in the other services, and others may find useful or interesting. *On Point* will not be the last word or the definitive history of this operation that, as we went to publication, is still unfolding, but we believe that it will be cited in that effort and will help to explain the role the Army played. That is the goal of this effort—to kindle the discussion on what happened and why.

Where possible, we let soldiers tell their own stories, and while we sought a balanced accounting, *On Point* is not a proportional history of OIF. Some units are mentioned more than others and some soldiers are singled out—that does not mean that the efforts of units and soldiers not mentioned did not merit telling, only that time, space, and purpose forced some hard decisions. However, it was immediately clear to us that the American people have much to be proud of in the service and performance of America's Army as part of the joint team.

GREGORY FONTENOT
Colonel (Retired),
 USA

E.J. DEGEN
Lieutenant Colonel,
 USA

DAVID TOHN
Lieutenant Colonel,
 USA

Acknowledgments

Historians prefer to write about people long dead for a number of reasons. For one thing, the dead can't criticize what is written. More important, it takes time for the record of events to be completed, and generally it takes the perspective of time to come to grips with happened and what it meant. For all of these reasons, those of us who wrote *On Point* depended upon help from many people to attempt to elucidate the record and to make some sense of what happened.

There are far too many to mention them all and we will certainly have left out some key folks, but we need to take a moment to acknowledge a few of the many persons who supported us.

First and foremost, we are grateful to the chief of staff of the Army, General Eric Shinseki, and his successor, General Peter Schoomaker, for mandating and sustaining this effort. We are also grateful to them for looking after the effort without looking over our shoulders. General Kevin Byrnes, commanding general of US Army Training and Doctrine Command, made sure we got the proper resources, in particular, the right people to get the job done. Brigadier General Mark O'Neill, deputy director of Strategy, Plans, and Policy, Army G3, and Colonel Jim Greer, director of the School of Advanced Military Studies, led the team in Iraq and provided us with their own insights and assisted when there were rough spots. Colonel Chuck Taylor, chief of staff, Initiatives Group, supported the team and made sure the Army staffers who needed access to determine policy insights got what they needed without turning the collection effort into a "staff study."

Lieutenant General Jim Riley, commanding general of the Combined Arms Center, Brigadier General Tim Livsey, Combined Arms Center-Training, and Brigadier General Jim Hirai, deputy commandant of the Command and General Staff College, provided superb support to the team. Reasoning they could learn by doing, General Hirai released several Command and General Staff Officer Course (CGSOC) and School of Advanced Military Studies students early so they could join the team. He was right—and they did. He also gave us his aide de camp, Major Travis Rooms, without whom the team would have never gotten off the ground.

Colonels Dave Buckley, Combined Arms Center chief of staff, Greg Lynch, dean of the Command and General Staff College, and Steve Spataro, deputy chief of staff, Resource Management pulled together the team, provided space and information technology support and supported budgets, travel, and contracting to get the team housed, equipped, transported, and sustained. Without them we could not have gotten off post, let alone to Iraq.

Ruth Eckert, Fort Leavenworth Resource Management, helped us prepare a budget on the fly and then accounted for what we spent and ensured we stayed within budget. She did all of that and managed to smile throughout. She also helped produce the mountains of orders and documents we needed to travel. Candi Hamm, secretary at the School of Advanced Military Studies, and Rose Cantrell, Fort Leavenworth Transportation Office, did the work of several folks helping us get orders processed and passports issued and supported the effort in every way from helping personnel process vouchers to getting us started on maintaining what grew to a huge archive.

Colonel (retired) Lynn Rolf, director of Educational Technology at the Command and General Staff College, begged, borrowed, or bought the gear we needed to manage the archives and develop our data. At one point his team installed, configured, and linked 60-odd computers and then moved them back into classrooms when we were done. They also set up the classified archives and built from the ground up the electronic archives architecture and hardware to support the archive. Fort Leavenworth's Directorate of Information Technology pitched in to provide encrypted phones and standard phones.

Several CGSOC students joined the team and remained at Fort Leavenworth following their course's completion to support the rest of us. Major Glenn Reed served as officer in charge in the rear and assured we got what we needed forward and reported our activities as required. Major Cindy Dillard served as adjutant and made sure spouses and the Army knew where everyone was. She managed our travel and generally accounted for all of us. Keeping track of the team was no mean feat since we often had folks in several different countries at once. Major Audrey Hudgins took on the task of determining how to archive the material so it could be found and searched with reasonable utility. Staff Sergeant Warren Reeves, who served with the team from April until October as our supply sergeant and operations sergeant, received and accounted for every piece of property from laptops to digital recorders. He was patient, thorough, indefatigable, and when required, he had the endurance of a bloodhound in tracking down a lost piece of gear.

Major C.P. Watkins did quality control on information technology gear and jumped through flaming hoops to acquire encrypted Iridium phones for the team's use in the theater. Only when he had all of the equipment we needed did he get to Kuwait and Iraq. Once there, he made sure things worked and helped ensure we got things back home. Major Ike Wilson, Major Travis Rooms, and Captain John Townsend ran the forward command post in Camp DOHA, and woe to the team member who failed a formation or time to move out. They kept us on track, on time, and in compliance with CFLCC regulations.

Within theater, Captain Scott Emmel, executive officer of the V Corps G3 Plans section, was singularly responsible for our care, feeding, and movement throughout Iraq. Coordinating the disparate movements of 30 team members at a time to various locations across the theater required patience and impressive powers of persuasion. We also thank the many soldiers who drove, guarded, and mostly waited for us at the various unit locations while we did our collection. Finally, we thank the units who hosted and supported us without hesitation or reservation.

Lieutenant Colonel Kevin Farrell and the Combat Studies Institute supported us in a number of ways, but most important they lent us Master Sergeant Phil Davis, Missouri Air National Guard, who in his day job is a first-class editor. Between the Air Force and *On Point,* Phil worked seven days a week for most of the summer and fall. In October, he retired from the Air Guard but retained his day job. If occasionally we called him unkind names and questioned his convictions about the Air Force, it is only because he discovered and red inked the many awkward sentences. The CSI editor Robin Kern did a masterful job of laying out this book.

In mid-July, the collection team members returned to their assigned units, leaving only three writers through 1 October 2003, and two after that. Even so, we continued to require support unstintingly provided by Colonel Larry Saul at Center for Army Lessons Learned. Travis Rooms, who stayed on to support phase two assessments in theater along with Sergeant Gregory Chancey, provided our administrative support.

In July, Colonel Jay D. Wells from the Joint Forces Command Lessons Learned Cell, moved in with us to provide liaison between our effort and theirs. He assured a two-way flow of information between the Army study group and Joint Forces Command's team. Lieutenant Colonel Kevin Woods and Commander Mike Pease from the Joint Advanced Warfighting Program supported our efforts to understand what the other side may have been thinking. Colonel Phil Exner, Lieutenant Colonel Dave Wessner and Mr. Daryl Gibson from the United States Marine Corps Combat Assessment Team helped us to understand I MEF operations and provided valuable information.

The Army's Center of Military History provided us contacts advice and access to their collection. Brigadier General John Brown, chief of Military History, Lieutenant Colonel (retired) Bill Epley, Center of Military History, and a number of command historians provided responsive—often immediate—help when asked. Randy Talbot of Army Materiel Command and Lieutenant Colonel Steve Holcomb of Third Army were particularly helpful. Dr. Charles Kirkpatrick, the V Corps historian, traded interviews and documents and offered helpful criticism throughout the effort, often serving as a sounding board as well. Rick Atkinson read our work and provided useful feedback and positive reinforcement. He graciously looked the other way when we claimed to others that we were "consulting with our Pulitzer Prize-winning colleague."

More than 120 people read the first draft and took time to provide feedback. Major General Hank Stratman, former deputy commanding general-support for CFLCC, and Colonel Dan Bolger, chief of staff, 2nd Infantry Division, in particular, took a great deal of time to read our work critically and provide useful feedback. A great many others gave freely of their time to answer follow-up questions and work with us to make sure we got things right. Some of these soldiers, still in Iraq, nonetheless made time to help us get information we required despite the fact they continued to work seven days a week in a difficult environment.

Several senior retired soldiers also gave freely of their time to assist in our research. General Fred Franks, who commanded VII Corps in DESERT STORM, went to the theater with us as our senior mentor, conducted interviews, and helped us identify significant themes. General Gordon Sullivan and Brigadier General Hal Nelson answered questions and provided information pertaining to the development of *Force XXI*. General Dennis Reimer patiently answered questions and helped us find resources to address his tenure as chief of staff.

In June, Lieutenant Colonel (retired) Quent Schillare brought in a team of transcriptionists and an archivist to support transcribing interviews and archiving material.

For the most part, they are retired soldiers who understood what they were transcribing and so could help not only by transcribing, but also by identifying important interviews. Given the speed with which we worked, their assistance in helping us sort through 2,300 interviews proved invaluable. Mr. Ed Burgess and the staff of the Combined Arms Research Library unhesitatingly turned a large part of the classified archives of the library into a workspace for us. They worked to make the archive accessible and kept it open literally seven days a week through most of July and August. Lieutenant Colonel (retired) Jack Burkett served as research assistant and unearthed clues with the panáche of Sherlock Holmes. When asked to verify a fact, he always came through with multiple sources and cross-references when the facts seemed in dispute.

We had problems peculiar to the era of digital cameras. Units gave us literally thousands of digital photographs. Then we had to determine who took them, since some looked too good to be GI photos. Sergeant Jeremiah Johnson from the Army's 55th Signal Company (US Army Combat Camera) spent a week using "gee whiz" software finding the copyrighted photos. Rose Dawson, who joined the team in October, scouted out sources and submitted copyright requests. Sergeant Johnson also brought thousands more images that combat camera took. To date, there are some 79,000 images in the archive.

Mark Osterholm did a superb job of developing graphics to illustrate operations. Although Mark never served in the armed forces, he learned rapidly and can identify units and develop operational graphics with speed that would make a School of Advanced Military Studies student envious. Sandi Miles worked copyright issues, helped develop the bibliography, and saw the project through the editing process.

We were blessed with an enthusiastic and thorough editorial board, led by Major General Jim Dubik of Joint Forces Command. Lieutenant General (retired) Dan Petrosky served on the board, as did Brigadier General John Brown, chief of military history, Dr. Williamson Murray, and Colonel (retired) Rick Sinnreich. They all carefully read the manuscript and, in an intense all-day session at Fort Leavenworth on 14 November 2003, gave us the benefit of their assessment. What emerged was clear guidance.

No one sets out to write a bad book or to make errors in fact or interpretation. We expect there are some in *On Point*. For those, we take full responsibility.

Table of Contents

Introduction

Every values-based institution has an image of itself at its purist, most basic level. It is a single mental snapshot—a distillation of all that is good and right. Reaching back to the institution's foundation, it evokes a visceral, emotional response from the members.

For the Army, the self-image is the small squad of infantry, maybe fewer than 10 soldiers, patrolling a hostile and unknown territory—whether jungle, woodland, or urban. The foremost soldier walks *on point*—the lead; sometimes moving cautiously to develop the situation, other times moving with great speed and purpose in order for the squad to accomplish its mission.

The point man focuses on picking out the path forward—identifying the dangers and opportunities along that path. The compass man, providing direction and guidance, travels behind, responsible for keeping the squad moving toward its objective. Success or failure rests on how well these two soldiers work together. A safe path to nowhere is as useless as a direct route into a fatal ambush. Serving on point is a position of honor, responsibility, and great danger. Only the most trusted, most skilled, most field-wise soldiers earn this responsibility. Selecting a point man is a difficult choice.

Leading, but not alone, the point man moves as part of a vast team of warriors. Above is the Air Force, controlling the skies and attacking ground targets with speed, violence, and purpose. Attacking from overhead and offshore, the Navy brings its considerable capabilities to bear and assures unimpeded supply that comes from undisputed control of the sea. Working alongside the Army, sometimes leading and other times in support, the Marine Corps brings its unique combined-arms team to the fight. The relationship between who leads, follows, and supports changes to accommodate the mission. The crux is that, even when leading, the point man is part of a team, both literally in the squad and among the services.

On Point tells the compelling story of America's Army in OIF and is of interest to a broad audience. However, it aims at a specific audience—soldiers and defense professionals. Within the Army, *On Point* has two specific goals: to educate soldiers on the conduct of combat operations in OIF and to suggest some preliminary implications for the Army's continued transformation.

Because it focuses on the *Army* and its role in this ongoing campaign, *On Point* is not the seminal history of OIF. It unabashedly argues that the Army played a central role in the joint team. Along with its sister services, the Army brought down the Ba'athist regime in decisive ground combat, took the enemy's capital city, destroyed the bulk of the Iraqi army and paramilitary forces in the fields and valleys of the Euphrates River, and liberated the Iraqi people from decades of oppression. Moreover, the Army continues the American presence in Iraq, striving to turn battlefield victories into strategic success.

Despite this deliberate Army point of view, OIF is not an *Army* victory. OIF demonstrates the maturation of joint concepts and the intent embodied in the Goldwater-Nichols Department of Defense Reorganization Act of 1986. It is a joint victory for the United States and its coalition partners. It is also just one of several campaigns undertaken and ongoing in the Global War on Terrorism.

Finally, as an integral part of the joint team, the American soldier has been *on point* in securing global, regional, and domestic security. OIF was executed against a backdrop of Army and joint military operations around the world. As American soldiers crossed the border into Iraq, fellow soldiers secured the peace in the Balkans, trained and assisted the Philippine army, executed counternarcotics operations in Central and South America, protected key facilities and infrastructure within the homeland, patrolled alongside an Afghani people liberated from the repressive and threatening Taliban, and conducted a myriad of missions globally in support of the Global War on Terrorism and to further the US national security and interests. Representing American resolve, power, interests, and values, an American soldier stands a post in a foreign land—*on point* for the nation.

A Campaign of Liberation

While combat operations began on 17 March 2003, preparations for Operation IRAQI FREEDOM began on 1 March 1991—the day after the first Gulf War ended. In the broadest context, OIF marks the latest chapter in the continuous US involvement in the Middle East and Southwest Asia theater. America's national security is directly tied to the region's stability and prosperity. As such, the nation has been applying the elements of national power—diplomacy, information, military action, and economics—to reach this elusive goal. From enforcing sanctions and international inspections, to protecting the Kurds and Muslims, to responding to Iraqi violations of the no-fly zones, the military has been a central element of the US policy toward Iraq since the end of DESERT STORM.

These efforts have supported regional strategy. The combined and coordinated regional presence set the conditions for OIF's military success. The United States ensured its forces had adequate access to the theater and could establish the necessary infrastructure to allow large-unit staging and employment while maintaining the necessary military capability to deter the Iraqi threat. Occasionally, of course, this regional engagement was not as effective as it could have been, as illustrated by Turkey's refusal to allow ground forces to stage for a northern front and NATO members' failure to achieve agreement regarding support for American military action in Iraq. Yet, commanders demonstrated unprecedented flexibility and agility in adapting to these types of challenges. Without the fruits of the 12-year engagement effort, OIF would have been impossible.

The formal military campaign to liberate Iraq was a four-phase operation. This phased construct recognized that the operation would cross the entire spectrum of conflict, from combat to peace support to humanitarian and security assistance. As such, strategic success would require success in *each* phase, inextricably linking actions into a campaign that is truly an extension of politics by other means.

The military campaign supported the strategic goal that transcended removing

Saddam Hussein and the Ba'athists from power. The strategic goal included establishing a stable, secure, prosperous, peaceful, and democratic Iraqi nation that is a fully functioning member of the community of nations.[1] Within this context, the end of major combat operations did not signify the end of combat or operations, just the transition to the next phase of the long-term campaign.

- Phase I. *Preparation* secured regional and international support, degraded the Iraqi regime's ability to resist, established the air bridge and secure lines of communications (LOCs) to the theater, sought to interdict tactical ballistic missiles (TBM) and weapons of mass destruction (WMD), and alerted, deployed, and postured American forces. In short, this phase set the conditions to neutralize Iraqi forces.
- Phase II. *Shaping the Battlespace* included posturing coalition forces to conduct sustained combat operations, beginning initial operations to degrade Iraqi command and control and security forces, and seizing key pieces of terrain. These actions were in addition to the ongoing diplomatic and counter-TBM/WMD operations.
- Phase III. *Decisive Offensive Operations* marked the beginning of conventional combat operations. It included the air campaign, preparatory ground operations, and the attack north to Baghdad. This phase culminated with securing Baghdad and removing Saddam Hussein and the Ba'athist regime from power.
- Phase IV. *Post Hostilities* operations encompass the transition from combat to stability operations and support operations, including humanitarian assistance and reconstruction. Interestingly, planners realized early on that as coalition forces liberated sections of Iraqi territory, operations in those sections would transition to Phase IV while Phase III combat operations continued elsewhere. This 'rolling transition' to Phase IV is the hallmark of true full-spectrum operations and is one of the defining characteristics of this campaign. The distance between forces conducting Phase III and Phase IV operations varied from meters to miles, requiring remarkable flexibility, initiative, and maturity of the leaders and soldiers.

The Army: On Point in Operation IRAQI FREEDOM

During the 12 years since DESERT STORM, the Army and the other services attempted to adapt to the post-Cold War era, adopt lessons learned during operations, anticipate changes or trends in the operational environment, and finally to take advantage of technologies that could improve combat capability. *On Point* addresses several skeins of effort in this adaptation and evolution of capability.

For example, soon after Operation DESERT STORM, the Army realized the potential of information-based warfare.[2] The Army transformed whole divisions into a digitally linked force capable of waging network-centric warfare, designing and building *Force XXI* on the hypothesis that digital links would increase the tempo of ground operations and thus the lethality and survivability of ground forces. Blue Force (friendly units) Tracking (BFT), a system that provided commanders a picture of where their subordinate units were and enabled commanders to pass commands and geographical measures, battle command on the move (BCOTM) technology, and the Army Battle Command System (ABCS) enabled the Army to realize that vision in OIF.

To support joint operations and training, the Army established an operations group in the Battle Command Training Program (BCTP) to teach joint doctrine in 1992. The new operations group was intended to bridge the gap in training until a joint training capability could be established. BCTP's Operations Group D remained following formation of the Joint Warfare Training Center to support training Army service components within joint contexts. In the fall of 2002, Operations Group D deployed to Kuwait to support training and then stayed on for the war, in which its soldiers served with distinction on the Combined Forces Land Component Command (CFLCC) staff.

In the decade following DESERT STORM, the Army reorganized its training and rewrote its doctrine to assure that it met its challenges and, when appropriate, led the way for the joint team. Joint doctrine grew rapidly as Joint Forces Command morphed from US Atlantic Command, gaining training and joint doctrinal development responsibilities. Along with the other services, the Army worked to support the development and training of increasingly "joint" capable organizations.

The Army changed its own basic doctrine not only to accommodate joint doctrine, but to accommodate apparent changes in the environment. The Army developed doctrine designed to wage noncontiguous, full-spectrum warfare. Published in June 2001, Army Field Manual 3-0, *Operations,* reflected an assessment of the operational environment in the years following DESERT STORM based on a body of evidence accumulated in operations and on careful consideration of what future operations might be like. After much study, the Army conceived the contemporary operating environment (COE), which describes the current environment and provides the context for future training and combat developments. The COE possesses complex battlefield environments populated with intelligent and adaptive enemies who seek asymmetric advantages across the battlespace. Training in this environment and operating with the increasingly better-networked systems that supported battle command on the move (BCOTM) allowed the Army to "operationalize" the vision encompassed in FM 3-0. In the COE, the Army estimated what operations in the early 21st century might be like. Combat in Iraq validated that estimate, but also demonstrated that the Army still has work to do in structuring and training to operate in this dynamic operational environment.

The Army also invested enormous effort and resources as the ground component for the US Central Command (CENTCOM) in the face of the ongoing Iraqi threat in the region. The Army, at the direction of CENTCOM, revamped and reorganized Third Army to operate as a land component command. The Army developed the infrastructure in Kuwait—airfields, seaports, laagering facilities, headquarters, and command posts at a cost of over $500 million to support contingency operations. Moreover, in conjunction with Operation SOUTHERN WATCH forces, the Army provided the bulk of the CENTCOM direct theater engagement effort, setting the conditions that enabled the successful conclusion of decisive combat operations in less than a month. Obviously, other components of CENTCOM made important investments as well.

Army special operations soldiers, as part of the joint special operations team, led the way into Iraq. US special operations forces (SOF) excelled during OIF. They did so on the basis of intense efforts made by the joint community, US Special Operations Command, and the services to develop capability and, more important, to integrate capabilities among SOF units and between SOF and conventional units. Integration of SOF operations in the campaign plan paid enormous dividends.

Coalition soldiers and marines led the ground attack on D-day, cutting lanes and destroying Iraqi observation posts prior to the main body attacks of V Corps and First Marine Expeditionary Force (I MEF). All of America rode with 3rd Squadron, 7th Cavalry as it led the fight up-country on point for the 3rd Infantry Division ("Rock of the Marne"), V Corps ("Victory Corps"), the CFLCC, and the nation.

The Army supported the other services as mandated by Title 10.[3] The Army embodied the concept of a truly joint force, providing ballistic missile defense theaterwide, as well as providing artillery and rocket fires and more than six battalions' worth of engineers, logisticians, military police, transporters, and medical evacuation support to its Marine Corps comrades.[4] In each of these cases, and in many more that will go without mention, the Army—and America's soldiers—served on point as the campaign unfolded.

A Campaign of Firsts

OIF is a campaign with a number of firsts. Arguably, it is the first "jointly" coherent campaign since the Korean War. American joint forces executed a large-scale, complex operation while simultaneously continuing active operations in Afghanistan, the Balkans, and in support of Homeland Defense.

In OIF, a combined and joint land component directed all ground operations for the first time since the Eighth Army did so in the Korean War. The US Third Army formed the core of what became a joint and combined headquarters—the CFLCC— charged with conducting ground operations, integrating air-ground operations, and directing theater support operations.[5] Also for the first time since the Korean War, Army National Guard (ARNG) infantry battalions participated in combat operations as units. Seven ARNG light infantry battalions deployed to secure Patriot missiles and guard vital supplies. Ultimately, six of them went "up-country" and conducted combat operations in Iraq.

There were other important firsts. Not since World War II have the armed forces of the United States operated in multiple theaters of war while simultaneously conducting security operations and support operations in several other theaters. As an example, on 9 June 2003, 369,000 soldiers were deployed overseas, of which about 140,000 were from the Reserve Components. These soldiers were serving in 120 countries, conducting missions ranging from combat to deterring adversaries, to training the nation's allies, to protecting the nation's vital assets.

OIF also provided the opportunity for a number of firsts in the integration of special and conventional operations. Emerging ideas on the integration of special operations and conventional operations that debuted in Afghanistan came close to their potential in OIF. OIF marked a watershed in the evolution of SOF-general purpose (conventional) force integration when CENTCOM assigned conventional units to the operational control of SOF units.

The unprecedented degree of air-ground coordination and integration is also a key first. While ground maneuver began simultaneously with air operations to preclude the Iraqi regime from undertaking a scorched earth campaign or turning the oil fields into a WMD, it is difficult to overstate the importance of air operations in the context of OIF. By dominating the air over Iraq, coalition air forces shaped the fight to allow for rapid dominance on the ground. Air power decisively turned the tide in tactical operations on the ground on several occasions. Air- and sea-launched precision-guided munitions (PGMs) and cruise missile strikes responded rapidly to the targets developed by improved intelligence, surveillance, and reconnaissance systems. Equally important, effective integration of artillery and Army attack aviation produced, in several instances, the kind of synergy conceived in joint manuals and practiced in training over the decade since DESERT STORM.

OIF forces employed emerging concepts in the body of joint doctrine. The establishment of the CFLCC represents the maturation of joint doctrine developed since Goldwater-Nichols and tested through Army and joint simulations and training. The "running start" stemmed from the recent US policy of preemption and also from the joint concept of rapid dominance. Finally, integration of precision munitions with ground operations, supported by a largely space-based command and control network, enabled combat operations to occur in ways only imagined a decade ago.

Within this context of "firsts" and the execution of emerging joint concepts, there are strong threads of continuity in OIF. First, ground combat remains physically demanding. Ground operations remain central to toppling a regime by defeating its armed forces, seizing and holding territory, and controlling the population. While the campaign clearly took advantage of breathtaking technology, in the end, individual soldiers and marines took the fight to the enemy in a personal, eyeball-to-eyeball manner. Humans, not high-tech sensors, remain indispensable, even in the 21st century.

Themes of Operation IRAQI FREEDOM

From the Army's perspective, these firsts and the threads of evolution after DESERT STORM are a crucial part of the story in *On Point*. Yet within the story, several other themes recur. The quality of the American soldier and the quality of decision making from private to lieutenant general is arguably the most important insight that emerged from battle narratives, reports, and eyewitness accounts. There are other themes, but the outstanding performance of soldiers is at the top and accounts for the speed and relatively low human cost of major combat operations. Soldiers revealed themselves to be brave, skilled, and innovative in a unique and decisive manner. Similarly, their enemy, although often unskilled, proved courageous and adaptive.

In the months since the end of major combat operations, some observers tried to explain the rapid coalition success only in terms of inferior Iraqi equipment and incompetence. That does not account for the disparity. Coalition soldiers, sailors, airmen, and marines demonstrated they were better trained and that they could adapt faster than their opponents.

A number of other themes warrant discussion. Each of these broad areas of investigation tends to overlap, both in terms of understanding what happened and in raising questions for further study or considering possible implications for the Army and the armed forces generally. For organizational purposes they are considered in five broad areas:

- **Command and Control.** This area encompasses technological means, including BFT, satellite communications, and various aids that supported communications and situational awareness which enabled effective command and control. But it also includes how the various echelons from CFLCC to company operated and contributed. The influence of doctrine, training, and experience on decision making is part of this discussion as well.

- **Combined Arms Operations.** Combat vignettes illustrating the synergy of combined arms operations in Operation IRAQI FREEDOM are numerous. In *On Point,* the term "combined arms operations" includes the efficacy of joint integration, especially special operations and conventional operations. But it really focuses on combining maneuver and fires to create specific effects and the combination of small tactical units, including engineers, infantry, attack helicopters, artillery, and armor, to create tactical effects. Combined arms operations stem from the way the services train, but also from the maturation of doctrine in the services and in joint tactics, techniques, and procedures. Integration of effects and the separate arms or branches of the Army produced enormous benefit on the battlefield

- **Joint Integration and Support.** Although this area could be subsumed in combined arms operations, joint integration deserves separate examination in the context of higher tactical and operational realms inherent in a multicorps campaign. It enables the examination of operational-level warfare from the perspective of CFLCC. This campaign is arguably the first campaign in which the initiatives inherent in the Goldwater-Nichols legislation bore full fruit.

- **Deployment and Sustainment.** Getting the forces into the theater and sustaining them while attempting to apply principles developed in the decade since DESERT STORM produced both success and failure. The acquisition of fast sealift and the C-17 and the development of concepts such as single port managers to streamline deployment paid dividends. On the other hand, the effort to supersede the joint deployment system and the arcane time-phased force and deployment list (TPFDL) and the deployment sequence that stemmed from it did not reap the benefit anticipated. Similarly, concepts such as "just-in-time logistics" briefed better than they performed. Opening and sustaining the theater depended on Reserve Component units that simply did not get to the theater as rapidly as required. These and other issues made sustaining units in the field difficult.

- **Information and Knowledge.** The services made strides both in the ability to move information and translate information into knowledge, but they did not attain the goal or capacity to wage "network-centric" warfare. Equally important, although the services made concerted efforts to wage information operations, gauging the success of those efforts remains elusive partly because the data is still unclear, but also because the concept remains immature.

Two other areas warrant separate consideration, both to set the context of operations in Iraq and to consider possible implications for the future:

- **Preparation.** The 12-year effort to build the theater infrastructure; maintaining long-term regional engagement; conducting significant investments in Command, Control, Communications, Computers, Intelligence, Surveillance, and Reconnaissance (C^{4}ISR); and completing significant materiel fieldings in the six months leading to execution were critical in setting the stage for success. Conversely, the very success within this theater raises questions about how the joint force would operate in a less mature theater, suggesting key shortfalls in the joint expeditionary capabilities.
- **Urban Operations.** The Army's updated doctrine and training, as well as detailed, focused preparation for leaders, planners, and soldiers, created a highly capable urban-combat force. Tanks and Bradleys proved survivable and effective in the grueling environment, augmented by rapidly fielded equipment expressly designed to operate in an urban environment. Planners employed an innovative systems-based approach to urban combat that fundamentally reshaped how soldiers and commanders approached the mission. The result was that soldiers dominated the urban terrain without significant casualties, destruction, or collateral damage.

One or more of these themes is in every story, narrative, or discussion in *On Point*.

Generally, OIF is a "good news" story, but any operation reveals areas that require improvement. American soldiers adapted and improvised to overcome five key shortfalls identified during OIF. As with the keys to success, these problems are evident in many of the same stories, narratives, and discussions.

- **Combat Service Support (CSS).** The CSS difficulties cross all aspects of Army operations—doctrine, organization, training, materiel, leader development, personnel, and facilities (DOTMLPF). From the recent shift to "just-in-time" logistics to the training and equipping of CSS soldiers and units, the CSS community and the Army must rethink how they conduct operations. The current system emphasizes efficiency over effectiveness—from parts and supply distribution to the physical equipping of CSS units. In combat, however, effectiveness is the only real measure of success; many CSS units struggled to perform their mission due to "savings" realized in recent changes in organization, equipment, training resources, and doctrine.

- **Ability of every unit to fight and win.** A noncontiguous operating environment has, by definition, no secure areas. Every unit in the theater must be prepared to fight to accomplish its mission. OIF drove this idea home and is fraught with implications for how ground forces are manned, equipped, and trained.
- **Tactical Intelligence.** The current Intelligence Battlefield Operating System (IBOS) is optimized for upper echelons and effectively supported the corps and higher echelons. However, in the COE, brigades and below need the capability to sense and analyze the threat to their immediate front. The historic emphasis at the corps and above, exacerbated by inadequate communications and analytic aids, often forced maneuver commanders literally to fight for information about the enemy to their front—or rear and sides.
- **Active Component/Reserve Component Mix.** The current mix is inappropriate to meet post-Cold War realities. The demands on the Reserve Components—to support a crisis contingency force while simultaneously supporting homeland security, major combat, and stability operations and support operations requirements, require a full review of missions and force structure. Moreover, the mobilization and employment process must be updated to meet the current and projected operational concepts, to wit—short-notice/long-duration deployments.

None of these areas requiring improvements will surprise anyone with any depth of experience within the Army. However, OIF provides hard and unambiguous data about the depth, breadth, and scope of these challenges. This clarity was lacking in previous, more theoretical venues of analysis and debate. While the past 12 years showed improvement in each of these areas, there is much more to do. Themes in these broad areas will affect how the Army continues transformation toward the future force. In this sense, the lessons of the most recent war will help guide the Army's preparation for the next war.

Issues and Implications

This study of Army participation in OIF reveals three larger, interrelated concepts that are also woven throughout this work: *campaigns, preparation*, and *seams*. Much of what is good—and bad—about Army and joint performance in OIF can be traced to some aspect of these three issues.

Simply stated, as the major ground component of the US armed forces, the Army demonstrated that it is the premier land combat force for sustained campaigns and operations. The Army provides this fundamental, defining quality to joint campaigning—*sustained* operations.

Sustained operations are more than just "clean up" after a series of standoff precision and ground engagements. While these actions are necessary and set the conditions for success, they do not equate to success. Presenting the adversary with an overwhelming combat power that will seek him out anywhere, outlast his ability to hide, deliver a decisive defeat, and bring positive change to the region are the attributes that transform successful battles and engagements into a successful campaign.

Without the Army, the world's best Navy, Air Force, and Marine Corps could not successfully conclude this, or any similar, campaign. Sustained land operations are more than just combat; they are *operations* that include the combination of decisive military actions and the ability to exploit that victory to achieve theater strategic objectives and advance national policy. Sustaining operations included providing common user logistics, supporting theater air and missile defense, providing for the security of enemy prisoners of war, supporting psychological operations, civil affairs, and many other tasks that afford the troops that execute them few opportunities for glory, but without which joint campaigns generally can not be concluded successfully.

Preparation is one of the keys to successful campaigning. It is fundamental to understanding the victory of OIF. Although discussed above, it requires additional detail here as a basic element to a successful campaign. As illustrated throughout this story, preparation takes on many nuanced meanings and took place from the diplomatic to the tactical level.

Preparing—or in the current vernacular, "setting the conditions"—has reemerged as a core component of the American way of war. For the most part, preparations were well reasoned and generally "80-percent solutions," given the resources, time, and political/diplomatic constraints at the time. How the Army capitalized on, integrated, or recovered from these varying levels of preparation is a fundamental part of every soldier's story and the Army's success.

The concept of seams emerged during the analysis for this work. Seams may be vertical, horizontal, organizational, and structural. Unless deliberately secured, seams expose weakness and may make the joint force vulnerable to enemy exploitation. In other cases, seams represent points of strength as two or more organizations reinforce and focus deliberately on a smooth transition. Perhaps one of the most vexing seams is how military forces posture for the "Three-Block War"—shorthand for full-spectrum operations within a single battlefield or even a single city block. Even calling it three-block war creates seams in what is an inherently seamless spectrum of conflict. How the ground forces contended with a "rolling," or even "blurring" transition to Phase IV operations is a major characteristic of this ongoing campaign.

These themes transcend the Army and are found throughout the campaign. As such, this work is not the appropriate forum for a detailed analysis or discussion. A more comprehensive study of OIF at the operational, joint campaign level would offer the necessary depth, breadth, and scope for this analysis. Yet, as in every war, there are many implications that will affect the Army's evolution. In any case, it is probably an understatement to say that there is much to learn from OIF.

On Point is more than a title; it is the central theme of this work, and soldiers are central to this theme. Soldiers on point demonstrated their quality and showed their flexibility, courage, and initiative as their antecedents have in every fight from Bunker Hill to Baghdad. Equally important, they remain on point from Mosul in the north to

As Samawah in the south. They are doing the important work of creating the conditions of an Iraqi democracy and sustainable peace—America's stated strategic goal.

Book Structure

As a first account, *On Point* tells the story of the Army in a joint and combined force. Yet the soldiers of V Corps did not simply appear on the Iraqi border on 21 March 2003. Nor was the campaign limited to the combat soldiers fighting their way to Baghdad. Victory on the battlefield required the efforts of all of the armed forces acting in concert. A host of preparatory and supporting events, spanning more than a decade, brought the soldiers to the line of departure. Moreover, the support effort was at least as impressive and challenging as the combat itself. To do these soldiers, sailors, marines, airmen, and coast guardsmen justice would require several volumes beyond the scope of this work.

The book is structured in three general parts: The first part—the introduction, Chapter 1, and Chapter 2—discusses how the Army prepared for Operation IRAQI FREEDOM. The preparation started the day after the end of Operation DESERT STORM and ended with the first soldiers crossing the line of departure in Operation IRAQI FREEDOM. The introduction provides the Army's context among its sister services and in the joint community. Chapter 1 describes how the Army evolved from 1991 to 2003. The Army that won in Iraq in 2003 was different from the Army that won in Kuwait in 1991. It is critical to understand how the Army managed its growth and evolution over that time to create the Army of IRAQI FREEDOM. Chapter 2 addresses the final preparations for combat, from the summer of 2002 to D-day. This last effort put almost all of the pieces in place for the campaign, from inside the Continental United States (CONUS) to Europe and, of course, in Southwest Asia.

The second part, Chapters 3 through 6, focuses on the ground campaign through the end of major offensive operations, roughly 10 April, depending on which unit one looks at. The chapters strike the balance between describing big, sweeping arrows and telling the individual soldier's story. They start with a general summary of events during that phase of the battle—the sweeping arrows, followed by a detailed, almost stand-alone description of three or four key events. The opening summaries also introduce parallel and supporting actions that affect the fight or have some other significance. The summary also seeks to set the joint and coalition forces land component command context of the fight.

To say "phase of the battle" is somewhat of a misnomer in that the chapter structure suggests an ex-post facto delineation of operations and purposes. No formal operations order discusses completing the "running start" before starting the "march up-country" or "isolation of Baghdad" or even the "regime removal." More accurately, operations overlapped in time, location, and purpose, with many engagements changing character as they evolved. However, in a complex, distributed battlefield marked by multiple, simultaneous operations across a country the size of California, a simple sequence of events would force the reader to jump all over the battlefield, possibly losing the context for why any specific operation was undertaken.

Therefore, for the sake of clarity, operations and engagements are grouped by purpose rather than by time. This allows the reader to understand why an action occurred, even if it presents some challenges in following the sequence of events. The timelines at the beginning of each chapter are designed to help the reader through any confusion in the sequence of events and helps to retain operational context. Moreover, times noted in the text have been adjusted from Greenwich Mean Time ("Zulu") to local Kuwait time (+ 3 hours).

Throughout the work, the soldier stories and vignettes serve a variety of purposes. First, they help the reader better understand the trials and tribulations of soldiers on the battlefield. Second, they offer a detailed discussion of a particular aspect of the war as an example of the actions occurring all across the battlefield. And finally, the stories and vignettes introduce the reader to the individual soldiers who fought the battle. The men and women who served in Iraq represent a cross-section of America and illustrate all that is good about the American soldier and citizen. Their success is the Army's success and America's success.

The final section of *On Point* is a discussion of some of the campaign's implications. Operation IRAQI FREEDOM marks the most integrated joint force and joint campaign American armed forces have ever conducted. It is also the second war of the new millennium and carries weight as such. For the Army, it marks the first major campaign since Operation DESERT STORM. It is the first time the decade's worth of investments in digitization and interservice interoperability has been put to the test. This quick look at the war from an Army perspective suggests implications for the Army's continued transformation to the future force. These implications are organized in the broad categories discussed earlier and may serve as a starting point for further discussions and ultimately, programmatic decisions.

As of this writing, the campaign in Iraq continues. Soldiers continue to work with other agencies and organizations to help stabilize Iraq and assist with the transition to civilian rule. Yet despite the declared end of major combat operations, soldiers continue to fight—and die—as they pursue the remnants of the Ba'athist regime and other groups who oppose the coalition's presence. This mission is neither new nor unique to the Army's tradition. In this sense, the Army continues its role as the service of decision—ensuring that battlefield victories translate into strategic success.

NOTES

1. President George W. Bush, "Address to the American Enterprise Institute, " 26 February 2003, accessed from http://www.whitehouse.gov/news/releases/2003/02/iraq/20030226-11.html, on 15 June 2003.

2. Alvin and Heidi Toffler, *War and Antiwar: Survival at the Dawn of the 21st Century*, (Boston: Little, Brown, and Company, 1993).

3. "Title 10" refers to US Federal Code, Title 10, which delineates the services' responsibilities in providing forces and support to the joint commander and the other services. During OIF, the Army fulfilled its Title 10 responsibilities in many ways, to include providing a majority of logistics and CSS to the other services for common user items.

4. Colonel Kevin Benson, CFLCC C5 (for OIF), interview by Major David Tohn, 12 August 2003.

5. Technically, with the Marine Corps providing ground forces, the CFLCC is actually a CJFLCC— Combined Joint Forces Land Component Command. However, this work adopts the theater's common naming convention.

Chapter 1

Operation DESERT STORM to ENDURING FREEDOM
The Army's Continuing Evolution

It was a JANUS war—it was the trailing edge of industrial-age warfare and the leading edge of knowledge-based, information-age warfare. Some of the old continued, and some of the new emerged.

General Frederick M. Franks, Jr.
Commanding General,
US Army Training and Doctrine Command[1]

The history of the US Army experience during the 1990s is the history of adaptation to new threats and challenges within an ambiguous, changing global security environment. It is a chronology of how the Army would conceive of and conduct itself in future wars. The Army's odyssey through the 11 years from the close of DESERT STORM in 1991 to the close of decisive combat operations in ENDURING FREEDOM in 2002 is remarkable and a testament to a traditional institution's commitment to deliberate, introspective change. In some cases, change came because the Army anticipated requirements, while in other cases the Army adapted to conditions it had not anticipated. Finally, the Army had not completed transformation by Operation IRAQI FREEDOM (OIF). The Army that went to war in March 2003 included modernized forces well on the way toward transformation and forces still organized and designed for the Cold War. The two Gulf Wars are bookends to an amazing, compelling, and frequently painful era of transition and growth.

In retrospect, this era can be loosely divided into three periods, denoted by gradual transitions in understanding and focus. The periods are: the immediate postwar euphoria following the end of the Cold War and DESERT STORM; the extended debate on how the Army should respond to an evolving and unfamiliar security environment; and finally, the decision and efforts to "transform" to a "Future Force" capable of operating within that rapidly changing environment. These changes occurred against a backdrop of accelerated development of joint doctrine and the maturation of joint training led by US Atlantic Command (ACOM), which later became Joint Forces Command (JFCOM). These three periods define the Army's intellectual, physical, and moral evolution as it transitioned from its Cold War posture to the force that fought and won in OIF. Of course, although divided into periods for logical reasons, the reality was constant and continuous change.

The era is notable in how, following an apparently sweeping victory, the institutional Army demonstrated a remarkable willingness to reexamine itself critically. The result was an often-winding path of evolution rather than revolution. While officers, soldiers, and civilians clearly did the hard, typically unappreciated "nug work" to make the evolution a reality, this chapter of the Army's story focuses on the general officers who led the Army's institutional engines of change. As the Army's senior leaders, these general officers were dedicated both to the Army's long-term survival and relevance for the nation. They provided the vision, direction, and "horsepower" to push against considerable inertia—and some outright resistance—from soldiers in the field.

The Army took this path in parallel with the joint community. Moreover, this effort ensued while the Army reacted to a complex and challenging domestic and international environment. Tracing this evolution is critical to appreciating how the victorious Army of 2003 is different from the victorious Army of 1991. What follows is a discussion of the US Army's growth, learning, and transformation from the 'certain victory' in Operation DESERT STORM (ODS) through the end of major combat operations in OIF and the transition into peace support operations—a transition that continues even today.

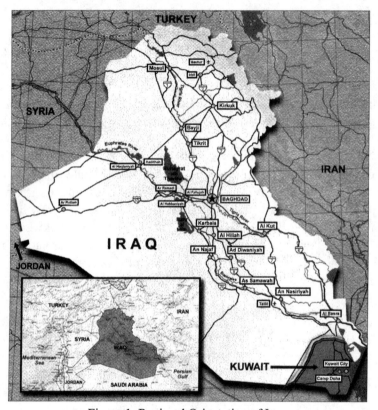

Figure 1. Regional Orientation of Iraq

Before and After the "Storm"

The success of the United States-led coalition against Saddam Hussein's invasion of Kuwait in 1990 in retrospect seemed a certain victory. Strategically, the conditions of war that brought the Gulf War coalition together and carried through the conflict were certain—the unprovoked violation of Kuwaiti sovereignty provided textbook justification for collective action. The threat to regional stability, the global economy, and environmental security, as well as Saddam's appetite for Kuwaiti and Saudi oil fields, only solidified the clear and present danger of the moment. The result was an unambiguous charter for staunch, swift, and severe collective action against Iraq.

The operational and tactical nature of DESERT STORM was equally certain. The battles and engagements of the first Gulf War were set-piece battles, reflective of World War II European combat. The US Army's AirLand Battle-tailored conventional force and its coalition partners met the fourth-largest 20th-century army in large-scale, open-quarter combat supported from above by air forces who found the air space largely uncontested. The resulting victory was so sweeping and complete as to be almost beathtaking in its nature. In short, the victory seemed to validate the Army's Cold War doctrine, equipment, training, and organization.

However, DESERT STORM, like all wars, proved Janus-like: some aspects were familiar, while others hinted at the nature of future combat. Precision munitions and the Global Positioning System (GPS) suggested that technology, and in particular, information technology, would fundamentally affect the course of future combat operations. As Alvin and Heidi Toffler argued, DESERT STORM contained the seeds of "Third Wave" warfare, in which information technology would dominate.[2] The war suggested elements of future warfare while validating service investments in high-technology systems such as precision munitions and the M1 Abrams Main Battle Tank. Yet, some argued that DESERT STORM would be the last of the symmetrical, large-machine wars.

At the moral and psychological levels, Operation DESERT STORM clearly demonstrated that the services could decisively fight and win the nation's wars. The speed with which the armed forces ejected the Iraqis effectively erased the painful memories of North Vietnamese tanks trundling about on the lawn of the South Vietnamese presidential palace or the charred corpses of the failed hostage rescue attempt at *Desert 1* in the Iranian desert. DESERT STORM was, in some ways, a catharsis for both the nation and its armed forces.

But the path from Vietnam to DESERT STORM did not present the Army with an easy journey toward change and adaptation. Although all of the services bore the burden of Vietnam, the weight rested most heavily on the US Army. The Army returned from Vietnam with its confidence shaken and wanting to put the experience behind it. But as a profession, the Army did not brood on that failure or attempt to excuse itself. Rather, a core group of officers quickly sought to learn from the experience. Even before the tanks rolled in front of the Vietnamese presidential palace, the "Big A" Army had shifted back to NATO and the defense of West Germany with conventional combat operations.

The Army found little comfort in Europe. The Soviets, or at least their weapons and tactics, seemed ascendant. The Egyptian army's successful use of Soviet gear and tactics in the 1973 Arab-Israeli war boded ill for the defense of Europe. Israel, after its great victory in 1967, seemed unbeatable— yet they nearly lost the Yom Kippur War six years later. Arguably, the Israelis' arrogance of victory prevented them from critically learning from the 1967 war. As a result, they were fundamentally surprised—tactically, operationally, and psychologically. Worse still, the Arab-Israeli War seemed to validate the Soviet approach to war, causing a collective chill in the US Army and Air Force.

Accordingly, both turned their energy to considering how to counter the apparent advantages that Soviet weapons and tactics seemed to have conferred on the Arabs and Egyptians specifically. The results were impressive. In the 1970s and 1980s, the Army's leadership wrought changes in doctrine, training, materiel development, and acquisition that amounted to a renaissance of the force. At the same time, the Air Force's Tactical Air Command aggressively sought the means to counter the air defense threat apparent in the Yom Kippur War.

DESERT STORM illustrated both the effectiveness of the Army's effort to reform itself in the 1980s and the appearance of technologies that might redefine the nature of war. The Army took the fight to the Iraqis armed with its "big five" weapon systems: the M-1 Abrams tank, M-2 Bradley Infantry Fighting Vehicle, the Multiple Launch Rocket System, the Patriot Air Defense Missile System, and the AH-64 Apache attack helicopter. These systems were originally fielded to meet the Warsaw Pact, using the AirLand Battle doctrine that was rehearsed in hundreds of bloodless fights at the National Training Center (NTC), Fort Irwin, California. Indeed, many soldiers returning in 1991 observed that the 32nd Guards Motorized Rifle Regiment, the NTC Opposing Force (OPFOR), proved a far tougher foe than the Iraqi Republican Guard. Following the 7 March 1991 cease-fire, the Army basked in the warm glow of success and public accolades.

However, the "big five" Army that had just won DESERT STORM would be forced to weather a new and gathering storm with a myriad of challenges—foreign and domestic, defense and security based, political, and economic. The character of emerging threats and potential future fights did not neatly match the Army's just-proved capabilities. While digesting this dilemma, the Army focused on maintaining a capable and effective force in the face of the downsizing trends of the 1990s that, as General Gordon R. Sullivan, the 32nd chief of staff of the Army (CSA), put it, required nothing less than "transformation" of the Army.[3]

The 1990s: Describing the World and Redefining the Future Army

From the early hours of 20 March to 1 May 2003, when President George W. Bush declared the end of major combat operations, soldiers, in concert with sailors, marines, airmen, coast guardsmen, and foreign military brothers and sisters in arms, fought what is already being recognized as the first information-age war. The previous 12 years of debate—theoretical, doctrinal, and political—that tried to predict the best way ahead had been tested in the battles of OIF. The following section is the story of the Army's sometimes-painful journey of learning, debating, changing, and growing in that chaotic and challenging dozen-year period.

The Domestic and International Environment

Defining and achieving the transformation that General Sullivan espoused became the central purpose of the institutional Army throughout the 1990s. The question was how best to adapt—whether to "leap ahead" technologically to a distinctively new pathway of force modernization, or gradually move ahead in an incremental manner involving a recapitalization of the big five-based legacy system. The question had to be answered not only from the Army's point of view, but from a joint perspective as well. The Army found its answers in testing and analysis and eventually demonstrated the results on the battlefield in OIF.

The domestic and international environment played a key role in shaping—both positively and negatively—this ongoing debate. Internationally, the world was breaking free of the relatively rigid structures of the Cold War era, presenting a dizzying array of security challenges to the nation and the armed forces. US engagement in the fields and cities of Somalia, Rwanda, Haiti, the Balkans, Central and South America, the Philippines, and East Timor had a direct and lasting impact on how the Army viewed itself: its role, its missions, and required capabilities.

The domestic political landscape in the immediate aftermath of the first Gulf War was equally challenging and reflected the typical American postwar reaction. The nation expected a lasting peace following the back-to-back defeat of its old Cold War nemesis and the new Iraqi threat. Moreover, Americans eagerly anticipated a "peace dividend" that could be applied to pressing domestic needs as the economy emerged from recession. Indeed, given the overwhelming military success, America's leaders and citizens considered the armed forces to be overly capable for the perceived future security environment.

The absence of any clear threat encouraged the perception that it was prudent to reduce the armed forces. Strategic ambiguity made it difficult for decision makers and the citizenry to reach a consensus on just what the military requirements should be. Amid this ambiguous political-military environment, the defense budget became the game ball of competing partisan-political and service rivalries and a lucrative resource to support domestic initiatives. The resulting policies placed enormous pressures on America's military in general, and the US Army in particular, to man, equip, train, field, and sustain an effective force in a new security environment.

Thus, budget constraints forced the military to balance its efforts between maintaining readiness and fielding new capabilities to deal with the growing array of unknown, but suspected, threats. These conditions compelled the Army to man, equip, and train a military force capable of providing for the common defense, but "on the cheap." The net result was a series of relatively inexpensive investments in doctrine development, experimentation, and certain key technologies that vastly improved capabilities without a wholesale overhaul of the big-five force. In doing so, the Army, along with its sister services, took on the task of doing much more with much less—to adapt and innovate in an environment of relatively scarce resources not experienced since the days of Generals George Marshall and Dwight Eisenhower in the hiatus between world wars.

Managing Downsizing and Setting the Stage for Transformation

Immediately following the 1991 victory, Sullivan, then the vice CSA, put things in perspective for the Third Army staff when he noted, "The American people expect only one thing from us: That we will win. What you have done is no more than they expect. You have won."[4] But as Sullivan knew very well, the Army would need to change significantly to remain relevant in the coming years. Moreover, he understood that coming fiscal and resource constraints would affect the pace and scope of that change.

First and foremost, the demobilization of the Cold War Army that had already begun with the 4th Infantry Division (ID), 5th ID, 9th ID, and the 2nd Armored Division (AD) would pick up speed. As it turned out, 3rd AD returned to Germany in the summer of 1991 and cased colors in the spring of 1992, joining the 2nd Armored Calvary Regiment (ACR), 8th ID, and VII Corps among the deactivated units in Germany. The pace of demobilization accelerated so that by the summer of 1993, the Army had drawn down its end strength from 786,000 to 500,000 soldiers.

But demobilizing the Cold War Army was not the only impetus for change. Sullivan, who succeeded Carl E. Vuono as CSA in 1991, perceived an absolute requirement to change fundamentally how the Army organized, equipped, trained, and employed units to reflect emerging trends. Sullivan spoke of "change and continuity" as the hallmarks of his tenure as CSA. He envisioned effecting change where it seemed warranted, while preserving the enduring qualities and values of the Army. Simply put, the Army needed to change from focusing on the Soviets to focusing on the emerging global threats. He believed the Army must anticipate change in the operational environment and incorporate the lessons learned in Panama and DESERT STORM.

Moving rapidly to establish momentum for change, Sullivan assigned General Frederick M. Franks, Jr. as commanding general of TRADOC in the summer of 1991. Both Sullivan and Franks grew up as commanders during the Army's post-Vietnam renaissance. Generals Creighton Abrams, William Depuy, and Donn Starry had led that effort. Sullivan and Franks understood that, as in the post-Vietnam era, the national strategy must inform and drive doctrine, combat development, and training. In his guidance to Franks upon his assumption of command, Sullivan specified, "You will be informing us and, in turn, teaching us *how* to think about war in this proclaimed 'New World Order,' Goldwater-Nichols era in which we are living. What we think about doctrine, organizations, equipment, and training in the future must be the result of a vigorous and informed discussion amongst seasoned professionals."[5]

Both also understood the Army's essentially conservative nature and the need for soldiers to embrace their vision of the future for any change to take root. This was particularly important in the absence of a shock to the Army system similar to the Israelis' shock of the Yom Kippur War. Rather, they had to build momentum against the self-satisfied inertia of the post-DESERT STORM Army. To achieve this, they developed several initiatives in parallel:

At the Department of the Army level, Sullivan organized and funded the Louisiana Army Maneuvers Task Force (LAM-TF) as the "general headquarters" tool for experimentation.[6] LAM-TF, led by a young up-and-coming brigadier general named Tommy Franks, "stood up" in the spring of 1992 at Fort Monroe, collocated with TRADOC. LAM-TF's role included both experimentation and general "pot stirring" to promote thinking about the future and leading change.

Having served as executive to former TRADOC commander Starry, General Fred Franks knew TRADOC and understood how it functioned. He used a variety of venues to define and divine early insights into future challenges. These venues included conferences on DESERT STORM and on the apparent changes to warfare suggested in that war, consulting experts and futurists, assigning talented officers the responsibility to consider apparent trends in warfare, and researching how the US and other armies experimented and considered the future. He concluded that there were five key areas in which the Army needed to consider change:

- Early or forced entry (since the Army would no longer be forward based in the most likely theater of operations)
- Mounted and dismounted maneuver
- Fires across the depth of the battlespace
- Battle command
- Combat service support

Franks disbanded the entrenched combat development offices that were "stovepiped" organizations serving their parent branches and replaced them with battle labs whose function was to experiment to anticipate changes concerning these ideas or domains. The battle labs deliberately crossed the traditional Army branch boundaries, breaking the previous vertical development patterns and forcing more holistic and innovative solutions.

To this mix, Sullivan and Franks resolved to effect changes to doctrine and unit training. Changing doctrine began with rewriting Field Manual (FM) 100-5, *Operations*, the Army's baseline doctrinal manual. The Army's combat training centers: the NTC, Joint Readiness Training Center (JRTC) (then at Fort Chaffee, Arkansas), and the Combat Maneuver Training Center (CMTC) at Hohenfels, Germany, each began to consider how to adjust training to anticipate the future. These initiatives, and the twin themes of *change* and *continuity,* started the Army down the path that ultimately led it to the palaces of Baghdad and to an Army very different from the one that returned from Kuwait in 1991.

Adapting AirLand Battle to Full-Spectrum Operations

The Army redeployed from the sands of Kuwait confident in AirLand Battle as a successful and effective doctrine. However, as the applause died down and the leadership looked toward the future, it was clear that the doctrine would need to change to meet a new reality. Importantly, the Army did not merely react; it *anticipated* change. Generals Sullivan and Franks moved rapidly to deliver on their vision of change along three axes: doctrine, organization and training, and materiel.

Developing the Doctrinal Foundation for Change

Even *before* DESERT STORM, then-CSA Vuono and his TRADOC commander, General John W. Foss, began to change the way the Army viewed warfare and doctrinal development. Both had seen the ground shifting as the Soviet Union moved from outright confrontation to "openness" and imminent collapse. The nature of future US commitments would change correspondingly. Accordingly, in 1990, Foss, in coordination with the Air Force Tactical Air Command, began the process of revising FM 100-5.[7] FM 100-5 would move from an operational-level manual to one that was firmly grounded in tying military operations to strategic considerations. The new doctrine was attempting to look 15 years ahead. That span allowed time to develop solutions across TRADOC's domains—doctrine, organizations, training, materiel, leadership, personnel, and facilities (DOTMLPF). As part of that effort, Foss concluded the Army would be involved in more than combat operations as the threat and conditions changed.[8]

General Franks' purpose for revising the doctrine stemmed from his conviction that the "glimmerings" of fundamental changes in the nature of warfare must be accounted for across the domains of DOTMLPF. Like General Sullivan, he perceived the need for transformation. Franks believed the Army would require changes across DOTMLPF to avoid arriving at merely a smaller version of the Cold War Army. Both Sullivan and Franks intended that the new FM 100-5 would serve as the intellectual "engine of change," while the newly formed battle labs conducted experiments with promising technologies and concepts and the LAM-TF invested effort and dollars in cutting-edge technologies. In short, both generals perceived the need to transform. Moreover, they believed that the Army would need to lead change not only internally, but within the joint community as well. What followed was a coordinated and driven effort to build on the successes of DESERT STORM, particularly those characterized as the nascent beginnings of information-enabled warfare.

The Army published FM 100-5 in June 1993. As promised, the new operations manual started to shift the focus from the operational level to the strategic level; or rather, it recast the doctrine in the strategic and joint context. The manual also addressed "the shift to stronger joint operations prompted by the *Goldwater-Nichols Act of 1986.*"[9] It did so by discreetly introducing the concepts of joint capabilities and missions and devoting chapters to joint operations and combined operations. The manual also addressed force projection and battle command as new topics.

Most important, the manual introduced and described "full-dimensional operations." The term captured the concept of joint and combined operations along a spectrum of conflict, perhaps at several points on the spectrum at once. To deal with the fundamentally changed problem of fighting and moving up and down the spectrum of conflict, the manual included an entire chapter devoted to operations other than war.

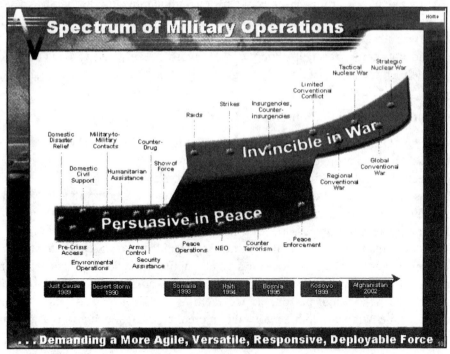

Figure 2. Spectrum of Military Operations ("Full-Spectrum Operations")

Additionally, the authors, led by Franks, chose operationally focused historical vignettes to illustrate joint and combined integration, including the Inchon Landing, Operation JUST CAUSE, and the Battle of Yorktown. Convinced of the importance of joint and combined integration, Franks led the TRADOC staff on a staff ride that reviewed the connections between the French defeat of the British off of the Virginia Capes and the combined American and French operations at Yorktown. He chose this specific campaign to convey to the TRADOC staff, by example, the fundamentally joint nature of successful operations and the absolute interdependence of joint forces at the operational and strategic levels. General Franks argued that this was so historically and would be so in the future.[10]

The authors also attempted to account for transition at the end of a conflict. In a section titled "Conflict Termination," the manual noted, "Success on the battlefield does not always lead to success in war."[11] Finally, for the first time, FM 100-5 devoted an entire chapter to operations other than war (OOTW). By no means complete in anticipating the difficult operations to come, FM 100-5 clearly articulated fundamental and important changes to the way the Army thought about what it might be asked to do and how to do those things in the post-Cold War era.

Organizations and Training: Experimenting with the Force

The LAM-TF and the battle labs played roles in creating a climate of change. They produced insights into how to leverage technology to meet emerging requirements. The battle labs supported experiments that featured new technologies which might have a high payoff as well as effect dramatic changes in formations and organizations. For example, in 1994 and 1995 LAM-TF and the battle labs teamed up with BCTP and the Command and General Staff College (CGSC) to conduct experiments in the CGSC *PRAIRIE WARRIOR* exercise series. Their intent was to test new technologies and radical combat formations embodied in an organization called the Mobile Strike Force. Air mechanization and digitally enabled battle command were central themes in both of these experiments. Additionally, the labs produced several concepts and equipment that the Army eventually incorporated; from the mundane "smart" identification card to auxiliary power units for tanks. But most important, the labs supported advancing the most important material idea emerging from DESERT STORM—Digital Battle Command and *Force XXI*.[12]

Digitizing the Force: Enabling *Force XXI*

Force XXI described both the concept and intent for digital battle command in the Army. Convinced that this was the way to enhance combat capability without building new combat systems from the ground up, Generals Sullivan and Franks sought to digitally link combat systems based on a straightforward working hypothesis. They believed that if the Army equipped units with the means to see each other and to see the enemy, those units would be able to operate at higher tempos than opponents. This, in turn, would make them more lethal and thus more survivable. All of this could be achieved without adding more armor or building new systems. The labs sought to test this hypothesis and find means to improve the ability of units to see the enemy. This led to a fair number of sometimes-bizarre efforts ranging from hand-launched unmanned aerial vehicles (UAVs) to various non line-of-sight strike capabilities. A suite of digital communication systems and software to aid decision making and shared situational awareness supported all of these emerging capabilities.

They did not develop their working hypothesis out of whole cloth. It came in stages. In the summer of 1993, General Franks visited Aberdeen Proving Grounds, where prototype M1A2 tanks were being tested. The M1A2 had on board a developmental system called the Inter-vehicular Information System (IVIS). IVIS contained the seeds of digitally enabling the crews to see each other and share information. But Franks was skeptical. He was not convinced that tank crews really could fight the tank and communicate with each other by looking at very crude computer screens. Franks asked the program executive officer (PEO) whether he could field a single platoon of tanks in a coming NTC rotation to enable a test under what Franks described as the most competitive environment short of combat. Major General Pete McVey agreed and shipped a platoon to the 1st Cavalry Division to be used in a test in the fall.

Consequently, in September 1993, one of the first experiments that ultimately delivered a digital Army to OIF occurred at the NTC. General Franks visited one of the platoon's after-action reviews. The tank crews, and in particular Sergeant First Class, Phillip H. Johndrow, were effusive about IVIS and what it could do for them in a fight. The future of the Army could be discerned in Johndrow's enthusiasm for the potential of IVIS. With it, all four tanks had computer screens that enabled them to "see" one another and pass email digitally. But the system was fragile, hard to use, and the racket produced by the constant warbling noise of the digital carrier wave was almost unbearable. Despite this, Johndrow was enthusiastic in his praise for the possibilities to Franks. Despite the flaws and the relatively primitive state of the system, Franks understood as he listened to the tankers explain that their ability to share information nearly instantly "magnified their combat power." To Franks, it was an epiphany, "I could see the potential for the entire combined arms team."[13] Johndrow and his platoon represented a major step in the Army's journey toward *Force XXI*. Ten years later, Johndrow served in Iraq as the command sergeant major of the digitally linked, air-transported 3rd Squadron, 2nd ACR (Light).

A Digitally Linked Battle Command System

To reach its *Force XXI* objective, the Army conducted a series of live, virtual, and constructive simulations to test the root hypothesis—battlefield visualization and digitized communication for all units would enhance the Army's warfighting effectiveness. It also developed combat requirements, not only for communication systems, but also for decision making and situational awareness aids as well. Together, these aids constituted the Army Battle Command System (ABCS), key elements of which provided the blue (friendly) common operational picture.

The *Force XXI* efforts were critical toward maintaining the Army's status as the most capable land force in the world. The relatively inexpensive investments in technology and battle command promised an exponential return in capabilities that would overwhelm any conceivable adversary. However, as General Sullivan often reminded soldiers—there were "no time-outs." While the Army moved toward *Force XXI*, it conducted operations in Somalia, Rwanda, and Haiti. Moreover, while FM 100-5 was an excellent—even prescient—start in describing how and where the Army fit into the nation's national security structure and strategy, ultimately it required revision to address the challenges imposed by these ongoing operations.[14]

The Army in the New Global Context

The first operations the United States faced following DESERT STORM were antithetical to the traditional concept of war. The contingency operations expanded "warfighting" beyond the context of the traditional maneuver battles and engagements. The new threats resided all along the full spectrum of conflict, from low-grade political and social instability within a nation-state to major combat operations. The 1990s did not break this trend.

Moreover, America has a history of "first battle" experiences where initial setbacks or near-failures on the battlefield set the essential conditions for the innovation that eventually

The SIPRNET Revolution

In addition to the work to digitize the tactical Army forces, the Army was a full participant in the Department of Defense's program to field the Secret Internet Protocol Router Network (SIPRNET). SIPRNET is a classified Defense Department network that is functionally equivalent to the civilian World Wide Web. Over the decade, SIPRNET became ubiquitous, with units at every echelon having access to a secure network where classified plans, discussions, and information could be shared freely.

SIPRNET quietly enabled a revolution in how the Army, sister services, and the joint community planned and operated. Collaborating without the constraints of mailing classified data or talking over a secure telephone was a quantum leap in efficiency and effectiveness. In addition to desktop access to the latest plans and intelligence information, the secure email and chat rooms fostered crosstalk at all levels. Planners at home stations could follow current operations and conduct parallel planning to anticipate requirements. Conversely, an overeager command could monitor every potential contingency and plan for commitments that would never be levied—creating unnecessary confusion and fatigue.

prevailed. As Franks anticipated, these operations challenged the Army's existing capabilities and exposed obsolescence in the AirLand Battle doctrine. Meeting the new reality with a smaller force, equipped and proficient in a doctrine that was increasingly outdated and overcome by the changing security environment, forced solutions that were innovative, if occasionally painful or disastrous. The decade's worth of experience delivered several key lessons learned that paid dividends during OIF. Some lessons were self-evident and readily incorporated into the force. Others were not fully appreciated at the time but were eventually learned, practiced, and applied in Iraq to great effect. Still others would prove elusive, demanding more operational introspection and organizational learning. The result was an Army crossing the border into Iraq with many— but not all—of the lessons of the past decade explicitly or implicitly incorporated into the force.

Somalia, Haiti, and Rwanda—A Painful Education Process

The histories of these operations have been chronicled; the causes and effects of where the nation and its Army succeeded or fell short in these experiences have been extensively debated. However, regardless of the verdict of success or failure, what is clear is that the Army was able to learn from these early experiences in 1990s' warfare. Each contingency operation presented a unique scenario that led to some specific lessons. As OIF unfolded, the Army encountered elements of all these contingencies and was able to apply many—but not all—of the lessons gathered along the way. Arguably, the Army was able to assimilate many of the lessons from Somalia, Haiti, and Rwanda in ways that have only become apparent in the aftermath of OIF.

Somalia

Operation RESTORE HOPE began as the first significant humanitarian assistance operation following the Cold War and DESERT STORM. However, it culminated as the first real US experience in the warlord politics so prevalent in much of the developing world. Though characterized since 1993 as a case of mission creep in the extreme, capped by the searing pictures of dead US soldiers being dragged through the street, there was a positive Army legacy from Somalia.[15] For better or worse, that yearlong stability and support campaign was effectively reduced to a single engagement on 3-4 October 1993. The Army was, in fact, hugely successful in the humanitarian assistance phases of the Somalia expedition. Some US

Agency for International Development (USAID) reports attribute US Army-led humanitarian aid with preserving over 10,000 Somali lives. Though not obvious at the time, particularly in the aftermath of the loss of 18 soldiers, the Army learned how to wield combat power to stabilize a region and set the conditions for humanitarian assistance.

The Army also gained experience in operating in the unfamiliar political and cultural environment of clan and warlord politics. Moreover, in the aftermath of the Battle of Mogadishu, the Army learned about the rapidly changing and diverse nature of a single combat operation. The Task Force *Ranger* raid demonstrated the need to maintain a robust and multifaceted force, conditioned to transition rapidly from peace operations to full combat operations. This lesson played in virtually every subsequent expedition.

Haiti

Operation RESTORE DEMOCRACY in Haiti (1994) was the Army's first post-Cold War experience in regime change operations. However, only in later years would the Army add to its positive legacy as a full-spectrum force. The mere threat of a pending airborne invasion by the 82nd Airborne Division brought about the final collapse of General Raoul Cedras' regime. Soldiers of the 10th Mountain Division on the streets of Port-au-Prince and Cap Haitian maintained stability to facilitate the first democratic elections that country had known for many years. The Army relearned the lesson that the tactical actions of the Army soldier have powerful strategic, diplomatic, and informational effects. This lesson, gathered then, would be applied to great effect in the desert towns and cities of Iraq.

Rwanda

Like Somalia, Rwanda (1994) started as a humanitarian relief operation that had great potential to devolve into another clan warfare experience. The Army and the nation reluctantly approached the crisis in Rwanda with the memories of Mogadishu fresh on the collective consciousness. Lacking a doctrinal base that placed these types of operations within the proper context of the Army's mission, the Somalia experience lingered and had a palpable effect on future operational and strategic decisions.

Once on the scene, the US Army contributed to improving conditions in Rwanda. In doing so, it gathered valuable and long-lasting lessons that, unfortunately, were marginalized or overlooked amid the noise of downsizing and other missions. Perhaps the greatest lesson was that the Army led its deployment not with combat units and equipment (tanks and armored vehicles), but rather with combat support and combat service support personnel and systems. The tip of the spear was not a mechanized infantry company led by a burly male Ranger second lieutenant; it was a water purification platoon led by a female second lieutenant. The Army demonstrated an understanding of warfare in its broadest and most holistic context; that is, sometimes force may be applied to organize a solution rather than to impose one. The Army demonstrated the ability to tailor forces, doctrine, techniques, and lethal force to the environment. This flexibility would be required on the battlefields of Iraq in 2003.

The Balkans

The disintegration of the former Yugoslavian republic led to the Army's first long-term involvement in aftermath wars of self-determination, or "ethno-religious-based wars" since before World War I.[16] The extended Balkan experience, from its beginning to its status today, marked the beginning, albeit initially slow, of a fundamental change in the Army's core concept of war. The various experiences in the Balkans were disturbingly reminiscent of the previous contingency operations, yet were laced with new and even more challenging problems.

Bosnia

By 1995, as Army forces crossed the Sava River, the US Army was nearly 300,000 soldiers smaller than it had been coming out of the Gulf War. With less infrastructure and capability, it faced a much more complex environment and a more complicated and unconventional enemy. Moreover, it had several less-than-successful experiences in "other than war" operations under its belt and was not institutionally excited about a similar experience in the Balkans. The unfolding Balkan crises (1990-1995) presented the nation and the Army with a set of complex, multifaceted, and ambiguous security challenges for which there were few political, legal, or doctrinal guideposts.[17] These unknowns fed the Army's expectation of an unpleasant experience in the region. Attempts to minimize the strategic risk by imposing an arbitrary end date exacerbated operational ambiguity.[18] At the same time, the political leadership set conditions for the Army's entry into Bosnia-Herzegovina by garnering international support and securing signatures of the three factions on the Dayton Accords. In this environment of legitimacy—diplomatic, informational, military, and economic—the Army had the relative luxury to experiment with, and evolve, the doctrine and equipment left over from AirLand Battle.

In executing its mission, the Army had the opportunity to wrestle with the challenge of applying overwhelming conventional force as an instrument of peace enforcement and peacekeeping. Soldiers relearned how to wield a broadsword as a rapier, using a series of small strokes and precise blows to defeat an elusive threat indirectly over a longer period of time. Yet, based on the previous half-decade's lessons, the Army also had to maintain the soldier's ability to decisively destroy any threats if the situation changed. In short, the Army learned, reluctantly at times, how to apply an AirLand conventional force across an expanding spectrum of conflict with finesse and patience.

Kosovo

By the 1999 Kosovo crisis and intervention, the US Army was well versed in its role as a combined and joint team 'service of employment'—the headquarters and command and control organization for multiservice and multinational campaigns. The Army served as a supporting effort to the air component's strategic bombing campaign. The air campaign and diplomatic pressure forced the Serbians to withdraw from Kosovo, enabling ground forces to enter unopposed and consolidate the victory. Several key lessons from the Kosovo experience were brought to bear in OIF.

The first lesson was that the air component produced the combat victory, but the Kosovars did not return until the combined ground forces secured the province—achieving the US strategic objective. In every way that mattered, air power won the fighting in Kosovo, while ground units served to consolidate that victory. The services learned important lessons in joint and combined cooperation and coordination that continued effectively during OIF. Other lessons include movement away from prescriptive time-phased force and deployment data

(TPFDD) force-deployment management system toward a more flexible request for forces (RFF) packaging system. The Task Force *Hawk* (an attack helicopter task force from US Army Europe) deployment to Albania in support of operations in Kosovo offered valuable lessons in air-ground integration and capability-based task organizing later applied in Iraq. Task Force *Hawk* failed to produce tangible benefit beyond driving home integration and training issues associated with deploying and employing forces. Kosovo drove home the lessons learned for stability operations and support operations in Somalia, Rwanda, Haiti, and Bosnia.

Fielding *Force XXI*

Against this background of a changing environment and a growing body of lessons gathered, the journey to *Force XXI* approached the final objective. In the summer of 1997, the Army executed a series of exercises designed to certify the 4th ID—the first fully digitized unit in the Army's future digital force. The 4th ID spent most of the summer of 1997 in the field under the leadership of Major General William Wallace, testing the concepts for employment, new organizations, and required technologies. On the basis of those division-level exercises, and supported by the BCTP, the Army determined final adjustments of the division, its equipment, and its organization prior to a final round of certification exercises in the spring and fall of 2001. The Army delivered a certified, fit-to-fight, "digital" division in more than enough time to see combat in Iraq.[19] But then-CSA General Dennis J. Reimer, an interested participant in the exercises in the summer of 1997, fully understood that *Force XXI* was not an end state. As he put it, "The Army is combining industrial age equipment—like M1A1 tanks and AH-64 attack helicopters—with information-age technology to vastly improve our warfighting capability."[20]

Reimer went on to add, "Army XXI is an intermediate step."[21] The Army moved rapidly to reorganize all of its divisions in the *Force XXI* model. Called the Limited Conversion Division (LCD), the new organization was smaller than its predecessors but was structured to take advantage of the increased lethality afforded by digitally linked units. Additionally, the LCDs fielded more capable weapon systems, including the M1A2 and Paladin howitzer. The plan was to field the advanced weapon systems into the LCD structure as funding and development allowed. Yet, even with less-than-optimum digital links, units that deployed for OIF without the full suite of proposed materiel improvements still proved significantly more lethal than their DESERT STORM predecessors.

Institutionalizing the Lessons

In the 1990s, events moved fast—faster than the Army could adjust DOTMLPF. Nonetheless, there were many notable successes. TRADOC developed and matured a process to draw lessons from the field and apply them to DOTMLPF:

- The Center for Army Lessons Learned (CALL) served as the primary tool for taking these lessons back to the institutional Army for analysis and incorporation into the training base.
- The COE, the notional training environment, replicated the potential threats an Army unit might face as well as the overall security environment in which such operations might take place. Unlike the rigid and template-driven Soviet doctrine-based Cold War-era OPFOR, the COE is dynamic and represents a realistic amalgamation of the various threats and conditions in the world. The work to conceptualize the COE forced

commanders to consider the battlespace across the spectrum of conflict in ways rarely considered over the previous 50 years. The Army's adoption of the COE is remarkable because it is largely the result of an acceptance of the idea that the Army had to change *how it viewed* the operational environment following the Cold War. The COE is an estimate of the possibilities and an accounting for known variables that forces intellectual and physical agility.

- The Combat Training Centers (NTC, JRTC, CMTC, and BCTP) adjusted their representations of the battlefield to reflect experiences learned on the fields of Somalia, Haiti, Rwanda, and the Balkans. For a variety of reasons, JRTC was the most successful in replicating the environment experienced in Iraq, although the other centers were not far behind. Both JRTC and CMTC mobilized resources to train for environments other than the Soviet Central Front model earlier than the NTC and BCTP. At the outset, the JRTC training featured contingencies that in the 1980s were less dangerous than the Cold War's worst case, but in some ways more complex. In the early 1990s the CMTC embarked on changes to accommodate possible missions in the Balkans. BCTP made similar adjustments, including civilians on the battlefield, more complex scenarios, and greater emphasis on SOF within the limitations of the simulations used. The NTC also responded to changes in the environment but retained a requirement to train for major regional contingencies, so change there was more incremental than at the other centers. By the late 1990s the NTC attempted to account for changes in the operational environment. These centers reinforced the lessons gathered in the field, turning many of them into valid lessons learned.

- Deployment Readiness Exercises (DREs) served to reinforce these lessons learned just before the forces deployed to the operations. One of the benefits of the high deployment operations tempo was that a vast percentage of soldiers rotated through the DREs and the subsequent contingency operations, leading to a wide distribution of these lessons and skills.

Thus, the Army suffered a swirling mix of initiatives, lessons, bureaucratic dynamics, policy and fiscal challenges, and a myriad of realized and unrealized opportunities as it approached the end of the 1990s. However, many of the conditions for a dramatic leap forward in capabilities were resident in this chaotic and frequently quixotic environment. But before discussing how these vectors coalesced to produce a successful and dominant force, it is necessary to describe the changes going on in the joint community and within the sister services. Indeed, these initiatives, coupled with the experiences of the 1990s, set the necessary conditions for much of the Army's evolution. Just as the Army absolutely depends upon the joint team to get to, and execute, the fight, the joint team depends on the Army to consolidate tactical gains—to link tactical engagements with the nation's strategic objectives. With this concept firmly implanted, changes in the joint community gave context, weight, validity, and a sense of urgency to the Army's introspection.

Evolution of the Joint Community–The Army in a New DOD Context

The Army's institutional and organizational response to the challenges of the 1990s did not occur in a vacuum. The sister services, joint community, and the entire Department of Defense were equally aggressive in changing to meet the new security environment. Their changes fundamentally altered the Army's operating environment and had far-reaching consequences in how, when, and where the Army would operate.

Joint and Service Vision and Doctrine

At the joint level, the regional combatant commands (RCCs) (formerly the unified commands) matured into true joint force headquarters for their areas of responsibility. DESERT SHIELD/STORM marked the first multicorps, truly joint operation since the Goldwater-Nichols Act of 1986. CENTCOM established the initial standard for what joint operations could and should be. In the following years, all of the RCCs matured and gained experience in organizing and commanding joint operations. Concurrently, the service components gained experience in integrating into the RCCs' operations plans (OPLANs) to better field a joint force.

Training Together

The chairman of the Joint Chiefs of Staff from 1989 to 1993, General Colin L. Powell, among others, knew the key to meeting challenges of the future depended on refining how US services work together in joint operations. He believed that a single, US-based unified command should be responsible for training forces from all services for joint operations. This unified command would supply ready joint forces to other unified commanders anywhere in the world. In 1993, US Atlantic Command fulfilled Powell's vision and became the first unified command to serve as a US-based force trainer, integrator, and provider. Under the 1993 Unified Command Plan, Atlantic Command assumed combatant command of the Army's FORSCOM, the Air Force's Air Combat Command (ACC), the Marine Corps' Forces Command Atlantic, and the Navy's Atlantic Fleet.

In October 1999, Atlantic Command changed to JFCOM to emphasize the command's role in leading transformation of US military forces. JFCOM gained a functional mandate to lead transformation of US military joint warfighting into the 21st century. The designation reflected the command's commitment to experimentation with new warfighting concepts, doctrine, and technologies. Thus, the joint community had a powerful and effective headquarters designed to integrate and harmonize the respective services' capabilities to achieve a truly joint force. OIF reflected the flexibility and capabilities inherent in such a force.

While the joint community moved to establish the necessary infrastructure to transform all of the armed forces, each service went through a similar renaissance in adjusting to the new environment. To meet the challenges of global engagements from peacekeeping to major combat operations, the US Air Force transformed itself into Air Expeditionary Forces (AEFs). The AEFs are tailored and configured to respond across the full spectrum of aerospace operations. Airmen from across the Air Force contribute to the expeditionary capability—from those who support the nation's deterrent umbrella, to those who deploy, to those who operate the fixed facilities to which the military reaches back for support. This reorganization gave the Air Force and the nation true highly responsive and agile "global reach."

Similarly, the US Navy and Marine Corps refocused to develop and mature their expeditionary capability. *Forward...From the Sea*, first published in 1994, reflected the Navy's shift from solely control of the sea to projecting power ashore. Naval and Marine Corps forces serve as America's constant forward presence, especially in areas where a substantial land or air presence is not possible. Moreover, they frequently serve as "first responders," helping to shape and manage a crisis in support of subsequent sustained operations. Over the decade, the Navy developed the doctrine and capabilities to project combat power deep inland, with the Marine operations more than 200 miles overland into Afghanistan as the seminal example. Coupled with the US Air Force's reach, these capabilities offered the nation the ability to project power virtually anywhere in the world. Moreover, the mix of capabilities ensured that forces could be tailored to meet the specific requirements of a contingency operation.

Service Enabling Investments

Each service made significant capital investments to enable this evolved vision, doctrine, and organization. Most of the investments focused on extending and improving the nation's strategic reach. Remarkably, both the Navy and Air Force made major investments in strategic lift capacity that would directly enable the Army to conduct sustained operations far from the United States. These purchases include the following:

- The US Navy's eight Fast Sealift Ships are the fastest cargo ships in the world. The ships can travel at speeds of up to 33 knots and are capable of sailing from the US East Coast to Europe in just six days, and to the Persian Gulf via the Suez Canal in 18 days, thus ensuring rapid delivery of military equipment in a crisis. Combined, the eight Fast Sealift Ships can carry nearly all the equipment needed to outfit a full Army heavy division.

Figure 3. US Navy fast sealift ship

- Military Sealift Command's newest class of ships—Large, Medium-speed, Roll-on/Roll-off Ships, or LMSR—has vastly expanded the nation's sealift capability in the 21st century. Twenty LMSRs have been converted or built at US shipyards. Each LMSR can carry an entire US Army battalion TF, including 58 tanks, 48 other tracked vehicles, plus more than 900 trucks and other wheeled vehicles. They have a cargo carrying capacity of more than 380,000 square feet, equivalent to almost eight football fields, and can travel at 24 knots.

US Treansporation Command

Figure 4. US Navy LMSR

- The Army's Theater Support Vessel (TSV) provides the operational Army commander lift assets that bypass predictable entry points and obstacles. Its shallow draft capability frees it from reliance on deep-water entry ports. For example, the 530-km Albanian coast has four major seaports, more than 20 naval ports and a few fishing ports. None of these are accessible by the LMSR, but the TSV can discharge troops and equipment at all but the smallest port. In fact, with the appropriate gradient, it will access the many lagoons and beaches along portions of the world's coastlines. One TSV equals 23 C-17 sorties and can travel at an average speed of 40 knots, self-deploy over 4,726 nautical miles, carry 350 fully loaded soldiers, has a helicopter flight deck, and can load/discharge in less than 20 minutes. The TSV's flexibility maximizes access, creates the greatest insertion uncertainty for an enemy, and provides a significant increase in efficient and effective operational reach.

US Treansporation Command

Figure 5. US Army TSV

- The Air Force's C-17 Globemaster III is capable of rapid strategic delivery of troops and all types of cargo to main operating bases or directly to forward bases in the deployment area. The aircraft can also perform tactical airlift and airdrop missions when required. The inherent flexibility and performance of the C-17 improves the ability of the total airlift system to fulfill the worldwide air mobility requirements of the United States. Its payload capacity of 170,900 pounds can carry an M-1A2 main battle tank or up to 102 combat-loaded paratroopers directly into the forward area. The fleet of 134 aircraft, including 14 especially equipped for special operations, provides rapid, agile reach to almost anywhere in the world.

Figure 6. US Air Force C-17 Globemaster

- The present National Military Strategy (NMS) calls for forward presence, but with primary reliance on US-based contingency forces. With 60 percent of the Army divisional force stationed in the Continental United States (CONUS), the Army Pre-positioned Stocks (APS) represent a significant investment to enable the rapid employment of a credible ground force on short notice. The APS fleet consists of seven pre-positioned brigade sets (two in Central Europe, one in Italy, one in Korea, two in Southwest Asia, and one afloat). These stocks shorten the employment timeline and offer a credible power-projection capability.

- Similar to the APS, the Marine Corps' 16 ships of the Maritime Pre-positioning Force (MPF), forming three squadrons (Mediterranean Sea, Indian Ocean, and the Pacific Ocean), bolster the USMC's force-projection capacity. Each Maritime Pre-positioning Squadron (MPS) carries sufficient equipment and supplies to sustain 17,000 Marine Corps Air Ground Task Force personnel for up to 30 days. Each ship can discharge cargo either pier-side or while anchored offshore using lighterage carried aboard. This capability gives the Marine Corps the ability to operate in both developed and underdeveloped areas of the world.

Thus, the mid to late 1990s marked a significant investment, both intellectually and fiscally, in creating a more agile, responsive, and capable joint force, able to project overwhelming combat power anywhere in the world. However, by their very nature, the Army's sister services were able to reorganize to meet these requirements without a significant reinvestment in their core combat capabilities and systems. The very nature of air and naval combat power lends itself relatively easily to global mobility and strategic reach. Unfortunately, the "big five" Army

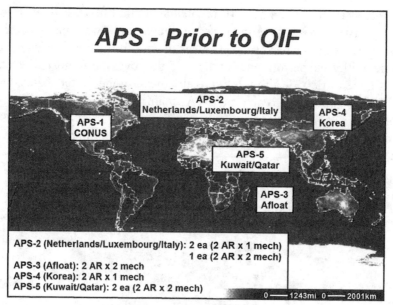

Figure 7. Army pre-positioned stocks

did not enjoy this luxury. Instead, it had to deliberately address the evolution of its fundamental combat systems. It is within this environment that the Army's efforts to change and evolve crystallized, bringing to a close the second period of the interwar era.

The Army's Transformation

> *If you don't like change, you're going to like irrelevance even less.*

> General Eric Shinseki,
> Chief of Staff of the Army[22]

Upon assuming the duties of Army chief of staff in June 1999, General Eric K. Shinseki quickly assessed that, despite all of the doctrinal evolution of the 1990s, the Army's core capabilities remained rooted in the "big five" systems. As such, regardless of the amount of work on the margins, the force would be unable to deploy in a manner that was both timely and relevant to the strategic environment. Task Force *Hawk*'s challenges in deploying to Kosovo later in 1999 reinforced this perception. It appeared that the sister services were capable of operating effectively in the new environment, while the Army would be relegated to "cleanup operations." All of these factors, and more, added a sense of urgency to the Army's transformation.

What followed was a sweeping vision and initiative to accelerate the transformation process begun with *Force XXI*. The goal was to develop a more capable and employable Army while retaining the ability to fight and win the nation's ground wars. Shinseki drove the institutional Army at an almost frenetic pace to ensure the force evolved rapidly yet logically. He approached the challenge on several fronts, marking the beginning of the final period in the Army's interwar era.

Doctrinally, the Army published FM 3-0, *Operations*, in summer of 2001. The new manual replaced the venerable but obsolete FM 100-5 series with a holistic vision of how the Army

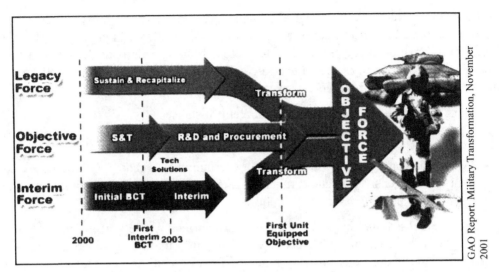

GAO Report. Military Transformation, November 2001

Figure 8. Army path to the future force

and ground operations fit into the nation's strategic application of military power. The doctrine holds warfighting as the Army's primary focus but further recognizes that the ability of Army forces to dominate land warfare also provides the ability to dominate any situation in military operations other than war. The foundation of FM 3-0, the Army's keystone doctrine for full-spectrum operations, is built on global strategic responsiveness for prompt, sustained Army force operations on land as a member of a joint or multinational force.

By establishing a comprehensive structure for offensive, defensive, stability, and support operations, FM 3-0 provides the context for conducting extended ground campaigns rather than mere battles and engagements. Indeed, the core competency to *campaign* is a defining characteristic of the Army and captures the requirement to conduct operations across the spectrum of war, from major combat operations to the peace enforcement and peacekeeping operations that typically follow. Clearly, campaigning is more than just extended combat operations. As the ongoing operations in Iraq illustrate, the Army remains a key component of the nation's ability to influence foreign powers well past the end of conventional combat. In short, Army forces sustain operations to make permanent the otherwise temporary effects of fires alone and must be able to plan and operate across the spectrum to achieve that strategic goal.

Across DOTMLPF, the Army adopted a three-prong approach that was both radical and conservative at the same time. In choosing to retain the "legacy" force as the guarantor of American security during the transformation period, the Army deliberately forfeited a more rapid and sweeping change that additional resources would have provided.[23]

Meanwhile, to ensure a capability to meet the requirements posed by the changing strategic environment, the Army developed the Stryker Brigade Combat Teams (SBCTs). The SBCT is designed to fill the gap between the legacy light and heavy forces—offering more protection and mobility than a light division while being far more deployable than an armor or mechanized infantry division. Of course, the SBCTs enjoy—and suffer from—all of the characteristics of any compromise capability. Their projected employment in Iraq will prove to be the first live test of the concept and weapon system.

Both of these vectors were designed to maintain an adequate capability to meet the nation's needs while the real transformation work was being done. On a highly aggressive timeline, Army transformation involves the directed research and operational design of a force and capability that will result in the future force. The future force marks a fielded force that is fundamentally different from the current capabilities. It will be able to:

- Conduct operational maneuver from strategic distances.
- Conduct forcible entry at multiple points, with the ability to overwhelm enemy anti-access capabilities.
- Operate day or night in close and complex terrain in all weather conditions.
- Win on the offensive, initiate combat on its terms, gain and retain the initiative, and build momentum quickly to win decisively.

The intent is a force that is physically light and deployable but presents overmatching combat power by applying advanced technology, information dominance, and advanced operational concepts to defeat a wide range of forces as an integral part of the joint force fight.

The Army was well on the way to implementing this three-prong strategy when the enemy struck. The terrorist attacks of 11 September 2001 interrupted the Army's deliberate plan for innovation and unavoidably truncated some ongoing organizational learning. However, the attack served to refocus and crystallize the Army's transformation efforts to meet more critical and time-sensitive demands.

11 September 2001

Today, our fellow citizens, our way of life, our very freedom came under attack in a series of deliberate and deadly terrorist acts. The victims were in airplanes, or in their offices; secretaries, businessmen and women, military and federal workers; moms and dads, friends and neighbors. Thousands of lives were suddenly ended by evil, despicable acts of terror.

The pictures of airplanes flying into buildings, fires burning, huge structures collapsing, have filled us with disbelief, terrible sadness, and a quiet, unyielding anger. These acts of mass murder were intended to frighten our nation into chaos and retreat. But they have failed; our country is strong.

A great people has been moved to defend a great nation. Terrorist attacks can shake the foundations of our biggest buildings, but they cannot touch the foundation of America. These acts shattered steel, but they cannot dent the steel of American resolve. . . . America and our friends and allies join with all those who want peace and security in the world, and we stand together to win the war against terrorism.

President George W. Bush
11 September 2001[24]

If there was any question of the commitment of the US Army to being active in 21st-century security affairs, it was answered on 11 September 2001 when four jetliners were transformed into weapons of mass destruction directed against the United States homeland. Though not explicit at that time, the US Army, in fact, already had its marching orders delivered that day.

On 20 September 2001, President George W. Bush addressed a joint session of Congress and a nation in mourning, laying forth a final articulation of what would become the Bush Doctrine:

> Americans are asking: Who attacked our country? The evidence we have gathered all points to a collection of loosely affiliated terrorist organizations known as al Qaeda...Our war on terror begins with al Qaeda, but it does not end there. It will not end until every terrorist group of global reach has been found, stopped and defeated...These terrorists kill not merely to end lives, but to disrupt and end a way of life. With every atrocity, they hope that America grows fearful, retreating from the world and forsaking our friends. They stand against us, because we stand in their way...
>
> Americans are asking: How will we fight and win this war? We will direct every resource at our command—every means of diplomacy, every tool of intelligence, every instrument of law enforcement, every financial influence, and every necessary weapon of war—to the disruption and to the defeat of the global terror network.
>
> This war will not be like the war against Iraq a decade ago, with a decisive liberation of territory and a swift conclusion. It will not look like the air war above Kosovo two years ago, where no ground troops were used and not a single American was lost in combat.
>
> Our response involves far more than instant retaliation and isolated strikes. Americans should not expect one battle, but a lengthy campaign, unlike any other we have ever seen. It may include dramatic strikes, visible on TV, and covert operations, secret even in success. We will starve terrorists of funding, turn them one against another, drive them from place to place, until there is no refuge or no rest. And we will pursue nations that provide aid or safe haven to terrorism. Every nation, in every region, now has a decision to make. Either you are with us, or you are with the terrorists. From this day forward, any nation that continues to harbor or support terrorism will be regarded by the United States as a hostile regime.[25]

The Bush Doctrine, later incorporated in the 2002 National Military Strategy (NMS) (draft), fundamentally changed the way the United States would ensure its national security. The shift from the previous "shape, respond, prepare" posture to the new "assure, dissuade, deter forward, and decisively defeat" had fundamental implications for how the armed forces, and the Army in particular, mans, trains, and equips itself. The new strategy requires a fully expeditionary force capable of rapidly imposing America's will on hostile foreign soil and then maintaining a robust presence to ensure the change is lasting. This implies the inextricable linkage between the postconflict peace and the conduct of the combat operations—the campaign. Again, while all of the service capabilities are necessary to the successful combat, the Army offers the follow-through capability vital to achieving the national strategic objectives.

The themes and implications within the new NMS resonated neatly with the Army's ongoing transformation efforts. And while some have argued that this new threat arose "while America slept," the "sleeper" was arguably already dreaming about a solution. The events of 9/11 did not place the Army on a new pathway toward change, but it did give that trek a tangible focus and sense of urgency. While already walking, the Army began to sprint toward true full-spectrum, 21st-century warfare.

Less than two months following President Bush's 20 September speech, the US Army found itself in the mountains of Afghanistan as part of the joint and interagency team, deposing the Taliban regime that had provided the sanctuary from which al Qaeda launched its attacks. Operation ENDURING FREEDOM (OEF) would become the first operational phase of what the president had confirmed to be a long campaign against global terrorism and the harboring state regimes. Moreover, OEF marked the first commitment of American forces in what would become simultaneous combat operations across multiple theaters of war since World War II.

Operation ENDURING FREEDOM

OEF illustrates the continuity of change within the joint force and the Army, tracing all the way back to the end of ODS, through the evolutions described above. OEF validated many of those underlying concepts and experiences of the transformation. Moreover, it validated the complementary vectors described in the joint community and its maturing doctrine. It clearly demonstrated the overwhelming effectiveness of a truly joint force leveraging all of the unique, complementary capabilities that the services bring to the fight. The initial Army presence, in the form of special operations forces (SOF), entered the fray with a rough vision of conducting an integrated, synchronized fight. All of the services matured in that pattern as the fight progressed. The learning that took place there played directly into how the force fought and won OIF.

As a test bed and demonstration platform for these futuristic visions, Afghanistan was almost as "worst case" as one could imagine. It was an austere theater about as far from the United States as one could get. The enemy was fleeting and unconventional. The terrain was rugged in the extreme. The infrastructure was almost nonexistent. And finally, the surrounding region was unstable and characterized by a variety of competing interests. Within this environment, the US Air Force, Navy, Marine Corps, and SOF learned and demonstrated precisely those characteristics and capabilities that the conventional Army was building toward. They reached deep into formerly denied territory and applied overwhelming combat power in a highly focused manner against a dispersed and challenging enemy. Further, they operated in a unique coalition environment arguably not seen since the days of Lawrence of Arabia.

During OEF's initial decisive combat phase, the Army's participation was generally limited to its contribution to the SOF community. The fight started on 7 October 2001 with an air campaign to secure air supremacy. By 15 October, Army SOF were in theater and established the initial contacts that led to a coalition force of US and UK forces and Afghani rebels. With these conditions set, the joint-coalition fight began in earnest. In a celebrated mixture of the old and new means of warfare—horsebacks and lasers—US forces orchestrated and brought to bear the unique and complementary powers of the services to destroy the Taliban regime.

The first coalition combat action took place on 21 October when Afghani forces under the command of Northern Alliance General Abdul Rashid Dostum seized the village of Bishqab with the assistance of US precision fires supported by SOF terminal guidance. The Marine Corps projected combat power several hundred miles farther than its doctrine posited and coalition aircraft provided highly effective close air support and aerial interdiction in ways previously considered unconventional. In another mix of legacy forces being functionally recapitalized into the 21st century through advanced technology, B-52 strategic bombers served as close air support platforms for the Joint Direct Attack Munitions System (JDAMS).

All of these efforts led to a sweeping and utter defeat of the Taliban forces, marked by Mullah Omar and the senior Taliban leadership fleeing Kandahar on 6 December 2001. However, coalition actions at Tora Bora (1-17 December) demonstrated a key shortfall in relying solely on coalition partners for the credible ground force; it appears that the coalition forces did not aggressively pursue or block the fleeing Taliban forces after the combat began. Failing to capture these senior leaders was a blow to US strategic goals. Nonetheless, these actions opened the path for an extended US effort to reshape the region to be more stable and economically successful.[26]

Conventional Army forces, primarily the light forces from the 10th Mountain Division, 101st Airborne Division, and the 82nd Airborne Division, arrived in sequence after the bulk of the decisive operations were completed. Operation ANACONDA (March 2002), the first major employment of conventional forces against remaining Taliban forces, had the Army employing the joint fires procedures pioneered by the SOF over the previous weeks. These forces defeated the remnants of the Taliban quickly in a series of engagements and separate battles lasting for almost a month.

Despite succeeding in Afghanistan, there remained lessons to learn. Joint fires, despite the successes alluded to above, were by no means uniformly timely and accurate. Ground commanders complained that they did not always get the support they needed on time. Operation ANACONDA also demonstrated a continuing requirement for organic immediate suppressive fires that, despite their best efforts, fighters could not deliver. Seams also developed between SOF and conventional forces in execution. In the months leading up to OIF, the services strove to improve on their record in Afghanistan.

The subsequent transition to stability operations and support operations revealed the Army's forte and unique capabilities. Winning the combat was necessary but not sufficient to meet the nation's strategic goals. Transitioning Afghanistan to a stable and secure state that did not harbor terrorists required a long-term presence by an agile force capable of rapidly moving from stability operations to combat and back again. While not required to participate substantively in the initial combat operations, the conventional Army served—and continues to serve on point as part of the coalition force—conducting sustained operations to secure the hard-won victory and achieve the nation's long-term goals.

In retrospect, OEF illustrates several key vectors that combined to make that campaign unique while having a tremendous influence on OIF. Unlike its experience in Southwest Asia, the United States had not spent a considerable amount of energy, time, and resources toward improving its access and influence in the vicinity of Afghanistan. Indeed, when the airliners destroyed the World Trade Center, the US had an active embargo against Afghanistan's two major neighbors: Iran and Pakistan. Suffice it to say, the conditions were not set to facilitate an "easy" introduction of combat power into that region.

Oddly though, Afghanistan's isolated geography relative to America's previous political interests set the conditions for some very positive operational developments. Arguably, the lack of a robust theater, coupled with the daunting terrain, vast distances, and the unique challenges of the enemy and coalition forces created conditions that forced the separate services and other government agencies to cooperate and integrate in ways never previously thought possible or practicable. With minimal guidance or directives from their bureaucracies, the various forces and agencies in theater synchronized their operations out of necessity and a sense of urgency and outrage. And while the joint targeting effort was not without its shortcomings, the results were stunning and provided the nation's first clear glimpse of the power and capabilities of a truly joint, combined, interagency force.

Conclusion

In years following DESERT STORM, the Army largely transformed itself. This transformation stemmed partly from a succession of senior officers who understood that DESERT STORM and the end of the Cold War produced conditions that required rapid change. That change came sometimes against considerable internal resistance and sometimes as a consequence of failure, as in Somalia and Task Force *Hawk*. But much of that change stemmed from the general flexibility of the Army and the persistence of soldiers such as Generals Dennis Reimer and William Hartzog, who replaced Sullivan and Franks respectively. Change in the other services, the Department of Defense, and the Congress stimulated transformation, or in some cases, enabled the change the Army desired. The Army also responded to and anticipated change that the increasingly dynamic operational environment required. Much remained to be done, as will be seen in succeeding chapters. Nonetheless, the Army that crossed the berm on 21 March 2003 did so with a tradition of nearly 228 years of service to the nation, but it was also an Army a dozen years into a journey of transformation and fully committed to dynamic change to anticipate and prepare for future challenges.

NOTES

1. General Frederick M. Franks, Jr., "TRADOC at 20: Where Tomorrow's Victories Begin," *ARMY*, October 1993, 51.

2. Alvin and Heidi Toffler, *War and Antiwar: Survival at the Dawn of the 21st Century* (Boston: Little, Brown, and Company: 1993), 64-80.

3. General (Retired) Gordon R. Sullivan and Michael V. Harper, *Hope is Not a Method* (New York: Times Business, Random House, 1996), 5.

4. Richard M. Swain, *Lucky War: Third Army in Desert Storm* (Fort Leavenworth, Kansas: CGSC Press, 1997), xv.

5. Gordon R. Sullivan, General, CSA, SUBJECT: "Reshaping Army Doctrine," Memorandum for Lieutenant General Frederick M. Franks, Jr., 29 July 1991.

6. Personal Message for General Galvin, et al. (senior Army commanders), "Louisiana Maneuvers, 1994," DTG 091415MAR92.

7. John L. Romjue, *American Army Doctrine for the Post-Cold War* (Fort Monroe, VA: TRADOC, 1990), 26-27.

8. Ibid., 21-27.

9. US Army Field Manual 100-5, *Operations*, June 1993, vi.

10. Romjue, 113-127.

11. US Army Field Manual 100-5, *Operations*, 6-23; and Romjue, 113-128.

12. TRADOC Pamphlet, *Battle Labs, Maintaining the Edge* (Fort Monroe, Virginia, 1994). On the development of the LAM-TF, see *Hope is not a Method* and General Jack N. Merritt, US Army, Retired, "A Talk With the Chief," *ARMY*, June 1995, 14-24. The major directives to establish these efforts include General Sullivan's letter to General Franks dated 29 July 1991; General Sullivan's letter to the field titled "*Force XXI*," dated 12 March 1994; and General Sullivan's memorandum titled "*Force XXI* Experimental Force Prime Directive," dated 14 February 1995. This last memorandum took the effort from concepts in labs to a fielded force experimentation program that ultimately resulted in fielding and certifying 4th ID as the first "digital" division. *Force XXI* is the carrier that produced the digital battle command systems that are discussed in this study.

13. General Frederick M. Franks, Jr., US Army, Retired, Telephonic interview conducted by Colonel Gregory Fontenot, US Army, Retired, 12 August 2003.

14. The 1993 edition of FM 100-5 did a first-rate job of describing the future strategic environment and the range of operations that the Army would have to conduct. The manual also identified places where the conduct of warfare seemed to be changing and accounted for those changes by advancing concepts such as depth and simultaneous attack. FM 3-0, which succeeded the 1993 edition, built on that work and the discussion that followed. Finally, experience in operations enabled the realization of the vision posited in the 1993 FM 100-5 in FM 3-0, published in 2001.

15. Steven L. Arnold, "Somalia: An Operation Other Than War," *Military Review,* December 1993, <"http://calldbpub.leavenworth.army.mil/cgi-bin/cqcgi@doc_exp_.5555.evn>, accessed 11 February 2003.

16. Allen Buchanan, "Self-Determination, Secession, and the Rule of Law," in Robert McKim and Jeff McMahan, eds., *The Morality of Nationalism* (New York: Oxford University Press, 1997), 301-323.

17. US Army Peacekeeping Institute, Bosnia-Herzegovina After-Action Review Conference Report (Carlisle Barracks, PA: US Army War College).

18. There are a number of good sources for understanding the history of the disintegration of Yugoslavia. Of these, Susan L. Woodward's *Balkan Tragedy* (Washington, D.C.: The Brookings Institution Press, 1995) is perhaps the most comprehensive. See also Lori F. Damrosch, *Enforcing Restraint: Collective Intervention in Internal Conflicts* (New York: Council on Foreign Relations Press, 1993), 22-26; *Peacekeeping and the Challenge of Civil Conflict Resolution*; David A. Charters, ed. (Center for Conflict Studies, University of New Brunswick, 1994); William J. Durch and James A. Schear, "Faultlines: UN Operations in the Former Yugoslavia," in William J. Durch, ed. *UN Peacekeeping, American Policy, and the Uncivil Wars of the 1990s* (New York: St. Martin's Press, 1996), 199-200; Max G. Manwaring, "Peace and Stability Lessons from Bosnia," *PARAMETERS,* Winter 1998.

19. Certification of the 4th ID occurred in two parts. In the spring, Phase 1 put a brigade of the division through a certification exercise at the NTC. The division executed Phase 2 at Fort Hood in October 2001. It was a long road from inception to combat ready. From the time that General Sullivan issued his prime directive in March 1995 until the conclusion of the final certification exercise in October 2001, the division either served as a test bed or was fielding and testing objective equipment for *Force XXI*. It took six long years, but it produced thoroughly tested systems that are fielded widely in the Army.

20. General Dennis J. Reimer, US Army, Retired, and James Jay Carafano, ed., *Soldiers Are Our Credentials* (Washington, DC: Center of Military History, 2000), 161. *Soldiers Are Our Credentials* are General Reimer's edited papers.

21. Ibid.

22. Prepared remarks by the Chief of Staff, US Army, General Eric K. Shinseki, at the Association of the United States Army Seminar on 8 November 2001, Washington, DC.

23. Shortly after General Peter J. Schoomaker followed General Shinseki as the CSA on 1 August 2003, he updated the Transformation concept from the depicted three-prong approach to an "Objective Force" to a continuous evolution from the "current force" to the "future force." The Army's concept paper states: "Transformation occurs within a context of continuous change. We will provide for the accelerated fielding of select future force capabilities to enable the enhancement of the current force. The goal of Army Transformation is to provide relevant and ready current forces and future forces organized, trained, and equipped for joint, interagency, and multinational full spectrum operations. Army transformation occurs within the larger context of continuous change brought about through the interaction of constantly evolving capabilities between current and future forces."

"The current force is the operational Army today. It is organized, trained and equipped to conduct operations as part of the Joint Force. Designed to provide the requisite warfighting capabilities the Joint Force commander needs across the full range of military operations, the current force's ability to conduct major combat operations underscores its credibility and effectiveness for full spectrum operations and fulfills the enduring obligation of Army forces to fight wars and win the peace. The future force is the operational force the Army continuously seeks to become. Informed by national security and Department of Defense guidance, it is the strategically responsive, precision maneuver force, dominant across the full range of military operations envisioned in the future global security environment." From <http://www.army.mil/thewayahead/quality6.html>, accessed 17 December 2003.

24. President George W. Bush, public radio address, 2030, 11 September 2001, Capitol, Washington, DC. Transcript from <http://www.whitehouse.gov/news/releases/2001/09/20010911-16.html>, accessed 15 July 2003.

25. President George W. Bush, Address to Congress, 20 September 2001, Capitol, Washington, DC. Transcript from <http://www.whitehouse.gov/news/releases/2001/09/20010920-8.html>, accessed 15 July 2003.

26. Stephen Biddle, *Afghanistan and the Future of Warfare: Implications for Army and Defense Policy* (Carlisle Barracks, PA: Strategic Studies Institute: November 2002), 8-12.

Chapter 2

Prepare, Mobilize, and Deploy

From today forward the main effort of the US Army
must be to prepare for war with Iraq.

General Eric Shinseki
Chief of Staff of the Army,
9 October 2002[1]

During the 12 years following DESERT STORM, the deliberate preparation for operations against Iraq focused primarily on defensive preparations in the event of a second Iraqi invasion of Kuwait and operation of the northern and southern no-fly zones. The US-led coalition maintained a presence in the region to serve as a deterrent, a "trip wire," and to confirm the continuing US commitment to the Kuwaiti people. The Army maintained near-continuous presence by rotating small, battalion-size forces to Kuwait to conduct combined training with Kuwaiti and other Gulf Cooperation Council armed forces.

Folded into the CENTCOM exercise *INTRINSIC ACTION*, these rotations served several purposes. First, *INTRINSIC ACTION* demonstrated resolve and a continuing commitment to the defense of Kuwait and Saudi Arabia from another attack. Second, the deployed task forces exercised the Army's brigade set of equipment pre-positioned in Camp DOHA, Kuwait. Although deploying units rarely used the entire set, rotational use and maintenance of the equipment ensured it would be fully mission-capable when called upon. The 2nd Brigade Combat Team (BCT) of the 3rd Infantry Division drew and used this equipment to fight its way up the Euphrates valley and into Baghdad. Similarly, constant practice in receiving new units into Kuwait, marrying personnel with pre-positioned vehicles and equipment, staging those units, and then moving them out to desert training areas developed the expertise, standing operating procedures, and organizations necessary to conduct reception, staging, onward movement, and integration (RSOI) of large formations into the theater.[2] Third, these exercises built proficiency in desert warfighting. Ten years of rotations by units from each of the armored and mechanized divisions of the Army into Kuwait, combined with more than 100 rotations to the NTC in the Mojave Desert, built expertise across the Army in desert combat. Finally, *INTRINSIC ACTION*, in conjunction with the ongoing Operations NORTHERN and SOUTHERN WATCH, helped to educate America's soldiers and leaders in the culture, politics, and social aspects of the Arab world.

Building on a dozen years of engagement, much of the success in OIF stems from the planning, preparation, mobilization, and deployment that took place from the fall of 2001 until major combat operations began on 19 March 2003. During that period of intense activity, soldiers and organizations around the Army built on the foundation laid down during the 12 years since DESERT STORM. When President Bush named Iraq as part of the "axis of evil," it rekindled speculation about war with Iraq. Slowly, yet steadily, America moved ever closer to its second war of the millennium. Although coalition forces remained engaged in combat operations in Afghanistan, CENTCOM shifted focus toward a possible offensive campaign to remove Saddam's regime. Although often accused of preparing to refight the last war, soldiers attempt to prepare for the next war. And because all campaigns are joint and interagency, the

Army prepared in conjunction with the Air Force, Navy, and Marine Corps under the command of CENTCOM. Planning included the key agencies of the nation's security team: the State Department, Department of Defense, Central Intelligence Agency, National Security Agency, the National Security Council, and other national agencies. Even without orders or assigned missions, alert leaders started to think through the immense challenges of a campaign in the deserts and river valleys of Iraq.

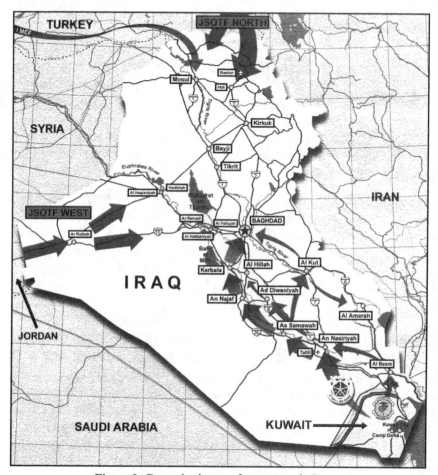

Figure 9. Ground scheme of maneuver in Iraq

As OIF changed from possible to probable, the Army and the rest of the nation's armed forces undertook a number of important tasks designed to prepare for war. From the Army's perspective, these included preparing the theater infrastructure, determining the ground forces command and control architecture, planning the campaign, training the staffs and soldiers, fielding new equipment, providing theaterwide support, mobilizing the US Army Reserve (USAR) and Army National Guard (ARNG) forces, deploying forces into the theater, and moving to the border. Equally important, preparing the theater had joint implications for the Army and the other services meeting their obligations to each other and preparing for their roles in increasingly likely operations in Iraq. Although *On Point* focuses on the Army's effort, the Army did not act alone, but in concert with the other services and in response to CENTCOM. Joint Forces Command, Transportation Command, European Command (EUCOM), and other joint organizations played central roles in training, preparing, and working with other nations' military and civilian authorities to set conditions for the possibility of a campaign in Iraq. This effort continued through execution of combat operations during operations in Afghanistan and elsewhere in CENTCOM's area of responsibility. CENTCOM and its subordinate commands found themselves stretched to assure they accomplished all of their missions.

Prepare—Building the Theater Infrastructure

For most of the 12 years following DESERT STORM, CENTCOM assumed that both Saudi Arabia and Kuwait could be used to mount a campaign against Iraq. More accurately, CENTCOM assumed a defense of Saudi Arabia and Kuwait from Iraqi attack. In conjunction with the *INTRINSIC ACTION* exercises, the Army improved the logistics, training, military support, and command and control infrastructure in Kuwait with this in mind. CENTCOM always made improvements for the next rotation but did so with an eye to a possible rematch with the Iraqi dictator. Training improvements included building the Udairi Range complex, located about an hour's drive from Camp DOHA and set in a wide-open expanse of desert. The Army steadily improved and upgraded the firing range and training resources, and experienced training support personnel created a first-class training facility. All of the services operating in the CENTCOM area of responsibility also sought to improve communications and command and control infrastructure so they could meet wartime requirements. The services also sought to improve facilities to better sustain combat operations. Third Army worked to develop the capability to receive and sustain units in Kuwait and elsewhere in the theater. As a general principle, Third Army focused on joint requirements for support in theater rather than on US Army operations. Prior to the war, for example, Lieutenant General David McKiernan, the Third Army and CFLCC commander, asserted, " There will never be a Third Army fight. We will always be in a combined [and] joint contest."[3]

By the end of the 1990s, planning in CENTCOM included branches to defensive plans that assumed counteroffensive operations. After the attacks on the World Trade Center and the Pentagon, the concept of operations in Kuwait shifted from a presumption of Iraqi invasion of Kuwait or Saudi Arabia to mounting offensive operations from Kuwait. Major General Henry "Hank" Stratman, the deputy commanding general for support of Third Army and CFLCC observed that from 9/11 on, the assumption in Third Army concerning war with Iraq was not whether, but when. According to Stratman, whatever doubts anyone in Third Army might have had evaporated when the president gave his "get ready" remarks. Of the general officers assigned to Third Army when it became CFLCC, Stratman had the longest tenure, having arrived in the summer of 2001. Stratman brought considerable experience to his task. He commanded a battalion in DESERT STORM and served on the Task Force *Eagle* staff in Bosnia during the operations by the Implementation Force (IFOR).[4]

Among the key planning assumptions that Stratman and his staff made, perhaps the most important was that they would not be able to stage in Saudi Arabia. Thus, Third Army had to augment existing Kuwaiti facilities or build what was required. Stratman and his engineers, logisticians, and training support staff developed a set of preparation tasks required to support opening and operating a theater within Kuwait. That meant building or improving everything from "bed-down" sites to training facilities to theater support facilities. Theater support facilities ran the gamut from aerial and sea ports of debarkation to bases for mobilizing theater support command (TSC) units. Stratman remembered well what the euphemism "austere theater" really meant in the northern Saudi desert in 1990 and in Bosnia in 1995. Accordingly, he sought to improve on what he believed would always be a difficult proposition—joint reception, staging, onward movement, and integration—in short, receiving the inbound units and preparing them for combat. Where possible, Stratman and his commander, Lieutenant General Paul T. Mikolashek, took advantage of the growth in forward presence of Army troops from a task force to a brigade combat team. That growth enabled them to build Camps VIRGINIA, PENNSYLVANIA, and NEW YORK, all named for states that suffered attacks on 9/11. Equally important, the growing crisis enabled them to draw and prepare two brigade sets of equipment from the Army pre-positioned stocks to increase combat power on the ground.[5] Other Army organizations also began to lean forward and to build capability on the back of the incremental deployment into the theater.

RSOI Infrastructure Improvements

To support developing and justifying requirements, Stratman brought in Major General Bill Mortensen, commander, 21st Support Command. Together, the two generals and key staff officers made some assumptions about throughput, bed-down, and storage requirements. Virtually all of these requirements support joint logistics. Accordingly, Mortensen and Stratman worked with Major General Dennis Jackson, the CENTCOM J4. Jackson consolidated the various requirements of the functional components and supported validating those requirements for approval by the joint staff and the Department of Defense. The bill was $550 million for preparation that included developing an airfield that could accommodate 250 rotary-wing aircraft, fuel pipelines, improvements at Kuwait Naval Base, housing and warehousing at Arifjan for 15,000 soldiers and various classes of supply to accommodate the TSC. CENTCOM validated virtually all of the preparatory tasks and the Army funded them so that, in the summer of 2002, they could begin in earnest. Although work did begin in the late summer of 2002, the pace quickened following Lieutenant General McKiernan's assumption of command on 7 September 2002. In October, after completing his mission analysis, McKiernan briefed the Army chief of staff on his requirements, already vetted at CENTCOM and approved by the Department of Defense. As a consequence, General Shinseki made Third Army's preparation tasks the number one priority in the Army. General Shinseki's decision was important since Army dollars paid the bills.[6]

In execution, General Stratman found he had to approach the task as though he were a project manager. His team included elements of the Third Army staff and the early-entry command post of the 377th TSC. The US ambassador, the government of Kuwait, and the Kuwaiti armed forces also played essential roles. Stratman believes their enthusiastic and unwavering support, and that of the Kuwait National Oil Company, made a gargantuan task feasible at the least possible cost. To illustrate this point, Third Army made more than 130 requests for support from Kuwait, and not one request was turned down. More important, the Kuwaitis took the initiative to help solve fundamental problems. For example, one key task involved laying a pipeline to move fuel to northern Kuwait. The Kuwait National Oil Company did the work, asking only that Third Army buy the pumps. At the time of this writing, Kuwait continues to provide the fuel at no cost. In Stratman's view, the support from both the American diplomatic team in country and from the Kuwaitis could not have been better.[7]

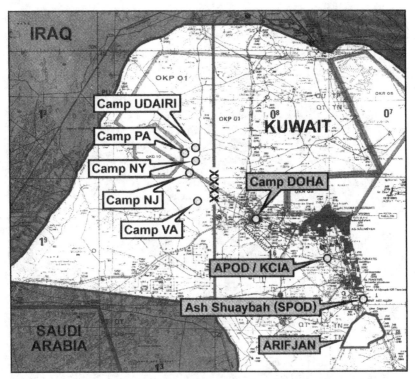

Figure 10. Key coalition camps and locations

Figure 11. Sea port of debarkation bed-down facilities, Kuwait Naval Base, Kuwait

Port Operations and Joint Logistics Over the Shore (JLOTS)

At the receiving end of operations, the Army is the lead service responsible for operating common-user seaports, which is executed under Military Traffic Management Command (MTMC) as the single port manager. The single port manager concept grew out of lessons learned during operations in support of DESERT STORM. Although the Army is the lead service, port operations are a joint operation. During Operation IRAQI FREEDOM, Colonel

Figure 12. Troop housing complex, Arifjan, Kuwait

Figure 13. Supply storage facility, Arifjan, Kuwait

Victoria Leignadier and her troops from the 598th Transportation Terminal Group led operations for the services as the single port manager and ran port operations in Bahrain, Qatar, and Kuwait to support OIF and troops in Afghanistan. The group also operated in Djibouti to support operations in the Horn of Africa. The 598th, in Leignadier's words, provided the "single face of port operations to the warfighter [and] to the port authority."[8] In the three Kuwaiti ports, Leignadier's soldiers collaborated with their counterparts in the Military Sea Lift Command and with a USMC Port Operations Group. The Navy also supplied a coastal warfare unit that provided "waterside" security. Finally, a Coast Guard port security unit patrolled the harbor waters.[9]

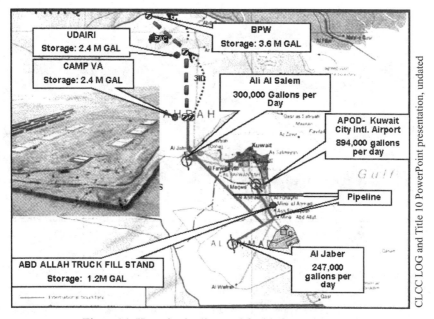

Figure14. Kuwait pipeline and fuel infrastructure

Figure 15. Sea port of debarkation facilities, As Shuaybah, Kuwait

The 143rd Transportation Command, USAR, assumed responsibility subordinated to the 377th TSC (USAR) to work in the port in support of the 598th. The 7th Transportation Group operated the ports for the 143rd. The 7th Group, a unique and valuable resource for the joint team, is normally composed of four battalions—the 6th Transportation Battalion (the only "truck" battalion in the group), and the 10th, 11th, and 24th Transportation Battalions (Terminal). The 24th assumed control of all Army watercraft in the theater. Additionally, the 106th Transportation Battalion (a line haul truck battalion) joined the group in theater.[10]

35

Figure 16. Kuwait Naval Base supporting US Army vessels

The 7th Group operated both in EUCOM and in CENTCOM. The 10th Transportation Battalion originally deployed to Iskendrun, Turkey, but ultimately redeployed to Kuwait. In Kuwait, the 7th Group supported terminal operations in three ports: Shuwaikh for containers, As Shuaybah, the principal port, and Kuwait Naval Base (KNB) for unloading I MEF, ammunition, and JLOTS. The 7th Group tasked the 24th Transportation Battalion with controlling watercraft to support port operations and JLOTS. The 24th had operated periodically at KNB since 1998 and had maintained at least one Logistics Support Vessel (LSV) at KNB since 2000. Accordingly, they were on reasonably familiar turf. The 24th began to ramp up its efforts in the spring of 2002 when 7th Group received an alert to transfer selected watercraft to the theater.[11]

In August 2002, the 24th Transportation Battalion soldiers loaded five Landing Craft Utility (LCU) vessels belonging to the 824th Transportation Company (USAR) onto the semi-submersible vessel *Tern*. They also loaded one large and one small tug assigned to the 10th Battalion and five of their own Landing Craft Mechanized-8 Mike boats. These vessels and associated crews joined the LSV forward. Finally the 24th's 331st Transportation Company (Causeway), the Army's only modular causeway system company, also deployed forward to support offloading equipment over the shore.[12]

To this mix, the Army added the theater support vessel (TSV) *Spearhead*. As noted, the Army acquired the TSV as an offshoot of the Army transformation effort and as a possible solution to Army requirements for lift within a theater. The *Spearhead* and its naval counterpart, the High-Speed Vessel (HSV) X1, *Joint Venture*, which was commanded by a naval officer and manned by a joint Army-Navy crew, provided first-rate high-speed lift for use in theater to make runs within the gulf and, as required, to the Red Sea and back.[13]

During OIF, Army watercraft, the TSV, and Army causeways all contributed to the theater efforts in important, if generally unheralded ways. Army watercraft sailed nearly 57,000 miles supporting ship handling, cargo hauling, passenger ferrying, and combat operations, including seizing the gulf oil platforms. The *Spearhead* sailed 30,000 of those miles, moving what amounted to 1,000 C-130 sorties of cargo. Army units supported 12 separate JLOTS

OCT/NOV 02
• 7th Trans Group uploaded the Heavy Lift Ship TERN
• 5 LCU 2000s, 5 LCM8s, Large Tug, and Small Tug
• Also 8 KALMAR RTCHs and unit equipment loaded as secondary loads
• Sailed to Kuwait and downloaded in late NOV 02 at KNB

OCT-NOV 02

7th Transportation Group

Figure 17. *Tern* delivers Army watercraft

ELCAS (Elevated Causeway) with Barge Ferry alongside for loading operations.

7th Transportation Group

Figure 18. The 331st Transportation Company (Causeway) in operation in Kuwait

operations and enabled the Marines to close at a single port, thus facilitating their consolidation and movement forward. Although the Army provided support, the Marines have world-class capability of their own and discharged the bulk of their equipment without assistance from 7th Group units. Finally, an Army tugboat helped clear the channel for the first humanitarian assistance supplies to be delivered by the UK cargo vessel *Sir Galahad*.[14]

Figure 19. *Joint Venture* and *Spearhead* at Kuwait Naval Base

Figure 20. Sea port of debarkation operations, Kuwait

MTMC terminal units, marines, navy cargo units, and a battalion of 7th Transportation Group offloaded 199 vessels at the sea ports of debarkation (SPODs), handling 880,000 short tons of goods and materiel. The 11th Battalion's assigned Army stevedores offloaded 51 of these vessels. As a general rule, if it came through Kuwait, someone in MTMC or 7th Group handled it or moved it.[15]

None of these US armed forces operations could have been achieved without the support and collaboration of the Kuwait Port Authority. Leignadier, as General Stratman had earlier, found the Kuwaiti authorities to be first-class partners. Similarly, her counterparts in the European ports she operated in strove to help when and where they could. Recognizing the threat to the ports posed by Iraqi missiles, Leignadier was also determined to protect contract stevedores from the threat of chemical weapons. Accordingly, the 598th soldiers equipped the contract stevedore teams with masks and protective garments in the event of a chemical strike.

More important, they trained their stevedores on donning the chemical equipment so that when missile alarms sounded, the stevedores donned their gear and remained at the port, prepared to return to work the moment the "all clear" sounded.[16] The record of the 598th, the troops of all services, and their Kuwait and third country nationals involved in the ports during Operation IRAQI FREEDOM speaks for itself.

Aerial Port Operations

On one side of Kuwait International Airport, life seemed to go on as usual. The exception was the occasional coalition trooper in desert camouflage sipping a cup of Starbucks coffee while sitting next to a Kuwaiti in long flowing gowns reminiscent of Arab herdsmen. But despite this odd and somewhat disorienting picture, the civil side of the airport was calm in contrast to the frenetic pace and apparent chaos on the far side, where the coalition's military airlift and charter airliners were disgorging people and gear at high speed.

Soldiers arriving in Kuwait by air did not pass through the civilian terminal, but rather entered the country through Camp WOLF. The Army built Camp WOLF right outside the airport as a reception, staging, and onward movement facility for soldiers and equipment arriving by air. A sprawling facility, it served as a holding area for troops awaiting transport to marry up with their equipment and their units. It also served as a trans-load point where equipment and supplies were transferred from aircraft pallets to trucks ready to move the equipment forward 24 hours a day. The Army's 3rd Theater Army Movement Control Center provided movement control for all of the services. More than 200,000 soldiers, sailors, airmen, marines, and coast guardsmen came through the aerial port of debarkation (APOD) between 1 January 2003 and the end of major combat operations. Movement troops processed and handed off 85,218 tons of air cargo for transportation. Obviously, the arrival airfield was a joint and combined operation, with all services and coalition forces, including the Kuwaitis, working together. All of the airmen, whether US or otherwise, and soldiers and civilians who operated the arrival airfield did a difficult job superbly.[17]

377th TSC

Figure 21. Aerial port of debarkation operations, Kuwait International Airport

Pre-positioned Equipment

In Europe during the Cold War, the Army had, at one point, two forward-deployed corps available to fight on short notice and supported by an enormous stockpile of gear in the Pre-positioned Equipment Configured in Unit Sets (POMCUS). The plan was that, in the event of war, CONUS units would deploy their soldiers to Europe, marry them up with the POMCUS, and head for the front lines. POMCUS greatly

> ### The Best I Have Ever Seen
>
> We drew tanks in UDAIRI. They were excellent; best I have ever seen! If we had used our tanks from Fort Benning, we would have lost the war.
>
> Staff Sergeant Michael Brouillard
> Alpha Troop, 3-7 Cavalry

reduced the deployment problem since equipment did not have to be moved from CONUS. Since the end of the Cold War, the Army reduced its footprint in Europe and has sought to pre-position equipment where it might be needed. Today, some equipment remains in Europe and is therefore closer to possible theaters than CONUS. Other equipment is pre-positioned at sea, following studies mandated by the Congress. The Army study, called the Army Strategic Mobility Program, focused on the deployment triad of airlift, sealift, and pre-positioned equipment. Among other things this study led to moving some equipment from Europe to other sites, including the Gulf region and its Army pre-positioned stocks (APS) APS-3 (afloat) and APS-5. Each set contained the bulk of gear required to equip a heavy brigade composed of two mechanized infantry battalions, two armor battalions, and supporting units.[18]

Figure 22. Army pre-positioned stocks, Arifjan, Kuwait

CONUS Facility Improvements

In addition to TRANSCOM, EUCOM, and Third Army efforts, the Army had to ensure that its units could use their installations as power-projection platforms. This meant investing in the infrastructure to move rapidly from home stations to sea or air ports. The Army identified and assigned priorities to the sites from which it would deploy or support deployments. Based on this analysis, the Army made improvements to railhead capacity and deployment facilities to ensure it could deliver units to ports of embarkation from which TRANSCOM would take them to the theater of operation. To that end, over the past 12 years, the Army invested $800 million to improve capability at 15 posts, 14 airfields, 17 seaports, and 11 ammunition plants to improve deployment posture. In short, the Army modernized its platforms and altered the focus of its thinking from forward basing to force projection.[19]

European Command

EUCOM also contributed to Operation IRAQI FREEDOM in a number of ways. In the fall of 2002, CENTCOM conceived the "Northern Option," which intended to produce concentric ground attacks on Iraq from all points of the compass. In the Northern Option, the coalition would introduce forces from Turkey. Because Turkey is in EUCOM's area of responsibility, EUCOM assumed responsibility for supporting CENTCOM's effort. Both commands already collaborated effectively to support operations in Afghanistan.

EUCOM assigned the mission of establishing a Joint Rear Area Coordinator to US Army Europe. Ultimately, US Army Europe (USAREUR) and V Corps assigned the mission to Major General John Batiste's 1st Infantry Division (Big Red One). In the end the Joint Rear Area Command mission evolved into a service component requirement. Specifically, the Big Red One provided command and control as Army Forces-Turkey. The division provided the core of this headquarters, two battalion task forces. USAREUR further augmented the 1st ID with units from the 21st TSC, 66th Military Intelligence Group, 18th Engineer Brigade, 7th Signal Brigade, 38th Personnel Support Battalion, and 313th Rear Area Operations Command. Ultimately, some 2,200 troops deployed to Turkey starting in January 2003 to prepare to receive, stage, and support units (primarily the 4th Infantry Division) that CENTCOM planned to employ from Turkey. The troops, in coordination with Turkish authorities, developed a 700-kilometer route, including three convoy support centers, four rest stops, 32 checkpoints, and six traffic control points, in addition to the work done to prepare staging areas near the ports. In the end, this capability was not required and the troops assigned to support the effort began redeployment to Europe in April 2003.[20]

However, EUCOM provided other important support, some of which stemmed from EUCOM engagement in NATO's Partnership for Peace Program and a EUCOM program called "In the Spirit of Partnership for Peace." Both programs originally existed as a means of engaging former members of the Warsaw Pact as it began to collapse following the disintegration of the Soviet Union. Over time these programs produced benefits as nations sought to join NATO. Basing rights, overflight, and other means of cooperation are in part benefits of more than a decade of NATO and EUCOM efforts in the newly democratic states of central Europe. Access to infrastructure and support in building communications links that CENTCOM needed could be found in countries eager to help as part of the continued effort to join NATO or to demonstrate support based on relations generated, at least in part, as a result of military-to-military engagement through Partnership for Peace or EUCOM's "Spirit" program. Lieutenant General Dan Petrosky, who served as chief of staff at EUCOM from 2000-2002, summed it up this way, "What (engagement efforts) did [is] set the stage for our war on terrorism and how we could support it."[21] Refueling rights in central Europe were among the benefits Petrosky believed stemmed from these efforts.[22]

EUCOM supported CENTCOM in other ways, including contracting support along the main air and sea deployment routes, developing communications infrastructure along the air and sea routes for example. Despite political differences of opinion, EUCOM had help from allies in the region in providing security in the Mediterranean. EUCOM's service components supported the operation from sites as diverse as Ramstein Air Base and Rhein Ordnance Barracks in Germany to bases in Spain and in the Azores.[23]

Prepare—Building the Command and Control Relationships

In any campaign, the design of the command and control architecture is extremely important. For large-scale ground combat operations, such design is critical. In DESERT STORM, the CENTCOM commander, General Norman Schwarzkopf, elected to command the ground operations himself, without a land component commander to integrate ground operations. In contrast, for IRAQI FREEDOM, General Tommy Franks decided to establish a Combined Forces Land Component Command (CFLCC) to command and control the operations of all Army, Marine, and coalition ground forces. Although General Anthony Zinni, who preceded General Franks at CENTCOM, had declared Third Army the joint land component command, Third Army had never been assigned the people required to enable it to function in that role.[24] On 20 November 2001, Franks designated Third US Army, based at Fort McPherson, Georgia, as the CFLCC.[25] Franks' order provided Third Army the basis to organize and man the headquarters as a joint forces land component command. During the previous winter and spring, Third Army had served as the CFLCC for OEF in Afghanistan and throughout the region. Much of the Third Army Headquarters (HQ) deployed to its forward command post at Camp DOHA, Kuwait, but by late spring 2002 had redeployed to Fort McPherson.

Filling the CFLCC's Empty Chairs

Commanded by General George Patton during WW II, Third Army has a proud history and tradition and had focused on the CENTCOM area since the late 1980s. But it was manned in peacetime at about half strength. As the potential for war grew in the fall of 2002, the Army began filling the Third Army HQ to full strength. Lieutenant General David McKiernan assumed command in September 2002. McKiernan, commissioned in 1972, had commanded a tank battalion, an armored brigade, and 1st Cavalry Division. He served with VII Corps in DESERT STORM, where he ran the corps tactical command post. As G2/G3 Intelligence and Operations in the Allied Rapid Reaction Corps, McKiernan learned NATO and coalition staff procedures. Finally, he served as the deputy chief of staff for operations (G3) for the Army prior to arriving at Third Army. McKiernan's experience and understanding of both coalition and joint warfare ideally suited him to the task of commanding CFLCC.

Shortly after McKiernan assumed command, he decided he needed to ramp up the experience level of his primary staff. Accordingly, he asked for a number of officers by name. With General Shinseki's support, McKiernan handpicked several generals and placed them in the key staff positions in Third Army, including Major General James "Spider" Marks as the CFLCC intelligence officer (C2), Major General James "JD" Thurman as the CFLCC operations officer (C3), and Major General Claude V. "Chris" Christiansen as the CFLCC logistics officer (C4). Colonel Kevin Benson, recently assigned to CFLCC as the C5 plans officer, remained at his post. Major General Lowell C. Detamore joined as the C6 communications officer. Before McKiernan took command, Shinseki provided a second deputy commanding general to the CFLCC. Major General William "Fuzzy" Webster joined the headquarters as deputy commanding general for operations (DCG-O). Major General Henry "Hank" Stratman, who arrived earlier, served as the deputy commanding general for support (DCG-S). Colonels normally headed the Third Army staff sections, but for OIF McKiernan and Shinseki wanted the most experienced team possible.

Joint and coalition members also joined the team. Major General Robert "Rusty" Blackman, USMC, arrived from CENTCOM to serve as the CFLCC chief of staff in October 2002. Blackman, who commanded the 2nd Marine Division and served as the president of the Marine Corps University, brought a wealth of experience to the team and amply demonstrated his skills as a leader. One Army colonel observed of Blackman, "I would follow him anywhere."[26] Major General Daniel Leaf, USAF, joined the CFLCC to direct the Air Component Coordination Element in February 2003, coming from the Air Staff. Leaf, a command pilot with more than 3,600 flying hours, had multiple combat experiences, including Operations NORTHERN WATCH and SOUTHERN WATCH in Iraq. He was intimately familiar with US Army operations, having been an honor graduate of the Army's Command and General Staff Officer Course and a graduate of the Army's pre-command course. Leaf and his team represented the Combined Forces Air Component Command (CFACC) and supported integrating air and space operations with ground operations. Finally, Brigadier, later Major General, Albert Whitley, British Army, rounded out the CFLCC corps of generals. Whitley replaced Brigadier Adrian Bradshaw as senior adviser to CFLCC for British land forces. McKiernan, who had served with Whitley in the Allied Rapid Reaction Corps, asked Whitley to lead a planning team that focused on operations in the northern part of Iraq.

Moving the Third Army staff toward a genuine joint and coalition headquarters could not be achieved by assigning a handful of generals. When Major General Blackman joined CFLCC in October 2002, he found "four or five" marines on the staff against a joint manning document calling for 90 or so marines. Blackman weighed in with his service to assign marines to CFLCC. In January 2002, Lieutenant General McKiernan also sought to have marines assigned. Although the Marine Corps could not immediately produce 90 marines in the grades required, it did assign more than 70 marines to serve with CFLCC.[27] Transitioning any service headquarters into a truly joint headquarters takes both time and effort to assure the result functions usefully. McKiernan and Blackman turned their attention to that task as well.

Staff Organization

Lieutenant General McKiernan also reorganized his staff. McKiernan wanted to move away from the traditional structure of administrative, intelligence, operations, and logistics and toward the operational functions that CFLCC would perform. In Blackman's view this meant transitioning from a "Napoleonic staff system" to a functional staff system. These functions included operational maneuver, effects, intelligence, protection, and sustainment. This organization required developing staff organizations, coordination boards and cells within the headquarters, new processes, and new digital architectures. For example, Blackman developed an Effects Synchronization Board that, among other things, attempted to examine whether CFLCC efforts achieved their intended outcomes.[28] Major General Marks, the C2, led the reorganization of the intelligence staff to meet the requirements of operational intelligence. At the same time, he built a new operational-level intelligence architecture that linked tactical and strategic intelligence functions while providing interoperability with all the various agencies and capabilities of the intelligence community. In plain English, Marks developed the organization to leverage joint intelligence and to provide intelligence support both to V Corps and to I MEF, which used different tools to move intelligence than did the Army. McKiernan's vision in developing a 21st-century functional staff organization contributed significantly to the successful battle command of complex simultaneous joint operations by CFLCC during the IRAQI FREEDOM campaign.[29]

Prepare—Planning the Campaign

CENTCOM did not plan the campaign in Iraq in isolation. Ongoing operations in Afghanistan, Yemen, and the Horn of Africa all required resources and supervision. To develop a campaign based fundamentally on a concentric attack against the regime, CENTCOM needed to work with EUCOM, whose regional area responsibility included northern Iraq and much of the Middle East as well as friendly nations in the region. CENTCOM also needed support and services from TRANSCOM and United States Space Command (SPACECOM). CENTCOM's task required more than a little finesse.

Figure 23. CFLCC to V Corps training and preparation schedule—
linkages between plan evolution and deliberate training events

As the winter of 2001 gave way to the spring of 2002, planners at CENTCOM and the supporting functional component headquarters including CFLCC, continued the dynamic process of planning contingencies in the region, now focusing on operations ranging from the isolation of the regime to the toppling of Saddam. Colonel Mike Fitzgerald and Colonel Kevin Benson led the plans cells at CENTCOM and CFLCC, respectively. Colonel Fitzgerald, an artilleryman, had been at CENTCOM headquarters since before 9/11. As chief of the CENTCOM Long-Range Planning Element, he had been the chief architect of the Operation ENDURING FREEDOM campaign in Afghanistan. A proven planner, Fitzgerald had a keen understanding of the strategic context in which the campaign would unfold. Benson, a cavalryman who had just finished a fellowship at the Massachusetts Institute of Technology, served as chief of plans at CFLCC. Benson had served at Third Army before and knew the CENTCOM region, Kuwait, and Iraq very well.[30]

Together, and in cooperation with planners of the other service components and special operations forces (SOF), Fitzgerald, Benson, and their two planning staffs laid out the broad outline of what would eventually become the campaign known as Operation IRAQI FREEDOM. However, the planning was not a top-down effort. In the information-age era that enables distributed, parallel planning, V Corps, I MEF, and subordinate divisions were near-equal architects for the final plan. V Corps and I MEF developed base plans and fed them up the chain. These plans, VIGILANT GUARDIAN and CONPLAN WOOD, were designed to thwart any Iraqi offensive action toward Kuwait or the Shiite population of southern Iraq. The planning process, led by Lieutenant Colonel James Danna, then chief of plans for V Corps, and his lead OIF planner, Major Kevin Marcus, paralleled both the I MEF and Third Army from the beginning. Among the key considerations later affecting the execution was how many units would deploy before combat operations began and how many axes of advance ground forces would use.

> ## Ripple Effects
>
> With the release of a draft prepare to deploy order (PTDO) in April 2002, there was an immediate ripple effect throughout the Army.[31] In addition to giving V Corps responsibility for lead planning instead of the XVIII Airborne Corps, the divisions considered how to refocus their training and maintenance posture to be ready for the possible deployment.
>
> The 101st Airborne Division, for example, was in the middle of planning an expected relief in place of its brigade in Afghanistan, along with a possible relief of the 10th Mountain Division's headquarters. However, as a unit specified on the draft PTDO, then-commanding general Major General Cody directed his staff to develop and resource 30-, 60-, and 90-day training and maintenance plans, as well as refocus from other contingency planning operations. The division staff had to balance the new requirements with what was already on its plate.
>
> Major William Abb,
> Chief of Plans, 101st Airborne Division

Planning Considerations

The planners considered several major factors to determine how many forces would deploy before the offensive began. Part of the consideration was the tension between the historic American penchant for large-scale, deliberate deployments of overwhelming force and the more efficient approach of "just-in-time" operations. Logistic requirements for large Army and Marine Corps formations and relatively limited strategic lift argued for a deliberate deployment, while strategic surprise argued for a no-notice deployment. From that tension flowed three options: a deployment scheme similar to DESERT STORM; an almost no-notice deployment in which the war would start with very few forces on the ground in Kuwait; and a hybrid that combined elements of both approaches.

The planners, in fact, developed a course of action for each of these three approaches. The DESERT STORM-like "generated start" plan required a lengthy deployment but carried a heavy price in both time and resources. By the fall of 2002, US diplomatic efforts in the United Nations demonstrated to the world that an American-led campaign to remove Saddam from power was becoming not just possible, but probable. Diplomacy in this case forfeited strategic surprise but allowed a gradual buildup of combat forces in the Persian Gulf region that exerted pressure on the Iraqi regime and its military forces. While the possibility of strategic surprise evaporated, opportunities for operational and tactical surprise remained.

Although no one in the command thought the regime would immediately collapse under the pressure of simultaneous attacks along multiple lines of operation, CENTCOM did attempt to create the conditions that might produce a sudden collapse. Planners thought it possible that the combination of effects from Tomahawk missiles, air attacks, ground attacks, and robust information operations would either render the regime irrelevant or cause it to collapse very early in the fight—in effect, like a balloon pops when poked. There were three iterations of planning based on differing sets of conditions. Each included the idea of simultaneous attack from the air and on the ground, with the number of units available as the key variable. Planners labeled the first option "generated start," which assumed a buildup of forces until all the forces required had arrived in theater. Since no one could be sure whether or when they would be told to go to war, planners developed a "running start" option, which assumed launching combat operations with minimum forces and continuing to deploy forces and employ them as they arrived. The final option stemmed from wargaming the running start. The hybrid plan reflected an assessment that the minimum force required reached a higher number of troops than envisioned in the running start option. In the end the plan reflected a compromise solution between the hybrid and running start options that provided more forces than planned in the running start, but fewer than estimated as required for the hybrid plan. Although most of those officers developing the plan would have preferred the simultaneous attacks afforded by the "hybrid" plan, they perceived the possibility of achieving operational surprise by way of the "running start." Further, operational surprise could offset the risks inherent in sequencing forces into the fight.[32]

The number of forces required to conduct the operation was the single most important variable around which all of the variants revolved. The end was never in question—remove the regime; but the specific method, or way, required to achieve this strategic goal was the subject of contentious debate. Without agreement on the way—simultaneous or sequential—there rarely was agreement on the amount of force or means required. Yet, correctly balancing mass, surprise, and sustained operations kept the two (way and means) entirely interrelated. The amount of available force affected the proposed course of action, which invited reevaluations of force requirements. This friction is not uncommon and can be found in virtually every modern US campaign. In the end, CENTCOM and CFLCC successfully concluded major combat operations with the forces allocated.[33]

General Scheme of Maneuver

Both General Tommy Franks at CENTCOM and Lieutenant General Dave McKiernan at CFLCC wanted to avoid making the main effort along the direct approach between the Tigris and Euphrates rivers. This approach is not only the obvious and most heavily defended approach; historically, armies using this direction of attack had been defeated. Also, the planners had concerns about Saddam's ability to flood the valleys, limiting coalition mobility. Yet to close on Baghdad from all directions required CENTCOM to commit forces into the Tigris-Euphrates valley to mount an attack along the Tigris to approach Baghdad from the east. Coming up the Euphrates also posed problems. Forces advancing along the southern approach would have to fight through or bypass the heavily populated urban areas along the Iraqi rivers. And finally, entering Iraq only from Kuwait would limit the coalition's ability to generate and sustain combat power through Kuwait's relatively limited ports and airfields. So, planners examined the southwest axis from Jordan and the northern axis from Turkey. Both axes were operationally difficult, but executable. That said, both axes were also subject to the restrictions imposed by the governments of Jordan and Turkey. These countries supported the effort against Saddam Hussein, but both restricted the use of their land and airspace for ground operations into Iraq.[34]

As planning continued through the summer of 2002, the campaign's basic outline took shape. CENTCOM's main effort would be a ground attack out of Kuwait to defeat Iraqi forces, isolate the regime in Baghdad and, if necessary, the Ba'ath Party home city of Tikrit, remove the regime from control of the country, and transition to security operations after major combat operations were complete. The main effort ground attack would be supported by significant air and special forces operations. To some extent the air component had already achieved a key goal for any campaign. Operations NORTHERN WATCH and SOUTHERN WATCH effectively precluded any Iraqi effort to challenge the coalition in the air or even to use helicopters. Again, as in DESERT STORM and in Afghanistan, the coalition owned the airspace. Air support to ground forces and the air campaign in Operation IRAQI FREEDOM are a model of responsiveness and precision, from strikes to air mobility operations. Obviously, the air component had other tasks besides supporting the ground component. The air component developed and ultimately executed an air campaign in support of CENTCOM objectives. Eventually some 1,800 coalition aircraft supported operations in OIF, ranging from B-2 bombers flying from Whiteman Air Force Base in Missouri, to aircraft operating from US Navy aircraft carriers.

The coalition maritime component provided support to the air component and operated to assure the safe transit of vessels en route to the theater. The US Navy fielded five carrier task forces, two amphibious task forces, and a dozen submarines. Britain's Royal Navy provided the next largest contingent based on a task group formed on the aircraft carrier HMS *Ark Royal*. Australia deployed two frigates and other supporting vessels. Naval units from other coalition countries supported operations by executing security operations at maritime choke points on the sea lanes into the theater.

Building on lessons inferred from Kosovo and confirmed in Afghanistan, SOF would mount two major supporting operations. In the north, SOF and conventional and Iraqi Kurdish forces would attempt to fix Iraqi army formations along the Green Line separating the Kurds from the rest of Iraq, attack south to isolate Tikrit, and maintain stability in the Kurdish region. SOF and the CFACC would conduct the other supporting operation in the western region of Iraq to deny the Iraqi forces the ability to engage Jordan, Turkey, or Israel with ballistic missiles. This would be a far more robust and visible "Scud hunt" than the one conducted during DESERT STORM. SOF also would insert "deep" to provide reconnaissance and execute direct action missions as required.

Baghdad—Planning for an Urban Fight

As planning matured, the challenge of urban combat loomed as a major issue. Not only was Saddam's regime centered in Baghdad, a city of approximately 5 million people, there were approximately 40 other cities that held significance for both the Iraqis and the coalition

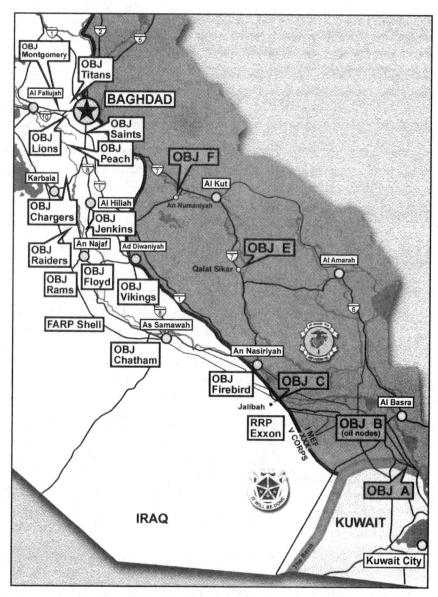

Figure 24. V Corps objectives

in any potential campaign. These cities differ from Western cities in that the buildings are generally less than five stories tall, but like cities everywhere, they "sprawl."

Urban operations are traditionally difficult, deadly, and destructive. House-to-house fighting usually leads to large numbers of friendly, enemy, and civilian casualties, and battles conducted in cities usually result in the destruction of large numbers of buildings and infrastructure. Unwilling to repeat the horrors of Stalingrad, Berlin, Aachen, Hue, and Grozny, the Army began a serious planning effort for combat operations in Baghdad and other critical cities of Iraq. In the years immediately preceding OIF, the Army and Marine Corps had focused on tactical operations in urban environments, but neither had devoted as much effort thinking about large-unit operations in cities. The Russian experience in Grozny sparked a more deliberate consideration of this problem. There, the Russian army experienced relentless attacks from guerilla forces positioned with vertical depth in urban infrastructure that made penetrating the city difficult and deadly. The Russians solved their problem by reducing Grozny to ruins. US planners strove to avoid anything resembling a Grozny-type operation in Baghdad.

Systems-Based Planning

In Atlanta, Colonel Benson led his operational planning team through a multiservice/ multiagency planning effort focused on urban operations. In a parallel effort, Major E.J. Degen, who became the chief of plans at V Corps in July 2002, directed his planning staff to begin examining the cities in the potential V Corps area of operations, focusing on Baghdad.[35] Major Degen assigned Major Lou Rago, newly arrived from the School of Advanced Military Studies (SAMS) at Fort Leavenworth, the mission to lead the detailed planning effort for urban operations in Iraq. Over the next six months, Rago would combine Armywide intelligence, engineering, and planning support with assistance from government and civilian agencies to refine the analysis, planning, and target selection.

Major Rago approached the problem of urban operations from a systems-based analysis of the city and of how Saddam exercised control over the population. Under Rago's direction, a team of soldiers, airmen, and marines attacked the problem of urban operations. Rago's team also included a group of officers from the SAMS. The corps planning team included a robust contingent from I MEF led by Lieutenant Colonel Mike Mahaney and Major Phil Chandler. The Marine planning team also included representatives from the MEF's air wing. Together the planners developed a methodology to identify key nodes in the regime's system of control.[36] The regime used the security forces, secret police, Special Republican Guard (SRG), the media, cultural and religious icons, and even the water, sewage, and power systems to control the population. The regime lavished wealth and quality of life incentives on those

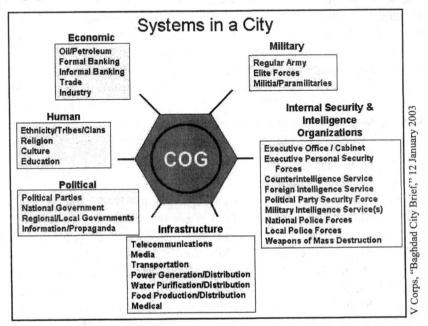

Figure 25. Saddam's systems of control over Baghdad and Iraq

neighborhoods that supported them, while denying the same to those they feared or hated. In cooperation with the Army, Department of Defense, and national intelligence agencies, the planners worked to identify the most lucrative targets. Destroying or seizing the most critical nodes would theoretically chip away at the regime's control.

The corps planners and their hired help from SAMS drew inspiration from several sources. First, all had read and considered the implications of arguments advanced by Dr. Roger Spiller in *Sharp Corners*. Commissioned by the chief of staff of the Army in 1999 to develop a study on urban operations and possible implications for the Army, Spiller published the results of his efforts—*Sharp Corners*, in 2001. In succinct clear language, Spiller did a survey of sieges and assaults on cities from Sargon the Great at Baghdad to the Russians at Grozny. He offered several conceptual solutions that influenced the planners. Spiller argued that cities could be spared if the right targets could be attacked with precision. Colonel James Greer, the director of SAMS, provided the second key influence. Greer published a "white paper" on urban operations drawing on Dr. Russ Glenn's notions on the environment of cities, including physical, cultural, and economic variables. Based on the work of Dr. Tom Czerwinski at the National Defense University, Greer came to see the city as a self-adapting system. Greer argued that cities operated as a system of systems, and as such, they had relationships among the systems that produced vulnerabilities. In advancing this case, he borrowed from Dr. Joe Strange, teacher and military theorist at the Marine Corps University, ideas on the relationships between nodes or points of critical vulnerabilities related to centers of gravity. Since the regime's primary control mechanisms lay in Baghdad, some or all of these could be construed as critical vulnerabilities, which, if exploited, could weaken the regime or even cause its collapse.[37]

By attacking the real and symbolic levers of control with precision, Major Rago's team hoped to avoid a house-to-house fight for the city. Historically, that type of fight carried an overwhelming human, political, and financial cost that would be unacceptable in a campaign of liberation. Aside from the inevitable American casualties, images of Berlin, Hue, and Grozny— wanton physical destruction, rampant human misery, and post-fighting devastation—haunted everyone associated with the planning. The relatively surgical application of force held the promise of avoiding that politically, militarily, socially, and morally unacceptable outcome. Admittedly theoretical and wholly untested, this approach informed the corps' target selection and mission planning. Eventually, V Corps briefed Lieutenant General McKiernan and General Franks on the systems approach to urban warfare. Both generals endorsed the approach and then designated V Corps to lead the effort to plan and execute operations in Baghdad.[38]

In preparing for IRAQI FREEDOM, the Army and the Marine Corps remained conscious of the Army's experiences in Mogadishu and those of the Russians in Grozny. *Black Hawk Down* and Grozny cast a long shadow. Determined to repeat neither experience, the Army, the Marine Corps, and JFCOM accelerated the publishing of essential doctrine for urban operations in the summer of 2002. The Infantry Center at Fort Benning produced the *Combined Arms Operations in Urban Terrain* tactical doctrine manual (FM 3-06.11). The Army's Combined Arms Center at Fort Leavenworth published FM 3-06, *Urban Operations*, and the Marine Corps, under the auspices of JFCOM, produced Joint Publication 3-06, *Urban Operations*. A number of papers and pamphlets published by everyone from the Rand Corporation to the Marine Corps Combat Developments Command added to this body of newly published doctrine.

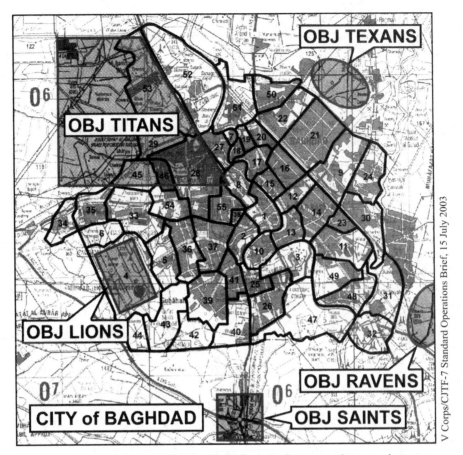

Figure 26. Map of Baghdad with V Corps' urban operations overlay

Obviously the planners did not operate in a vacuum or some monkish retreat cut off from others, or more important, from their commanders. They collaborated with their commanders and with each other not only because it made sense, but also because they belonged to a community. Most of the planners were graduates of the Army's School of Advanced Military Studies or the Air Force or Marine equivalent. Founded in 1983, SAMS graduated its first class in 1984. Later, both the Air Force and Marine Corps established similar programs. Educated in the theory and practice of planning, graduates of these advanced military studies courses are assigned to important assignments specifically as planners. Often these are iterative assignments. Major Degen for example, served as a division planner prior to joining V Corps as the corps chief of plans; similarly, Colonel Benson served as a planner at XVIII Airborne Corps and at Third Army in an earlier tour as well. As an experienced marine planner, Colonel Chris Gunther, the I MEF planner, moved easily in this circle along with his two lead planners, who were graduates of the Marine Corps Advanced Amphibious Warfare School.

The planners knew each other and networked because it makes difficult work less difficult. They also enjoyed their work, so many engaged in theoretical and practical debates on the art and science of war on Internet lists that they managed expressly for that purpose. Their community included some of their superiors at CFLCC as well, including Generals Fuzzy

Webster and Spider Marks. Marine Brigadier General Chris Cowdrey, who joined CFLCC as deputy C3, did a fellowship at SAMS that included one year of study and a second year on the faculty, so he was both a graduate of and teacher in the Army's course. All of this facilitated parallel planning and reduced friction; as the planners came to know each other, they also passed on information, which they called "FLAGINT" or intelligence generated by their "flag or general officers."[39]

The top tier of generals in the land component participated actively in the planning process. They worked closely with each other and with their own planners. McKiernan made a point of assuring that he remained closely tied to Lieutenant General Wallace at V Corps and to Lieutenant General Conway at I MEF. More important, McKiernan understood the operational tasks CFLCC needed to accomplish and kept his staff on track. He coached his planners "not to plan the V Corps fight, not to plan the I MEF fight, but to shape (them)."[40] McKiernan wanted his subordinate commanders to have "freedom of action within their zone," so he focused at the operational-strategic level and worked with his planners and his subordinates in a de facto, "adaptive planning process" that accounted for the dynamic variables in the theater.[41] At V Corps, Wallace engaged frequently and at length with his planners in a comfortable relationship, encouraging debate and issuing guidance as required.[42]

McKiernan had clear ideas on a number of important operational issues. For example, he did not like the notion of sequencing I MEF and V Corps into the fight. An early iteration of the plan called for I MEF to lead the attack with a relatively small force composed of units from 1st Marine Division and a BCT from 3rd ID. Ultimately a CENTCOM wargame confirmed McKiernan's view and the plan changed. McKiernan also wanted one commander in charge at Baghdad. Initially, he determined that Lieutenant General Wallace would command the forces assaulting Baghdad. In the end, however, he divided the responsibility for Baghdad between V Corps and I MEF. Finally, in response to guidance from General Tommy Franks, McKiernan began considering how to open a northern front if 4th ID could not enter through Turkey.[43]

Prepare—Training the Staffs and Soldiers

With the chain of command and general scheme of maneuver emerging, the next step in preparation included training the troops and headquarters. Preparing to operate at a scale and scope not seen since DESERT STORM with units not used to working together, a series of exercises served to advance the planning and develop procedures, teamwork, and familiarity across the divisions, corps, CFLCC, and CENTCOM. CENTCOM began to host a Component Commanders Conference monthly to build the team. The CFLCC commander ensured his major subordinate commanders also attended these events. These events not only enabled CENTCOM to convey guidance and information, they helped build the command team. Lieutenant General Wallace at V Corps began to build his team by hosting a seminar on command and control in August of 2002. The senior mentors of the seminar were General (retired) Fred Franks and his VII Corps operations officer, Brigadier General (retired) Stan Cherrie, both of DESERT STORM fame. The seminar included the commanders from all the subordinate divisions and separate brigades that were matched against any possible war plans for Iraq.

C2 Seminar

Heidelberg, Germany (26-28 Aug 02)

Participants
SROs – GEN (R) Franks & BG (R) Cherrie
Commanders – V Corps, 3ID, 101st, 1AD, 1ID
Staff representatives – V Corps, 3ID, 101st, 1AD, 1ID

Discussion Topics
Deployment
RSOI
Battle Command
Logistics

V Corps Command Brief, 15 July 2003

Figure 27. V Corps command and control seminar, 26-28 August 2002

Training Exercises

In September 2002, V Corps and selected subordinate command posts deployed to Poland and conducted Exercise *VICTORY STRIKE*. This exercise enabled the V Corps staff to practice planning, preparing, and executing corps operations with a focus on the deep fires and maneuver that would be critical to the coming campaign. VICTORY STRIKE enabled the corps to train with airmen in a "live" training environment. Conducting the exercise proved difficult since the V Corps staff was simultaneously planning for the actual IRAQI FREEDOM campaign. V Corps also used this exercise to test its deployment systems, as it deployed a large portion of the corps to Poland and back again. VICTORY STRIKE led the way for a series of exercises through the fall and winter that resulted in completed and rehearsed plans.

CFLCC conducted the next critical exercise, *LUCKY WARRIOR*, in Kuwait. It was McKiernan's first opportunity to plan and conduct operations with his new staff and new general officers and to exercise the new organizations. *LUCKY WARRIOR* also provided the first opportunity for CFLCC's major subordinate elements—V Corps, I MEF, and coalition forces—to practice operations under the CFLCC HQ. Much of the exercise focused on team building and establishing standing operating procedures (SOPs) that would enable the CFLCC to integrate the operations of forces with differing capabilities, doctrine, languages, communication capabilities, and historical modes of operation. The exercise also provided an opportunity to practice a variation of the still-evolving plan, thus contributing to commanders' and staffs' understanding of the challenges and complexity of the environment, terrain, and enemy they would soon confront.

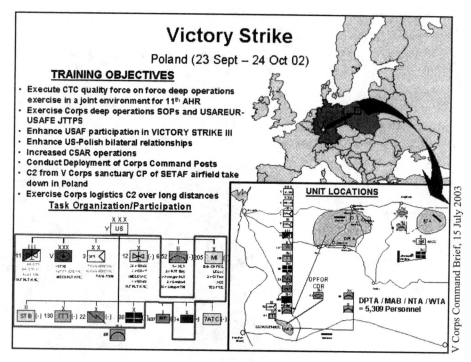

Figure 28. V Corps *VICTORY STRIKE* summary

CENTCOM conducted the next major exercise, its annual *INTERNAL LOOK*, which had a long history for the command. A dozen years earlier, shortly before Saddam invaded Kuwait in 1990, General Schwarzkopf led CENTCOM through an *INTERNAL LOOK* exercise. The 1990 iteration contributed significantly to CENTCOM's rapid and effective response to Saddam's invasion on 2 August 1990. But that *INTERNAL LOOK* occurred without foreknowledge of the impending war. In contrast, CENTCOM executed the 2002 *INTERNAL LOOK* in an atmosphere of growing likelihood of war with Iraq. Accordingly, *INTERNAL LOOK* 2002 focused on joint and coalition operations specifically for the OIF campaign.

As the services turned to the final preparations for the anticipated campaign, *INTERNAL LOOK* provided the venue for the functional components of the command to examine their plans. Air Force, Marine, and Navy air units combined to form the Joint Force Air Component Command (JFACC), while Special Operations Command for CENTCOM (SOCCENT) formally established two Joint Special Operations Task Forces (JSOTF): JSOTF-North and JSOTF-West. McKiernan also won an important point with General Franks on the minimum US force required to execute the running start option. CFLCC would have at least I MEF with part of its air wing, 1st Marine Division with two regimental combat teams, and V Corps with all of 3rd ID, an attack helicopter regiment, and part of the corps artillery.[44] This decision laid the cornerstone for the final version of the war plan for Iraq to evolve. McKiernan decided he would attack into Iraq with V Corps and I MEF simultaneously.

Lieutenant General McKiernan identified the regime's ability to control and direct the country as the principal target. Since most of the regime's control mechanism resided in

Baghdad, he believed Baghdad to be the center of gravity. In consonance with General Franks at CENTCOM, McKiernan envisioned a simultaneous and synchronized ground attack from multiple directions aimed at isolating the regime within Baghdad and ultimately at striking sites in the city. He directed V Corps to attack along the west bank of the Euphrates River as the main effort and the I MEF to make the supporting effort up the Tigris-Euphrates river valley. Because CENTCOM joint special operations task forces in the north and west mounted offensive operations, Saddam had to cope with concentric attacks. McKiernan further specified the method he desired as simultaneous, multidirectional, continuous effects using combined arms maneuver, operational fires, and information operations, synchronized within the context of the CENTCOM plan. The plan dictated that the two corps control liberated portions of Iraq as they progressed toward Baghdad to minimize the damage to infrastructure, ensure security of lines of communication, assist with the exploitation of sensitive sites, and to control the populace. In short both corps would, in McKiernan's words conduct a rolling transition to stability operations and support operations as they advanced on Baghdad.[45]

V Corps conducted the last significant series of exercises at the Grafenwoehr, Germany, training area in late January and early February 2003. The first of these was called *VICTORY SCRIMMAGE*. Like *LUCKY WARRIOR*, *VICTORY SCRIMMAGE*'s primary purpose was team building as it provided Lieutenant General Wallace and his staff the first opportunity to work with the units they would employ in the coming campaign. All of the subordinate divisions and separate brigades were represented for this exercise. Supported by the Army's BCTP, the corps and its units fought a campaign similar to the one that would shortly unfold. The exercise allowed the corps to plan and execute combat operations using a corps battle simulation in computers against the Army's World-Class Opposing Force (an element within BCTP trained to portray various types of enemy forces—in this case the Iraqi armed forces). *VICTORY SCRIMMAGE* accomplished Wallace's training objectives of building a cohesive team, refining SOPs and rehearsing various aspects of the plan.

Parallel to *VICTORY SCRIMMAGE* in nearby Vilseck, Germany, the V Corps Support Command conducted a weeklong rehearsal of the entire range of logistics efforts required by the vast distances, large formations, and major combat operations of the coming campaign. The logistics rehearsal identified a number of challenges that logisticians were able to adapt to during deployment and before the beginning of hostilities. V Corps also sponsored an urban-focused exercise named *GOTHAM VICTORY* immediately following *VICTORY SCRIMMAGE*.[46] Colonel J.D. Johnson, commander of 2nd Brigade, 1st Armored Division, tested the corps' newly developed tactics, techniques, and procedures for urban warfare in an interactive simulation against a "thinking" enemy. The results of this simulations-driven exercise seemed to validate the corps' new concepts for urban warfare and generated tools useful to the commanders who would eventually fight in As Samawah, An Najaf, Karbala, and Baghdad. The results of *GOTHAM VICTORY* were so pertinent to impending operations that Lieutenant General Wallace brought Johnson to Kuwait to brief the urban operations lessons to all key leaders in the corps just prior to the war.

Collective training by units from the smallest sections all the way up to CFLCC continued right up until the attack. Numerous command post exercises were conducted to verify communications and validate plans. V Corps actually conducted a corpswide exercise just days

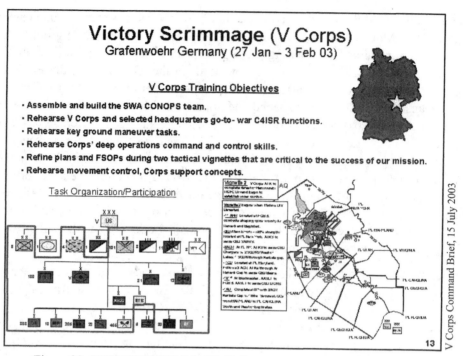

Figure 29. *VICTORY SCRIMMAGE*, V Corps training exercise summary

prior to the actual attack to rehearse movement plans to attack positions and the initial breach plan of the Iraqi border. The corps also validated the initial deep fires plan and logistic support structure during this last exercise. Time was seen as a valuable but perishable resource, therefore it was managed meticulously to ensure units were given ample time to prepare for the fight ahead.

BCTP Training Support

By late summer 2002, CENTCOM and its major subordinate commands were actively planning urban operations for what became OIF. To General Shinseki, the possibility of combat in Iraq required him to get the US Army up to speed on current urban operations doctrine and materiel requirements. Urban operations had not been an area where the Army had focused its energies since the end of the Cold War, but leaders anticipated Iraqi operations would include significant city fighting. Shinseki took several steps, including directing General John Abrams, the TRADOC commander, to form teams to train units on the anticipated troop list for OIF and to determine any materiel requirements for combat in the complex and urban terrain of Iraq.[47]

TRADOC responded by organizing a fifth, temporary, operations group in the BCTP—Operations Group F (OPS F). TRADOC tasked OPS F to conduct seminars in urban operations focused on JP 3-06 and FM 3-06 for division and higher echelons. Simultaneously, Operations Group C (OPS C) developed and executed seminars in military operations in urban terrain (MOUT) at brigade level and below.[48] Additionally, TRADOC planned to support mission rehearsals for V Corps and Third Army and ultimately to deploy BCTP soldiers to augment the V Corps and Third Army staffs. JFCOM also moved to support required training by augmenting OPS F for the V Corps seminar as well as supporting all OPS F seminars with "targeteers" from the JFCOM J7 targeting school at Dam Neck, Virginia. Two British officers (a brigadier and a lieutenant colo-

Figure 30. V Corps urban operations seminar, 4-6 November 2002

nel) also supported development of the seminars, as did Dr. Russell Glenn, an expert in urban operations from the Rand Corporation. Two senior mentors, retired Generals Ed Burba and Jim Lindsay, and retired USMC Lieutenant General Paul "PK" van Riper, who served as a "Red" or enemy subject-matter expert, supported the team in developing and executing the seminars.[49]

OPS F's deputy commander, Lieutenant Colonel Al Watts, came from OPS C and served with OPS F long enough to lay the groundwork for the seminars and to set conditions to execute brigade training with OPS C. OPS F finished with a seminar for 1st Cavalry Division that ended on 17 December 2002. In just over three months, OPS F formed, developed its training products, coordinated training with the planned troop-listed units, and conducted seminars for CFLCC, V Corps, I MEF, and associated divisions in CONUS, Europe, and Kuwait. It is impossible to say with certainty what OPS F achieved for the training units. Major General Blackman, the CFLCC chief of staff, may have said it best when he observed that the "seminar was helpful, but not critical."[50] Clearly units appreciated the opportunity to consider the problem and discuss solutions useful since the demand for OPS F events exceeded the supply. Two units—1st Marine Division and 10th Mountain Division—ran their own training seminars and invited members of OPS F to participate after its dissolution. OPS F also set the stage for brigade level training by OPS C.

OPS C received the mission to prepare training seminars for brigades while in Korea training the forward-deployed maneuver brigades of the 2nd Infantry Division. Preparation for OPS C's work with the brigades included lessons garnered by a small team that visited Israel in November 2002. OPS C built on the work begun by OPS F and eventually conducted tactical-level military operations in urban terrain seminars for every maneuver brigade on the planned troop list. OPS C supported training for units in the United States, Europe, and Kuwait, completing its work in February. BCTP managed this unplanned addition to its training load without canceling other events, including both routine training and special events planned to accommodate anticipated operations.

Unit and Soldier Training

As the soldiers flowed into the theater, they quickly completed the reception and staging process and moved out to the various camps and facilities in the Kuwaiti desert. However, rather than relaxing in the not-yet-too-hot sun, most of the troops embarked on an aggressive individual and collective training program to further hone their combat skills. Although it was far away from their families and the comforts of home, the Kuwaiti desert offered vast training space. Moreover, with the Army gearing up for combat, the usually scarce training resources — ammunition, time, and fuel—were abundant.

Lieutenant Colonel John Charlton assumed command of 1-15 Infantry Battalion in July 2002. His battalion, part of the 3rd Brigade, 3rd Infantry Division, had already completed a six-month rotation in Kuwait, returning to Fort Benning, Georgia, in October 2002. They redeployed to Kuwait in January, and their efforts are representative of the typical training regimen for units in 3rd ID:

> TF 1-15 IN arrived in Kuwait on 9 January 2003 and immediately moved to Camp NEW JERSEY, located deep in the Kuwaiti desert. After the soldiers got their feet under them in the crowded camp, they moved out to a bare spot in the desert, designated Assembly Area MAINE, about 20 km from the border with Iraq. The soldiers spent three austere months in hard training with daily force-on-force exercises, live fires, urban combat training, and operating in a chemically contaminated environment. The task force took advantage of the extensive live-fire ranges at the Udairi Range complex as well as the numerous mock-up villages and trench complexes. Additionally, the soldiers learned how to use the bevy of new equipment that the Army accelerated through the procurement process to bring to the field. While the soldiers and junior leaders trained relentlessly, the staff and senior leaders continued to plan and prepare for the task force's expected missions. As they moved closer to D-day, security relaxed and the soldiers were "read on" to their specific missions. The platoons and companies then went through as many rehearsals as time would allow. The six weeks of training went far to build the critical esprit de corps that the soldiers would rely on in the pending combat.[51]

Prepare—Equipping the Force

In the fall of 2002, the Army senior leadership was convinced that war with Iraq would come early in 2003. General Shinseki used the opportunity provided by the annual 4-Star Army Commanders' Conference to assemble key corps, division, and separate regiment commanders. Shinseki used the conference to determine requirements and assign priorities. The conference also provided Lieutenant General McKiernan the opportunity to describe to his potential subordinates his vision for the campaign that lay ahead. Due to extremely tight security measures during the initial planning, many of these commanders learned for the first time that their units were among those anticipated for use in the mission. The conference also gave these commanders the opportunity to coordinate directly with the senior Army staff to articulate their

U.S. Army

Figure 31. TF 1-30 IN practicing bunker clearing training, Kuwait

requirements. Finally, TRADOC presented the Army's plan for battle command interoperability, urban operations training, and a host of other actions to prepare for the campaign ahead.[52]

One of the key outcomes of this conference was the decision to create from within the Army staff an Army Strategic Planning Board (ASPB). The ASPB formed on 14 September 2001 to help manage the Army's rapid transition to a wartime focus, as well as to sustain the Army's support to homeland defense and the global war on terrorism (GWOT). To support equipping the field Army for the upcoming fight, the ASPB managed priorities, tracked over 485 discrete tasks, and obligated over $3 billion to field urgently needed capabilities and technologies to units deploying or otherwise engaged in the GWOT. The Army staff's work to prepare units and infrastructure proved critical to the future success. The ASPB managed the Army's effort to abridge the ponderous acquisition cycle and bring selected equipment and systems to the field in time for the campaign.[53]

Fielding New Systems

Accelerating fielding required a delicate balancing act between getting the best capabilities into the hands of soldiers against the risks of incomplete training and integration into the receiving unit's SOPs. Under the direction of the Army G3, Lieutenant General Richard Cody, the Army changed the priorities for the fielding of numerous systems to ensure those units designated to participate in OIF got the best equipment available. All avenues were explored by Army staffers to ensure that these new systems and equipment got to the units in time for their employment in war. The new systems achieved varying levels of success in striking this balance. Systems such as the Blue Force Tracking (BFT) and AN/MLQ-40V Voice Collection System (PROPHET) earned rave reviews and worked very well. Others, such as the AN/PRC-150 Harris high-frequency radio or the Counterintelligence and Human Intelligence

Figure 32. Soldiers posing with a D9 armored bulldozer

Management System did not meet operational expectations because they reached units too late for the recipients to learn how to use them effectively.[54]

The D9 armored bulldozer was one of the more visible successes. It represented a concerted effort to bring enhanced capabilities to the Army in anticipation of a specific combat operation—urban warfare. TRADOC moved rapidly to develop the mission needs statement for the D9 armored bulldozer. The D9 is enormous—nearly 20 feet tall with an add-on armor kit that protects the driver's compartment against small-arms fire and rocket propelled grenades (RPGs). Inspired by the utility that the Israelis found in the D9, the Army began to think seriously about acquiring it in the summer of 2002. By October 2002, TRADOC was convinced and actively expedited acquisition. Ultimately, the Army acquired 12 of the behemoth dozers, fielding eight in V Corps and providing four to I MEF.[55] Troops who used the D9 swore by them.

Fielding Information-Age Battle Command and Control

The Army that fought OIF was an information-age army, one determined to leverage the power of information to gain effectiveness. Accordingly, the Army, as an institution and individual units, had invested in, experimented with, and employed a wide array of digital C2 systems since DESERT STORM. These separate initiatives coalesced into the Army Battle Command System (ABCS). ABCS consists of 11 subsystems that enabled digital command, control, and coordination of various battlefield functions ranging from maneuver and fires to intelligence and digital terrain support.

Acquiring such systems is expensive, so the Army had not completed fielding them to the entire force. To bridge the gap, some units bought alternatives to meet their needs. For example, USAREUR units spent the last half of the 1990s in peacekeeping deployments in the Balkans with a significant requirement for digital battle command. But because it was not high on the Army's priority list, USAREUR bought commercial systems as surrogates for the ABCS equipment it had not yet been issued. Additionally, as in home computers, hardware and software upgrades continually outpaced the Army's purchasing ability. For example, as the lead digital division, only the 4th Infantry Division had the latest equipment and software. Because other units had various versions and surrogates, the Army had to move aggressively to bridge the gaps.

To further complicate matters, the Army needed to be interoperable with the other services and coalition partners. Joint battle command at the CENTCOM level would be conducted using the Global Command and Control System (GCCS). As a completely new organization, the CFLCC had to create a C2 architecture where one had never existed. After significant discussion and analysis, CFLCC chose to combine joint systems with the ABCS and commercial systems the Army had been using, most notably Command and Control for Personal Computers (C2PC).

In anticipation of the looming challenge of achieving interoperability with the other services and coalition partners, the TRADOC commander, General John Abrams, brought together three organizations in August 2002. These included the TRADOC Program Integration Office for ABCS (TPIO-ABCS), directed by Colonel John Bartley; the Army's Battle Command Battle Lab (ABC-BL), directed by Colonel Jim Connelly; and a team of representatives from various Army program managers responsible for the development, acquisition, and fielding of the ABCS equipment. Bartley's organization synchronized requirements for the 11 ABCS components and their integration into Army units. Connelly's battle lab developed future battle command systems through experimentation and in coordination with commercial ventures. The program managers did the actual work of acquisition and fielding. Bartley, Connelly, and the various program representatives met at Fort Leavenworth and set about finding a solution for the interoperability challenge.[56]

First, the group identified what hardware and software the other services, coalition partners, and Army units currently used. Then, they looked at courses of action to redistribute systems or field new systems to ensure interoperability. Time was of the essence since there were only a few months to field systems that normally take years to distribute. Whatever they selected, or rather recommended for selection, had to be issued, and then training teams had to train the receiving units. Once they had some answers, Colonels Bartley and Connelly traveled to the Pentagon and briefed the proposed solution to the Army's deputy chief of staff for operations, Lieutenant General Dick Cody, who set the Army in motion to acquire and distribute the needed hardware and software.[57]

The Army solution also provided for joint and coalition interoperability. The Army and Marine Corps already shared the same field artillery battle command system, but IRAQI FREEDOM required interoperability in other key tactical systems. Accordingly, the Army provided the deploying Marine Corps units with BFT and the Air and Missile Defense Warning System (AMDWS)—which provided an integrated picture of enemy aircraft and missiles as well as friendly aircraft. The Army also provided systems to participating British forces. The Kuwaiti Patriot missile force was already interoperable with US Patriots, using the AMDWS linkage already in place.

Figure 33. V Corps assault command post with command vehicles

Tactical Communications and Battle Command on the Move (BCOTM)

Yet for these systems to work, they must be able to talk to each other, whether the units using them are halted or on the move. Communications in combat are notoriously difficult but absolutely necessary to enable commanders not merely to control their units, but to exercise command over them—tell them what must be done and provide them the means to do it. Not surprisingly, armies historically put significant energy into developing systems to support command and control (C2). However, the Army of 2002 remained tied to line-of-sight terrestrial equipment—30-50 km range FM radios or Mobile Subscriber Equipment (MSE). Although the Army and the Department of Defense had been investing in satellite communications for some time, ground forces generally had lower priority than space, air, naval, or strategic forces. The scope and depth of the pending operation would clearly exceed this capability. As a result, following the October 2002 Army Commanders' Conference, the Army moved rapidly to purchase and field special-built BCOTM vehicles and satellite phones, radios, and bandwidth to ensure adequate communication capabilities.

The V Corps' 22nd Signal Brigade, commanded by Colonel Jeff Smith, took on the task of providing the communications for the hundreds of commanders, command posts, and units that would be spread across an area larger than California. Smith, an experienced "signaleer," also enjoyed the benefit of an innovative staff that reflected his own drive for new solutions to tough problems. Together, they planned a series of "bands of communications" that would open as V Corps marched up-country. Command posts moving through the bands and in proximity to signal nodes would be able to use the wideband and multichannel communications Smith's signal troops would make available. In addition, the Army rapidly invested in tactical satellite radios for voice communications by commanders and their staffs. These TACSATs, as they are called, enabled commanders from corps to brigade to communicate across the vast distances over which they would operate.[58]

Blue Force Tracking and the Common Operational Picture

The BFT system is a revolutionary component to the ABCS and the Army's effort to fight as an information-age army. BFT is the software and hardware that enable the Army's *Force XXI* Battle Command Brigade and Below (FBCB2) system to operate via satellite communications rather than ground-based radios. BFT-equipped vehicles carry transponders that transmit the vehicle's location and receive the locations of similarly equipped vehicles, which are then displayed on a small screen in the vehicle. BFT includes limited text messages and, more important, populates the common operational picture shared at all echelons. The common operational picture shows blue icons depicting BFT-equipped units and their location on a digital map. In short, the common operational picture is a map with friendly units displayed in real time. Red icons, representing enemy units, can be added to the system as well, but they are not automatically updated. The BFT-generated common operational picture enables units to "see" friendly units and to "see" the enemy if enemy information is available. BFT also produced an unintended, but happy, surprise; it helped reduce fratricide in this nonlinear fight since objects that could be seen but not identified, could, with high reliability, be discriminated by looking at the screen. In short, a tank equipped with BFT that can be seen at a distance, but not recognized, can be identified as friendly by its icon on any BFT monitor.

BFT provided the common operational picture, augmented communications, and allowed the Army's combat units to fight digitally enabled in OIF. BFT also permitted commanders to generate graphics rapidly that all of their units could see. This helped them to articulate concepts rapidly and clearly. Notwithstanding all of the capability inherent in BFT, there are things BFT did not enable units to do. BFT is a tool, but it does not provide the means to receive detailed images or other products that require large bandwidth. BFT displays relied on a library of preloaded images and maps as a background for the icons. While better than anything the units had before, the images were typically months old. BFT did not support disseminating current intelligence products to tactical units. It is important to recall that not all combat vehicles, or platoons for that matter, were equipped with BFT. Equally important, not all logistics units fielded the logistics equivalent of BFT. While taking a large and effective step toward becoming a fully digital force, the Army had not reached that goal.

Prepare—Additional Considerations

In addition to these specific infrastructure, organizational, planning, and equipping preparations, the Army leadership focused on several other areas in preparation for the campaign. These included providing much of the intratheater logistics support to the entire joint force, as required by law and interservice agreement; building the theater missile defenses; preparing the complex military intelligence architecture; preparing to process the expected enemy prisoners of war; preparing to respond to any oil field disasters, whether accidental or as the result of sabotage; and supporting the integration of Iraqi exiles who would participate in the upcoming campaign.

Theaterwide Support

The Army provided combat, combat support (CS) and combat service support (CSS) to the other components in the theater in accordance with legal requirements or because it was the right thing to do. More than 6,200 soldiers supported special operations, and another 33,220 soldiers executed critical missions throughout Kuwait, Saudi Arabia, Qatar, and elsewhere, in a wide variety of units and organizations. Some of these include the 32nd Army Air and Missile Defense Command, the 244th Theater Aviation Brigade, the 204th Air Traffic Service Group, the 416th Engineer Command, the 52nd Ordnance Group, the 377th TSC, the 335th Theater Signal Command, the 352nd Civil Affairs Command, the 513th Military Intelligence Brigade, the 3rd Medical Command, and the 75th Field Artillery's Sensitive Site Exploitation and WMD Discovery teams.[59]

These soldiers distributed bulk fuel, water, and ammunition and managed mortuary affairs, enemy prisoner of war operations, theater communications, transportation, air and sea port operations, and combat support hospitals. Many soldiers wore "purple" uniforms, working solely in a joint environment, while others remained "Army Green" but nonetheless supported all of the services and theater personnel. For example, in support of I MEF, the 377th TSC transported more than 4,266 containers from 16 January to 19 April, 9,572 short tons of cargo and just under 10 million gallons of bulk fuel from 20 March to 19 April 2003. During the same period, soldiers provided similar support to the Air Force, including handling more than 18 million gallons of fuel.[60]

Support to I MEF

By design, Marine Corps forces are not organized or equipped for sustained land combat, and certainly not for a campaign ashore lasting months in an offensive hundreds of miles into the interior of a country with a poor infrastructure and virtually no coastline. Accordingly, the Army provided significant reinforcement from both active duty and reserve units to round out or—in the case of rocket artillery, Patriots, civil affairs, and psychological operations—provide the I MEF capabilities they required for a sustained campaign.

So as Army forces flowed into the theater, Marines assigned to and supporting I MEF also arrived and prepared. The I MEF, commanding 1st Marine Division (1 MARDIV), 1 Air Wing, the 1st Armoured Division (UK), and other supporting units, made the supporting attack on the right flank of CFLCC's advance to Baghdad. At the time the Marines executed their initial operation to secure the southern oil fields in Iraq on 20 March 2003, the Army had attached more than 2,700 soldiers to I MEF to provide the capabilities not resident in Marine forces, including: a Patriot missile brigade and five Patriot batteries; an engineer group with two engineer battalions and three bridge companies; a military police (MP) battalion; a nuclear, biological and chemical (NBC) defense battalion; an air medical evacuation company; a signal battalion; a civil affairs brigade; a psychological operations (PSYOP) battalion; a corps support group with seven transportation companies; and numerous smaller units.[61] These units contributed to the success of the I MEF in OIF.

Theater Missile Defense Employment

The Army also supported theater air and missile defense (TAMD) as part of a joint theater air and missile defense effort. TAMD had to be provided not only over Army, Air Force, Marine Corps, and coalition forces, but also over the nations of Kuwait, Jordan, Turkey, Qatar, Bahrain, Saudi Arabia, and Israel. The 32nd Air and Missile Defense Command (AAMDC), based in Fort Bliss, Texas, provided the Army component of joint theater air and missile defense.

The 32nd fulfilled several roles. First, it provided the Army Forces (ARFOR) and the CFLCC an organization for theater air and missile defense planning, integration, coordination, and execution. Second, the 32nd deployed liaison officers to the other components to facilitate integration of the Army air defense systems in the theater. In this capacity, the commander of the 32nd served as the Army's theater army air and missile defense coordinator, commanding all Army echelon above corps air defense units, and served as the air component commander's deputy for air defense. Simply stated, the 32nd represented one-stop shopping for access to and execution of Army TAMD. Equally important in fulfilling these roles, the 32nd relieved an air defense brigade commander from wearing all of these hats and commanding a brigade as well.

The Army air defense artillery worked hard to correct technical deficiencies perceived in theater missile defense based largely on Operation DESERT STORM. First praised as the "bullet that could hit a bullet," the Patriot soon came under fire after DESERT STORM. Upon analysis of the results, Patriot had not performed as well in DESERT STORM as the Army first believed. Army air defenders and their colleagues in the other services worked to develop systems that would solve the problems identified during DESERT STORM. Some of the solutions proved to be technical, while others were organizational or doctrinal. Technical solutions included better ways to detect launches and more effective communications to facilitate destroying missiles on the ground or in flight. Organizational changes included weaving together ground, air, naval, and space-based capabilities to provide a seamless capability. The air defense artillery and its joint colleagues capitalized on 12 years' worth of experience in the region, developing tactics, techniques, and procedures to defend against the missile and WMD threats.

In the end, two general threads led to a far better missile defense in OIF. One was technological, including the development of the Patriot Advanced Capabilities Version 3 (PAC 3) air defense missile. When combined with various software and hardware that enabled better linkage with the US Navy's AEGIS Combat System, the theater early warning and command and control improved dramatically. The second thread was the creation of a deliberate theater air/missile defense plan and assigning the 32nd as the force protection headquarters.

The services worked together to improve technical solutions to the problem of air and missile defense as well. The Army, for its part, chose to develop and implement incremental improvements to the Patriot system. Patriot Advanced Capabilities Version 2 (PAC 2) improvements included software upgrades and hardware changes that enabled better acquisition and tracking. After PAC 2, the Army took an even more deliberate approach, developing and testing "configurations" designed to assure an affordable and highly reliable PAC 3 that would account for changing threats and solving system deficiencies discovered in testing or in use. After more than a decade, the result is that air defenders can say with certainty they destroyed nine out of nine missiles engaged. Moreover, the improved missile and command and control structure enabled a truly joint and coalition effort featuring effective early warning from the Aegis Destroyer USS *Higgins* and the integrated Kuwait Patriot batteries. Problems persist, including two fratricides, but the performance of the joint and coalition team remains extraordinary given the inherent difficulty of the problem.

Brigadier General Howard Bromberg, commanding the 32nd, wore four hats and led the organizational solutions to the problem. In addition to commanding the 32nd, he served as the deputy area air defense commander (DAADC) for JFACC, the theater army air and missile defense coordinator (TAAMCOORD), and the CFLCC chief of operational protection. He devoted much of his time to maneuvering the Patriot brigades, battalions, and batteries to generate a "strategic set" that protected the nations of the coalition while enabling a "tactical set" that protected the military forces as they attacked into Iraq. To meet these requirements, the Army deployed the majority of its Patriot systems to the Iraqi theater.

Military Intelligence (MI) Preparation

The Army Military Intelligence Corps reaches from the tactical to the strategic level—literally from mud to space. In the mud, the MI Corps' focal point is a young intelligence analyst working in a battalion S2 section. However, that soldier integrates information drawn from the entire intelligence community through "reach" operations. In reach operations, an intelligence soldier must draw on the intelligence and information available from the entire intelligence community. The organizational and communications architecture to enable this is complex and requires deliberate planning and execution to be effective. Although the Army had started work to build this capability during DESERT STORM, these efforts came to fruition just in time for OIF.

Army intelligence maintained a steady, if small, presence in-theater throughout the previous dozen years in support of the *INTERNAL LOOK* and *INTRINSIC ACTION* exercises. However, by the summer of 2002, the intelligence units supporting Army Central Command (ARCENT) and V Corps started enlarging their presence in the theater. From the national intelligence agencies to the Army's National Ground Intelligence Center (NGIC), to the intelligence professionals within the V Corps, Europe, and the United States, the entire intelligence community focused on the Iraqi conventional military threat. What followed was a steady growth in capabilities and manning until, by January 2003, the Army component of the joint intelligence system was ready to go to war.

National, Joint, and Army Intelligence

The US Army Intelligence and Security Command (INSCOM) is the Army's "echelon above corps" intelligence organization. Historically considered a "strategic intelligence" organization with little direct connection to tactical combat operations, INSCOM, commanded by Major General Keith Alexander, transformed itself into the organization responsible for bringing the national intelligence capabilities to bear on the tactical commander's problems. INSCOM also coordinated linguist support for all military forces in theater, eventually hiring more than 3,500 linguists.[62]

INSCOM "plugs" into the national intelligence organizations through its subordinate brigades. Among its many subordinate units, the 704th Military Intelligence Brigade works with the National Security Agency (NSA); the 902nd Military Intelligence Group works with the nation's counterintelligence organizations; the NGIC is the nation's expert knowledge center for ground combat; and the 66th Military Intelligence Brigade directly supports USAREUR it its operations. In a symbiotic relationship, these INSCOM units support the host organizations in their national missions, while they act as a network for the Army to meet its particular needs. All of these capabilities complement and reinforce the tactical intelligence units organic in the Army's divisions and corps.

Under Alexander's direction, INSCOM moved to integrate and synchronize its vast capabilities to meet the CFLCC and V Corps requirements. The 18 months from 11 September 2001 to 19 March 2003 mark the "operationalization" of INSCOM to support the soldiers in the field.[63] Alexander instituted often twice-daily video teleconferences with the subordinate commanders and eventually included representatives of the CFLCC and V Corps. His main purpose, aside from improving synergy and integration, was to "find out where the data sits [in the national intelligence community] and getting it to V Corps."[64]

Through the various subordinate commands, INSCOM leveraged the information and capabilities of the nation's various intelligence agencies. For example, through the hard work of Army military intelligence experts such as Chief Warrant Officer 5 Walter Price, Lieutenant Colonel Alexander Cochran, and Lieutenant Colonel Ian French, the NSA was a full partner supporting the soldiers in the field. They served as the points of contact to whom intelligence soldiers "reached back."[65]

Moreover, under the close direction of the operations officer, Lieutenant Colonel David Grogan, the NGIC shifted from its historic mission of long-term analysis to developing a highly focused knowledge center concentrated on tracking the Iraqi Republican Guard, conducting detailed hydrology studies in support of the CFLCC, and analyzing urban areas, including Baghdad. NGIC created products that anticipated specific requests from the field and adjusted its hours to assume the theater's battle rhythm. To ensure a responsive relationship, it dispatched liaison officers, including Captain Ruey Newsom to CFLCC and Major Mike Bowling to V Corps. Specialized collaboration software allowed analysts in Kuwait to work with NGIC's analysts in real time. Regular secure video teleconferences augmented the communications and cooperation between NGIC and the theater.[66]

US Army Europe

Within Europe, INSCOM's 66th Military Intelligence Group, commanded by Colonel Gus Greene, Sr., added its capabilities to support the forces deploying from—and through—Europe to Southwest Asia. In addition to the ongoing requirement to support Army operations in the Balkans, the 66th surged to help meet the deploying forces' requirements. As the European theater intelligence support unit, the 66th cooperated with America's European allies to provide force protection and counterterrorism intelligence support to the units moving through Europe.[67]

First and foremost, the 66th, and specifically 2nd MI Battalion under Lieutenant Colonel Hugh Smith, had to plan and provide counterintelligence support to V Corps ' deployment from Germany along ground lines of communication at convoy support centers, and at sea and air ports of debarkation in Germany, Belgium, and Italy. The 66th's counterintelligence troops focused on counterintelligence and force protection requirements. Moreover, the 66th simultaneously supported out-load requirements in the European Central Region while supporting deployable counterintelligence, all-source, and specialized communications capabilities to Joint Task Force *Cobra* in Israel, Joint Task Force *Free Iraqi Forces* in Hungary, Army Forces-Turkey, JSOTF-North, the 10th Special Forces Group, and 173rd Airborne Brigade. The group's military intelligence detachments, located throughout USAREUR, had "pre-established direct coordination and liaison procedures with their supporting area support groups and base support battalion leadership, with the USAREUR leadership, and with their local host nation contacts," contributing to the successful force protection and counterintelligence mission.[68]

In support of the original plan for the 4th Infantry Division to launch from Turkey into northern Iraq, the 66th prepared to provide the necessary intelligence support for northern Iraq. The 66th's Analysis and Control Element (ACE) conducted detailed intelligence studies to meet the expected 4th ID requirements while still maintaining its support to ongoing European missions. Although the 4th ID ultimately entered the theater through Kuwait under CENTCOM's control, the 66th and EUCOM intelligence posture continued to support the JSOTF-North and 173rd operations along the "Green Line," the semi-permanent de facto border between the Kurdish Autonomous Zone in northeastern Iraq and the areas under the Ba'athist regime's control.[69]

Additionally, at the joint level, EUCOM brought its intelligence capabilities to bear. The Joint Analysis Center (JAC), under the direction of Colonel Sharon Mack and coordinated by Major Matthew Glunz, established a 24-hour watch capability to provide intelligence and targeting support to forces in and around Iraq.[70] Further, to ensure the steady flow of requirements and intelligence, the JAC provided liaison officers to the various units operating in the region. These liaison officers were selected based on their experience, education, and ability to provide the most value-added to supported units.[71]

V Corps

V Corps' 205th Military Intelligence Brigade, commanded by Colonel Gary Parrish, aggressively laid the groundwork to provide intelligence to Lieutenant General Wallace and the soldiers of the corps. Normally a three-battalion unit, the 205th grew to seven battalions, including several reserve intelligence units from Utah and California. As the brigade worked to deploy its organic battalions, it integrated these additional units.[72]

In the late summer, the brigade started cycling its long-range surveillance teams into the theater to train and acclimate soldiers to the environment. Normally trained in the western and central European woodlands and fields, the soldiers found that the desert environment posed an entirely different set of challenges. Trained to infiltrate deep into hostile territory and maintain 24-hour coverage of a targeted area without being detected, the soldiers had to adjust to the temperature, terrain, soil, and cultural differences between Europe and Iraq. Five months of cycling units through the theater went far to improve their readiness.[73]

Similarly, the tactical human intelligence collection teams and linguists started rotating into the theater in late fall 2002. Organized into highly flexible four-soldier teams, these intelligence collectors developed the familiarity necessary to support the force protection requirements for the corps. Moreover, they honed language skills and conducted mission-specific training to prepare for the possibility of a campaign in Iraq.[74]

Additionally, the brigade deployed its specialized, advanced imagery systems into the theater. Under the direction of Major Laura Potter, the brigade's imagery systems were integrated into the theater architecture. Under her leadership, the Army's exploitation of theater and national imagery collection proved so exceptional that they were given responsibility for all in-theater imagery production. Collocated with a fighter wing, Potter's team provided targeting folders to pilots before they launched on close air support (CAS) missions.[75] Armed with this intelligence, the pilots consistently reported that they were far more effective than their less-fortunate brethren.[76]

Military Police and Enemy Prisoner of War Planning

Figure 34. 18th MP Brigade headquarters, Baghdad

One of the coalition's fundamental assumptions was that the Iraqi military would not resist. Indeed, most strategic intelligence assessments predicted large-scale surrenders and capitulations on the order of those experienced during DESERT STORM.[77] This assumption was central to the decision to limit the amount of combat power deployed into the theater and played a significant role in the development of the CFLCC's campaign plan. Given the anticipated numbers of enemy prisoners of war (EPWs), CFLCC required a robust military police capability. Moreover, as the combat forces moved north, Lieutenant Generals McKiernan and Wallace appreciated the need for military police to help stabilize the liberated territories. Clearly, military police would be critical in the campaign, both in Phase III and IV.

CFLCC EPW Capture Rate Estimate

Iraqi Unit Operational Ready Rates

Regular Army Infantry Units = 65% Ready Rate
Regular Army Mechanized Units= 75% Ready Rate
Regular Army Armor Units= 80% Ready Rate
Republican Guard Units= 90% Ready Rate
Special Republican Guard Units= 90% Ready Rate

Projected Capture Rates

50% of Regular Army Units
20% of Republican Guard Units
10% of Special Republican Guard Units

Estimates of EPWs by Iraqi Defensive Strategy

Iraqi Units in Positional Defense In Depth
49,000 to 57,000

Iraqi Units in Urban-Centric Defense
31,000 to 35,000

Early Regime Collapse
16,000 to 18,200

CFLCC EPW Methodology Briefing,
CFLCC G2 plans

The 18th MP Brigade, stationed in Mannheim, Germany, began planning for OIF in December 2001.[78] Identifying the specific MP units to deploy and fight proved difficult since the FORSCOM list of available units fluctuated daily based on worldwide MP obligations. The war on terrorism, in particular, absorbed many MP units from both the Active and Reserve Components. Their missions ranged from airport security to force protection at the Pentagon and military installations all over the world to detainee operations in Bagram, Afghanistan, and Guantanamo Bay, Cuba.

Originally, the 18th MP Brigade planned to have two battalion headquarters and 8-10 MP companies available when combat operations commenced.[79] This formation, in addition to the division MP companies, would enable the 18th MP Brigade to execute all of its specified and implied tasks, including EPW operations, high-value asset (HVA) security, area security operations, and main supply route (MSR) regulation and enforcement. To bring combat units into the theater more quickly, CFLCC assumed risk and moved the MP units toward the tail end of the force flow. As additional MP units arrived, they immediately moved north and joined the fight.

As planning progressed and execution neared, it became obvious that there would be significantly fewer MP units in-theater when the war started than originally planned based on the new force packaging decisions. These decisions had the greatest effect on the division provost marshals, who were responsible for coordinating MP support to the divisions with only half of the required police forces. As the provost marshal for the corps' lead division, Lieutenant Colonel John Huey, the 3rd ID provost marshal, developed the EPW handling plan for the offensive. His main concern was that he would not be able to relieve maneuver commanders of EPWs in a timely manner. After analyzing the mission, he concluded that the three general support platoons (each with 21 soldiers) of the division's 3rd MP Company would have to limit their operations to one specified task: EPW operations. He also realized he could not afford to operate in accordance with current doctrine, which calls for holding EPWs for 12-24 hours until the corps MPs moved them to a corps holding area.[80]

To manage the problem, Huey formed Task Force *EPW*. In addition to the division's MP company, the task force received the 546th Area Support Hospital, the 274th Medical Detachment (Field Surgical Team), a tactical human intelligence (HUMINT) team, a mobile interrogation team, a criminal investigation division (CID) division support element, and an adviser from the Staff Judge Advocate.[81] With the 3rd MP Company, the task force had the resources necessary to receive, process, and safeguard prisoners. This proved to be a highly successful, responsive task force that relieved maneuver commanders of the burden of prisoners across the full breadth of the battlefield.

Preparing for the Worst: Task Force *Restore Iraqi Oil (RIO)*

Based on Saddam's performance during DESERT STORM, planners at all echelons from the Department of Defense down to V Corps and the I MEF assumed that the Iraqis would set fire to their oil fields. Destroying the oil production infrastructure would produce both an ecological and economic disaster of huge proportions for the region and the Iraqi people. In anticipation, the Department of Defense assigned the Army responsibility for developing a plan and the means to put out the fires and rebuild the oil infrastructure, even as CENTCOM considered plans to attack rapidly to seize the oil fields if the Iraqis moved to set them ablaze.[82]

The Army assigned the task to the Corps of Engineers, Southwest Division, in Dallas, Texas, commanded by Brigadier General Robert Crear. Crear assembled a joint team of military and civilian personnel, including contractors from Kellogg, Brown, and Root, which had already demonstrated expertise in fighting difficult oil field fires during DESERT STORM. Task Force *RIO*'s missions included: extinguishing any fires; safely shutting down oil facilities to prevent accidents prior to full restart of the Iraqi oil industry (because the Iraq oil reserves are under pressure, an uncontrolled shutdown can be as disastrous as setting fires); conducting environmentally sound reduction of spills; repairing and restoring facilities; and assisting the Iraqis in restarting their oil industry after the war.[83]

In February and March, Task Force *RIO* mobilized and deployed both military and contract personnel focused on the worst-case scenario of hundreds of fires. In the first two weeks of March, four sets of firefighting equipment arrived. In the end, *RIO* did not have to confront hundreds of fires. The Iraqis damaged nine wells, setting seven afire. Two gushed oil onto the ground. By the middle of April, Task Force *RIO* had put out all of the oil field fires in the southern fields. In late April, *RIO* got access to the northern fields, where damage proved insignificant.

The lack of damage stemmed from several factors. First, coalition forces responded rapidly at the first hint of Iraqi sabotage, reaching the southern fields by 23 March. Second, Iraqi oil workers took matters in hand, safely shutting down facilities before departing. For example, at the refinery in Basra, Iraqi oil workers executed safe shutdown and welded doors shut to prevent looting. Finally, coalition engineers executed safe shutdown of several wells and facilities.[84] The combination of combat operations, courageous decisions by Iraqi oil workers, and Task Force *RIO* helped preserve the southern oil fields for the future, democratic Iraq.

Free Iraqi Forces

The Army program to recruit, train, deploy, and employ Iraqi citizens as Free Iraqi Forces (FIF) had operational and tactical implications. This effort actually began with the Iraqi Liberation Act, passed in 1998, which provided for assistance to Iraqi democratic opposition forces.[85]

In June 2002, the Army received the mission to train up to 5,000 FIF for employment during a future campaign to liberate Iraq. The Army assigned the mission to TRADOC, due to its expertise with training initial-entry soldiers for the US Army—that is, changing civilians into soldiers. During the fall of 2002, a TRADOC task force created a program of instruction and prepared to train the incoming FIF recruits. The planners selected Taszar, Hungary, as the site for FIF training. By January 2003, the trainers, primarily USAR civil affairs soldiers, were mobilized and ready.[86]

The task force arrived in Taszar on 25 January and began preparing to train the Iraqis. The first class of 55 Iraqi citizens started their 10-day course on 17 February. While training was ongoing, planners coordinated with CFLCC and Army units in Kuwait to determine where the FIF could best be employed. By 4 March, the initial class of FIF arrived in Kuwait. Meanwhile, a second class of 23 FIF started training back in Hungary.[87]

Upon arrival in Kuwait, FIF were assigned to V Corps, I MEF, and the 352 Civil Affairs Command. During the war, the FIF trained various coalition units on the culture, politics, and environment of Iraq. They conducted negotiations with local civilians and served as interpreters for the same purpose. FIF assisted in searches and performed initial evaluation of captured documents, at times enabling rapid exploitation of information that led to capture of senior Ba'ath Party members. Following major combat operations, the FIF were released, and the task force redeployed to the US. While the total number of FIF was small, their strategic, operational, and tactical impact was significant.[88]

Mobilizing the Reserves

Throughout the winter of 2002 and the spring of 2003, ARNG and USAR units mobilized for OIF. Many of these units were CSS or logistics units, providing the bulk of the soldiers who operated ports, hauled fuel, repaired equipment, and sustained the theater in general. As well, some CS units, including military police battalions, engineer bridge companies, civil affairs detachments, and psychological operations units, mobilized and met vital requirements. For these critical assets, rapid mobilization and deployment was the goal, but not one that the Army always achieved. Generally, the Army met its reserve mobilization timelines.

But whether the planned timelines were adequate depended partly on how quickly the unit was required. In OIF, the timelines and requirements did not always match up. For example, the 299th Engineer Company, a multirole bridge company, received its mobilization order in September 2002. Activated on 1 November 2002, the 299th left Fort Belvoir, Virginia, three days later for Fort Leonard Wood, Missouri. By prewar planning, the engineers should have conducted their mobilization training at Fort Eustis, Virginia, but because there was a bridge available for training in Missouri, the company headed west. Soon, four more bridge companies mobilized and joined the 299th at Fort Leonard Wood. Eventually, the bridge companies were validated as trained and ready for deployment to Kuwait and Iraq. The 299th Engineer Company experience was repeated all across the United States as ARNG and USAR units mobilized.

The 19th Army Special Forces Group was another key Reserve Component unit mobilized due to the heavy SOF requirements after 9/11. The 19th SF Group deployed much of its force to Kuwait in 2002 for Operation DESERT SPRING, along with elements of Special Operations Command and Control Element—Kuwait (SOCCE-Kuwait) and the 3rd ID. During OIF, the 19th SF would operate under the command of JSOTF-West in support of both V Corps and I MEF in the first large-scale use of Reserve Component special forces since the group was formed. The 19th SF's missions included reconnaissance and direct action in support of the Marine Corps' TF *Tarawa* battles in the vicinity of An Nasiriyah.[89]

Individual Reserve mobilization was another critical effort. The Army was authorized to mobilize over 34,000 Reservist soldiers to fill vacant positions. Contacting, recalling, training, and deploying individual Reservists proved to be a management and leadership challenge. After mobilization, each Reserve soldier cycled through one of the Army's CONUS Replacement Centers (CRCs) to receive training and equipment. The CRCs also served government and contract civilians deploying into the theater. The CRCs themselves were run by USAR formations, often mobilized with short notice and still in need of training to perform their mission.

Week after week, hundreds of soldiers and civilians passed through the CRCs at Fort Benning, Georgia, or Fort Bliss, Texas, en route to IRAQI FREEDOM. Operating a CRC was a trying mission, made more difficult since such centers only existed in wartime or during crisis operations. Soldiers and civilians processing through CRCs were often frustrated by their experience. Standing in lines for shots or to draw equipment has never been anything other than frustrating. Staying in old World War II-style billets only added to the soldiers' frustration. At times, after an almost immediate response to their mobilization, the mobilized solders stayed at the CRC for weeks with little to do as they awaited orders assigning them to a specific unit and position. As trying as the CRC system was, in the end it worked effectively.

Deployment to Theater

As summer gave way to the fall of 2002, the center of gravity of Army preparations for IRAQI FREEDOM shifted from CONUS to the theater. In addition to the BCT from 3rd Infantry Division already in Kuwait for Operation DESERT SPRING, a second BCT from 3rd ID deployed from Fort Stewart to Kuwait. Deploying a second BCT increased pressure on Saddam Hussein to comply with UN WMD inspections and to pre-position for potential combat operations. An attack helicopter squadron, 2-6 CAV, deployed from Germany into Kuwait to support the troops in the field. Additional logistics units also deployed. The two major Army headquarters, Third Army and V Corps, deployed their respective forward command posts to Kuwait from Atlanta and Heidelberg, Germany, respectively and joined the 3rd Infantry Division, I MEF-Forward, and the CENTCOM Forward Command Post, already in theater. The V Corps' Rear Command Post and the headquarters of the 377th TSC deployed as well. These two staffs would be critical for coordinating deployments and logistic support during the campaign. With the arrival of these command posts, the essential theater land operations infrastructure was complete.

Deployment Planning

With the coming of the new year, activity shifted into high gear and focused on three critical components of the operation: deploying forces to the Iraqi theater of operations, mobilizing ARNG and USAR units and individuals, and developing the theater logistics infrastructure necessary for the campaign. Deploying V Corps' combat units began in earnest as political rhetoric heated up and war inched ever closer.

The shifting strategic landscape of coalition and supporting partners, as well as the lack of a specific date and troop list for the operation, complicated deployment, mobilization, and logistics. The Joint Operations Planning and Execution System (JOPES) provided the framework and structure for handling these three components of the campaign. As planners developed courses of action, they built a Time-Phased Force and Deployment List (TPFDL), using the JOPES automated systems, of which units would deploy and in what priority sequence. Once approved, a TPFDL flows forces into the theater automatically until turned off by the command. While very structured, this system forces detailed planning. It ensures, for example, that logistics and support units are available as combat units arrive in the theater. However, because of the complexity of synchronizing units, limited transportation assets, and time, a TPFDL is frustratingly difficult to modify in response to changing requirements.

Led by Lieutenant Colonel Tom Reilly of Third Army and Major Kevin Marcus of V Corps, planners did tremendous work building the TPFDL. They worked hard to maintain the proper mix of combat, CS, and CSS units to fulfill the war plan requirements. Although this system worked very well for deliberate planning, it lacked the flexibility and responsiveness required by senior leaders. Accordingly, after six time-phased force deployment data (TPFDD) conferences at TRANSCOM headquarters, CENTCOM resorted to a different approach.

The new approach required planners to group units into force packages that could deploy in the order required as the campaign unfolded. This system allowed CENTCOM to hold units for deployment at a later date. However, it required that every force package be approved by CENTCOM. As a result, force packaging as executed in OIF reduced the ability to plan the integration of units since the commanders depended on approval from higher headquarters to flow the force. Additionally, deviating from the detailed TPFDL had unintended consequences as logistic units fell farther back in the force flow. This affected not only Army units, but also those from sister services that depended on Army supporters.[90] For example, the Army provided much of the long-haul ground transportation used by the Marine Corps. However, because Army planners were directed to move those units into later force packages, I MEF compensated by contracting civilian trucks in Kuwait until the Army units were allowed to deploy in country.

From a national strategic perspective, there was another impact of using force packaging to deploy the force. The ability to adjust the deployment sequence rapidly did not match the requirement to schedule the finite strategic lift assets—the airlift and sealift fleets—well in advance. The careful, detailed management of the lift assets could not readily adjust to meet the relatively rapid adjustments to the deployment timelines. As the campaign progressed, the force flow never caught up with the operational requirements; the approach ultimately failed to provide either the flexibility or responsiveness anticipated.

Deployment Execution: Planes, Trains, Ships, and Automobiles

The difficulties in planning a deployment are equally evident at the unit execution level. To give a sense of perspective of the magnitude of the challenge, imagine that one day, without warning, the manager of the Wal-Mart in Clarksville, Tennessee, adjacent to the 101st Airborne Division at Fort Campbell, was told to move everything in the store—merchandise, displays, equipment, computers, and all employees—to Kuwait within three weeks, and to be ready to open the store within days of arriving. That is a miniature example of the problem—miniature because the 101st is bigger than 100 Wal-Marts.

While this sounds, and is, chaotic, confusing, and often inefficient, it is not the result of indifference or poor planning. The deployment system is large, complex, and sensitive to mistakes and serendipity. A unit showing up at the airfield out of sequence or late causes a ripple effect that can take days to overcome. Weather delays, vessel breakdowns at sea, and a host of other problems are common and have similar effects on the unit's arrival in the theater. Many things can go wrong, and even when they go very well, cargo and passengers usually arrive at facilities not designed to receive an army on the move. Even the cardinal rule of not separating soldiers from their gear can be difficult to follow. Units, personnel, and equipment are often cross-loaded in different aircraft or ships to maximize loading efficiency, but causing those units to arrive at different locations and times and separated from their equipment. Moreover, since deployment occurs in several stages as units move from their home station to the theater, these events can occur at multiple points in the deployment sequence.

Units are not necessarily located adjacent to either aerial or seaports, so a move is required to get from "fort to port" then from "port to port," and finally RSOI in the theater. This stage, or "port to foxhole," is perhaps the most fragile part of the entire deployment process. RSOI starts with receiving arriving unit passengers who, in most cases, arrive by air and must be met and transported to a place where they may be reunited with their equipment. Ultimately it includes uploading ammunition and other supplies, test-firing weapons and, as time permits, training and rehearsing for missions.

"Fort to Port"—Deployment

Packing up an entire unit and its soldiers is akin to packing the family into the car for the summer vacation—with the associated frenetic pace, urgency, and chaos. Tactical units all have deployment SOPs with slews of checklists to assist and order the process. But reality and checklists do not always match. Seemingly endless changes in the transportation timelines and availability, combined with changes to the tactical plan, ripple throughout the units. In addition to validating load plans, finalizing deployment rosters, and physically preparing the equipment to load onto rail cars or aircraft, the units must also prepare the families for the ordeal to follow. Deploying is even more intense for USAR and ARNG units that have not had the time, resources, or experience to prepare accordingly.

That said, the Army's 12-year investment in deployment infrastructure paid dividends for OIF. From improved railhead facilities at individual posts to the improvements at the ports, the units were able to move their equipment to the ports far more efficiently than for DESERT STORM. As well, the investment in training unit movement officers and sergeants in the technical aspects of rail and aircraft loading down to the company level helped to smooth the process even more. Finally, modernized deployment and unit movement software tools improved the management process significantly. With the Army's steady rate of deployments over the previous dozen years, virtually every unit had a cadre of soldiers who were experienced with the art and science of getting "down range."

"Port to Foxhole"—RSOI

Units normally arrive in a theater of operations by a combination of surface and air delivery methods. By experience, approximately 95 percent of personnel arrive by air. Conversely, 95 percent of materiel arrives by sea. The soldiers, arriving at an airfield with just their personal bags, must then meet up with their unit equipment and vehicles in designated staging areas near arriving seaports (ports of debarkation). Through this synchronization of airlift and sealift arrivals, soldiers prepare their equipment for movement forward to the battlefield. Essentially, this means arriving unit personnel must be met and transported, hopefully with their baggage, either to the port of debarkation to pick up their unit equipment or to the forward assembly area where their equipment will later arrive.

Even this is not as straightforward as it sounds. Anyone waiting for a bag on a turnstile at an airport has discovered and indeed is told by convenient announcements that many bags look alike. Well, in the Army, they all look exactly alike. Passengers on a deploying military aircraft, say 300 or so, typically disembark from about 25 hours in transit. The unwritten rule is that units usually arrive in pitch dark and no one is there to meet them. The exhausted soldiers, who are entirely disoriented now, rummage through bags to find their own. This little vignette, or ones like it, repeated hundreds of times during the buildup and execution of OIF.

Given all that can go wrong, the performance of the US deployment system in OIF was superbly efficient, rapid, and generally effective as a consequence of thoughtful analysis of previous deployments and important investments in infrastructure and equipment since Operation DESERT STORM. TRANSCOM and its major subordinate commands, including the Army Materiel Command (AMC), Military Sealift Command (MSC), and the MTMC, are responsible for deployment transportation, literally from point of origin to final destination. Their tasks are enormous, require intensive management, and depend on Active and Reserve Component service members and a great many civilians. The Army depends on TRANSCOM and its subordinate commands to move everything from tanks to troops to paper clips to support operations around the globe.[91]

Soldiers on the Move

So, the divisions and supporting units destined to fight the Iraqi army began to flow into the theater. The first four divisions on the move, and the only ones to participate in Phase III combat operations, included the 3rd Infantry Division, 101st Airborne Division (Air Assault), 82nd Airborne Division, and the 4th Infantry Division. They were all in different stages of deployment when combat operations began.

3rd Infantry Division

The 3rd Infantry Division was the first into Kuwait. The 2nd BCT was already in Kuwait, having deployed for Operation DESERT SPRING in the fall of 2002. In December 2002, the remainder of the 3rd ID began to deploy from Fort Stewart, Georgia, to Kuwait. The soldiers of the division flowed into the theater by air and linked up with the pre-positioned heavy brigade equipment sets of APS-3 and APS-5. The soldiers and leaders of 3rd ID found the APS vehicles and equipment to be in excellent shape (many said better than their own), but some equipment did not exactly match the model and version the soldiers had back at Fort Stewart. That was, however, a minor difficulty and one quickly overcome by soldiers and noncommissioned officers.

The division drew the APS equipment and deployed out to camps in the desert of Kuwait. Brigades began training in earnest, using the Udairi Range complex and the vast expanse of desert to practice offensive operations. Training right up until they attacked into Iraq, during the next four months the division would fire, drive, and fly the equivalent of two years of training ammunition and fuel, roughly *six times* what they would have experienced in peacetime. This precious training opportunity, afforded only to 3rd ID because of the unique buildup in this campaign, contributed significantly to the division's success.

101st Airborne Division

The second major unit to deploy into Kuwait was the 101st Airborne Division. Alerted for deployment in January 2003, the division began deploying on 6 February 2003. Based at Fort Campbell, Kentucky, the division deployed its equipment by rail, truck, and air to the port of Jacksonville, Florida, including self-deployment of over 250 helicopters. After loading, the division's equipment made the 9,000 mile voyage to Kuwait. As the ships approached Kuwait, more than 20,000 soldiers from the reinforced division flew to Kuwait International Airport and began to link up with their equipment at Camp WOLF. For many of the soldiers, particularly from the division's 3rd Brigade, deploying to Kuwait followed closely on the heels of their deployment in Afghanistan from January to August 2002 and their subsequent JRTC

Figure 35. Udairi Airfield, Kuwait

training rotation in November. Indeed, some of the division's CH-47 *Chinook* pilots were at Fort Campbell for only 22 days before departing again.[92]

The division's rapid deployment is a testament to the hard work and planning by both the division staff and the Fort Campbell garrison soldiers and civilians. During the fall as the V Corps and CFLCC plan evolved, the 101st executed a series of deployment and load-plan validation exercises to prepare for the anticipated movement. Colonel Kim Summers, the Fort Campbell Garrison commander, brought all of the fort's capabilities to bear in pushing the division "out the door." The division off-loaded its first ship in Kuwait less than 30 days after its receipt of the deployment orders.[93]

The last planeload of "Screaming Eagle" soldiers arrived on 10 March. Despite a remarkable effort, the division closed in theater less than 10 days before hostilities commenced. The division conducted RSOI in significantly less time than planned, including moving to the desert, acclimatizing soldiers, pilots, and equipment to desert operations, drawing ammunition and test-firing all weapons, and performing the thousand other tasks required to prepare a division for war in a distant land. Still, because the formal order to deploy had come so late, when the CFLCC offensive commenced, the last elements of the 101st were still completing their preparations for war.

4th Infantry Division

In the northern portion of the theater, the deployment was not going as well. In January, CENTCOM and EUCOM began setting the stage for a northern front. During planning and coordination, operating from Turkey into northern Iraq was considered integral to the campaign's success. EUCOM had been in close consultation with the Turkish armed forces and civilian leadership throughout the fall. In early January, EUCOM designated the 1st Infantry Division, based in Germany, to serve as the Joint Rear Area Command (JRAC) in Turkey. The

Jeremiah Johnson, Combat Camera

Figure 36. CH-47 helicopters and assorted rolling stock

JRAC would perform coordination, logistics support, and force protection to enable the 4th ID to deploy to Turkey, position in assembly areas close to Iraq and, on order, attack south toward Tikrit. The 1st ID moved elements to Turkey and began coordination and preparations for the 4th ID's arrival. At the same time, elements from the Army's 10th Special Forces Group, under command of Colonel Charlie Cleveland, formed the core of JSOTF-North and began coordination and staging for future operations from Turkey. Meanwhile, the 4th ID loaded its equipment on ships bound for the Mediterranean Sea and Turkey. Soon, more than 40 ships carrying tanks, aircraft, and supplies were flowing into the "eastern Med."

While the JRAC continued its preparations and 4th ID ships arrived outside the ports, the Turkish government refused to allow offensive operations from its soil. As the United States and Turkey tried diplomatic means to resolve the impasse, preparations for operations into Iraq from Turkey slowed and then halted. While negotiations continued, the ships carrying the equipment of 4th ID awaited permission to enter port and discharge their cargo. When hostilities commenced, it became clear that the 4th ID was not going to be able to operate from Turkey. Eventually, General Franks ordered the ships to move through the Suez Canal to Kuwait, and the 4th ID joined V Corps in the attack from the south. Meanwhile, JSOTF-North was forced to deploy by air into northern Iraq without transiting Turkish airspace, leading to dangerous infiltrations by air as SOF C-130 aircraft negotiated the dense Iraqi air defense umbrella. The Turkish government finally granted limited use of their airspace and ground for logistics only. This would help sustain the campaign in the north over time, but the initial damage was done.

Without the 4th ID in the north, the Third Army resorted to a backup plan. The 173rd Airborne Brigade, based in Vicenza, Italy, as part of the Southern European Task Force (SETAF), had been part of the planning for the northern front since mid-December. Although the 173rd was intended to serve under the 4th ID, the plans quickly changed to employ the brigade as a

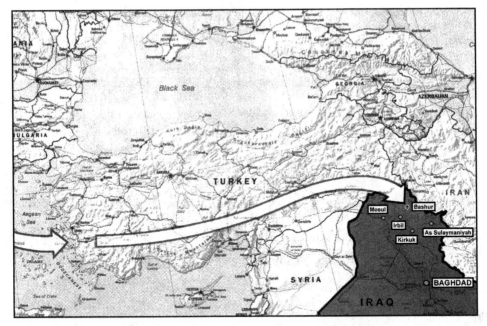

Figure 37. 4th Infantry's route was to take it through the Mediterranean Sea
and Turkey to attack into Iraq from the north.

conventional force under command of JSOTF-North. The 173rd fielded two infantry battalions provided with a few high-mobility, multipurpose, wheeled vehicles (HMMWVs), an artillery battery, and other support elements. Because the 173rd had no armored or mechanized forces, USAREUR contributed its medium ready company (MRC) of infantry in M113 armored personnel carriers (APCs) and its heavy ready company (HRC) of M1 Abrams tanks and M2 BIFVs. With those two companies placed under command of 1st Battalion, 63rd Armor, the 173rd became a light-heavy BCT.[94]

JSOTF-North identified Bashur Airfield in the Kurdish area of northern Iraq as the best place to bring the 173rd BCT into the theater. After reconnaissance by SOF and Kurdish *Peshmerga* Freedom Fighters, the "Pathfinders" of the 173rd moved into Bashur, followed shortly by the first brigade-size airborne assault since Operation JUST CAUSE in Panama in 1989. Once the airborne troops secured the airfield, C-17s brought in the heavy equipment, tanks, and Bradleys of Task Force 1-63rd AR. After building combat power and preparing for combat, the 173rd BCT participated in the final ground operations that sealed the fate of Iraqi Regular Army forces in northern Iraq. Operations in the north could not, however, attain the effect hoped for with the 4th ID's heavy forces. Nonetheless the brigade did contribute to JSOTF-North operations.

82nd Airborne Division

The 82nd Airborne Division initially endured an "on again/off again" experience with IRAQI FREEDOM. While the division's airborne assault capability offered tremendous operational flexibility, the "All Americans" already had a BCT and part of the division headquarters deployed in Afghanistan for OEF. Still, CENTCOM and CFLCC planners needed to be able to place a large force anywhere in Iraq rapidly, either to take advantage of opportunities such as a sudden collapse of the regime or to meet unforeseen challenges as the campaign unfolded. So, in early January the rest of the division was alerted for deployment to Kuwait.

The division's advance party arrived by air and established the All-American Base Camp adjacent to Camp WOLF and the Kuwait International Airport, from where they would depart on any airborne operation. Because the Kuwaitis had no facilities for rigging the 82d Division's heavy equipment for airborne drop, the division's engineers created the same capability in the desert that they had back at their home—Fort Bragg, North Carolina. Breaking ground on 16 February, the engineers completed a world-class heavy drop rig site on 7 March—capable of rigging every piece of the division's equipment. As the 82nd's heavy equipment arrived by sea, they quickly positioned it at the All-American Base Camp and prepared for operations. Meanwhile, the division's ground and air troops conducted desert operations training at Udairi Range and at the Faylaka Island training site. By 17 March, the 82nd was ready for war in Iraq.[95]

Prelude to War: "Final Planning and Preparation"

As mid-March approached, the Army began to position for war. The 3rd ID, as the lead element of V Corps, moved out of its base camps and into assembly areas along the Kuwait/ Iraq border. This was in part to be closer to their jump-off point, but also to make room for follow-on units arriving in the theater. Even the desert can fill up when over 200,000 soldiers, marines, and their vehicles and equipment deploy into a relatively small country. According to the V Corps situation report on the evening of 19 March 2003, the corps had the following combat systems ready to attack:

Unit	M1 Abrams	M2/3 Bradley	Paladin How.	Towed How.	MLRS	AH-64A/D	OH-58D	UH-60	CH-47
3rd ID	247	264	54		18	18	16	15	
101st				60		72	24	126	34
2/82nd							12		
11 AHR						61			
12 AVN								37	28
TOTAL	247	264	54	60	18	151	52	178	62

As the 3rd ID left camp, the 101st BCTs moved in to replace them. Likewise, artillery units moved to positions from which Army Tactical Missile System (ATACMS) and MLRS batteries would fire the opening salvos of the war. The huge fuel tank farms that had been built began to fill up and everywhere command posts and signal nodes sprouted antennas as the Army set up the communications architecture that would enable the campaign. Throughout Kuwait, there was last-minute training, resupply of ammunition, fuel, and other supplies, and soldiers engaged in their own mental and physical preparation for war. By 18 March, Third Army, V Corps, and their subordinate units were prepared to open the campaign.

NOTES

1. Taken from personal notes of Colonel James K. Greer, director, US Army School of Advanced Military Studies. Colonel Greer attended the Army Commanders' Conference and was one of the principal briefers.

2. The RSOI process is critical to the rapid deployment and then employment of large units in a theater. See also JP 4-01.8 and FM 100-17-3 for joint and Army doctrine on RSOI.

3. Lieutenant General David McKiernan, commander, Third Army ARCENT/CFLCC, interview by Major John Aarsen, 17 November 2002.

4. Major General Henry Stratman, deputy commanding general for support (DCG-S), CFLCC interview by Colonel Gregory Fontenot, US Army, Retired, 19 May 2003.

5. Stratman. See also Stratman input to *On Point* assigned tracking number 031027. Colonel Kevin Benson, who served as the Third Army plans officer for then Lieutenant General Franks, believes the turning point for planning operations under the assumption that Saudi Arabia would not be available came in 1997. Benson accompanied Franks on his first trip to the theater as commanding general, Third Army. Franks told Benson as the two of them "stood on a dune looking into Iraq," that in the rewrite of the war plan, Benson should assume starting from Kuwait. See also Colonel Kevin Benson, C5, CFLCC interview by Colonel Gregory Fontenot, US Army, Retired, 20 November 2003.

6. Stratman.

7. Stratman.

8. Colonel Victoria Leignadier, commander, 598th Transportation Group (Terminal), interview by Colonel Gregory Fontenot, US Army, Retired, 24 November 2003.

9. Ibid.

10. Lieutenant Colonel David Kolleda, "Chapter Prep Mob Deploy, Section 2. SWA Theater Prep and JLOTS" 15 July 2003 OIFSG. Developed from after-action reviews and interviews collected in April and May 2003. Lieutenant Colonel Kolleda joined the OIF-SG in theater, where he served with the 377th TSC.

11. Kolleda. Much of this information could also be found on 7th Transportation Group unit web pages in summer 2003.

12. Kolleda, "Port Operations and JLOTS.," 15 July 2003.

13. Ibid.

14. Ibid. See also Leignadier. USMC MPS vessels, in the end, did not employ Army JLOTS or their own on-board lighters. The Marines did use their excellent hovercraft.

15. Major General Ann Dunwoody, commanding general, MTMC. In the operational summary Lieutenant Colonel Kolleda prepared, he argued that Army watercraft played important roles in enabling rapid unloading and supporting JLOTS. Neither Major General Dunwoody nor her staff agreed with this assessment. Colonel Leignadier, whose Transportation Terminal Group provided port management believed that they could have done the job without the watercraft, but having them reduced the burden. Some of the data cited here came from 7th Transportation Group web pages. See also Major General Bobby Dail email to Lieutenant Colonel Dave Kolleda, 3 July 2003.

16. Leignadier.

17. Kolleda.

18. Ibid. (section titled APR Master Plan) APS-1 includes equipment stored in the US. APS-2 includes three brigade sets, one in Germany, one in the Netherlands, and one in Italy. APS-3 includes a brigade set afloat in Diego Garcia and one in Saipan. APS-4 is a brigade set in Korea. APS-5 includes a brigade set in Kuwait and one in Qatar.

19. Kolleda.

20. V Corps Rear (Provision), "AAR Draft," December 2002.

21. Lieutenant General Dan Petrosky, US Army, Retired, interview by Colonel Gregory Fontenot, US Army, Retired, 20 November 2003.

22. Ibid.

23. Ibid.

24. Technically, with the Marine Corps providing ground forces, the CFLCC is actually a CJFLCC—Combined Joint Forces Land Component Command. However, this work adopts the theater's common naming convention.

25. "CJFC FRAG ORDER, 02-015."

26. This remark made to Gregory Fontenot on 13 November 2003 by an Army colonel who served on the CFLCC staff.

27. Major General Robert Blackman, chief of staff, CFLCC, interview by Brigadier General Robert Cone, 17 and 31 March 2003.

28. Ibid.

29. Major General J.D. Thurman, C3, CFLCC, interview by Colonel James K. Greer, 25 April 2003. See also Major General J. D. Thurman, C3, CFLCC, interview by Colonel Gregory Fontenot, US Army, Retired, 21 May 2003. Specifically, Thurman recalled they had to train the staff to conduct a battle update assessment.

30. Benson.

31. Major Kevin Marcus, G3 planner, V Corps, email to Lieutenant Colonel E.J. Degen, 8 September 2003.

32. Benson.

33. Ibid.

34. An operational planning team (OPT) formed at Fort Leavenworth, Kansas, spring 2002, in support of the Army Staff and CENTCOM for the purpose of examining the logistic considerations for deployment and sustainment of Army forces through the three axes of advance (Kuwait, Jordan, and Turkey). Briefing prepared by SAMS Deployment OPT, undated, held in Combined Arms Research Library, Fort Leavenworth, Kansas.

35. Major E.J. Degen was later promoted to lieutenant colonel by Lieutenant General Wallace in Baghdad on 26 April, 2003.

36. In October and November 2002, SAMS deployed a team of six students to Heidelberg, Germany, to assist V Corps in planning the Baghdad operation. These students planned side by side with the V Corps staff in an example of the successful marriage of education and actual operations. On Marine participation, see email Rago to Degen, 5 January 2003. According to Rago, the marines brought a "platoon" of planners to every planning session to assure the MEF understood the plan and could collaborate effectively.

37. See Dr. Roger J. Spiller, *Sharp Corners: Urban Operations at Century's End* (Fort Leavenworth, Kansas: Combat Studies Institute, 2001). Colonel Greer's white paper essentially formed the core of the concept that V Corps built in preparation for Operation IRAQI FREEDOM. Dr. Russell Glenn is a Rand analyst who has published a number of studies on urban operations. A frequent speaker at the School of Advanced Military Studies, Glenn enjoys wide respect in the Army and in the USMC. A retired Army officer, graduate of School of Advanced Military Studies and a past faculty member, Glenn's major publications on urban operations include several Rand studies, the most important of which is *Heavy Matter: Urban Operations Density of Challenges* (Santa Monica, CA, RAND, 2001). See also Tom Czerwinski, *Coping with Bounds: Speculations on Non-Linearity in Military Affairs* (Washington, DC: NDU Press, 1998). Dr. Joe Strange's ideas on critical vulnerabilities are detailed in Joe Strange, *Centers of Gravity and Critical Vulnerabilities,* Marine Corps University Perspectives on Warfighting No. 4, 1997.

38. Major E.J. Degen from notes taken at the CENTCOM Component Commanders' Conference held at Camp DOHA, Kuwait, September 2002.

39. Much of this paragraph is planners' "tribal wisdom" but facts cited stem either from list of graduates of School of Advanced Military Studies or from Benson.

40. Lieutenant General David McKiernan, commanding general, CFLCC interview by Major John Aarsen, 30 November 2002.

41. Ibid.

42. Lieutenant Colonel E. J. Degen to Colonel Gregory Fontenot, US Army, Retired, 12 November 2003.

43. Ibid. See also Lieutenant General David McKiernan, commanding general, CFLCC, interview by Major John Aarsen, 19 December 2002. See also Benson.

44. V Corps G3 Plans notes. Major John Aarsen, 19 December 2002.

45. "CFLCC OPLAN COBRA II Base Plan," Camp DOHA, Kuwait, 13 January 2003.

46. Exercise timelines referenced from V Corps/CJTF-7 Standard Operations Brief, or MOAB (Mother of All Briefings), 12 July 2003.

47. General Shinseki came to this conclusion while at Fort Leavenworth, Kansas, during a visit to the Pre-Command Course. Shinseki received a briefing on "The Way Ahead for Urban Operations" from Lieutenant General James Riley, commanding general of the Combined Arms Center, and his staff. The CSA determined to publish FM 3-06, *Urban Operations,* immediately and to distribute it to the field with priority to troop listed units. Second, he directed that TRADOC field a mobile training team to educate the field in the new urban operations doctrine, including both joint and Army doctrine.

48. The Battle Command Training Program (BCTP), formed in the late 1980s by General Carl E. Vuono, CSA, originally focused on providing flagship training for divisions and corps. In the beginning BCTP included two operations groups (A and B), each commanded by a colonel. Subsequently, BCTP formed Operations Group C to support the training of Army National Guard brigades as part of the Army's effort to improve training in the

Guard. Finally, as Atlantic Command transitioned to become JFCOM, BCTP formed Operations Group D to support joint training until the Joint Warfare Center could form. In the end, Operations Group D supported Army service component training. Starting with ODS and since, BCTP has supported mission rehearsal exercises and augmented Army staffs in the field during DESERT STORM and IRAQI FREEDOM.

49. Memorandum for BCTP commander, "OPS Group F After-Action Review," 20 December 2002. Three other senior mentors supported execution, including Generals Crouch, Franks, and Hendrix, all of whom had commanded at the four-star level. Crouch commanded US Army Europe and served in Bosnia in a NATO command. Franks, who commanded VII Corps in DESERT STORM, commanded the US Army Training and Doctrine Command. Hendrix, who led V Corps in support of operations in Kosovo, later commanded US Army Forces Command.

50. Blackman.

51. Lieutenant Colonel John Charlton, commander, TF 1-15 IN, interview by Lieutenant Colonel Arthur Durante, US Army, Retired, 22 August 2003.

52. Personal notes of Colonel James K. Greer.

53. Department of the Army (DAMO-SS) Information Paper, "Army Strategic Planning Board Functions and Organizations," 28 August 2003.

54. United States Army Intelligence Center "Operation IRAQI FREEDOM Consolidated Lessons Learned (DRAFT)," 22 August 2003, 34.

55. Army engineers did the analysis of the D9's use in Israel and developed the requirement for the Army, processing it through all of the required acquisition steps.

56. Taken from personal notes of Colonel James K. Greer, director of the US Army School of Advanced Military Studies. Colonel Greer participated in Colonels Bartley and Connelly's efforts and was one of the principal briefers in the decision brief to Lieutenant General Cody.

57. Ibid.

58. "V Corps Command and Control Briefing," presented to Army staff team by Colonel Jeff Smith, commander, 22nd Signal Brigade, 19 June 2003.

59. "US Army Contributions to the Iraqi Theater of Operations," Department of the Army briefing to the secretary of defense, 4 June 2003.

60. Ibid.

61. Ibid.

62. Colonel Clyde Harthcock, chief of staff, INSCOM, interview by Major Daniel Corey and Major David Tohn, 19 June 2003.

63. Major General Keith Alexander, commander, INSCOM, interview by Major Daniel Corey and Major David Tohn, 19 June 2003.

64. Ibid.

65. Harthcock.

66. Major Daniel Corey, OIF-SG, "OIF-SG Operational Summary: Intelligence," 15 July 2003.

67. Lieutenant Colonel John McPherson, deputy commander, 66th Military Intelligence Group, interview by Major David Tohn, 14 June 2003.

68. 66th Military Intelligence Group, "History Of Operation IRAQI FREEDOM," 25 May 2003.

69. McPherson.

70. Major Matthew Glunz, operations officer, JAC, interview by Major David Tohn, 16 June 2003.

71. Major Robert Mooney, senior Russian analyst, JAC, interview by Major David Tohn, 16 June 2003.

72. Colonel Gary L. Parrish, commander, 205th Military Intelligence Brigade, interview by Major Daniel Corey and Major David Tohn, 30 May 2003.

73. Ibid.

74. Ibid.

75. Major Laura A. Potter, Operations Officer (S3), 302nd Military Intelligence Battalion, interview by Major Daniel Corey and Major David Tohn, 29 May 2003.

76. Major Michael Millen, A-10 pilot, 190th Expeditionary Fighter Squadron, USAF, to Major David Tohn, 4 September 2003.

77. Major Anthony Cavallaro, S3, 800th MP Brigade, interview by Captain Michael Matthews, 1 June 2003.

78. Lieutenant Colonel Erik Nikolai, MP planner, V Corps, interview by Captain Michael Matthews, 9 May 2003.

79. Colonel Teddy Spain, commander, 18th MP Brigade, interview by Captain Michael Matthews, 10 May 2003.

80. Lieutenant Colonel John Huey, provost marshal, 3rd ID, interview by Captain Michael Matthews, 13 May 2003.

81. 3rd MP Battalion memorandum for record, "Subject: MP Chronology, Operations ENDURING FREEDOM and IRAQI FREEDOM," 16 March 2003.

82. Lieutenant Colonel James Knowlton, OIF-SG, "OIF-SG Operational Summary: Task Force *RIO*." Developed from Engineer News Record, TF *RIO* History and CFLCC SITREP. OIF-SG and TF *RIO* happened to be assigned adjacent office space so that the study group had some first-hand opportunity to observe TF *RIO*'s planning and execution efforts.

83. Ibid.

84. Ibid., TF *RIO*'s efforts continue as of the development of this study. *RIO* confronted serious challenges due to looting and long-term neglect of facilities, from pipelines to well heads. Prior to the war, the Iraqi oil industry employed a security force of as many as 12,000. As these security forces departed, looters moved in. Lack of adequate security required coalition troops to secure key facilities. Stretched thin already, security remained a problem as late as June 2003.

85. "Mission Overview, Free Iraqi Forces," produced by Task Force *Warrior*, Colonel James D. Doyle, 26 April 2003.

86. Ibid.

87. Ibid.

88. Ibid.

89. Members of SOCCE-Kuwait and 19th SF Group, interviews by Colonel James K. Greer, 20 April 2003. Of note, several ODAs from 19th SF were being debriefed from missions in support of TF *Tarawa* in the vicinity of An Nasiriyah, and the interviewer had the opportunity to take unclassified notes.

90. CFLCC planning staff, Camp DOHA, Kuwait, interview by Colonel James K. Greer, 25 April 2003.

91. James K. Matthews and Cora J. Holt, *So Many, So Far, So Fast: United States Transportation Command and Strategic Deployment for Operation Desert Shield/Desert Storm* (Washington, DC: Joint History Office, 1992), 318, provides an excellent overview on the previous desert war's deployment issues and is essential to understanding the complexities and scale of strategic deployments.

92. Major William Abb, chief of plans, 101st Airborne Division to Lieutenant Colonel David Tohn, 4 September 2003. Major Abb visited the OIF Study Group after having reviewed first draft material. This passage reflects corrections to the draft that he offered.

93. Ibid.

94. Colonel Blair Ross, public affairs officer, US Army Europe, "A Transformed Force in Legacy Clothing" (Unpublished).

95. Colonel Carl Horst, chief of staff, 82nd Airborne Division, interview by Colonel James K. Greer, 3 May 2003.

Chapter 3

The Running Start

We were expecting jubilation, not RPGs!

Captain Robert L. Smith
Commander, A Company
2nd Battalion, 7th Infantry

Missiles are cheap; soldiers are expensive.

Colonel Charles A. Anderson
Chief of Staff, 32d AAMDC

An Unlikely Flotilla—The Army at Sea

No one would confuse the US Army's *Mechanicsville* Landing Craft Utility (LCU) 2027 with a "greyhound of the sea," but it is indicative both of the maturity of joint operations and the Army contribution to joint operations at sea. At 1800 on 20 March 2003, *Mechanicsville*, previously redesignated as coalition *Vessel 2027*, sailed with the US Navy High Speed Vessel (HSV) X1, *Joint Venture*, and a flotilla of US Coast Guard boats. The HSV led the LCU and a convoy of Coast Guard boats into Iraqi waters, becoming the first coalition vessels to enter Iraqi territorial waters in the North Arabian Sea. The *Mechanicsville* sailed with Navy special operations personnel embarked and a mixed crew of US Army Reserve and Regular Army mariners under command of Vessel Master (Skipper) Chief Warrant Officer 2 (CW2) Mia Scotia Perdue. The *Mechanicsville* headed into harm's way to support a direct action seizure of two gulf oil platforms to prevent the Iraqis from destroying them.

US Transportation Command

Figure 38. Landing Craft Utility at sea

The *Mechanicsville* served multiple purposes, including diverting Iraqi attention from US Marine Corps operations on the Al Faw Peninsula and providing support to naval special operations forces. For the next eight days, *Mechanicsville*, ultimately joined by the US Army Vessel Large Tug (LT) 1974, *Champagne Marne*, served as the forward operating base for operations in and around the platforms. It performed a variety of tasks from cross-decking cargo and refueling the USCG *Walnut* to providing a staging area for enemy prisoners of war. Its evacuation of an injured Coast Guard sailor is emblematic of the joint and coalition nature of OIF. To evacuate the sailor, *Mechanicsville* called the USS *Tarawa* for air evacuation support. The *Tarawa* then sent an Australian helicopter to take the injured sailor to the Navy hospital ship, USS *Comfort*.

Summary of Events

Saddam Hussein and his sons must leave Iraq within 48 hours. Their refusal to do so will result in military conflict.

President George W. Bush
17 March 2003

My fellow citizens, at this hour, American and coalition forces are in the early stages of military operations to disarm Iraq, to free its people and to defend the world from grave danger.

On my orders, coalition forces have begun striking selected targets of military importance to undermine Saddam Hussein's ability to wage war. These are opening stages of what will be a broad and concerted campaign.

President George W. Bush
Address to the Nation
19 March 2003

President Bush made the decision to launch OIF on 16 March 2003 and issued an ultimatum with a 48-hour deadline on the 17th. That decision was the beginning of the end of 12 years of cat-and-mouse between Saddam Hussein and the international community. CENTCOM's and the services' years of hard work and preparation in the Southwest Asia (SWA) theater gave the president the flexibility to make that announcement—to draw a line in the sand—with a credible military force ready and able to enforce that decision. While regional and European governments attempted last-minute diplomacy, the United Nations and international aid agencies, anticipating war, cleared out of the future combat zone. America's strategic goal was embedded in the president's numerous addresses—establish a free, democratic, prosperous, and nonthreatening Iraqi state. The first step in achieving that goal was removing Saddam Hussein's Ba'athist regime, by force if necessary.

The path from 17 March to Iraq's new future started at the berm along the Kuwait-Iraq border and ended in Baghdad, the regime's seat of power and control. To accomplish this, the coalition focused on the capital city as the key to removing the regime. Crossing the berm and pushing north into Iraq was the first task. Coalition troops breached the berm on the 20th of March and conducted a series of maneuvers and attacks to secure the Rumaila oil fields and to set the conditions for their march up-country.

The running start began with the president's decision to execute the "decapitation strike" on the 19th of March, intending to kill Saddam Hussein and the senior regime leadership in one fell swoop. Subsequent Iraqi attempts to sabotage the oil fields led CENTCOM to begin the coalition's ground forces border crossing 24 hours earlier than originally planned.

Over the next few days, coalition aircraft averaged between 1,500 and 2,000 sorties a day, with about 50 percent of those flown in support of CFLCC or on-call missions. During these early days of the campaign, the US Air Force launched 100 air-launched cruise missiles. Coalition warships also launched another 500 cruise missiles. Coalition air attacked senior Iraqi leadership, air defense systems, surface-to-surface missiles, and artillery batteries to

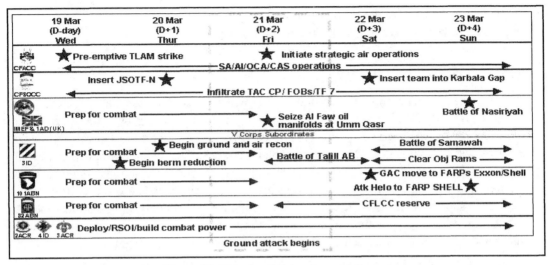

Figure 39. Running Start sequence of events

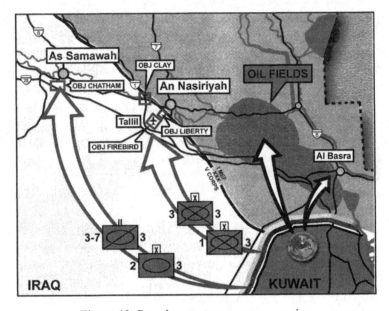

Figure 40. Running start maneuver overview

reduce the threat to coalition air and ground forces in Kuwait. The full wrath of coalition air power was on display during the night of "shock and awe," 21-22 March. As maneuver forces advanced, the air component shifted emphasis toward close support missions beginning on the night of 22-23 March.[1]

Major Combat Operations of the Running Start

In the first four days of ground operations, 20-23 March, the 3rd Infantry Division spearheaded the V Corps' drive into Iraq. The initial stages of ground operations included three critical events:

- Breaching the berm at the border with Kuwait
- Seizing Tallil Air Base and areas around An Nasiriyah
- Isolating As Samawah

Breaching the Berm

Completing a difficult night breach of a 10-kilometer (km)-wide obstacle belt, the division moved three Brigade Combat Teams (BCTs) and a large portion of corps units north into Iraq. Crossing the berm was a major combat operation. Erected to defend the Kuwaiti border by delaying attacking Iraqi troops, the berm now had the same effect on coalition troops heading the other way. Breaching in the presence of Iraqi outposts required rapid action to deny the Iraqis the opportunity to attack vulnerable coalition units while they were constrained to advance slowly and in single file through the lanes in the berms. Finally, orchestrating the movement of literally thousands of vehicles through a relatively small number of openings required detailed planning and rehearsal, all adjusted quickly to meet the accelerating timetable.

Colonel Pat Donohue, V Corps operations officer, and Lieutenant Colonel Pete Bayer, G3 of the 3rd ID, coordinated, synchronized, and orchestrated the breach. Donohue, commander of Operations Group Bravo (OPS B) of the Battle Command Training Program (BCTP), on loan to V Corps, led the breach planning for V Corps. The 3rd actually had to execute the breach and accommodate not only its troops but corps and CFLCC units as well. Pete Bayer's practical approach to planning, along with his appreciation of 3rd ID's role in the fight, led to a palpable attitude of cooperation in planning and executing the breach. Bayer and 3rd ID accommodated the requirements of a host of other units that also needed to pass through the bottleneck at the breach. The importance of the detailed planning of the movement through the berm cannot be overstated. This initial uncoiling would set the tone for the entire operation. The tasks included staging and coordinating the movement of 10,000 V Corps vehicles through these passage lanes and integrating the movement of TF *Tarawa*'s convoys within the V Corps' serials. Although marines also breached to support I MEF, TF *Tarawa's* units needed to cross with 3rd ID to facilitate their operations in the An Nasiriyah area. V Corps and I MEF collaborated, as did their subordinate units, to ensure that this operation was executed to near perfection. Any mistake in the sequence of unit departures or routes could have taken days to overcome.[2]

Seizing Tallil and Crossing Sites over the Euphrates

After breaching the berm, the 3rd ID attacked more than 140 km to secure objectives in and around Tallil Air Base just outside of the Euphrates town of An Nasiriyah. CFLCC needed Tallil Air Base to provide a site for the logistics and aviation facilities necessary to support the long march up-country. Seizing Tallil Air Base was an important moment not only because the CFLCC needed the base, but also because it was adjacent to An Nasiriyah, the first Iraqi city the corps would encounter. The soldiers would glean some sense of how the Iraqi soldiers and civilians would react. Additionally, V Corps required 3rd ID to seize a crossing site on Highway 1 over the Euphrates River northwest of An Nasiriyah and defeat elements of the 11th Iraqi Infantry Division within their zone. As rehearsed in multiple CFLCC drills, V Corps seized the Highway 1 bridges intact west of the city at Objective CLAY. Never assigned the mission to clear An Nasiriyah, the 3rd ID blocked the town, secured the bridge northwest of the town and handed it off to the I MEF's Task Force *Tarawa* on 23 March.[3]

Isolating As Samawah

The 3-7 Cavalry Squadron of the 3rd ID made the corps' first substantial contact with the paramilitary forces about 210 km north of the berm in As Samawah and got a glimpse of the future fight to secure the lines of communication (LOCs) and possibly Baghdad itself. Fighting in As Samawah, Umm Qasr, and Basra all served to illustrate that the Iraqi army would fight and that not all Iraqis assumed the coalition forces were liberators. At the same time, the 101st Airborne Division conducted three sequential operations to extend Army attack aviation's reach as far north as southern Baghdad. All of this was completed by 23 March.

The Darkest Day

By any definition, 23 March 2003 proved a dark day for the coalition forces fighting in Iraq. CFLCC's maneuver units fought from As Samawah to the Al Faw peninsula. The Iraqis' initial tactical surprise had dissipated and their defense, as it was, crystallized. Coalition ground troops fought a determined enemy, while supply convoys moving forward over difficult terrain literally ran a gauntlet of ambushes. Several things went wrong on the 23rd. In the air war, the Patriot missile, which until that moment seemed to function perfectly, destroyed a British *Tornado* fighter-bomber, killing its two-man crew. In An Nasiriyah, TF *Tarawa* fought a sharp engagement with the enemy, losing 18 of its own, with many others wounded.[4]

Early that morning, one of two serials of the 507th Maintenance Company of the 5th Battalion, 52nd Air Defense Artillery (Patriot), drove into An Nasiriyah. Between 0700 and 0830, the 507th ran into a hail of fire, during which the Iraqis killed 11 soldiers, captured seven, and wounded nine, to include some of those captured. One of those captured, Private First Class Jessica Lynch, became the object of a dramatic rescue later in the campaign. The 507th's story tells much about the fog, friction, bravery, and carnage of combat and is described in the next chapter.

The day closed with the 11th Attack Helicopter Regiment's unsuccessful deep attack against the *Medina* Division near Karbala. There, the regiment lost two aircraft (one to hostile fire), had two aviators captured, and saw literally every AH-64 *Apache* helicopter come back riddled with holes. Worse, the targeted *Medina* units remained relatively unscathed from the attack. The Army's vaunted deep-strike attack helicopters appeared to have been neutralized by the Iraqi air defense tactics.

Taken together, these incidents had a palpable effect on the morale of the higher-echelon headquarters. To loosely quote one planner, "We all knew Baghdad would be a hard and ugly fight; but if it was *this* hard before we even got close to the city, how hard would the fight really be and did we have enough force?"[5] That question was on the minds of people literally all over the world. Yet, however grim things may have seemed on the 23rd, the "running start" set the conditions for the subsequent march up-country and was critical in extending CFLCC's operational reach into Baghdad.

Supporting and Parallel Operations

As V Corps advanced north toward Baghdad, I MEF, supported by the 1st (UK) Armoured Division, conducted amphibious and ground operations toward Basra and successfully secured the oil infrastructure. US Marines seized the port of Umm Qasr to facilitate delivery of humanitarian assistance supplies, while US and Royal Navy minesweepers began to clear the waterways leading to Umm Qasr of mines. UK forces succeeded in preventing any reinforcement of Basra and, along with the Marines, secured the southern oil fields. Special forces troops operated throughout the theater. In the west, Joint Special Operations Task Force-West worked to reduce the theater ballistic missile (TBM) threat to Iraq's neighbors. In the north, Joint Special Operations Task Force-North, along with Kurdish troops, maintained pressure on the northern Iraqi forces.

Throughout it all, CFACC continued to degrade the regime's ability to command and control its forces and provided exceptional CAS to the coalition ground forces in contact. Coalition air forces roamed the skies over Iraq at will, providing CAS, interdicting enemy forces, and striking strategic targets across all of Iraq. Coalition ground forces maneuvered with impunity, knowing that the coalition determined what flew. Coalition air attacks were responsive, accurate, and precise.

In addition to operations on the ground and in the air, several related and associated actions took place that either enabled the fight or prepared the battlefield for future operations. Those actions ranged from the anti-tactical ballistic missile fight to efforts to meet logistics requirements of units in the field.

The events over the next five days reflected Lieutenant Generals McKiernan's and Wallace's constant balancing of rapid maneuver against the need to secure the LOCs and ensure the forces did not reach a culmination point due to logistics shortfalls. Factors playing on this balancing act included the scope and distance of the operation and the reality of initiating combat operations before the logistics base was fully established. That they were successful in achieving this balance is a testament to the depth and breadth of planning; the command's clear sense of operational and strategic objectives; and of course, the hard work and dedication of the soldiers on the ground.[6] At the end of this series of operations, V Corps had uncoiled nearly 400 km into Iraq and was ready to take the fight to Baghdad. What followed was an operational ground maneuver at impressive speeds.[7]

Triggering the Running Start

On 19 March 2003, "D-day," Phase II "Shaping" operations started. Combat operations began with a combined F-117 and Tomahawk Missile strike to decapitate the regime by killing the leadership and forcing an early disintegration of the Iraqi defenses. According to open media reporting, the decision was based on highly perishable intelligence reporting that Saddam Hussein and several key subordinate leaders were gathered together in a known location. Unsure if such an opportunity would present itself again, the president authorized the strike. Although the strike failed, it presaged the remainder of the phase's operations and resulted in major ground operations preceding the initiation of the air campaign.

Concurrent with the decapitation strike, other operations occurred across Iraq. In the south, SOF secured gas and oil platforms and other key objectives. CFLCC conducted reconnaissance and screening operations along the border. V Corps and I MEF units continued to prepare for combat operations. In the west, special operations troops prepared to secure key airfields and facilities and moved to preempt the Iraqis' use of WMD and tactical missiles. In the north, SOF worked with the Kurdish opposition to fix Iraqi forces on the Green Line as well as to deter

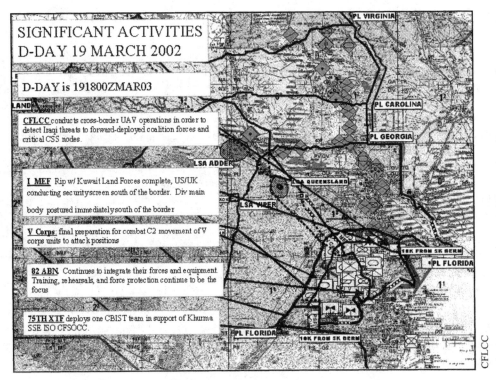

Figure 41. CFLCC common operational picture, D-day, 19 March 2003

Turkish intervention. Across the entire theater, CFACC attacked strategic targets, including leadership, air defense systems, and other Iraqi military systems.

Making the Call—Starting Phase III: Decisive (Ground) Operations

Early on the morning of 19 March, a small group of intelligence analysts located at Camp DOHA, Kuwait, made the key intelligence call that launched the ground war on the 21st. Protecting and preserving the Iraqi oil wells was one of the coalition's

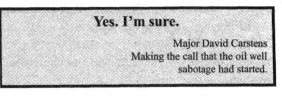

Yes. I'm sure.

Major David Carstens
Making the call that the oil well
sabotage had started.

strategic objectives. In fact, it was so important that detecting indications of sabotage was a "priority intelligence requirement," or PIR for McKiernan. A commander designates a question as a PIR because the answer to that question will drive a critical decision. The intelligence system then focuses its collection and analysis capabilities to answer the question. Determining if the oil wells were in danger of destruction—before they were destroyed—was a vital question and difficult to answer. The decision on when to start the ground war rested on that answer.

The responsibility to answer the question fell on the Joint Analysis and Control Element (JACE) Joint Term Fusion Cell (JTFC), led by Colonel Michael Gearty, a seasoned military intelligence officer with experience in both tactical and strategic intelligence. The JACE, the CFLCC's focal point for intelligence collection and analysis, drew on subordinate, theater, and national intelligence to develop a comprehensive picture. Moreover, the JACE controlled

---

Intelligence Supporting Operational Decisions

The JTFC monitored imagery and noted that the oil stopped flowing during the night. Normal flares stopped burning and were replaced by fake flares designed to confuse intelligence sensors. The JTFC oil team had studied the fields so thoroughly that they were not fooled by these dummy flares and understood that these activities were indicators that rigging for demolition was under way. At about 1000 on 19 March, General Franks talked with Lieutenant General McKiernan to determine if the attack could launch on the night of the 20th, 24 hours earlier than planned. McKiernan said that the CFLCC could launch early, but the CFACC reported that they could not move the air attack forward on such short notice. Franks gave the order for CFLCC to go, and I MEF attacked to seize the oil fields on the night of the 20th (morning of the 21st in local time). V Corps launched simultaneously. The I MEF achieved tactical surprise and quickly secured the oil fields, preventing the Iraqis from igniting more than a few small fires.

From the "C-2 Evolution Study"
Prepared by Lieutenant Colonel Steve Peterson

---

collection in-theater to ensure McKiernan's questions would be answered. As a small section within the JACE—ultimately growing to about 40 analysts—the JTFC was originally conceived as a cell that could draw on all sources of intelligence to provide a coherent and complete intelligence assessment.[8] However, because the entire JACE was so consumed in maintaining the *current* intelligence picture in the run-up to the war, eventually no element was looking at long-term issues and intelligence problems.

The JACE proved unable to develop the expertise and perspective necessary to fully understand the most complex issues.[9] The JTFC evolved to fill that analytical gap—a cell that provided a long-term, all-source focus on very specific issues: the defense of Baghdad proper, targets and objectives designated for special site exploitation (looking for chemical or biological weapons), Republican death squads, hydrology, and of course, the oil fields.[10]

Because the JTFC was a new concept, it required strong, focused leadership at all levels to succeed. Major David Carstens, an intelligence officer with 15 years of experience, who had honed his skills during deployments to Haiti, the Balkans, and Afghanistan, led this team. In 25 months of deployments between September 1999 and February 2003, Carstens developed an uncanny ability to see intelligence from the combat soldier's perspective—clear and focused.[11]

Assuming his position as the JTFC production manager on 4 December 2002, Carstens instituted an aggressive training plan to ensure the team of analysts had the requisite skills and backgrounds in their assigned areas. With Colonel Gearty running interference and keeping the administrative requirements to a minimum, the JTFC matured. Major General Marks also demonstrated patience and forethought in developing and protecting the JTFC, enabling it to grow into one of the standout intelligence organizations in the war.

The JTFC and Major Carstens were quickly recognized as experts in the theater, and they and their products were in high demand. For example, Carstens personally spent more than 20 hours with Lieutenant General Wallace, briefing the estimate of the Iraqi defense of Baghdad one on one.[12] Moreover, the JTFC's intelligence products, aggressively distributed across the theater, were universally considered some of the best in the theater. As an example of successful reach operations,[13] infantry brigades in Iraq executed operations using products developed by this small organization, although it was three echelons removed from the brigades and operated far to the south in Camp DOHA.[14]

In the months prior to the war, CFLCC received frequent reports of the Iraqi oil wells being set afire, causing the headquarters to react accordingly. Generated by sources or analysts unfamiliar with oil well operations, none proved accurate. Generally the reports stemmed from analysts who mistook normal "burn-offs" of combustible gasses as sabotage. After several mistaken reports, Chief Warrant Officer 4 Henry Crowder instituted a deliberate training plan whereby the JTFC analysts met with oil industry experts and worked with video and pictures of the burning oil wells from DESERT STORM. The JTFC analysts learned to differentiate between normal burn-off and sabotage. Crowder trained a mix of soldiers with a variety of unrelated specialties to be expert analysts of oil field imagery.[15]

This training bore fruit on the morning of 19 March. Images from a *Predator* UAV showed oil well fires with pressure-backed flames reaching 60-310 feet into the air—a much different flame than a typical maintenance burn. Major Carstens called Colonel Rey Velez, the officer in charge of the JACE, with an initial report. Velez then called Major General Marks, and the report "spun around the world for about 30 minutes."[16] In that time, Mr. Cliff Fowler, CENTCOM's civilian expert on the oil fields, confirmed the read. Colonel Steven Rotkoff, the deputy C2, and Marks, the CFLCC C2, called Carstens back at approximately 0830, and the following conversation ensued:

> "Dave, what do you think this is? Do you think it is the beginning of the sabotage we talked about?"
>
> "Yes sir."
>
> "Dave, I just want you to be sure because we are getting ready to launch 60,000 Marines across the border."
>
> "Yes. I'm sure."[17]

Shortly thereafter, McKiernan issued the order to execute G-day 24 hours earlier than originally planned.

A True "Running Start"

CENTCOM originally planned to initiate air operations (A-day) 16 days before the start of major ground combat operations (G-day). This would have afforded more time for the ground forces to complete their deployments and prepare for operations. However, Marks had been one of the primary advocates of an early attack to seize the oil fields to prevent their destruction. Rotkoff had even suggested a "G *before* A" approach as the best way to achieve tactical surprise. Colonel Kevin Benson, the CFLCC C5 (plans), developed and forwarded to the CENTCOM staff a series of position papers advocating adjusting the G-A day sequence. Over time, the plan evolved to a 15-hour gap between A-day and G-day. As these discussions progressed, CFLCC alerted I MEF and V Corps to the potential for a short-notice start, and they prepared accordingly.[18] The decapitation strike reversed that gap so that the ground war actually started two days *before* formal air operations began.[19]

Moving the start of the ground campaign ahead of the air attack resulted in CENTCOM achieving tactical and operational surprise. The premise for G-day preceding A-day from the onset was that A-day would trigger the destruction of the oil fields. As long as they were operating, the southern fields generated close to $50 million a day for Saddam. Because of this, the CFLCC intelligence officers expected Saddam to wait to the last possible minute to put them out of action—particularly if he was unsure if or when the attack would come.

In addition to allowing the CFLCC to seize the oil fields intact, executing G-day before A-day seems to have put the Iraqis off their game from the start. Seizing the oil fields, while important, is almost ancillary to the greater achievement of desynchronizing any plans the Iraqis might have had. As Colonel Rotkoff noted, "Surprise Matters!—it is incumbent on leaders to find a way of introducing surprise despite the massing of 250,000 soldiers on the border." In fact, the air component struck the first blow when a target of opportunity arose against the regime's leadership. The real difference between DESERT STORM and OIF is that to attain operational surprise, G-day did not follow a lengthy air campaign in OIF. Instead, the air component, blessed with more precision munitions than during DESERT STORM, proved able to attack targets successfully with fewer munitions and no longer needed a discrete air campaign to set the conditions CENTCOM and CFLCC desired. Accordingly, this enabled CENTCOM and CFLCC to break the "operational pattern" set in DESERT STORM. "'G before A' was this war's equivalent of the 'left hook' of DESERT STORM."[20]

A second great contrast with DESERT STORM is that CENTCOM ordered G-day prior to completing the flow of forces into the theater. Ground operations commenced while follow-on forces continued to flow into the theater. When 3rd ID's main body crossed the berm on 21 March, it was the only Army division ready to fight out of the four that the original plan required. The remaining units were still moving into the theater, linking up with their equipment, or moving forward to attack positions.

The 101st Airborne Division, completing the last stages of its deployment, moved into the assembly areas just cleared by 3rd ID but would not be ready for commitment until 22 March.[21] The 1st Armored Division was still in the preparation stages, and the 4th ID's equipment remained afloat in the Mediterranean Sea. The 3rd ACR had weeks before it expected to enter the theater, as did the 2nd ACR (L). Three of the 7th UK Armoured Brigade's four battle groups had completed their integration, but the last one was not expected to be ready until 21 March.[22] The support forces, from logisticians to military police, were in similar states of deployment.

With a clear understanding of the strategic situation and of the CFLCC's combat power, General Franks made the deliberate decision to start the ground fight before some of the designated forces were available and ready for combat. He balanced the strategic, operational, and tactical benefits of a rapid, early advance against the risk inherent in not having sufficient combat power to achieve the campaign's objective at the start of operations. The tensions within this balance affected the campaign's execution and are a defining characteristic of the entire operation.

Quite apart from whether there were adequate combat forces, repercussions of starting the war with an immature logistics, long-distance communications, and transportation capabilities surfaced. As the soldiers and marines leapt forward, the logisticians, communicators, and transporters struggled to keep up. Meticulous planning for fuel, water, and ammunition

---

Ordering the Early Start

(DECL IAW USCENTCOM OPLAN 1003-V, Classification Guidance, 31 October 2002)

CENTCOM FRAGO 09-009 (DTG 200433Z March 2003):

"This FRAGO promulgates early attack, planned operational timing in support of CFC Operations in the ITO [Iraqi Theater of Operations]."

CENTCOM FRAGO 09-009, Subject: CFC FRAGO 09-009,
200433Z March 2003

CENTCOM FRAGO 09-012 (DTG 201121Z March 2003):

"Execute CENTCOM FRAGO 09-009 (DTG 200433Z March 2003) with the exception of A-Day... that continues on time line for 1800Z, 21 March 2003. The following are major timing events:"

- D-Day/H-Hour: 19 MARCH/1800Z.
- On D+1 at 1700Z Aerial Recon into Southern Iraq.
- On D+1 at 1800Z Ground Recon in the South.
- On D+1 at 1900Z Seize GOPLATS [gulf oil platforms], Al *Faw* Manifold.
- On D+2 at 0300Z, G-Day: Seize southern oil fields; Brigade Recon; Main attack

CENTCOM FRAGO 09-0012, Subject: CFC FRAGO 09-012,
201121Z March 2003

CFLCC EXORD:

"Mission. CFLCC attacks to defeat Iraqi forces and control the zone of action, secure and exploit designated sites, and removes the current Iraqi regime. CFLCC conducts continuous stability operations to create conditions for transitions to CJTF-Iraq."

CFLCC EXORD, Subject: EXORD to COMCFLCC OPORD 03-032,
CFLCC Cobra II OPLAN Conversion to CFLCC OPORD Cobra II,
190900Z March 2003

---

paid off, yet at a cost. Delivery of just about every other commodity, to include repair parts, suffered as a consequence of inadequate means, limited ability to track supplies, and lack of an effective distribution system. These challenges became significant as the fight progressed toward Karbala and southern Baghdad.

Securing the Oil

As noted, preserving the Iraqi oil fields was a major strategic objective to protect Iraq's future and to prevent a replay of the DESERT STORM environmental disasters. The oil production facilities included the oil fields in southern Iraq and the oil platforms in the Gulf of Arabia. Poised, the marines rapidly secured the oil fields, supported by Army rocket artillery firing 13 unitary and an additional 44 standard ATACMS rounds.[23]

An aggressive Army-executed psychological operations (PSYOP) campaign supported the goal of preserving the oil fields. In addition to radio broadcasts and other uses of public information, the coalition executed a deliberate leaflet program to encourage the defending Iraqis to protect the petroleum production and processing facilities within Iraq. The combination of the PSYOP leaflet program and accelerating G-day prevented Iraqi forces from repeating the kind of environmental catastrophe they visited on the region in 1991.

Figure 42. PSYOP leaflets distributed to protect the oil fields

Figure 43. LT-1974 USAV *Champagne Marne*

To prevent Iraqi sabotage, the coalition not only seized oil fields in Iraq, but also used SOF to seize the gulf oil platforms, which required complex and integrated joint operations, including SOF, Navy, Coast Guard, and Army forces. The opening vignette describes how Army watercraft supported the special operations direct action to secure the oil platforms. Additionally, the Army tug *Champagne Marne* supported these operations.

The *Marne,* a large tugboat that operated throughout the region, earned the Navy Commendation Medal for its work in clearing derelict vessels from key navigation ways in the North Arabian Sea. On the evening of 21 March, the *Marne*, captained by Chief Warrant Officer 2 Jay Dehart, led two Navy 1600-class LCUs through the coalition warship screen beyond the most-forward mine sweepers and linked up with the forces that had secured the Mina Al-Bakr oil terminal. Establishing communications with prearranged flashing light signals, the *Marne* secured a lighterage working platform to the structure at 2309. With 24 Coast Guard security personnel aboard, the *Marne* then moved on to the Khor Al-Amaya platform to do the same, finishing the work by 0034 on the 22nd. After dropping the security team at the second platform, the crew picked up 22 marines and transported them to one of the Navy LCUs. The *Marne* completed the troop transfers and returned through the mined waterway, crossing back through the coalition warship screen at 0630 on the 22nd.[24]

Once the marines and SOF captured the oil wells and gulf oil platforms, the original fires were confirmed as sabotage, albeit an unsophisticated attempt. The wells were rigged with two explosives—the first to destroy the "Christmas tree" rigging and the second to set the oil on fire. The JTFC was unsure if the rigging of the demolitions was so poor because the Iraqis thought they had more time (given the expected 30-day air campaign) or if they were trying to preserve the oil for the future and were only making a token effort. Regardless, of the more than 1,000 oil wells in the south, only nine were set afire, and all were extinguished by the end of April.[25]

Enemy Response—TBMs and Patriots

The 32nd Army Air and Missile Defense Command's (AAMDC's) hard work in setting up comprehensive anti-tactical ballistic missile (ATBM) coverage paid off in the early hours of the war. When the fight started, there were 27 US Patriot batteries and five coalition Patriot batteries in Kuwait, Jordan, Qatar, Bahrain, and Saudi Arabia, with additional batteries in Israel and Turkey. This marked the culmination of 12 years of hard work developing the right technology, training the crews, and training and supporting allied Patriot units. Moreover, years of successful diplomacy allowed the US and the coalition to establish coverage, protect the allies, and ensure continued regional support as the campaign unfolded. Now, with reasonable assurance of protection from TBMs, regional allies were far more ready to provide the support necessary for a successful campaign.

Iraq responded to the decapitation strike with the first of 17 TBM attacks on coalition forces. At 1224 on 20 March, an Ababil-100 surface-to-surface missile streaked out of Al Basra, targeting the 4,000 soldiers and 100 helicopters of the 101st at Tactical Assembly Area (TAA) THUNDER. This launch broke the pattern Iraq

> **Patriot saved the 101st.**
>
> Major General Dave Petraeus
> Commander, 101st Airborne Division

Figure 44. Patriot missile launchers protecting key facilities

established in the first Gulf War, when all TBMs were launched at night—affording the Iraqis a measure of self-protection and taking advantage of more favorable temperatures and winds for chemical weapons employment. The USS *Higgins*, an AEGIS destroyer off the coast of Kuwait, detected the launch, providing a 90-second warning. D/5-52 ADA, one of the three SHORTSTOP batteries deployed to extend TBM protection to the Army formations, destroyed the missile. This was the first of five TBM attacks on that first day.

The Iraqis fired a second missile, aimed at Camp DOHA and the CFLCC headquarters, at 1330, from the vicinity of Al Basra. E/2-43 ADA, firing the newest PAC-III missile, destroyed it just 3 miles from the camp. Of the other three Iraqi missiles fired, two fell harmlessly in the Arabian Gulf or Kuwaiti desert and US Patriot missiles destroyed the other one.

Missile Strikes on the Headquarters

During the [briefing], they're giving the Battle Update Assessment [BUA] Brief, sure enough, you can pick it up on the [Air and Missile Defense Work Station], [we] got early warning from AEGIS . . . there's another ABABIL [missile] coming right at us, impact point Doha.

The CG, I'm talking about Lieutenant General McKiernan, said "everybody put their mask on" and they sat there and they continued with the BUA. There was so much confidence in this weapon system that nobody moved. Then suddenly, you heard the walls rumble and you heard the sound of those missiles take off, and there it went, two more missiles in the air. Then you heard a loud explosion. This time pieces of metal actually fell on the roof of our headquarters. That was a high-five moment.

Colonel Charles Anderson
Chief of Staff, 32nd AAMDC

Terrain Description

This early phase of the ground war started in the soft sands of the Kuwaiti-Iraqi desert and closed in the Euphrates River valley. Throughout the fighting, soldiers had to contend with the best, and worst, of each type of soil and hydrology. Crossing the berm into Iraq led directly into soft, shifting sands that were 2-4 feet deep, wreaking havoc with movement timelines and convoy operations. Moving north and west toward the river valley, the ground firmed up but was heavily compartmentalized by waddies and gullies that were difficult to see and impossible to drive through.

Due north of the berm lay an area soldiers described as "the far side of the moon," because it was so broken and difficult to traverse. However, there was generally freedom to maneuver once out of the constricted and rough terrain. Within the river valley, the terrain became complex and canalizing. Many farms, villages, and small groupings of houses broke up the ground and impeded movement. Generally constructed of the soft concrete and cinder blocks common to the region, buildings in the area rarely reached three stories. The farm fields were muddy and soft, crisscrossed with irrigation ditches and small canals. The primary highways ran roughly parallel to the river and were generally improved paved roads. The secondary roads were narrow, in various states of pavement and repair, and frequently bore no resemblance to the map as far as trafficability and routes. In short, units operating in the river valley found themselves compelled to rely on the road network.

The Enemy Disposition

The Iraqi leadership focused defensive planning against expected coalition actions in the Tigris-Euphrates Valley (Highways 1, 6, and 7) and on defending Baghdad proper. Iraqi dispositions reflected a clear expectation of the coalition main effort along Route 6 in the east through Umm Qasr. Saddam's generals planned to conduct a defense in depth, using the oil fields as sanctuaries. They embedded forces in the vicinity of gas/oil separation plants to shield them from coalition strikes and to ensure control over these key facilities. Forces were generally arrayed to defend key routes and population centers.

To defend Iraq, Saddam and his military leaders fielded 17 regular army (RA) divisions and six of the better-equipped and better-trained Republican Guard (RG) divisions. In Baghdad, the Special Republican Guard (SRG), a force of approximately 15,000 soldiers, had the specific task of defending key sites and repressing popular unrest in Baghdad. In addition to these conventional forces, Saddam organized a host of paramilitary and militia forces, including the infamous *Saddam Fedayeen* and Ba'ath Party militia. Iraq fielded no significant naval or air forces following their destruction during Operation DESERT STORM. However, the RA and RG forces had a few rotary-wing aircraft to conduct ground-attack or airmobile operations.

Southern Iraq: Kuwait to Baghdad

Iraqi defensive preparations along the Kuwaiti border were minimal. In the main, they consisted of a string of border observation posts offset several km north of the complex ditch-berm-wire obstacle that ran along the border. Clearly designed only to provide early warning, the outposts lacked the manpower, armor, or artillery required to conduct a defense.

IRAQI Ground Forces From ODS to OIF	
Operation DESERT STORM	**Operation IRAQI FREEDOM**
• 950,000 troops serving in 60 divisions. • Republican Guard estimated at 150,000 troops. • Over 5,000 tanks, 5,000 APCs, and 3,000 artillery pieces.	• 280,000 to 350,000 troops serving in 17 divisions. • Republican Guard estimated at 50,000 to 80,000 troops. • Over 2,200 tanks, 2,400 APCs, and 4,000 artillery pieces.

Figure 45. Comparison of Iraqi ground forces in ODS and OIF

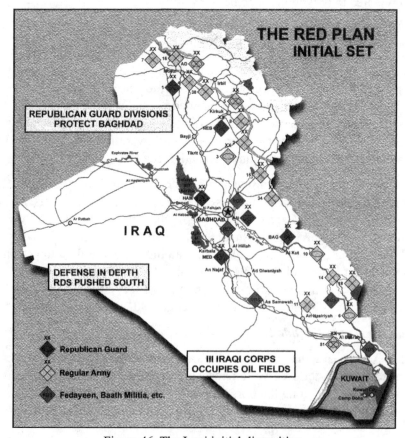

Figure 46. The Iraqi initial disposition

On 19 March, Iraqi ground forces were in position to defend the Tigris-Euphrates Valley, weighting the eastern (Highway 6) approach to Baghdad with six divisions. Beginning at Basra, Iraqi formations echeloned along the Highway 6/Tigris River avenue of approach, with the 51st Mechanized Division south of Az Zubayr, supported by reinforcing armor to the southwest of the city. The 6th Armored Division defended from just north of Basra, with the 18th Infantry Division in Qurnah, the 14th Infantry Division in Qurnah and Al Amarah, and the 10th Armored Division in Al Amarah. Farther up the Tigris River, the *Baghdad* RG Division concentrated at Al Kut, its brigades echeloned from northwest to southeast.[26] Along the western Euphrates (Highway 8) approach, the 18th Infantry Division positioned the 704th Brigade in the Rumaila oil field, along with elements of two RA armor brigades and an RA mechanized infantry brigade. The 11th Infantry Division defended An Nasiriyah and As Samawah to the southeast on the approaches to An Nasiriyah.

Irregulars and Popular Forces

The list of anticipated paramilitary forces included:

- *Saddam Fedayeen,* "Saddam's Martyrs"—fanatically loyal but relatively poorly trained paramilitary forces
- *Al Quds*—local militia, many of whom are Ba'ath Party members or responsive to Ba'ath Party direction
- Ba'ath Party militias; loyalists from the security services
- Intelligence services
- The *Lions of Saddam* youth organization

These organizations prepared to fight as irregulars rather than as standing conventional forces. The regime used many of these troops in the south, with approximately 2,000 operating in Basra. Some assumed responsibility for defense of the urban areas along Highway 8 and the Euphrates Valley, to include An Najaf (12,000-14,000 fighters) and Karbala (2,000-3,000 fighters). Additional irregular forces operated in An Nasiriyah, As Samawah, and elsewhere.[27] Unanticipated and not accounted for, other (non-Iraqi) paramilitary fighters entered the country and turned up among the combatants.

This extensive use of paramilitaries may have reflected an Iraqi plan to rely on a "popular army" and on an effort to generate popular support for the defense of key urban areas. There were references in the Iraqi open press to *Black Hawk Down* and indications that the Iraqis were preparing elements of this "popular army" to engage coalition forces in that manner.[28] There were significant amounts of cached arms and ammunition to support just such an effort—the regime clearly planned for their use, or at least intended to telegraph such a plan to observers.[29]

Conclusion

V Corps and I MEF attacks across the border into Iraq demonstrated effective operational planning, flexibility, and agility. After building on 12 years of theater preparation, followed by approximately nine months of planning, preparing, and deploying into the theater, coalition armed forces sought to liberate the Iraqi people, preserve Iraq's natural resources, and supplant a 30-year dictatorship. The ensuing campaign quickly achieved the first of several national goals— securing the Iraqi oil fields to preserve the future prosperity of the country. At the tactical level, the first 72 hours marked a lightning advance of over 400 km (in the case of Objective RAMS) to secure the first two primary objectives. Yet the coalition did not merely attack from Kuwait. Special forces operated against the Iraqi western and northern areas, undermining the regime, supporting US allies, stabilizing the Kurdish Autonomous Zone, and protecting Iraq's western neighbors from Scud launches. So, in addition to forces advancing from Kuwait, Iraq faced mounting pressures from its other three borders, and in the center, from relentless coalition air attacks.

Violating virtually all of the traditional wisdom about how to prepare for a campaign of this scope, the V Corps and I MEF forces appear to have achieved operational and tactical surprise when they started their attack before all of the "necessary" forces had arrived and without a lengthy air effort. Accepting the inherent risks, General Franks and Lieutenant General McKiernan understood the necessity and value of attacking early and aggressively. The running start appears to have thrown the Iraqis off of their defensive plan, and they were never able to regain their footing. Coalition forces moved farther and faster than any Iraqi—and even many in the coalition —believed possible. The force was on its way to Baghdad.

Of course, no plan survives contact with the enemy, and the Iraqi defenders offered a few surprises of their own. The widely expected mass capitulation of the regular army never materialized. Generally, they did not surrender or even vigorously defend. Instead, the majority of Iraqi soldiers just melted away, offering relatively light, if any, resistance. Yet, it was unclear whether this was a deliberate tactic to preserve the force, the result of the extended PSYOP campaign, the result of the ongoing attacks on their command and control systems, the result of their fear of coalition combat power, or simply as close as the soldiers could come to a formal capitulation given the tight control imposed by the layers of security services.

More surprising, the *Fedayeen* and other paramilitary forces proved more of a threat than anyone had expected. While the paramilitaries were always considered part of the enemy capabilities, the intelligence and operations communities had never anticipated how ferocious, tenacious, and fanatical they would be. The attacks were never able to interrupt the coalition's advance, but they did disrupt operations in An Nasiriyah and As Samawah and inflicted the first startling casualties of the war.

The "darkest day," 23 March, marked the soldiers', marines', airmen's, and the American people's true baptism under fire—when all were reminded that the liberation of Iraq would not be accomplished without spilling coalition blood. Clearly, at least some element of the Iraqi nation was willing to close with and engage the overwhelming Coalition ground forces. Worse, they were attacking in a manner that avoided traditional American strengths—high-technology, stand-off weapons. An Nasiriyah and As Samawah offered the first inklings of how the Iraqis would attempt to defend through the conclusion of major combat operations and after.

Iraqi tactical ballistic missile strikes on coalition forces and facilities in Kuwait came as no surprise. In a pleasant and confidence-inspiring surprise, the coalition's Patriot missiles were 100-percent effective in destroying threatening inbound missiles. The Patriots' success cemented the support of America's regional allies and lent the ground commanders the confidence to maneuver aggressively against the Iraqis. Thus, with the fight joined and several successes already under the coalition's collective belt, the world watched and waited for the first major force-on-force engagements closer to Baghdad. The scope, scale, and character of the Iraqi defense were just becoming apparent, and no one yet knew how the fight would play out. The threat of chemical weapons was palpable as missiles streaked southward and coalition forces raced northward.

Camp PENNSYLVANIA—The Alleged Murder of Two Officers

Two days prior to crossing the border into Iraq, in what it believed to be a secure location in its desert encampment in Kuwait, the 1st BCT, 101st Airborne Division, was preparing for combat operations when it suffered an emotionally devastating nighttime attack on the soldiers who operate the tactical operations center (TOC). The attack on the sleeping men, however, was not due to enemy action; it was apparently perpetrated by one of their own.

Captain Christopher Seifert, the assistant brigade S2, and Major Gregory Stone, the air liaison officer, were killed in the attack. Their deaths and the injury of 14 other staff members shocked the brigade to its core. In this attack, every staff section received injuries, but losing Captain Seifert was particularly devastating to the S2 Intelligence section. Seifert was a well-liked and respected officer within the staff and among subordinate battalions. An outstanding officer, he possessed all the strengths of character and professional competence that anyone could hope for in a subordinate. Perhaps most significantly, Seifert was the perfect counterpart to the brigade S2, Major Kyle Warren. They complemented each other's strengths and weaknesses. In eight months, they built a relationship based on mutual respect and admiration.

Captain Seifert was, as Major Warren recalled, his tall center around whom the rest of the team revolved. Losing him in the final hours before war affected the S2 section so deeply that it literally took most of the war for the section to recover. Warren, like most Army officers, had built his team around his strongest officer. Seifert was a meticulous operator who did not tolerate sloppy work. He was also an expert on intelligence systems who knew how to leverage the architecture to meet requirements. As the intelligence planner, Seifert maintained a forward look to support planning.

Although this was his official capacity as the senior intelligence captain, there was more to it than that. Captain Seifert carried a natural air about him that expressed confidence, know-how, and a passion to train. Seifert's death affected the S2 section in several ways. The first was obviously the loss of the soldier. The war was literally two days away and Major Warren knew he had to maintain the section's focus on the fight while dealing with a host of emotional and operational issues. Warren simply asked his team to "take commands from the tower" and to trust his leadership in the days to come. The only way they could move forward—figuratively and emotionally—was with a strong unity of effort. Anything less than a total commitment would have been a disservice to Captain Seifert and Major Stone.

Major Warren reflected on how to deal with a death that is so close and personal and yet still maintain the focus to fight. Captain Seifert's personal items were a reminder of the magnitude of the unit's loss. His uniforms with his nametape sewn on, his books, and personal photos were still with the section, and these had to be packed and sent home, and Warren still had to write a letter to Seifert's widow, Terri. Some of Warren's soldiers were just plain afraid and struggled to sleep through the night. Warren recalls how God gave him strength to get through it. He was blessed to have a strong NCOIC and to have had the composure that was truly "beyond himself."

The day following the attack, the Army's Criminal Investigation Command conducted its investigation, followed the next day by a short memorial service. Upon its conclusion, the BCT mounted its vehicles and, following 3rd ID, began its attack into Iraq toward the city of An Najaf. Within 60 hours, they were in combat. Here, they faced a deliberate foe in the streets of An Najaf, a city of 800,000 citizens. The S2 section had to describe and predict an enemy who held nearly every asymmetric quality as the brigade committed to the urban fight.

A replacement S2 planner arrived on the third day of the An Najaf fight, and the section began the arduous task of training a new team. Rebuilding the team focused on reworking SOPs and shifting Captain Seifert's work to others. Scores of things that resulted from his death were a constant challenge, like finding the threat studies he had produced, operating intelligence systems, and maintaining the high standards that Captain Seifert so diligently enforced. The brigade excelled in the fight for An Najaf, proceeded to Al Hillah, Karbala, and continued to execute SASO in northern Iraq. In Major Warren's words, "it certainly was not pretty, but Captain Seifert would have been proud of the results."

Compiled from interviews with Major Kyle Warren
1st BCT brigade intelligence officer
101st Airborne Division

Crossing The Berm

They are coming to surrender or be burned in their tanks.

Mohammed Saeed al-Sahhaf
Iraqi Information Minister
"Baghdad Bob"

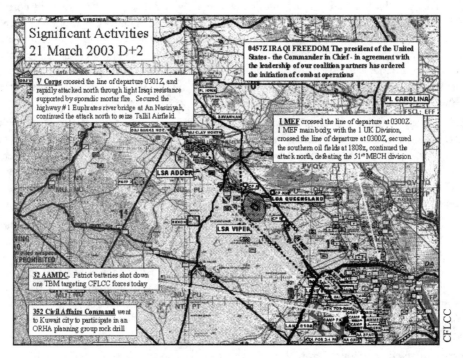

Figure 47. CFLCC common operational picture, D+2/G-day, 21 March 2003

The first task of the ground war was to penetrate the 10-km-deep defensive linear obstacle complex along the Kuwait-Iraq border. Literally a line in the sand, the berm was a combination of massive tank ditches, concertina wire, electrified fencing, and of course, berms of dirt.

The breaching operation required four major tasks: reducing the berms, destroying the defending Iraqi forces along the border (mostly observation posts), establishing secure lanes through the berm, and then passing the follow-on forces through to continue the attack into Iraq. The division planned eight lanes. In coordination with the Kuwaiti forces, the 1st and 2nd BCTs would conduct the actual breaches. Once the lanes were clear and the security zone was established, the division cavalry and the 3rd BCT would pass through and press the attack north. The 1st and 2nd BCTs would follow, expanding the division's presence on Iraqi soil.

Reducing the Berm

As noted, the deliberate breaching operation had been carefully planned and rehearsed. Still, the decision to execute early rippled through the force so that, by the time word reached the brigades and battalions, they ended up moving directly from the attack positions to the border. The 1st BCT's Task Force (TF) 2-7 IN, for example, was assigned the mission to assist

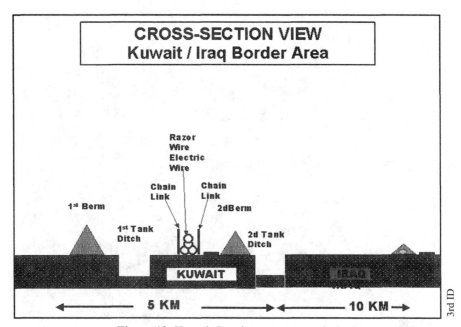

Figure 48. Kuwait-Iraq berm cross-section

Figure 49. Berm to first tank ditch, Kuwait-Iraq border

in preparing the berm approaches in support of 1st BCT's breach (along Lanes 5, 6, 8A, 9, and 10). On 19 March 2003, the task force occupied an attack position less than 11 km from the border. As it moved into the attack position, TF 2-7 believed it would be there for 24-48 hours, but literally as it arrived, the BCT commander ordered the reduction teams forward.[30]

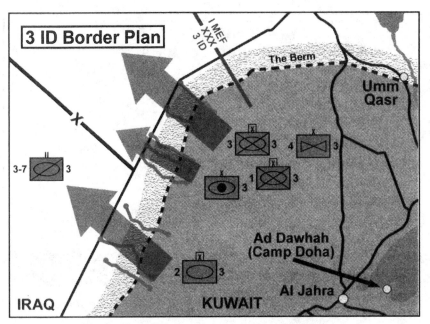

Figure 50. 3rd ID border breach scheme of maneuver

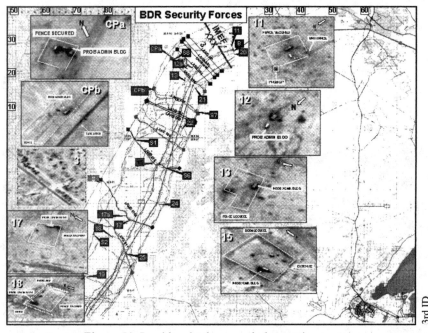

Figure 51. Iraqi border lanes and observation posts

The TF 2-7 IN reduction team consisted of two combined arms company teams to secure, assist, and supervise the Kuwaiti nationals actually reducing berms.[31] The Kuwaitis plowed in the berms, filling the tank ditches with the dirt. Armored combat earthmovers supporting TF 2-7 IN reinforced and constructed roads across the tank ditches. The plan called for tracked vehicles to use the newly constructed roads, while wheeled vehicles crossed on armored vehicle-launched bridges. Once this work was completed, there was a clear, marked route crossing the border. Positioned on the border and poised for war with all inspections complete, drills rehearsed, and rounds chambered, TF 2-7 IN was ready for war.[32] Similar actions occurred at each breach lane for both BCTs.

Preparing to Breach the Berms

The first critical mission of the war was the breach of the border obstacles. Lieutenant Colonel Ed Jackson, commanding the 54th Engineer Battalion, was responsible for the breaching operations. The entire operation had been rehearsed in detail before the attack, with all the key leaders in the division driving through a full-scale mock-up of the border and the lane marking system. Coalition engineers were prepared to reduce the series of obstacles, creating lanes through the berm, tank ditch, wire fence, electrified fence, wire fence, second berm, tank ditch, and then the third berm 10 km from the start point. The whole complex was colloquially known as "the berm."

Along each lane, combat engineers and MPs manned traffic control points, with construction equipment and recovery vehicles nearby to repair damage or remove any blockages. As units passed through the border, control of the crossing transitioned from division (937th Engineer Group) to corps (130th Engineer Brigade and the 864th Engineer Battalion), allowing the 3rd ID headquarters to focus on the advance north. Following the passage of the main body, the 864th Engineer Battalion would close all but two lanes. These lanes would be left open for follow-on forces.

As combat operations drew near, the Kuwaitis decided that they wanted to be the ones that breached the obstacles at the Iraq-Kuwait border. This was a very prestigious mission, and they would be able to accomplish it under the guise of border maintenance. This would also allow them to limit the amount of damage to the obstacles. With the help of Colonel Gregg Martin, commander of the 130th Engineer Brigade, and Captain Chris Miller, V Corps liaison officer for the border reduction, Kuwaiti civilians began breaching the obstacles. At one point, they suspended operations when the press heard about the project, but restarted after the press moved on to other issues.

On 20 March, the day before coalition forces would cross the border, the Kuwaiti heavy equipment operators were trying to finish the last obstacles in each of the 12 lanes. Problems with the language barrier, haul assets for the dozers, and fuel were making the task a difficult one. Colonel Martin was personally escorting dozers from lane to lane to ensure that the work would be done prior to crossing the line of departure. His goal was to get maximum effort from the Kuwaitis, because anything they did saved valuable engineer resources to use later in the fight. As darkness approached, there were still four lanes in the marines' zone to the north that were not complete. Colonel Martin pushed the dozers forward and picked locations for the last four breaches. It was dark by the time the last lane was completed and the opening shots of the war were fired. There was now nothing between Iraq and the Kuwaiti operators and US engineers but a berm and tank ditch that had now been breached. As the Kuwaitis refueled and moved out of the area, the 3rd ID MLRS and 155mm rounds were flying overhead in preparation for the attack on the border guard posts.

Based on "Victory Sappers: V Corps Engineers in Operation IRAQI FREEDOM" by Colonel Gregg F. Martin and Captain David Johnson; and interviews with Colonel Martin, commander, 130th Engineer Brigade, Lieutenant Colonel Fehnel, commander, 864th Engineer Battalion, and Colonel Hildenbrand, commander, 937th Engineer Group.

Destroying Iraqi Border Opposition

With the conditions set to pass through the berm, coalition forces shifted their efforts to denying the Iraqi leadership early warning of the actual invasion. The corps developed a deliberate fire and maneuver plan to destroy the thin line of Iraqi observation posts and covering forces rapidly and simultaneously. Once the corps breached the obstacle, the lead units intended to rush forward to destroy any remnants of the Iraqi forward forces.

Artillery and PSYOP Support

Five artillery battalions supported the breach, firing simultaneously against 11 targets with a total of 458 artillery rounds.[33] The direct support battalions, assigned to provide artillery fires primarily for their respective BCTs, fired from positions that facilitated their ability to move with the units they supported. Thus the artillery could provide fires for the infantry and armor units during the breach and on through the attack.

> ### Sometimes Even a Nonlethal Attack Can be Lethal
>
> "The cause of death was a box of leaflets that fell out of a *Combat Talon* aircraft when a static line broke. The box impacted on the Iraqi guard's head, and 9th PSYOP Battalion may have achieved the first enemy KIA of Operation IRAQI FREEDOM."
>
> Lieutenant Colonel Carl Ayers, commander of the 9th PSYOP Battalion, describing the death of an Iraqi border guard in western Iraq

For example, the 1st Battalion, 9th Field Artillery Battalion (1-9 FA), fired the opening rounds of the ground war in direct support of the 2nd BCT. The division artillery assigned the battalion four targets and directed that a "battery six" (36 rounds) be fired against each of them. The battalion fired 132 rounds and destroyed three of its four assigned targets—observation posts in the southern portion of the crossing sector.[34] They engaged the fourth target, an observation post, with only limited results due to probable target location error. Attack helicopters and ground elements of TF 3-15 IN combined to destroy the target. Rocket fires from 1-39 FA Battalion (MLRS) and the 2-4 FA Battalion (MLRS) augmented the entire effort. The 1-39 FA, for example, delivered 63 MLRS strikes deep into Iraq, shaping the battlefield by destroying critical command and control nodes and enemy headquarters.

Figure 52. PSYOP capitulation leaflet

The psychological operations leaflet effort, somewhat less successful than the oil well preservation campaign, attempted to convince the Iraqi forces to capitulate. Prewar intelligence indicated that the Iraqi army might be susceptible to an aggressive campaign to promote capitulation or mass surrender. Unfortunately, the surrender leaflets did not work as well in OIF as they did in DESERT STORM. Of course, one major difference between the two wars was that during DESERT STORM, Iraqi soldiers suffered through an extensive bombing for a month before receiving ground forces. As a result of the bombing, those forces were far more receptive to the surrender appeals. In DESERT STORM Iraqi troops were not defending their homeland, and the motivation to stay—and die—in Kuwait was arguably much weaker.

The leaflet effort to induce capitulation was a high priority prior to breaching the berm. But, due to the speed of the subsequent ground advance, the program did not have adequate time in which to work. "In many cases, efforts to deliver capitulation instructions to units failed outright, or the target audience did not easily understand messages that were delivered."[35] Moreover, the regime conducted a massive counterpropaganda campaign against this PSYOP operation. The regime threatened death to soldiers who deserted or surrendered. Although the 3rd ID would eventually take in some 2,600 EPWs, there was no massive capitulation of entire units. However, there is plenty of evidence to suggest that many of the Iraqi regular forces deserted their units and abandoned their equipment. Although it is still too early to determine with precision the efficacy of the PSYOP effort, it clearly did not have the effect anticipated.

Crossing the Line of Departure

Before we were going to LD, I arranged for what we called a Patriotic Oath Service. It was the last time that TF 1-64 AR would be together until we met in Baghdad. I arranged for the 3rd ID band to be present and our Brigade Chaplain, who offered the invocation. I gave the Oath of Office to the commander, LTC Schwartz. In turn, he then gave the Oath to the officers in the task force. After the completion of the Oath, he gave the Oath of Enlistment to all the soldiers. After that, the Commander and Command Sergeant Major spoke to the task force, reaffirming our mission. We ended with a prayer offered by me. This was a very moving service which built cohesion in the task force and reaffirmed our commitment to our vocations as soldiers.

Chaplain (Captain) Ron Cooper,
TF 1-64 AR

Shaping Operations

In addition to using artillery to reduce the Iraqi outposts, Lieutenant General Wallace moved to preclude either a counterattack or defense by the Iraqi 11th Infantry Division, located in the vicinity of Tallil Air Base. The 11th ID was the closest Iraqi ground unit to the breach points. To eliminate this threat, Wallace tasked the 11th Attack Helicopter Regiment (AHR) to destroy 11th ID's artillery and armor in the vicinity of An Nasiriyah and Tallil Air Base. The 11th AHR is a lethal and agile force of 21 AH-64As and 21 AH-64D *Longbow Apache*[36] attack helicopters, augmented with an additional 18 AH-64Ds from 1-227th Aviation Battalion out of the 1st Cavalry Division. The regiment was V Corps' most powerful and agile deep-strike capability. The 11th and its *Apaches* were designed to penetrate deeply into enemy terrain to destroy enemy formations before they can affect the battle. Destroying the Iraqi 11th ID would provide the 3rd ID freedom of maneuver and secure its eastern flank.

The 11th AHR launched on time, with two UH-60L *Black Hawks* providing command and control and personnel recovery and two CH-47Ds providing fuel support. As they crossed the border, the UH-60 and CH-47 pilots reported poor visibility from the dust and haze, even though they were using their night vision goggles. The AH-64 crews, however, could continue on by using their advanced Pilot Night Vision System, which employs thermal sights that could see through the haze. Lieutenant Colonel Michael J. Barbee, the commander of the 6-6 Aviation Squadron, aborted the mission since the UH-60s and CH-47 s needed for command and control and refueling could not continue safely.[37]

After the aborted mission, morale sank. Some pilots had compared this attack to the 101st Aviation Brigade's legendary deep attack in Operation DESERT STORM; they, too, were going to be heroes. Their frustration continued to build, adding to the 11th AHR's collective desire to get into the fight, and possibly played a major role in the unsuccessful deep attack later in the war. In any case, the 3rd ID crossed the border without the 11th AHR having destroyed the threat to its north and east.[38]

Securing Lanes

With the preparatory actions in motion, the division was set to penetrate the berm along the eight lanes assigned to the 1st and 2nd BCTs, with the marines crossing through the remaining four lanes to the east. They all acted in parallel to bring the maximum combat power to bear on the Iraqis simultaneously. The 2nd BCT's breaching operations are an excellent example of the deliberate breaches done across the entire border obstacle.

The 3rd ID ordered the 2nd BCT to establish three lanes through the obstacle (Lanes 10A, 11, and 12) to support movement of the division cavalry squadron, followed by substantial elements of the division and V Corps. Task Force 3-15 IN, commanded by Lieutenant Colonel Stephen Twitty, led the 2nd BCT's breaching operations. The task force consisted of two organic mechanized infantry companies (Alpha and Bravo, 3-15 IN), one attached tank company (Bravo Company, 4-64 AR), one engineer company (Alpha Company, 10th EN), and a PSYOP team. The task force organized into two elements. Lieutenant Colonel Twitty led Team *China*, composed of tanks and Bradley fighting vehicles. The remainder of TF 3-15 IN, all the wheeled logistics and administrative vehicles, formed Team *Dragon*, led by the battalion executive officer, Major Denton Knapp.[39]

After 19 days of intense rehearsals at Camp NEW YORK, the task force completed its final preparations early on 20 March, expecting to breach on the 22nd. B/3-15 Infantry opened the

Figure 53. Crossing sign, 2nd BCT, 3rd ID, entering Iraq

lane through the Kuwaiti side of the border defenses and established an outpost to maintain visual contact with the Iraqi border observation posts.

While waiting, the soldiers assumed mission-oriented protective posture (MOPP) 4, wearing all of their chemical protective clothing, in case the Iraqis responded with a chemical or biological weapon strike.[40] At 1224, a Patriot missile fired from D/5-52 ADA, located at Camp VICTORY, intercepted an inbound Iraqi missile about 15 km from Camp NEW YORK. Throughout the day, the Iraqis fired a total of five surface-to-surface missiles. Each time, the soldiers donned their protective masks and hunkered down in trenches. As elsewhere on the battlefield, unit chemical officers used point-of-impact data calculated from the Patriot missile battery and AN/TSQ-36 and AN/TSQ-37 *Firefinder* radars and automatically transmitted across the battlefield via the ABCS.[41] With this information, the chemical officer added the effect of the wind and determined the possibility of any chemical contamination reaching the unit. However, in this case, the missiles were targeted at Camp DOHA, and the TF 3-15 IN returned to MOPP 0 and resumed preparations for combat.[42]

Less than 3 hours later, at 2100, the direct-support artillery battalions began 20 minutes of 155mm fire directed on Iraqi border observation posts. TF 3-15 IN crossed the line of departure (LD) at 2120, with Bravo and Alpha Companies in the north and south, clearing lanes 10A and 11, respectively.[43] Alpha Company "Gators," under the command of Captain Joshua Wright, drew first blood when, at 2138, it engaged and killed seven Iraqi soldiers at observation posts 18 and 19. In the course of the breaching operation, the task force destroyed three observation posts, four tanks,

> **Soldiers Looking Out for Soldiers**
>
> As the 603rd continued to move north beyond As Samawah, it passed two soldiers walking along the road. They were in the middle of nowhere, walking north. The convoy stopped and picked up the soldiers and took care of them until their commander recovered them personally. The two soldiers were cooks on the commanding general's mess team who had somehow become separated from their unit.
>
> 603rd Aviation Support Battalion
> unit history

three armored personnel carriers, and five trucks. It then established a 10-km-deep security zone and prepared to pass 3-7 CAV, the corps refuel package, and the rest of 2nd BCT through the lanes.

Following the successful passage of lines, the 2nd BCT followed 3-7 CAV north. To facilitate movement and to clear the breach quickly, Colonel David Perkins, the BCT commander, split his BCT into two groups. Perkins moved armored vehicles, accompanied by the minimum required support vehicles such as tankers, as a separate grouping that he called *Heavy Metal*. Perkins' executive officer led *Rock and Roll*, composed of all of the wheeled vehicles.[44]

Passing Follow-on Forces

Conducting the passage of lines was far from routine. Several of the lanes were not as trafficable as expected. Moreover, the sheer physics of pushing the 10,000-plus V Corps vehicles through eight functioning lanes led to some early problems. For example, the 450 vehicles of the 603rd Aviation Support Battalion, commanded by Lieutenant Colonel Rich Knapp, were rerouted to lane 5 instead of 8A shortly after starting movement. Due to the size of the convoy, communication from the lead vehicle to the trail vehicle exceeded FM range, and the simple act of passing the change of route proved difficult. With hard work and only a bit of confusion, the battalion made the adjustment. Similar little dramas played themselves out elsewhere in the breach—almost nothing goes as planned, even in the most routine evolutions in combat zones. As the 603rd convoy drivers finally exited the passage lane, they drove by a dead Iraqi soldier on the road and they knew they were not in Kuwait anymore. For the next three days, the ground convoy encountered rugged desert terrain, traffic jams, fatigue, and more. Other units across the battlefield faced similar challenges.

Trafficability Past the Berm—the 603rd ASB's Story

The 3rd Division provided the 4th (Aviation) Brigade with three heavy equipment transporters (HETs), which were to be used to move the bucket-loader and forklift assigned to the 603rd Aviation Support Battalion. During mission planning, the 603rd Battalion commander, Lieutenant Colonel Knapp, decided to leave two of the HETs empty so that they could be used to recover vehicles and equipment during the road march.

Shortly after clearing the passage lane through the berm, recovering the HETs became the sole focus of the recovery team leader, the support operations officer, the battalion commander, and the three wrecker crews. As the brigade convoy continued north to Objective BULLS, the radio call *"HET stuck, grid XXXXXX"* would become all too familiar.

In the space of about 3 miles of open desert, the three HETs were each recovered more times than any of those involved can remember. It became a mindless drill and a remarkable display of human endurance. HETs have a lot of wheels and that means a lot of digging when they get stuck up to the axles. Each recovery involved various combinations of shovels, wreckers, snatch blocks, and other HETs. Several times a 10-ton wrecker left the ground, bouncing as it strained against its winch cables. At that point, more sand was shoveled and another wrecker was added. Self-recovery with another HET using its winch worked sometimes, until the cables became hopelessly snarled from the strain. On occasion, some HETs became stuck 50 meters from where they were just freed from the clutches of the Iraqi desert.

The 603rd moved slowly across the desert throughout the night. While moving, it discovered a stuck HET from another unit and helped to recover the vehicle. The HET and crew joined the 603rd convoy. It took nearly 24 hours to travel 30 km from the attack position to Objective BULLS.

603rd ASB Unit History

Corps units passed bumper to bumper through the breach for two days and began the long, tiring movement north.[45] The combat elements led, with 3-7 CAV in the west, 2nd BCT moving north in the desert, and 3rd BCT driving straight north after passing through 1st BCT. The rest of V Corps followed, traveling over 100 km, sometimes in 600-vehicle convoys moving at only 3-5 miles per hour along a single main supply route (MSR). Nonetheless 3rd ID reached attack positions from which it attacked its first objective, Tallil Air Base, Objective FIREBIRD, in 24 hours.

Extending Aviation's Reach

While 3rd ID forces moved north, the 101st Airborne Division maneuvered to extend the corps' reach into Iraq. The 101st, as an air assault division, is built around three infantry brigades and two helicopter brigades, providing lift and attack capabilities and allowing the division to lift maneuver formations great distances with tremendous flexibility. The 101st, in extending its own reach north, would also establish the infrastructure for the rest of the corps' aviation assets. Getting the aviation as far north as possible was the key to reaching out and shaping future battles early. Naturally, fuel is the key to aviation availability. Thus, while much of the 3rd ID's and 11th AHR's attack aviation supported the breaching operations, the 101st prepared for the next phase of combat by pushing the fuel and attack helicopters forward.

The corps' concept of the operation centered on the desire to position 101st combat power near Baghdad quickly. To accomplish this, the division integrated ground and air operations to move fuel points as far forward as possible.

As Figure 54 illustrates, the 101st planned air assault operations to set up a

Ghosts of 1991

Earlier in the evening of 20 March, the brigade reconnaissance troop, *Bushmaster*, reported enemy vehicles in TF 2-7 IN's sector. They believed that T-72 tanks were firing on their vehicles. This report reached the task force and everyone keyed up for contact, contrary to what the most recent intelligence reports claimed.

The brigade reconnaissance troop reports turned out to be grossly false and inaccurate. In the darkness, the thermal sights of the scouts had picked up hot spots, largely from fires, earlier artillery explosions, and a day's worth of sun beating down on hulks. *Bushmaster* fired on the "T-72s" as they crossed the border.

Hours later, the rising sun cleared up the confusion, revealing T-55 hulks remaining on the battlefield from the 1991 conflict.

TF 2-7 Infantry Unit History

"daisy chain" of support locations—Rapid Refuel Point (RRP) EXXON, Forward Arming and Refueling Point (FARP) SHELL, and Forward Operating Base (FOB) 5. Establishing EXXON and SHELL would extend aviation's reach to the Karbala Gap and southern Baghdad. To support these long jumps forward, four CH-47D *Chinook* helicopters from A/7-101st AVN (159th Aviation Brigade) would conduct FAT COW operations to help reach SHELL. FAT COW operations use the CH-47D helicopters' internal 800-gallon tanks to refuel other helicopters, allowing the small, armed OH-58D helicopters from 2-17 CAV to move forward to the edge of their range, refuel, and establish security.

On 20 March 2003, the RRP EXXON team of fuel and ammunition handlers crossed the berm and entered Iraq under the control of TF 2-187 IN. It took almost 16 hours to travel the 200 km to their release point. They arrived at EXXON, already secured by an air assault, and established a 12-point RRP within 1 hour of arrival. The service support troops built a fully operational fuel system supply point (FSSP)

Sir, Blades are turning (230853ZMAR03), should have liftoff for AASLT to SHELL in the next 3 minutes.

E-mail from Captain Tim O'Sullivan, 101st Airborne Division battle captain

within 3½ hours of arrival. This marked the first step in extending the reach of attack helicopters into central Iraq. Eventually, the corps would establish FARPs across the entire country, enabling the attack helicopters to strike virtually every corner of Iraq, as shown in Figure 56.

To provide security to the helicopter fleet, the 101st attached 136 door gunners to the 159th Aviation Brigade alone. The gunners came from the three maneuver brigades in the 101st Airborne Division after they had received a 40-hour block of formal training on aviation operations and aeromedical factors. Attaching infantry as door gunners not only supported security but also facilitated maintenance. With infantrymen serving as door gunners, only one

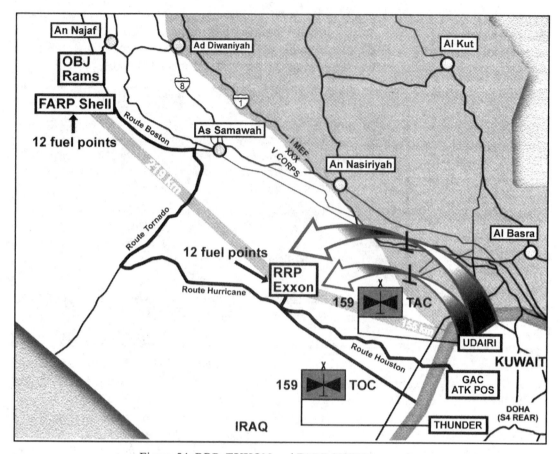

Figure 54. RRP EXXON and FARP SHELL concept

Figure 55. 101st Airborne Division FARP operations

crew chief flew with the aircraft during missions. The second crew chief remained behind and conducted ground maintenance on aircraft not assigned a mission. Thus, the division maximized the availability of its most maneuverable and responsive asset.[46]

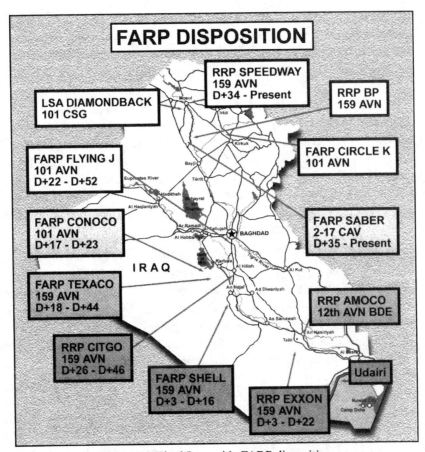

Figure 56. Final Iraq-wide FARP disposition

Attacking North to Tallil Air Base

The 1st BCT, 3rd ID, led by TF 2-7 IN, passed through the berm and started its maneuver north as one of the lead combat elements. As TF 2-7 IN moved through the lanes, engineer soldiers stood atop the berm, welcoming the task force into Iraq, waving enormous American flags. Traveling north through the Iraqi desert, the task force passed small Bedouin encampments. The families emerged from their small tents as the vehicles thundered by. Confused adults stared and excited children waved happily. This was the extent of contact south of Highway 1.

As the day turned to night, the TF 2-7 IN continued north into the darkness. Moving through the desert in a modified wedge formation, the task force was flanked by the remainder of 1st BCT. With TF 3-69 AR on one side and TF 3-7 IN on the other, the BCT continued attacking north. Shortly after darkness swallowed the formation, an order came down to switch on "white light" headlights for driving. Now, moving with three task forces abreast, 1st BCT, along with other division elements, made the Iraqi desert resemble a crowded Los Angeles freeway. Even though it facilitated movement, attacking deep into Iraq with thousands of pairs of high beams blazing into the night was counter to years of training.[47] The 1st BCT moved north to the Jalala Airfield, just to the south of Tallil, and then passed the 3rd BCT through to the north. The 3rd BCT would attack in zone to defeat the Iraqi 11th ID in the vicinity of Tallil

Air Base (An Nasiriyah), seize the air base, and then seize the Highway 1 crossing site on the Euphrates River in support of the I MEF advance.

The Fight at Tallil Air Base

Tallil Air Base is situated southwest of the town of Tallil and adjacent to An Nasiriyah, at the bend of Highway 1 where the highway turns northward to cross the Euphrates River. The Battle of Tallil opened this critical LOC for the corps and the Highway 1 bridges for I MEF. The attack at Tallil also supported the deception story that the corps' main effort would be east of the Euphrates River. The V Corps operations order directed Major General Buford "Buff" Blount's 3rd ID to seize the air base to develop a logistics support area (LSA) to sustain the corps as it moved north. Securing the air base also provided a position to block Iraqis from interdicting Highways 1 and 28 from the town of Tallil.

Accordingly, Blount assigned the mission to 3rd BCT (the *Hammer* brigade) and its four maneuver battalions. Colonel Daniel Allyn, commanding the 3rd BCT, designated Tallil Air Base as Objective FIREBIRD. Blount also required the brigade to seize and secure the Highway 1 bridge over the Euphrates River (Objective CLAY) to continue the attack north. The 3rd ID would eventually hand over the bridge to I MEF. At 0600 on 21 March, "MARNE 66" (the 3rd ID assistant division commander for maneuver, ADC-M), Brigadier General Lloyd Austin, authorized the brigade to initiate the attack to seize Tallil Air Base.

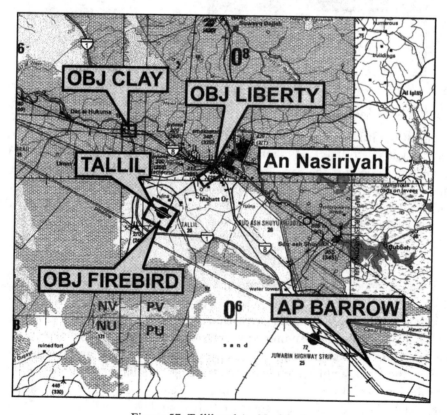

Figure 57. Tallil and An Nasiriyah

Prior to crossing the line of departure, estimates of the enemy varied from a strong defense in depth to a complete collapse. Units assigned to the 11th ID of the Iraqi Regular Army constituted the bulk of enemy forces in the vicinity of Objective FIREBIRD. The 3rd ID designated the 11th ID's garrison northeast of the airfield as Objective LIBERTY. The three brigades of the Iraqi 11th ID occupied positions east and northeast of An Nasiriyah, defending the approaches to town rather than Tallil or the air base. Other Iraqi forces that could threaten the 3rd ID included 21st Tank Regiment in the vicinity of An Nasiriyah and paramilitary forces, including *Saddam Fedayeen*. Intelligence did not assess the defenses as robust. Surveillance by SOF inserted prior to G-day reported on the Highway 1 bridge (Objective CLAY) and the area around Objective FIREBIRD. The immediate defenses around Objective CLAY included a dismounted infantry company defending the Highway 1 bridge, a T-55 tank company at the air base, an infantry battalion northeast of Objective FIREBIRD positioned to block the southern approaches to Tallil (on Objective LIBERTY), and about 25 vehicles on and around the airfield itself.[48]

The Approach

Strung out from the congested choke point through the berm, 3rd BCT had not closed all of its units and supply trains when the lead elements reached Assault Position (AP) BARROW (southeast of Objective FIREBIRD), at 1045 on 21 March. Fatigue

> If I had tried this attack at the NTC, I would not survive the after-action review.[49]
>
> Colonel Daniel Allyn
> Commander, 3rd BCT, 3rd ID
> commenting on the attack into Objective FIREBIRD

also became a factor as the brigade closed on BARROW. Colonel Allyn, for example, recalled that he slept for about half an hour at the assault position and really did not rest again until 24 March. The troops did not rest either. Lieutenant Colonel John Harding, commanding Allyn's direct support artillery, recalled that at one point the battalion moved only to discover that it had left a battery asleep by the side of the road.[50]

Tired or not, the brigade's advance guard cleared BARROW of a small Iraqi force consisting of a few trucks and fighting vehicles. Despite the fact that 3rd BCT did not have its units and supply trains closed up, Brigadier General Austin ordered the brigade to attack at 1145 with available forces. Colonel Allyn quickly executed his planned combined arms attack, employing ground maneuver, fires, and attack aviation. The essence of his plan was to envelop the air base from the south and northeast, with TF 1-30 IN attacking from the south and TF 1-15 IN moving to a blocking position in the northeast. TF 2-69 AR would attack to seize the bridge across the Euphrates—Objective CLAY. Allyn issued a warning order to 1-10 FA to prepare the objective with fires while the remainder of the brigade closed on AP BARROW.[51] Allyn was concerned that the brigade's approach to FIREBIRD might be so aggressive and so close to the Iraqis that they would be compelled to fight rather than capitulate, as anticipated. Accordingly, his subordinate battalion commanders devised plans to position themselves to either accept a surrender or fight, as appropriate.[52]

The 3rd ID provided further support from the 4th Brigade's attack aviation. Attack helicopters from 1-3 Aviation attacked targets in advance of 3rd BCT, destroying one SA-6 air defense missile system, two tanks, and six BTR-70 infantry fighting vehicles. The attack helicopters emerged nearly unscathed despite having to avoid shoulder-launched surface-to-air missiles. However, small-arms fire wounded one aviator.[53]

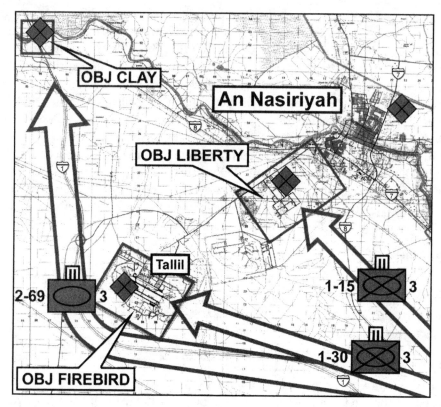

Figure 58. The 3rd BCT scheme of maneuver, Tallil Air Base

The 3rd BCT attacked at 1400, with the brigade reconnaissance troop leading and reconnoitering the zone, moving up Highway 1. The troop made contact with the enemy 25 minutes later—a small party of approximately 20 soldiers emplacing land mines. The cavalrymen drove the enemy off, killing one soldier, capturing four others, and destroying one of their four trucks. The captured soldiers claimed they had come from Tallil Air Base but were leaving because they knew the Americans were coming.[54]

At 1540, TF 2-69 AR, supported by 1-10 FA, using the same route as the reconnaissance troop, advanced north to seize Objective CLAY SOUTH, the southern side of the Highway 1 bridge crossing the Euphrates River. The task force reported contact with Iraqi dismounted infantry about 5-6 km outside of Objective FIREBIRD and began receiving Iraqi artillery at 1645. In what would become *de rigueur* all the way to Baghdad, the armor task force and the artillery fought off dismounted infantry and fired counterbattery and suppressive fires all along the route to CLAY SOUTH. The Iraqis defended from vantage points along roads and from overpasses and highway ramps. TF 2-69 reported contact with tanks and dismounted infantry on CLAY SOUTH at 2115. By 2350, the task force secured the southern objective. Throughout the fight, 1-10 FA responded to calls for fire against enemy vehicles and infantry positions, later firing the first sense and destroy armor (SADARM) munitions of the war in support of TF 1-15 IN at Objective LIBERTY, destroying a T-55 tank.[55]

With TF 2-69 AR en route, TF 1-15 IN and TF 1-30 IN departed BARROWS by 1826. The 1-41 FA and 1-39 FA (MLRS) had arrived and occupied firing positions from which they could

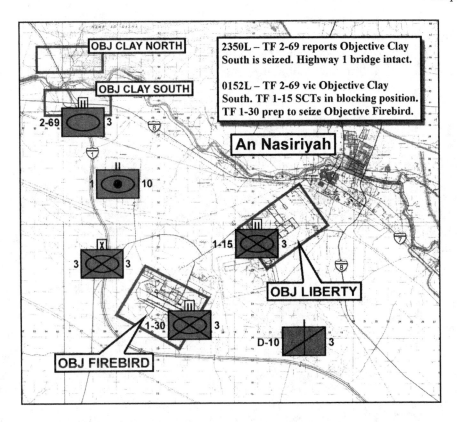

Figure 59. The 3rd BCT at Objective FIREBIRD, blocking positions set

support the assault. By 2200, TF 2-70 AR, the BCT reserve under Lieutenant Colonel Jeffrey Ingram, closed on Position Area (PA) TROOP, 6 km outside Tallil, completing the brigade's positioning for the final attack on the air base itself. TF 2-69 AR secured the bridge, while TF 1-15 IN occupied Objective LIBERTY to block movement between Tallil and the air base.[56]

The Attack

Shortly after midnight on 22 March, B/1-15 IN occupied a position from which they could block the northeastern approach to Objective FIREBIRD. An hour later, the company reported soldiers and armed men in civilian clothes accompanied by tanks and pickup trucks mounting automatic weapons evacuating Objective FIREBIRD south of its blocking position. Bravo Company, 1-15 IN, engaged and destroyed several of the fleeing vehicles, including two T-55 tanks. The Iraqis appeared to be abandoning the airfield before the ground attack even started. B/1-15 IN then returned to its blocking position to support TF 1-30 IN's pending attack. Leaving B/1-15 IN in its blocking position, the rest of TF 1-15 IN advanced toward Objective LIBERTY at 0143. B/1-64 AR identified five tanks occupying dug-in defensive positions within Objective LIBERTY. The tank company destroyed the closest four tanks with direct fire from the M-1 tanks; the fifth was destroyed with SADARM rounds after the scouts located and targeted it with their newly fielded Long-Range Advanced Scout Surveillance System (LRASSS).[57]

TF 1-15 IN secured Objective LIBERTY at 0551, suffering only one soldier wounded in action. The task force destroyed five tanks and killed several dismounted soldiers and also captured more than 200 EPWs, including an Iraqi brigadier general who commanded the regional air defenses. The brigadier carried with him Iraqi war plans for operations from Kuwait to Turkey and information about the senior Iraqi leadership.[58]

Tanks! Out.

Captain Dave Waldron's tank team (B/1-64 AR, attached to TF 1-15 IN) moved closer to Objective LIBERTY. This was part of Lieutenant Colonel Charlton's plan to put units into position to be able either to accept a unit's surrender or to engage a unit that was combative. Charlton did not know what the situation was, or what the enemy forces were, in Objective LIBERTY, so he sent up the heavy team to look. What Waldron's tankers found gave him the first shock of the night.

As soon as B/1-64 AR moved to where it had line-of-sight to Objective LIBERTY, it discovered that the Iraqis had moved an armored force into prepared fighting positions around the perimeter. These tanks were hot spots in the thermal sights of the M1 Abrams, proof that their engines were running and they were combat-ready. The message Waldron sent was short and sweet. It didn't need to be any longer; everyone who heard it knew exactly what he meant. Charlton remembered the message vividly. It came over the radio loud and clear, *"Dragon 6, Knight 6. Tanks! Out."* With that, the fighting kicked into a higher gear.

The Iraqis in the tanks dug in around Objective LIBERTY never had a chance, not that B Company was planning on giving them one anyway. With the superior fire control and night vision sights of the Abrams main battle tank, the ancient T-62s of the Iraqis were sitting ducks. They could still be dangerous, especially to the infantrymen in their Bradley Fighting Vehicles, but the Abrams made quick work of them.

As soon as Waldron sent his short contact report to Charlton, he issued a platoon fire command to his lead platoon. With his tank adding its firepower to the four others in the platoon, in less than 30 seconds after the radio call, the massive 120mm cannons on five tanks roared in unison. The firing continued for 2 minutes as the gunners and tank commanders traversed left and right, seeking out and destroying the tanks and other vehicles dug into supporting positions around the perimeter. In less time than it takes to tell, they destroyed four T-62 tanks, several other armored vehicles, and some trucks that were moving behind the bunkers.

Derived from interview with Lieutenant Colonel John Charlton,
Commander, TF 1-15 IN

As TF 1-15 IN concluded the attack on Objective LIBERTY, TF 1-30 IN breached FIREBIRD's (Tallil Air Base) southeast perimeter berm at 0411. Following intense artillery (192 rounds of high explosive ammunition) and attack aviation strikes, and concealed by 97 rounds of artillery-fired smoke, TF 1-30 IN seized its objective against light resistance. The task force cleared the airfield and brought in a sensitive-site exploitation team, which confirmed that the Iraqis had no chemical weapons stored in bunkers on the base.[59]

Consolidation

Fighting through the night of 21-22 March, the 3rd BCT concluded this action late in the morning of the 22nd. TF 2-69 AR moved north across the bridge, seizing Objective CLAY NORTH by approximately 0500 and securing a route across the Euphrates. TF 2-70 AR, the

BCT's reserve, relieved TF 2-69 AR at 1330. TF 2-69 AR moved south to rendezvous with 1st BCT to support its forward passage of lines through 3rd BCT. With Tallil Air Base secure and routes from An Nasiriyah blocked, the fighting shifted to the outskirts of the town itself, where 1-10 FA engaged two counterbattery targets identified by the *Firefinder* radars. Having secured the objectives and set blocking positions between Highway 1 and An Nasiriyah, the 3rd BCT and 3rd ID had met all of their mission objectives. The 3rd BCT then began the process of handing off the bridge at CLAY to TF *Tarawa* in the early hours of the 23rd. Once that was completed, 3rd BCT moved out to secure the LOC as far as As Samawah.[60]

Handling the Enemy Prisoners of War (EPWs)

The Battle of Tallil presented the 3rd ID with its first substantial numbers of EPWs. Handling the prisoners was a major task that the division and corps had been working for months. This would be the first test of that effort. At 0900 on 22 March, Captain Joe Hissom, the 3rd MP Company commander, led the advance party of Task Force *EPW* to AP BARROW and established the first EPW collection point. Shortly thereafter, the main body arrived and received and processed the first three Iraqi EPWs. All three prisoners had gunshot wounds. The 274th Medical Detachment (Forward Surgical Team) treated all three and performed surgery on one of them.[61]

While processing the prisoners at BARROW, Lieutenant Colonel John Huey, 3rd Infantry Division provost marshal, received a message from 3rd BCT asking for assistance with the prisoners taken at Tallil Air Base (Objective FIREBIRD). Huey and a small advance party moved north on MSR TAMPA to take control of the prisoners, established a hasty collection point, and accepted 3rd BCT's prisoners. The following morning at 0900, TF 1-30 IN of the 3rd BCT cleared a building complex planned as the location of Division Central Collection Point HAMMER. Task Force *EPW* occupied the complex in the early afternoon.

Figure 60. The 274th Medical Detachment (Forward Surgical Team) located near An Nasiriyah

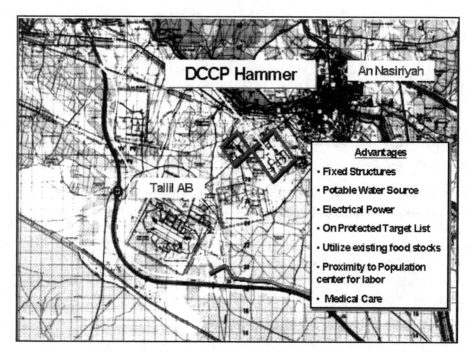

Figure 61. Division Central Collection Point *HAMMER*

By the morning of 24 March, Lieutenant Colonel Richard Vanderlinden, the 709th MP Battalion commander, arrived at Tallil Air Base, coordinated and effected a relief-in-place with TF *EPW*. This freed Task Force *EPW* to continue movement north following the 3rd ID brigades. However, Vanderlinden quickly realized that he did not have adequate combat power to relieve Task Force *EPW* and conduct his second mission of escorting critical logistics convoys to the fighting forces. The only available forces at his disposal were two platoons and the company headquarters of the 511th MP Company from Fort Drum, New York, all of which had arrived ahead of the unit equipment.

Lieutenant Colonel Vanderlinden decided to commit this force to conduct the EPW mission at Tallil. On 24 March, Captain Travis Jacobs, commander of the 511th MP Company, led 80 soldiers in six *Black Hawk* helicopters from Camp PENNSYLVANIA to Tallil Air Base, with only their weapons, rucksacks, a picket pounder, and two days' supply of food and water.[62] They immediately augmented the 709th MP Battalion and effectively relieved Task Force *EPW*. The 709th MPs renamed the collection point Corps Holding Area *WARRIOR*. With limited equipment and supplies, the 511th MP Company expanded the collection point and processed and safeguarded over 1,500 EPWs until the 744th MP Battalion (Internment and Resettlement) relieved them on 6 April 2003.

The holding area at Tallil Air Base ultimately became Camp WHITFORD, a trans-shipment point where all coalition ground forces brought EPWs pending movement by the 800th MP Brigade to the theater internment facility at Camp BUCCA at Qasr. On 9 April, coalition forces had over 7,300 EPWs in custody. Most of these prisoners ultimately made it to the theater internment facility. However, coalition commanders released prisoners who they determined

Figure 62. EPWs being cared for early in the war

did not have ties to the Iraqi armed forces or the Ba'ath Party. As coalition forces transitioned to peace support operations, the internment and resettlement mission also transitioned. Shortly after 1 May 2003, when President Bush declared the end of major combat operations, the 800th MP Brigade began paroling approximately 300 EPWs a day. As the prisoners were released, criminals replaced them in the camps as coalition forces began to establish law and order throughout the country.[63]

The Fight at As Samawah

As Samawah is a moderate-size city, approximately 265 km west-northwest of Al Basra and 240 km south-southeast of Baghdad. The town is on the Euphrates River and is also astride Highway 8, a main improved road leading northwest to Baghdad. Highway 8 parallels the Euphrates River and turns north at As Samawah, crossing to the east side of the river. As Samawah itself lies mostly to the south of an east-west leg of the river, with some built-up areas to the north of the river. Additionally, the rail line between Al Basra and Baghdad passes around the town to the south and west. A man-made canal runs northwest to southeast approximately 5 km south of the town.

Intelligence reported fighting positions covering a large portion of the circumference of the town, on both sides of the river, as well as behind existing water obstacles. The Iraqis built other fighting positions forward of apartment blocks that afforded sniper and machine gun positions capable of firing over the heads of troops in the fighting positions below. While some mortar pits were noted, no artillery positions had been identified before 3rd ID made contact. There were no clear indications of the paramilitary threat in the town. Figures 65 and 66 provide an overview of the enemy within the town.[64]

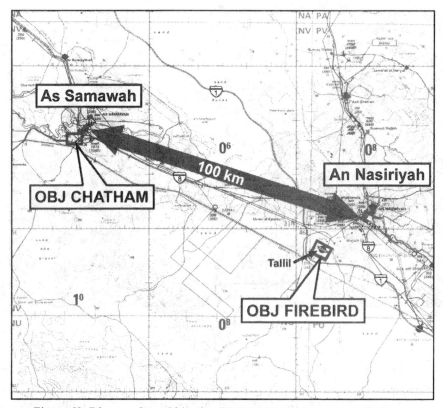

Figure 63. Distance from Objective FIREBIRD to Objective CHATHAM

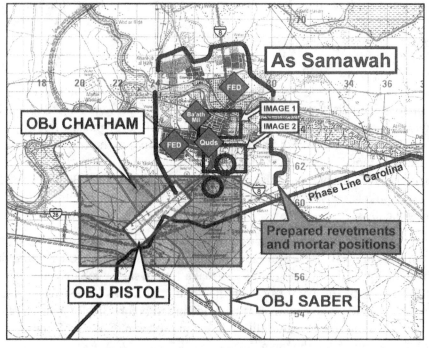

Figure 64. As Samawah prepared defenses

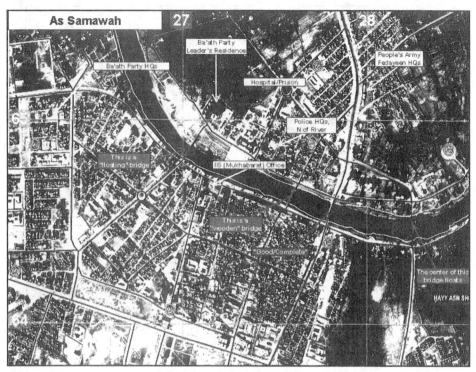

Figure 65. (Image 1 from Figure 64.)
Downtown As Samawah with US annotations

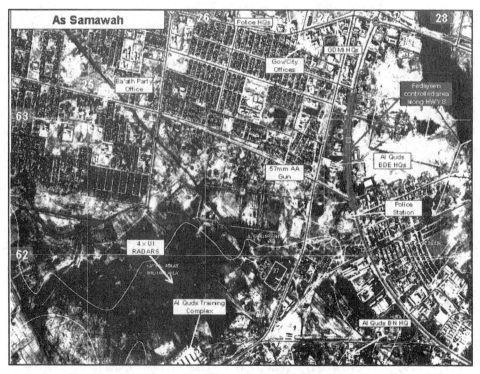

Figure 66. (Image 2 from Figure 64.)
As Samawah where Highway 8 turns north, with US annotations

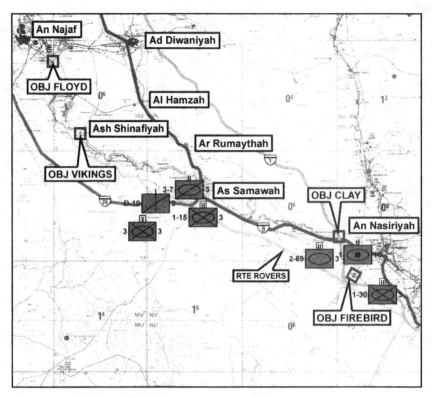

Figure 67. Routes of march north to As Samawah

The original V Corps scheme of maneuver envisioned containing any enemy forces in the town to allow the division to move around the western edge, north toward Objectives RAIDERS and RAMS near An Najaf. Lieutenant General Wallace intended 3rd ID to strike deep and did not want it tied down clearing towns along the way. The 3-7 CAV, leading 2nd BCT's Team *Heavy Metal*, had the mission to contain As Samawah.[65] Seizing Objective CHATHAM, the two bridges crossing the canal southwest of the town, would effectively isolate Iraqi forces in the town and ensure that Highway 28 remained clear. The squadron did not expect significant opposition based on division and corps intelligence summaries. In fact, Lieutenant Colonel Terry Ferrell half-jokingly told his unit to "expect a parade." However, "the only flags were white flags that they shot from behind [referring to Iraqis feigning surrender and then engaging coalition forces]."[66]

The squadron scheme of maneuver divided CHATHAM into two smaller objectives—Objective PISTOL, the western bridge, and Objective SABER, the eastern bridge. Although PISTOL saw the most action, SABER was the main effort, because that bridge would support about 60 percent of the division's logistics traffic.

The Approach

On 21 March, after breaching the berm, the OH-58Ds of D/3-7 CAV conducted a zone reconnaissance 200 km forward of the ground troops to confirm the terrain and the bridges at CHATHAM. They did not see any enemy forces. The ground troops arrived at As Samawah at 0747 on 22 March. When the lead troop, C/3-7 CAV, "*Crazy Horse*," neared the southwest approach to the bridges, it came across 1-64 AR, from the 2nd BCT, resting in a depression off the side of the road about 3 km outside the city. The soldiers were sleeping atop their tanks and Bradley Infantry Fighting Vehicles (BIFVs), uniform tops off because of the heat. They were resting after almost two days of moving and were waiting for their logistics to catch up.[67]

As *Crazy Horse* moved forward toward Objective PISTOL, a group of small pickup trucks mounted with large machine guns greeted them. The trucks raced toward them from the town with large American flags flying off the backs of the vehicles; they were an SOF team conducting linkup. The team had been in the town for several days conducting reconnaissance and surveillance of key terrain. The SOF troopers effected the linkup in accordance with an established recognition signal worked out with the special forces liaison element (SFLE). The SOF team confirmed that the bridges were intact and not wired for demolition. The SOF troops had developed a contact in town who reported on the infiltration of Republican Guard troops in town and the presence of paramilitary forces as well.[68]

The Attack

Expecting a positive reception, with the enemy surrendering or capitulating, Sergeant First Class Anthony Broadhead, the platoon sergeant for 1st Platoon, C/3-7 CAV, led a hunter-killer team of three Bradleys and two M-1 tanks toward the bridge where some Iraqis had assembled. As his tank approached the bridge at 0900, Broadhead waved at the Iraqis. Rather than waving back, the Iraqis responded with AK-47 fire. The fight quickly escalated as paramilitary forces engaged *Crazy Horse* from pickup trucks; armed with small arms, machine guns, rocket pro-pelled grenades and mortars. For the first, but not the last time, well-armed paramilitary forces—indistinguishable, except for their weapons, from civilians—attacked the squadron.[69]

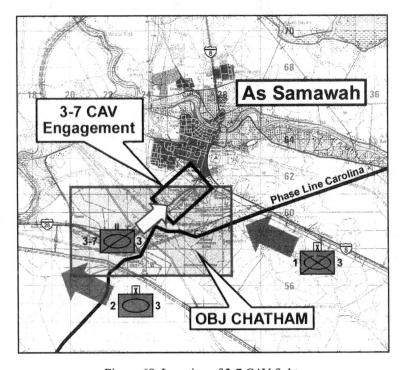

Figure 68. Location of 3-7 CAV fight

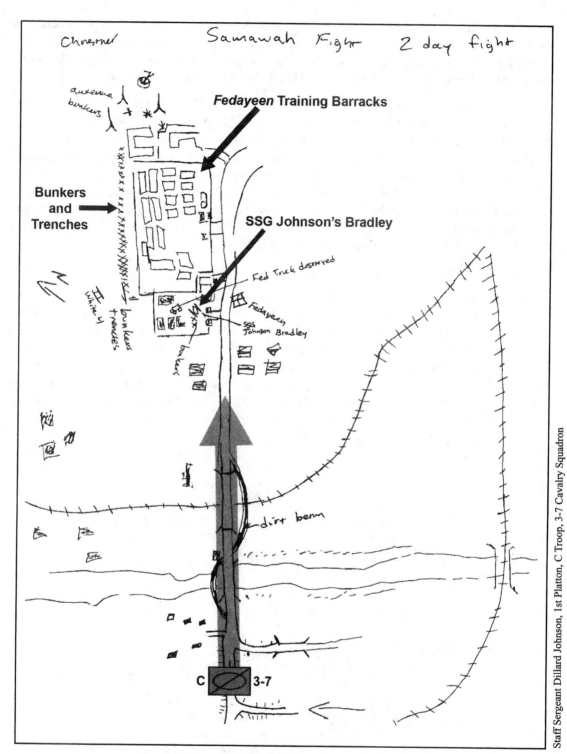

Figure 69. Drawing, C/3-7 CAV actions at As Samawah

Staff Sergeant Dillard Johnson, 1st Platton, C Troop, 3-7 Cavalry Squadron

As they moved up close to the canal bridge on Objective PISTOL, the two lead vehicles, Broadhead's M1 and a Bradley commanded by Staff Sergeant Dillard Johnson, the squadron's lead scout, identified a Ba'ath Party police station and *Fedayeen* training barracks on their left and right, respectively. Both compounds had walls, and the facilities were swarming with *Fedayeen* troops, firing primarily small arms and mortars from a tree line off to the north. [70]

As the team began to destroy the enemy mortar positions, it noted that the enemy soldiers came in waves in an almost suicidal manner. Subsequent waves replaced men shot down just moments before. When the team moved up parallel with the *Fedayeen* compound, it drew heavy fire from inside the facility. The two vehicles moved inside the walls and began moving around the compound, firing into any buildings where they saw a muzzle flash. Dillard Johnson describes his fight:

> We were closing from the west in a HKT (Hunter Killer Team). I identified a large number of dismounts near the bridge, which was our objective. Due to the [Rules of Engagement], (there had been no engagements during the war to this point), we could not fire on them. We signaled them to surrender and they immediately opened fire on us. I was told to move up to the bridge with [Broadhead's] M1 tank. While we were moving up, the M1 engaged the dismounts with coaxial and .50-caliber machine gun, which had no effect. So, I opened up with the 25mm High Explosive (HE) that literally laid them out. [Note: 65 KIA later identified at the location]. We then moved up to the bridge and secured it. . . .

> An Iraqi military truck then came down the road from the military compound. A privately owned vehicle got between us, so I could not engage him. So we chased the truck into the compound and the M1 remained at the gate. The guys in the truck then opened up on me with small arms and RPGs. One of the RPGs' backblast set one of the Iraqis on fire and he fell out of the truck onto the road. . . . A guy with an RPG then ran into a bunker by the M1 tank. The tank fired a 120mm HEAT round into the bunker and killed him. I then fired four rounds of 25mm HE into the truck. This caused the truck to break in half and burst into flames [Note: 25-30 KIA later identified in and around the truck].

> Now is when total mayhem broke out! We began to receive a huge volume of fire from the right side and the M1 withdrew outside the gate. Between 150-200 guys then began to pour out of the buildings. They engaged us with small arms and a few RPGs. They were so close that my M240 coax [machine gun] was destroyed by small-arms fire. Also, literally dozens of RPGs were bouncing off the vehicle because the Iraqis were too close! The RPGs did not have enough range to arm so were just non-explosive projectiles. I had rigged a [second] M240 on the cargo hatch and my observer began to engage the dismounts. I engaged with my M9 (9mm pistol) and M4 (5.56mm assault rifle) while the [BIFV] gunner used the 25mm. This went on for 25 minutes or so. When the shooting stopped, there were 13 EPWs and the rest were dead. I then took an AK round to the chest, which knocked me down into the vehicle. I thought I was dead and was surprised that I was not [due to the body armor, even though he was not equipped with the ceramic plate that affords additional protection] [Note: 167 KIA later identified at this site].

> I then dismounted with the observer and began to provide first aid to the wounded EPWs. I was really sore from where the AK round had hit me. That is when eight trucks full of *Fedayeen* came down the road outside the compound and stopped. They did not see me and began to fire on the rest of the platoon. We were less than 30 meters

away. My gunner then engaged the trucks with 25mm and placed 13-15 rounds in each. I hit one with my M203, [and it] burst into flames. . . .

Then 70 guys came running out of another building and engaged the M1 with small arms. . . .The M1 engaged them with its .50 cal [machine gun]. I grabbed the two Iraqis with the best-looking uniforms and dragged them to the BIFV. That was when a mortar round landed among the rest of the prisoners. The mortar round killed 13 of the EPWs and I told the other two to run away. I used hand signals, which they must have understood because they ran away into a building.

We mounted up and took off. At this moment, a mortar round hit the palm tree we were under and exploded. It knocked me down into the turret and the observer down into the cargo compartment. I had shrapnel wounds in both legs, both arms, and my right eardrum burst. The observer had shrapnel wounds in both of his hands. . . . We hauled ass out of there and the M1 crossed the bridge. I got in a hull down position on our side of the river and kept returning fire. We reported the [battle damage assessment] and the assessment of the situation. . . .

This is when the missile flew out of the town. I am not sure it if was a surface-to-air or surface-to-surface missile. We now began to take heavy mortar fire and spotted the mortar crews in the tree line. I radioed the platoon sergeant and he called our internal mortars on them, which killed all of them. The platoon sergeant then told me to sit tight while the platoon came to us. This forced the Iraqis to withdraw temporarily.

We then all moved back to the original start position. Unfortunately, the last Bradley hit one of the mortar craters, spun around, and fell into the ravine. This caused it to hang by its tracks on the edge of the ravine. Now all the Iraqis came running back and began to engage the stuck Bradley. He could not fire at them because of the angle the vehicle was stuck in. . . . We raced up, dropped the ramp, and the crew ran inside my Bradley. I then saw an ambulance with a Red Crescent pull up into the compound. About 10 soldiers in uniform jumped out and ran into the building. They immediately began shooting at my vehicle, so we engaged the houses with 25mm HE and killed all of them [Note: 10 enemy KIAs later identified at that location]. I then re-crossed the bridge and provided overwatch on the stuck Bradley. A van then pulled up full of armed Fedayeen. I engaged the van and killed all of them also . . . we [continued to] overwatch with the rest of the platoon [Note: 221 enemy KIA identified around the bridge from Staff Sergeant Johnson protecting the stuck Bradley].[71]

During the fighting the enemy used innocent men, women, and children as human shields. Iraqi forces also used trucks, taxis, and ambulances to transport fighters onto the battlefield. These tactics, along with the *Fedayeen* practice of "retreating" into homes and forcing the civilians at gunpoint to engage the Americans with small arms, challenged the soldiers' application of the Rules of Engagement (ROE). The soldiers had no choice but to return fire.[72] This pattern of operation became routine as the war wore on.

Shortly before *Crazy Horse*, C/3-7 CAV reached the bridge, *Demon Troop*, D/3-7 CAV (equipped with OH-58D *Kiowa Warrior* armed reconnaissance helicopters) had maneuvered over and around the town. Conducting mission coordination with Ferrell via a commercial satellite telephone, *Demon Troop* moved to reconnoiter the bridges over the Euphrates north of CHATHAM. At approximately 0800, Captain Thomas Hussey and Chief Warrant Officer 2 Jeff Pudil flew the lead aircraft into As Samawah, drawing small-arms and RPG fire from dismounted forces in the town. The ground fire was heavy, so the OH-58D crews flew low along the river, 20 feet above the water but still 10 feet below the banks. Whenever they gained altitude to observe the town, the helicopters drew small-arms and RPG fire from the palm groves on the banks. Pilots reported feeling the heat of the glowing orange rounds as they passed by the open helicopter doors. The air cavalrymen developed the practice of flying one *Kiowa Warrior* over a built-up area to draw fire, and the wingman, standing off, would then engage the shooters with rockets and machine guns.[73] The firing diminished after the pilots engaged with rockets, only to intensify once the Iraqis reseeded their positions with new fighters.[74]

On 23 March, 3-7 CAV identified and engaged the Ba'ath and other paramilitary headquarters in As Samawah, with CAS as a result of information provided by SOF and from EPW interrogation. Technical Sergeant Mike Keehan led the enlisted terminal attack controllers (ETACs) assigned to the squadron. ETACs are the Air Force's forward air controllers assigned to ground

Two Shots—One Kill

A C/3-7 CAV hunter killer team identified a T-55 tank on a rail car west of the city. The [HKT] developed a tactic to destroy the tank with a sabot followed by a high explosive antitank (HEAT) round, because the sabots were too powerful and would shoot right through the tank. The HEAT rounds would explode the tank, therefore illustrating that the tank was "dead."

3-7 CAV Unit History

units and trained and equipped to call in CAS. The ETACs and *Kiowa Warriors* guided F-15s onto the Ba'ath Party headquarters, eventually marking the building with a *Hellfire* missile to ensure the pilot knew the exact target. Within a few minutes, the F-15 identified the mark and destroyed the headquarters.

The *Kiowas* also identified various targets, to include a surface-to-surface missile in the vicinity of a factory downtown. When the cavalry reported the discovery, corps ordered division to use ATACMS to destroy the target. As a standard safety precaution, friendly forces within 2 km of the target had to depart the impact area. This meant that all of C/3-7 CAV had to withdraw to a safe distance, relinquishing the ground they had spent the previous day and that morning taking. Although 3-7 CAV withdrew, the missiles never came due to the complex process to clear fires in such a way as to avoid both fratricide and damage to the civil infrastructure. After 6 hours of waiting, the call came back over the "net" to allow the squadron to engage the targets, and A/3-7 CAV destroyed the large missile.[75]

The Fight Disrupts the LOCs

While the fighting at CHATHAM continued, 1st BCT, "*Raider,*" moved north along Highway 8 from An Nasiriyah to As Samawah, en route to Objective RAIDERS. Iraqi civilians had been coming out to greet the soldiers from the *Raiders* once they were in the Euphrates River valley. However, as lead units traveled along Highway 8 where it neared the southern edge of As Samawah, they found themselves under fire.[76] The 1st BCT maneuvered out of the engagement area and passed through 3-7 CAV to the west at approximately 1200, continuing its mission to the north. On 23 March, it became clear that paramilitary troops in As Samawah posed a threat to the LOC. V Corps ordered logistics traffic and soft-skinned vehicles to divert from Highway 8 to Route ROVERS (Highway 28) via a bypass that avoided the danger zone near As Samawah.

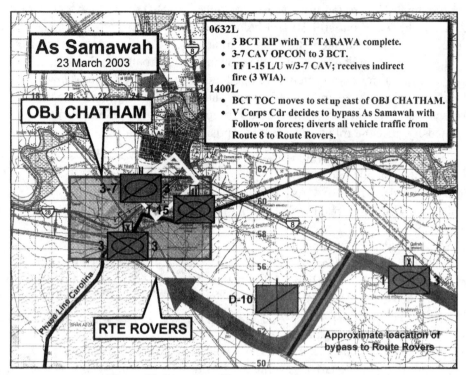

Figure 70. Location of bypass to Route ROVER

In support of this bypass, 3-7 CAV cleared the Iraqis from the area 1 km north of Highway 8. Throughout the fight in the town, 3-7 CAV estimated that it killed more than 550 Iraqis and destroyed 30 antiaircraft systems, 30 civilian vehicles, and three command and control facilities.[77]

Transition of As Samawah to 3rd BCT

After TF *Tarawa* relieved 3rd BCT at the Euphrates bridge on 23 March, 3rd BCT could now continue north. Leaving one battalion to secure Tallil, Colonel Allyn assumed control of the fight at As Samawah. The 3rd BCT's mission at As Samawah was to prevent Iraqi forces from interdicting logistics traffic along Highways 8 and 28. The 3rd BCT moved toward As Samawah, with TF 1-15 IN leading. The rest of the BCT was strung out along Highway 8 as far south as Tallil Air Base. Allyn had to exert command and control over the BCT across 240 km. Three TACSAT radios with only limited access to a single frequency provided the chief means he had to do so.[78] The BFT system, using a satellite link to share unit positional information across the battlefield, enabled Allyn to maintain a picture of his widely dispersed units as he approached As Samawah.

Initially, Allyn planned to employ his two battalion task forces along the highway to clear the LOCs from Tallil to As Samawah, and then later, north to An Najaf.[79] Given the intensity of fighting in the town, Allyn changed his mind and used his HMMWV-mounted brigade reconnaissance troop along the highway away from the heaviest fighting. He used the more heavily armored infantry task forces to isolate As Samawah itself.[80]

At 1430 on 23 March, 3rd BCT took control of the fight at As Samawah from 3-7 CAV. The division resumed control of the cavalry and ordered it north toward An Najaf, the next major city on the route to Baghdad. The 3-7 CAV would seize the bridge on Objective FLOYD and isolate An Najaf from the east and north.[81] This mission would also serve as a second feint against the *Medina* Division, presenting the Iraqis with the prospect of the main effort crossing east of the Euphrates River in An Najaf. After briefly refitting, the squadron moved north along Highway 9, which amounted to running a gauntlet that the soldiers dubbed "Ambush Alley."[82] The 3-7 CAV's fight on Highway 9 is discussed in the next chapter.

Better Intelligence

The intelligence picture in As Samawah improved as the 3rd BCT's fight evolved. Naturally, as soldiers gain and maintain contact with the enemy, they develop a better understanding of the environment and the threat. Captured Iraqis revealed that paramilitary forces were forcing civilians to fight, executing those who refused. They also stated that every school had been taken over and was being used as a command post or staging base. The pattern in As Samawah appeared to mirror that in An Nasiriyah, where a captured Iraqi captain claimed the *Fedayeen* assassinated 50 Iraqi soldiers because they were not fighting hard enough.[83]

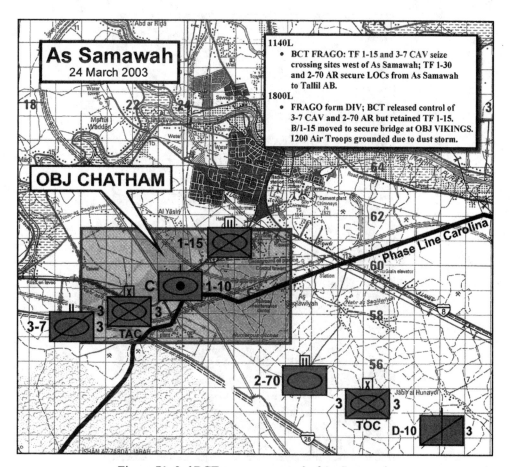

Figure 71. 3rd BCT assumes control of As Samawah

The SOF continued to provide critical information from inside the town, sending reports of from 500 to 1,000 Republican Guard forces reinforcing As Samawah. Special Forces Operational Detachment-Alpha (ODA), the SOF team in the town when 3rd BCT assumed the fight, had one contact, a taxi driver who provided two reports daily via cell phone on enemy disposition and command and control nodes.[84]

Psychological Operations and Civil Affairs in Support of 3rd BCT Operations

The brigade employed psychological operations in As Samawah, but the effective range of a loudspeaker in high winds and sandstorms was only 300-1,000 meters. The primary message was for civilians to stay put and get off the road. Civil Affairs (CA) teams were very busy making contact with the locals in the small towns on the outskirts of the city to determine who were hostiles or otherwise posed a potential problem for friendly forces.

The SOF passed this type of information to the 3rd BCT several times a day, sometimes using the BCT's radio nets. They also provided a liaison team to TF 2-69 at the bridge on Highway 8. In Colonel Allyn's opinion, the integration with SOF at As Samawah was the best of the whole war and helped shape the fight decisively.[85]

U.S. Army

Figure 72. Army vehicles in a sandstorm

During the fighting at As Samawah, the brigade realized that the enemy was fundamentally different from what had been expected. Though fierce and relentless in their attacks, the Iraqi paramilitaries did not fight competently, nor did they adapt to changing conditions.[86] Colonel Allyn noted that the division considered ordering 3rd BCT into the town to destroy the defending Iraqis. However, he kept the purpose of his mission foremost in his mind—"To prevent interdiction of the LOCs." By coming out to attack the 3rd BCT, the Iraqis forfeited the advantages afforded them by defending in urban terrain. Accordingly, Allyn decided to conduct a series of demonstrations, keeping the Iraqis "interested" and effectively fixing them in As Samawah, where they could not attack elsewhere along the LOC.[87]

Transition to 82nd Airborne Division

The 3rd BCT fought in As Samawah until relieved by the 2nd BCT of the 82nd Airborne Division on 29 March.[88] The 3rd BCT then moved to Area of Operation *HAMMER*, northwest of An Najaf, and prepared for offensive operations in Karbala. Committing the 2nd BCT of the 82nd Airborne released the bulk of 3rd ID's combat power and allowed the division to focus on the first major conventional fight it expected—the destruction of the *Medina* Division of the Iraqi Republican Guard at the Karbala Gap.

"Soldiers are our Credentials"
Rangers Lead the Way: Specialist Manuel Avila

Born in Mexico, Specialist Manuel Avila grew up in El Paso, Texas. Growing up, Avila recalls, "I always thought about joining the Army." Avila enlisted in 2000, joined the Ranger Regiment in late 2000 and earned his Ranger Tab in the summer of 2001. Subsequently, he deployed with his unit to Afghanistan and then to OIF.

On 27 March 2003, Specialist Avila was hit in the shoulder by a bullet that caromed off a bone and through his chest, lodging in his flak vest. Badly wounded, he was evacuated ultimately to Walter Reed Medical Center, where on 5 April, General Eric Shinseki awarded him the Nation's oldest medal—the Purple Heart.

Figure 73. Specialist Avila receives Purple Heart from General Eric Shinseki

Michael E. Dukes, US Army

Determined to get fit despite his serious wound, he worked hard to get back into shape so he could rejoin his unit. In June 2003, Avila ran a 12-km team race with his unit. Although others marveled at the speed of his recovery, Avila expressed disappointment that he could only manage an average pace of 6 minutes per mile.

NOTES

1. Williamson Murray and Major General Robert H. Scales, Jr., *The Iraq War, A Military History* (Cambridge, MA: The Belknap Press of Harvard University Press, 2003). Murray and Scales' chapter on the air war is a first-rate review of how air campaign planning evolved from DESERT STORM to OIF. Re: numbers of missions and level of effort, see 166-172.

2. Lieutenant Colonel E.J. Degen, chief of plans, V Corps, interview by Major David Tohn, 19 August 2003.

3. "CFLCC OPLAN COBRA II," 13 January 2003, 24.

4. Rich Connel and Robert J. Lopez, "A Deadly Day for Charlie Company," *Los Angles Times*, 26 August 2003, cites 18 marines killed in action on 23 March 2003 in An Nasiriyah. Apparently all 18 marines were members of Company C, 1st Battalion, 2nd Marine Regiment and Task Force *Tarawa*.

5. Major Lou Rago, V Corps planner, interview by Major David Tohn, 8 May 2003.

6. Rago.

7. It is tempting to compare the speed of operations in OIF to the first Gulf War or to operations in Korea or World War II. Such comparisons are faulty for a host of reasons, and the scale and pace of operations in OIF are impressive without resorting to these comparisons. Coalition troops reached Baghdad on 5 April, about 500 kilometers from their starting point. By any measure that is a rapid advance.

8. The JTFC was not part of the doctrinal JACE, so the analysts and resources had to be reassigned from within the JACE or donated by other units with an interest in the mission.

9. Major Julius Washington, CFLCC C2 planner, reviewed a draft of *On Point* with Major David Tohn, 8 August 2003. This passage reflects Washington's recommended revision to the draft.

10. Brigade S2s, 3rd ID and 101st Airborne Division, summary of individual interviews by Major Daniel Corey, 9–30 May 2003. These are notes from interviewing the brigade S2s of these divisions by Major Daniel Corey, OIF-SG. Cory produced several summaries for OIF-SG, and all of the discrete interviews are available in the OIF archive. Republican Death Squads was the generic term used to describe the mix of *Fedayeen*, Ba'ath Party militia, foreign mercenaries and volunteers, and other assorted armed civilians. Although the intelligence types used the term "Republican Death Squads" to describe the amorphous collection of paramilitary forces, the troops did not.

11. Major David Carstens, Early Entry Command Post, CFLCC, interview by Major David Tohn, 9 May 2003. Although Carstens did serve in the CFLCC early entry command post, his correct job title is CFLCC C2 fusion cell production chief.

12. Ibid.

13. "REACH Operations" refers to a maturing doctrinal use of "sanctuary" capability to augment capabilities in the field. Using the advanced communications capabilities, units in the field and in the rear area share data and distribute analytic requirements and production. In this manner, a small forward element can leverage the substantial capabilities of a unit in a safe haven. Conversely, the rear unit can reach into forward units' databases and perform analysis to support their respective requirements.

14. Brigade S2s of 3rd ID and 101st Airborne Division.

15. Carstens by Tohn.

16. Colonel Steven W. Rotkoff, deputy C2, CFLCC, interview by Major Weisler, commander, 50th Military History, Detachment, and Major Daniel Corey, OIF-SG, 7 May 2003.

17. Carstens by Tohn.

18. CFLCC C2 History, Lieutenant Colonel Peterson.

19. To understand the scale of the air effort, see "Operation IRAQI FREEDOM—By the Numbers," CENTAF-PSAB, KSA, Commander's Action Group, 9th Air Force, Shaw Air Force Base, SC, 30 April 2003.

20. Colonel Steven Rotkoff, deputy C2, CFLCC email to Major David Tohn, 6 August 2003.

21. "CFLCC Executive Summary (200400ZMAR03-210400ZMAR03)" [SECRET/REL USA, GBR, AUS, CAN]. Although the entire document is classified, the material cited here is not.

22. "CFLCC Executive Summary (190400ZMAR03-200400ZMAR03)" [SECRET/REL USA, GBR, AUS, CAN].

23. The Unitary Missile is an advanced guided missile with a range in excess of 60 km. It distributes over 400 Dual-Purpose Improved Conventional Munitions bomblets over the target area, with great effect against personnel and lightly armored vehicles; "Operation IRAQI FREEDOM Operations Summary: Fire Support," Lieutenant Colonel William Pitts, 15 August 2003.

24. Chief Warrant Officer 2 Jay Dehart, commander, USAV *Champagne Marne*, interview by Lieutenant Colonel David Kolleda, June 3, 2003; and LT-1974 USAV *Champagne Marne* unit history (undated).

25. "USCENTCOM OIF Chronology and Facts (SECRET NOFORN)," 6 May 2003.

26. Colonel Michael Gearty, chief, Joint Analysis and Control element (JACE) Term Fusion Cell (JTFC), Interview by Major David Tohn, 25 May 2003; interview with Iraq Team, Forces Directorate, National Ground Intelligence Center (NGIC). It is too soon after the fighting to be entirely certain of what the Iraqis intended or even to confirm with certainty physical locations of Iraqi units. As a result, the summary of Iraqi actions represents a combination of extant estimates made during the fighting and an analysis by the OIF-SG of such evidence. Joint Operational Analysis Center Joint Forces Command is working to develop an understanding of Iraqi operations and intent, but their work is ongoing and classified, and so it cannot be cited here.

27. Ibid.

28. A reference to the TF *Ranger* Raid of 3-4 October 1993, during which 18 US soldiers were killed in intense urban fighting in Mogadishu, Somalia.

29. Caches of ammunition continue to turn up in Iraq to the present day. The data cited here comes from summary notes by Colonel Charles Green, US Army, Retired, OIF-SG, stemming from interviews done with Colonel Steve Boltz, V Corps G2; Colonel Michael Gearty, deputy C2 CFLCC; Major Chris Parker, chief of staff, 7 UK Brigade; Captain Chris Medhurst-Cocksworth, G2 7 UK Brigade; and several Iraqi brigadiers and staff colonels held at Camp BUCCA, Iraq. Green conducted these interviews during the period 23-28 May.

30. First Lieutenant Mark K. Schenck, TF 2-7 Infantry, 3rd Brigade Combat Team, 3rd Infantry Division (Mechanized), "Unit History, Operation IRAQI FREEDOM," 5.

31. Team *Bushmaster* was B Company, 2nd Battalion, 7th Infantry; Team *Bulldogs* was B Company, 11th Engineer Battalion (Source: Unit History of Operation IRAQI FREEDOM, First Lieutenant Mark K. Schenck).

32. Schenck.

33. Firing units included: 1-9 FA BN (155mm), 1-10 FA (155mm), 1-41 FA (155mm), 1-39 FA (MLRS), and 2-4 FA (MLRS).

34. 1st Battalion, 9th Field Artillery, Operation IRAQI FREEDOM, "Unit History,"(undated).

35. Major David A. Converse, "Psychological Operations Field Collection Team Operational Assessment, Operation IRAQI FREEDOM,"35. Converse drew this conclusion from his review of after-action reviews, but this is a conclusion of an OIF-SG collector and not a primary source. There is evidence that PSYOP achieved success in precluding massive destruction of the oil fields. For example, in an interview on 7 May 2003 with 50th Military History Detachment and Major Daniel Corey, Colonel Rotkoff, deputy C2, CLFCC, reported that "IO" worked, but only when there were "boots on the ground." PSYOP loudspeaker teams did prove effective, but the jury is still out on the efficacy of the leaflet campaign.

36. The AH-64D *Apache Longbow* has increased lethality due to advanced avionics, a fire control radar, and the capability to launch fire-and-forget *Hellfire* missiles.

37. Captain Karen Hobart, S2, and 1st Lieutenant Aaron Anderson, 11th AHR, interview by Major David Tohn, 8 May 2003.

38. Captain John Cochran, battle captain, 11th Attack Helicopter Regiment, interview by Major James Brashear, undated. Lieutenant Colonel Jerry Pearman, executive officer, 11th AHR, confirmed that frustration in a telephone call to Colonel Gregory Fontenot, US Army, Retired, and in notes passed via facsimile on 17 December 2003. Frustration was particularly keen among 2-6 CAV aviators, who felt they could have executed the mission since they had more flying time in the desert than their colleagues.

39. "Unit History, Task Force 3-15 Infantry (TF *China*) 2nd BCT, 3rd Infantry Division (Mechanized) in Operation IRAQI FREEDOM, 20 March through 1 May 2003,"5.

40. MOPP: Mission-oriented Protective Posture—determines the level of chemical protective clothing and equipment worn. In MOPP 0, soldiers carry their full equipment, but do not wear it. In MOPP 1, soldiers wear the overpants and overshirt; MOPP 2 adds the overboots; MOPP 3 adds the mask and hood; and MOPP 4 includes the gloves, providing full protection. There is an inverse relationship between MOPP level and mission effectiveness, due to fatigue, discomfort, and bulkiness of the protective equipment. Commanders are very deliberate in balancing the need for rapid transition to a fully protected posture against the need to remain mission-effective over time.

41. The ABCS is a suite of automation tools that support maneuver, intelligence, fire support, air defense, and logistics operations. When operating properly, they are networked together to provide a seamlessly integrated ability to track and manage the battle. The AMDWS, or Air and Missile Defense Work Station, is the terminal that runs the Air and Missile Defense Planning and Control System, the air defense component of the ABCS.

42. "Unit History, Task Force 3-15 Infantry," 5 (Note: The unit history states that this missile was targeted at Kuwait City, but information contained in the final report from 32nd Army Air and Missile Defense Command and the accompanying overlay from the Air Missile Defense Work Station reflects an *Ababil*-100 missile targeted at the area around Camp DOHA and Camp COMMANDO at approximately that time).

43. Each company team was organized with a tank platoon and an engineer platoon for the mission. The mortar platoon followed Alpha Company to provide immediate indirect fire support.

44. Not all were tracked vehicles. Force *Heavy Metal* did include some high-mobility support and sustainment vehicles.

45. Major Kevin Marcus, V Corps planner, interview by Lieutenant Colonel William Connor, US Army, Retired, 8 May 2003.

46. Captain Sean Connely, 159th Aviation Brigade, 101st Airborne Division, interview by Major James Brashear, 21 May 2003.

47. TF 3-15.

48. "Operational Summary of 3rd BDE in Operation IRAQI FREEDOM", 1. This is the unit history of 3rd BCT, 3rd ID. 3rd BCT's history discusses the Tallil Air Base fighting in the context of Iraqi forces defending An Nasiriyah. Specifically, the history reports that Iraqi forces in the area of An Nasiriyah included the 45th and 47th Brigades east of the town, with the 23rd Brigade in the town. The brigade estimated that elements of the 21st Tank Regiment, a commando battalion and Ba'ath and *Fedayeen* paramilitary forces might offer a moderate defense of the city.

49. Colonel Allyn initiated the attack against Tallil Air Base with just TF 1-15 Infantry in position to assault. He was still waiting for the rest of the 3rd BCT to close into position.

50. Colonel Daniel Allyn, commander, 3rd BCT, 3rd ID and multiple BCT officers, interviews by Colonel Tim Cherry, 13 May 2003.

51. 3rd Brigade, 3rd ID, Unit History.

52. Lieutenant Colonel John Charlton, commander, 1st Battalion 15th Infantry, 3rd BCT, 3rd ID, interview by Lieutenant Colonel Arthur Durante, US Army, Retired, 22 August 2003.

53. 3rd Brigade, 3rd ID, Unit History.

54. Ibid.,1.

55. SADARM is a newly fielded advanced munition that seeks out and destroys armored vehicles by attacking through the relatively thin and vulnerable top armor plating. 3rd BCT Operational History, 1-2.

56. 3rd Brigade, 3rd ID, Unit History 2-5.

57. TF 1-15 Infantry Unit History Operation IRAQI FREEDOM. See also 3rd BCT, 3rd ID and Operation HAMMER COBRA II briefing. Determining with precision when events described occurred is not possible with the data available. Times cited are derived from comparing times in all three sources.

58. Ibid. TF 1-15 IN reported destroying 6 tanks, 4 BMPs, 12 technical vehicles and killing an estimated 200 enemy. The TF also captured some 250 of the enemy.

59. 3rd Brigade, 3rd ID, Unit History.

60. Ibid.

61. "3rd Infantry Division, Task Force EPW—Tallil AB to Objectives Rams and Raiders," undated.

62. Captain Travis Jacobs, commander, 511th MP Company, interview by Captain Michael Matthews, 22 May 2003.

63. Major Anthony Cavallaro, S3, 800th MP Brigade, interview by Captain Michael Matthews, 1 June 2003.

64. From redacted National Ground Intelligence Center reports.

65. After 3-7 CAV entered As Samawah, 2nd BCT continued north to Objective RAMS, west of An Najaf.

66. Lieutenant Colonel Terry Ferrell, "S2 Editorial 3-7 CAV," and "3-7 CAV Command Briefing," 25 May 2003.

67. Ibid.

68. Ibid.

69. Ibid.

70. 3-7 CAV Unit History, and 3-7 CAV Command Briefing.

71. Johnson. Events were corroborated by separate interviews with the remainder of C/3-7 CAV, to include the troop commander. The estimated enemy KIAs for Staff Sergeant Johnson's BIFV during this fight was 488. The informal estimate from the troop was that Johnson and his crew killed at least 1,000 Iraqis on 23 March. Later in the move north, Johnson engaged and destroyed 20 trucks and tallied 314 KIAs in the vicinity of An Najaf. At Objective

FLOYD, Johnson's platoon fought yet another bitter fight against what they claim was a thousand paramilitary troops. In that engagement, Johnson's BIFV fired 2,800 25mm HE rounds, 7,200 COAX 7.62-caliber rounds, and 305 25mm depleted uranium rounds.

72. Soldiers frequently reported to their leaders that they could tell which Iraqis were fighting because they wanted to and which were fighting because they were being coerced. Soldiers claimed to shoot to wound those they believed were coerced. The practice of using civilians as shields and forcing unwilling participation in the fighting was widely reported by Iraqis themselves.

73. This was a standard practice of "pink" teams of the air cavalry units in Vietnam. The OH-6 *Cayuse* (White) would draw fire while AH-1 *Cobras* (Red) remained overhead and close enough to engage targets when they fired at the OH-6.

74. 3-7 CAV and 3-7 CAV Command Briefing.

75. Ibid.

76. Colonel William Grimsley, commander, 1st BCT, 3rd ID, interview by Colonel Gregory Fontenot, US Army, Retired, 19 November 2003.

77. "3rd ID Consolidated Division History and After Action Review."

78. Colonel Daniel Allyn, commander, 3rd BCT, 3rd ID, "Command Briefing," 12 May 2003.

79. TF 2-70 AR had been taken from the BCT and placed under control of division rear headquarters to secure Objective RAMS.

80. 3rd BCT Command Briefing. See also Lieutenant Colonel William Connor, US Army, Retired, notes from 3rd BCT Command Briefing, 12 May 2003.

81. 3rd ID Consolidated Division History, and Allyn.

82. This was not the only time this term was applied by soldiers in a unit. The men of TF 3-15 Infantry also used it to describe the route north out of Objective SAINTS into central Baghdad. There may have been other references to this term used at other times.

83. Allyn, command briefing. See also 3rd BCT, 3rd ID.

84. Ibid. See also Allyn and 3rd BCT officers, by Cherry.

85. Ibid.

86. According to the 3rd Infantry Division's G3, Lieutenant Colonel Pete Bayer, "We overrated his army, but we underrated the irregulars. They were fierce, but not too bright. They were evil men who deserved to die. They didn't adapt to our forces. They would continue to impale themselves on our BIFVs and tanks." Notes taken from 3rd ID command briefing by Lieutenant Colonel Arthur Durante, US Army, Retired, 12 May 2003.

87. 3rd ID Consolidated Division History and Durante notes.

88. Ibid.

Chapter 4

The March Up-Country

I don't like to say we were surrounded, but we were being fired at from all directions.

Captain Jeffrey McCoy, Commander, C/3-7 CAV
commenting on fighting at An Najaf

Saved by the Helmet

The 2nd Squad, 1st Platoon, 511th MP Company was involved in a firefight at a manufacturing plant near Al Iskandariyah. Staff Sergeant Daniel Small led his squad to a known arms and ammunition cache, where they discovered several men looting the materials. Small directed his squad into defensive positions.

A man immediately began to approach Sergeant Anthony Cassetta's team, consisting of the driver, Private First Class Hunter Cloke, and the gunner, Private First Class Chad Hicks. Cassetta motioned for the man to get into the prone position, but the man refused and began to run at the team. Cassetta then shot the man with his 9mm pistol, killing him. Shortly thereafter, the team began to take small-arms fire from about 300 yards away; Cassetta ordered the HMMWVs to move to form a defensive perimeter.

At this time, Cloke had stopped a vehicle with two Iraqis in it and placed them in the prone position. One of the individuals took out a grenade and threw it toward the team. Cloke grabbed the unexploded grenade and threw it from his position, saving his team. The grenade exploded just feet from his head, spraying shrapnel into his Kevlar helmet and hitting him in the eye.

Simultaneously, Cassetta engaged the man with his M-4 Carbine. The man went down but came back up with another grenade and threw it as well. The second grenade did not explode. Cloke, with shrapnel in his eye, engaged the man with his 9mm pistol, finally killing him.

As all of this was going on, Small and the rest of the squad were in a firefight against an unknown number of attackers. Ultimately, the squad defeated them, killing one and critically wounding another with well-aimed M-4 fires.[1]

Summary of Events

The chapter title is borrowed from Xenophon's account of the ill-fated campaign of Cyrus I of Persia. Following Cyrus' defeat and death in 401 BCE, Xenophon successfully led a Greek contingent of the Persian army as it fought its way out of Mesopotamia marching up-country home to Greece. Xenophon's narrative is a classic on the difficulty of campaigning in Mesopotamia, or what we now know as Iraq.

Although hampered by severe sandstorms, coalition aircraft continued to attack air defense, command and control, and intelligence facilities in the Baghdad area. Coalition aircraft continued to achieve high sortie rates despite the weather. The focus of strike missions began to shift to the Republican Guard divisions in the vicinity of Baghdad. Control of the air allowed the employment of slow-moving intelligence-gathering aircraft such as the E-8C Joint

Surveillance Target Attack Radar System (JSTARS) and the RC-135 *Rivet Joint,* which gathers signals intelligence and UAVs. In the days just prior to the sandstorms, the air component flew an average of 800 strike sorties daily. The majority of the effort was against discrete targets designed to achieve specific effects against the regime, to interdict enemy movement, or in close support of ground forces.[2] Even during the sandstorms, surveillance aircraft continued to provide data that enabled the coalition to target Iraqi units over an area of several hundred square miles during weather the Iraqis thought would shield them from air attack. On 28 March, the weather cleared, allowing coalition forces to increase the number of strikes on Baghdad and Republican Guard units. Coalition air forces operated against strategic, operational, and tactical targets, demonstrating both the efficacy and flexibility of air power.

Coalition maritime forces continued their efforts to expand the width of the cleared channel in Khor Abdullah. The channel was opened with about a 60-yard-wide pathway up to Umm Qasr. During operations to widen the cleared pathway to 200 yards, coalition forces identified "bottom-influence" mines. The Iraqis clearly had thought through denying the use of Umm Qasr to the coalition.[3]

Lieutenant General McKiernan and the CFLCC staff had reason to breathe a bit more easily in the days after V Corps and I MEF breached the berm. Both the corps and the MEF had moved out rapidly. SOF operations to seize the Gulf oil platforms and to generate threats against the regime from 360 degrees were under way and apparently with good effect. CFLCC's theater reception system seemed able to keep pace. In some ways, CFLCC now had to await events as its major formations undertook operations in Basra and in oil fields and began the march up-country. At An Nasiriyah, I MEF encountered and defeated an enemy attack in the sharpest engagement of the war thus far. The 3rd Commando Brigade of the 1st (UK) Armoured Division launched an offensive near Basra that secured Abu al Khasib. British forces continued aggressive patrols and engaged in sharp firefights with paramilitaries in the Al Faw and Basra areas. The Brits prevented any reinforcement of Basra while maintaining the security of the southern oil fields and the port of Umm Qasr.

V Corps had breached the border and secured its initial objectives. Now Lieutenant General Wallace directed several parallel actions to bring the corps forward to where it could threaten Baghdad proper. So far, the attack was "on plan," with the possible exception of the congestion along the restrictive LOCs as the corps uncoiled into Iraq. Casualties were minimal and the first fight, against the Iraqi 11th Infantry Division, had gone very well.

With the initial objectives secure, shifting the combat power north was necessary to prepare for the attack on Baghdad. It involved three distinct actions: moving the actual fighting forces—the 3rd Infantry Division, elements of the 101st Airborne Division, and the 11th Attack Helicopter Regiment (AHR)—north; moving the logistics base north; and securing the vital LOCs. These related actions needed to be completed before the corps could engage in heavy fighting anticipated in and around Baghdad.

Lieutenant General Wallace and the corps planners knew that, after the 400-km assault north, it would be necessary to refuel, rearm, and refit the 3rd ID before it continued north.[4] Accordingly, the corps planned to seize Objective RAMS, west-southwest of An Najaf and roughly two-thirds of the way between the border and the Karbala Gap. At RAMS 3rd ID and

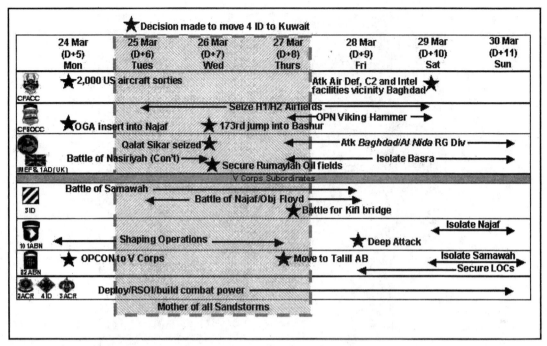

Figure 74. March up-country sequence of events

other corps units could refit to continue the attack while continuing to shape the enemy with deep fires. Establishing the logistics foundation became the proverbial "long pole in the tent" and drove the operations to seize RAMS, secure the LOCS, and neutralize the threats in As Samawah, An Najaf, and the surrounding areas.

The corps originally planned to move north along improved roads, bypassing the dangerous urban areas along the way. The 3rd ID would punctuate this maneuver with several feints across the Euphrates River to present the picture of a main effort east of the river. Following the combat troops, the corps logistics units would move forward to establish an LSA near Objective RAMS to sustain the upcoming phases of the operation. Moving north also enabled Wallace to bring his hard-hitting attack aviation forces, the 11th AHR and 101st Division's Aviation Brigade, into the fight, taking the first swipes at the *Medina* Division. These attacks would degrade the *Medina* and preclude any moves south to interrupt the corps' advance. Finally, they would thin the defense of Karbala Gap, supporting the 3rd ID's eventual attack.

Positioning 101st Airborne Division attack helicopters within striking distance of the *Medina* required the establishment of a series of intermediate fueling stops, or "lily pads." The division plan called for the ground emplacement of rapid refuel point (RRP) EXXON, approximately 150 km north of Camp UDARI, Kuwait, into a remote area of the Iraqi desert where the terrain offered reasonable access for 5,000-gallon fuel tankers. The second stop would be the bed-down location at a forward arming and refuel point (FARP) SHELL, just south of RAMS.

The 101st had to integrate its FARP personnel and equipment into 3rd ID's early convoys if they were to reach EXXON and SHELL in time to set up. 101st CSS units to support rearm-

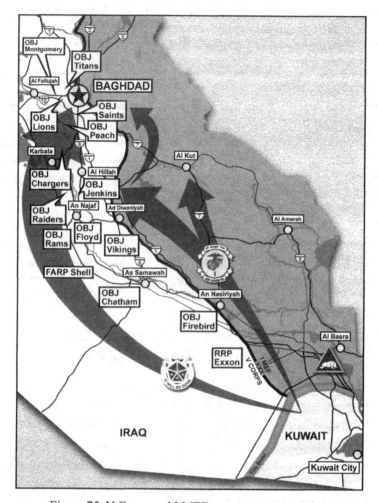

Figure 75. V Corps and I MEF maneuver to Baghdad

refuel points crossed the berm on 22 March. The mission of building and securing the refuel points fell to the 101st's 3rd BCT. Fresh from a nearly eight-month deployment to Afghanistan, followed by a training rotation at the JRTC, 3rd BCT built the aviation support facilities with FARP assets detached from the two aviation brigades. These lily pads supported not only the 101st's movement north, but eventually supported almost all aviation traffic transiting Iraq on the left bank of the Euphrates.

However, as in any battle, the enemy had a vote, and their tactics and their will to fight proved different than expected. For example, 3-7 CAV, which led the way for the 3rd ID, anticipated a relatively simple move north along the Euphrates River. Instead it became involved in a 100-km running fight against persistent, if generally ineffective ambushes. The 2nd BCT's attack to seize Objective RAMS also proved more difficult than expected. After seizing RAMS, the soldiers spent the next several days fending off waves of counterattacking Iraqi paramilitary forces coming out of An Najaf. Just as the enemy had to be prevented from exiting towns farther south, so too would An Najaf have to be isolated to ensure the troops working in the LSA and units moving on the LOC could do so unmolested. Isolating An Najaf developed into one of the hardest-fought actions in the campaign, eventually absorbing two BCTs and the division cavalry. In the end the 3rd ID handed An Najaf off to the 101st Airborne Division. Elsewhere, the ambush of the 507th Maintenance Company demonstrated the danger on the ever-lengthening LOCs.

While fighting continued along the corps' axis of advance, the CFLCC continued to build the logistics and sustainment base necessary to support extended combat operations in and around Baghdad. While perhaps not as exciting as the combat operations, these actions were among the most complex and critical to ensuring the campaign's overall success. The fighting in An Nasiriyah and As Samawah demonstrated the risk paramilitary forces posed to the LOCs. With 1st Armored Division unavailable to secure the LOCs as planned, McKiernan and Wallace had to find a way to secure the LOCs. Ultimately, McKiernan released the 82nd Airborne to V Corps and Wallace committed it, along with the 101st, to clean up the enemy forces that threatened to interdict the LOCs.

The march up-country included a series of combat and support operations to set the tactical and logistic conditions necessary to secure the corps' rear area and isolate Baghdad. Adding to the complexity and risk, the region suffered through a sandstorm of biblical proportions. The four major events described in detail are: [5]

- The use of Army attack aviation in deep attacks
- The battle to isolate An Najaf
- The operations to secure the LOCs
- The airborne insertion of the 173rd Airborne Brigade into northern Iraq

These were, by no means, all of the operations that occurred during the march up-country. The coalition executed a series of parallel, sequential, and simultaneous operations across the theater designed to increase the pressure on the Iraqis while moving the sustainment base forward.

Following Turkey's refusal to allow US combat forces to stage an invasion from its territory, CENTCOM and CFLCC determined to use the 4th Infantry Division in the south. Once on the ground, the "Ivy Division" assumed a "follow-and-support" mission, coming up from Kuwait behind the 3rd ID and 101st Airborne Division, ultimately securing part of northern Iraq. While the original plan was not executed, the extended threat of 4th ID attacking through Turkey may have fixed Iraqi conventional forces in the north, preventing them from repositioning south against V Corps and the MEF.

Without the 4th ID operating from Turkey, the coalition instead employed a powerful combination of SOF, Kurdish forces, and conventional US forces in northern Iraq. This included the first US airborne operations mounted from the European theater since World War II and 173rd Airborne Brigade's first combat operation since the Vietnam War. These forces continued to fix the Iraqi forces well north. SOF units worked aggressively in the west and north to interdict any theater ballistic missile capabilities, isolate Iraq from neighboring Syria, and destroy strategic targets throughout Iraq.

In addition to ground attacks from the south, CFLCC kept pressure on Baghdad and Saddam's regime directly by keeping the 2nd BCT of the 82nd Airborne Division, the theater reserve, available to employ deep in Iraq—specifically Baghdad. The 82nd could jump or fly into Baghdad to restore order and demonstrate a coalition presence if Saddam's government fled or imploded. In the meantime its presence in the theater gave Saddam another problem to contemplate.

Finally, as 3rd ID marched north, operations continued in the areas it passed through. The coalition's strategic goal was to establish a free, democratic, and prosperous Iraq, and this work started in earnest as soon as combat was over in the towns to the south. In what Lieutenant General McKiernan described as a "rolling phase IV transition," Army forces began stability operations and support operations in towns and cities from the Kuwaiti border all the way up to the frontline forces. Spearheaded by SOF, the coalition began linking up with local leaders and started the hard work of reestablishing basic public services and some degree of local governance.

Logistics–Setting the Conditions to Win

At this point in the advance to Baghdad, V Corps and I MEF had nearly reached the end of their organic logistics tether. To continue beyond the range of onboard stores, V Corps and I MEF would require the entire theater's focused logistics efforts. The cliché that amateurs study tactics, while professionals study logistics proved to be quite true. Here is where the true "graduate-level" work of the campaign's design and execution paid off—*after* the initial push into Iraq.

There are certain hard facts that apply to even the most modern and best-equipped armies. Soldiers must eat, drink, and sleep. Tanks, Bradleys, and other vehicles require fuel and at least some maintenance or they will grind to a halt. For modern armies, fuel is perhaps the greatest single supply burden. For example, OIF planners estimated a daily fuel requirement approaching 2 million gallons through about day 14, when they expected the total requirement to exceed that amount. An armored move of this scale and scope placed an almost overwhelming logistics burden on theater and corps logistics units supporting V Corps and the MEF.

Wallace had believed in the months leading to OIF that the corps would need to slow or even pause somewhere "just to the west side of An Najaf" to "build our logistics power to continue to project our combat power."[6] No stranger to the desert or to fighting a resourceful enemy in difficult terrain, Wallace did not just happen upon this conclusion. As a Vietnam veteran and an experienced cavalryman, including regimental command and six years at the NTC in California's Mojave Desert as a trainer and ultimately the commanding general, his planners' estimates made sense to him. Moreover, he knew the capabilities of his units, having commanded the 4th ID and having trained every kind of unit the Army fields during his tour at the NTC. Based on this experience, he knew the corps could win the tactical fights; his concern was adequate fuel, ammunition, and maintenance for future operations. An established LSA at Objective RAMS would be critical to future operations toward Baghdad.

Fuel, water, and food are the greatest burdens for logisticians to bear. To meet the 2 million gallons of fuel per day required—from tanks to aircraft—the Third Army had worked for two years to develop the infrastructure that a potential war with Iraq would require. Among other things, the Kuwaiti national oil company had, at the request of Third Army, laid pipeline nearly to the border. Third Army augmented this largesse by supplying the pumps. But in execution,

Colonel Melvin Frazier, who commanded the 49th Quartermaster Group (fuel and water), was the man who brought it all together. Frazier and his troops, working with the 377th Theater Support Command (TSC) and Third Army, started planning in earnest in the fall of 2001. By March of 2003, he had assembled engineers and petroleum units that laid pipeline and built bag farms to store fuel. Between January and March 2003, seven line-haul truck companies arrived and reported to the group. Ultimately, Frazier's units—with support from Army and Marine units—had a system in place that could store 7.3 million gallons of fuel. Moreover, Frazier assigned one truck company to support V Corps and one to support the I MEF. Together with trucks organic to the corps, this meant that V Corps could refuel every 100 km, or five times between crossing the line of departure and arriving at Baghdad.[7]

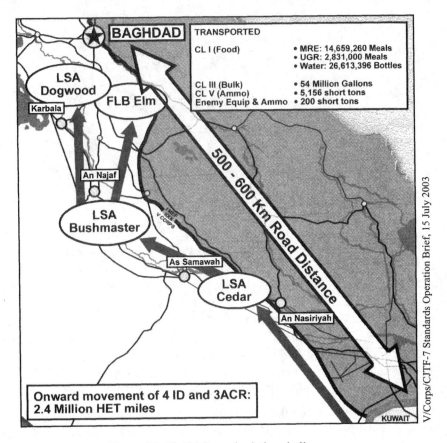

Figure 76. The V Corps logistics challenge

The plan to sustain the force further envisaged staging storage forward to reduce the length of the line haul. This would, in turn, reduce the time on the road for truckers and ensure that the demands of I MEF, V Corps, and nearby air bases could be met. To understand the scale of this effort, CFLCC expected to consume 40 million gallons of fuel by D+20, or about 10 April. By comparison, the Allies in WW I consumed 40 million gallons of gasoline during the four years of the war, a war that Winston Churchill described as having been won "on a sea of oil." By contrast, during World War II, the Allied fuel reserves in Normandy reached 7.5 million gallons only on D+21.[8]

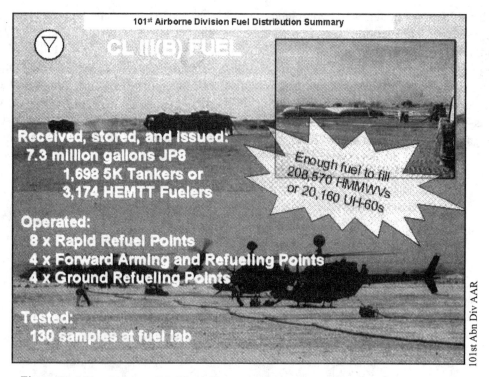

101st Airborne Division Fuel Distribution Summary

CL III(B) FUEL

Received, stored, and issued:
7.3 million gallons JP8
1,698 5K Tankers or
3,174 HEMTT Fuelers

Enough fuel to fill 208,570 HMMWVs or 20,160 UH-60s

Operated:
8 x Rapid Refuel Points
4 x Forward Arming and Refueling Points
4 x Ground Refueling Points

Tested:
130 samples at fuel lab

101st Abn Div AAR

Figure 77. 101st Airborne Division fuel consumption summary as of 30 April 2003

Clearly, Colonel Frazier and the V Corps and I MEF logisticians were no pikers in setting the conditions to feed the aircraft and fighting vehicles of an entirely mechanized force. Moreover, they planned to travel and fight across a theater to seize a hostile capital almost as far as Remagen on the Rhine River was from the Normandy beaches. To provide historical context, in summer and fall 1944, to keep up with a consumption rate of 800,000 gallons per day for First and Third Armies, General Dwight D. Eisenhower's logisticians created the Red Ball Express. The Red Ball Express required 132 truck companies to move the fuel over its 400-mile route. Frazier and the soldiers and marines of CFLCC, by means of trucks, pipelines, and fuel storage bags, aimed to more than double that accomplishment on a route that exceeded the length of that used by the fabled Red Ball Express.[9]

Three general officers shared the responsibility of assuring that trucks got forward to the right place and that logistics bounded forward. Major General Claude V. Christianson, the CLFCC C4, Major General David Kratzer, commanding the 377th TSC, and Brigadier General Jack Stultz, commanding the 143rd Transportation Command, responsible for transportation, focused considerable energy on the issue. Stultz attacked the problem vigorously. In the end everyone involved in logistics in Operation IRAQI FREEDOM found that personal leadership and hands-on management proved essential to coping with the scale of the problem.[10] To this team, Brigadier General Charles A. Fletcher, commanding the 3rd Corps Support Command (COSCOM), and his counterpart in I MEF added their efforts to assure that bulk fuel and other supplies made it to the tactical units. The marines also extended their hose and reel pipeline system to Jalibah air base south of Tallil, where they built an LSA.

Figure 78. 101st Airborne Division water summary

Regardless of these generals' hard work, they all laid the credit for the fuel movement success at the feet of the soldiers and marines who drove the trucks and laid the pipeline, including 240 km of the Marine Corps' hose reel system. Truckers and logistics soldiers drove themselves to the point of exhaustion. They kept on driving and fighting to get supplies forward. Christianson, not given to hyperbole, claims that these ". . . guys were incredible."[11]

CFLCC and the corps logisticians managed water, food, and ammunition as intensively as the fuel, with the result that units ran low but never out of any of these vital commodities. The theater did not do as well with repair parts. Generals Christianson, Kratzer, and Stultz all agree that the parts distribution system never worked, despite heroic efforts.[12] More than enough parts reached the theater and were duly processed, but almost none reached the intended customers during the fighting. Forward, the troops made do by cannibalizing broken-down equipment and towing what they could not repair. So, as the force moved north toward Baghdad with adequate fuel, water, and food, its ability to sustain an adequate maintenance readiness rate began to suffer. Fortunately, major combat operations ended before the failure of the parts distribution system affected operations in a meaningful way.

Fundamentally, the problem with parts is emblematic of a larger problem in the matter of distribution generally. A requisition for parts has to make its way through a fairly complex system and must be handled several times before it reaches the division where it is needed, let alone the platoon in which the part is required. In General Christianson's view, the real problem is that there is no single agent for managing "cargo distribution," whether it is water or a bolt needed on a tank.[13] OIF highlights a problem identified during DESERT STORM that remains to be solved.

Deserts and Rivers—the Terrain

V Corps conducted operations in both desert and river valley terrain on the way to the Karbala Gap. In the western section of the area of operations, the terrain is typical desert—dry and broken with waddies and gullies that disrupt and canalize movement when traveling cross-country. Within the river valley, the terrain is similar to that around As Samawah—plowed fields dissected with irrigation ditches and interspersed with palm groves. Wheeled movement is possible along the canal dikes and roads, but they are generally not wide or strong enough to support armored vehicles. The desert area is generally not populated, while the farmlands between the towns on the Euphrates River are dotted with small villages and farming communities. The terrain was a known factor that the corps could plan for; the weather, on the other hand, was not.

The Mother of All Sandstorms

On 25-27 March 2003, a strong weather system in the Middle East triggered a series of dust/sandstorms that became nearly continuous and slowed operations throughout the theater. On the first day, several moderate to strong thunderstorms swept west to east through Iraq and Kuwait. In front of and behind these storms, strong winds caused blowing sand, reducing visibility to near zero at times. Sand, dust and raindrops mingled to form what troops described as a mud storm. On the second day, the storm center passed across northern Iraq and moved into Iran by midnight.

Strong west and southwesterly winds from this low-pressure system blew across central and southern areas of Iraq, keeping the sandstorms going throughout the theater. On 27 March, most of Iraq's skies cleared as the dust settled under an approaching high-pressure area. But Kuwait and the Persian Gulf were still experiencing blowing dust, hindering ground and air operations around Kuwait and naval operations in the gulf.[14]

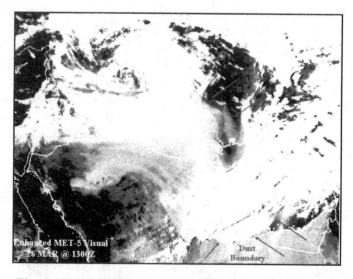

Figure 79. Satellite photograph of sandstorm, 26 March 2003

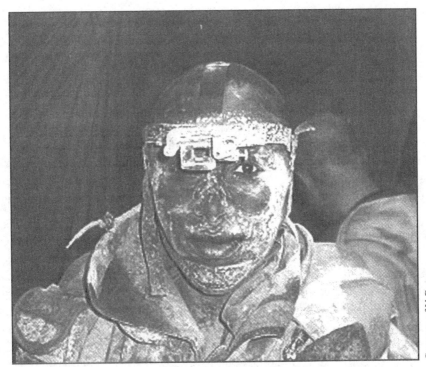

Courtesy of V Corps

Figure 80. 3rd ID soldier during the sandstorm

101st Abn Div AAR

Figure 81. 101st Airborne Division OH-58D *Kiowa Warrior* after the sandstorm

While the weather threw its wind-borne surprises at the coalition forces, the Iraqis did the same on the ground. The enemy disposition, tactics, and threat were, at times, as murky as the dust-filled air.

Enemy Disposition

CFLCC and V Corps had no evidence of a significant conventional Iraqi force between An Nasiriyah and Karbala. Intelligence officers believed the next conventional forces would be encountered farther north, defending the immediate approaches to Baghdad itself. Here the Iraqis apparently had arrayed three Republican Guard divisions, the *Hammurabi*, *Medina*, and *Al Nida* Divisions from west to east. The Special Republican Guard Division remained in Baghdad, with the bulk of its troops west of the Tigris River and in position to protect essential regime personnel and facilities. During the opening three days of operations, the CFLCC and corps had not detected any significant movement. However, it remained unclear how the Iraqis would respond to the ongoing air and information operations campaigns. Intelligence proved even less precise on tracking or estimating what the various paramilitary troops might do.

As the fight in As Samawah indicated, approximately 3,000-5,000 paramilitary fighters of all sorts defended from the towns and cities along the Euphrates River valley. Generically described in intelligence and operational estimates as Republican Death Squads, these fighters included Ba'athist Party militia, *Saddam Fedayeen*, foreign fighters, and some elements of the Republican Guard forces. Moreover, as discovered during the fighting, they included Iraqi civilians coerced into fighting against coalition forces by *Fedayeen* or militia who threatened their families at gunpoint. Although the estimates accounted for these forces, they did not anticipate their intent. As Major General Marks, the CFLCC C2 put it, "We did not predict that they were going to come out of the cities and expose themselves to up-armored vehicles and armored formations without similar protection."[15]

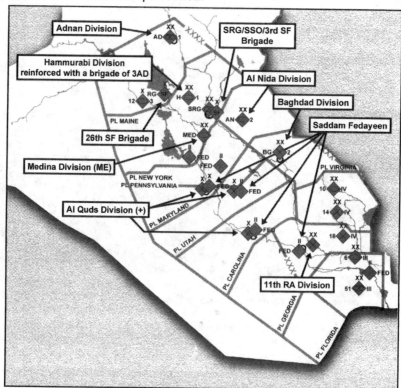

Figure 82. Iraqi force disposition

All of the estimates accurately assumed the *Fedayeen* were the most dangerous of the paramilitary forces, but they were thought to be in Baghdad in large numbers to bolster the capital city defense. As events unfolded, it appears that Saddam sent them south along the approach routes from Kuwait to stiffen the conventional defense, maintain political control over the southern cities, delay coalition momentum, and induce significant casualties. More surprising, these irregular forces chose to come out of the relatively safe urban areas to engage coalition armored forces out in the open. In doing so, they forfeited the tactical and propaganda advantages offered by fighting from the complex urban terrain—where fighting could result in significant civilian casualties and damage to buildings and infrastructure that could be used to sway international opinion. Even more surprising, the paramilitaries chose to attack the lead armored forces in waves rather than waiting for the soft-skinned, logistics convoys that would follow. Because the paramilitary forces were essentially untrained, if dedicated, their tactics were suicidal in that they literally ran, and drove, to their deaths.

In northern Iraq, two-fifths of the Iraqi conventional forces defended the "Green Line," across from the Kurdish Autonomous Zone, along the border with Turkey, and along the border with Iran (see Figure 83). Stiffened with two Republican Guard divisions, *Saddam Fedayeen*, and Ba'ath Party militia, these forces secured northern Iraq and posed a significant obstacle to the Kurdish forces. Moreover, if they moved south to reinforce the defense of Baghdad, they would greatly increase the challenge to the coalition forces moving up from Kuwait. V Corps and I MEF advanced north against this enemy disposition.

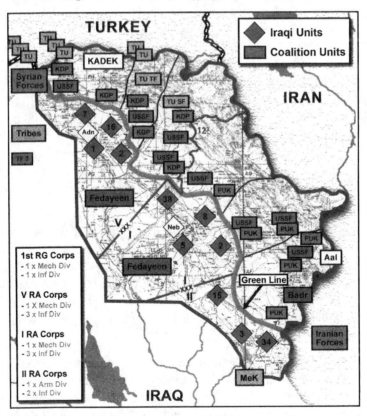

Figure 83. Iraqi forces disposition, northern Iraq

The 507th Maintenance Company

When OIF began, many Americans viewed warfare with almost clinical detachment, assuming that the war could be concluded rapidly, with precision and with few casualties. They also believed that American troops armed with the latest technology and precision munitions could not possibly become lost or surprised in combat. They continued to believe this despite the evidence of *Black Hawk Down* and the inconclusive results of the air war in Kosovo, possibly because, with the exception of *Black Hawk Down,* all they saw were gun camera tapes accompanied by cocksure appraisals of the incredible precision of American weapons.[16] Americans believed in the apparent precision of our armed forces without considering adaptation by the enemy or the frequent fallibility of the best technology or, for that matter, the human condition.

Humans tire and make mistakes, even if their weapons do not. When theorists and experts describe the modern battlefield as nonlinear, fast-moving, and noncontiguous, they fail to account for the implications of that assessment. If modern warfare is nonlinear—it means just that—there are no lines and no visible demarcation between the "front" and "rear." If there is no front and no rear, then nowhere on the modern battlefield is truly safe. An adaptable enemy may not wear uniforms and may not behave in a manner consistent with conventions developed in the West. If there are no rules—then there are no rules. In March 2003, the condition of the battlefield at An Nasiriyah, the town controlling the major southern crossing on the Euphrates River, was truly "noncontiguous," "nonlinear," and very much occupied by an adaptable enemy prepared to fight "asymmetrically."

Moving Out

The 507th Maintenance Company arrived at An Nasiriyah just over 60 hours after it had started out to join the 3rd Forward Support Battalion (FSB), 3rd ID convoy to Objective RAMS. RAMS lay some 350 km northwest of the 507th's base camp at Camp VIRGINIA, which was near the Kuwait-Iraq border. The 507th departed Camp VIRGINIA at 1400 on the 20th with 64 soldiers and 33 vehicles. Driving cross-country almost due west, it arrived in Assault Position DAWSON at 2100. There, the unit refueled and rested until departing the next morning at 0700. The second leg of the convoy took the 507th from DAWSON to Assault Position BULL, where it would link up with the 3rd FSB. The company drove some 35 km, crossed the Iraqi border, and arrived at BULL at noon on the 21st.[17]

At BULL, Captain Troy King, commanding the 507th, met with the operations officer of the 3rd FSB, who provided him a CD-ROM disk containing orders and route information. Although 3rd FSB intended to travel cross-country for a part of the way, ultimately it would travel up Highway 8—called Route BLUE—to a point just south of An Nasiriyah where Highway 8 met Route JACKSON, or Highway 1. There, soldiers at a traffic control point would direct the 600-vehicle convoy from Route BLUE to Route JACKSON. Somehow, King only understood that he would travel Route BLUE.[18]

In any case, the 507th departed as part of the 3rd FSB column at 1800 on 21 March, moving cross-country to Assault Position LIZARD, which lay to the northwest, across 80 km of difficult terrain. During the night, vehicles in the convoy had trouble due to breakdowns, getting stuck in the sand, or becoming separated from their unit in the dark. Falling behind, Captain King decided to break his convoy into two serials. He led the first serial, consisting of vehicles that could keep up. First Sergeant Robert Dowdy recovered mired or broken-down vehicles and assembled them into the second, slower serial to continue the movement north.[19]

Captain King and the lead serial arrived in LIZARD at 0530 on 22 March. First Sergeant Dowdy and the second group finally reached LIZARD at 1600. Meanwhile, King reported his situation to his Commander, Lieutenant Colonel Joseph Fischetti, and to the 3rd FSB, which confirmed there would be no changes to the route. The 3rd FSB also advised King that the convoy would depart as scheduled at 1400. Rather than leave at the scheduled time, King opted to wait for Dowdy and the trailing vehicles, sending his executive officer on with the remainder of the company.[20]

At 1930 on the 22nd, King and Dowdy departed LIZARD with 33 soldiers, including two (Sergeant George Buggs and Private First Class Edward Anguiano) who were assigned to 3rd FSB. King had 18 vehicles, including two that were being towed. The serial contained three HMMWVs, two of which were towing trailers, and eight 5-ton tractor-trailers, one of which was being towed. There were also five 5-ton trucks, including a wrecker towing a water trailer, two cargo trucks towing trailers, a fuel truck, and a disabled 5-ton cargo truck. Finally, there were two 10-ton wreckers, one towing the broken-down 5-ton shop van and the other towing the broken-down 5-ton tractor-trailer.[21]

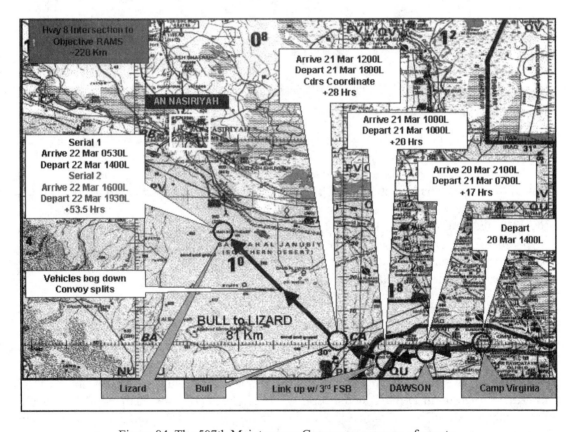

Figure 84. The 507th Maintenance Company sequence of events

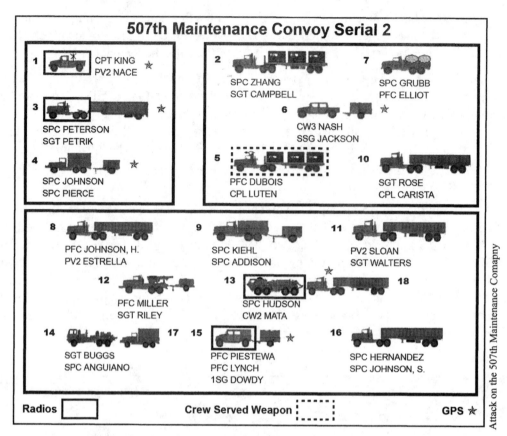

Figure 85. Captain King's serial, 507th Maintenance convoy

Missing the Turn

Captain King decided to take the most direct route to intersect Route BLUE, some 15 km cross-country from LIZARD. Unfortunately, the terrain proved nearly impassable. It took some 5 hours to reach Route BLUE. Sometime after 0100, the 507th drove through the traffic control point at the intersection of Route BLUE and Route JACKSON. Although there were troops in the area, no one manned the traffic control point. King, believing he was supposed to stay on Route BLUE, continued on rather than turning onto Route JACKSON. Because his next GPS waypoint was generally to the west, there was no cause yet for alarm. Just after 0530, King missed a left turn on Route BLUE. As yet unaware he had missed the turn, he headed north along the eastern side of An Nasiriyah.[22]

Entering An Nasiriyah

Captain King, First Sergeant Dowdy, and the 31 other soldiers drove north through the eastern edge of An Nasiriyah, passing armed "civilians" and traveling through two Iraqi military checkpoints without incident. When the convoy reached Highway 16 on the northern outskirts of An Nasiriyah, it turned left, thinking it was turning onto Highway 8 south of the city. King turned north at the T-intersection where Highway 16 ends, realized his error and, after consulting with Dowdy, turned the convoy around. By now, after more than 60 hours on the move, King, Dowdy, and the soldiers were exhausted. Nevertheless, they got their vehicles

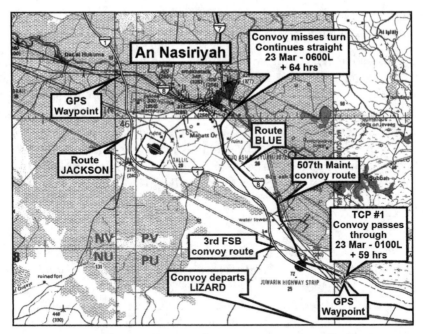

Figure 86. The 507th route of movement toward An Nasiriyah

turned around and made their way back and turned left, or east, onto Highway 16, and started looking for the right turn which would take them back south to safety and Route BLUE.

Almost from the moment they turned back onto Highway 16, they came under fire. First Sergeant Dowdy recommended that the serial pick up the pace to escape the fire. With only five radios, passing the word must have consisted, in part at least, of setting the example and exhortation by hand and arm waving. Dowdy's efforts to get the word out apparently included driving up alongside trucks and yelling instructions at the vehicle commander and driver.[23]

Moving fast, Captain King now missed the turn south. First Sergeant Dowdy saw the error and called King to have him turn around a second time. By now, the entire serial had passed the turn. Sergeant First Class Pierce sped up and caught Captain King to advise him that he could find the turn. King told Pierce to take the lead. At this point, still under fire, the 5-ton tractor-trailer, driven by Private Brandon Sloan and commanded by Sergeant Donald Walters, broke down. Sergeant James Riley and Private First Class Patrick Miller, in the following vehicle, the 5-ton wrecker towing the water trailer, slowed down so that Sloan could leap aboard. It is unclear what became of Walters. He may have fought his way south of Highway 16 for some distance, but at some point he was killed in the action.[24]

The serial, now disintegrating, had to travel some 3 km past the missed turn to find enough room to turn the large tractor-trailers around. As they made the U-turn, Sergeant Buggs and Private First Class Anguiano mired their wrecker and its tow in soft sand. Stuck and taking fire, the two needed help. First Sergeant Dowdy, who for more than two days had been policing up the trail of the 507th, slowed his HMMWV and picked them up. Dowdy reported to Captain King that the trail element had turned around and that he had Buggs and Anguiano and that they needed to get out of the city as soon as possible. Dowdy's HMMWV now had five people aboard, including Private First Class Lori Piestewa, Private First Class Jessica Lynch, whose supply truck had broken down, the two soldiers from 3rd FSB and Dowdy himself.[25]

Driving fast, taking fire, doing a U-turn, and making a hard left off Highway 16 all contributed to breaking the serial into three groups. The first group, led by Captain King, included his HMMWV, a 5-ton tractor-trailer, and a 5-ton truck towing a trailer. The second group of three 5-ton tractor-trailers, one HMMWV, and one 5-ton truck followed some distance behind King. The last group, by now fairly far behind and badly strung out due to problems turning around and making the turn to the south, included First Sergeant Dowdy's HMMWV, two 5-ton tractor-trailers, one 5-ton truck with trailer, one 5-ton wrecker with a water trailer, and one 10-ton wrecker towing a 5-ton tractor-trailer. The company had abandoned three vehicles back on Highway 16.[26]

Running the Gauntlet

Shortly after 0700 as the 507th sped south, separated into three dispersed groups, it now had to run a gauntlet of small-arms fire, RPGs, possible indirect fire, and at least one Iraqi tank. To add to the convoy's troubles, the Iraqis were placing obstacles—including vehicles—in the road. The beleaguered Americans had to maneuver the lumbering cargo trucks, made less agile by towing other vehicles or trailers, around obstacles. Captain King and his group of three vehicles cleared the city, raced south and made contact with marines of the 8th Tank Battalion assigned to Task Force *Tarawa*. The marines immediately moved out to rescue the rest of the company, heading back north the way King had come.[27]

Meanwhile, the Iraqis continued to pound the two trailing groups of vehicles. The second group made it 5 km south of An Nasiriyah before their luck, such as it was, ran out. Taking multiple hits from RPGs and small-arms fire, the tractor-trailer crewed by Specialist Jun Zhang and Sergeant Curtis Campbell came to a stop. Zhang leapt aboard the trailing tractor-trailer crewed by Private First Class Marcus Dubois and Corporal Damien Luten, who had just been shot in the leg. Campbell, also wounded, caught a ride on the HMMWV crewed by Chief Warrant Officer 3 Mark Nash and Staff Sergeant Tarik Jackson. Like Campbell, Jackson was already wounded. Nash, carrying his two wounded passengers, managed to get a bit farther south before Iraqi fire stopped his HMMWV.

Private First Class Dubois, Corporal Luten, and Specialist Zhang turned their slow, awkward tractor-trailer around and returned to help CW3 Nash and his two wounded NCOs. Shortly after this, Private First Class Elliot arrived in his 5-ton fuel truck, carrying Specialist Grubb, who was already wounded in both arms. Sergeant Matthew Rose, driving the last tractor-trailer, and his co-driver, Corporal Francis Carista, also joined at this point. Together, the soldiers formed a defensive perimeter while Rose, a combat lifesaver (trained in combat first aid), supervised three other combat lifesavers in treating the wounded. The marines arrived in time to rescue this group of soldiers.[29]

The Final Moments

First Sergeant Dowdy's group never cleared An Nasiriyah. They reached their end about 3 km north of where the marines rescued their colleagues. The end, when it came, was quick. First, the 5-ton tractor-trailer crewed by Specialist Edgar Hernandez and Specialist Shoshana Johnson veered off the road, swerving to avoid an obstacle. Dowdy, coming from the rear,

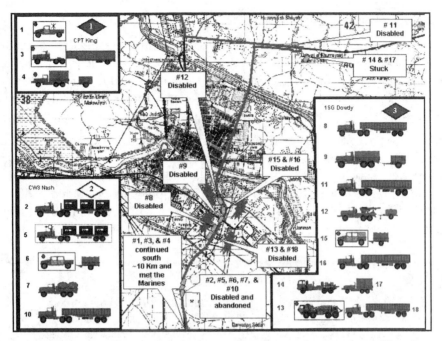

Figure 87. The 507th Maintenance Company ambush summary[28]
(The highlighed numbers depict actual locations where vehicles were left)

passed Miller's 5-ton wrecker and ordered him to pick up speed and keep moving. Soon afterward, an Iraqi round, possibly an RPG, struck Dowdy's HMMWV. Private First Class Piestewa lost control and crashed into the rear end of Specialist Hernandez's 5-ton tractor-trailer. The redoubtable First Sergeant Dowdy died on impact. Piestewa, seriously injured, died after capture. Anguiano and Buggs died as well, like Piestewa, under circumstances that remain unclear. Alive but unconscious, Lynch remained in the wreck.[30]

Iraqi fire stopped Private First Class Miller's wrecker some 400 meters north of where First Sergeant Dowdy died. Private Sloan, whom Miller had picked up minutes earlier, was killed at this time. Miller and Sergeant Riley moved south to assist Dowdy and the soldiers with him. Riley, now the senior man, took charge and attempted to organize a defense but had little to work with. Private First Class Johnson and Specialist Hernandez were wounded, so he had them take cover. No one in Dowdy's HMMWV could help, and Riley couldn't get a weapon to fire consistently. With no good options, Riley elected to surrender. Miller apparently made his way away from the scene and continued to fight until he too was surrounded and compelled to surrender.[31]

Farther south, Specialist Joseph Hudson and Chief Warrant Officer 2 Johnny Mata maneuvered their 10-ton wrecker past several obstacles and a tank. They reached as far south as the edge of the city before Iraqi fire brought them to a stop. Mata died soon after, killed by multiple rounds after the vehicle stopped. The Iraqis pulled the wounded Hudson from his vehicle and took him captive. The remaining two vehicles of the 507th did not make it quite as far south. Private First Class Howard Johnson and Private Ruben Estrella-Soto were driving a 5-ton tractor-trailer. They, along with Specialist Jamaal Addison and Specialist James Kiehl traveling in a 5-ton truck, were killed just north of where the Iraqis killed Mata.[32]

The Rescue of Private First Class Lynch

On the evening of 1 April 2003, SOF, supported by marines, assaulted the hospital in which Private Jessica Lynch was being treated. Although there have been news stories subsequently suggesting that the assault was unnecessary since Iraqi troops had left the day before, one fact is clear—the SOF troops brought Lynch out. Her capture, her captivity, even her return home stimulated speculation and enormous media attention.

Less than two weeks later, marines, apparently notified by locals of the presence of American captives nearby, rescued the remaining survivors of the 507th Maintenance Company, as well as two *Apache* pilots being held with them. The small-unit tragedy of the 507th that began on 23 March had finally ended. The ripples of what happened to the 507th and, for that matter, the 11th Attack Helicopter Regiment, will affect how the Army trains and equips units for years to come.

Civilians on the Battlefield

Specialist Eric Huth, a 22-year-old infantryman assigned to B/3-15 IN, witnessed an incident where a Bradley from his company engaged a van loaded with 19 civilians, killing and injuring many of them. Huth was driving the company executive officer and was able to monitor the radio conversations between the company Commander, Captain Ronny Johnson, and the platoon leader manning the roadblock.

The van approached a checkpoint but would not stop, even though the soldiers at the roadblock held up their hands as a "HALT" signal. Captain Johnson reiterated his order for the soldiers to halt all vehicles and not to let that van approach American positions closely enough to cause casualties, should it be filled with explosives.

When the van ignored the signal to halt, Captain Johnson ordered the platoon leader to shoot at the van's radiator and tires to make it halt. The platoon leader did that, but the van continued to advance without slowing at all. As it approached the US position, the 1st Platoon leader made the decision to initiate 25mm High Explosive fires to disable the van.

Specialist Huth drove the executive officer to the site within a minute or two of the van being engaged. He witnessed the medics treating the survivors from the van and their medical evacuation. Huth thought the unit had done the right thing, that there was no other way to protect US soldiers from the suicide bombers. The 1st Platoon leader felt very badly about killing the noncombatants, but the consensus within the unit was that it was regrettable but unavoidable, given the situation they were in.

Specialist Eric Huth,
based on an interview with Lieutenant Colonel (retired) Arthur Durante,
24 May 2003

Moving North

> *During planning, Objective RAMS, [in the] vicinity of An Najaf, was supposed to be a maintenance stop for the unit, but it turned into a 72-hour fight precluding any planned maintenance.*

Based on Interview with Captain James Mazurek and Chief Warrant Officer 2 Roger Guillemette
TF 1-64 AR battalion maintenance officer and maintenance technician

With 3rd BCT, 3rd ID securing the logistics and staging facilities at Tallil, the scheme of maneuver required the 1st and 2nd BCTs to move north to secure Objective RAMS as the LSA in the vicinity of An Najaf. The 2nd BCT would secure the actual Objective RAMS, while 1st BCT would move through and north to isolate An Najaf from Baghdad. The 3-7 CAV would close the ring around the town from the south and east, ensuring the Iraqi defenders could not molest the logistics and aviation operations within Objective RAMS.

The 2nd BCT at Objective RAMS

The 2nd BCT, the division's lead element, arrived at RAMS late in the afternoon on 22 March, after moving north and passing 3-7 CAV as it fought in As Samawah. TF 1-64 AR, leading the brigade, traveled 141 km along Highway 28, with the task force's scout platoon and brigade reconnaissance troop (BRT), leading. The task force prosecuted several contacts, including one when the BRT encountered a roadblock about 50 kilometers south of Objective RAMS. Four to six paramilitary troops fired small arms on the troop at a range of about 800 meters. The reconnaissance troop dispatched the defenders and four more who attempted to flank the troop in a pickup truck. The reconnaissance troops then continued toward RAMS and at about 1800, just south of RAMS, handed off the fight to TF 1-64 AR.[33]

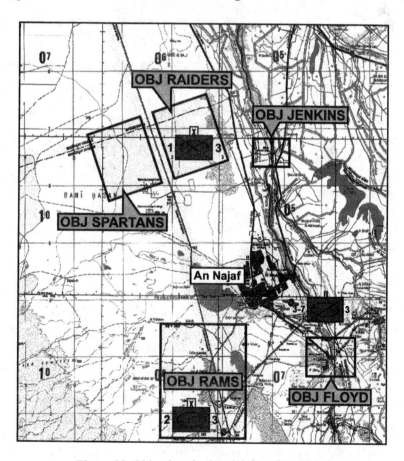

Figure 88. Objectives in the vicinity of An Najaf

TF 1-64 AR, commanded by Lieutenant Colonel Phillip DeCamp, seized RAMS against light resistance and then spent several hours clearing the area. Ultimately the task force fought off counterattacking Iraqi forces throughout the night, using direct fire, indirect fire, and CAS to retain the critical terrain on RAMS. The Iraqis used tactics similar to those 3-7 CAV experienced at As Samawah—suicidal attacks using RPGs and civilian vehicles against armored vehicles. Paramilitary forces swarmed all over RAMS in civilian trucks. They also fought from spider holes along Highway 28 in the restrictive terrain.[34]

After destroying more than 20 vehicles and killing approximately 350 paramilitaries, 2nd BCT secured RAMS by 2245 but had not cleared it of all enemy defenders. The brigade human intelligence teams immediately interrogated 27 captured EPWs. The questioning revealed the local enemy unit to be Ba'ath Party militia sent to secure a radio tower in RAMS and to defend against an expected airborne assault. They were completely surprised to see armored vehicles that far north so early in the war. Though poorly trained, the militia fought fanatically, occupying the brigade throughout the night. By 1000 on the 23rd, 2nd BCT had cleared the enemy from RAMS itself and turned its focus to defending against the steady flow of counterattackers streaming out of An Najaf. The 2nd BCT would remain at RAMS until called on to relieve 3-7 CAV south and east of An Najaf two days later.[35]

> ### The Iraqi Defense at Objective RAMS
>
> There were two types of enemy [at RAMS], the *Fedayeen* wearing black pajamas, and the regulars. I would not have known a *Fedayeen* from a regular at that point. . . .
>
> We captured some of their officers. They were expecting an attack from the sky, with the 82nd dropping in. They thought there was going to be an airborne drop. They positioned their forces as such. Two days before the fight, a general came in and said this is the overview of the land, and left. The next day, the officers came in and drew a circle on the ground, mapping out where defensive positions should be, and then left. Then the soldiers came in. About 6 hours after the soldiers came in, we (TF 1-64 AR) came in.
>
> There was no [command or control] for these guys; they were fighting independently. You could literally see a circle on the ground where the officer had drawn for the RPG guy to shoot from; that is exactly where he died. They were in a wedge formation; I remember seeing five guys in a wedge...that is where they died.
>
> Lieutenant Colonel Eric "Rick" Schwartz,
> Commander, TF 1-64 AR,
> interview, 18 May 03

Long-Range Surveillance Teams

The 2nd BCT did not attack into RAMS blindly. In addition to estimates developed prior to crossing the line of departure, V Corps attempted to insert reconnaissance deep on RAMS itself. V Corps has a unique, specialized capability to conduct sustained surveillance of an area to support decisions and targeting. Running counter to the trend for high-technology systems and remote sensors, the corps' long-range surveillance (LRS) company consists of the corps' most elite infantrymen, whose mission is to go deep into enemy territory and maintain constant "eyes on" a key piece of terrain. LRS teams are trained in infiltration, hide-site construction, enemy equipment and tactics, advanced communications, and a staggering host of survival and evasion skills. The selection process is brutally competitive to ensure only the very best, most capable, and experienced soldiers make the team. The small LRS teams are the corps' only all-weather, 24-hour-a-day capability to watch a critical piece of terrain.

However, employing LRS is not a haphazard decision. Helicopter infiltration, extraction, and emergency recovery so deep in enemy territory require a staggering amount of planning and preparation. A typical planning cycle is 48-72 hours and includes coordination with the Air Force, the corps aviation units, and the entire targeting community. Even more challenging, once the team is on the ground, it is not mobile. A vehicle would be nearly impossible to hide, and any foot movement is necessarily slow and meticulous to prevent detection. Once the team is at the site, the terrain must support digging ideally undetectable hide sites. A typical hide site is large enough for four soldiers to live in for a week at a time without ever breaking cover. If they are compromised, the lightly armed soldiers have a redundant evasion and extraction plan to reach safety.

> **Long-Range Surveillance Team Insertions**
>
> We never knew where 3rd ID would end up on any given day. The speed of the advance complicated the collection management process. I think we should have gone into Iraq before G-day to collect [far enough ahead of the division's advance].
>
> Sergeant First Class Kevin Ricks
> operations sergeant, E (LRS)/165th MI BN

For these reasons, the V Corps intelligence collection manager, Major Matthew Littlejohn, needed to select the LRS objectives with great care. The collection manager, responsible for coordinating the corps' array of intelligence collection capabilities to answer the corps commander's key questions, recommends the proposed sites with an eye to where the corps would need to look three to four days out.[36]

Because of the rapid pace of the corps' advance,

> **LRS Team Compromise—10 Feet Away**
>
> Despite all of the planning, not all insertions go as planned. Staff Sergeant Peter D. Armstrong's team, Team 1-2, E/165th MI BN, was one of three teams inserted for the campaign. Bedouin dogs compromised the team soon after its insertion into central Iraq. After the dogs followed the team to its secondary site, the team quickly moved to its tertiary site and went to ground. As an example of how disciplined the soldiers are and how effective their hide techniques are, Armstrong's team spent over 48 hours in an 18-inch-deep hole with a sheet covering six soldiers. Iraqis, actively searching for them, came within 10 feet of the team hide site. Staff Sergeant Armstrong lay flat on his back, peering through a small hole in the camouflaged sheet with his weapon tracking the Iraqi leader who was looking for them. Once the Iraqis moved off, the team exfiltrated to an alternate extraction site and was picked up safely.
>
> Lieutenant Colonel Robert P. Walters, Jr.
> Commander, 165th Military Intelligence Battalion
> 1 June 2003

site selection proved to be difficult. The corps started the fight with 27 potential LRS sites, of which 17 were specifically to support the 3rd ID; however, the corps only inserted three teams. Indeed, the LRS teams' relative inability to contribute was due to the speed of the maneuver units' advance. After the initial three insertions, the pace was too fast to make an educated guess on where the corps would be—and what it would need to know—three to four days out.[37] Moreover, the 11th AHR's experiences on 23 March in going deep, along with the sandstorm, cast a pall on aviation's percieved ability to support and made planning and execution more difficult.

Despite the inability to employ LRS after crossing the border, two of the three teams inserted provided some basic intelligence. Since the corps planned to use RAMS as a major LSA, it had to know what was there before the first combat troops approached. LRS Team

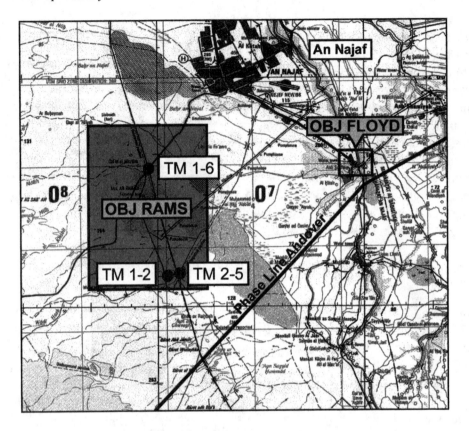

Figure 89. LRS team positions around Objective RAMS

1-6, led by Staff Sergeant Travis Prohaska, inserted on G-day. The corps expected 3rd ID's 2nd BCT to take two days to reach RAMS; Team 1-6's insertion was planned for two days prior. However, the team was on the ground for only one day before 2nd Brigade *"Spartans"* rolled into RAMS. While on site, the team reported 10 technical vehicles on the objective and about 60 paramilitary fighters, believed to be a mixture of Ba'ath Party militia and *Fedayeen*, some of whom came close to Prohaska's position.[38] In fact, the team remained hunkered down while 2nd Brigade engaged and destroyed the paramilitaries, only coming out of their hide site after fighting ended.[39] Team 2-5, led by Staff Sergeant Timothy Barnwald, inserted to observe the airfield in the vicinity of An Najaf. After an 8-10 km ground infiltration from where the helicopters dropped them off, the team sat in place and maintained continuous coverage until extracted after linking up with the advancing 3rd ID soldiers.[40] In OIF, LRS teams achieved little in return for the risks that they took and the effort expended to insert them. SOF units produced far more information but even they could not be inserted everywhere. LRS units assigned to conventional maneuver units also produced very little in DESERT STORM, suggesting that their role and viability should be reassessed.

1st BCT to Objective RAIDERS

At 1120 on 23 March, 1st BCT passed through 2nd BCT on RAMS and proceeded north to seize Objective RAIDERS. 3rd ID wanted RAIDERS as the site from which they would mount the attack on Baghdad. Practically adjacent to An Najaf, RAIDERS also afforded protection for the LSA at RAMS. From RAIDERS, 3rd ID could position forces to preclude attacks against either RAMS or the LOC. To reach RAIDERS the division had to attack through the An Najaf escarpment. The escarpment, a natural shelf nearly 250 feet high running roughly west to east, could only be negotiated via a lone road. On the approach to the escarpment, the road formed a single-lane causeway between a marsh on one side and an inland lake on the other. The climb up the hill was at an 11.6-percent grade in some areas. The Iraqis appreciated the tactical value of terrain and dug in artillery and infantry to take advantage of the narrow approach and steep grade, emplacing fighting positions along the crest and at points along the face of the cliffs.

Colonel Will Grimsley's 1st BCT had the mission to seize RAIDERS. Commissioned as an infantryman in 1980, Grimsley brought a wealth of theoretical and practical experience to commanding a brigade. A graduate of the School of Advanced Military Studies and an Advanced Strategic Arts Fellow at the Army War College, he had tours in Germany, Korea, Fort Hood, and Fort Stewart and served as a planner on the joint staff. He was a veteran of many bloodless battles at the National Training Center, the Combat Maneuver Training Center, and the Joint Readiness Training Center. Grimsley also served as an observer/controller for some 30 rotations

---

212th Mobile Army Surgical Hospital in the Attack

Lieutenant Colonel Kenneth Canestrini and the advance party of the 212th MASH arrived in Objective RAMS at 0400 on 24 March, prior to the conclusion of fighting on the objective. V Corps developed RAMS as an objective to provide space to concentrate forces for the attack on Baghdad. The 212th and other combat service support units needed space at RAMS to support that attack. Canestrini and his troops first had to wait until the fighting on RAMS stopped. They did not wait long. By 1600 that day Canestrini had done his reconnaissance and had a forward surgical team in place and operational. His main body closed at 1800. The sandstorm and the realities of the nonlinear battlefield moved in at roughly the same time. Canestrini's small hospital unit of 160 troops, including doctors, nurses, medics, drivers, and support personnel, found that they had to "erect" their 44-bed hospital during the mother of all sandstorms while securing their own perimeter.

Commenting on the experience, Canestrini observed, "At one point all (assigned) enlisted soldiers were on the perimeter. The key point is that all medical units must train on this basic task." For Canestrini and his troops, the problem become more difficult when the 212th had to develop a ward for enemy prisoners of war that they also had to secure without help.

Despite sand, manning the wire, and guarding prisoners, the 212th operated at RAMS for 15 days. They treated 100 surgical cases, more than 700 emergency treatment cases, and evacuated more than 200 patients. On two occasions the 212th went from 44 beds to 56 beds by using cots.

Lieutenant Colonel Canestrini
Interviewed by Lieutenant Colonel Judith Robinson
24 May 2003.

at the NTC. Because the terrain confined the brigade to the causeway that skirted the lake through soft ground, Grimsley expected a sharp fight at the escarpment. Intelligence placed an Iraqi regular army air defense battalion defending the escarpment and guarding an ammunition dump on the plateau. Grimsley also expected *Fedayeen* and Ba'ath militia in the area because An Najaf was a Shia city, so the *Fedayeen* would be there to assure the Shiites stayed in line. In the end his brigade confronted what amounted to two battalions. The regular army air defense battalion defended the An Najaf Ammunition Storage Facility on the top of the escarpment. A second battalion size force composed of about 250 *Fedayeen* and special republican guard troops with supporting mortars, dug in at the top and into the face of the escarpment.[41]

Colonel Grimsley assigned the task of assaulting the escarpment to Lieutenant Colonel "Rock" Marcone commanding TF 3-69 AR. Grimsley and Marcone had "rehearsed" this operation at the National Training Center in the fall of 2002 in anticipation of this very mission. On the basis of that experience and others, Marcone had decided opinions on how to do things. A veteran of DESERT STORM and Kosovo, Marcone had 17 blue force rotations at the NTC. He had participated in several rotations in support of an Army study on the wisdom of tracked versus wheeled scout platoons. Although the Army cited the study as the reason to mount scouts on HMMWVs, Marcone reached a different conclusion. Accordingly, he took the M113s assigned to company maintenance teams and gave them to his scout platoon in return for three HMMWVs for the maintenance teams to use. A firm believer in combined arms, he organized his tanks and Bradleys in what he called "combat patrols" of two tanks and two Bradleys accompanied by an engineer squad, thereby creating his own combined arms platoons and training them that way. Like Grimsley, Marcone believed in combined arms including using fires to support maneuver. Finally, Marcone liked to fight "two companies in relationship to each other. That is the key to success. It is to fight two company teams in relationship to each other because it is an unstoppable force."[42]

Figure 90. The 1st BCT moving along Highway 28 to Objective RAIDERS
after clearing the An Najaf escarpment

Marcone and Grimsley justifiably expected trouble attacking through the defile that led to the top of the escarpment. So did the division and corps. Accordingly, Grimsley had his own direct support battalion, 1-41 FA, and a second artillery battalion, 1-10 FA, reinforcing the direct support battalion positioned forward to support the assault up the escarpment. Further, Grimsley placed B/1-10 FA in Marcone's task force so Marcone had immediate support. To cover his advance Marcone ordered B/1-10 FA to lay in a 1,000-meter smoke screen. Grimsley also cued up air support and asked Colonel Dave Perkins and his 2nd BCT to help where they could. Perkins moved part of his brigade up to where they could support by fire.[43]

Despite the screen, the Iraqis still shelled Marcone's task force, which was stacked up on the road since the terrain prevented dispersal. Iraqi mortar and later artillery fell within 50 meters of vehicles. Nonetheless, TF 3-69 AR's assault force quickly gained the heights. The lead unit, a tank company team, went deep while Captain Dave Benton's team B/3-7 IN, the *Bandits*, turned east and swept the escarpment, destroying the dug-in mortars that harassed the brigade. The remainder of the task force dealt with the air defense troops, who served as the guard force at the ammunition storage site. As 1-41 FA moved over the escarpment, each battery shot fire missions, mostly counterbattery, to protect the brigade's movement. Despite a brisk fight, neither the artillery nor the brigade sustained casualties.[44]

U.S. Army

Figure 91. The 1st BCT climbing the An Najaf escarpment en route to Objective RAIDERS

Close air support assured TF 3-69 AR's success. As Marcone's troops advanced under fire, Grimsley's tactical air control party opened kill boxes on the escarpment. Grimsley used A-10s to "fly the road and get as close to the escarpment (as possible) ... [then] react to contact left and right all the way down the ridgeline . . . It was almost like opening a breach laterally for us."[45] The fighters also began reporting what they believed was armor moving to reinforce the fighting, but it eventually proved to be truck-mounted paramilitary troops. Marcone's troops and aircraft from all four air forces (USMC, USN, USAF and RAF) supporting the brigade that day quickly dispatched the reinforcements. The airmen also assisted in destroying enemy artillery. For a time the brigade could not locate enemy artillery firing on them because one of their counterbattery radars broke down. Brigade fire support officers estimated enemy artillery locations from crater analysis. CAS aircrew flew over the estimated locations and detected D 30 howitzers from their muzzle flashes and destroyed them. Reflecting on that fight and those to come, Will Grimsley noted that there are a "host of Marine Corps, Navy, Air Force, and Royal Air Force pilots I would love to meet some day."[46]

Ground Surveillance Radars and the Sandstorm

Animal 24 and Animal 26 [A/103rd MI BN ground surveillance radar teams], in direct support to the brigade reconnaissance team (C/1 CAV/1st BCT), finally had a chance to prove the worth of the Ground Surveillance Radar (GSR), specifically the new and improved AN/PPS-5D.

Throughout this week, 3rd ID was swarmed with the most intense and blinding sandstorms we had yet experienced. While all other reconnaissance assets were severely degraded, GSR consistently reported enemy targets. GSR's greatest accomplishment during the war was on 26 March when Sergeant Perez's team, consisting of Specialist Apostolou and Private Vasquez, detected 40 enemy targets during a sandstorm. Many of these targets were also confirmed when Corporal Kottwitz's team, consisting of Specialist Russell, Private First Class Showers and Private First Class Schexayder, detected them.

The targets were reported to Raider X Ray and subsequently destroyed by indirect fire and CAS assets.

A/103 Military Intelligence Battalion
Unit History

While 2nd BCT secured Objective RAMS and 1st BCT advanced to Objective RAIDERS, 3-7 CAV departed As Samawah and moved north along the river to isolate An Najaf. Major General Blount wanted to prevent the Iraqis from moving additional reinforcements into the city and to prevent the Iraqis from interdicting operations at Objective RAMS. It was clear that the town could not be bypassed and left unattended. Although the BCTs advanced along the relatively clear highways west of the Euphrates River, the squadron hugged the valley and moved through some of the more densely populated and heavily defended areas south of Baghdad.

3-7 CAV—Ambush Alley

After returning to division control on 24 March, 3-7 CAV marched north on Route Appaloosa (See Fig. 92) paralleling the Euphrates en route to a bridge designated Objective FLOYD. FLOYD was east and south of An Najaf; securing it would prevent Iraqi forces from entering or leaving the town from those directions. The squadron took Route Appaloosa to avoid congestion with 2nd BCT, still moving north to secure Objective RAMS.[47] During the movement, the squadron ended up stretched out over an extended distance, beyond radio range. The satellite-based BFT email system provided the only reliable means of communications throughout the squadron. Communications proved essential as the enemy compelled the cavalry to fight through a series of well-prepared ambushes. Paramilitary forces fought from the side of the road and from ramps using small arms, automatic weapons, and RPG teams. They also attacked from armed vehicles that the troops called technicals, and a mix of ordinary cars and trucks. After the fact, soldiers dubbed the route "Ambush Alley." Ultimately, the squadron fought through a series of ambushes throughout the night. Complicating matters, visibility dropped precipitously with the start of the now infamous three-day sandstorm.[48]

At 2100, as the squadron continued north out of As Samawah, it hit the first ambush. As the A/3-7 CAV scout platoon leader, First Lieutenant Matt Garrett, moved past a mosque on the western side of the road, he radioed, "Hey look, we're in Florida, it's Middle Eastern Times,"[49] referring to the popular restaurant in Orlando, Florida. The mosque caught his attention

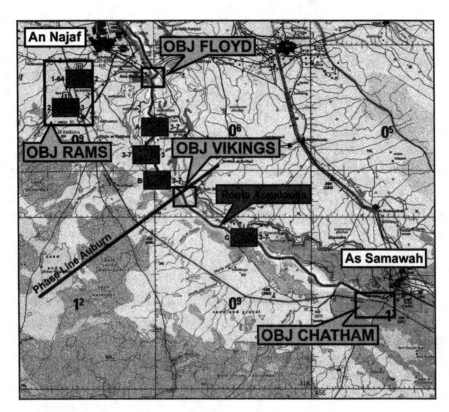

Figure 92. Ambush Alley—officially known as Route Appaloosa from As Samawah to An Najaf

because of its design and complementary lighting that accentuated the architecture. Just as he commented on the radio net, Iraqis emerged from the mosque and engaged the platoon. Alpha Troop's fire support officer, First Lieutenant Wade, said it looked like "Star Wars, with the tracer bounce off of the vehicles." [50] The ambush lasted approximately 2 hours as Alpha Troop fought through the extended engagement area. Artillery proved useful only in the early stages of the fight as the enemy closed to within 15 meters of the vehicles; so close the troop could not use artillery. Nonetheless, the heavily armed and armored cavalry cleared the engagement area with no casualties or losses.

Because the terrain did not permit maneuver, the following cavalry troops had to fight through the same ambush area as they moved north. The squadron confronted other difficulties during the running ambushes. After a canal bridge collapsed, dropping an M1 tank about 15 feet into a canal (with no injuries), A/3-7 CAV had to turn around on the narrow road and retrace its steps to the original route. Narrow roads and soft ground compounded the misery and resulted in an overturned truck and three mired vehicles. The collapsed bridge stranded a five-vehicle hunter-killer team of tanks and Bradleys on the far side. They had to wait until daylight before maneuvering back to the squadron. [51]

The ambushes continued intermittently all the way up the road, but they were particularly intense at Fasillyah and other towns along the river. At sunup, the Air Force weighed in with A-10 *Warthogs* using missiles, 500-lb bombs, and their 30mm GAU-8/A Gatling gun. 3-7 CAV finally consolidated south of Objective FLOYD at 0550 on the 25th, after 9 hours of fighting through one ambush after another. 3-7 CAV learned some important lessons during the fight up "Ambush Alley" and refined tactical techniques on the way. For example, their supporting artillery reacted to calls for fire quickly because they "went to ground" and laid the guns on the direction of potential targets as soon as they heard a spot report. Therefore, when they received an immediate call for fire, the guns responded very

---

Dodging RPGs

The operations M577 armored vehicle in the TOC, commanded by Captain Brett Bair, fought through one of the ambushes along [Ambush Alley]. Inside the M577, Major John Keith, the ground executive officer, and operations officer Captain Adam Beard controlled the squadron's fight through the multiple, simultaneous ambushes extended over 20 km. Suddenly, a large explosion twisted Bair completely around in the track commander's hatch. As he fell back into the track, Beard was dragging him down into the compartment. Beard breathed a sigh of relief as Bair glanced up at him; he had expected Bair's face to "not still exist." Bair offered a few choice words and climbed back up into the hatch. The RPG that was marked for their track had collided with a tree a few feet off the roadside, saving Bair and possibly the rest of the vehicle's occupants.

3-7 Cavalry Unit History

---

quickly. Lieutenant Colonel Terry Ferrell remembered that the all-night fight through the ambushes "traumatized everyone." According to Ferrell, "We do own the night, but we also train to own the night with standoff. When you have the guys crawling up beside your tank and you are using the 9 mil (Beretta 9 mm pistol) or stepping off to draw an AK to shoot somebody, your average tank crew does not train to do that."[52]

The fighting at RAMS, at the escarpment, and on the way to FLOYD demonstrated that the enemy would fight with courage, even dedication, but not with great skill. For one thing the enemy did not shoot accurately. They did, however, fill the air with bullets. The Iraqis literally attacked in waves against far-better-armed coalition units. On the other hand, the enemy reached sound conclusions on where to fight as at the escarpment. They also used other techniques suggesting more sophistication

---

M88A1 Recovery Vehicles

The M88A1 fleet issued to 3-7 CAV could not perform as the unit's tank recovery unit. It was too slow and prone to breakdown to tow M1 tanks over desert terrain for anything more than a very short distance. [Doctrine for recovery requires units equipped with the M88A1 to use tandem towing vehicles to tow M1 tanks.] The unit performed like-vehicle towing of disabled equipment, with M1s towing M1s. . . .In the vicinity of An Najaf, one squadron unit had three M1 tanks mired after the shoulder of the road along a canal they were traveling on collapsed and mired the tanks in the canal. The unit could not free the tanks with like-vehicle recovery or the unit's M88s. I directed a D9 bulldozer operator from the engineer unit attached to the squadron to fill in the ditch, creating a ramp so the tanks could drive out of the canal.

Interview with Chief Warrant Officer 4 Rocky Yahn,
3-7 CAV Squadron Maintenance Officer

---

than some might credit them with, including turning city lights on and off to signal an ambush of the 11th Attack Helicopter Regiment. Grimsley observed that at night, as the Americans approached towns, the lights went off, suggesting the Iraqis perceived they might have an advantage in fighting in the dark. By 23 March when Grimsley's brigade seized RAIDERS, a not unexpected, but more sinister phenomenon was revealed. Grimsley's troops captured the commander of a nearby Iraqi ammunition plan, who advised Grimsley that he knew the army commander in An Najaf and that he was not in charge, "others were." At An Najaf the paramilitary troops used a cemetery to stage attacks and ambushes from and used human shields to protect them as they did so. This enemy's soldiers may not have been well trained, but they were not unsophisticated.[53]

Countering Iraqi WMD And Ballistic Missile Strikes

While the coalition forces moved north, the Iraqis continued to exercise their only deep-strike capability—surface-to-surface missiles—with virtually no effect. After firing five missiles on the first day, the Iraqis launched an additional 12 missiles between 21 March and 3 April. The missiles included Ababil-100s, Al Samouds, and antiquated Soviet FROG-7 rockets. Of these 17, the Kuwaiti Patriots destroyed one, US Patriots destroyed seven, one was engaged simultaneously by US and Kuwaiti Patriots, and eight were not intercepted because they were not aimed at anything of value, fell well short of their targets, or blew up on launch. Aside from the four ineffective missiles, the Iraqis fired the remainder at Army and Marine staging camps within Kuwait and Camp DOHA, site of the CFLCC headquarters. Regardless of the Patriots' effectiveness, ground forces within a certain distance of the projected impact point continued to respond to the threat of a chemical weapons strike.[54]

The threat of chemical weapons attack was not limited to surface-to-surface missiles. The coalition believed that the Iraqis had an artillery-delivered chemical attack capability that presented a significant threat to coalition forces. US combat actions also could lead to a chemical threat. For example, south of Objective RAIDERS on 28 March, JSTARS identified 10 Iraqi tankers heading south from Baghdad. The Latifiyah Phosgene and solid propellant production facility was their suspected point of origin. The contents of the tankers were unconfirmed, but intelligence believed that they might be filled with Phosgene, a dual-purpose industrial product and confirmed chemical weapon (choking agent). The Air Force attacked and destroyed the tankers approximately 10 km north of Objective RAIDERS, where 1st BCT, 3rd ID was located. The brigade assumed full chemical protective posture due to the potential downwind hazard. Since the unit's organic chemical defense equipment could not detect Phosgene, the brigade had to wait for the chemical reconnaissance platoon of the 3rd ID's chemical company to arrive and complete its specialized tests before receiving the "all clear."[55]

Regardless of whether a missile or artillery attack triggered the chemical warning system, soldiers and marines donned their chemical protective equipment. Clearly, gaining control of the Iraqi's WMD capability was critical to ensuring coalition effectiveness, as well as meeting a national objective. These operations were generally termed "sensitive-site exploitation" (SSE) operations.

Sensitive-Site Exploitation

As coalition forces moved north into the heart of Iraq, they continuously conducted SSEs to support the elimination of Iraqi WMD, regime change, and the destruction of terrorist networks. More specifically, SSE consisted of selectively seizing and searching facilities associated with Iraqi WMD programs and other points of interest. The purpose was to collect intelligence or WMD samples for analysis and, if necessary, secure sites until final disposition

---

Soldiers Caring for Soldiers

BACKGROUND NOTE: On 26 March, the M2 Bradley that Specialist Ryan Horner and Private First Class Anthony Jackson, both of 1st Platoon, Charlie Company, 2-7 IN, were assigned to as dismounted infantrymen, had an electrical fire and was completely destroyed. When interviewed, they were wearing other soldiers' uniforms.

On 28 March 2003, the platoon was in a blocking position near the "Airfield." Both Horner and Jackson had just awakened and were eating MREs in the back of the company's cargo truck. The unit received artillery fire, and an adjacent chemical unit's alarms went off. It also received warning to don protective overgarments and masks immediately. As their masks had been destroyed [in the vehicle fire], their squad leader (Staff Sergeant Carver) had them run to the back of one of the M2s to have some protection. He also had them pull the hoods of the NBC suit as tightly as possible over their heads. By this time the entire company, as well as the chemical unit, was in MOPP 4. Staff Sergeant Carver then opened the rear personnel hatch and had a mask in his hand. At this point Private First Class Jackson stated "Give it to Horner, he has a wife and kids." Twenty minutes later all clear was sounded.

On two more occasions in the next three days they received indirect fire and went to MOPP 4. Every time, Jackson insisted that Horner use the mask. On the fourth day, the company gave Jackson a mask from a soldier who had been MEDEVACed.

Jackson's actions may sound trivial, but one must take into account that everyone thought that a chemical attack had just occurred. Jackson did not hesitate with his decision. When asked why he gave up the mask, Jackson replied, "[Specialist Horner] is my friend and he does have a wife and a little girl. . . . He is really a great guy and I know how much he loves his family. . . . I have a family but it is father, mother, you know, and that is not the same. . . . all I can say is that it was the right thing to do."

Of his friend, Specialist Horner said, "That was the most unselfish act I have ever seen in my life. . . Jackson did not even hesitate when the mask was placed in the vehicle. . . .I was absolutely stunned."

Interviews with Specialist Horner and Private First Class Jackson
conducted by Sergeant Major Victor LeGloahec, OIF Study Group
15 May 2003

---

could be determined. Sensitive sites varied in size, scope, and composition. They included, but were not limited to, research and development (R&D) facilities, laboratories, weapons production facilities, and storage sites. Not all sites were strictly military. Some were dual-use facilities, such as fertilizer and pharmaceutical plants that were suspected of producing WMD. Other locations were associated with individuals or organizations involved in WMD programs.

While most sensitive sites were associated with WMD, a significant number included known terrorist camps, universities, and government-sponsored commercial ventures, locations associated with individuals involved in terrorist activities, infrastructure that supported terrorist activities, presidential palaces, command centers, and headquarters. Other sites of interest, such as prisons and confinement sites suspected of holding personnel characterized as missing in action (MIA), hospitals believed to have treated MIAs, organizations associated with MIAs, and intelligence centers that could have held information regarding the existence, treatment,

Figure 93. The 101st Airborne Division chemical staff surveys a mobile laboratory

Robert Woodward, US Army

and location of MIAs, were searched. Intelligence identified more than 900 sites, not including a large number of sites that troops reported as suspicious.

To execute this task, the CFLCC used every available resource in the theater from the tactical to the national level. CFLCC employed maneuver units from the 3rd ID, 82nd Airborne Division, and the 101st Airborne Division and personnel from other government agencies as well. On a daily basis, the CFLCC approved or identified sensitive sites for exploitation based on current intelligence estimates and staff recommendations. The CFLCC C3 then tasked one of the major subordinate commands to seize and secure the approved sites. Once a maneuver unit secured a site, specialized teams of Army and other government agency personnel moved in to assess and exploit the sites.

Not only did seizing and securing sites divert combat power, most of these missions required combat support and combat service support from the divisions as well. Divisions provided NBC reconnaissance, decontamination teams, medical response, engineers, and military police. Furthermore, divisions provided force protection, life support, and transportation for the theater-level specialized teams.

Two specialized organizations exploited the sites: the site survey teams (SSTs) and the mobile exploitation teams (METs). SSTs focused primarily on conducting initial assessments of chemical, biological, radiological, and nuclear (CBRN) production locations, R&D facilities, storage sites, equipment, and other WMD infrastructure. Each SST, approximately 26 personnel, consisted of subject matter experts from the Defense Threat Reduction Agency (DTRA); explosive ordnance disposal (EOD) technicians; nuclear, biological, and chemical reconnaissance specialists; and a support element. Based on its initial assessments, an SST

Courtesy of 75th FAB

Figure 94. NBC reconnaissance specialists assigned to SST 4

would recommend sites for further exploitation by the MET. The MET elements were much larger and could conduct sample collection, perform computer and document exploitation, interrogate captured personnel, render safe munitions, and evacuate samples and materials to a laboratory or collection center for further evaluation and exploitation.

Despite the number of specialized teams in the theater, the number of sites, coupled with the velocity of the march north—exceeded the capacity of CFLCC to conduct SSE exclusively with specialized teams. To span the gap, divisions organized, trained, and conducted limited sensitive sight exploitation with assigned personnel and equipment. The majority of these newly formed teams came directly from each division's organic chemical company. Much like the SSTs, the divisional teams made initial assessments of suspected WMD sites, reported their findings to higher headquarters, and made recommendations on further exploitation.

Although finding and destroying Iraqi WMD capabilities was a major strategic objective, coalition forces had not found any by the conclusion of Phase III combat operations. Of course, during the combat operations, V Corps could not divert significant combat power to secure and exploit the overwhelming number of suspected sites. Troops continued to support SSE after the conclusion of major combat operations.

Communicating or Not

As the corps stretched out toward Baghdad, the corps and theater communications started to falter. The modernization undertaken in the 12 years since DESERT STORM had closed part of the gap, enabling the Army to build a force (*Force XXI*) that could fight digitally connected. The Army Battle Command System (ABCS) enabled commanders to pass orders, intelligence, real-time awareness of everything flying, logistics information, and many other bits of useful or vital information. However, even modernized communication systems proved inadequate to support the speed of advance attained over long distances.

Most of the ABCS information is passed over an aging component of the communication system called Mobile Subscriber Equipment (MSE). The key to understanding MSE is that the name is literal. The subscriber may be able to communicate on the move, but the equipment

Figure 95. Chemical soldiers from the 101st Airborne Division
investigate a research and development facility

on which the system is based cannot. The MSE "backbone" is based on stationary nodes dependent on line-of-sight antennas. Although satellite linkage is available, subscribers reach it via ground-based nodes. Consequently, it is easier to sustain the backbone while defending than attacking. If an MSE-equipped unit is attacking, the nodes must bound forward to assure continued service. Signal units have no organic security forces, so the same soldiers who install, service, and man the signal nodes must also defend those nodes.

The problem of keeping up with the fight and keeping MSE users happy fell to Colonel Jeff Smith, commander of the 22nd Signal Brigade. Smith's challenge was not unlike that which confronts his civilian counterparts who provide "wireless" service, except that Smith had no "roaming" capability. When a subscriber passed outside of Smith's coverage, there were no adjacent nodes to carry the signal. In OIF, that meant turning to FM radio or a combination of commercial and military satellite radios and phones.

Undismayed, Smith and his troops set to work to solve the problem. In addition to Smith's organic battalions, the theater assigned two more and placed a third under the 22nd's operational control. Armed with six battalions and the ability to analyze the terrain and the operational plan, Smith and his staff developed a system that would bound node centers forward and congregate enough resources at preplanned sites to support what they called "wide band belts." The 22nd developed a set of positions along the anticipated axis of advance, from which their nodes could link to satellites and thus back to Kuwait (or to anywhere else) and provide adequate bandwidth to support the operation.[56]

In the end, despite feverish efforts and signal units attempting to operate under fire, the 22nd proved unable to provide MSE support to the lowest levels. The 3rd ID, operating in the vanguard, fought the war "push to talk," using radios, satellite phones, and BFT delivered by satellite. V Corps' separate brigades and other units that relied on MSE and had fewer backup capabilities found themselves on the wrong side of the digital divide. Major General Marks, the C2, described one outcome of the digital divide when he noted that, although he could acquire "oven-fresh imagery," he could not necessarily get it to the units advancing on Baghdad.[57]

National Guard and US Army Reserve Troops

As V Corps advanced north, it was far more than an active duty-only force. A true "Army of One," the corps included Army Reservists and National Guard soldiers who served throughout the combat zone. These soldiers were vital, indispensable members of the team and, unless asked, were wholly indistinguishable from active-duty solders. This marks a revolutionary change for the better toward achieving a fully integrated Army.

Operation DESERT STORM and the subsequent demobilization of the Cold War Army produced a divide between the Active and Reserve Components that seemed to many too wide to bridge. Acrimonious debates over the size of the reduction of each of the components eventually forced Congress to get involved. At first, congressional mandates and internal Army agreements pleased none of the components, but the Army—all of it—weathered the storm. Thanks to the energy of the leadership, all three components—Active, US Army Reserve (USAR), and US Army National Guard (ARNG)—reached a point during recent years when the Army could honestly describe itself as "the" Army—meaning *everyone* who wore the uniform or served as a civilian in any of the three components.

The tempo of operations driven by commitments in the Balkans, the Sinai, and elsewhere forced unprecedented deployments of reserve troops. Guard and reserve military police, civil affairs, and PSYOP units deployed at previously unheard-of rates. ARNG infantry units deployed routinely to secure Patriot units rotating in and out of the CENTCOM area of responsibility. Post-9/11 deployments increased astronomically to support everything from combat operations to providing security at housing areas near Army installations in Germany. On 9 June 2003, 143,000 reservists were on active duty. In short, by the time of OIF, saying the Army could not go to war without the Guard and Reserve was demonstrably not merely a slogan.[58]

For the first time since the Korean War, ARNG infantry units went to war as units. Seven ARNG infantry units deployed in support of OIF. All were intended to secure sensitive sites, including Patriot units, theater support units, and air and seaports. Generally, because CFLCC expected to use them in local security roles, these battalions deployed in pieces and parts. Only one of them, 1-293 IN, Indiana Army National Guard, deployed as a whole battalion. Most deployed one or two companies, and others deployed with their headquarters but without their heavy weapons, a fact most came to regret. One unit, the 92nd Separate Infantry Brigade of the Puerto Rico Army National Guard, provided some 1,400 troops as on-board security to both commercial and Military Sea Lift Command vessels.[59]

In fact, all of the ARNG infantry battalions that deployed were light infantry. Light infantry's distinguishing characteristic that makes them "light" is that they have almost no vehicles—in short, they are foot-mobile. Moreover, none of these battalions deployed with their parent brigades so they came without their organic support and, some might argue, without an advocate. The experience of the 1st Battalion, 293rd Infantry Regiment, is emblematic of all of them. From a broader perspective, it is emblematic, in many ways, of the experiences of the "orphan" active Army battalions, including the 2-70 AR, 1-41 IN, and the 2-14 IN. In overcoming the difficulties of being "orphaned," these units demonstrated the flexibility and initiative of American soldiers.

The 1-293 IN, commanded by Lieutenant Colonel Ivan Denton, mobilized at Camp Atterbury, Indiana. During their mobilization process, the soldiers worked through every holiday in the winter of 2002-2003. Mobilized on Veterans Day, they were "federalized" or brought on active federal service at Fort Knox, Kentucky, during Thanksgiving week, and the advance party deployed to Kuwait on New Year's Day. The battalion closed on the theater over the next couple of weeks, with the last unit (D Company) arriving on 20 January 2003. B Company arrived on 2 January and began conducting rear area security missions the next day. Supporting the 377th TSC, the battalion found itself spread all over Kuwait securing port facilities, Camp UDAIRI on the Iraqi frontier, the military side of the Kuwait International Airport, and convoys across the entire country.[60]

But the battalion's real challenge came on 25 March 2003. CLFCC planned to establish a LSA south of Tallil Air Base (Objective FIREBIRD). Brigadier General Jack Stultz, commanding the theater transportation command, arrived at the air base on the heels of 3rd ID and immediately began setting up logistics support and working to return the airfield to service in support of coalition operations. On the 25th, Stultz learned that the Active Army infantry battalion task force, TF 1-41 IN, which had been defending the air base and assuring that any bad actors in Tallil remained in Tallil, would be moving north. TF 1-41 IN deployed from Fort Riley, Kansas, as part of the solution to the dilemma posed when V Corps learned 1st AD would not be flowed in time to secure the LOCs as planned. Now they had to move on to perform the same role farther up the LOC. Stultz needed infantry to relieve the TF 1-41 IN, and he needed them fast. Major General Kratzer, commanding the 377th TSC, had only one complete infantry battalion, the "Hoosiers" of the 1-293 IN.[61]

That evening, Kratzer ordered Lieutenant Colonel Denton to move his battalion to Tallil as soon as possible. Because all three infantry companies were out on missions, Denton ordered his support platoon to issue tube-launched, optically tracked, wire-guided (TOW) antitank missiles to his antitank company, Delta Company, 1-293 IN. He then ordered Delta Company to depart Camp UDAIRI for Tallil Air Base as soon as it completed loading its TOW missiles.[62]

Lieutenant Colonel Denton, with a small command post, his mortar platoon, one scout team, and two rifle platoons, departed Camp ARIFJAN at 0600 on the 26th. Delta Company trailed Denton by 2 hours, departing Camp UDAIRI at 0800. Denton linked up at Convoy Support Center (CSC) CEDAR, located south of the air base near Highway 8. There, the CSC commander claimed that the battalion's mission was to secure CEDAR and not Tallil Air Base. Denton did not believe that to be the case, but he left his operations officer and most of the troops at CEDAR and went on to Tallil Air Base with an antitank section and scout team where he reported to Brigadier General Stultz. Stultz confirmed the mission to relieve TF 1-41 IN in-place. After talking with Stultz, Denton concluded that he could relieve TF 1-41 IN and secure the CSC with the resources on hand. Out of radio range, Denton could not talk to his operations officer down at CEDAR. Accordingly, he sent a written order, delivered by his scout team, which directed his operations officer to move out smartly and to leave the two rifle platoons to secure CEDAR.[63]

The following morning, Delta Company, the scout team, and mortars did the necessary reconnaissance and handoff with TF 1-41 IN. Lieutenant Colonel Denton did his own reconnaissance and conferred with the commander of TF 1-41 IN as well. The remainder of his battalion arrived on the 28th. At 1600 that day, 1-293 IN assumed the mission, thus becoming the first ARNG infantry battalion since Korea to enter combat as a unit. It was not the last. Ultimately all but one of the seven ARNG infantry battalions deployed into Iraq.[64]

Conclusion

At the end of the march up-country, the corps had reached positions from which to launch north through the Karbala Gap and begin the isolation of Baghdad. The LSA at Objective RAMS was well on the way to achieving full operational capability, and the CFLCC had freed up the 82nd Airborne Division and the 2nd ACR (L) to start cleaning up the threat along the lengthening LOCs.

Although many perceived the war as "in a pause," V Corps and I MEF did not cease operations. V Corps continued to fight in several directions, from As Samawah to An Najaf and elsewhere to defeat the mix of paramilitaries and conventional forces to set the conditions required to attack to Baghdad. I MEF was doing much of the same within its zone, and both corps were busily transitioning their support structures forward to support future operations to the north. The fighting to protect the LOC revealed the real nature of the Iraqi defense. Corps units adapted their fighting techniques to match. Immediately behind the fighting, soldiers quickly transitioned to stability and humanitarian relief operations while they tried to stabilize the liberated areas. The 11th AHR, which conducted the first Army aviation deep strike of the war, learned that its tactics were inappropriate and helped lead the effort to adapt appropriately. And finally, a sandstorm of biblical proportions swept through the theater, shutting down most aviation and inhibiting ground maneuver.

Elsewhere in the theater, JSOTF-North supported Kurdish attacks toward Kirkuk, Irbil, and the vital oil facilities in the region. In the west, the JSOTF-West searched for surface-to-surface missiles and WMD while denying the Iraqis the use of the entire western desert. SOF troops in JSOTF-West or in TF 20 seized a key dam and several airfields. Taking the dam protected V Corps and I MEF from a deliberate inundation, while seizing the airfields extended JSOTF-West's reach across the barren desert regions. Finally, the CFACC transitioned from its initial strategic air focus to concentrate on destroying the Iraqi ground forces. With a level of air-ground integration not seen before, the CAS and air interdiction operations destroyed threatening Iraqis and enabled ground maneuver.

During the march up-country, the implications of the scope and scale of the campaign became apparent. Reaching operational ranges greater than anything the US Army had executed since World War II, the speed and distance started to tell on the Army's logistics and combat support systems. While never out of fuel, ammunition, or food and water, the systems designed to deliver repair parts, tactical communications, and tactical intelligence support faltered under the strain. Moreover, after the initial coalition surge up-country, the enemy actions influenced events and to some extent forced the CFLCC to adjust. Soldiers, of course, immediately adapted and continued toward their objectives. Behind and beside them, the logistics troops demonstrated that they too could get the job done under difficult conditions.

While never perfect, the Army and entire coalition force carried on despite the enemy and miserable conditions.

Army Attack Aviation
The 11th Attack Helicopter Regiment and 101st Attack Aviation

The 11th Attack Helicopter Regiment's deep strike of 23 March remains one of the key components of the "darkest day." On the night of 23-24 March, the Army sent its most powerful deep-attack system, the AH-64D *Apache* attack helicopter, to destroy *Medina* Division armor and artillery before they could affect the maneuvering ground forces. However, the regiment returned with 31 of 32 aircraft damaged, one downed in enemy territory, and two pilots captured, without decisively engaging the *Medina*. While marines eventually rescued the pilots, and the aviators repaired many of the damaged aircraft rapidly, it took 30 days to restore the regiment to full capability. The mission cast a shadow over deep-attack operations throughout the duration of major combat operations. In fact the Army only attempted one other deep attack. Moreover, the incident placed in question the efficacy and utility of attack helicopters in Army doctrine. Soon after the sandstorm cleared, the 101st Airborne Division successfully executed a deep attack. On that mission, two aircraft crashed in brownout conditions on takeoff, marring even this achievement.

But the mission is significant and important for other reasons, chief among which is that 11th AHR quickly assessed what went wrong and shared their assessment with the 101st and others. More important, all of the attack aviation units in theater learned lessons from the unsuccessful mission and applied them to great effect. A close review of the attack suggests the failed mission suffered from a classic "first-battle" dynamic. Specifically, *Apaches* ravaged Iraq formations during DESERT STORM. As a consequence, the Iraqis adjusted and prepared a defense specifically against attack helicopters going deep. No one detected their dispositions, with the result they achieved surprise and defeated one of the best-trained attack aviation units in the world. The aviators flew against these defenses using tactics, techniques, and procedures inappropriate to the combat environment. It took the hard lessons of the night of 23 March to change these tactics.

To be sure, the 11th AHR did not fail solely because of inappropriate tactics. As with most failures, there was a chain of events—a "failure chain"—that led to the ultimate outcome. In this case, the failure chain links the inevitable fog and friction of combat with a series of individual and collective decisions and the human ego in war. From delayed convoys to confusing terrain management to an indomitable warrior spirit to get into the fight, a variety of dynamics contributed to the unsuccessful mission. Yet even with the loss and damage of equipment, the capture of two aviators, and an unmolested enemy, the mission triggered an amazing revision of tactics and procedures that is a testimony to the integrity, flexibility, and perhaps most important, persistence of Army aviators.

The 11th AHR Attack

The 11th AHR, commanded by Colonel Bill Wolf and composed of two attack helicopter squadrons—2-6 CAV and 6-6 CAV—began planning for OIF in October 2002. At that time,

2-6 CAV was already in Kuwait supporting Operation DESERT SPRING, and the aircrews and planners were comfortable with conducting operations in the desert environment. By the time the rest of the regiment arrived in Kuwait, 2-6 CAV had flown some 4,000 hours training in the Kuwaiti desert. In January 2003, the rest of the regiment alerted to deploy to Kuwait and learned that it would receive attachment of the 1-227 Attack Helicopter Battalion (AHB). The 1-227 AHB, commanded by Lieutenant Colonel Dan Ball, an AH-64D *Longbow*-equipped attack helicopter squadron joined from Fort Hood, Texas.[65] Thus, the regiment would consist of three attack squadrons fitted with the most advanced attack helicopters in the world.

The AHR aborted its first planned deep-attack mission against the Iraqi 11th ID in the vicinity of Tallil Air Base due to haze, dust, and poor visibility. The mission would have been a "JV [junior varsity] fight," preparing the 11th AHR for the "varsity fight" with the *Medina* Division.[66] Frustration over aborting their first mission was palpable within the staff and aircrews. In particular, the 2-6 CAV aviators felt tremendous frustration. Not assigned to fly that night, they harbored the idea, with their longer experience in the desert that they might have been able to execute the mission had they flown. Second, the running start option reduced the number of ground combat units available to V Corps so the regiment, as Major John Lindsay, the operations offer put it, "felt significant obligation to alleviate as much pressure as we could on the 3rd ID."[67] But, when the regiment received the mission to destroy the Republican Guard *Medina* Division's artillery and armored maneuver units, it was determined to succeed.[68]

The Plan

The 11th AHR planned to move forward to Objective RAMS immediately after 2nd BCT had cleared it. The initial quartering party and command post would fly into the assembly area, followed by the regiment's support units bringing fuel and ammunition forward. The attack helicopters would arrive last. Moving would position the corps' deep-attack capability well forward, extending their reach ahead of the rapidly advancing ground forces. Moreover, it would enable the corps to continue combat operations unabated while the ground forces refitted from their 200-km dash north from the border.

Intelligence on how the *Medina*'s three maneuver brigades and its artillery were arrayed for battle was incomplete and led to debate between the corps and regimental staff officers. Intelligence estimates reported the *Medina* brigades in the vicinity of their home garrisons but their actual disposition for battle was unclear.[69] Although corps intelligence painted a fairly clear picture for the 10th AR Brigade of the *Medina,* the corps directed the regiment to attack the *Medina's* 2nd AR Brigade because it appeared to be astride the avenue of approach north of Karbala that 3rd ID planned to use.[70] Unfortunately, the corps could not accurately locate the units assigned to the 2nd AR Brigade

The original mission, purpose, and endstate were:

> On order, 11th AHR attacks to destroy the artillery and armor of the Medina Division to facilitate 3rd ID freedom of maneuver through the Karbala Gap and seizure of Objective SAINTS.

> The purpose is to shape the Corps' battlespace and thereby provide the 3rd ID freedom to maneuver in the Karbala area by destroying the artillery and armor forces of the 14th, 2nd, and 10th Brigades of the *Medina* Division.

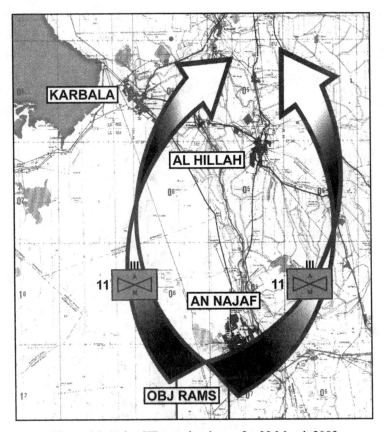

Figure 96. 11th AHR attack scheme for 23 March 2003

> The endstate is the destruction of the Artillery and Armor of the 14th, 2nd, and 10th Brigades, 3rd ID freedom of maneuver maintained, and 11th AHR postured to conduct shaping attacks against the Republican Guard's *Hammurabi* Division in support of V Corps establishment of the inner cordon [around Baghdad].[71]

The 11th AHR estimated that the destruction of the *Medina* would take two nights of deep attacks, employing three battalions each night.[72] Planning, already contentious because of inexact intelligence, became more contentious on the matter of routes. Regimental planners repeatedly requested to attack into their objectives from the west, avoiding the urban areas to the north and east of RAMS.

The western avenue of approach crossed Milh Lake north of Karbala, followed by a sparsely populated Iraqi army maneuver training area. Because the 101st's division boundary was to the west, the 11th AHR had to request these routes through the corps. V Corps denied the western avenues because to use them would have required establishing a FARP near Milh Lake to refuel the attack helicopters. This FARP would have been well forward of the advancing 3rd ID's forward line of troops and thus vulnerable. The corps had already received multiple reports of Iraqi forces maneuvering in the area where the FARP would have to go and did not believe the risk was acceptable. Even if the corps had approved the western approach and the

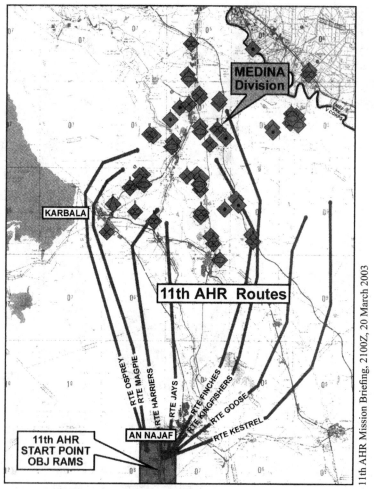

Figure 97. Overview of 11th AHR planned routes

forward FARP, it is clear that 11th AHR could not have executed such a plan. As it turned out, the regiment only got enough fuel at RAMS to refuel part of two battalions. On 23 March they had no means to establish a FARP north of RAMS, let alone as far north as they imagined prior to departing Kuwait. As it was, attacking the Iraqi 2nd Armored Brigade required a south-to-north approach, directly over the Iraqi equivalent of urban sprawl.[73]

In any case, a route near the lake may not have solved the problem. Chief Warrant Officer 3 Troy Templeton recalled that "we templated all this ADA expecting us to come up the lakes."[74] Templeton believed that the 1-227 AHB routes reflected concern about possible ADA that could engage units attempting to use the lake to reach targets. In short, the enemy may well have anticipated that attack helicopter units would use the lake as a means to avoid ADA and so placed ADA where they thought the aviators would have to come to use the lake on their approach to the *Medina*. Templeton liked the idea of avoiding the ADA at the lake. As he put it, "They (the routes) were fine with me. We didn't start getting shot until we were right over the city—and what is a good way to enter a city?"[75]

Still, the regiment planned routes that avoided the towns and villages along the way to the target. To do this they used *FalconView, which* enables route planning and rehearsal using high-resolution imagery. *FalconView* is first-class software that essentially supports a "magic carpet ride" over the terrain. Of course the utility of the tools is entirely dependent on the imagery. The relatively open areas the regiment planned to fly were not devoid of habitation. As Wolf put it, "We avoided any idea of a village at all. I will tell you once you cross the Euphrates everything is lit up. Every farm has a light and every farmhouse has a brick wall around it. Everything became a hiding place for whoever wanted to be there." [76]

Captain Karen Hobart, the regimental intelligence officer, understood the threat urban terrain posed to the aircraft. In her intelligence estimate for OPLAN 1003, she explicitly described the threat to rotary-wing aircraft operating over the Iraqi urban terrain. Her intelligence summary described how Iraq's air defense systems enjoyed advantage in urban areas. Iraqi guns had the advantages of high rates of fire and high gun elevations, and they were light and easy to deploy and move on civilian vehicles.

In general terms, the regimental intelligence summary also addressed how smaller-caliber weapon systems, such as antiaircraft artillery, could be placed on rooftops and on mobile trucks for hit-and-run operations. Moreover, the summary assessed that the air defense assets could be placed around schools, mosques, and hospitals, indicating Iraq's awareness of coalition attempts to avoid collateral damage. Finally, Hobart described Iraq's air defense ambush techniques along friendly routes, to include massing small-arms fires on low-flying and hovering aircraft. At the final rehearsal for the mission, Wolf highlighted the small-arms threat, noting that he told his aviators that small arms "would ruin their day." But after the fact he recalled, "nobody in their right mind would have envisioned what we ended up facing."[77] In fact the Iraqis had perhaps as many as a dozen air defense teams deployed along possible routes. The teams included light air defense artillery cannon, and shoulder launched surface-to-air missiles.[78]

The coalition intent to avoid destroying the Iraqi power grids also concerned Hobart. City lights could silhouette aircraft against the night sky and hinder the pilots' use of their night vision goggles. Thus placing their air defense artillery in the well-lit population centers reduced one of the Iraqi's major weaknesses—the lack of night-capable air defense artillery. What Captain Hobart and others did not know was that the Iraqis planned to use city lights as an early-warning system, turning an entire town's lights off and on to signal the approach of helicopters.[79]

All aviators and intelligence personnel "knew" of the *theoretical* risk of small arms in an air defense role. But with the exception of Somalia in 1993, the Army had no contemporary experiences to weigh the *actual* risk, and very few of the aviators who flew that night had flown in Vietnam, where ground fire took an awful toll on helicopters. So the 11th AHR—and its supporting intelligence soldiers—seriously underestimated the small-arms and light ADA cannon threat to attack aviation operations. The commanders, pilots, and planners generally tried to avoid flying over urban terrain where possible, but after years of training on benign live-fire ranges and in computer simulations that do not adequately represent the small-arms threat, no one really understood that small-arms and light ADA cannon could be showstoppers.

Coordinating deep artillery fire for suppression of enemy air defenses (SEAD) along the routes is a critical element of any deep strike. SEAD missions are historically among the most complex and challenging to execute, as ideally the artillery hits suspected air defense sites along the planned route only minutes before the aircraft traverse the area. Timing and accuracy are critical, made all the more difficult by typically imperfect knowledge of exactly where the air defense systems are. For this mission, the corps planned to fire 32 Army Tactical Missile System (ATACMS) missiles.[80] The corps also panned joint SEAD, primarily coming from electronic warfare aircraft and air strikes on suspected air defenses.[81]

The Preparation

Based on the pace of 3rd ID's advance, the corps ordered the regiment to attack the *Medina* a day earlier than originally planned. Adding to the sense of urgency, a severe sandstorm was bearing down on the region,

Figure 98. ATACMS missile fires in support of combat operations

US Army, Redstone Arsenal

expected to hit on the 24th. Many in the regiment felt that if the attack didn't occur on the 23rd, the 11th AHR might not get into the war in a meaningful way.[82]

The regiment failed to meet several of the doctrinal conditions for the attack. First, it operated from an unsecured assembly area on Objective RAMS. Some Iraqis appear to have driven around the flight line during mission preparation.[83] Second, the MSE Small Extension Node (SEN) that would have provided high-bandwidth digital communications for the TAC could not be sling-loaded forward due to weight and atmospheric conditions. Finally, less than half of the regiment's refueling and rearming capability made it to RAMS in time for the mission preparation. The rest of the fuel and ammunition handlers crossed the berm on 21 March and were still making their way north.[84] Nonetheless, against the pressure of the looming sandstorm and despite a shortage of fuel, communications, and security, the regiment prepared to execute.

Aircraft started landing at 1400. As the regiment assembled into a mile-long line of aircraft, the implications of the lack of security were quickly apparent. Pilots watched as one group of Iraqi civilians traveled throughout the area in a pickup truck. This scene repeated itself several times as Iraqi civilians moved about unimpeded and in plain view of the assembled attack helicopters. This raised concerns that the regiment's impending attack would be reported to Iraqi combatants in the surrounding villages and along the attack routes.[85]

Powdery dust, distance, and lack of fuel also started to affect operations. Refueling operations took an exceptionally long time as the fuelers traveled down the long line of aircraft.

Moreover, with less than half of the planned fuel trucks on hand, the regiment could not refuel all of the attack helicopters, the command and control aircraft, or for that matter the CH-47s that needed fuel for their return trip south.[86] Although only two battalions were scheduled to go, getting the right amount of fuel in the right place proved difficult. The regiment had enough fuel to refuel fully 1-227 AHB, but could only partially refuel 6-6 CAV. With 31 aircraft refueled the regiment leadership believed they had adequate resources to attack the Iraqi 2nd Armored Brigade.

> **A Failure of Imagination**
>
> We could have highlighted the small-arms threat [to the 11th AHR], but it would have been a failure of imagination for people to understand the magnitude.
>
> Captain Karen E. Hobart,
> S2, 11th AHR,
> commenting on the small-arms
> threat to the deep attack

The GO/NO GO Decision

Doctrinally the first step in the decision to launch is to confirm that there is a target to strike. Forward at RAMS and without the mobile subscriber digital communications, Captain Hobart could not contact her staff at the main regimental command post in Kuwait. She used her only communications means, a satellite telephone, to contact Captain Bret Woolcock, her liaison officer, whom she had embedded with the V Corps Fires and Effects Coordination Cell. Once in contact, Hobart, Colonel Wolf, the operations officer, and a few others stood around the satellite telephone out in the open, intently listening to receive the latest intelligence verbally. Woolcock could only provide 1,000 square meter estimates of the center of mass of company-size units. Exacerbating the problem, the *Hunter* UAV, the V Corps' only dedicated UAV, was not available. It was currently moving by air and ground convoy up to Objective RAMS and would not support the deep attack. The theater's *Predator* UAV was also unavailable, as it was still busy flying for the Air Force.[87] Taking Woolcock's report, Hobart believed she had a 75-percent picture on the enemy disposition. She so advised Colonel Wolf.[88]

Surprisingly, Woolcock also passed three Iraqi communications intercepts. Until now, the Iraqis had made infrequent use of their communications to avoid detection. Subsequent to the attack, Hobart thought that the increased communications might have been related to the regiment's pending attack, which she believed the Iraqis were expecting. While the Iraqis did not know the timing or the targets, they did know American tactics. The US Air Force had been attacking Iraqi forces for days, and 3rd ID was pressing the Iraqi army and paramilitary forces hard in the west. The enemy knew that the US almost always leads ground forces with the Air Force, followed by attack aviation.[89]

At this point, Wolf and the 11th AHR had a partial intelligence picture, some fuel, and were postured at Objective RAMS, secure or not. At 2200, Wolf assembled his battalion commanders to present the final GO/NO GO analysis to the V Corps chief of staff via the tactical satellite radio.[90] Wolf, with grids to "20 or 25" targets generated from signals intelligence and updated

> **They Would Not Be Denied**
>
> But with all the problems, they felt they could get the job done. Everyone was past the point of "can't." It did not matter; every ounce of energy was devoted to making the mission work.
>
> Major Kevin Christensen
> S3, 6-6 CAV
> Interview with Major Jonathan Gass

imagery, believed he had enough to find and attack the 2nd Armored Brigade, but only by "search and attack techniques."[91] The go-no go briefing included Wolf, Brigadier General Dan Hahn, the corps chief of staff, G3, G2, effects, and air support representatives. Despite fuel problems, delayed liftoff, and uncertainty about the precise location of the enemy, there was no dissent.[92]

The Execution

Delayed 2 hours and 15 minutes as the troops sorted out who got fuel, helicopters began lifting off at 0115 on 24 March.[93] From the start things did not go well. Colonel Wolf returned to his command and control aircraft to find that he lacked the fuel to make the mission. He waited an additional 45 minutes to get more fuel. He was not the only one having problems. Some crews swapped aircraft to assure that key leaders boarded aircraft that had fuel. In the end, only 30 of the 31 *Apaches* left the assembly area, as one crashed on takeoff due to severe brownout conditions caused by the "moon dust."[94]

Poor communications plagued the regiment throughout the mission with obvious effects on execution. When Colonel Wolf delayed the launch by 2 hours and 15 minutes, the regiment could not alert supporting fixed-wing units. The ground SEAD fired at the adjusted time and in accordance with the corps standard of 30 minutes before the helicopters' time on target. Even this success proved a mixed blessing since many of the pilots considered 30 minutes too early and wondered if it acted more as a warning to the Iraqis than a suppression. Worse still, the fighters assigned to support the mission never received the adjusted mission time and departed as originally scheduled, which meant they were not on station during the actual attack. The corps Fire Effects Coordination Cell and air liaison officer did obtain some help. For example, B-52s dropped 26 JDAM bombs in support of the effort to rescue the pilots of the lone downed aircraft. Reportedly, some ground-attack aircraft engaged targets in a supporting kill box, but there are no specifics available.[95] Whatever problems the regiment experienced with the SEAD and CAS execution, the Iraqi air defense "system" was arguably not vulnerable to traditional SEAD operations—26 ATACMS and 26 JDAMS could not realistically *suppress* several hundred Iraqis distributed throughout a densely populated urban area firing small arms and light air defense artillery.[96] Fundamentally, the attack helicopters attacked alone and unsupported.

As they traveled up the route, although the lead troop of 6-6 CAV had no contact, 1-227 AHB was already reporting enemy fire. En route to the target, when B/6-6 CAV oriented west at approximately 0100, all of the lights in the area, to include the cities of Al Haswah and Al Iskandariyah, blinked out for approximately 2 seconds.[97] Immediately thereafter, the sky erupted with all manner of ground fire, which was apparent by the red, yellow, and white tracers. Initially unaimed, the fusillade of fire created a "wall" between the aircraft and their objectives. Although the *Apaches* were running with lights out, the lights from farms and town silhouetted the attack helicopters against the night sky. Crews reported damage to their aircraft and difficulty maneuvering due to the volume of enemy fire.[98]

In the *Apache,* one of the two crewmen flies wearing helmet-mounted night vision goggles to see things thermals do not, including, for example, wires and tracers. The second crewman flies with thermals and the 30mm chain gun slaved to his head-up display. When the sky "lit" up with tracers, the aviator with goggles could see them, but the aviator who had immediate control of the gun could not. Therefore, to add to their problems, one crewman had to talk the other on to the source of fire to suppress it.

Igor Paustovski, US Army

Figure 99. *Apache* attack helicopter in dust-created brownout at FARP SHELL

The following account drawn form the battle summary of 6-6 CAV details how difficult this mission became and conveys a sense of what flying that mission was like for one crew.

Chief Warrant Officer 2 John Tomblin and First Lieutenant Jason King were in the second aircraft to depart for the *Medina* fight, and when they finally took off to the north, the aircraft shuddered from the weight of the ammunition. Vehicle traffic trying to refuel the regiment's aircraft had created 6 inches of talcum powder dust—making it very difficult for everyone trying to depart the assembly area. The crew was not surprised when it monitored radio traffic that an A Troop aircraft had crashed on takeoff. Along the 53-nautical mile route, *Palerider 16* received very little small-arms fire but noticed heavy tracer fire to the west in the vicinity of its sister battalion, 1-227 AHB. As they began to turn west into the objective area, Tomblin and King noticed how bright the lights were in the nearby town; it seemed odd considering it was midnight [unit reports suggest time was actually 0100]. As they climbed to clear a set of 200-foot wires, the lights went out for about 2 seconds. When the lights came back on, they started receiving aimed AAA fire at the aircraft. It had been a coordinated ambush directed at taking out the *Apache* aircraft. *Palerider 16* conducted evasive maneuvers and returned fire. Tomblin stated "fire was coming from all directions." He could tell the aircraft had been hit when he smelled electrical equipment burning. Looking down, Tomblin saw a man with a rifle shooting at the aircraft. He engaged with the 30mm, killing the man and hitting a nearby fuel tanker. There was a tremendous explosion that lit up the sky.

As Tomblin maneuvered the aircraft, King was calling in [a] report that they had taken fire. In the middle of his report, a bullet entered the cockpit and went through his throat. His transmission stopped and Tomblin asked, "Sir are you ok?" There was no response. King's throat had filled with blood, and although he could hear everything that was going on, he was unable to answer. Tomblin turned the aircraft to the south and reported that his front-seater had been hit, condition unknown. Ahead of them was the 53-nautical mile route they had just come up, with other aircraft trying to reach their objective area.

By now the air defense ambush was waiting, and the aircraft continued to receive heavy fire. The flight controls seemed sluggish and uncontrollable. Major Christensen (6-6 CAV S3) was in a C2 aircraft several miles to the south. The plan was to link with the *Black Hawk* at a designated location and transload King for a flight to the nearest field surgeon team. Tomblin continued to ask First Lieutenant King if he was OK—still no answer, although he could hear him breathing. Chief Warrant Officer 4 Robert Duffney and Chief Warrant Officer 3 Neal served as their wingman. Tomblin pulled in behind them and noticed a tremendous amount of smoke coming from one of Duffney's engines. A hydraulic line on Duffney's aircraft had been severed and fluid was flowing into the engine. This same hydraulic system controlled the weapons on his aircraft; Duffney was unable to return fire. Tomblin pulled back and, as Duffney's aircraft received fire, he laid down suppressive fire in the enemy's direction.

Earlier, before the flight, King had taken his pressure bandage out of his load-bearing equipment and placed it on the dash of the aircraft. Usually this would be placed in the rear storage bay of the aircraft, unreachable by its owner. Now he was applying pressure to the wound and was finally able to speak. "I am ok, I am ok, you're taking fire from the right." King could see tracer fire through his night vision goggles and continued to direct fire for his back-seater and other aircraft. Together the two aircraft continued down the route, receiving heavy fire. The plan to link up and land with the *Black Hawk* had been changed. They would fly back to the assembly area and load King into a waiting vehicle that would take him to a MEDEVAC aircraft. As they approached the assembly area, the small-arms fire stopped. Now they had to land the crippled aircraft at an assembly area that had several other damaged aircraft attempting to land. Both aircraft flew past the assembly area and allowed landing aircraft to touch down while locating the awaiting transport vehicle. While they were waiting, numerous reports from other aircraft could be heard on the radio. One from their sister battalion was transmitting on the emergency guard frequency; this aircraft was badly damaged and lost all navigation and night vision equipment. [Airborne Warning and Control System] was vectoring the aircraft to the south; the crew was noticeably shaken up.

Once on the ground, King was loaded into the waiting vehicle and was moved to the MEDEVAC aircraft. Knowing other pilots may have been shot, King would not allow the MEDEVAC to leave. Finally, the pilots of the MEDEVAC told King, "Sir we need to go now!" This was the last thing King would remember; he later woke up in the aid station. After receiving initial treatment, he was transported to the rear, where the surgeon told him he was very lucky. The bullet had just missed his windpipe and trachea, and he very easily could have permanently lost his voice or bled to death. King's wife was notified that her husband had been shot and was in critical condition. As King's condition improved, he was to be transported to Germany, where his wife would meet him. Instead of flying home, he convinced a sergeant major to coordinate a ride for him back to his unit. When he rejoined the unit, the soldiers could not believe their eyes. King continued to fly security missions in support of OIF north of Baghdad.[99]

The 6-6 CAV reached its objective but had to abort before engaging any ground targets due to the heavy fires. The 1-227 AHB made it to its objective and engaged some targets but eventually had to break off and return for fuel. They never found the 30 T-72 tanks they hoped to find. One of 1-227 AHB's helicopters made an emergency landing after taking serious damage. Lieutenant Colonel Dan Ball attempted to provide support to the crew as it sought to evade capture, but he took heavy fire that set a weapons pod alight. Ball finally had to jettison the pod and return home, unable to rescue his crew.[100]

Returning shot up and in some cases with wounded aboard, the *Apaches* had to land on the same plowed ground that had dried to dust, which the pilots found vexing even during daylight the afternoon before. Having positioned himself at the center of the flight line, the operations officer, Major John Lindsay had a ringside seat as aircraft returned alone or in small groups, turned into the wind and did their best to avoid mid-air collisions and wrecking their aircraft as they sought the ground in a haze of blinding dust. The pilots executed running landings to give themselves some hope of staying just ahead of the dust cloud they generated. Lindsay recalled that it was terrifying to watch as aircraft rolled "100, 200, 300 feet right toward us," attracted to light and heat sources generated by Lindsay's little command post group.[101]

Of the 30 aircraft that departed Objective RAMS for the mission, 29 returned with small-arms and some antiaircraft artillery damage. One aircraft force-landed due to ground fire and was subsequently destroyed to prevent compromise. The Iraqis captured both pilots. On average 1-227 AHB aircraft returned sporting 15-20 bullet holes each, and one had a total of 29 holes. The unit performed an average of 70 small-arms damage repairs per day until all damaged areas were repaired in accordance with applicable aircraft technical manuals. A typical repair of damage incurred from small-arms fire is portrayed in Figure 1. If nothing else, the *Apache* demonstrated how tough an aircraft it is. As one pilot put it, "that airplane is resilient. It is amazing! We got back and looked at all the airplanes and it is incredible that we were able to fly those things home. It is an amazing aircraft."[102] On the other hand, no one was claiming a victory that night.

Enemy Battle Damage

Assessing battle damage is always difficult, but fundamentally aside from killing some air defense systems, a few gun trucks, and a number of enemy firing small arms, the regiment achieved very little.

Repairing the Apaches

That all but one of the *Apaches* returned to RAMS is a testimony to the aircraft's durability and survivability. The pilots owed their lives to engineers who designed the *Apache* and to those who built and maintained them.

Despite significant damage, all of the aircraft were repaired well forward in the field and returned to service. On 24 March three CH 47s came forward, bringing the regiment's executive officer, maintenance officer, and others. The aircraft also brought spare parts carried as sling loads. En route Iraqis engaged the CH 47s. Two of the helicopters jettisoned their loads, including all of 1-227's spare parts.[103] Despite that latest bit of bad news, mechanics returned two aircraft to service within 24 hours, 12 of 17 within 96 hours, 15 of 17

> ### Making the Abort Decision
>
> The first 10 minutes of the flight were okay, but Lieutenant Colonel Barbee [Commander, 6-6 CAV] noted the amount of lights that came from the built-up areas. . . .Then they started to receive tracer fire; at first not aimed, but then as they flew north it became more focused. . . .The Alpha Troop commander radioed him and asked if they should abort the mission. Barbee said no, given that aircraft were dispersed all along the route. He ordered the squadron to fly east of the assigned route, away from the built-up areas.
>
> But Barbee could not make radio contact with the Bravo Troop commander and Colonel Wolf, the regimental commander, was still not on the radio. Many calls from other Alpha Troop aircraft began to come in reporting that they were "taking heavy fire" as they entered the objective area.
>
> Barbee had to get Bravo Troop out of the area; he was in contact with some of the crews. He called mission abort, but now they had to fly back through the gauntlet again. He ordered the troops to fly as far east as possible. But due to the [adjacent] CAS maneuver box and the I MEF's boundary, their freedom of maneuver was limited.
>
> Lieutenant Colonel Mike Barbee
> Commander, 6-6

within a week, and the remaining two within 30 days.[104] The 2-6 CAV, which had not flown the mission due to the fuel shortage, remained fully mission capable. The corps assigned 2-6 to support 3rd ID.[105] The 11th AHR flew its first battalion-size mission only nine days after the ill-fated attack.

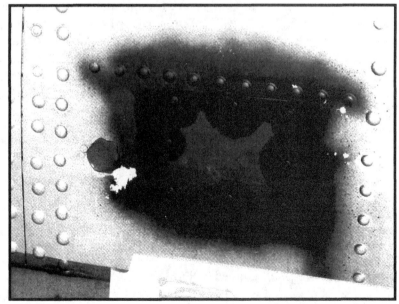

Figure 100. Photograph of repaired small-arms damage

Adaptations

Following the attack, Army aviators took a collective step back to assess what had happened and to determine the causes and develop solutions. To be sure, the Iraqi air defense technique clearly proved effective in countering the helicopters as they were employed. After 12 years of experience with the Americans targeting their air defense systems, Iraqis had adapted. They developed a simple, yet sophisticated air defense "system" virtually impossible to detect and suppress.

Because US forces are very effective at destroying air defense radars that radiate and missile/gun systems, the Iraqis avoided using these as cornerstones in their network. Rather than using radar, the Iraqis appear to have relied on ground observers who reported on cellular phones and low-power radios. Finally, flickering the city lights warned the shooters to be prepared to engage. Rather than relying on easily targetable missile or gun systems, the Iraqis' main weapon systems were the small arms widely distributed among the general population.

At the time of the 11th AHR's attack, the Iraqis in the area had not been subjected to any coalition ground or air actions. As a result, shooting up into the sky at the American helicopters could be viewed as a no-risk proposition, even for the most reluctant armed Iraqi civilian. With rudimentary training on where to shoot (at the apex over power lines), even paramilitary troops could contribute to an air defense engagement area. Moreover, with no visible concentration of air defense equipment prior to mission, SEAD was ineffective. Once the fight started, the fires were so dispersed and distributed among populated areas that they were virtually impossible to suppress. The American pilots' restraint in returning fire into the urban areas to avoid civilian casualties also hampered their response. For Colonel Wolf this point loomed as particularly important. His crews needed to identify a target before returning fire, "because there were people out there we did not want to kill."[106] They could not, as he put it, "spray indiscriminately."[107]

Consequently, the Iraqis executed an air defense operation in which the early warning and tracking systems operated below the US ability to detect and destroy; equally important, the Iraqis distributed their air defense weapons so widely that they could not be tracked or suppressed; and they decentralized their command and control so that it could not be effectively disrupted. The Iraqis, in this instance at least, used the decade between the wars to develop tactics that produced a highly survivable and effective air defense capability that, in turn, forced adaptation in Army aviation tactics.

In addition to reviewing the enemy's actions, Army aviators reviewed mission planning, tactics, techniques, and procedures to determine what they could learn from this. The next day while maintenance crews repaired the aircraft, the command group conducted a conference call with the 101st Airborne Division aviators to share lessons learned and discuss countermeasures. 11th AHR presented its assessment in 11 major areas ranging from internal security while airborne to the rules of engagement (ROE). The ROE in effect prevented the aviators from using rockets to suppress targets given the possible proximity of civilians. On another topic, the 11th advised its colleagues that go/no go briefings focused on target fidelity inadequately accounted for en route air defenses—doctrine requires an assessment of en route air defense, and the 11th attempted to do that, but the defenses it faced were outside the model they anticipated.

This deliberate effort to learn from the first deep attack of the war paid off, as evidenced by the successful 101st Aviation Brigade, deep attack on 28 March, after the sandstorm cleared. Whatever else the aviators learned, they were reminded that small arms and light cannon are effective against attack helicopters. After the fact, the decision to go seems incomprehensible on the basis of inadequate fidelity in target locations. On the other hand, even with absolute accuracy on the 2nd Armored Brigade it is hard to see how the regiment could have overcome the fierce resistance it encountered. As more information on the enemy in OIF becomes available, the Army will need to consider under what conditions flying attack helicopters deep will produce the kind of benefits that warrant the potential risk.

The 101st Goes Deep

When OIF commenced, 101st Aviation Brigade's first planned mission was to destroy the 14th Mechanized Infantry Brigade of the *Medina* Division, projected to occur on 24 March. The mission would complement the 11th AHR's attack on the rest of the *Medina*. However, the division postponed the mission when the sandstorm grounded all Army aviation. Moreover, after the 11th AHR's experience, the corps leadership debated whether to attempt the mission at all.

By the time the weather cleared, the 101st Aviation Brigade had done its homework on the 11th AHR's experience.[108] That experience suggested that the enemy was using observers linked by cell phones to provide early warning to a dispersed air defense. Pilots, planners, and commanders had a frank and detailed exchange to share insights, observations, and recommended changes in tactics and procedures.[109] With the lessons disseminated, chief among which was to avoid the built-up areas, and the enemy still able to menace the 3rd ID's advance through the Karbala Gap, Lieutenant General Wallace authorized the 101st's attack. Thus, on 28 March, the 101st Attack Brigade conducted the operation's second deep attack—this time against the 14th Brigade of the *Medina* Division.

130th Engineer Brigade

Figure 101. Using oil for dust abatement at FARP SHELL

Planning

The planned 101st attack against the *Medina* division was one of the few missions that survived each evolution of the base plan. This attack required the early entry of the 101st force package on the TPFDL. The scheme of maneuver, refined in Grafenwoehr, Germany, during the corps' preparatory exercise, *VICTORY SCRIMMAGE*, required the division to establish an additional forward operating base (FOB 5) or FARP southwest of Karbala to assure the *Apaches* could remain on station long enough to accomplish their mission.

Based on the discussion with the 11th AHR, Major Bill Gayler, the 101st Aviation Brigade S3, devised a plan that combined CAS, artillery, and direct fires from helicopters within the formation in support of the brigade's maneuver. Gayler planned to use artillery and CAS to prepare the battlefield prior to the attack. Once the aircraft were en route, ATACMS would fire 4 minutes in front of the aircraft, while CAS remained on station to suppress any enemy encountered. The brigade relied heavily on its air liaison officer, who in turn requested an airborne forward air controller (AFAC) on the mission to ensure CAS could be coordinated directly between fixed- and rotary-wing aircraft.

The *Apache* crews planned constant movement, with variations in airspeed and altitude to increase their survivability by decreasing the enemy's ability to track and engage them. Additionally, the lead/wingman concept would be used to provide supporting fires in and around the more populated urban areas or areas where they expected enemy contact. Crews intended to suppress immediately any ground fire with direct fires, develop the situation and then engage with CAS as needed. Based on the 11th Regiment's comments, they decided to fly using these techniques from the moment they lifted off. In short, they assumed they would have to fight all the way to their objective.

The brigade S3, along with Chief Warrant Officer 3 Brendan Kelly, the brigade tactical operations officer, felt development of the routes was as important as the engagement areas. They focused a great deal of time accounting for fuel efficiency, enemy locations, and deception. For example, based on threat assessment, several routes were developed with frequent heading changes over known or suspected enemy observers. This technique aimed to confuse observers as to the actual direction of travel. Aviators are trained to fly to the least-lit areas. The enemy knew this and focused air defenses on those areas. In response, the pilots thought that flying over populated villages might not be a bad idea. The pilots and staff used both *FalconView* and *Topscene* flight visualization tools in planning and rehearsals. Once the brigade developed the plan, aircrews came to the brigade TOC to "fly" the mission in *Topscene*, allowing them to refine and adjust the routes.[110] Both tools enabled rehearsal over terrain generated from imagery. Of *FalconView*, one pilot observed, "The only thing that I did not see in *FalconView* that I saw in the gun tapes afterward was the amount of palm trees.[111]

Execution

Two battalions executed the attack on 28 March. The 1-101st Aviation (AVN) attacked to the north as the main effort, while 2-101st AVN feinted to the south. The brigade Commander, Colonel Greg Gass, commanded from a command and control *Black Hawk* supported by his brigade fire support officer and air liaison officer.[112] Gass positioned himself near 1-101st, the main effort. As it turned out, 1-101st encountered very little enemy contact, while 2-101st found what they sought.[113]

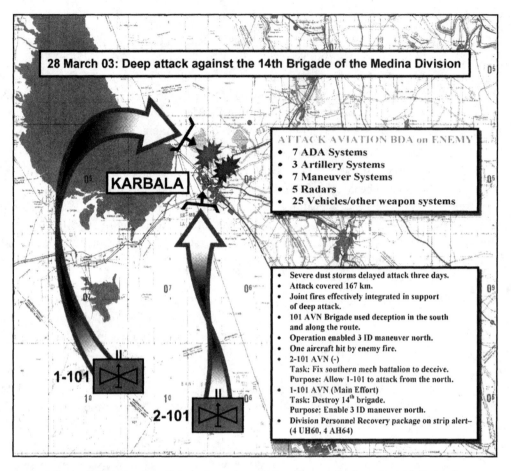

Figure 102. 101st Attack Aviation scheme of maneuver against the 14th Brigade

The 1-101st departed from FARP SHELL at 2145, following a route north, then east across the Karbala Lake and maneuvering out into the Karbala Basin. At 100 km in length, the route to the objective area was long, requiring a flight time of 40 minutes. As the battalion aviators flew the route, communications problems prevented them from calling for the fires to suppress enemy air defenses. Upon arrival at the objective, B/1-101st conducted a movement to contact to locate the Iraqi 14th Brigade, with no luck. Alpha and Charlie companies departed 30 minutes after B/1-101 to complete the planned destruction. After handing off the empty engagement area to Alpha and Charlie companies, B/1-101 returned to base. Alpha and Charlie companies continued the search for targets and returned after 30 minutes on station with no contact. Apparently, the 14th Brigade had already departed the objective area.[114]

While maneuvering through the objective area, all three companies took ground fire. The Iraqis acted as described in 11th AHR's "lessons learned"—civilian vehicles tried to maneuver along routes of flight to engage the aircraft, and dismounted Iraqis fired small arms and RPGs. Dedicating aircraft to security succeeded. With an aircraft maneuvering around the rear of the flight and one on either flank, the remaining aircraft focused on target detection and engagement. The battalion destroyed five pickup trucks, four of which had heavy machine guns mounted in the back. The battalion estimated it killed 15 armed people on the ground.[115]

The 2-101st intended to attack the southernmost two battalions of the 14th Brigade. The concept of operation assigned two companies in continuous attack with a third company as the battalion reserve, ready to continue the attack or to suppress the enemy in support of a self-extraction of any downed aviators. Their routes took them literally to the edge of Karbala. Alpha and Bravo companies conducted the mission, with Charlie Company in reserve. A/2-101st led, followed by the battalion Commander, Lieutenant Colonel Stephen Smith, and trailed by B/2-101st.[116]

Alpha Company departed FARP SHELL at 2204 on the 28th. After some initial confusion when one aircraft turned left instead of right, the battalion re-formed and headed for the objective. As the flight approached the line of departure, Smith took up an overwatch position behind the company. On the way to the target, the lights in Karbala went off and then came back on, just as the 11th AHR had reported. About this time Alpha Company acquired targets along Highway 9 southeast of the city of Karbala. As planned, the pilots passed the target grids to Smith, who in turn tried unsuccessfully to contact the brigade's air liaison officer in the command and control aircraft. After making several attempts, Smith, tried to contact the F/A-18s and AWACS directly. Finally, he transmitted on the emergency frequency and contacted *Gospel 01*, a pair of F/A-18s, and passed the target information. *Gospel 01* then contacted the lead *Apaches,* which conducted a target handover, leading to several CAS runs on the targets. Handover went smoothly because A/2-101st had already started engaging the armor forces on Highway 9 using the running-fire techniques. Of course, a linear road with burning tanks presents a good mark for fixed-wing aircraft.[117]

Lieutenant Colonel Smith remembered, "The rest of the night was amazing."[118] Smith watched tracers coming up, saw fighters dropping 500-pound bombs and listened to one pilot report that people were waving to him from a rooftop. According to Smith a second pilot corrected this misapprehension, saying, "Dude, they ain't waving."[119] Despite receiving ground fire, the *Apaches* continued to attack tanks and other fighting vehicles along Highway 9 and antiaircraft artillery in the open terrain west of the highway. Gun camera tapes verified that the crews engaged the enemy, running in from 8 to 5 km. As one aircraft ran in toward the target, his wingman provided overwatch and suppressive fires. Once the lead aircraft completed the engagement, the wingman would then begin his run-in toward the target. The fight continued as the attack aviation alternated with CAS to destroy the forces along the highway.

Army, Air Force, and Navy pilots destroyed six armored personnel carriers, four tanks, five trucks, and a fiber-optic facility. They also killed approximately 20 troops. Although not a high count by "exercise standards," the attack marked an effective use of deep-strike Army attack aviation against a highly adaptive enemy. Moreover, it illustrates how quickly Army and fixed-wing aviators adapted to an enemy that had caused significant damage to the pervious deep strike.

The Battle of An Najaf: 25-28 March 2003

Like As Samawah, An Najaf is located along the Euphrates River with several key bridges across the river. Highway 9 parallels the river and runs directly through the town. Highway 28 also parallels the river but runs several kilometers to the west of the town. Any Iraqi forces in the town, conventional or paramilitary, could interdict travel along both highways and disrupt the corps' planned attack through Karbala.

Figure 103. Destroyed Iraqi tank on Highway 9

The Iraqis defending from An Najaf included paramilitary and some regular troops. As had their colleagues in As Samawah, they forfeited the relative security and defensive advantages within the built-up areas to come out and attack the approaching 3rd ID soldiers. Learning from the two previous fights in An Nasiriyah and As Samawah, the 3rd ID decided rather than simply blocking and bypassing the town, it would contain An Najaf from the southwest and northwest and isolate from the north and east. This would prevent enemy paramilitary forces from interdicting logistics operations in Objective RAMS and position the division to prevent other enemy forces from reinforcing An Najaf.

The division aimed to secure the two key bridges on the north and south sides of An Najaf and then place forces on the eastern and western sides, effectively isolating the city from all directions. The division designated the northern bridge at Al Kifl as Objective JENKINS and the southern bridge Objective FLOYD. 3rd ID assigned JENKINS and FLOYD to 1st BCT and 3-7 CAV, respectively. Complicating execution, the sandstorm took helicopters out of the equation. The 3-7 CAV lost the use of its OH-58D *Kiowa Warriors* eyes and weapons. En route and looking for a safe place to land, the *Kiowas* saw other helicopters on the ground below and landed. The helicopters turned out to be the 11th AHR, recovering from their deep attack. Rotary-wing aviation would not contribute to the upcoming fight.[120]

Setting the Cordon—1st BCT in the North at Objective JENKINS

Late on 24 March 2003, while consolidating his brigade in Objective RAIDERS, Colonel Will Grimsley received an order from Brigadier General Lloyd Austin, the assistant division commander for maneuver, to seize Objective JENKINS, a bridge over the Euphrates River at the town of Al Kifl. The division had designated every class-70 bridge (rated at 70 tons capacity)

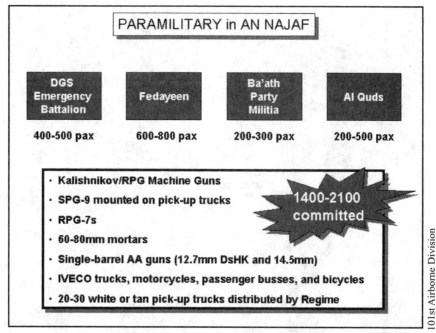

Figure 104. 101st Airborne Division estimate of paramilitary forces in An Najaf
(PAX refers to the estimated number of paramilitary troops assigned)

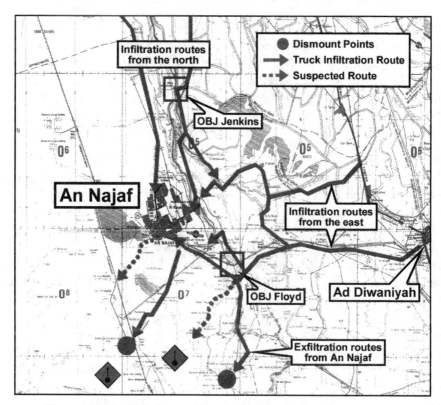

Figure 105. An Najaf paramilitary infiltration/exfiltration routes,
developed by 101st Airborne Division soldiers

Figure 106. Bridges at Objectives JENKINS and FLOYD

as an objective to enable a quick orientation of the force if the division required the bridge as a crossing site and to orient forces on possible threats to the division's flank as it advanced. But intelligence had gathered information suggesting that the enemy was using the highway that ran south from Al Hillah to An Najaf to reinforce Najaf and points south. Austin wanted Grimsley to seize the bridge and interdict the highway to prevent reinforcements from getting south. Seizing JENKINS would isolate An Najaf from the north while the 3-7 CAV completed isolating the town at FLOYD from the south and from the east by crossing the river and advancing north.[121]

But Grimsley had no one readily at hand to execute the mission. He had troops spread from RAIDERS all the way back to An Nasiriyah. He assigned the mission to Captain Charles Branson and his Alpha Battery 1-3 ADA, the brigade's air defense battery equipped with the LINEBACKER missile system.[122] Grimsley augmented the battery with a combat observation lasing team (COLT) and a section from the brigade reconnaissance troop. Branson assembled his troops and gave a quick order supported by back brief. The troops moved out about midnight. Grimsley also tasked Lieutenant Colonel Marcone and TF 3-69 AR to provide a quick-reaction force in the event Branson got in trouble.[123] About 0200, as Branson's team approached the bridge, it ran into heavy contact, primarily from paramilitary troops. Along Highway 9 west of the bridge, Branson encountered dug-in troops armed with what Grimsley described as the "whole works."[124] Over the course of the night, Branson's troops fought their way forward, but as they reached the west bank of the Euphrates they encountered more enemy. Branson whistled for help. Grimsley called on Marcone to commit the quick-reaction force just before sunup.[125]

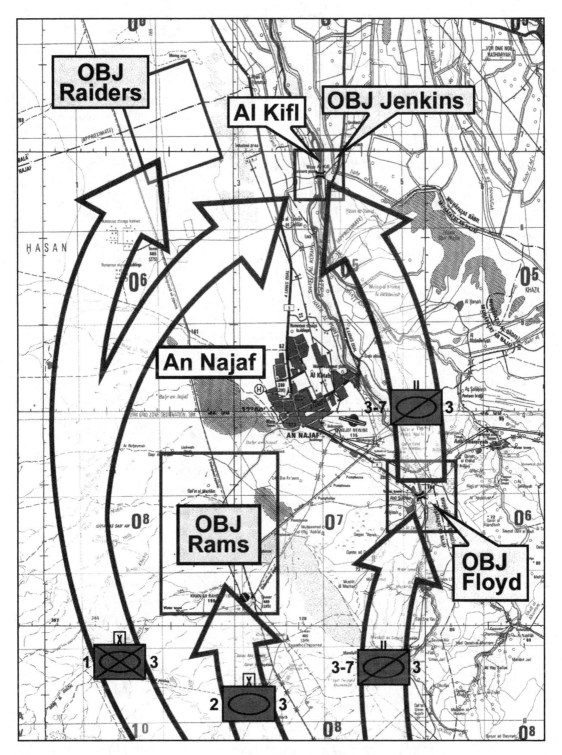

Figure 107. 3rd ID's scheme to encircle An Najaf

Captain Benton's Team B 3-7 IN, composed of two mechanized infantry platoons and one tank platoon, moved out just before 0600 heading for the bridge some 17 kilometers away. Like Branson before him, Benton met opposition as he reached highway 9. Major Mike Oliver, Marcone's operations officer, followed Benton by about 1 hour to assume command of the two-company operation. Oliver caught up

---

True Combined Arms Forces

An air defense battery commander leading a Bradley and tank company team in an attack is unprecedented. Just after midnight on March 25th, Captain Branson's company team reached the service road leading to the [Al Kifl] bridge and immediately started receiving heavy RPG, small-arms, and mortar fire from enemy positions well established in prepared defensive positions on the near side of the bridge. Captain Branson pulled his forces back. . . and called in artillery fire to suppress the enemy fire. . . . For the next eight hours, Captain Branson maintained the momentum of the attack, calling for artillery fires on three separate occasions. . . [until B/3-7 IN arrived].

Award citation narrative
for Captain Charles Branson

---

with Branson just before 0800. Branson had thrown a track in rough terrain near the road leading into Al Kifl. Oliver took a quick update from Branson and continued on, now traveling east, where he met Captain Benton about 0830. Benton's company was fighting to clear the route into Al Kifl. Oliver ordered the ADA battery to orient to the south along the road to prevent the enemy from reinforcing the outlying buildings in Al Kifl.[126]

Oliver planned to attack across the river and control the eastern bank from high ground near what the map showed as a second bridge. But first Benton's troops had to clear the way. The company engaged numerous dismounted Iraqis armed with small arms and RPGs and supported by mortars. Infantrymen cleared buildings along the way. At one point the infantry could not gain access so the tank platoon blew a hole in the offending building, enabling the infantry to enter. The opposition included both uniformed troops and paramilitary in civilian clothes. Oliver assessed the enemy defending the near side or west bank as a reinforced platoon supported by mortars. The company team stopped at the bridge and destroyed several targets on the far side while the infantry cleared nearby buildings. Benton's troops completed clearing the west bank at 1030.[127]

Now Oliver ordered the section from the brigade's reconnaissance troop forward to determine whether the ground would support his plan to defend the bridge from the high ground on the east bank. Oliver specifically ordered the scouts not to cross the bridge just yet. Meanwhile, Captain Branson rejoined and began moving his battery into position to prevent the enemy from reinforcing from An Najaf. Shortly thereafter, the scouts reported that there was only one bridge, not two as indicated by the map, supporting a similar assertion made by Branson. The scouts also reported they had killed several enemy infantrymen on the bridge and on the east bank. About 1100 the ADA battery reported the north-south road on the west bank clear, so Oliver ordered Benton to assault across the bridge.[128]

At about 1100 Benton attacked with the tank platoon leading while the Bradleys provided overwatch. The four tanks of Second Lieutenant John Rowold's platoon (the 1/A/3-69 AR, attached to B/3-7 IN) approached the bridge in a staggered column.[129] Private First Class Alfeiri, driving A13, used his mine plow to clear several destroyed trucks from the bridge. Tank

A14 followed. The third tank, Lieutenant Rowold's A11, driven by Specialist Price, was on the bridge when the Iraqi defenders detonated explosives rigged along the span. Price increased his speed, clearing the damaged section by maintaining the tank's momentum. As the dust from the explosion cleared, the soldiers saw that the bridge section had pancaked straight down, with three tanks isolated on the eastern bank.[130] Oliver recalled, "Temporarily stunned by the blast, it took us a few seconds to realize what had happened. The first thought that flashed through my mind was, how far was the bridge over the water, then how deep was the river; and finally, could they survive the fall from the bridge into the water."[131] Lieutenant Rowold reported that they were alright, with three tanks on the east bank and no one injured. Oliver reported to Marcone what had happened and that he would assess the condition of the bridge.

Thoroughly alarmed and not realizing the entire span had not gone in the river, both Grimsley and Marcone moved out traveling separately. Grimsley had his engineer battalion commander bring their tele-engineering rig, planning to look for a good place to get an assault bridge across the river, because "I've got a *Black Hawk Down* scenario here. I have American soldiers on tanks on the far side with no way to get back."[132] Major Oliver ordered engineers supporting Benton to determine whether the partially destroyed span was safe to cross. The scout section drove a HMMWV across with no problems, so at least wheeled vehicles could cross. The scouts could see wires on the bridge that presumably led to explosives to blow up the rest of the span. When told to cut the wires, the scouts demurred although after some discussion they did cut the wires and moved to the river's edge to prevent the enemy from regaining access to the explosives still on the bridge.[133]

When Lieutenant Colonel Marcone arrived, he went immediately to the bridge. He could see no damage, so he asked one of the brigade scouts where the enemy blew the bridge. The scout replied, "right here." Marcone said, "You've got to be kidding me, this little indentation," so Marcone ran down the stairs at the side of the bridge and looked underneath, concluding it would hold a tank[134] Marcone walked out to the mid point of the bridge and called his own tank across, expecting the tank to pick him up on the way, but the tank crew drove on past him. Crossing was one thing, but hanging around to pick up the boss was another. While the bridge span sank a bit, it held the weight. Following Marcone's example, Rowold's fourth tank and Benton's Bradleys crossed the bridge to reinforce the tanks on the east bank.[135]

The Iraqi defenders continued to engage the tanks on the eastern bank while the task force assessed the bridge status. Once on the far side, Lieutenant Colonel Marcone participated in securing the bridgehead, shooting and capturing one enemy soldier, and disarming another in hand-to-hand combat. As Marcone shoved a weapon away from a wounded paramilitary trooper who lay near a low wall, a man in civilian clothes brandishing a weapon stood up on the other side of the wall. Marcone wrestled away the man's AK-47 and used the rifle like a bat on his still-struggling opponent. The man dropped and Marcone's medics treated him and his wounded colleague and took them away.[136]

Unwilling to give up the bridge, the Iraqis charged the armored vehicles on the far side in pickup trucks and vans. Grimsley crossed the bridge on foot and joined Marcone. "There are firefights going on all over the place around us and that is when the vehicles start coming, driving down the highway trying to ram the Bradleys. Vehicles (trucks) with explosives and knuckleheads in them. Rock, Tom Smith (Commander, 11th Engineer Battalion), and I are

Figure 108. From left to right, Lieutenant Colonel Marcone
Lieutenant General Wallace, and Colonel Grimsley

standing in the intersection (just east of Al Kifl) watching this go on over and over again."[137] Marcone's infantry expanded the bridgehead and began engaging enemy on the highway to the east of Al Kifl with artillery. As the weather worsened, the sand blew so hard it became difficult to see the traffic on the highway. But Marcone's fire support officer registered the guns on two linear targets on the highway, enabling him to fire concentrations on the highway as required.[138]

As Marcone's troops organized their positions, the Iraqis also began shelling them with mortars. At about sunset while Marcone was walking his positions, a mortar round struck nearby knocking him unconscious for about 45 minutes. Once he recovered and resumed control of the fight, he ordered the tanks to withdraw back across the bridge due to the limited fields of fire on the far side. The tanks withdrew to the west bank and provided overwatch for the two Bradley platoons that had crossed and remained on the far side. Team B/3-7 IN established a strongpoint and continued to defend against suicidal Iraqi attacks, supported by artillery and by the Air Force in the person of Technical Sergeant Crosby, who called in CAS throughout the defense. The enemy technique was both simple and suicidal. Mike Oliver recalled that they attacked by coming south from Al Hillah in pickup trucks carrying 8-10 people. Benton's Bradleys would destroy the trucks, but the survivors continued forward, using buildings for cover. Generally poor visibility enabled at least some of them to close to 10-15 meters, where they fired RPGs and assault rifles until Benton's troops killed them. Benton's troops fought nearly continuously until relieved by TF 2-69 at 1900 on 26 March.[139] By controlling the bridge at JENKINS, 1st BCT prevented Iraqi paramilitary reinforcements from entering An Najaf from the north, successfully closing the top of the cordon.

Setting the Cordon—3-7 CAV in the East

The division assigned 3-7 CAV the mission to isolate An Najaf from the south and east. 3-7 CAV moved straight from its "march" up from As Samawah into the attack. At As

Samawah, the division elected to block the exits from the town, but at An Najaf, Blount needed to interdict traffic flowing south from Baghdad reinforcing An Najaf and possibly points farther south. The airborne JSTARS indicated heavy movement south along Highway 8 /80. Crossing the Euphrates south of An Najaf at Objective FLOYD and attacking north would isolate An Najaf from the south and east, and with TF 3-69 AR crossing at JENKINS, the division could interdict enemy movement along the Euphrates.[140]

B/3-7 CAV, "*Bone*" Troop, led 3-7 CAV to the bridge on Objective FLOYD at 0600 on 25 March, at about the same time Captains Branson and Benton linked up at JENKINS. The storm had reduced visibility to 25 meters or less, so the cavalrymen relied on their night vision and thermal sights to provide some limited ability to see and respond to the Iraqis' continuous small-arms, RPG, and suicidal attacks. At 1043, *Bone* secured the western side of the bridge, and engineers determined it was not prepared for destruction, although they had discovered almost 10,000 pounds of plastic explosives cached on the far side.[141]

At 1100, *Bone* crossed the Euphrates and attacked north. While *Bone* halted east of An Najaf, *Apache* Troop (A/3-7 CAV) attacked due north to secure a concrete dam and large bridge over the river. En route, they encountered several hundred dismounts and roads choked with technical vehicles and all types of military equipment. The fight up the east side of the town was intense. The sandstorm reduced visibility, allowing the Iraqis to approach to within a few feet before they could be identified. Consequently, the fighting was very close. Hundreds of paramilitary fighters in technical vehicles or on foot attacked in waves, using small arms, RPGs, and mortars.[142]

> **Hunter-Killer Teams**
>
> The hunter-killer team concept works fantastic!. . . The M1/M3 combination is outstanding. What you get when they work together is lots and lots of dead folks.
>
> Sergeant First Class Jason Christner
> Charlie Troop, 3-7 Cavalry

Crazy Horse Troop (C/3-7 CAV), provided security for the remainder of the squadron. Placed in the rear to give it a respite following its intense fight at As Samawah, *Crazy Horse* positioned one platoon on the bridge at FLOYD and the other two at a key intersection 3 km to the north along Highway 9. Ironically, *Crazy Horse* would end up in yet another fierce fight, never getting the intended break. At this point, the squadron was spread over 30 km. Consequently, *Crazy Horse* was out of FM radio range. Filling the gap, the Air Force cleared the CAS radio net, and the Air Force liaisons assigned to each troop used their organic tactical satellite radios to provide communications support to the squadron.[143]

The cavalry's attack continued through the night against increasingly fierce resistance. The intensity of the sandstorm prevented the air cavalry troops from supporting, so the ground troops fought through on their own with help from the air component, which could still drop precision munitions from above the sand. After seizing the bridge, B Troop continued east then north to a position just east of An Najaf, periodically fending off attacks from Iraqis either trying to ram them or firing on them from civilian vehicles or from the side of the road, generally at point-blank range as blowing sand reduced visibility to a few feet.[144]

As B Troop moved north it was ambushed. Two 2nd Platoon tanks took hits to the turrets that started fires involving ammunition. In both cases, the blow-off panels worked as designed,

Figure 109. Vehicles from the Third Infantry Division roll through
the powdery Iraqi sands, March 2003

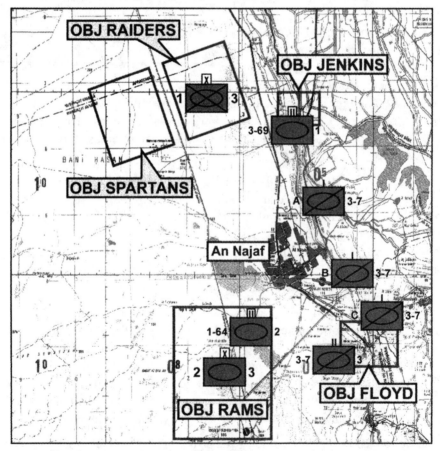

Figure 110. Force disposition around An Najaf, 25 March 2003

3-7 CAV Fighting in An Najaf

As the [C/3-7 CAV] troop set up a traffic control point, cars began to charge up the highway toward the position. Some charged just because they could not see the combat vehicles due to the weather, but some others had different intentions. The tank and Bradley crews manning the northern TCP were the first in contact. They fired warning shots indicating for the traffic to turn around. Many turned and "ran" the other direction, while others paused, then jumped out of the cars and trucks, engaging the soldiers with small-arms fire. Quickly, the threat was neutralized. Still other vehicles began suicide-charging the combat vehicles. They were eliminated as well. But due to the mass of the onslaught, a few others made it up to the tanks and Bradleys. Usually they only made it that far because of the momentum of their automobile, since the drivers and passengers were already dead from the massive amounts of fire delivered by *Crazy Horse*.

The scout [platoon sergeant], Sergeant First Class Jason Christner, watched as his platoon leader, First Lieutenant McAdams, fired his 9mm at a charging bus that rammed his vehicle, knocking the fighting vehicle back a few feet while almost knocking the crew unconscious. The enemies in the bus were already dead. The driver of the bus was expelled out the side door while still on his seat, as a Bradley main gun round pierced the windshield. Even a fuel tanker rammed the TCPs. It was destroyed and burned brightly, helping to illuminate *Crazy Horse*'s fields of fire through the storm, the oncoming night hours and then the following two days' storms as well.

The fight escalated to the point that *Crazy Horse* called in artillery and CAS strikes from B-1 bombers using GPS-guided JDAMs [the B1 flew above the sandstorm and was able to provide support]. The artillery and CAS destroyed two T-72 tanks and a variety of other targets.

Extracted from 3-7 Unit History

---

venting the flames from ammunition propellant upward and out of the crew compartment. Stunned tankers abandoned their tanks. The 3rd Platoon stopped to recover the crews and secure the site. Sergeant First Class Anderson, tank commander of tank B24 and platoon sergeant of 2nd Platoon, recalled, "I thought the 23 crew (the other tank that was hit) was killed, and that was the worst thing that could happen. After my tank first got hit, my vehicle didn't have power. I made the call to evacuate the tank as we were still taking hits. I didn't know what I was hit by. I couldn't call anybody, as I didn't have power to transmit. There was fire coming out of the TC's hatch. I got out and drew my nine (9 MM pistol.)"[145] But things were worse than Anderson yet knew.[146] Bravo 23's driver could not get his hatch open far enough to exit the tank. Sergeant First Class Javier Camacho, platoon sergeant of B Troop's 4th platoon, put it this way, "All hell broke loose. We were the trail platoon so all we could see was tracers hitting the middle of the troop. That is where two tanks were destroyed." Camacho now found three crewmen from B23, " We could see tracers going over their heads. We brought them to the low ground and Sergeant Median (tank commander of B 23) said, 'Could you get my driver out, as he is in the tank alive?'[147] Camacho and his gunner now undertook to rescue the driver of the stricken tank under fire. Camacho recalled hearing rounds strike the ground and the tank and he could hear "the zinging of the bullets (going) over my head."[148] After expending six fire extinguishers gathered from three vehicles, all while under fire, Camacho and his gunner reduced the fire to the point they could pry away the obstruction that kept the driver in his tank. They took the dazed and nearly asphyxiated driver to a nearby vehicle and mounted their own tank to find that Iraqis were crawling around the two burning tanks. According to Camacho, "We fired them up."[149] Eventually, B Troop did reach its blocking position, as did A Troop, but they all fought hard to get in position and harder still to stay.

TeleEngineering

TeleEngineering provides soldiers and commanders access to solutions and subject matter experts to help them solve complex problems. The TeleEngineering Kit (TEK) provides a reach-back to experts in the US who can access information and develop solutions to be transmitted back to the field for implementation. The US Army Engineer Research and Development Center (ERDC), located in Vicksburg, Mississippi, developed a deployable communications system that supports a wide range of voice, data, and video teleconferencing services. Compact and highly mobile, the system combines a suitcase-size satellite terminal with a laptop, camcorder, and roll-around secure videoconferencing unit.

The 54th Engineer Battalion, "*Jungle Cats*," sported a TEK. With the TEK in hand, the battalion had the task to assess and make recommendations for both hasty and permanent repairs to damaged bridge sites that could impact the mobility of the 1st BCT, 3rd ID, and all follow-on forces. The TEK was put to the test on 27 March 2003. In the advance to isolate An Najaf, 1st BCT pushed a platoon across the Euphrates River, at Objective JENKINS. Iraqi defenders detonated explosives at one of the bridge piers, dropping two sections on top of the damaged pier and cutting off the platoon on the far side.

Figure 111. The damaged pier at the bridge site north of An Najaf

Lieutenant Colonel Marcone determined that the damaged bridge could support his immediate requirements, but he needed to know how long the bridge would support the heavy, sustained traffic of the following corps.

To meet this requirement, the *Jungle Cats* conducted a complete technical evaluation of the damage using the TEK. They sent the information back to the TeleEngineering Operations Center in Vicksburg, which, in under 4 hours, provided technical advice on how and where to add wooden cribbing to the failing support. After additional video teleconferences that evening, the operations center recommended further, permanent repairs using sections from a medium girder bridge. However, the scope of work was beyond the *Jungle Cats'* resources and current mission.

While the *Jungle Cats* had to move north with the advancing 1st BCT and did not conduct the repairs, the bridge held for all of 3rd ID's missions at JENKINS, under the *Jungle Cats'* strict control measures. Moreover, the TEK brought virtually limitless technical engineering expertise to the battlefield and greatly enhanced engineer support to the combined arms team. The TEK and TeleEngineering were validated as a powerful resource to draw on engineer knowledge outside of the battlefield and were employed elsewhere with exceptional results.

Extracted from "TeleEngineering"
by Debbie Quimby, ERDC PAO
and 54th Engineer Unit History

Relieving 3-7 CAV

Nearly from the moment C Troop occupied its positions at FLOYD and north of FLOYD on Highway 9, it came under intense attack from all points of the compass. At 1824 on 25 March,

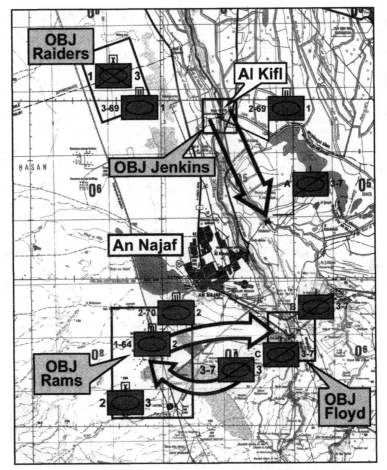

Figure 112. Relief in place of 3-7 CAV around An Najaf, 26-27 March 2003

3-7 CAV reported that C Troop, under heavy counterattack, needed reinforcement. Shortly after this call the Division ordered 2 BCT to send help to C Troop. Colonel Perkins ordered Lieutenant Colonel Rick Schwartz's TF 1-64 AR to assist C Troop. The task force moved out at sunset, relieving C Troop after dark, crossing the Euphrates and continuing throughout the night, reaching B Troop the next day. Fierce fighting continued on the 26th, although by nightfall the TF felt it had the situation in hand, but as the unit history reported, "That night, nobody slept."[150]

Iraqis attacked at JENKINS and everywhere there were Americans east of the Euphrates throughout 26 March. At sunset that day, Lieutenant Colonel J. R. Sanderson's TF 2-69 AR relieved Dave Benton's Team B 3-7 IN at Jenkins. Sanderson's task force had been reassigned to Grimsley's 1st Brigade since the remainder of his own brigade remained in action at As Samawah. Sanderson had just closed on JENKINS when Grimsley ordered him to mount a limited objective attack from JENKINS south to relieve pressure on *Apache* Troop, 3-7 CAV. Captain Stu James, accompanied by Major Ken Duxbury, the task force operations officer, leading a tank company team based on his A/2-69 AR, attacked after dark south toward *Apache* Troop. That did the trick for the moment. With the situation stabilized but still dangerous, 3rd ID elected to leave 3-7 CAV in place until 27 March. That morning Grimsley assigned

Sanderson an area of responsibility east of the river called Area of Operations PANTHER. Grimsley ordered Sanderson to operate in this 10 kilometer by 10 kilometer box extending south from JENKINS on the east side of the river to allow no penetration of the area of operations to prevent movement between Al Hillah and An Najaf, as well as to deny movement through JENKINS toward the Karbala Gap to the west.[151] Sanderson and his battalion now assumed the chief responsibility for preventing enemy reinforcement of An Najaf and endured what he described as 60 hours of hard fighting.[152]

Colonel Dave Perkins' 2nd BCT completed clearing the routes south and east of An Najaf to effect the relief of 3-7 CAV, using TF 1-64 AR and TF 2-70 AR on the afternoon of 26 March against what the division described as "nonstop suicide attacks."[153] At noon on 27 March, 3-7 CAV

> ### Negative Illumination
>
> We initiated the attack [into An Najaf] in "negative illumination"; it was worse than zero illumination. It was a mud storm—a thick cloud of dust in the sky, blowing sand, and then it started to rain and the rain would run through the mud and cover everything in mud. You couldn't read a map, you couldn't wear glasses, couldn't use your [night vision goggles]. It was the worst weather I ever saw.
>
> Lieutenant Colonel Eric "Rick" Schwartz,
> Commander, 1-64 AR,
> commenting on the sandstorm

withdrew after nearly 120 hours of continuous fighting. The division expended considerable effort using the best part of four battalions to effect the actual isolation of An Najaf rather than

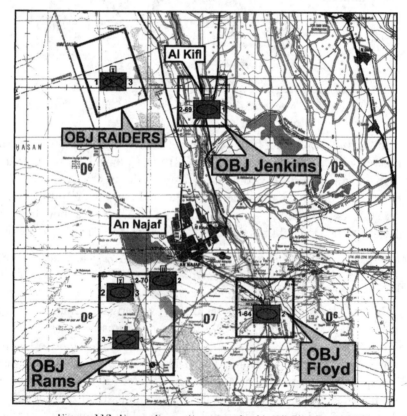

Figure 113. Force disposition near An Najaf, 28 March 2003

merely containing the enemy as they had at As Samawah. Artillery had supported throughout, including 12 danger-close rocket missions, but CAS had provided the lion's share of support with 182 sorties. In intense fighting the enemy managed to destroy two tanks and one Bradley. The division reported an estimated 2,000 *Fedayeen* killed and 100 "technical" vehicles destroyed. More important, they captured an Iraqi brigadier who commanded the southernmost of three military districts in An Najaf. He reported he had lost most of his 1,500 fighters, but claimed 800 more remained in the other districts. In any case, the division had reduced the flow of *Fedayeen* south, and the fighting tapered off on 27 March.[154]

101st and 82nd relieve 3rd ID, 29-30 March

Although Lieutenant General Wallace had hoped to avoid fighting in towns such as An Najaf along the Euphrates, he had anticipated the possibility. He "reasoned that the enemy would have *Al Quds*, *Fedayeen*, and Ba'ath Party militia in the towns in a defensive set." What he had not anticipated was their "tenacity and fanaticism."[155] Wallace had also hoped to avoid a fight in An Najaf, in particular, due to "cultural, religious, and historical" considerations. Containing, among other things, the Tomb of Ali, An Najaf is a significant holy site to the Shiite Muslims.

However, the constant stream of attacks that threatened the logistics at RAMS required that the corps continue to contain An Najaf. Similarly, attacks all along the LOC, and from As Samawah in particular, required the corps to contain or isolate the towns. So far, two-thirds of the 3rd ID was consumed in containing the threat between these two towns. Locked into this fight, the division could not disengage and prepare to lead the corps into Baghdad. The corps situation reports effectively mark the change in view concerning the *Fedayeen*. Until 23 March, the enemy situation began with a review of what the corps knew about conventional units. On 23 March, the tone changed, with the situation report noting that *Fedayeen* and "loyal security forces...seem to be offering the most resistance."[156] V Corps needed to solve this problem. Ultimately, Wallace asked for and received the CFLCC's 82nd Airborne Division. He also employed his 101st Airborne Division to relieve the 3rd ID. The 82nd relieved 3rd BCT at As Samawah; the 101st relieved the 1st and 2nd BCTs at An Najaf.

Lieutenant General McKiernan's decision to release the 82nd stemmed from the larger strategic decision to apply combat power to finally—and fully—secure the LOCs and enable the corps to move decisively on Baghdad. The combination of the 3rd BCT's continuing operations farther south, the intensity of the fight in and around An Najaf, and the challenge of consistently and securely running logistics convoys all pointed to a need to deliberately secure the corps' area south to Kuwait. Secure LOCs were a fundamental precondition for the corps to launch its attack on Baghdad. The decision to focus combat power on the LOCs was critical—arguably *the* decision of the ground campaign—and deserves a detailed discussion.

Securing the Lines of Communication

There was no discrete set of attacks on specific dates by which to neatly describe the fight to secure the LOCs. Moreover, no one at any echelon of command really viewed the LOC fight as a separate mission. Rather, it was viewed as part of the efforts to concentrate the force for the coming attacks to isolate Baghdad, to assure the LOCs remained open, and finally, to deal with several cities that the 3rd ID had bypassed in the march up-country.

As the V Corps and I MEF fights in An Nasiriyah, As Samawah, and An Najaf progressed, Lieutenant General McKiernan reached the same assessment that Lieutenant General Wallace had—it was time to slow down and shift gears from the rapid move north to securing the areas

> ### Decisive FRAGO
>
> **"82 ABN DIV (-):** EFFECTIVE 260001Z MAR03, REPORT OPCON TO V CORPS."
>
> CFLCC FRAGO 102 to OPORD 03-32
> 262200Z [260100L] March 03

already taken. McKiernan had already done what he could to provide the logistics resources and to ensure that his two major tactical formations—V Corps and I MEF—had adequate maneuver room. McKiernan and his C3, Major General J. D. Thurman, now refocused their efforts on ensuring that the I MEF and V Corps had the resources to control what they owned, particularly the LOCs. I MEF, although confronted with serious problems of its own, actually had more combat troops available than V Corps at this point. McKiernan had one remaining tool—the 82nd Airborne and its one brigade of three airborne infantry battalions—to add to the fight. The 82nd's planning priority was to reinforce early success by conducting airborne operations into Baghdad should the Saddam regime collapse in the opening days of the war. By this time, it was clear that contingency no longer applied. Accordingly, McKiernan released the 82nd to V Corps early on 26 March.[157] He also asked CENTCOM to accelerate the planned deployment of one squadron of the 2nd ACR. In retrospect, McKiernan believed that giving V Corps the 82nd was the most important decision that he made during the war. Wallace, McKiernan, and Thurman independently reached the same conclusion. Thurman recalled that it was crucial that they "took the time to deal with the threat against their rear area."[158]

Led by Major General Chuck Swannack, Jr., the storied 82nd Airborne would give Lieutenant General Wallace a combat-ready brigade with a division headquarters that could control additional units as required. Having Swannack and his headquarters was as important to Wallace as having the troops that came with them. Wallace would assign them to the now-very long LOC. With Swannack dealing with the LOC issues, the corps could focus on offensive operations across a growing and increasingly complex area of operations. General Swannack understood this as well. As early as 23 March, when it became clear that the regime would not immediately collapse, Swannack contacted Wallace to see if the 82nd could contribute to the corps' fight. This discussion set the corps and division planners into motion so that if, and when, the CFLCC released the division, it would know exactly where to go in the fight.[159] Ultimately, the 82nd freed the corps to focus on continuing the attack. When the 2nd ACR arrived and joined the 82nd, the "All American Division" assumed responsibility for even more ground and began clearing and opening additional LOCs.

In addition to the 82nd Airborne and the in-bound 2nd ACR, Wallace had additional internal resources to apply to the problem—the 101st Airborne Division's maneuver brigades had closed in Kuwait and remained uncommitted. Originally, he had planned to apply the 101st's unique air assault capabilities as a key element in isolating Baghdad, while the 1st Armored Division would secure the LOCs and start transition operations. However, at this point in the fight, with 1st AD unavailable and with much of 3rd ID committed to securing the LOCs rather than attacking north, it was unclear if the corps would be able to bring enough combat power to bear on Karbala and Baghdad. The 101st would be of little value if the corps

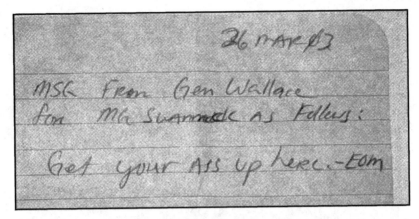

Figure 114. Lieutenant General Wallace's order to Major General Swannack

could not get its heavy forces into the fight. Thus, while the CFLCC commander considered releasing the 82nd, Wallace was already adjusting plan for the 101st.

Leaning Forward

Major Degen and the V Corps planners started working on a course of action based on Lieutenant General Wallace's directive on 24 March. They exploited their relationships with the planners at the 82nd and 101st, most of them classmates or fellow graduates of SAMS, to keep the divisions informed of future planning requirements. Before receiving the CFLCC fragmentary order to release the 82nd, the corps and divisions had collectively conducted a mission analysis, developed a course of action, and wargamed it against the threat. CFLCC released the 82nd at midnight on 26 March, and Wallace approved the plan for employment early that same morning.[160]

The corps issued the FRAGO that day, and the divisions started executing. The 101st was already favorably positioned at FARP SHELL to execute its mission around An Najaf, with one brigade on site and another closing while the third completed its deployment into the theater. As soon as its brigades closed, the 101st could relieve 3rd ID. The 82nd, on the other hand, was not favorably postured or located, but the paratroopers moved with fierce determination to get into the fight sooner rather than later. Apparently, to meet the mission timelines, the 82nd initiated the preparatory actions to move north even before the CFLCC released the order.[161] The division derigged equipment that had been prepared for an airborne drop and moved by ground assault convoy (GAC) and C-130 aircraft. The paratroopers sent everyone with a driver's license to Camp ARIFIJAN, where they drew a menagerie of trucks ranging from cargo to dump trucks to haul the troops. Meanwhile they started moving, using two C 130s that were available to make quick turns between Kuwait and Tallil Air Base. Using this combination, the last units of the brigade reached As Samawah on 29 March.[162]

All of this activity occurred during the so-called pause, but it constituted exactly the kind of activity consistent with a pause designed to build combat power and prepare for future operations. In any case, an operational pause does not mean ceasing operations, but rather

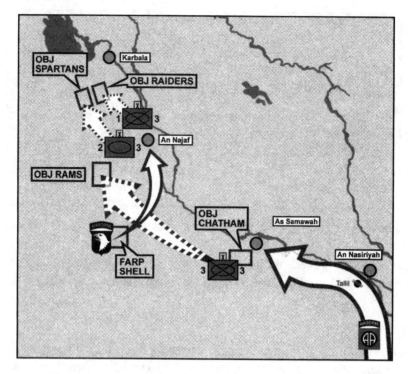

Figure 115. V Corps' scheme to consolidate 3rd ID forward

focuses on those operations required to transition a large formation from one phase of an operation to another. In this case, the V Corps and I MEF transitioned from an approach march to setting the stage to isolate Baghdad.

For the American logistics and combat troops alike, there was no time-out. From their perspective, the pace slowed from outrageous to merely brutal. The only aspect of the pause that caused concern in the corps was whether the Iraqis might be able to take advantage of the shift in momentum and the reduction in the pace of the operation. In the end, the Iraqi army did not take wholesale advantage of the slowing advance—and perhaps did not detect it. They did, however, use the sandstorm to reposition some units, including two brigades of the *Adnan* Republican Guard Armored Division into the Karbala Gap and astride Highway 6 southeast of Baghdad.

The 82nd Airborne Division Isolates As Samawah

By releasing the 82nd Airborne to V Corps on 26 March, Lieutenant General McKiernan provided Lieutenant General Wallace the key enabler he required to concentrate the 3rd ID south of Karbala. The 82nd could assume the mission at As Samawah that had consumed the 3rd ID's 3rd BCT. The 82nd responded to the change of mission with alacrity. Because the paratroopers planned to conduct an

> ### The Will to Get Into the Fight
>
> The success of the 82nd Airborne Division getting into the fight was not attributable to the plan so much as the 82nd's execution—their will to get into the fight.
>
> V Corps Planners
> Interview by Lieutenant Colonel (retired) William Connor,
> 8-9 May 2003

airborne assault, the units had begun to rig their equipment and vehicles for a heavy drop.[163] However, on 26 March, V Corps ordered the division to As Samawah. The 82nd also was told that it would be reinforced with TF 1-41 IN, a mechanized infantry unit originally from the 1st AD but currently located at Tallil Air Base, and a lift helicopter company, A/9-101 of the 159 Aviation Brigade, from the 101st Airborne Division.[164] This would give the brigade greater combat capability and mobility for the projected fight in and around As Samawah. The paratroopers derigged their equipment in record time and departed Camp CHAMPION on 27 March in three large ground convoys for the long, dusty drive to Tallil Air Base. Simultaneously, the Air Force began to move the brigade's troops by C-130 to the Air Base, an operation that took 24 hours.[165] The 2nd Brigade, commanded by Colonel Arnold "Arnie" Bray, reached As Samawah on the 28th and closed on the 29th to relieve the 3rd BCT.

A career paratrooper, Bray and his soldiers were eager to get into the fight and glad to have the tank and Bradley troopers of the 1-41 IN with them. Together, paratroopers, tankers, and mechanized infantry provide commanders the agility, armor, firepower, and endurance that produce synergy career soldiers refer to as "combined arms." Bray's team had firepower, attitude, and the tactical mobility to protect the LOCs and take the fight to the enemy. They soon had the opportunity to do both.

Based on V Corps' order, the 82nd Airborne Division assumed responsibility for isolating As Samawah and for protecting the LOCs from the V Corps rear area to Phase Line (PL) OAKLAND (see Figure 116). Colonel Bray intended to locate and destroy the enemy paramilitary force in As Samawah; secure the ground supply routes in his sector; identify pro-coalition supporters within his sector; and conduct vigilant force protection operations. He saw the end state as friendly forces able to move unhindered along the ground LOCs and the paramilitary forces destroyed, unable to either conduct organized operations or to influence friendly operations on the MSR. He also wanted to have his unit positioned to conduct additional operations outside of the town.[166]

TF 1-41 IN moved north first to meet the 3rd BCT. The two units linked up on the evening of 28 March. On 29 March, TF 1-41 IN officially relieved TF 1-30 IN at the town.[167] 3rd BCT, happy to be done with As Samawah, promptly moved north to RAMS and began preparing for offensive operations near Karbala.[168]

Prior to departing, Colonel Allyn and his staff provided Colonel Bray their assessment of the enemy. Essentially the mechanized troopers advised the paratroopers that, although the enemy force was large, it was neither well trained nor well led. Allyn's intelligence staff estimated that the Iraqis had a company of Republican Guards, some local *Fedayeen* (estimated at approximately 300 to 350), about 200 to 250 Ba'ath Party militia, and approximately 100 to 150 *Al Quds*.[169] There were other enemy forces, however, that the 3rd BCT had not discovered. Hundreds of Arab volunteers had entered Iraq from Syria and Jordan in recent weeks. US troops would soon be fighting non-Iraqi Arab fighters in several districts. According to eyewitness reports, 40 to 50 volunteer fighters from Syria had joined the forces battling US troops in As Samawah. These Syrians entered the city on 3 April, taking up positions in a residential area.[170]

Adding to its intelligence picture, the 2nd BCT, 82nd Airborne took over Colonel Allyn's contact with SOF in an around As Samawah. A SOF representative attended the brigade's

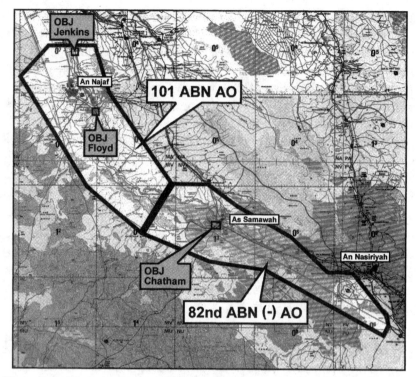

Figure 116. 82nd and 101st Airborne Divisions areas of operations along LOCs

daily staff meetings. This greatly aided in targeting the enemy command and control structure. The paratroopers quickly learned that the Iraqis in As Samawah were using schools, mosques, and hospitals as headquarters and logistic sites. They did not use radios to direct operations but instead relied on runners to issue orders and coordinate combat actions.[171]

Colonel Bray and his troops knew that the enemy was equipped with mortars, light and heavy machine guns, and RPGs. . . lots of RPGs. After the AK-47, the RPG was the most ubiquitous weapon of the war. Based on the SOF and 3rd ID experience, the "All Americans" thought the Iraqis would operate in 3- or 4-man groups, often using civilian pickup trucks fitted with automatic weapons.[172] Armed with information passed by 3rd Brigade, 3rd ID, and the SOF, the paratroopers immediately started probing As Samawah. TF 1-41 made the first enemy contact at As Samawah late in the day on 27 March, before it had officially assumed control of the area. TF 1-41 IN maintained continuous contact from then on. Generally, TF 1-41 dealt with small groups of Iraqis making forays against the US blocking positions, often in taxis or civilian cars. TF 1-41 IN and other units in the brigade killed about 50 paramilitary fighters in similar attacks each day that they occupied the triangular crossroads southeast of the city.[173]

On the night of 29 March, 3-325 IN and TF 1-41 IN mounted the first probes into the town from the southwest. In the process, the airborne and mechanized infantry developed familiarity with each other and practiced light-heavy integration while gleaning information about the enemy and taking the fight to the Iraqis. Quickly, Colonel Bray's paratroopers and mechanized troops shifted their effort from terrain-focused attacks to enemy-focused attacks. The brigade's operations evolved into raids against specific enemy positions where the paramilitaries were congregating. This kept the defenders off balance and unable to interfere with logistics traffic.

From 29-30 March, the 82nd conducted probing attacks to gain information about enemy locations, dispositions, and intentions. By maintaining contact over time, Bray's troops began discerning enemy patterns of operation and developing "actionable" intelligence. These operations also set the conditions for their attack to clear the town on 31 March, as part of the V Corps' five simultaneous attacks.[174]

101st Airborne Division Contains An Najaf

The 101st Airborne Division was also on the move. Unique among all the infantry in the Army and in the Marine Corps, the infantry troops assigned to the 101st are exclusively air assault. The concept of vertical envelopment by helicopter, first experimented with by the Marines in Korea and later amplified by the Army in the early 1960s, became the mainstay of operations in Vietnam. The 101st mastered the art of air-assault operations in Vietnam and transitioned to air-assault infantry in the 1970s.

The heliborne 101st enjoys tremendous operational mobility, able to move battalions very long distances rapidly. Almost everything in the division can be carried to the fight by air if need be. Once on the ground, the paratroopers fight as light infantry. The potential of the air-assault division—first demonstrated by the 1st Cavalry Division (Airmobile) in Vietnam—was achieved during DESERT STORM when the 101st moved from Saudi Arabia to the Euphrates Valley in two bounds, covering more than 300 km and enabling it to cut Highway 8. Now the 101st had returned to the Euphrates Valley prepared to show its other great capability: the ability to mount an attack from several directions at once using helicopters to envelope the enemy.

Major General Dave Petraeus, commanding the 101st, planned to advance by stages, establishing refueling points along the way to sustain the 250 helicopters that provided the chief tactical and operational mobility to the division. By this time, the division had completed the moves north, establishing RRP EXXON and FARP SHELL near An Najaf. The main body of Petraeus' infantry arrived on 28 March, having been on the road for 42 hours.[175]

The decision to commit the 101st to contain and eventually clear An Najaf caused a flurry of activity within the 101st planning section. The size of the newly assigned area of operations to contain An Najaf and tie in with the 82d ABN north of As Samawah required committing both remaining infantry brigades, 1st and 2nd BCTs. 3rd BCT remained committed to securing EXXON and SHELL while maintaining a battalion prepared to seize a northern forward operating base near Karbala in support of continued deep attacks against the *Medina* and *Hammurabi* Divisions.

Clearing operations are inherently manpower intensive, and with significant threats from the north and east, putting a force on the ground to clear An Najaf would quickly consume the 101st's two BCTs. With the two BCTs in An Najaf, Petraeus and Wallace would not have an uncommitted force to respond to unforeseen requirements. The planners developed contingency plans to extricate forces from An Najaf as required, building them around the 3rd BCT's headquarters. As the 101st division staff monitored 3rd ID's progress in resupplying its brigades, the need to find ways for the 101st to support the corps' maneuver through the Karbala Gap became more and more pressing.[176]

Although the division assault command post arrived by helicopter into SHELL on the 24th, the sandstorm precluded moving the rest of the division's combat forces until the 28th, when 24

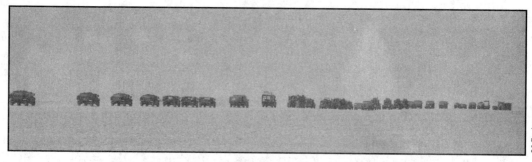

U.S. Army

Figure 117. Infantry of the 101st Airborne Division convoy
through the desert near Desert Camp New Jersey

Black Hawks started moving the remainder up. The original plan had assigned the "Screaming Eagles" the task of supporting the isolation of Baghdad. The flow of events and conditions on the LOCs led Lieutenant General Wallace to change his plan.

By 28 March, the weather improved, and so did V Corps' posture vis-à-vis the enemy and the security of its LOCs. With the arrival of the 82nd and 101st at As Samawah and FARP SHELL, Wallace now had adequate forces not only to secure his LOCs, but also to start cleaning up the bypassed towns. Accordingly, with the 82nd engaging in As Samawah, he ordered the 101st to contain and later to clear An Najaf. Clearing An Najaf would not only reduce the threat to the LOCs, but also would open the highway for follow-on operations, to include clearing Al Hillah, north of An Najaf. Clearing Al Hillah would also support isolating Baghdad from the south. Wallace's orders to the 101st thus achieved LOC security and also shaped the battlespace to meet his ultimate operational objective in Baghdad.

The 101st troopers are big on panache and dash. Regardless of their style, Petraeus' division plans meticulously. It is partly air-assault culture; people who fly lots of troops inside hundreds of helicopters and expect to do it in the dark are not casual about planning. Beyond air-assault culture, the 101st developed detailed plans because Petraeus believed, quite rightly, that detailed planning saves lives. Although committed to detailed planning, the 101st is also able to plan quickly. The division reduced many of its planning procedures to drills to facilitate rapid planning. This approach to planning enabled the division to transition rapidly from isolating An Najaf to clearing, using combined arms forces attacking from multiple directions.

In developing the scheme of maneuver, the 101st planners developed estimates of exfiltration routes that the Iraqis were using to exit An Najaf and attack US units and LOCs from the south (see Figure 105). Their analysis also included determining the routes into An Najaf from the north. Using imagery, combat information generated by 3rd ID, and SOF information, the division developed a plan that envisaged using two brigades to relieve the 3rd ID. Petraeus and his planners anticipated follow-on missions after An Najaf and wanted to retain the two brigades and the flexibility they provided. This enabled the division to sustain the cordon initially set by 3rd ID and eventually to enter and clear An Najaf, if that became necessary.[177]

There is no doubt that the coalition forces had not estimated enemy intentions and capabilities in An Najaf accurately. But on 28 March, when the lead elements of the 101st moved into the town, everyone had a much better picture. To assist in the operation, 3rd ID

Figure 118. 101st Airborne Division soldiers in the attack

Figure 119. Major General Petraeus, 101st Airborne Division commander,
and Brigadier General Ben Freakley, assistant division Commander for Operation

handed off TF 2-70 AR (*Thunderbolts*) to Petraeus. The *Thunderbolts*, who had relieved TF 1-64 AR on Objective RAMS on 26 March, had been in the area for several days. Alpha Company, 2-70 AR, as part of the effort to relive 3-7 CAV, had assumed responsibility for a blocking position at the southeastern edge of An Najaf known as "Checkpoint Charlie" on 26 March. Petraeus assigned the *Thunderbolts* to 2nd BCT, commanded by Colonel Joseph Anderson. The *Thunderbolts*, one of two "orphan" battalions of the 3rd Brigade, 1st Armored Division, now went to work for their second division in the war.[178]

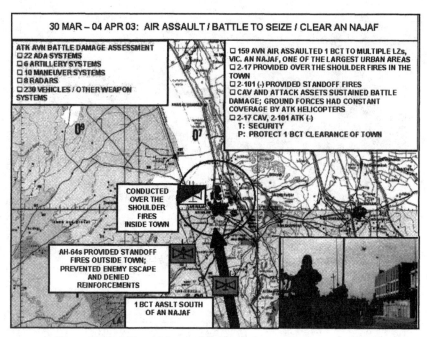

Figure 120. 101st Airborne Division air assault into An Najaf

Brigadier General Ben Freakley briefed Colonel Ben Hodges, commanding the 1st BCT, and Colonel Joe Anderson, commanding 2nd BCT, on their mission at FARP SHELL mid-morning on the 28th. The two brigade commanders refined boundaries and graphics and then moved out to execute. Colonel Anderson and his artillery battalion Commander, Lieutenant Colonel Henry "Bill" Bennett, went to the vicinity of Objective JENKINS at Al Kifl. There they met with Colonel Will Grimsley of 3rd ID's 1st BCT and one of his battalion commanders. According to Bennett, they "had a good exchange of information [through] HMMWV crosstalk."[179]

RPG Showers

Colonel Hodges drove up to An Najaf. When he first arrived, his mission was to secure the LOC. According to Hodges, "So that's what we thought we were going to do, stay up there almost like a picket line to keep those *Fedayeen* trucks from coming down out of the city."[180] When he arrived to effect the relief of TF 1-64 of 2nd BCT, 3rd ID, he met his West Point classmate Colonel Dave Perkins, who commanded that brigade. Perkins announced, "Come on, let's do a recon," Hodges was astounded. "I had been hearing about these RPG showers." But Perkins had his own armored personnel carrier, "So I rode with him, we rode all through the southern part of An Najaf and I got a much better appreciation for what was out there."[181] Perkins' brigade staffers also passed on the information they had.

Colonel Ben Hodges,
Commander, 1st BCT, 101st Airborne Division

Passing the word between 3rd ID and 101st occurred routinely and included intelligence and tips on how to fight. TF 2-70 AR now added to the lore regarding techniques on how to integrate heavy and light forces in an urban area. TF 2-70 actually linked up with 2nd BCT on the afternoon of the 29th. Lieutenant Colonel Jeff Ingram task-organized on the fly, leaving A

Company at Checkpoint Charlie, subordinated to 1st BCT, 101st, and picking up C/1-502 IN. His mechanized infantry company, C/1-41 IN, was en route so he had only his B Company and the newly acquired rifle company, which came with an antitank platoon. Ingram cross-attached a tank platoon to the infantry company and an infantry platoon to the tank company.[182]

TF 2-70 AR moved out on the 29th with only its HHC and one tank company—Bravo—to the vicinity of JENKINS. Assembling the fighting team was a model of flexibility on the fly. Lieutenant Colonel Ingram started the day with only a third of his battalion. In the course of the fight, he received and integrated two more companies and an antitank section. Specifically, C/1-502 IN joined TF 2-70 AR, and the *Thunderbolts* became a task force again in fact, as well as in name. Then on the 30th, the *Thunderbolts* and their airborne infantry cleared the northern part of Al Kifl, establishing a blocking position with B/2-70 AR. Bravo Company, now organized as a company team of two tank platoons and one air assault infantry platoon, set up north and east of the town to stop the flow of paramilitary forces south from Al Hillah. Team C from the 502 defended the all-important bridge.[183] The next day C/1-41 IN joined the task force in the middle of a fight, completing Ingram's task force.

TF 2-70 AR and the infantry brigades of the 101st demonstrate the flexibility of the Army's tactical units. The *Thunderbolts* task force, composed of units from three different battalions from two different divisions, also illustrates the inherent tactical agility of Army formations. Now Anderson's direct support artillery settled in to support the *Thunderbolts*, a unit with whom they had never trained, but confident—as were Anderson and Ingram—that all would go well. Lieutenant Colonel Bennett's artillery settled in on the west side of the river along Highway 9 and could range north to Al Kifl and still cover the remainder of the 2nd BCT sector. By the evening of the 30th, Bennett's troops included his own three batteries of 105mm howitzers, a fourth from another battalion, and a 155mm battery from still another battalion. In the south, outside of An Najaf, Colonel Hodges' 1st BCT assumed responsibility for preventing the Iraqis from reaching the LOC or RAMS. A/2-70 AR, now part of 1-327 IN, remained at Checkpoint Charlie. Together, the tankers and air-assault infantrymen of the 101st secured their part of the LOC and dealt handily with Iraqis who challenged them.

2nd ACR to the Lines of Communication

As the 82nd and 101st got into the fight to secure the LOCs, the 2nd ACR (L) prepared to join them. Lieutenant General McKiernan asked for 2nd ACR at about the same time he elected to release the 82nd. The 2nd ACR (L), equipped with armored HMMWVs, combined firepower with high mobility. Too lightly armored to slug it out with tanks, the 2nd ACR (L) was perfect for the LOC security mission since it could respond rapidly and had the firepower needed to execute security missions. Receiving its deployment order on 26 March, the ACR, under the command of Colonel Terry Wolff, moved out smartly. The regiment's 2nd Squadron, the regimental tactical command post, and an air cavalry troop made the move by air. Within 96 hours they were on their way. The regiment's first flight departed at 1615 on 30 March. The cavalry closed in Kuwait on 4 April and completed processing equipment and uploading ammunition and test firing weapons by 6 April. They joined up with the 82nd at As Samawah, arriving on 8 April. The 2nd ACR (L) commenced operations nearly immediately, conducting route reconnaissance and security along the LOC from As Samawah to An Najaf on the same day they arrived. The rest of the regiment followed by sea and air.

Mortars at Checkpoint Charlie:
The American Soldier's View of Senior Officers

American soldiers expect their senior leaders to exhibit physical courage and to face the dangers of combat without flinching. They have an informal network that passes information about leaders quickly, far beyond the immediate area of an incident. Nothing a senior officer does in combat is ever really hidden from his soldiers. They see. . . They hear. . . They know.

The details of one such incident involving several senior officers' actions under fire were soon known across V Corps and positively affected the confidence and morale of soldiers far from the actual fighting. On 30 March, the 101st Airborne Division was assaulting through An Najaf. Mortar fire began impacting near a crowded road intersection known as Checkpoint Charlie. There was a group of senior officers and other personnel at the checkpoint, including the V Corps Commander, Lieutenant General Wallace, the 101st Airborne Division Commander, Major General Petraeus, the ADC-O, Brigadier General Freakley, and a special forces liaison team. The senior officers huddled around the hood of a HMMWV, using it as a desk while they discussed the ongoing battle.

The initial mortar rounds landed 300 meters away. Rounds started walking in at 100-meter intervals. The three general officers continued their hood-top meeting, seemingly oblivious to the creeping mortar fire. A round suddenly landed unannounced less than 30 meters away, causing everyone to jump a little. One sergeant recalled that generals backed up about 10 feet and continued with their business.

Without warning, a sudden burst of small-arms and automatic weapons fire broke out near the checkpoint. Lieutenant General Wallace and the other general officers moved immediately to the sound of the guns, with their MP squad security detachment running to keep up. Another mortar round landed not 20 yards away from them as they ran. Fortunately, none of the group was injured. The firefight ended quickly, and a *Kiowa Warrior* (armed reconnaissance helicopter) finally spotted the mortar tube and initiated a call for fire that destroyed it.

The story of the calm way with which the generals reacted circulated quickly among soldiers. The military policemen assigned to protect Lieutenant General Wallace told their comrades about it and it spread from there. That the corps commander was willing to put himself up so near the fighting, and that he and Major General Petraeus seemed to move to the fighting instinctively, impressed many of the soldiers who heard of it. They said that it gave them a high regard for Lieutenant General Wallace and made them admire him as a leader.

Compiled from soldier interviews
conducted by Lieutenant Colonel Dennis Cahill and
Lieutenant Colonel (retired) Arthur Durante

The arrival and employment of 2nd ACR (L) are important events on several counts. First, although Lieutenant General McKiernan asked for them during the height of the sandstorm and during the two or three days when, to outside observers, the operation seemed to be slipping, he knew they could not come in time to affect the LOCs fights directly. Rather, McKiernan reflected the kind of thinking expected in senior operational commanders; he anticipated the conditions in April, when the lightly armored but highly mobile 2nd Cavalry would be in its element. It would provide additional flexibility and eventually release the 101st for follow-on operations. Organized to cover large pieces of ground and to conduct reconnaissance and security missions, the 2nd Cavalry was the perfect unit to arrive on the scene after the 82nd and 101st successfully concluded the street fighting. Attaching the 2nd ACR (L) to the 82nd gave the division enough combat power to control the whole LOC. In turn, Major General Swannack assigned TF 1-41 to the ACR, giving his most mobile unit the punch it might need. Finally, the arrival of the cavalry serves in some ways as a useful bookend to the LOC fights. Clearing the towns during the five simultaneous attacks really won the LOC fight, but it was when the 2nd Cavalry secured the lateral routes between the towns on 11 April that the LOCs could be said to be reasonably safe. That is arguably the right point at which to declare the "LOC fight" over.

Psychological Operations (PSYOP) Support to the Fight

As 3rd ID moved north, the PSYOP campaign changed its focus from protecting the oil fields and promoting an early Iraqi capitulation to helping manage the civilian population in the cities and towns coming under coalition control. From themes to reduce collateral damage and civilian casualties to efforts to undermine the paramilitary forces operating in and among the civilians, the PSYOP served as a nonlethal fire to help shape the battlefield for the soldiers and marines. Army tactical PSYOP teams (TPTs) supported both the V Corps and I MEF forces strung out over the vast expanse of the two areas of operations. The TPTs were generally in direct support, providing PSYOP support to the commanders in contact with the Iraqi population.

For example, on 23 March, TPT 1141, led by Sergeant Daniel Voss of the 305th PSYOP Company, supported TF *Tarawa* assigned to I MEF. At first Voss found it difficult to get the marines to use him—a phenomenon not unheard of from TPTs assigned to support Army units. On 25 March at An Nasiriyah, Voss and TPT 1141 got their chance. TF *Tarawa* was in a pitched battle with paramilitary forces sniping from both sides of the road leading into the town and from within the town as well. Two days earlier part of the 507th Maintenance Company had stirred up a hornets' nest at An Nasiriyah. Stiff resistance in An Nasiriyah threatened to bog down the marines' advance.[184]

That day, Sergeant Voss convinced his marine commander that TPT 1141 might be able to help deal with approximately 20 paramilitary troops hiding in the military hospital on the eastern bank of the river. From the hospital the Iraqis fired mortars and machine guns at Marines crossing the bridge over the Euphrates. According to Voss, "We set up the two vehicles and I gave a surrender appeal and a statement about the inevitability of their defeat. We told [them that] we would drop bombs and artillery on the hospital if they did not surrender. About 10 minutes into the broadcast, personnel started emerging, doing exactly what we told them to do."[185] Voss and his team also supported *Tarawa* by assisting them in controlling safe passage of civilians and gleaning information of value in the course of passing information from civilians to the combat troops during house-to-house clearing operations. The loudspeaker team enabled the marines to communicate with the population, which enhanced the safety of the marines and civilians.[186]

Courtesy of 9th PSYOP Battalion

Figure 121. Tactical PSYOP team accompanies mechanized infantry on move north

9th PSYOP Battalion

Figure 122. Tactical PSYOP team mounted on an M113

9th PSYOP Battalion

Figure 123. Loudspeakers mounted on UH-60 *Black Hawk* with members of C/9th
Psychological Operations Battalion

173rd Airborne Operations

Formerly the "Southern European Task Force (SETAF) Infantry Brigade," the unit reflagged as the 173rd Airborne Brigade in June 2000. The 173rd Airborne Brigade officially reached initial operating capability on 14 March 2003, following a three-year effort to stand up a second airborne infantry battalion. In addition to the second battalion, the 173rd reorganized to be a more capable and deployable force. Just 12 days later, on 26 March, the brigade conducted the 44th combat jump[187] in US history, dropping 965 paratroopers into northern Iraq to secure a lodgment at Bashur during OIF.[188] The 173rd augmented and provided a visible and credible

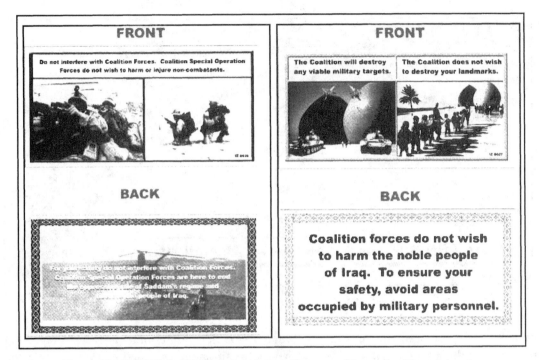

Figure 124. PSYOP leaflets to minimize civilian casualties and collateral damage

conventional capability to the already-robust SOF presence in the Kurdish Autonomous Zone, the area on the Kurdish side of the Green Line.

Planning

The 173rd Airborne Brigade's jump into Bashur was a far cry from its original concept of operation. The 173rd was originally to be attached to the 4th ID, providing a versatile and highly capable light infantry to the most modern mechanized force in the world. But when Turkey refused the US permission to move the 4th Infantry Division through its territory, EUCOM ordered the 173rd to plan an airborne operation into Iraq under the operational control of the Combined Forces Special Operations Component Command (CFSOCC).[189] Without the 4th ID, SOF troops would be wholly responsible for northern Iraq until the conventional forces could fight their way north from Kuwait.

With the ground route through Turkey denied, the brigade was an obvious choice to establish a stabilizing conventional presence in northern Iraq. Based in Vicenza, Italy, it is close to Aviano Air Base, the major US aerial port of embarkation in southern Europe.[190] Bashur was a relatively short 4¼-hour flight from Aviano. CENTCOM selected the airfield because it could handle repeated landings by the C-17 aircraft. Of course, once the force was on the ground, successfully supplying and supporting it without that ground route required a major, focused effort by CENTCOM, EUCOM, and the US Air Force.[191]

Political issues complicated the operation. Although under fire from Italian political factions opposed to the US effort in Iraq, Prime Minister Silvio Berlusconi's government provided absolutely crucial support to the brigade's deployment. Italian authorities actively assisted the

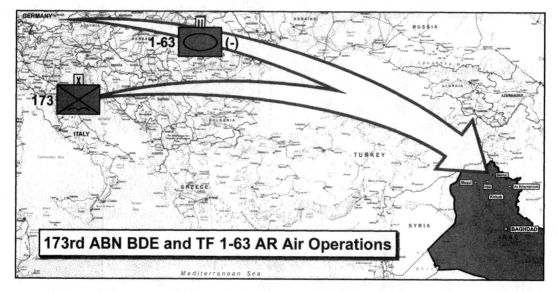

1-63 (-)

173

173rd ABN BDE and TF 1-63 AR Air Operations

Figure 125. 173rd and TF 1-63 deployed straight from Europe to Iraq

brigade with security and movement. The Italian ministries of interior and defense played key roles in coordinating all equipment movements by rail and vehicle convoy. With protesters physically trying to block the road and rail movement, Italian police conducted critical escort operations that allowed the brigade to move soldiers and equipment to the port without serious incident. Thanks to concerted efforts by the Italian government and police, protesters did not significantly delay the brigade's movements, to including 10 trains, 300 trucks, and more than 120 busloads of soldiers.[192]

Subordinating the 173rd to the JSOTF-North marked another first in the integration of special and conventional forces during OIF. It brought tremendous capabilities and flexibility to the CENTCOM commander. The conventional forces gave the JSOTF-North commander the ability to seize and retain ground, something SOF teams are inherently unable to do. Further, the 173rd served as a highly visible indicator of US presence and resolve—reassuring to both the Turks and Kurds. Finally, the 173rd gave the JSOTF-North commander the ability to seize Kirkuk and to control the key oil production facilities, a specified strategic goal.

Integrating these formations raised the kinds of issues expected when units do not habitually train together. SOF and conventional infantry approach the battlefield from two fundamentally different perspectives. Moreover, the Army's doctrine on how to integrate SOF and conventional units is not mature enough to provide adequate guidance. Additionally, since they had not trained with each other to any degree, they had not developed the trust and procedures so critical to working through the unknown issues. Finally, the command and control relationship created potential for disagreement since conventional forces are traditionally the *supported* force and not the other way around. Clearing up the nuances of this reversal required specific attention from the JSTOF-North to make it work properly. The infantry and SOF troops worked to establish the trust in each other's judgment necessary for the forces to work closely together. They did not readily accept each other's intelligence and operational assessments until they had developed a base of experience. But the troops worked through these friction points.[193]

The 173rd's combat capability also improved with the deployment of the United States Army Europe (USAREUR) Immediate Ready Force (IRF). The IRF is a C-17-transportable unit that includes a heavy ready company (HRC) of five Abrams tanks and four BIFVs, an M113-based medium ready company (MRC), organic fire support, and elements of a forward support battalion. TF 1-63 Armor of the 1st Infantry Division, commanded by Lieutenant Colonel Ken Riddle, served as the IRF when the war began. The first elements of TF 1-63 AR began deploying from Rhein Ordnance Barracks in Kaiserslautern, Germany, on the evening of 7 April 2003.[194]

Preparation

As the brigade prepared for the jump, a small drop zone support team of Army and Air Force personnel moved forward separately to link up with SOF soldiers already on the ground in the vicinity of Bashur. At 2000 on 23 March, 14 personnel, including Major Phillip Chambers, the brigade S1, Captain Tom McNally, 74th LRS Detachment commander, elements of the long-range surveillance detachment, and an Air Force tactical air controller, left Vicenza to meet the SOF detachment at its staging base in Constanta, Romania.

After flying a circuitous route to accommodate political restrictions, they arrived in Romania by 1000 on the 24th.

> On the morning of March 25th, we were pretty nervous about being able to get into Iraq before the jump on the 26th. We knew that we would need at least 24 hours to get everything in position and assessed to make a [go/no go] call back to Italy. Turkey had been giving our flights lots of trouble and had been turning them back night after night. On March 23rd, a plane got in through Jordan and had taken 15 good-size holes in the fuselage from air defense guns and had to divert to Turkey.

> That afternoon, after checking over our gear, weapons, and ammo, we boarded an MC-130 *Combat Talon*, a specially designed C-130 variant used by special forces. . . We got clearance to go through Turkey. It was a fairly uneventful ride. We dropped down nap of the earth inside of Iraq. Touchdown at Bashur Airfield was comforting.

> The plane stopped and the ramp went down. It was the darkest night I can remember. It was also raining sideways, hard like in the southern parts of America. And, it was cold. . . .We were soaked after about a minute. I tried stepping off the concrete ramp onto the dirt and sank up to the tops of my boots. I was trying to figure out where Captain McNally was going to set up our hide site in all of the mud.

> The other half of the SF team we went in with was waiting on the ramp for us and told us to get into trucks lined up on the road. . . .We got in and drove for about a half-hour. When we stopped, the rear tarp was lifted and we were in a military-type compound with lots of soldiers . . . They were the *Peshmerga*, the Kurdish warriors who had been fighting against Saddam most of their lives. . . This was a special forces safe house.

> It was about 0700 [on 26 March] and I wanted to get down to the drop zone at first light.... Two SF soldiers drove me back to the airfield. There was a long road, about a mile and a half long, that intersected the runway. On either end of the road was a hasty *Peshmerga* checkpoint that controlled access to the area. The drop zone was composed of rolling hills with a single runway down the middle. On the ends were what the map showed as "intermittent streams" that happened to be very full at the

Figure 126. The 173rd IN Brigade rigging HMMWVs for airdrop

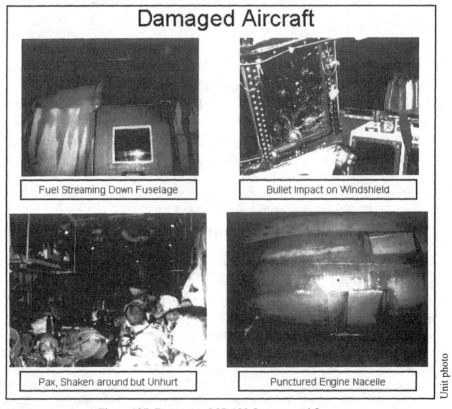

Figure 127. Damage to MC-130 from ground fire

moment. The ground had been plowed in the fall and was extremely soft. This is good for paratroopers to land in because it means fewer injuries, but it makes it very difficult to move to those who do get hurt or for paratroopers to move to an assembly point. We drove around the area and then returned to the safe house to call back a report to Italy on the TACSAT. We made the call and told them that the drop zone was good, but that the weather was not.

The jump was scheduled for 2000 and we had to have the TACSAT set up by 1800 to make a call to the inbound aircraft. We got to the airfield with little time to spare, and the LRS members performed superbly, moving the communications equipment and then setting it up in time to make our calls. The weather was not looking good. The winds were light but the ceiling was less than 1,000 feet, and we would need a minimum of 2,500 feet to call the drop. . . . Fortunately, the weather lifted to an unlimited ceiling and we waited with the *Peshmerga* on the edge of the drop zone.

Major Phillip Chambers,
BDE S1 and drop zone support team
officer in charge[195]

The Special Forces Operational Detachment Alpha, the element supporting the 173rd's jump, dryly noted that its "split element [was] conducting deployment prep with the 173rd."[196] Thus, with the drop zone team on the ground to control the jump, the remainder of the 173rd was en route from Italy.

Jumping

The C-17s entered Iraqi airspace at 30,000 feet, but descended to 1,000 feet for the actual jump. To reduce exposure to Iraqi air defenses, the aircraft literally dove down, with the paratroopers momentarily experiencing negative G-forces. At 2000 on 26 March, five C-17s dropped 10 heavy drop platforms of vehicles and equipment. One of the keys

> **Jumping the Red Light**
>
> During routine airborne training missions, soldiers frequently "jump the red light"— sneak out of the aircraft a second or two after the "stop" signal flashes. They do this because it took too long for the first paratroopers to exit the aircraft and the trailing paratroopers do not want to miss the jump or have to "go around." In training, it is a relatively safe practice because the aircraft typically maintain a straight and level flight path after dropping the soldiers. However, during the jump into Bashur, jumping the red light could mean death as a late paratrooper would get caught in the jet wash as the C-17s powered up to make their violent escape back up to altitude.

to successful airborne operations is to exit rapidly from the aircraft. Colonel William Mayville, commanding the 173rd, followed the heavy drop as the first paratrooper out the door at 2010.[197] 963 soldiers followed in 58 seconds. Only 32 jumpers did not make it out of the aircraft.[198]

With all of the US and coalition presence—the support team, SOF team, and *Peshmerga*—on the ground, the jump was considered "permissive," meaning the soldiers did not expect to be shot at as they descended. Parachute insertion made sense because it saved time given the relatively small ramp capacity on the airfield. While the jump was good, the aircraft "jumped long"; the brigade was strung out all over the airfield with some airplanes releasing 2,000-3,000 yards early, while others released that late. As the sun rose, it revealed "LGOPPs"—"little

17 C-17 cargo aircraft used to airdrop 1,000 paratroopers of the 173d Airborne Brigade and their vehicles and equipment.

Martin Fano, US Army

Figure 128. C-17s at the ready

groups of pissed-off paratroopers"—strung out all over a now-10,000-yard-long drop zone. LGOPPs form when paratroopers link up with whomever is closest, regardless of unit affiliation, and move as a group to the assembly points. If there is a fight on the drop zone, the LGOPPs are trained to move to the sound of the guns and still fight as a team. Although it took all night for the soldiers to move through the thick mud to consolidate on the objective, the brigade achieved combat readiness far more quickly than if it had done an air landing. At 2 hours the brigade had occupied all assigned blocking positions on the airfield, and by 15 hours after the jump the brigade had completed assembly; the LGOPPS had become a brigade again.[199]

The bulk of the jumping force came from the *Red Devils*, the 1-508 IN (Airborne), led by Lieutenant Colonel Harry D. Tunnell, and *The Rock*, the 2-503 IN (Airborne), led by Lieutenant Colonel Dominic Caraccilo. The *Red Devils*, the main effort, had the mission to secure the southeast side of the airfield and prepare the runway to receive C-17s within 6 hours of landing. The 2-503 would secure the northeast side of the objective. The remainder of the BCT included field artillery (D/319th Airborne Field Artillery Regiment), combat engineers, Stinger air defenders, the 74th LRS Detachment, medics from the 401st Forward Support Company, a surgical team from the 250th Medical Detachment (Forward Surgical Team), elements of the 10th SF Group, and Major Robert Gowan, the public affairs officer on loan from the JSOTF-North.

The brigade cannot jump by itself; it requires significant support from a variety of units and services to make a successful combat jump. The BCT included airmen from the 86th Combat Readiness Group, who are experts in runway repair and airfield operations. About 20 airmen participated in the jump and, along with 173rd combat engineers, worked together to prepare the airfield quickly for heavy follow-on traffic.

The brigade also jumped with a highly capable medical team led by Lieutenant Colonel Harry Stinger, a board-certified surgeon. Stinger and eight other medical personnel from the 250th Medical Detachment (Forward Surgical Team) jumped with the main body and were treating injured soldiers within minutes of landing. By the next morning, they had set up a working operating room, using equipment dropped in the heavy bundles. Fortunately, only 19 soldiers were injured during the jump, with only four requiring evacuation back to Italy due to broken bones and joint dislocations.[200] With the infantrymen on the ground and the airfield fully secured, the rest of the brigade closed quickly.

Consolidating

In the days following the jump, 12 C-17s landed per day, bringing in another 1,200 soldiers and the vehicles of the brigade's assigned and attached units. Because of the short turnaround from Aviano Air Base in Italy, the Air Force was able to move 2,160 soldiers and 381 pieces of equipment in only 96 hours. This remarkable joint effort was accomplished with a total of 62 sorties of C-17 aircraft flown from Aviano to Bashur, led by the 62d Airlift Wing from McChord Air Force Base, Washington. TF 1-63 AR flew in on an additional 27 C-17 sorties.[201] The 173rd closed the essential combat, CS, and CSS components of a fully capable BCT and began coordinated operations with JSOTF-North and the Kurdish elements with whom they were working.[202]

Operations

By 29 March, the 173rd, less TF 1-63 AR, completed its flow into the theater and was prepared to conduct operations. The paratroopers conducted reconnaissance of routes and key terrain beyond the airhead and within the Green Line that informally marked the boundary between Kurdish- and Iraqi-controlled territories. Throughout these operations, the brigade exploited the capabilities bestowed by a unique motorization and modernization package adopted over the previous two years.[203] The Enhanced Information System (EIS) improved the unit commanders' situational awareness. The EIS is a USAREUR-fielded initiative that provides the same satellite - based BFT as well as text messaging capabilities like V Corps had. The system is compatible with the larger joint tracking software, and the ubiquitous C2PC system. The ultimate challenge for the brigade's communications network came as its units began escorting convoys of "nonlethal" supplies, belatedly permitted access through Turkey, from the Turkey-Iraq border over a 180-km route through the Kurdish autonomous zone to Bashur.[204]

As a lone unit far from a traditional higher headquarters, the brigade S2 section brought a range of intelligence systems to gain access to the theater and national intelligence resources. Equipped with the Joint Deployable Intelligence Support System (JDISS), the *Trojan Spirit* communications system, and the Common Ground Station (CGS), and supported by elements of Bravo Company, 110th MI Battalion (attached from the 10th Mountain Division), the brigade had unparalleled access to intelligence products provided by higher headquarters and agencies. Although the brigade benefited from its unparalleled access to the technical intelligence resources, as well as the analysts throughout the intelligence community, the perennial shortage of linguists and the long-term focus on the Iraqis rather than the Kurds led to a gap in the intelligence preparation. The brigade would have to close the gap through direct collection and liaison with the SOF in the region who had developed extensive human contacts.[205]

The brigade also received two *Dragon Eye* UAVs shortly before deploying. Developed by the Marine Corps, the hand-launched *Dragon Eye* is a very small, very lightweight, user-friendly system that provided short-range video capabilities. The *Dragon Eye*, an essential element of the brigade's direct collection efforts, along with the reporting from unit patrols, human intelligence collection teams, and long-range reconnaissance teams, allowed the brigade to maintain a relatively accurate and complete picture of what was occurring in the area of operations.[206]

As the 173rd closed, it prepared for combat operations in the vicinity of Kirkuk and the neighboring oil fields. Kirkuk is a key northern population center, and the oil fields and associated oil-production infrastructure to the north and west of the city represent the most significant strategic asset in northern Iraq. Kurdish forces, supported by SOF advisers and coalition air forces, kept pressure on the Iraqi forces defending Kirkuk and its environs. The 173rd supported by executing two artillery raids. Using the 105mm howitzers of D/319th Field Artillery (Airborne), as well as newly fielded 120mm mortars, the brigade brought Iraqi ground units on the Green Line under conventional artillery fire for the first time in the war.[207] By the end of the first week in April, pounded by air strikes, continuously probed by the *Peshmerga*, and facing a growing conventional force to their front, Iraqi Regular Army and Republican Guard units began to come apart as their soldiers deserted.[208]

Sustainment

Placing the 173rd so deep into northern Iraq posed an insurmountable challenge to the Iraqi defenders. Placing the 173rd so deep into northern Iraq posed an *almost* insurmountable challenge to the Army and Air Force logisticians. With additional combat power come additional support requirements. Particularly when augmented by the 1-63 AR, the 173rd required continuous logistic support significantly greater than the SOF units to whom they were attached. Having to provide the support solely via an air bridge would have been almost unsustainable, particularly with the fuel requirements of up to 10,000 gallons per day. Moreover, bulky repair parts added to the difficulty.[209] Fortunately, EUCOM, USAREUR, and US Air Forces in Europe (USAFE) all were familiar with the region and so eventually they were able to negotiate contracts with Turkish companies to deliver fuel into northern Iraq. SOF troops, in conjunction with Kurdish *Peshmerga*, secured the movement of these shipments into northern Iraq. As the 173rd completed closing, it assumed the security mission for the ground convoys, relieving the pressure on the air transport for bringing the fuel. The solution for repair parts was ingeniously simple. Europe-based combat divisions are conveniently based near the Ramstein Aerial Port of Embarkation (APOE), only an 8-hour flight from Germany to northern Iraq. It became routine to resupply the 173rd's heavy forces from sustainment stocks resident within the 1st Infantry Division and flown into northern Iraq. In most cases, the time between order and receipt was less than 24 hours. Unlike the rest of the Army in OIF, the 173rd had a parts system that worked. Contract fuel and parts "workarounds" reduced the burden on the air bridge.

Although the 173rd played a crucial strategic role by establishing a significant conventional presence in northern Iraq, it did not engage in significant combat operations prior to the end of major combat operations. The brigade first saw action when it moved into Kirkuk on 10 April, following the JSOTF-North's successful efforts to evict the Republican Guard and Regular Army from the city. Once in Kirkuk, the 173rd was absolutely vital in establishing a secure environment for follow-on stability operations.

Figure 129. TF 1-63 AR Abrams tank offloads at Bashur Airfield, Iraq

Figure 130. TF 1-63 AR provides security with a Bradley on patrol in Kirkuk

"Can Do" Battalion Takes Bloom as One of Its Own

Several journalists died during major combat operations in Iraq. Each death brought with it a deep sense of grief for the reporter's family and friends. But the death of NBC reporter David Bloom, of a pulmonary embolism, had a profound impact on the soldiers he covered. David died on 5 April while embedded with the soldiers of the 3rd Battalion, 15th "Can Do" Infantry Regiment.

Who could forget those live updates Bloom provided from his specially equipped M88 recovery vehicle, which was nicknamed the "Bob Sled"? The soldiers remember him not only as a loving husband and father, but also as a professional journalist who felt honored to be reporting on TF 3-15 IN. Staff Sergeant Joe Todd, vehicle commander of the "Bob Sled," recalls that every night David would look at a picture one of his daughters drew for him prior to deploying.

Todd said Bloom was a "real guy" and would just sit down and talk to soldiers.[210] Bloom also allowed (with permission from the chain of command) soldiers to use NBC's satellite phones and Internet connection to call and e-mail home. What's more, Bloom and some of the other journalists would call the wives back at Fort Stewart to update them on what TF 3-15 IN was doing.

Lieutenant Colonel Stephen Twitty, commander of TF 3-15 IN, knew Bloom better than any other soldier in the task force. They had first met 12 years earlier when Bloom, as a young up-and-coming journalist, covered the 24th Infantry Division during Operation DESERT STORM. Twitty was then a captain, serving as aide de camp for then-Major General Barry McCaffrey, commander of the 24th Infantry Division.[211]

Bloom became an integral part of TF 3-15 IN. Twitty made Bloom his "media squad leader." David embraced his duties, and he performed as one would expect a sergeant to perform. He conducted precombat inspections of the reporters' chemical suits and ensured that everyone had sufficient food and water. He was also the "voice of the media" and would channel their concerns to Twitty for his action.

David Bloom's death hit the task force very hard. So much a part of the unit, he was included in the memorial service held for two battalion soldiers who had been killed in combat.

Dennis Steele, *Army Magazine*

Figure 131. David Bloom's flak vest and helmet
in memorial service conducted by TF 3-15

The relationship that Bloom struck up with the men of TF 3-15 IN was remarkable, and it demonstrates the utility of having embedded media with Army units. Bloom told the Army and the soldiers' story, and he did it in a professional and objective manner. The media gets a front-row seat to the action, and the Army gets to highlight its soldiers performing great deeds. In the end, the American people are better served when they get to see and, more important, understand and connect with their soldiers.

NOTES

1.   Captain Michael Matthews, OIF-SG, "OIF-SG Operational Summary: Military Police," 15 July 2003. See Sergeant Matthew Cassetta, Private First Class Hunter Cloke, 511th Military Police Company, interview by Captain Michael Matthews 22 May 2003. This incident occurred on 25 April 2003.

2.   Anthony H. Cordesman, *The Iraq War: Strategy, Tactics, and Military Lessons* (Washington, DC: The Center for Strategic and International Studies, 2003), 69-84. This book is arguably the best general source for understanding the scale of operations across all of the components of the coalition campaign.

3.   Cordesman, 80.

4.   Headquarters, 3rd Infantry Division, "3rd Infantry Division Historical and Lessons Learned Briefing," 20 May 2003, 22. See also Lieutenant General William Wallace, Commander, V Corps, interview by Colonel French Maclean, 15 April 2003

5.   Many operations, like the effort to clear As Samawah, An Najaf, and the lengthy ground LOCs started as early as the second full day of the campaign, during the "Running Start" phase, but continued in one form or another through every phase of the attack. These fights are discussed in the context of how they assisted in posturing V Corps for its push to the outskirts of Baghdad. Subsequent actions in these towns and along the LOCs that are more accurately part of the attack into Baghdad are discussed in detail in the "Isolation of Baghdad."

6.   Wallace by Maclean.

7.   Major General Henry Stratman, Deputy Commanding General for Support, CFLCC, interview by Colonel Gregory Fontenot, US Army, Retired, 19 May 2003; and Lieutenant Colonel David Kolleda, OIF-SG, "OIF-SG Operational Summary: Prep, Mob, Deploy," 14 July 2003. See also Colonel Melvin R. Frazier, Commander, 49th Quartermaster Group, interview by Lieutenant Colonel David Kolleda, 24 May 2003.

8.   There are a number of excellent sources for information on fuel consumption during World Wars I and II and on the Red Ball Express. Both the Quartermaster and Transportation Regiment museums have good references on their web pages. But to understand the scope and scale of the effort during WW II, see Joseph Bykosfsky and Harold Larson's book *The Transportation Corps: Operations Overseas*, (Washington, DC: Office of the Chief of Military History, 1957). This excellent single volume history details the story of truck companies and truckers in all of the theaters of war. It reports on less well known, but equally difficult operations in China, Burma, India and Persia, to name a few. It also reviews subsequent express routes in Europe.

9.   Bykosfsky and Larson.

10.   Major General David B. Kratzer and Brigadier General Jack Stultz, Interview by General Frederick M. Franks, US Army, Retired and Colonel Gregory Fontenot, US Army, Retired, 19 May 2003.

11.   Major General Claude "Chris" Christianson, C4 CFLCC, interview by Colonel Gregory Fontenot, US Army Retired, 19 May 2003.

12.   Christianson. See also Kratzer and Stultz.

13.   Ibid.

14.   Jim Keane, HQ AFWA/XOGM, Metsat Applications Branch.

15.   Major General "Spider" Marks C2, CFLCC, interview by Colonel Gregory Fontenot, US Army, Retired, 17 November 2003.

16.   Mark Bowden, *Black Hawk Down: A Story of Modern War*, (Boston: Atlantic Monthly Press, 1999).

17.   Executive Summary to the Army Investigation, *Attack on the 507th Maintenance Company*, An Nasiriyah, Iraq, 23 March 2003, 2-5. This account depends on the executive summary, as the Operation IRAQI FREEDOM Study Group was not authorized to interview anyone with respect to this incident because there were several ongoing investigations. The executive summary leaves a number of important questions unanswered as beyond the charter of the base investigation. Some things may never be known for sure. Times cited here stem from the executive summary. Charts used to illustrate are from this same document.

18.   Ibid., 5.

19.   Ibid., 5.

20.   Ibid., 5-6.

21.   Ibid., 7.

22.   Ibid., 7-9. After linking up with the 3rd FSB, Captain King loaded waypoints or intermediate locations in his Global Positioning System receiver. The GPS provides a direction arrow pointing toward the next waypoint and a distance to that point. It is difficult to be sure of the timeline here despite the official report citing 0100. King's serial departed for route BLUE at 1930 and took 5 hours to reach Route BLUE, arriving at 30 minutes after midnight, but the report doesn't show where the company intersected BLUE, so the times are likely approximate rather than exact.

23.   Ibid., 8-10. The 507th had some handheld radios, but apparently the batteries were dead.

24.   Ibid., 10-11.

25.   Ibid., 12.

26.   Ibid., 12-13.

27.   Ibid., 12-13.

28.   Ibid.

29.   Ibid., 13.

30.   Ibid., 14.

31.   Ibid.

32.   Ibid.

33.   E Troop, 9th Cavalry, "Unit History, Operation IRAQI FREEDOM" undated, 2. See also "Task Force 1-64 Armor Summary of Unit Actions from 20 March-11 April 2003, Operation IRAQI FREEDOM," undated, 6-12. TF 1-64 AR unit history is composed of short narratives for each subordinate unit. Most cite times in zulu.

34.   Ibid.

35.   Ibid. Numbers of enemy dead and vehicles destroyed are based on summaries from discrete unit reports and, therefore, suspect. No one misleads on purpose, but these figures are based on observation and can vary between observers.

36.   Major Matthew R. Littlejohn, collection manager, V Corps, interview by Major David Tohn, 9 May 2003.

37.   Ibid.; and Captain Brett T. Funck, Commander, E (LRS)/165th MI BN, interview by Major Daniel Corey, 1 June 2003.

38.   Ibid.

39.   Littlejohn.

40.   Funck.

41.   Colonel Will Grimsley, Commander, 1st BCT 3rd ID, interview by Colonel Gregory Fontenot, US Army, Retired, 19 November 2003. See also Lieutenant Colonel Rock Marcone Commander, 3-69 AR, 1st BCT, 3rd ID, interview by Colonel Gregory Fontenot, US Army, Retired, and Lieutenant Colonel E. J. Degen, 22 October 2003.

42.   Marcone.

43.   Grimsley. See also Marcone and 3rd ID Division Artillery Document "Fire Support In Support of OBJ RAMS/RAIDERS."

44.   Marcone. See also "Unit History For TF 3-69, Operation Enduring Freedom and Operation IRAQI FREEDOM," Re: Artillery Operations: Undated: see "1-41 FA Operation IRAQI FREEDOM Day-by-Day History", 13 May, 2003.

45.   Grimsley.

46.   Ibid.

47.   Lieutenant Colonel Terry Ferrell, Commander, 3-7 Cavalry, "3-7 CAV Command Briefing," Slides 7-11, undated.

48.   Ibid.

49.   "Fight of Apache," 3-7 CAV Unit History, undated. See also Platoon Leader, A/ 3-7 CAV, interview by Major Daniel George, 29 May 2003.

50.   Ibid.

51.   Ibid.

52.   Lieutenant Colonel Terry Ferrell, Commander, 3-7 CAV 3rd ID and Major Brad Gavle S3, 3-7 CAV, 3rd ID, interview by Colonel Tim Cherry. See also "Unit History, 1-10 FA."

53.   Grimsley. Many of the interviews of soldiers and their leaders reveal this combination of cunning and suicidal bravery. More important, however poorly trained the foot soldiers were they would freely trade their lives to kill Americans and that fact was not lost on their targets.

54.   32d AAMDC, "Operation IRAQI FREEDOM, Theater Air and Missile Defense History," September 2003.

55.   "Fire Support In Support of OBJ RAMS/RAIDERS."

56.   Colonel Jeff Smith, G6, V Corps and Commander, 22nd Signal Brigade, interview by Colonel Tim Cherry, 1 June 2003, and Colonel Jeff Smith by Lieutenant Colonel Edric Kirkman, 14 May 2003.

57.   Major General "Spider" Marks, C2, CFLCC, interview by Colonel Gregory Fontenot, US Army, Retired, 14 June 2003.

58.   Mathew Cox, "Stretched Thin," *Army Times*, 23 June 2003, 14-15.

59. Colonel Rodney Mallette, MTMC, email to Colonel Gregory Fontenot, US Army, Retired, 12 November 2003.

60. "1st Battalion, 293rd Infantry Locations and Missions for OEF and OIF," Notes by Lieutenant Colonel Ivan Denton, prepared for Lieutenant Colonel Scott Gedling, OIF Study Group. See also Lieutenant Colonel Scott Gedling, "OIF-SG Operational Summary: Army National Guard,"15 July 2003.

61. Marcus. See also 1-293 IN unit history.

62. 1-293 IN unit history.

63. Ibid.

64. Ibid.

65. Colonel Bill Wolf, Commander, 11th AHR, interview by Colonel Gregory Fontenot, US Army, Retired 13 November 2003.

66. Captain Gary Morea, S3 planner, 11th AHR, interview by Major Jonathan Gass, 13 May 2003.

67. Major John Lindsay, S3, 11th AHR, interview by Colonel Gregory Fontenot, US Army, Retired, 11 December 2003. Lieutenant Colonel Jerry Pearman, executive officer, 11th AHR, telephonic interview by Colonel Gregory Fontenot, US Army, Retired, 17 December 2003.

68. "Battle summary, 6th Squadron, 6th Cavalry, Operation IRAQI FREEDOM," 9 June 2003.

69. Captain Karen E. Hobart, S2, 11th AHR, interview by Major Daniel Corey, 31 May 2003.

70. Lindsay.

71. Battle summary, 6th Squadron, 6th Cavalry.

72. This estimate was in the original plan and confirmed by telephone conversation between Major John Lindsay and Colonel Gregory Fontenot, US Army, Retired, 10 February 2004..

73. Major John Lindsay, S3, 11th AHR, interview by Major Jonathan Gass, 11 May 2003; "Battle Summary, 6th Squadron, 6th Cavalry, Operation IRAQI FREEDOM," 9 June 2003, 13; Captain Gary Morea, S3 Planner, 11th AHR, interview by Major Jonathan Gass, 13 May 2003; Major Kevin Christensen, S3, 6-6 CAV, interview by Major Jonathan Gass, 15 May 2003; Lieutenant Colonel Trent Cuthbert, effects coordinator, Fires and Effects Cell, V Corps, email to Lieutenant Colonel E.J. Degen, 13 September 2003.

74. 1-227 AHB, 11th AHR, pilot interviews by Major Jonathan Gass, 22 May 2003.

75. 1-227 AHB pilot interviews.

76. Wolf.

77. Wolf. See also 11th AHR OPLAN 1003(V), Annex B (Intelligence), Appendix L (Intelligence Estimate).

78. Some prisoners of war have reported defenses of this kind as present and designed to take on *Apaches*. The Joint Center for Operational Analysis, Joint Forces Command is doing some of this work and analyzing other reports, but their work is neither complete nor declassified, so it will be some time before anecdotal reports from tactical units can be collaborated. The resistance the 11th AHR fought through cannot be explained solely as a consequence of dispersed air defense teams. It is likely that the defenses included "less formal" air defenses raised by troops in the area and perhaps paramilitary forces as well.

79. Hobart.

80. The ATACMS is a precision engagement weapon that integrates stand-off delivery accuracy with a submunition that can kill moving armor columns.

81. Wolf.

82. Battle summary, 6th Squadron, 6th Cavalry.

83. B/ 2-6 CAV, group interview by Major Ike Wilson, 2 May 2003. Pilots reported the area not secure. See also Barbee, who asserted that his crews observed a white pickup truck. Major John Lindsay, on the other hand, saw only a single van departing the area. Lindsay believed the reports of Iraqis around the flight line to be exaggerated. There is no way to verify whether Iraqis on and around the flight line compromised the mission.

84. To prevent total loss or delay, the regiment sent its fuel trucks on two different routes. The movement, scheduled to take 48 hours, eventually took 72 hours due to congestion and enemy contact on the roads. As it was, only half of the fuel made it to Objective RAMS in time to support the attack. See Lindsay, who discussed the fuel situation at length.

85. B/2-6 CAV. See also Barbee.

86. Lindsay.

87. Littlejohn.

88. Hobart.

89. Ibid.

90. Lindsay.

91. Wolf.

92. Hobart. See also Wolf.

93. Barbee.

94. Wolf and Lindsay. See also Barbee, who returned to find his aircraft also had no fuel. Like Wolf, he missed takeoff time, waiting to get fuel.

95. Major Michael Gabel, fire support officer, 11th AHR, email to Major Jonathan Gass, 9 August 2003.

96. Ibid. See also Wolf, Lindsay, and Hobart.

97. Battle summary, 6-6 CAV.

98. Ibid.

99. First Lieutenant Jason King and Chief Warrant Officer 2 John Tomblin, crew of Palerider 16, interview by Major John Gass, 16 may 2003.

100. Lindsay. Colonel Wolf and Major Lindsay believe that Lieutenant Colonel Ball showed great courage that night as he sought to find a way to rescue the downed aircraft's crew.

101. Lindsay.

102. Pilot interview, 1-227 AHB.

103. Lieutenant Colonel Jerry Pearman. See also Wolf and Lindsay. Unit AARs detail the effort. Pilot interviews for 1-227 noted they were ready and back in the fray in six days.

104. Ball. Pilot interviews for 1-227 AHB said they were ready and back in the fray in six days. Obviously they flew shorthanded until the all of the aircraft were repaired and the one they lost was replaced.

105. Cochran.

106. Wolf.

107. Ibid.

108. Many innovative tactics, techniques, and procedures (TTPs) were employed that resulted in a successful mission. These TTPs were adopted from prior experience in Afghanistan and AAR discussions with the 11th Regiment. Areas addressed included route planning, use of *Eagle I*, *FalconView*, BFT, and *Topscene*, actions on contact, movement techniques, use of deception, and integration of CAS and artillery.

109. 101st Airborne Division After-Action Report, 30 April 2003.

110. Ibid.

111. Captain Henry Perry, assistant S3, 1-227 AHB, interview by Major Jonathan Gass, undated.

112. A specially configured command and control *Black Hawk* with a suite of communications and battlefield visualization tools.

113. 101st Airborne Division after-action report. This AAR is very detailed, with several supporting interviews from pilots and staff officers not cited here, but used elsewhere. See also 101st Aviation Bde Deep Attack Against the *Medina* Division, 28 March 2003.

114. Ibid.

115. Ibid

116. Ibid.

117. Ibid. See also personal notes of Lieutenant Colonel Steve Smith, Commander, 2-101 AVN.

118. Smith.

119. Ibid.

120. "3-7 CAV S2 Editorial, Operation Iraqi Freedom," undated. The 3-7 CAV S2 editorial is a unit history occasionally embellished by the anonymous author who wrote it.

121. Grimsley.

122. The Bradley-mounted Stinger missile system.

123. Grimsley. See also Marcone.

124. Grimsley.

125. Ibid. See also Marcone.

126. Major Mike Oliver, S3, 3-69 AR Personal account of the JENKINS fight.

127. Ibid. See also "TF 3-69 Unit History as of Mid-April 2003," undated.

128. Oliver.

129. Ibid.

130. Ibid.

131. Ibid.

132. Grimsley.

133. Oliver.

134. Marcone.

135. Ibid. See also Oliver.

136. Marcone.

137. Grimsley.

138. Marcone.

139. Oliver.

140. "3rd ID Consolidated Division History and After Action Review."

141. 3-7 CAV S-2 Editorial.

142. Information compiled from several interviews, but primarily reliant on 3-7 CAV S2 Editorial and 3-7 CAV command briefing given on 25 May 2003. In that command briefing 3-7 CAV estimated 300 enemy killed in action.

143. Ibid.

144. 3-7 CAV S2 Editorial. Developing the time line for the engagements at FLOYD proved very difficult since unit reports and eyewitness accounts seldom agree.

145. 2nd Platoon leader and Platoon Sergeant B/3-7 CAV, interview by Lieutenant Colonel Dave Manning 25 May 03.

146. 4th Platoon Leader and Platoon Sergeant B/3-7 CAV, interview by Lieutenant Colonel David Manning

147. Ibid.

148. Ibid.

149. Ibid.

150. 1-64 AR summary of unit actions.

151. Lieutenant Colonel J.R. Sanderson, commander 2-69 AR, email to Colonel Gregory Fontenot, US Army, Retired dated 23 November 2003.

152. Sanderson.

153. "Operation Iraqi Freedom, Third Infantry Division (Mechanized) "Rock Of The Marne", After Action Report, Final Draft," 12 May 2003, 35.

154. Ibid.

155. Wallace interview by Maclean. See also Wallace by Cherry.

156. "V Corps Daily Staff Journal," 23 March 2003.

157. Commander, Combined Forces Land Component Command, "Fragmentary Order 102 to Operations Order 03-032, OPCON 82D ABN DIV(-) to V Corps," 252200Z March 03 [SECRET, RELEASABLE to AUSTRALIA and GREAT BRITAIN].

158. Major General J.D. Thurman, C3, CLFCC, interview by Colonel Gregory Fontenot, US Army, Retired and General Frederick Franks, US Army, Retired, 21 May 2003.

159. Lieutenant Colonel E.J. Degen, V Corps chief of plans, interview by Major David Tohn, 13 August 2003.

160. Major Lou Rago, Major Kevin Marcus, Lieutenant Colonel Chuck Eassa, V Corps planners, 8-9 May 03, and ACP OIC, 9 May 03, interviews by Lieutenant Colonel William Connor, US Army, Retired, and Degen.

161. Ibid.

162. Ibid. There were only two C-130 aircraft available so the brigade cycled troops on quick turnarounds between Tallil Air Base and Kuwait International Airport. See also, Colonel Arnie Bray, Commander, 2nd BCT, 82nd Airborne Division, interview by Colonel Gregory Fontenot, US Army, Retired, 5 November 2003.

163. Lieutenant Colonel Edward Rowe, Executive Officer, 2nd BCT, 82nd Airborne Division, notes from interview in Baghdad, 17 May 2003 by Lieutenant Colonel Art Durante, US Army, Retired.

164. Ibid.

165. Ibid.

166. Bray.

167. Ibid.

168. Lieutenant Colonel Wesley Gillman, Commander, TF 1-30 Infantry, Notes from interview in Baghdad, 12 May 2003.

169. Rowe.

170. Ben Arnoldy, "Syrian Volunteers Fought US Troops In Southern Iraq," *Christian Science Monitor*, 11 April 2003.

171. Bray.

172. Rowe.

173. Rowe. See also Bray.

174. These engagements are discussed in greater detail as part of the V Corps' five simultaneous attacks.

175. 101st Airborne Division, Operation Iraqi Freedom Chronology and Operational Data Report, 12 May 2003. 3rd Brigade reached FARP Shell on 25 March per 101st entry to V Corps assessment report for 26-28March. How long the convoys lasted varied by unit. Most reported being on the road anywhere from 40 to 60 hours.

176. Major William Abb, 101st Airborne Division Planner, interview conducted by Lieutenant Colonel William Connor, US Army, Retired, 23 May 2003.

177. Abb.

178. Memorandum for record, "2-70 AR Operation IRAQI FREEDOM Timeline," 22 May 2003, 2. The *Thunderbolts* ultimately were subordinated to two divisions in the corps as well as to SOF *TF 20*. To meet that requirement C Company, 2-70 AR road marched back to Tallil Air Base and then was airlifted to an air base in western Iraq and attached to the 3rd Ranger Battalion.

179. Lieutenant Colonel Henry "Bill" Bennett, Commander, 1-320 FA, interview by Lieutenant Colonel William Pitts, 22 May 2003.

180. Colonel Ben Hodges, Commander, 1st Brigade, 101st Airborne Division, interview by Lieutenant Colonel William Connor, US Army, Retired, 23 May 2003.

181. Ibid.

182. TF 2-70 AR timeline and Bennett. See also Lieutenant Colonel Jeff Ingram, Commander, TF 2-70 AR, interview by Lieutenant Colonel David Manning, 22 May 2003.

183. TF 2-70 AR timeline and Bennett. Bennett reported these events as occurring on 1 April; authors cited 2-70 AR timeline for the date of these events.

184. Major Robert Tallman, OIF-SG, "OIF-SG Operational Summary: PSYOP," 15 July 2003.

185. Ibid. See also Sergeant Daniel Voss, Tactical PSYOP Team 1141, interview by Major David Converse, 31 May 2003.

186. Ibid.

187. See <http://www.dropzonepress.com/usjumps.htm>. This total (44 combat jumps) excludes smaller-scale jumps conducted by special operations units in the period covered from World War II through Operation IRAQI FREEDOM. The site lists 43 jumps but does not list the 173rd's jump. Presumably it will do so ultimately.

188. Lieutenant Colonel Tom Collins, *Forward Deployed Army Force in Italy Proved its Worth During Iraq War* (Draft), unpublished. Portions of this draft appeared in an article in *ARMY* in June 2003.

189. Ibid.

190. Ibid.

191. Although CENTCOM directed operations in OIF, the 173rd Airborne belonged to the Southern European Task Force. Accordingly, they worked for US Army Europe and the US European Command, thus EUCOM. The boundary between EUCOM and CENTCOM areas of responsibility also put northern Iraq in EUCOM's area, thus the two regional commands worked together on employing the 173rd and in other ways as well.

192. Collins.

193. Lieutenant Colonel Robert S. Walsh, Army Special Operations Forces Field Collection Element "Operational Assessment: JSOTF-North, Northern Operations," 30 June 2003. Lieutenant Colonel Walsh served with OIF Study Group. This paragraph reflects his assessment of JSTOF-NORTH operations.

194. Collins.

195. Major Phillip Chambers, S1 and drop zone officer in charge, 173rd Infantry Brigade, email to Major David Tohn, 27 June 2003.

196. "Forward Operating Base 102 SITREP," 24 March 03 (SECRET).

197. Chambers.

198. Mr. Perry Doerr, Southern European Task Force G3 email to Colonel Gregory Fontenot, US Army, Retired. Each aircraft also had two troopers on board who assured safety but were not scheduled to jump.

199. Chambers. See also letter from Major General Thomas R. Turner, commanding general, Southern European Task Force, to Brigadier General Timothy D. Livsey, Deputy Commanding General for Training Combined Arms Center, Fort Leavenworth, Kansas, 23 October 2003. Times, of course, varied by unit; see also Captain Ned Ritzmann, A/1-508 IN, interview by Major Peter Kilner, 28 May 2003. Ritzman reports that his unit assembled in "5 or 6 hours" and then moved to its assigned blocking positions.

200. Chambers.

201. Lieutenant Colonel Bradley Wakefield, chief, movement operations center, USAREUR, email to Lieutenant Colonel E.J. Degen, 16 September 2003.

202.   Colonel Blair Ross, *A Transformed Force in Legacy Clothing;* and Lieutenant Colonel Tom Collins, *Forward Deployed Army Force in Italy Proved its Worth During Iraq War (Draft)*, unpublished.

203.   Ross.

204.   Ibid.

205.   Major Robert Sanchez, S2, 173rd Airborne Brigade, interview by Major David Tohn, 28 May 2003.

206.   Ross.

207.   Ibid.

208.   Ibid.

209.   Collins.

210.   Staff Sergeant Joe Todd, maintenance section, TF 3-15 IN, interview by Robert H. Tallman at TF 3-15 Headquarters, Baghdad, Iraq, 19 May 2003.

211.   Lieutenant Colonel Stephen Twitty, Commander, TF 3-15 IN, interview by Lieutenant Colonel Arthur Durante, US Army, Retired, 19 May 2003.

Chapter 5

Isolation of the Regime

One time, we had gotten the left track of our Bradley hung up on really heavy cable and wire. It was so bad that when we tried to get out of there, we couldn't. The other combat vehicles . . . started off to their next objective and we thought we could get ourselves unstuck, so we said we'll catch up because it wasn't that far away, but as we continued to try to drive and continued to try to cut the stuff out of our vehicle, it just somehow got worse.

So now we have our Bradley back up on the highway and it came to a point where the vehicle would no longer move forward or backward. So, my driver and gunner got out and tried cutting the stuff away, and as we were sitting there, we came under heavy machine gun fire, at least a 14mm machine gun, and [we] had electrical lines right next to our Bradley and big, huge explosions and electrical power lines flying everywhere and fire and smoke . . . pretty exciting.

And the Iraqi civilians coming down this highway saw what was going on and were parking their cars and getting out with pry bars and machetes and anything else they could find and helping my gunner and driver—they actually pushed my gunner and driver out of the way and took charge trying to untangle this stuff out of our Bradley's tracks—while we were under fire. It's just another signal to us that these people really appreciated us being there and they were really trying to take care of us.

Captain Mike Melito,
assistant battalion S3, 1-3 ADA, 3rd ID

Summary of Events

Coalition air operations began to focus more assets on the isolation and destruction of regime leadership and their ability to command and control units. The air component's attack priorities shifted to striking Iraqi ground units defending the approaches to Baghdad and providing close air support to coalition ground troops. The air component continued to strike strategic targets as ground units closed on Baghdad. On 4 April Tallil Air Base south of An Nasiriyah became home to coalition A-10 *Warthog* aircraft. The coalition air component's dominance of the air now allowed it to stack attack aircraft and await targets. *Warthogs,* Army *Apaches and* Marine *Cobras* flew low-altitude missions at will, providing excellent support over urban areas. On 6 April the coalition declared air supremacy over all of Iraq.[1]

The maritime component continued to clear and maintain the waterways, patrolled the Khor Abdullah, and discovered more weapons caches along the river. The maritime component handed over port operations of Umm Qasr to the land component. A British military port management unit assumed responsibility for running of the port. The coalition now had a fully operational port on Iraqi soil and began the steady flow of food and products for the Iraqi people.

CFLCC units seized objectives that isolated Baghdad, thus denying reinforcements or escape by regime military forces. Soon, V Corps took control of the corridor from Karbala to Baghdad in the east, and the I MEF gained control of the ground from Salman Pak to Baghdad. Ultimately I MEF advanced on Baghdad from the east, crossed the Tigris River, and drove through significant concentrations of troops, destroying the *Baghdad* Division of the Republican Guard at Al Kut and elements of the *Al Nida* Republican Guard Division between Al Kut and Baghdad. UK troops continued to secure the Al Faw peninsula and the southern oil fields while expanding their influence by advancing into Basra and ridding the town of regime death squads. Through aggressive foot and mobile patrols, British forces established control over a large part of the city of Basra. The performance of the British in Basra set the standard for future stability operations in large urban areas.

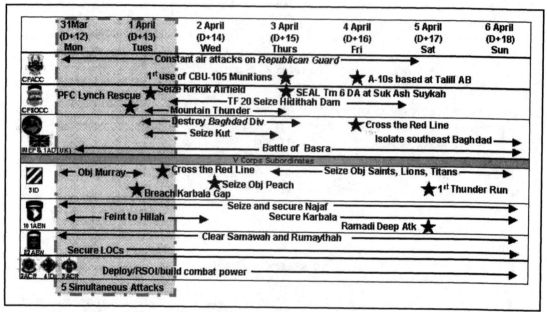

Figure 132. Isolation of Baghdad sequence of events

By 29 March, V Corps had concentrated 3rd ID and began to solve the problem of securing its LOCs. Lieutenant General Wallace had the corps within striking distance of the Republican Guard divisions defending the approaches to Baghdad. Moreover, the Corps was sound logistically and operationally. This was important since Wallace expected the effort to isolate Baghdad to be the start of the truly hard fighting. Nonetheless, he had reason to be confident about the immediate future. The corps was well on its way to being logistically able to sustain the expected fight in and around the capital: the 3rd ID had completed 3-5 days of replenishment and sustainment operations. Theater and corps support troops had brought fuel, ammunition, and food forward to Objective RAMS. Most important, 3rd ID had concentrated, and Wallace now had sufficient combat power—the 82nd Airborne Division and the 101st Airborne Division—dedicated to keeping the LOCs open.

While combat had by no means stopped or even slowed during the refit operations, the corps had all but ceased moving north from 25 to 29 March. Instead, the corps focused on refitting and on cleaning up the roads and key chokepoints between the Kuwaiti border and Objective RAMS, in the vicinity of An Najaf. While some of these actions had been planned

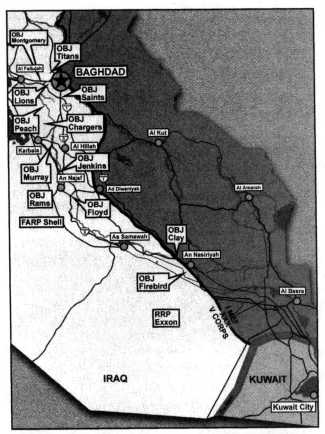

Figure 133. Objectives in the vicinity of Baghdad

in advance, committing the 82nd and 101st to the LOCs had not been in the original scheme of maneuver. Similarly, the MEF concluded a stiff fight in An Nasiriyah and cleaned their long and difficult-to-defend LOCs. Other important changes had occurred since Wallace had unveiled his plan to the commanders of Army and Marine Corps units on the troop list for the attack. For one thing, the I MEF would retain control of its units rather than subordinate part of 1st Marine Division to V Corps as originally planned. Second, 4th ID was rushing to get ashore and into the fight from Kuwait instead of attacking south from Turkey. Other units that Wallace originally envisaged joining the fight as part of V Corps either were no longer troop listed or would arrive too late.

Moreover, V Corps and I MEF knew a lot more about the enemy, including that the assumption that the Iraqis would not fight was wrong. On the other hand, assumptions on the quality of Iraqi regular force effectiveness had proved fairly accurate. The demonstrated ferocity and tenacity of paramilitary forces were important and unpleasant surprises. While the CFLCC, corps, and MEF all knew much more about how the enemy fought, they continued to have difficulty finding and tracking units, especially the paramilitary forces. Finally, the Iraqis had been able to force V Corps and I MEF to fight in cities that they had hoped to bypass or seize in stride. Regardless of the changes in task organization, forces available, and general conditions, defeating the regime still required attacking into the capital.

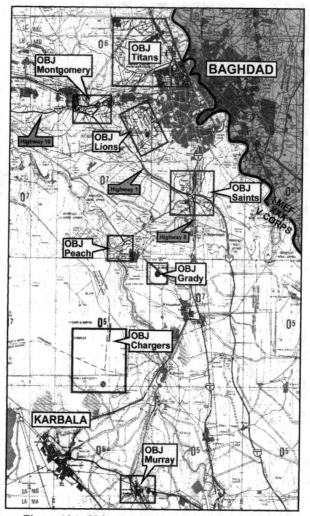

Figure 134. Objectives in the vicinity of Baghdad

As the corps' main effort, 3rd ID was poised in the vicinity of Objective RAMS and ready to surge forward. The 101st had closed on An Najaf and was ready and able to continue the attack. Finally, the 2nd BCT of the 82nd Airborne Division had assumed responsibility for much of the LOC, freeing the rest of the corps to focus on attacking. The isolation of the regime began with the move from RAMS. Establishing the cordon around Baghdad can be divided into four distinct but overlapping events:

- The five simultaneous attacks that set the stage for the assault through Karbala Gap
- The attack through the Karbala Gap to Objective PEACH
- The attacks to seize Objectives SAINTS and LIONS
- The attack to seize Objective TITANS

These actions, constituting the major moves to complete the isolation of Baghdad, are described in detail following this brief overview.

CFLCC Conference at Jalibah

On 28 March Lieutenant General McKiernan went forward to meet with his commanders on the ground. McKiernan traveled to General Conway's I MEF command post at Jalibah, where he met with Conway and Wallace. McKiernan wanted to hear directly from his subordinates how they assessed their "stance" for the transition from the march up-country to closing on Baghdad, which he had identified as one of the regime's two centers of gravity. He identified the second as the paramilitary forces. The sandstorm had finally abated, and the theater, corps, and MEF logisticians had brought supplies forward, but there was intense fighting ranging from Basra to An Nasiriyah and other points in the MEF zone. In V Corps' zone the fighting ranged from As Samawah north to An Najaf. The meeting began with McKiernan providing his assessment on enemy forces and asking some key questions of his subordinates, including their satisfaction with the level of risk along the LOCs. In McKiernan's words, "we did the wargaming and we looked at the running estimate" of the situation.[2] Both Wallace and Conway had some concerns they believed they needed to address prior to crossing the "red line or red zone" that referred to entering the inner defensive cordon outside of Baghdad. Wallace briefed his plan for a series of attacks designed to set the conditions for the assault to isolate Baghdad. McKiernan asked what he needed to set that stance. Wallace responded by saying he needed to position the corps by 31 March to launch his attacks on 1 April. Conway noted that the MEF was undertaking "a systematic reduction of the bad guys in An Nasiriyah" and he wanted 1 UK Armoured Division to execute some "pinpoint armor strikes" in Basra. Conway also observed that "Joe Dowdy (Colonel Joe Dowdy, commanding 1st RCT) was in a 270-degree fight."[3] After hearing his commanders, McKiernan made a decision, as he put it, to "take time to clean up and make sure we have the right stance in our battlespace before we commit into the Baghdad fight, because once we commit to the Baghdad fight, we can't stop."[4] That decision moved CLFCC into setting the conditions to isolate Baghdad.

Five Simultaneous Attacks

On the heels of the effort to secure the LOCs and resupply the corps, Lieutenant General Wallace wanted to position the corps to isolate Baghdad. Just prior to the meeting at Jalibah, he saw opportunity in a plan that Major General Blount at 3rd ID had developed to launch north to an objective near Karbala. He polled the rest of the corps units to see if they could conduct any complementary operations. Virtually every unit had coincidentally considered local operations within hours of one another. Wallace, along with the corps G3, Colonel Steve Hicks, took control and synchronized them. Attacking in five directions, the corps regained momentum, deceived the Iraqis as to the main effort, and completed securing of the LOCs. These actions enabled the attack through the Karbala Gap and the subsequent isolation of Baghdad.

The Karbala Gap

The corps expected its first major armor-on-armor fight to be against the *Medina* Division at the Karbala Gap. Although unrelenting air attacks by fixed-wing aircraft and attacks by the 101st Airborne Division's attack helicopters weakened the *Medina,* it remained a significant threat. The narrow gap between Bahr al-Milh Lake (Buhayrat ar Razazah) and the city of Karbala offered the only relatively open approach to the outskirts of Baghdad. Other routes crossed a river or entered the mazes of irrigation ditches and soft agricultural land along the Euphrates River valley. Attacking through the Karbala Gap also avoided the urban sprawl in the Euphrates Valley; the lake afforded protection of the corps' left flank, and once north of the gap, maneuver space opened to the west. To describe the Karbala Gap as "relatively open" does injustice to the problem of attacking through the gap. Colonel Will Grimsley, commanding 1st Brigade, 3rd ID, elucidated the conditions in the gap as follows: "We prepared for Karbala of course to be the end all, the chemical target from hell with a choke point 1,800 meters wide, which it is ... if you look at a map ... when you take the city [Karbala], when you look at a 1: 50,000 map, and you go all the way to the lake [Milh], what you quickly realize is that this is all agricultural land. It is very chopped up with rock quarries, and there are really only two or three little roads that lead through the Karbala Gap and across the irrigation canal that runs from the lake and feeds into the farmland, as well as the city water for Karbala. What that connects you down into is a one thousand, eight hundred-meter gap with two roads that you can cross ... a huge mobility challenge."[5]

This natural chokepoint, further cluttered by irrigated farm fields, offered obvious advantages to the defenders, having all of the attributes of a classic engagement area. That is to say the Karbala Gap afforded good fields of fire to the defenders and limited maneuver space and few exits for the attackers. Here, the Iraqis could bottle up the 3rd ID and destroy it with a combination of artillery, tank, and antitank missile fire. Moreover, intelligence had assessed the gap at Karbala as the start of the "Red Zone," the area where coalition forces expected the Ba'athist regime to employ chemical weapons in a last desperate bid to protect its seat of power.

For all of these reasons, Lieutenant General Wallace and his staff paid particular attention to creating an environment that would ensure the 3rd ID could maneuver safely through the gap. Establishing this environment, or in Army parlance—setting conditions—included a series of feints and the five simultaneous attacks. All were linked to a deliberate deep strike and air interdiction efforts. Wallace intended the feints to draw the Iraqis into believing the corps would actually push across the Euphrates River south of Karbala and approach Baghdad from due south, adjacent to the advancing marines. He believed this would cause the Iraqis to reposition their well-camouflaged forces to meet the expected threat, and thereby be vulnerable to air strikes and deep fires as they moved. The resulting destruction of the exposed Iraqi forces would clear the Karbala Gap of a significant artillery threat and much of its armored forces, allowing the 3rd ID to defeat the remnants of the defending *Medina* Division on its own terms.

Isolating Baghdad

Once through the Karbala Gap, V Corps would prepare for the final phase of ground combat—the isolation of Baghdad and attacks into the city designed to remove Saddam Hussein and the Ba'athist regime. The plan required effecting control of Baghdad; but V Corps, I MEF, and CFLCC hoped to avoid a house-by-house, block-by-block reduction of the defenses in the city.

The original plan envisaged the corps and the MEF advancing more or less abreast, with 4th ID attacking from the north to isolate Baghdad. The soldiers and marines would concentrate on the city and establish an inner cordon. Never intended to be a hermetic seal, this cordon would rather consist of five brigade-size operating bases placed on key terrain encircling the city and cutting the major roads in and out.

The Threat at Karbala

From: D101 ACE CHIEF

Sent: Sunday, March 23, 2003 12:33 PM

To: 101ABN G2 LNO

Cc: D101 DM G2; D101 DM G2 PLEX; D101 ACE BATTLE Captain; D101 ACE PRODUCTION; D101 ACE FAIO; D101 ACE CM&D

Subject: RE: 101 Special Product

Importance: High

We've seen a BTRY from the 124th (2nd AR) and the 132nd (14th MECH) reposition to form an *ad hoc* artillery group north of Karbala. With the advance of 3rd ID north of An Najaf, we think the *Medina* is going to reposition up to a MECH BN (+) force to help defend the gap. *Al Quds* and [*Saddam Fedayeen*] will likely man the defensive position we saw in the [deleted] assessment south of the town. This artillery group will provide DS fires to disrupt 3rd ID as it approaches the gap. What we're **missing is the MRLS**. We think the **gap is a rocket box**—and as soon as 3rd ID gets into the gap they'll close it, initiate rocket fire, then destroy remaining vehicles in the kill zone with flank fires from the city (RPG-7, AT-3, etc.). The MECH BN (I say plus because a . . . cable this morning had a company of tanks back on the west side of the river at *Mussiyab*, therefore we think task organized force) serves both as a blocking force with counterattack capability. Believe the rest of the brigade remains [in the vicinity of] Mussiyab to secure the Highway 9 Bridge, then to fall back to prepared defensive positions at Iskandariyah.

Best route for 3rd ID; therefore, is to go east of the Karbala Gap.*

AR column engaging 3rd ID now in the vicinity of Objective RAIDER is likely an advance guard/ screen line from the [Iraqi] 2nd AR Brigade. I haven't heard any reporting of BRDMs associated with the RECON company; therefore, I assume this is an armor unit.

No comms with 3rd ID, would be interesting to get their assessment and make sure they have this info. The 3rd ID [liaison officer] in our TOC does not have comms.

Also, we're in the RED ZONE as we approach Karbala. This is the trigger for chemical release (according to Intelligence estimates). Additional reporting of chemical release authority to regional commanders, coupled with chemical defense training and supplies [corroborates] this assessment.

Email from 101st Airborne Division
Analysis and Control Element chief

*Editor Note: Author was apparently unaware of corps plan to mitigate the threat.

Named after the planner's favorite National Football League teams, the operating bases at Objectives SAINTS, LIONS, BEARS, TEXANS, and RAVENS would position the corps to execute the final stage of the fight for Baghdad. The final battle for Baghdad would be a sequence of raids and limited-objective attacks to control, neutralize, or destroy the regime's symbolic and physical levers of power. Presumably, this could be done without a step-by-step reduction of the city, avoiding a slugfest that would produce large numbers of dead and wounded fighters and civilians.

Attacking through the Karbala Gap, V Corps planned to seize three objectives west of the Tigris River—LIONS, SAINTS, and BEARS. The 3rd ID assigned these objectives to its three brigade combat teams, 1st BCT, 2nd BCT, and 3rd BCT, respectively. The 1st BCT would initially secure Objective PEACH, the corps' actual crossing site over the Euphrates River. The 2nd BCT would pass through PEACH and attack to seize Objective SAINTS, a key intersection of Highways 1 and 8. Following 2nd BCT through PEACH, 1st BCT intended to move due north on the west side of Baghdad to seize LIONS, or the Saddam International Airport (later

> ## Regime Isolation
>
> "By the time we reached Baghdad we had conducted nearly 500 physical destruction information operations missions on Iraqi command and control nodes, links, and decision makers. Information operations took away the Iraqi leadership's ability not only to mass combat power, but to govern [the] nation."
>
> Major Prentiss Baker,
> CFLCC IO targeting officer,
> interview with Major Robert Foley.

renamed the Baghdad International Airport, or BIAP). Once relieved from the Karbala mission by the 101st, 3rd BCT planned to follow the rest of the 3rd ID and attack to seize Objective BEARS, but later they refined the position of this objective and called it TITANS, to the north of the city. The marines, remaining under the I MEF's control, would move up the east side of the Tigris and the Diyalah River, then cross the Diyalah and close the cordon at TEXANS and RAVENS.

The defending Iraqis continued to reposition, desert, or die in place. By 1 April, the *Medina* Division—originally composed of two armored brigades, one mechanized infantry brigade, and supporting assets—was largely destroyed. On 3 April, V Corps assessed the *Medina* as being down to only three maneuver battalions but noted that the 15th Mechanized Brigade of the *Hammurabi* Division was on the move to "backstop the *Medina*" south of Baghdad. The corps also believed a brigade of the *Nebuchadnezzar* Division had moved to a position in the vicinity of Al Hillah. Through 6 April, the Iraqis continued to move units to the Karbala Gap-Al Hillah area to reconstitute their defenses in the south, but they also moved units to Fallujah to block V Corps attacks from the west. Eventually, units from the *Adnan, Al Nida,* and the regular army all maneuvered south and west to reinforce the approaches to Baghdad.

Cleaning Up to the South

After V Corps completed its operations to attack through the Karbala Gap, it left one unfinished piece of business—cleaning up Al Hillah. After the 101st's feint toward Al Hillah as part of the five simultaneous attacks on 31 March, it kept the town isolated. The division deliberately did not force a fight and withdrew far enough to preclude being drawn into an ugly urban battle. Now, as the corps moved north some six days later, Al Hillah was the only part of the line running from the lake through Karbala to Al Hillah that had not been secured. Doing so would clear the last defenders that could interdict the Highway 8 approach to Baghdad. It would also protect the LOCs west of the Euphrates as the corps brought troops and supplies up through the Karbala Gap. Most important, Al Hillah remained, as Wallace described it, a "hornets' nest."[6]

The 101st's 3rd Brigade took the task in hand, leading off with a feint on 8 April, employing a force built on Lieutenant Colonel Ingram's TF 2-70 AR, *Thunderbolts*. Coming off an attack at Karbala on 5 April, the *Thunderbolts* had one day to prepare, continuing their growing tradition of task organizing on the fly. Attached to the 3rd Brigade on the 6th, they gave up an air assault infantry company and a tank company. In return, the *Thunderbolts* received an air assault company from 3rd Brigade on the 7th and retained a tank company and a mechanized infantry company. Despite the changes, the *Thunderbolts* remained an agile and deadly combined-arms, light/heavy-mixed force ready for an urban fight.

The newly reorganized task force moved to an assembly area about 18 kilometers west of Al Hillah. There, Ingram issued an operations order at 2230. The following morning, supported by artillery, CAS, and attack aviation, the *Thunderbolts* attacked east, crossing the Euphrates at Objective MURRAY and reaching the western edge of Al Hillah. Other 3rd BCT units reconnoitered toward Al Hillah, both on the same axis as the *Thunderbolts* and from the south as well.[7] At the close of operations, the 3rd Brigade soldiers had the town isolated.

The division followed up on 8 April with an attack at 0600. Although the Iraqis—and apparently Syrians—in Al Hillah fought hard, resistance collapsed the next day. The 101st reported capturing "huge numbers of weapons."[8] With its mission complete at Al Hillah, 3rd Brigade of the 101st consolidated and prepared to attack north toward Objective GRADY via Al Muhmudiyah and Al Iskandariyah, some 50 kilometers distant. The following morning, 3rd Brigade continued the attack, ultimately reaching Baghdad.

Following the fall of Baghdad International Airport (Objective LIONS), the corps developed information that the Iraqis intended to mount an attack to retake the airport—with the report first appearing in the corps' 7 April intelligence assessment.[9] However, the repositioning and counterattacking Iraqis fought essentially piece-meal, if they fought at all. Identifying specific Iraqi units became difficult with all the ad hoc mixing taking place. In most instances, coalition air forces had hammered units opposing V Corps and I MEF, and in some cases, the Iraqi soldiers simply walked away from their equipment. In other instances, combat systems presumed destroyed by air strikes remained capable of firing, and did so. Coalition ground units learned to re-engage any Iraqi tanks, armored vehicles, or guns to ensure that they really were "dead."

Parallel and Supporting Combat Operations

Of course, these maneuvers could not have been successful in isolation. The corps was confident of its ability to defeat the Republican Guard units in open combat, where all of the US advantages in sensors and precision long-range weapons could be brought to bear. These advantages would evaporate if the Republican Guard melted into the city to conduct a deliberate urban defense. Thus, while the corps advanced on Baghdad, a highly focused air interdiction effort hampered the remaining Republican Guard divisions from repositioning into the city. Equally important, I MEF fought a supporting effort on V Corps' eastern flank, destroying many Iraqi units and preventing others from affecting the main effort.

Close Air Support

The Air Force's and Navy's contributions to the campaign cannot be overestimated. Lethal combinations of A-10s, F-15s, F-16s, F/A-18s, B-1s, B-52s, and a host of other aircraft were absolutely essential to the ground campaign's success. The Air Force's investment of air liaison officers and enlisted terminal attack controllers embedded into the maneuver units paid off in spades. Throughout the entire campaign, 79 percent of air operations (15,592 of 19,898 attacks) were CAS or kill box interdiction—direct targeting of Iraqi ground targets in support of coalition maneuver.[10] These were generally effective in hindering the bulk of the conventional forces from reaching cities, either by destroying them en route or by inducing the soldiers to abandon the equipment. The only complaint the Army commanders had was that the clearance of fires process was sometimes unwieldy.[11]

JSOTF-North, the 173rd Airborne Brigade, and the Kurds

The SOF in northern and western Iraq continued to harass the Iraqi forces and inhibit them from repositioning against the main effort at Baghdad. The JSOTF-North, with its 173rd Airborne Brigade and the Kurdish forces, conducted a series of attacks to defeat the Iraqi 4th ID (30 March), 2nd ID (31 March), 8th ID (2 April), and the 38th ID (2 April). They also attacked and defeated a unit of the terrorist group *Ansar Al Islam* during Operation VIKING HAMMER (28-30 March). VIKING HAMMER produced a number of important effects, including securing the Kurds' rear area and perhaps causing the Iranian government to deny *Ansar Al Islam* sanctuary. VIKING HAMMER reinforced Kurdish trust in the US commitment and prompted the Kurds to reallocate combat power to attack Iraqi units defending the Green Line. Finally, they seized Khurma on 28 March. This series of operations, pressing and maintaining contact with the defending Iraqi forces through a combination of Kurdish direct action and US air power and deep fires, caused the Iraqi units to begin to melt away.

One of the last coordinated tactical Iraqi efforts against JSOTF-North occurred at Debecka Ridge on 6 April against a position known informally as "The Alamo." There, a small group of special forces soldiers held commanding positions overlooking a wide valley up which the Iraqis advanced.[12] Although greatly outnumbered by their attackers, the special forces troopers were heavily armed, with .50-caliber machine guns, Mk-19 automatic grenade launchers, 60mm mortars and, most important, the Army's newest antitank weapon, the *Javelin* missile. They were also able to call on supporting Air Force and Navy fighters and bombers armed with precision-guided weapons.

> ### *I've Got A-10s*
>
> The F-15s and F-16s were good. The A-10s were absolutely fantastic. It is my favorite airplane. I love those people. If I had enough coins, I'd send one to every A-10 driver in the Air Force just to tell them how much I appreciate them because when those guys come down and they start those strafing runs, it is flat awesome. It is just flat awesome.
>
> You can move, and when that A-10 starts his strafing run, you can do anything you want to do as a task force commander because the bad guy's head is not coming off the hard deck. His head is not coming out of the ground. If he is in a hole, he is hugging Mother Earth and praying to whatever God he can to that he lives through this. You can maneuver anywhere you want to maneuver as long as that cannon is firing. As long as that A-10 is flying above you and turning and moving, you can do anything you want to do.
>
> You could hear the roar of screams of joy when [the air liaison officer] would come over the radio and say, "I've got A-10s." When the A-10s came in, first of all you could see them, second of all the control, the positive control, over what we were shooting with was absolutely phenomenal.
>
> Lieutenant Colonel J.R. Sanderson,
> commander, TF 2-69 AR
> interview 12 May 2003 by Lieutenant Colonel David Manning

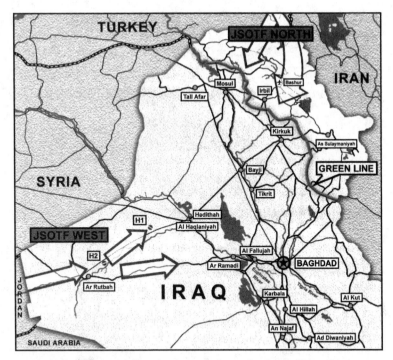

Figure 135. JSOTF-North operations along the Green Line

The Iraqis attacked during daylight with a platoon of T-55 tanks, two platoons of mechanized infantry mounted in tracked carriers, and an additional infantry force in trucks. Iraqi commanders supported the attack with artillery and mortars and at least one 57mm air defense weapon.[13] The T-55 tank platoon led the attack straight up the road toward the special forces position at the top of the ridge, with tracked vehicles arrayed in combat formations in the open fields on both sides.

Although the Iraqi attack may have appeared tactically sound, and it certainly had numerical superiority, it was doomed from the beginning. The special forces soldiers picked off the Iraqi armor with shoulder-fired *Javelin* missiles long before it could even close to within accurate range of the American positions. Enemy infantry died under withering heavy machine gun and 40mm grenade fire. The special forces troops destroyed the Iraqi supporting weapons either with their own mortars or by calling in CAS.

The defending special forces troopers stopped the Iraqi armored attack with no US casualties. Regrettably, a supporting bomber mistook a group of Kurdish *Peshmerga* and US special forces grouped on a ridgeline near the battle for the enemy. The aircraft mistakenly attacked the group, killing several and wounding others. The *Javelin* antitank missile proved its worth once again during this battle. Already employed by TF 2-7 IN against T-72 tanks in downtown Baghdad, it devastated the exposed T-55s in the fields of northern Iraq. One of the special forces soldiers became the Army's first *Javelin* "Ace" after he destroyed two personnel carriers and three troop trucks.[14] After this final spasm of Iraqi opposition, the coalition forces continued to move east and south. With the conditions now set, they liberated Irbil on 1 April and Kirkuk on 10 April, and cleared the way for the I MEF and 101st Airborne Division to secure Mosul.[15]

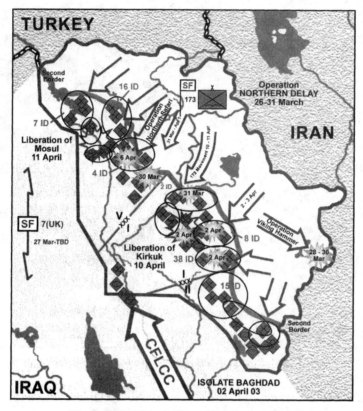

Figure 136. Enemy disposition in the north

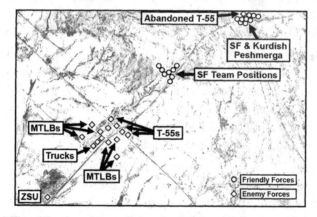

Figure 137. US and Iraqi positions during the Battle of Debecka Ridge, 6 April 2003

JSOTF-West and TEAM Tank

JSOTF-West continued its mission to destroy Iraqi forces in the area from the Jordanian border eastward. The SOF soldiers continued to prosecute intensive counter-TBM operations to ensure Saddam could not threaten Jordan or Israel with Scuds. Leap-frogging from air base to air base, SOF troops seized several key facilities, to include the Hadithah Dam. JSOTF-West seized the dam to prevent the Iraqis from releasing the water behind the dam. Had the Iraqis released the water, the resulting inundation of the Euphrates valley would have hampered movement. Troops from the 3rd Battalion, 75th Ranger Regiment fought for nearly three weeks against a determined enemy to retain control of the dam, thus preventing inundation and protecting a vital piece of infrastructure for the Iraqi nation. Subsequently, 1-502nd Infantry Battalion of the 101st Airborne Division relieved the rangers at the dam on 19 April 2003.

As the JSOTF-West forces edged closer to central Iraq, the commander determined that he needed additional mobility and firepower on the ground to meet the Iraqi threat. Company C, 2-70 AR, originally attached to 3rd BCT of the 3rd ID, got this mission. On 31 March, Captain Shane Celeen's company attached to TF 1-41 IN was fighting several hundred miles to the east-southeast with the 82nd Airborne Division in As Samawah. During that fight, C/2-70 AR supported seizing a key bridge crossing on Highway 8. One day later, on 1 April, Celeen's company was attached to a SOF task force in the west. Because it would have taken far too long for the unit to drive out to the west, the company immediately road-marched south to Tallil Air Base for an air movement.[16]

Arriving at Tallil early on 2 April, the company linked up with SOF personnel and transported 10 M1A1 tanks, three M113 armored personnel carriers, a FST-V fire-support vehicle, two fuel trucks, three cargo trucks, and an HMMWV by C-17 aircraft to H-1 Airfield in western Iraq. Air Force transports moved Celeen's company in 15 sorties over three days. The C-17s and their crews provided flexible and responsive support to a complex problem. They exemplified the exceptional agility the US joint forces displayed in applying the right units to the right mission.[17]

On arrival at H-1 Airfield, the company came under the control of the 1st Battalion, 75th Ranger Regiment. The rangers and the tank company road-marched 160 kilometers east,

Figure 138. Hadithah Dam

back toward Baghdad, and began conducting raids in the Bayji-Tikrit area. In addition to the raids, the company supported interdiction missions along Highway 1 to Syria, attempting to seal the border from fleeing Ba'athist and Iraqi military personnel. The company supported JSOTF-West from 2 to 24 April, until 4th ID assumed responsibility for the area.[18] This rapid intratheater movement and multiple task reorganizations integrating conventional and SOF units demonstrate the power of joint integration to meet the ever-changing tactical and operational situation in the theater.

Rolling Phase IV Transition

In addition to the combat operations along the LOCs and at the approaches to Baghdad, corps forces had to transition seamlessly to stability the operations and support operations for the areas already under control. More than just assisting in providing humanitarian aid, virtually every element of Iraqi civil society—from police to fire to basic utilities and food distribution—dissolved with the defeat of the Iraqi army and paramilitary forces. The liberated Iraqi civilians were happy to see the regime's representatives depart or die. However, they immediately looked to the coalition forces to provide basic life-support services.

The populace also drove the requirement for rolling transition because their needs could not wait for a tidy resolution of combat operations. They often confronted unit leaders with requirements while combat operations were going on just a few blocks away. At the risk of winning the battle but losing the campaign to liberate Iraqi civilians, the local commanders were torn between their fights and providing resources—soldiers, time, and logistics—to meet the civilian needs. Partially due to the scarce resources as a result of the running start, there simply was not enough to do both missions.

The SOF community, specifically the special forces and civil affairs troops, proved instrumental in mitigating this threat and challenge in the liberated areas. Working closely with the local civil and religious leaders in the towns and villages, the SOF soldiers helped the newly liberated Iraqis establish a modicum of order and discipline.

James Matise, US Army

Figure 139. Iraqis welcoming the 2nd Brigade, 101st Airborne Division

While not universally successful, outside of a few major cities, there were remarkably few instances of public disorder or popular resistance to coalition presence.

Iraqi Actions

By the last days of March, CENTCOM, CFLCC, and all of the troops had learned a number of things about the Iraqis. First, in stark contrast to what some had asserted, CFLCC had a real fight on its hands. The irony is that the same pundits who in 1990 had direly predicted 10,000 American casualties—and criticized the Army in particular as not up to the task—had now, in 2003, predicted utter collapse of the Iraqis. It appears that some in uniform may have also accepted this analysis, but the coalition soldiers and marines doing the fighting knew better. The Iraqis did not instantly melt away, and they had learned from their experience in DESERT STORM. They understood that if they massed formations in the open desert, the Americans would destroy them rapidly and from a distance. Their planned defenses did not array their forces in the open desert. Rather, they planned to fight from dispersed positions in considerable depth. Saddam planned to use his paramilitary units, both militia and *Fedayeen*, to further extend the depth of the battlefield to deny sanctuary to US logistics units and to bleed coalition forces as they advanced.

The Iraqis also sought to deny to the coalition's technical intelligence a clear picture of their dispositions and intent. They positioned inoperable equipment to deceive and to decoy coalition efforts and attract attacks on unmanned, derelict pieces. Where and when they could, they hid units and shielded them in groves of palms or positioned them in and around targets that the coalition would be loath to attack, such as hospitals or schools. To the extent possible, they protected their communications by using cell phones, low-power radios, and couriers. They were able to shield or hide air defense, maneuver systems, tactical headquarters, and tactical missiles with some success.

It appears that the running start and speed of advance achieved tactical and operational surprise. The pace of coalition operations in OIF appears to have surprised the Iraqis and

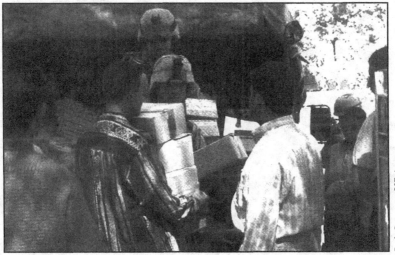

Luis Lazzara, US Army

Figure 140. A 101st Airborne Division soldier distributes humanitarian aid

Figure 141. Sample district council identification card

exceeded the rate at which they could respond effectively. Still, they did respond and demonstrated the ability to move brigade-size forces and to reposition whole divisions incrementally. V Corps attacks in the last week of March may have produced significant Iraqi maneuver, movement, and counterattacks in the first two weeks of April.[19]

V Corps detected some movements of Republican Guard and regular army units trying to reinforce the crumbling *Medina* Division south of Baghdad or at least to reinforce the Euphrates River line. The problem posed for the Iraqis at the end of March and in the first days of April stemmed directly from their failure to achieve anything useful during the sandstorm

Figure 142. Soldiers examine an Iraqi air defense artillery piece hidden in a palm grove

and "pause." Although the corps found it very difficult to maintain a lock on specific units, it was, for the most part, able to follow general movements. Discerning what the Iraqis intended or why they were doing some of the things they did remained illusory. Every echelon found it nearly impossible to track militia and *Fedayeen* movements. This was further complicated by new reports of Syrians, in groups as large as 150, operating south of Baghdad. Against this ambiguous background, the corps resumed its advance north to the capital.

Conclusion

CLFCC's maneuvers to isolate Baghdad occurred across the entire country and across the spectrum of modern conflict. In a country the size of California and populated by several separate and often antagonistic cultural groups, coalition forces simultaneously executed

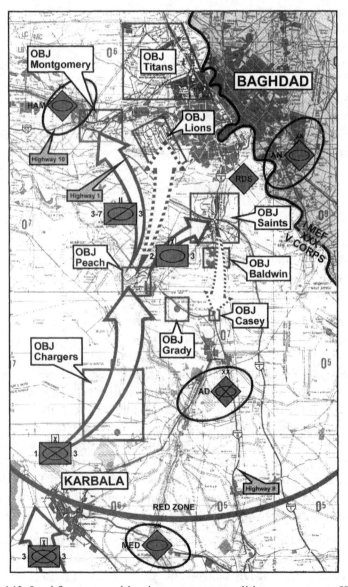

Figure 143. Iraqi forces reposition in response to coalition maneuver to Karbala

virtually every type of mission possible. Missions ranged from the attacks to seize SAINTS and LIONS, to classic river-crossing operations, to urban fights along the LOCs as far south as As Samawah, to humanitarian, security, and stability operations throughout southern Iraq, to searching for weapons of mass destruction and hunting the Iraqi senior leadership. The coalition did not focus merely on the physical isolation of Baghdad, but on making Saddam's regime irrelevant.

The V Corps sequence of attacks and maneuvers to isolate the capital exemplified distributed operations. Three separate divisional headquarters—82nd, 101st, and 3rd—operated simultaneously to finish clearing the LOCs, defeat remaining Iraqi forces south of Baghdad, and establish the inner cordon of Baghdad. Breaking into the "Red Zone," CFLCC had to take seriously the possibility that the Iraqis would respond with every weapon and capability they had—from the vaunted Republican Guard to chemical weapons. Most often, the troops in the field found the conventional Iraqi forces disorganized, ineffective, or simply not there. The paramilitaries, however, continued their fanatical, but suicidal, attacks. In any case, the corps had arrived at the city and was preparing for the end game, the slashing attacks to oust the regime and liberate all of Iraq. Every echelon of command, from Lieutenant General McKiernan at CFLCC to Lieutenant General Wallace at V Corps, to the division, brigade, battalion, and company commanders, all understood the final objective and could see how their mission fit in. Coordinating and synchronizing these various actions over such a large battlefield was a testament to the respective staffs' ingenuity, dedication, and just plain hard work.

V Corps' Five Simultaneous Attacks

At 1300 on 30 March, V Corps headquarters issued FRAGO 149M, which initiated a series of interrelated limited-objective attacks to begin early the next day. Beginning on 31 March, V Corps conducted an ambitious and extensive set of limited-objective offensive operations south of the Karbala Gap. These attacks would accomplish several tactical objectives, ending with the V Corps forces positioned to cross the Euphrates and isolate Baghdad.

Among other things, the 3rd ID's attacks aimed to deceive the Iraqi commanders as to where the corps' main effort would cross the Euphrates River—north or south of Karbala. If the Iraqi commanders bought the deception, they would reposition their artillery to meet the coalition threat. In repositioning, the artillery would be exposed to destruction from coalition airpower. Intelligence indicated that the Iraqis expected the coalition assault through the Karbala Gap, and the corps believed the Iraqis had turned the gap into a huge artillery and missile kill zone. Accordingly, Lieutenant General Wallace wanted to clear the gap and destroy any Iraqi artillery or missile units that could range it. He also wanted to destroy the enemy's reconnaissance capabilities, as well as any major maneuver forces south of Karbala. Doing so would eliminate the threat of a counterattack against his right flank as he maneuvered the corps. As the corps' main effort, the 3rd ID's attacks would restart the northward momentum. Last, upon culmination of the attacks, the division would be in position for the upcoming operations into the heart of Baghdad.

The 101st Airborne Division's several attacks would support the main effort by adding combat power and credibility to the 3rd ID's deception efforts. Additionally, the powerful attack helicopters of the 101st Division would strike at any Iraqi forces south and west of

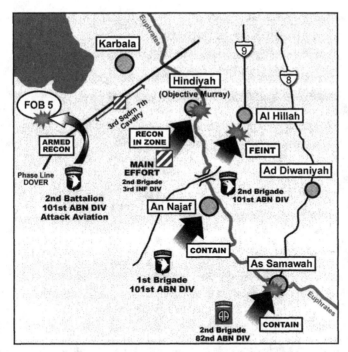

Figure 144. V Corps' five simultaneous attacks

V CORPS FRAGO 149M

(DECL IAW USCENTCOM OPLAN 1003-V, Classification Guidance, 31 October 2002)

V Corps conducts simultaneous limited attacks 310300Z March 2003 vic Al Hillah, Karbala, and As Samawah to deceive enemy units into repositioning and to destroy enemy reconnaissance capabilities.

3rd ID (ME) attacks to Objective MURRAY to cause enemy forces to reposition and to set conditions for future offensive operations.

- 300300Z Mar 2003 attack to establish screen along PL DOVER.
- Conduct reconnaissance in force 310300Z Mar03 to Objective MURRAY (WB 273018) to cause the enemy to reposition forces and reinforce deception objectives.
- Block traffic on Highway 9 and Euphrates River road to prevent reinforcement of An Najaf.
- Block Highway 28 to prevent enemy infiltration into AO. Occupy attack positions to prepare for an attack on the *Medina* Division.
- Be prepared to seize bridges over Euphrates River vic Objective MURRAY.
  101st ABN (SE) 310300Z Mar 2003
- Conduct a feint along Highway 9 from Objective JENKINS north toward Al Hillah to support the main effort.
- Conduct deep attack 31 Mar 2003 to destroy the *Medina* Division. On order, withdraw to prepare for future operations.
- Conduct reconnaissance in force (armed reconnaissance) 310300Z March 2003 vicinity of FOB 5 and quarries at 38SLA6985 to support the main effort.
- Conduct deep attacks to destroy repositioned forces of the *Medina* Division.

12th AVN Brigade provides lift to insert LRSC elements from the 205th MI Brigade to cover named areas of interest west of Karbala after the 101st AA's armed reconnaissance.

2nd BCT, 82nd ABN (SE) 310300Z March 2003 attack to continue to contain enemy forces in As Samawah and sever enemy eastern LOCs into the city.

Lieutenant General Wallace on the
Five Simultaneous Attacks

"All five of those actions, or six if you count the repositioning of the brigades of the 3rd Infantry Division, were to occur simultaneously at 0300Z [0600 local] on the morning of whatever day that was.... Now, the results of those five simultaneous actions, in my mind, caused the enemy to react. It was late that afternoon when all of those fights had run their course and we were sitting on Objective MURRAY, and we owned the bridge. The 3-7 Cavalry had repositioned, and the armed recon, I think, was probably still ongoing. The attack into As Samawah had run its course. The 101st was still fighting like a son of a bitch up at Al Hillah, because they really did run into a hornets' nest there. Late that afternoon, in beautiful sunlight, we started getting reports of the Republican Guard repositioning to what we believed to be their final defensive setup.

My current thinking is that those actions caused the enemy commander to think that series of attacks was our main effort, that our main attack had started, and that we were attacking from west to east across the Euphrates to gain Highway 8 [south of Karbala] so we could turn north into Baghdad. That was never our intention. But having done that, I believe our attacks caused him to react to our actions, fully knowing that if he did not react to them, given the limited successes that we had had in those actions, then he would be out of position. So he started repositioning—vehicles, artillery, and tanks on [heavy equipment transporters]—in broad daylight, under the eyes of the US Air Force.

I believe it was one of those classic cases of a maneuver action setting up operational fires, which in turn set up for a successful decisive maneuver, which took place the following day and over the following 48 hours. Just 48 hours later, we owned Baghdad International Airport and Objective SAINTS. We had begun the encirclement of Baghdad. From my perch, my perspective, my retrospection, that was a tipping point in the campaign."

Lieutenant General William S. Wallace
commander, V Corps
interview with Colonel French Maclean, 15 April 2003

Bahr al-Milh Lake, west of Karbala. This would add security to the corps' left flank from any possible Iraqi counterattack. The 101st's attack at An Najaf aimed to destroy the festering threat to the LOC.

The 2nd Brigade of the 82nd Airborne Division's continued attack at As Samawah would ensure that no Iraqis there could threaten the ever-lengthening network of roads linking the V Corps forces to their logistic bases in the south. Further, part of the brigade would attack to the northeast, cutting the routes being used by the Iraqis to reinforce from that direction. This would complete the isolation of As Samawah and eventually lead to its elimination as a threat to the LOCs.

Wallace's desired end state envisioned positioning the 3rd ID to attack through the Karbala Gap to Objective PEACH, the actual crossing site for the corps, with the division's flanks secure and the corps' LOCs open. The 101st would secure An Najaf and control the LOCs around that city, while the 82nd achieved similar results at As Samawah.

In the end, the corps accomplished all of this, and more, but only after what, to some who participated, seemed a very confusing three days of combat across the entire corps area. The corps cut key enemy LOCs, preventing reinforcements or resupply into the south (An Najaf, As Samawah, An Nasiriyah). The attacks by the 3rd ID to Objective MURRAY and the 101st toward Al Hillah appear to have deceived the enemy into believing that the US would attack along Highway 8 as well as through the Karbala Gap. Lieutenant Colonel "Rock" Marcone recovered the map (see insert pg C-10) from the body of the 10th Brigade *Medina* Division reconnaissance company commander at Objective PEACH. The map shows clearly that the 10th Brigade thought the main attack was coming from the south, with supporting efforts from the west and through the Karbala gap. The red circle in the center of the map is the bridge at Objective FLOYD. V Corps' action at that location clearly drew the attention of the Iraqis, who, either in response to V Corps or for reasons of their own, began repositioning artillery, armored, and mechanized infantry forces, which made them vulnerable to air attack. The corps and coalition air strikes destroyed dozens of individual systems and defeated several units. The Iraqis also defended their flank with only a reconnaissance battalion, no match for the "Marne" Division's march on Baghdad.

The 2nd BCT, 3rd ID Attacks Objective MURRAY (30 March – 1 April)

The attack to MURRAY aimed to "cause the enemy to reposition forces and reinforce deception objectives."[21] But as the first of the corps' five simultaneous attacks, it actually began on 30 March when 2nd BCT of the 3rd ID attacked northeast of RAMS to clear the enemy from some restrictive terrain

> **Feint**
>
> A feint, according to the Joint Army-Marine Corps Manual for Operational Terms and Graphics, is "a type of attack used as a deception to draw the enemy's attention away from the area of the main attack. Feints must appear to be real and therefore require contact with the enemy."[20]

and rock quarries and to position itself for the attack on Objective MURRAY the following day. The Spartans attacked with TF 1-15 IN and TF 3-15 IN abreast to clear the quarries north of Objective SPARTANS and to seize key intersections leading to a bridge over a canal outside of Al Hindiyah.[22]

The Approach

En route, the task forces met light resistance until nearing Al Hindiyah, where TF 1-15 IN destroyed several technical trucks and dismounted *Fedayeen*. The 2nd BCT maintained contact with the enemy and destroyed several artillery, armor, and infantry units hiding in the quarries. Upon reaching their limit of advance, the lead task forces established a secure position west of Al Hindiyah, designated Objective SPARTANS 2. The remainder of the BCT closed on the objective and prepared for the attack on MURRAY the next day. The 3-7 CAV passed to the west of 2nd BCT and established a screen along the division's flank at Phase Line DOVER.[23]

The 2nd BCT also repositioned its direct-support artillery. The 1-9 FA moved to Position Area Artillery (PAA) NIXON, approximately 30 kilometers south of Karbala and east of Highway 28, to provide fires in support of 2nd BCT's planned attack on MURRAY. The battalion arrived in NIXON at 1008 and immediately received a call for fire against a platoon-size enemy force in the quarries at SPARTANS 2. Accurate artillery fire killed most of one Iraqi squad and convinced the rest to surrender.[24] With the fight at SPARTANS 2 complete, the artillery and remainder of the brigade continued to prepare for MURRAY.

Starting 31 March, the 6-6 CAV of the 11th AHR provided one troop of AH-64 *Apaches* to 3rd ID as a quick-reaction force. The helicopters would address 3rd ID's concerns about the threat posed by any bypassed enemy forces on its eastern flank. Specifically, the division

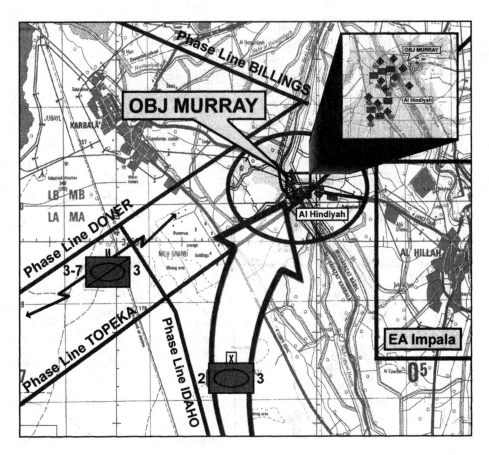

Figure 145. Objective MURRAY

worried about Iraqis crossing the Euphrates River near MURRAY to attack the sprawling concentration of forces to the south at Objective RAMS.[25] The 6-6 CAV provided continuous attack helicopter coverage, assigning each troop an 8-hour block of time and requiring a response time of no more than 45 minutes. Over time, the squadron's mission evolved into an area reconnaissance of Objective MURRAY. The 3rd ID eventually tasked the air cavalry to reconnoiter the main avenues of approach to MURRAY. Alpha Troop also launched a team of armed helicopters and reconnoitered the objective.

Attacking to MURRAY

The brigade employed a simple scheme of maneuver: Two infantry-heavy task forces, TF 1-15 IN and TF 3-15 IN, would secure the roads leading into MURRAY, while an armored task force, TF 4-64 AR (*Tuskers*) attacked into the town to seize the key bridge over the canal. The brigade's second armored task force, TF 1-64 AR, would remain in reserve and secure the area to the west.

At 0600 on 31 March, TF 1-15 IN, TF 3-15 IN, and TF 4-64 AR attacked to the east along three separate routes. Combat engineers moved with each task force, prepared to clear lanes if they encountered any mines or obstacles.[26] The *Tuskers*, under the command of Lieutenant

Colonel Phillip DeCamp, attacked along the main road leading to the bridge. Colonel Dave Perkins accompanied the *Tuskers* in his tactical command post (TAC).[27] Perkins aimed to fix any enemy forces in the vicinity of Al Hillah to the east and to allow the 3rd ID's artillery to identify Iraqi artillery positioned within range of the Karbala Gap.

Fedayeen and Republican Guard forces engaged the *Tuskers* with small-arms and RPG fire as the task force entered the town. Approaching the bridge at 0650, A/4-64 AR, under Captain Phillip Wolford, reported receiving sporadic fire from the buildings nearby. The task force quickly destroyed the defending forces, seized the west side of the bridge, and brought enemy forces on the far side under main-gun and mortar fire. Wolford's tank company destroyed several civilian trucks mounting crew-served weapons, several of which erupted in massive secondary explosions from the ammunition they were carrying. Captain Chris Carter's A/3-7 IN passed Wolford's company and actually seized the bridge. As one indicator of the intensity of the fighting, the 10th Engineer Battalion commander, riding in his track in company with the 2nd BCT TAC, reported being under fire much of the day. Iraqis firing on the engineer track struck and wounded one soldier in the leg.[28]

After TF 4-64 AR secured the bridge, B/10th Engineers identified wiring under the bridge and began to cut it. They searched carefully, but apparently the Iraqis had not yet installed any explosives. They did find telephones and wire in positions near the bridge, indicating a prepared defense.[29] The engineers also cleared ammunition caches, including one containing more than 1,000 mortar rounds. During the course of the attack and the remainder of the day, 1-9 FA fired 14 missions, destroying two buildings that were sheltering RPG teams, killing nine enemy fighters and effectively suppressing other targets. The artillery also fired five counterfire missions against Iraqi mortars.[30]

At about 0800, the *Tuskers* captured 10 enemy soldiers, including a platoon leader from the 2nd Battalion of the 23rd Republican Guards Infantry Brigade, a brigade of the *Nebuchadnezzar* Republican Guard Infantry Division.[31] As they continued to root out small pockets of resistance, the *Tuskers* identified other soldiers wearing the red triangle flash of the Republican Guard. The presence of combat units from the *Nebuchadnezzar* Division was surprising and indicated that Iraqi units were being moved from the north to reinforce the defenses south of Baghdad. The presence of troops from the *Nebuchadnezzar* also suggested the importance the enemy placed on defending bridges south of Baghdad following their loss of An Najaf. Throughout the day, the brigade had sporadic contact with enemy forces at almost all of the blocking positions west of Al Hindiyah.[32]

The fight at the bridge continued throughout the day. At 1045, the enemy began to reposition forces on the far side of the bridge. They moved behind buildings and in the areas blocked from the *Tuskers'* observation by the arch of the bridge itself. TF 4-64 AR maneuvered elements onto the bridge so they could better observe and engage the Iraqis.[33] Just after 1300, the task force reported that paramilitary forces on the east side of the bridge were using women and children as shields in front of their vehicles. The hapless civilians shielded the trucks from Americans reluctant to fire on civilians, allowing the enemy to reach positions near the bridge. One of the human shields, an elderly woman, attempted to run across the bridge but the Iraqis shot and wounded her in the back. Determined to rescue the woman, troops on the scene threw smoke grenades to cover their movement and evacuated her from the bridge while under fire.[34]

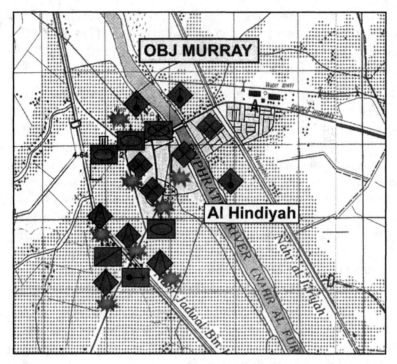

Figure 146. Enemy and friendly disposition in Objective MURRAY

One company from TF 4-64 AR cleared the police headquarters building near the bridge and confiscated a case of AK-47s and ammunition. Another company reported hundreds of AK-47s, RPGs, uniforms, 82mm mortar rounds, and 25mm ADA ammunition inside a large weapons cache located south of the bridge. The unit also captured documents outlining the defense of the city and the location of the military headquarters in that area.[35] As the afternoon waned, the *Tuskers,* having accomplished what they intended, pulled out of the town and returned to the positions they occupied prior to the attack.[36] The attack on MURRAY proved quite productive—killing some 46 Iraqi troops, capturing 23, and destroying 29 mortars and more than 1,000 mortar rounds. In addition, the troops destroyed one Iraqi 20mm AA gun along with a four-barrel self-propelled AAA vehicle. They captured or destroyed more than 50 AK-47s, 90 RPGs, and hundreds of RPG and mortar rounds. Finally, the attack into MURRAY fixed enemy forces east of the Euphrates River by demonstrating a threat to Baghdad from due south. This ultimately allowed 1st and 3rd BCTs to successfully attack north and seize the Karbala Gap, securing the actual route for the attack into Baghdad from the west.[37]

Artillery Support

As TF 3-15 IN withdrew, one of its tanks slid into a canal. The commander estimated it would take all night to recover the tank and assigned a company-size force to provide security for the area. To provide protection for the recovery operation, 1-9 FA established a critical friendly zone (CFZ) around the recovery area. A CFZ is a programming feature within the AN/TSQ-36 *Firefinder* counterbattery radar. The *Firefinder* can detect artillery shells in flight and plot the point of origin—the enemy artillery tubes. By creating a CFZ, if the radar detects any enemy rounds falling into that protected area, the American artillery is cleared to fire immediately. In short, a CFZ links fire-detection radar to the guns and defines the area the guns must protect and reduces the reaction time for artillery from minutes to seconds. The TF 3-15 IN fire support element (FSE) planned fires in support of the recovery operation in case of an enemy ground attack. During the night, 1-9 FA fired two counterfire missions, to include a response to Iraqi indirect fires into the CFZ. This mission silenced an enemy mortar firing on the tank recovery operation, and the tank was successfully recovered.

The attack at MURRAY was important for several reasons. MURRAY marked the first fight the 3rd ID had against organized Iraqi Republican Guard forces. The attack also helped the division identify and destroy enemy

---

Overrated—Underrated

"We overrated his army, but we underrated the irregulars. They were fierce, but not too bright. They were evil men who deserved to die. They didn't adapt to our forces. They would continue to impale themselves on our BIFVs and tanks."

Lieutenant Colonel Pete Bayer, G3, 3rd Infantry Division

Baghdad, 11 May 2003.

---

artillery units from Karbala to Al Hillah and to gain a clearer picture of how the enemy had arrayed their defenses south of Baghdad.[38] The 3rd ID also polished its ability to control simultaneously CAS and artillery. The 3rd ID artillery fired 20 counterfire missions and called 30 CAS and interdiction missions to support this engagement. The division continued to fight effectively and, more important, learn from each fight and adapt, while its opponents often failed to adapt. The 3rd ID rapidly communicated what the soldiers learned and assured that all of its units benefited from the experience of one of them.

While fighting at MURRAY, 2nd BCT also prepared to pass 1st BCT to the north. The 1st BCT was positioning itself for the planned attack to isolate the west side of Karbala. Although the 2nd BCT withdrew from MURRAY after defeating the Iraqi infantry battalion there, it maintained control of Highway 9 southwest of Al Hindiyah. That night, E Troop, 9th CAV led TF 2-69 AR of 1st BCT along Highway 9 to its attack position. This set the stage for the decisive attack through the Karbala Gap to the Euphrates.

The 1st BCT, 101st Airborne Division clears An Najaf (30 March – 4 April)

Coalition commanders hoped to avoid fighting in An Najaf, which, along with Karbala, is considered by Shia Muslims to be among the holiest places in the world. Inside the city cemetery is the Tomb of Ali, son-in-law and cousin to Mohammed and founder of the Shiite sect. Coalition leaders saw no benefit to getting into a possible street fight that could be portrayed as an attack on Islam. As Lieutenant General Wallace put it, "It was never our intention to go into any of the towns."[39] Prior to OIF, it also seemed reasonable to suppose that there would not be a fight for An Najaf. An Najaf is a Shia town where Saddam's regime was, to say the least, unpopular. None of the prewar estimates showed regular army or Republican Guard units defending the town. Moreover, none of these same estimates suggested much of a fight from the various paramilitary forces, including the *Al Quds* militia or the *Fedayeen*.

However, with little elaboration, the V Corps operations plan opined that the militia constituted a "ready reserve, with limited training and equipment..." and went on to add, "These forces are likely to defend the urban centers such as As Samawah, An Najaf, and Ad Diwaniyah."[40] And that is just what they did. As they had at As Samawah, An Nasiriyah, and other towns, paramilitary forces came streaming out of the town, attacking 3rd ID furiously as it rolled past. For this reason, Wallace ordered the 101st Airborne to contain An Najaf.

The Approach: Isolating An Najaf

After relieving 2nd BCT, 3rd ID, the commander of 1st BCT, 101st Airborne, Colonel Hodges, felt that he had to close his brigade in on An Najaf. Although his original guidance was "...don't get stuck in the city," Hodges recalled that he "felt a little naked out there so I moved my first battalion (1-327 IN) closer to the city where they had a better-covered area."[41] For this and a number of other reasons, An Najaf exerted a gravitational pull on the 101st. Some of the thinking that led to clearing An Najaf stemmed from the philosophical—potential slaughter of innocents—to the mundane—the 101st wanted an airfield to get their aircraft on hardstands, and An Najaf had an airfield.[42]

Anchored on Checkpoint Charlie astride the main road 6 kilometers southeast of the town and within sight of the airfield, 1-327 IN, commanded by Lieutenant Colonel Marcus Deoliveira, cleared the complexes of buildings on the southern end of the city. Clearing one complex brought the battalion under fire from the next, drawing it ever inward toward the center of the town. On Deoliveira's left, TF 2-327 IN would similarly attack into the town. A number of reports, apparently from special operations troops, of possible atrocities in the city fueled the momentum to go into the town. According to Hodges, "We started getting reports . . . that (the *Fedayeen*) were killing families to make guys come out and fight. So we started getting the sensing that there might be a disaster going on inside the city."[43]

Even before Hodges felt the pull into the town, Lieutenant General Wallace and Major General Petraeus discussed different options for dealing with An Najaf. They spoke or met daily as the division's efforts to isolate morphed into an outright attack to clear the city. Wallace recalled that the two of them arrived at the decision to clear the city, "partly as a consequence of enemy action. As the 101st took some ground, including the agricultural university [at the southwestern edge of town] and the airfield, to improve their security, they drew attacks from the Iraqis.... Over time, speaking daily with [Major] General Petraeus, we found that we would have to clear the town. An Najaf, in some ways, is to southern Iraq what Baghdad is to the entire country. It was important and it was big enough that we determined it would be a test case for fighting in Baghdad."[44]

Major General Petraeus also believed that attacking An Najaf had much larger implications for the corps than dealing with the city itself. In seizing An Najaf, the division employed precision tactics, techniques, and procedures (TTPs)—integrating,

> **Printing Maps at Battalion Level**
>
> We had decided months ago to use FalconView and put graphics on FalconView and print maps for each operation. We were able to print enough for platoon level.
>
> Lieutenant Colonel Marcus deOliveira
> commander, 1-327 IN,
> commenting on producing maps in the field
> for imminent combat operations,
> 24 May 2003.

precision attack by the Air Force on targets immediately followed by ground attacks. They would use these TTPs elsewhere along the fight to Baghdad.[45] This precision minimized collateral damage and maximized shock to the defenders. With the two senior commanders in accord, the "Screaming Eagles" transitioned to the attack.

Entering the Town: Clearing An Najaf

In developing the scheme of maneuver to clear the town, 101st planners built on the work they had done to contain forces in the city and subsequently isolate it from external reinforcement. "Screaming Eagles" planners developed estimates of exfiltration routes that they believed the Iraqis were using to exit An Najaf and attack US units and LOCs. Their analysis also included determining routes the Iraqis used to reinforce An Najaf from the north. Obviously, that told them something about the routes going the other way and where they should anticipate trouble.

Using imagery, combat information generated by 3rd ID and SOF, and other intelligence, the division developed a plan that envisaged a two-brigade operation.[46] The planners divided the city into rectangular sectors, providing a method for ready reference and a good means of coordinating fires and reporting cleared areas. Equipped with highly capable mapping software, battalions printed maps with their own "plotters." Thus, each battalion had the means to illustrate the plan clearly. Moreover, the battalion commanders could assure that every small unit had the detailed maps that an attack in a city demands.[47] With little time to plan the transition from isolation to attack, the ability to generate detailed maps and the constant situational awareness provided by BFT enabled the attack.

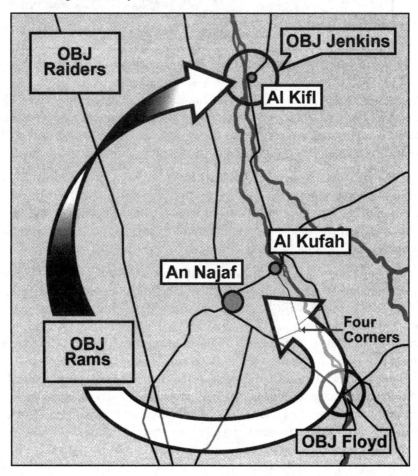

Figure 147. Scheme to isolate An Najaf

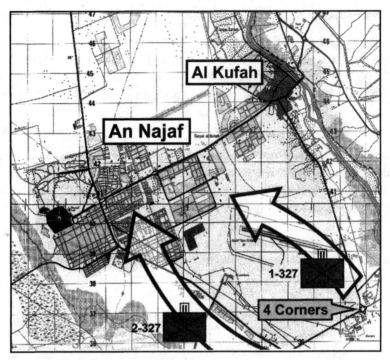

Figure 148. 101st Airborne Division's attacks into An Najaf

Clearing An Najaf also required a major change in the division's thinking. The staff had focused its planning originally against Republican Guard defenses in the Karbala Gap. As the focus changed to supporting the continued advance of the 3rd ID, it wound up fighting, as Petraeus put it, "the enemy they found, not the enemy they planned for."[48]

Although the division ultimately used two brigades to clear the town, with 2nd BCT attacking from the north and 1st BCT attacking from the southwest, the task of making the initial penetration of the city fell to Colonel Hodges' 1st BCT. Just before the attack, the unit made last-minute adjustments and drew ammunition for the battle that everyone believed would be fierce. Building on the foothold Deoliveira won, Hodges' brigade attacked on 31 March.

Changing the mission from isolation to clearing happened fast enough to preclude methodical planning at the battalion level. Lieutenant Colonel Chris Hughes, commanding the TF 2-327 IN on TF 1-327 IN's northern flank, quickly assembled an armed leaders' reconnaissance, using an attached tank platoon and a borrowed M113. Hughes brought rich experience to his battalion with five combat training center rotations at the JRTC and NTC under his belt. He also commanded an OPFOR company at the JRTC for 22 rotations and deployed as a "lessons learned" collector to Haiti. Hughes believed in combined arms and joint fires and now he set the conditions to put theory into practice. His reconnaissance party included the two company commanders who would lead the attack on 31 March. Hughes brought his D Company and its TOW antitank missile launchers forward to overwatch from just outside the city. He positioned himself about 5 kilometers outside of Najaf where he could see and control the fight. Hughes' team included both an Air Force Tactical Air Control Party (TACP) and a Combat Observation Lasing Team (COLT) from the brigade.

Hughes launched his reconnaissance at 1500 to place the sun at their backs and in the eyes of potential defenders. The reconnaissance party immediately came under fire from dozens of paramilitary troops operating from inside and around a mosque. They attacked the tanks and M113 energetically with RPGs, small arms, and even howitzers in the direct-fire mode. Hughes brought in fighters, artillery, and Army aviation to support the team, which also managed to enter a minefield. Eventually, the party returned safely, covered by the battalion's antitank company, artillery, and CAS.[49] The fight lasted nearly 4 hours. D Company, along with the reconnaissance party, had all the fight they wanted. D Company fired 56 TOW missiles against point targets, actually managing to hit one of the Iraqi towed howitzers. D Company fired on targets the tanks could not reach, adding their efforts to the 65 tank rounds the Abrams crews fired. British Tornados, and US F-16s, B-52s and B-1s dropped 12 500-pound bombs, seven 1,000-pound bombs and five JDAMs. Gunships fired several hundred rockets and unknown numbers of machine gun rounds. Finally, the reconnaissance party broke contact and, using plastic explosives, cleared a lane out of the minefield and returned unharmed.[50]

Using tanks and Bradleys attached from TF 2-70 AR, Hodges formed combined arms teams supported by artillery and air. Over the course of the fighting, he methodically carved out parts of the city and eventually reached the Ba'ath Party headquarters. Highly

The Weak, the Stupid, and the Brave

Lieutenant Colonel Hughes described the enemy in An Najaf as including ". . . the weak, the stupid and the brave." The weak they could force to run.

"The stupid would fire from a window and come back and fire from the same window. The brave were the ones that would let us bypass them and wait and attack us."

Lieutenant Colonel Christopher P. Hughes,
commander, TF 2-327 IN,
interview 23 May 2003.

Figure 149. 101st Airborne soldiers, south of An Najaf

Andres J. Rodriguez, US Army

130th Engineer Brigade

Figure 150. Engineers clear the streets with a D9 armored bulldozer

1st Battalion, 327th Infantry

Figure 151. Supporting fires south of An Najaf, 31 March 2003

accurate maps, with clear control graphics dividing the city into sectors, eased the challenge of coordinating the difficult handoffs between units and reduced the likelihood of killing innocent civilians or doing unnecessary damage to the city's infrastructure.

Hughes' battalion eventually fought its way into the city and to the Mosque of Ali. Convinced from his conversations with Colonel Perkins and what his battalion learned over the course of three days, Hughes believed that most of the people in An Najaf neither wanted to fight him nor obstruct his efforts. Hughes had a Free-Iraq Fighter who he felt provided good advice on how to work with the local clerics and the Ayatollah to reduce the fighting in the town. During the initial assault, his Free-Iraq Fighters recommended not fighting during the calls to prayer. Accordingly, Hughes brought up his PSYOP unit and had it broadcast a message announcing to the locals that the American forces respected their religion and would not prevent them from praying at the Mosque of Ali. According to Hughes, hundreds of Iraqis took him at his word and demonstrated it by waving white flags from the escarpment that led to the mosque. He believed that this gesture resulted in little resistance when 2-327 IN entered the city, and he also garnered an invitation to meet with the Grand Ayatollah Sistani later.[51]

Take a Knee

On April 3rd, 2003, the soldiers of the 2-327 Infantry moved into An Najaf, the home of one of Iraq's leading holy men, the Grand Ayatollah Ali Hussein Sistani, to gain his crucial support for their stay in the town. As the soldiers turned a corner, a group of men blocked their way, shouting in Arabic, "God is Great." The crowd grew into hundreds, many of whom mistakenly thought the Americans were trying to capture Sistani and attack the Imam Ali Mosque, a holy site for Shiite Muslims around the world. Someone in the crowd lobbed a rock at the troops, then another. Lieutenant Colonel Hughes was hit on the head, chest, and the corner of his sunglasses with rocks.

Appraising the situation as he was leading his troops, he thought: "Why does a guerrilla want to fight? Give him what he needs and he will not fight." Lieutenant Colonel Hughes lived by the philosophy of Sun Tzu: "A great commander is one who does not shoot a weapon." [Sun Tzu is reported to have put it this way, "To subdue an enemy without fighting is the acme of skill.]

Contemplating these thoughts, he yelled to his troops to "take a knee and point your weapons to the ground; smile, and show no hostility." Some of the Iraqis backed off and sat down, which enabled Hughes to identify where in the crowd the troublemakers were. He identified eight. Wanting to make sure that it would be clear where the shooting would come from, he gave the order: "We're going to withdraw out of this situation and let them defuse it themselves."

Hughes made sure his soldiers understood cultural differences and the meaning of restraint. With his own rifle pointed toward the ground, he bowed to the crowd and turned away. Hughes and his infantry marched back to their compound in silence. When tempers had calmed, the Grand Ayatollah Sistani issued a decree (*fatwa*) calling on the people of Najaf to welcome Hughes' soldiers.

"This gesture of respect helped defuse a dangerous situation and made our peaceful intentions clear," commended President George W. Bush during his weekly radio address.

Lieutenant Colonel Christopher Hughes,
commander, 2-327 IN,
interview with Major (CH) Peter Baktis, 11 July 2003.

When his battalion attacked into town, Hughes once again took Sun Tzu's counsel in mind. Sun Tzu offered the illusion of a golden bridge to defeat an enemy. In short, Sun Tzu held if a commander afforded the enemy an apparent means of escape, the enemy would use it. As Sun Tzu put it, "Show him there is a road to safety and so create in his mind the idea that there is an alternative to death. Then strike." Hughes intentionally did not interdict a route leading from the Mosque of Ali and then north toward Al Hillah. He planned, with 2-17 CAV, a *Kiowa Warrior* ambush on the route north of the town supported by his scouts, snipers, and TACP. The air cavalry executed the ambush with great success.[52]

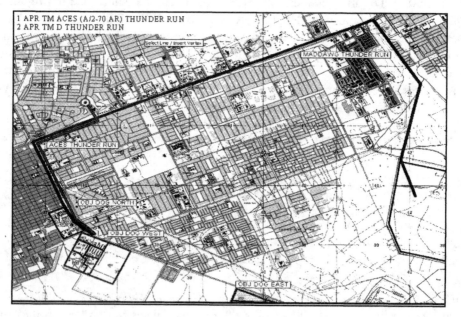

Figure 152. The 101st Airborne Division "Thunder Run" in An Najaf

Although the division's operation to take An Najaf took nearly five days to complete, the turning point may well have come on 1 April, when A/2-70 AR attacked to the center of town. Alpha Company's mini-"Thunder Run" demonstrated the power of the US forces and that, just as Colonel Dave Perkins had told Lieutenant Colonel Chris Hughes, American tanks could move anywhere they wanted without hindrance.[53] Leaders from platoon to corps took note of this. The next day, they conducted another run through the eastern side of the city. The combination of these two raids seemed to break the back of the resistance.

Joint Fires Support

But a handful of tanks did not assure success. A combination of guile, using tanks and infantry, supported by the 101st's organic air cavalry and attack aviation, coupled with CAS and artillery, that kept Hodges' brigade from, in his words, getting "stuck in a 'Stalingrad' kind of city fight."[54] The 101st employed all of the capabilities it could obtain from the joint and Army team. Using Air Force precision munitions to attack Ba'ath Party sites enabled the 101st to destroy centers of resistance while minimizing damage to the city. The division's own organic aviation provided valuable support as well. Both air cavalry and attack helicopters joined the fray, destroying more than 300 vehicles or weapon systems ranging from air defense artillery to "technical" vehicles.[55]

After the second armor raid, 1st Brigade maneuvered rifle companies using the sectors they had designated. They attacked deep into An Najaf against *Saddam Fedayeen* strong points, seizing important buildings and destroying massive amounts of captured equipment, ammunition, and weapons. Attacking the town from the north, the 2nd Brigade employed similar techniques with similar results. Coordinating the attacks, the division established a limit of advance to prevent fratricide as the two brigades converged. By the end of the day on 4 April, the 101st Airborne Division controlled An Najaf. What remained was to assure security and to transition from fighting on one block and handing out MREs on the next to assuring security and conducting stability operations and support operations.[56]

In An Najaf, the division started its adaptation to the enemy at hand. It learned from 3rd ID and subsequently from its own attacks in An Najaf, Al Kifl, and Al Hillah. At Al Kifl, the soldiers validated what they learned here—they "allowed the tanks to react to the initial small-arms fire [and then maneuvered] the infantry against the enemy once contact was made."[57] Eventually, the division fought in eight different cities, noting that each required slightly different approaches based on the terrain and prevailing conditions. But the essential lesson of these urban fights was that integrating combined arms, heavy and light forces, armored raids, and a liberal application of precision airpower applied in each case.[58] Their tactics evolved rapidly as the troops adapted to the enemy, and these fights proved useful as "dress rehearsals" for subsequent operations in Baghdad and elsewhere.

The 101st Airborne Division Feints toward Al Hillah (31 March)

After 2nd BCT took control of the bridge at Objective JENKINS, V Corps ordered the division to conduct a feint toward Al Hillah some 25 kilometers north. Accordingly, the 101st assigned this mission to Colonel Anderson and his 2nd BCT. Part of Lieutenant General Wallace's five simultaneous attacks, he intended for the feint to mislead the Iraqis as to the direction and composition of the main effort. By attacking north, the feint also would support 3rd ID's attack at Objective MURRAY. Thus, the division had to attack with sufficient force and for a sufficient duration to convince the Iraqis it was serious.

Task Organization and Planning

Since TF 2-70 AR was already at JENKINS and organized as a task force of two combined-arms company teams, Colonel Anderson assigned this mission to Lieutenant Colonel Ingram's well-traveled *Thunderbolts*. To support the feint, the division provided AH-64 *Apache*s from 3-101 AVN. Anderson's direct-support artillery, 1-320 FA, now composed of four 105mm howitzer batteries and a reinforcing 155mm howitzer battery, joined the fight as well. Ingram called this operation "Thunderbolt Fake." Although there was little time to plan, Ingram, who colleagues describe as unflappable, was not dismayed. In his mind, this is what tank battalions do. As he put it, "tank battalions are great at reacting. The NTC prepares you for that."[59]

The light infantry seemed undismayed as well. Their training also included combined heavy and light forces. For his part, Ingram believed that his attached light infantry company was "one of the best organizations I've seen. . . .with those guys behind me, I never had to look back. I knew where they were and what they were doing so. . . I could focus on the stuff to my front."[60]

The Feint

At 0600, the *Thunderbolts* launched north with C/2–502 IN attacking along the Euphrates River road, just east of the river. Two kilometers to the east, B/2-70 AR made the main effort, attacking due north along the highway leading to Al Hillah. Given the ferocity of counterattacks against the bridgehead, it is not surprising that the task force immediately came under fire across its front. The *Thunderbolts* nonetheless continued to advance against the defenders firing a mix of RPGs, small arms, and artillery from two Iraqi D-30 towed 152mm batteries.

The *Thunderbolts'* tactics were well adapted to urban fighting. Generally, a tank platoon led each of the two teams, with the infantry following. The tanks suppressed fire, and as the infantry came forward, the tanks ceased firing their main guns and passed the fight to the infantry—a straightforward tactic but hard to execute under fire. Not long after crossing the line of departure, B/2-70 AR suffered two casualties in its attached infantry platoon from C/2-502 IN, including one killed.

In the west, 1 hour into the attack and about 3 kilometers north of the bridge, Ingram ordered C/2-502 IN to assume hasty defensive positions. He further directed the infantry to deal with the enemy it was engaging and then to withdraw to the bridge. Faced with heavier contact in the east, Ingram called for attack helicopters and supporting artillery.[61]

Controlling and supporting the fight at TF 2-70 AR's command post located at Al Kifl, Anderson cycled artillery and air support as the *Thunderbolts* required. Heavy fighting persisted through the morning, but the *Thunderbolts* continued to make their way north toward the limit of advance, just 2 kilometers south of Al Hillah. Lieutenant Colonel Bill Bennett, commanding the supporting artillery, began his day at the 2nd Brigade command post south of Objective JENKINS to ensure that the preparation fires went off as planned. He now found that he had to

James Barker, US Army

Figure 153. Lieutenant General William Wallace (left) and Lieutenant Colonel Jeffrey Ingram, commander, 2nd Battalion, 70th Armor, standing in formation for a ceremony

bound artillery forward to continue to support the attack. By 1000, his 155mm battery and one of his 105mm batteries moved north on Highway 9 on the west bank of the Euphrates. The two batteries bounded by platoon, laying their guns and firing right from the highway to stay close enough to respond rapidly to calls for fire.[62]

Colonel Anderson, with Bennett in tow, moved out of Al Kifl at 1000 and joined Lieutenant Colonel Ingram forward. Bennett's 155mm battery silenced the D-30s, while the 105mm howitzers fired rocket-assisted projectiles (RAPs) for the *Thunderbolts*. Bennett had the opportunity to see his guns in action as *Thunderbolt* scouts some 400 meters to his front adjusted fire onto Iraqi targets. Bennett was delighted with the accuracy of his guns, given that they had not had time to calibrate muzzle velocities for the propellants they had been issued. Moreover, they lacked the weather data to determine winds aloft and other information that would enable them to do the arcane mathematics that assured the highest accuracy. In short, according to Bennett, it was just like training at the JRTC, "…civilians on the battlefield, (operating) with fragmentary orders, with rapid moves (no time to plan)…"[63]

Overhead, C/3-101 AV supported with close-combat attacks and armed reconnaissance. Some of Charlie Company's aviators had fought in Afghanistan, so they well knew the danger posed by ground fire. More important, they learned running fire in Afghanistan. Thus, they were at least moving targets when they approached danger areas. As the *Thunderbolts* moved north, attacking up a four-lane highway, they were constrained as they passed through built-up areas

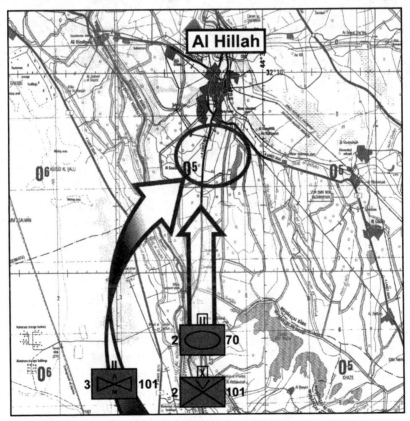

Figure 154. The 101st Airborne Division's attack to Al Hillah

on the way to Al Hillah. Accordingly, the task force asked the attack helicopters to reconnoiter the flanks as far as 5 kilometers north of the ground units. This proved dangerous as the Iraqis had S-60 air defense artillery guns hidden among palm trees. In the end, the aviators weathered intense fires, and along with Bennett's artillery, destroyed 26 S-60s, 12 D-30s, 6 mortars, and a "whole bunch of infantry."[64] The attack helicopters did not achieve this without cost. The Iraqis damaged eight aircraft and wounded the company commander. However, of the eight, all but one returned to action soon.[65]

Figure 155. An *Apache* from 101st Airborne Division over Al Hillah

Andres J. Rodriguez, US Army

Despite the relative success of the combined-arms team fielded that day, the fighting never really tapered off. The Iraqis stayed in the fight and used human shields with fairly good effect. More than once aviators, who could see planned artillery targets from overhead, waved off fire missions due to the presence of civilians on the scene and intermingled with militia or Iraqi troops. During the course of the day, the task force identified units of the *Nebuchadnezzar* Division among the Iraqi defenders. Finally, at 1830 the battalion concluded its feint, reporting some 250 enemy killed. The *Thunderbolts* also destroyed two tanks and 15 other vehicles.[66] With such an intense fight, the feint went far to convince the Iraqis that the rest of the corps would attack up this same route.[67]

The 101st Airborne Division Armed Recon South of Bahr al-Milh Lake (31 March – 1 April)

On 31 March 2003, 2-101st Attack Aviation Battalion received orders to conduct an early morning armed reconnaissance southwest of Bahr al-Milh Lake. The mission was also part of the V Corps' five simultaneous attacks. With the rest of the 101st moving on the eastern flank along the Euphrates River valley, the 2-101st would determine if there were any enemy forces on 3rd ID's western flank. The pilots took off just before sunrise, using night vision systems to fly to their objective, but the sun had risen by the time they arrived in the designated area.[68]

The pilots of 2-101st looked carefully but found only a small group of antiaircraft weapons set up to guard an ammunition supply point. As the AH-64s approached the Iraqi guns, the gun crews ran out of a building to man the systems to fire at the Americans. The pilots engaged and killed the crews and destroyed the guns before the Iraqis could man their weapons. Additionally, the flyers discovered large caches of ammunition,

> ## Those Guys Were Awesome!
>
> Working with tanks was pretty good; they let us be infantrymen; good combined arms team. We really liked them because they always had our back. . . . After this, I will never bad mouth a tanker again. Those guys were awesome.
>
> Corporal Richard Bergquist,
> C/2-7 IN, attached to 3-69 AR

which they reported but were unable to destroy because of low fuel. They continued reconnaissance flights southwest of Bahr al-Milh Lake the next day.[69]

On 1 April, just as the aircraft of 2-101st were returning to base after another long day of looking for enemy forces in the open desert, the unit received an order to send two attack aviation companies to conduct a hasty attack to the southwest side of Bahr al-Milh Lake. V Corps had received a report via JSTARS that was interpreted as a large number of enemy vehicles moving in the area. The corps feared the enemy was mounting a counterattack.[70] The battalion's ground crews immediately went to work rearming and refueling the aircraft. Charlie Company lifted off within 45 minutes of notification of the mission, a truly amazing feat. The company, along with the battalion commander in his aircraft, proceeded to the objective and conducted an armed reconnaissance of the area. Although they never found a large enemy formation (it probably was not there to begin with), the pilots took advantage of the situation and attacked the large ammunition supply point they had seen the day before.[71]

On the same day, the corps tasked 6-6 CAV to conduct a force-oriented zone reconnaissance of the western flank as far as Phase Line VERMONT. Fuel constraints did not permit the squadron to reconnoiter all the way to the designated phase line. However, it was able to make it to Phase Line CODY before the aircraft had to return to base. The squadron encountered no enemy forces. Wallace now knew that no significant Iraqi force could threaten his far western flank as he moved through the Karbala Gap toward Baghdad.

The 82nd Airborne Division Clears As Samawah (31 March – 6 April)

As Samawah had been a thorn in V Corps' side since the very beginning of the war. The 3-7 CAV, leading the corps' attack, had fought a tough fight there, as had the following task force, 3rd BCT's TF 2-7 IN.[72] Later the 3rd BCT defeated a long series of attacks launched from the city against the division's vulnerable and vital supply lines. The 2nd Brigade of the 82nd Airborne had relieved the 3rd BCT on 28 March and assumed the mission to keep the Iraqis from interfering with the logistics flow north. Colonel Arnie Bray's brigade would now remove the thorn by entering the town and clearing it once and for all as part of the five simultaneous V Corps attacks.

Colonel Bray felt ready for the task. He had no illusions about the fight and no pre-conceived notions about the enemy. Bray believed the enemy would fight differently than he expected. Bray's conviction stemmed from two rotations at the NTC, two more at the CMTC, and a fifth at the NTC as part of a Joint Forces Command exercise called *MILLENNIUM CHALLENGE*. In each of these experiences, along with his experiences in Bosnia and Panama, Bray learned that the adversary seldom behaves as expected. In short, the opposing forces cheat—they never play by the rules. Bray found that true again at As Samawah where the enemy "used mosques, fired from hospitals, used ambulances to resupply. They would surrender with a white flag and then duck behind a vehicle and fire. They took civilians and used them as hostages."[73] Bray anticipated this, telling his troops on arrival in Kuwait, "You know what? This damned OPFOR (enemy) cheats just like the guys back at CMTC."[74] Bray's comparison of the enemy to what the troops call the "lying, cheating, stealing OPFOR" is not unusual. Most commanders and troops found that their training centers replicated the enemy far better than they expected and, in any case, gave them fair warning of the possibility. Bray made no judgments about the enemy's behavior, but neither did it surprise him. He described it as "that is home field advantage."[75]

Ultimately Bray experienced each of these "OPFOR" tricks for himself, but he first learned of them from 3rd ID. Bray and his brigade had planned nearly every conceivable contingency for which they might be used from sudden regime collapse to operations on islands in the Gulf. One thing was always clear to him and the brigade—they would go north. Lieutenant General McKiernan made that plain when he briefed the 82nd's leadership in early March. According to Bray, McKiernan described the options for the 82nd as either the regime collapses and the 82nd is used to secure the area or the regime fights and the 82nd goes forward to "secure the LOCs, bridges or other things but you got to go north. The only constant is that you got to go north." [76] Bray anticipated the LOC security mission to be his most likely because at the CFLCC "rock drill" in Camp Doha in late February, General Wallace brought it up for discussion.[77] Getting the word to go north therefore came as no surprise. Every echelon of command from CFLCC to Bray's battalions ruminated on and planned for the possibility of committing the paratroopers to secure LOCs.

Bray arrived in the area of operations on the evening of 26 March. The following day he relieved Colonel Dan Allyn's 3rd BCT of responsibility for As Samawah. Allyn handed off TF 1-41 IN, good combat information on the town and introduced Bray to special forces troops operating in the area. The special forces troops also introduced Bray to "other government agency folks."[78] Bray now found what every unit that remained in the same area for a few days did. Units in contact produce combat information and are able to develop intelligence about an area over time. Generally in Operation IRAQI FREEDOM, units had by this time garnered information that proved accurate so that they could act on that information with confidence, as the 101st did in An Najaf. For example, on the basis of radar data and firing incidents, Colonel Allyn advised Bray that the enemy in As Samawah had about 20 mortars. Bray confirmed that by destroying approximately 20 mortars and the attacks ceased.[79] Bray's task ultimately included clearing As Samawah, but it began with guidance to open Highway 8 to coalition use. The end state from General Swannack was clear as well. According to Bray, Swannack said, "I don't want anybody or anything to touch a US or coalition force along this road." [80] Abundantly clear guidance and not attainable if the enemy remained in the southern part of the town.

The Approach

On the evenings of 29 and 30 March, the brigade probed As Samawah to gain information about enemy locations, dispositions, and intentions. The 3-325 Airborne Infantry Regiment (AIR) attacked from the southeast along with TF 1-41 IN. The units made good use of these initial attacks, learning how to integrate the light and heavy forces in urban terrain

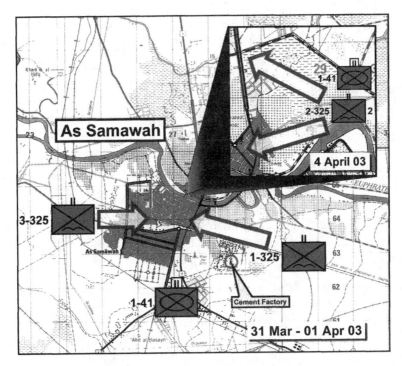

Figure 156. 82nd Airborne attacks in and around As Samawah

and confirming the superiority of US forces at night. The 3-325 AIR found that moving into positions at night to engage enemy forces when they moved at first light was an effective tactic. These probing attacks typically provoked Iraqi mortar and RPG fire, but the paratroopers countered with mortar and artillery fire of their own, with much greater effect. The first night's combat resulted in 14 enemy KIA and 3 WIA at a cost of one American WIA. More important, the brigade developed intelligence with each of these attacks. Generally, the heavy troops developed information on Iraqi TTP that saved the infantry from learning it on foot or in HMMWVs.[81]

The Attack

Beginning on the morning of 30 March, the brigade conducted a series of simultaneous limited attacks from the east, west, and south of the city. Colonel Bray based his plan on intelligence the brigade S2, Major Michael Marti, assembled from earlier operations, the special forces teams, and from local Iraqi citizens. These attacks and the earlier probes resulted in the brigade learning the local patterns of operation. According to Major Marti, these patterns were straightforward. At the outskirts of town the Iraqis, and perhaps some Syrians, employed suicidal attacks. In the city they fought house to house, employing human shields, and near the bridge over the Euphrates the paramilitary troops employed RPGs fired in volleys and mortars registered on the road and bridge. Marti observed, "They never changed the way they fought, so we were able to use appropriate tactics to counter. Fighting started at 0800 local every day and then stopped at 1800. It was like they were punching a clock like Wile E. Coyote in the cartoon." [82] Marti believed that the intelligence overlay provided to the 2nd Brigade by the 3rd ID's 1-30 IN proved invaluable in helping to discern patterns they could exploit. Based on what they learned from the 3rd ID, SOF troops operating in As Samawah, and on their own, Colonel Bray and his staff concluded they needed to focus on the Ba'ath Party leadership. Accordingly, they targeted and struck sites where they perceived Ba'ath command and control nodes would be.[83]

The attacks of 30 March and earlier probes prepared the brigade for the main attack to seize the city and the bridges to the north. Driving the enemy north of the river would preclude ground attacks against Highway 8. TF 1-41 IN, which had two mechanized infantry companies but no tank company, manned checkpoints south of the town and made some limited advances north. The 1-325 AIR attacked from the east, and 3-325 AIR attacked from the west to draw out the Iraqi defenders and kill them.[84] A special forces "A-Team", with considerable experience gained during operations in Afghanistan the year before, provided valuable targeting and intelligence support. The enemy in As Samawah attempted to reinforce with fresh troops coming down from the north along Highway 8. The AC-130 gunships and Air Force A-10 CAS aircraft hit targets north of the river, attacking these reinforcing units and the marshaling sites the Iraqis were using.

The brigade began its assault on 31 March to cut off Iraqi ground access to Highway 8, with the 1st and 3rd Battalions of the 325th AIR attacking from the east and west. TF 1-41 IN attacked from the southeast while simultaneously securing the ground LOCs south of As Samawah. CAS and AC-130 gunships also supported the attack.[85] *Kiowa Warriors* from division provided support as well. The light attack helicopters proved effective in attacking point targets in the city. In one instance, one of the companies identified an enemy mortar position to an attack pilot by first having him locate a particular blue door and then describing the target location in respect to the blue door. The pilot and some his friends destroyed the mortar position.[86] Although the Iraqis fought back with determination, the brigade continued to make steady progress advancing deliberately. The 1-325 AIR executed the initial thrust seizing a toehold on the city's southeastern outskirts. The troops encountered particularly stiff resistance when they stormed a cement factory the paramilitaries were using as a forward observation point and a weapons cache. The paratroopers supported the assault using their .50-caliber sniper rifles, to pick off defenders from great distances. They also fired TOW missiles to destroy a Ba'ath Party headquarters and against an Iraqi sniper in a tall smokestack near the cement factory.[87]

Many of the local Iraqi civilians did not leave the area during the fight. At one point, 4 hours into C/1-325 AIR's attack on the cement factory, battalion Command Sergeant Major Ortiz and his driver, Specialist Hutto, watched two mortar rounds pass directly over their heads, landing in the center of a flock of sheep and several shepherds that had not moved away from the area. In fact, both the sheep and shepherds were seemingly unconcerned about the battle raging around them. Sadly, the Iraqi mortar rounds killed several sheep and wounded two of the shepherds.[88]

The two battalions' pincer movements into the city appeared to force some pro-Saddam forces to flee from the north end of As Samawah. However, the "All Americans" closed the trap by using the division's *Kiowa Warrior* helicopters to attack the fleeing men and vehicles with accurate rocket and machine gun fires.[89] More important, by sunset on 31 March Bray's paratroopers had driven the Iraqi defenders away from Highway 8. At this point in the fighting, Bray felt frustrated by having inadequate intelligence from inside the town. The special forces troopers had not penetrated into As Samawah, so most of what they reported came from a contact in the town. Bray did have contact with one of the local tribal chiefs, who swore if Bray got tanks in town that he (the sheik) would produce 600 fighters of his own. In the end, Bray delivered, but the sheik did not. Still, information improved daily as the troops penetrated As Samawah.[90]

Squeezing As Samawah

On 1 April, the attacks continued against objectives within indirect-fire range of the corps' LOCs. The 2-325 AIR, which had arrived at As Samawah on 31 March, participated in this attack. The commander and staff had planned their operation in the 1-325 AIR headquarters only 3 ½ hours before going into action. On 2 April, 2-325 AIR then feinted westward along the river toward the bridges. This attack drew concentrated machine gun and mortar fire from Iraqi forces north of the river. The battalion estimated that it killed about 50 Iraqi fighters.[91] During this series of limited objective attacks, the brigade estimated that it killed from 300 to 400 Iraqis and destroyed approximately 30 civilian trucks mounting heavy machine guns.[92]

On 3 April, the brigade conducted several attacks within the city, while the long-range weapons of TF 1-41 IN's Bradleys contained the Iraqis attempting to exit the city to the south. Although he tried to avoid attacking hospitals, Colonel Bray had to launch an attack against one on the west side of town that was being used as a support area for the enemy. The soldiers also engaged a paramilitary force assembling on an athletic field, using *Kiowa Warriors*, field artillery, and CAS. TF 1-41 IN eventually drove through the city all the way to the bank of the Euphrates River.

Seizing the Bridges

On 4 April, the brigade ordered 2-325 AIR and TF 1-41 IN to seize the key bridges over the Euphrates River. Taking the bridges would enable convoys to move through As Samawah instead of bypassing it, fully opening up the LOC. At 0335, following a 30-minute mortar and artillery preparation, TF 1-41 IN attacked, followed by 2-325 AIR. Their combined attack flushed the Iraqi soldiers into streets and buildings on the northern outskirts of the city, where they were picked off in house-to-house combat. The Iraqis either surrendered or were shot. Shots from men in a taxi crossing the bridge crackled just a few feet from the US soldiers. The Americans returned fire and destroyed the taxi before it could escape across the Euphrates.[93]

"We have people surrendering in this next building," an 82nd Airborne unit commander called over the radio. In another radio transmission, a soldier announced discovering three Iraqi artillery pieces. By midday, three plumes of oily smoke from destroyed Iraqi vehicles drifted across the skyline.[94] Three US soldiers were wounded in the fighting and dozens of Iraqi soldiers were killed or wounded. Several civilians, wounded in the assault, sought medical help from US troops after the fighting.

The attack was successfully concluded, and the Bradleys of TF 1-41 IN moved north to set up blocking positions along Highway 8 toward Ar Rumaythah.[95] For much of the night, an Air Force AC-130 gunship pounded Iraqi positions along the north side of the river. The sound of .50-caliber machine guns, grenades, and *Hellfire* missiles from *Kiowa* helicopters firing on the Iraqi paramilitary soldiers rang through the city.[96] Seizing the bridges across the Euphrates kept the Iraqis from sending more fighters and supplies into the southern part of the city. The 2nd BCT now turned its attention to attacking north along Highway 8, toward Ad Diwaniyah.[97]

The protracted fighting in As Samawah apparently drew enemy forces down to the south, denuding Ar Rumaythah of Iraqi fighters. The townsfolk there threw the Ba'ath Party officials out of the town and celebrated the arrival of the American paratroopers.[98] By 6 April, organized resistance in the area collapsed and the townspeople came out in mass.

Setting the Baghdad Cordon

The 3rd ID planned operations for tomorrow [1 April 2003] will begin with a 2100Z LD by 3rd Brigade to isolate Karbala from the east. Two hours later, 1st Brigade will [depart] and 1-30 IN will follow. The 1st Brigade will have a TF screen to the east along the Euphrates River and a TF seize/secure Objective PEACH. 3-7 CAV will then collapse screen and move through the gap and form a new screen to the northwest. Once the screen is set, 2nd Brigade, on order, will pass through 1st Brigade and continue the attack to SAINTS and complete the destruction of the *Medina* Division.

The corps commander asked the division what were its plans if the division receives a chemical attack in Karbala. The division commander said they have numerous preplanned decon sites, but in the short run they would continue the mission and decon at the first opportunity.

The corps commander asked if there would be any combat power left between Karbala and An Najaf once the 3rd ID attacks. The 3rd ID plan is to keep two Linebacker [Bradley Stinger Fighting Vehicles] companies back to keep LOCs open.

The corps commander said he is not concerned about the fighting strength of the 3rd ID but that he has concerns about the logistics tail of the 3rd ID.

The corps commander asked how many [days of supply] the 3rd ID has to go forward with. The 3rd ID commander said most units have six [days of supply] and some have up to eight.

> Scribe notes of Lieutenant General Wallace's
> meeting with 3rd ID senior leaders
> 31 March 2003, 1715.

With the Iraqis off-balance from the cumulative effects of the five simultaneous attacks, the 3rd ID now prepared to execute the corps' main effort—breaching the Karbala Gap and attacking Republican Guard forces directly. Although the combined effects of Army aviation deep strikes and unrelenting Air Force strikes appeared to have weakened the *Medina* division, Major General Blount and Lieutenant General Wallace expected its remnants to present a credible threat. Moreover, the gap also marked the boundary for the Iraqi's self-declared "Red Zone," where intelligence reporting indicated Saddam had authorized chemical weapon strikes to check the advance. Thus, facing an expected combined-arms threat heavily reinforced with artillery, a ubiquitous paramilitary threat, and the potential for chemical weapons, the 3rd ID attacked north.

What followed was an exercise in command initiative, momentum, and classic exploitation of success. The 3rd ID did not find a coherent *Medina* Division capable of a coordinated defense. Rather, any organized conventional resistance was smaller than company-size. Much of the Iraqi equipment, although well placed in prepared positions, was abandoned. While the paramilitary troops continued to attack out of the towns, Karbala in particular, there were not as many as the division had seen in As Samawah and An Najaf. And, finally, the Iraqis did not employ chemical weapons. Thus once through the gap, the division continued on to Objective PEACH, a bridge on the Euphrates, crossed the river and advanced into objectives SAINTS, LIONS, and TITANS in a continuous series of attacks.

However, enemy intentions remained unclear to the division and corps as the events unfolded. Uncertainty abounded as to what available information and events said about the Iraqi defenses in and around Baghdad. Yet instead of slowing his division's tempo to better assess and understand the enemy situation, Major General Blount pushed forward relentlessly. As the division advanced through the Karbala Gap to Objectives SAINTS and LIONS, he accelerated the attack in order to exploit success. As the BCTs achieved each objective faster than projected, Blount and Wallace worked to keep the Iraqis off-balance and unable to respond effectively. Of course, they balanced aggressiveness against uncertainty stemming from what they did not know, but both understood the value of retaining the initiative. Aggressive and persistent attacks appear to have prevented the Iraqis from ever regaining their balance or their ability to operate coherently. The Iraqi's best-prepared defense of their most valuable piece of terrain—Baghdad—crumbled and did so rapidly.

Breaching the "Red Zone": Karbala Gap (2-3 April)

Yes, the American troops have advanced farther. This will only make it easier for us to defeat them.

Iraqi Information Minister
Mohammed Saeed al-Sahhaf,
"Baghdad Bob"

The Karbala Gap was, in military parlance, "key terrain." A narrow corridor with little room to maneuver, the Karbala Gap still offered the best high-speed avenue of approach to Baghdad. This gateway to outer Baghdad would also serve as the main supply route once the division and corps established the cordon positions. The Iraqis also realized this, and planned to defend at the gap with the *Medina* Division, eventually reinforcing with other Republican Guard units as the *Medina* withered under coalition strikes. However, the actual Iraqi disposition was hard to discern with clarity. The mixture of units and the confusion about whether any specific unit would fight, run, hide, or just evaporate, made it difficult to gauge accurately the conventional threat in the gap.[99] What is clear and is proven by the captured map discussed earlier is that the Iraqi defense shifted with more focus to the south, thus leaving the Karbala Gap lightly defended.

Moreover, the town of Karbala, on the eastern shoulder of the gap, promised to be a threat similar to that experienced at An Najaf and As Samawah. For these reasons, the 3rd ID had to fight its way through the gap, defeat any defending Iraqi conventional forces that stood between it and the city, and isolate and eventually neutralize any paramilitary threat to the force or the LOCs.

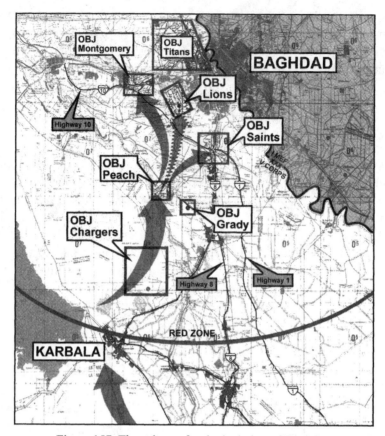

Figure 157. The scheme for the isolation of Baghdad

The division developed a relatively simple scheme of maneuver. The 3rd BCT would lead the attack with the mission of isolating the town of Karbala. As from the start, the plan intended for units to avoid entering the built-up areas that offered the paramilitary defenders obvious advantages. The 3rd BCT would isolate the eastern portion of Karbala, while 1st BCT would follow to isolate the western portion and seize key bridges on Highway 28 and a dam on the western side of the gap, designated Objective MUSCOGEE. Once it seized the dam, the 1st BCT would continue on, attacking through Objective CHARGERS slightly north of Karbala, where it expected to find the remnants of a *Medina* brigade. Finally, the plan required the 1st BCT to seize Objective PEACH, the division's real crossing site over the Euphrates River.

The 2nd BCT would leave Objective MURRAY, its previous feint objective, to follow 1st BCT and cross the Euphrates at PEACH to continue the attack on the east side of the river. After crossing the river, the 2nd BCT planned to seize Objective SAINTS, located at the intersection of Highways 1 and 8 about 15 kilometers south of the Baghdad city center. When he deemed the time right, Perkins planned to use one or more task forces to attack south from SAINTS toward Objective BALDWIN and then Objective CASEY to destroy Iraqi units located east of the river.

The division scheme of maneuver required 3-7 CAV to move through the gap and maneuver to the northwest to protect the 3rd ID's western flank. The division was concerned about a possible counterattack by the *Hammurabi* Division, then located to the west of Baghdad. The intended end state for these attacks envisioned 2nd BCT across the Euphrates, 1st BCT at the crossing site and prepared to attack north to Objective LIONS, and 3rd BCT containing Karbala. Once the 101st arrived to relieve 3rd BCT at Karbala, the 3rd would cross the river at PEACH and attack north to seize Objective TITANS to isolate the western side of Baghdad.

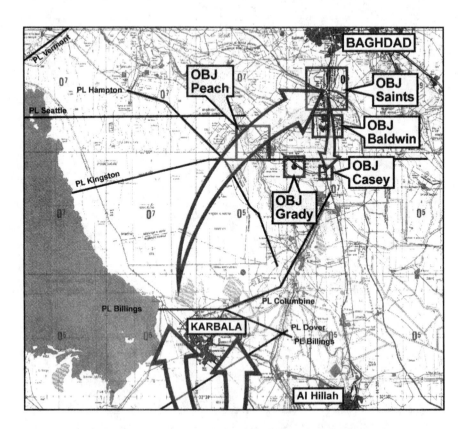

Figure 158. Scheme of maneuver from Karbala Gap through Objective PEACH

Launching the Attack

Having rearmed and refitted from the fight around As Samawah, 3rd BCT led 3rd ID's attack. Expecting a possible chemical attack, the division wore overgarments designed to protect against chemical weapons. At midnight on 1 April, TF 2-69 AR initiated the 3rd BCT's attack to isolate Karbala. TF 2-69 AR conducted a forward passage of lines through 2nd BCT and attacked to isolate the eastern side of the city. The TF 2-69 AR met minimal contact while working through the severely restrictive wetlands to the east of Karbala. TF 2-69 AR eventually established a blocking position on a paved road running south of Highway 9.[100]

At 0200 on 2 April, 1st BCT attacked with TF 3-69 AR on the right and TF 3-7 IN on the left to isolate the western side of Karbala and seize Objective MUSCOGEE. The brigade seized two crossing sites and then moved to contain Karbala from the west. They made contact with dismounted forces on the western outskirts of Karbala, fighting through the resistance quickly in an effort to get through the gap during the night. At 0533, TF 3-69 AR killed numerous dismounts and destroyed a mortar platoon in the vicinity of the Highway 28 bridge on Objective MUSCOGEE.[101] By 0600, TF 3-69 AR had seized both the bridge and dam on MUSCOGEE and cleared a minefield blocking Highway 8. Throughout the fight, an attack helicopter company supported 1st BCT by attacking targets north of the dam at MUSCOGEE and artillery east of the dam.[102]

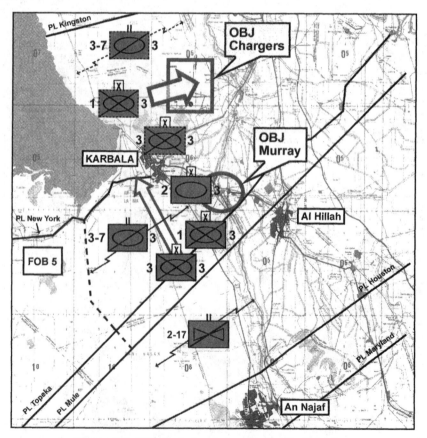

Figure 159. V Corps' plan to breach the Karbala Gap

As the battalions' parallel attacks progressed, the Iraqis responded with rocket and howitzer fire from the east. The brigade called in CAS to deal with the rocket artillery, and DIVARTY fired counterbattery missions in response to radar acquisitions. CAS and counterbattery silenced the Iraqi artillery, helping to protect the brigades as they transited the gap. Air Force and Navy aircraft flying in the vicinity of Karbala also contributed when they identified and destroyed an armored column moving from the north side of the city toward the dam on Objective MUSCOGEE.[103]

Exploiting Success

Sensing an opportunity, Brigadier General Lloyd Austin, the 3rd ID ADC-M, decided to maintain the momentum by continuing the attack to the river. He directed 3rd BCT to relieve 1st BCT at Karbala so that 1st BCT could attack to seize the bridges at Objective PEACH. Consequently, 3rd BCT's TF 1-30 IN relieved 1st BCT's TF 2-7 IN. At 0648 on 2 April, 3rd BCT assumed sole responsibility both for isolating Karbala and securing Objective MUSCOGEE. The division ordered the 937th EN group forward and attached it to 3rd BCT to control traffic flow over the bridge at Objective MUSCOGEE. With the gap secured and Karbala isolated, 3-7 CAV moved through at 0854 en route to protect the northwest flank. The squadron had its ground troops in their initial position within 2½ hours.[104]

The 1st and 3rd BCTs' quick successes in isolating Karbala and moving through the gap had cascading consequences, allowing Major General Blount to accelerate the 2nd BCT's timeline also. However, to do that the brigade had to change its route. Now, rather than following 1st BCT through the gap along congested roads, 2nd BCT planned a new route east of Karbala. Theoretically, this would allow the brigade to get through PEACH more quickly, increasing the pressure on the Iraqi defenses east of the Euphrates River. The 2nd BCT started moving north on 2 April.[105]

> **Finding the Way**
>
> The canal road became untrafficable and [I] rerouted the rest of the brigade. Each unit ended up moving on a different route. . . and attacked [through PEACH to SAINTS] from the march. The brigade did not close again until we got to Objective SAINTS.
>
> This would not have been the. . . course of action anyone would have selected. Everyone was under contact—1-64 AR destroyed several motorized rifle companies going through Karbala; 1-15 got into contact at 2100 when it turned into a swamp; and 4-64 turned west and got into a firefight. . . [but] the intent was to maintain momentum.
>
> What I think helped was that we had FBCB2 and BFT; I could track where the brigade was on all the "snail trails." I could conduct time-distance calculations to determine how long it would take for units to cover their respective routes.
>
> Colonel David Perkins
> Commander, 2nd BCT, 3rd ID
> command briefing, 18 May 2003

Unfortunately, the move to the east proved to be a tougher task than either Blount or Colonel Perkins had anticipated. The 2nd BCT quickly discovered that the new routes could not support its movement. The road east of Karbala was cratered in earlier fighting, and there were still paramilitary forces in the zone. The ubiquitous irrigation canals, soft soil, and narrow, unimproved secondary roads further impeded movement. The brigade bogged down, and at 1634, Perkins elected to turn the trailing four-fifths of his brigade around. They retraced their route and moved to the west of Karbala to get to PEACH.[106] Thus, only the lead units, TF 1-15

IN and the tactical command post—aided by an armored vehicle-launched bridge (AVLB)—negotiated the route east of Karbala. The remainder of the BCT, TF 3-15 IN, TF 1-64 AR, TF 1-64 AR, 1-9 FA, and the 26th FSB moved around to the west of Karbala on Highway 28. At one point, Perkins had units moving along four separate routes, all in enemy contact. As a result, 2nd BCT did not reach Objective PEACH until 3 April.[107]

Crossing the Euphrates: Objective PEACH (2 April)

While 2nd BCT maneuvered to take advantage of the division's success around Karbala, 1st BCT initiated its attack to secure PEACH, the crossing site over the Euphrates. At 1229 on 2 April, 1st BCT's TF 3-69 AR attacked from Objective CHARGERS, north of the Karbala area, to seize the bridge on Objective PEACH. Meanwhile, 3rd BCT continued to defeat enemy forces in and around

> ### Just like Vietnam
>
> We had just come out of a desert [going] through the Karbala Gap, through their [version of the] National Training Center and now the ground was like the middle of Vietnam—palm trees, rice paddies, and canals. We had done a good map reconnaissance with 1-meter resolution and nothing prepared us for this. We could not get off the road and had two tanks get mired.
>
> Lieutenant Colonel Rock Marcone
> Commander, 3-69 Armor
> interview 15 May 2003 by Lieutenant Colonel David Manning

Karbala, holding the right shoulder of the gap open while providing traffic control for the division's movement through the gap.[108]

Forty minutes later, the brigade reported that TF 3-69 AR, *Power*, had reached the southern edges of PEACH, and TF 2-7 IN had arrived in EA HANNAH. Lieutenant Colonel Marcone, the

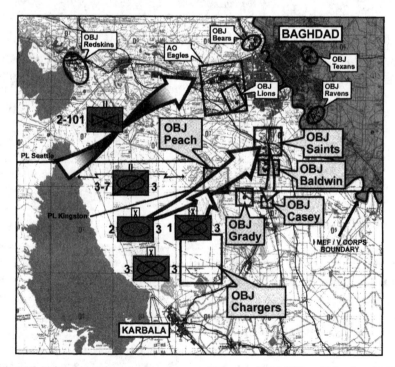

Figure 160. V Corps' Scheme of maneuver, Objective PEACH to Objective SAINTS

commander of TF 3-69 AR, planned the attack in two stages. First he planned to seize ground on the near side of the river from which he could suppress enemy on the far side and generate smoke to obscure the crossing site. Once Marcone had his suppression forces established, he intended for his assault forces to attack through the crossing site on the Euphrates and expand the bridgehead while securing other key terrain to facilitate follow-on V Corps operations to Baghdad.[109]

Marcone sent his scouts out first to develop the situation. The scouts immediately got into a fight beyond their means to win. The enemy had positioned a battalion of infantry on the western approaches to the bridges at PEACH. There were also elements of an enemy reconnaissance battalion in the area. Marcone committed his Alpha Company to clear the zone along the river up to the near side of the crossing site and used his mortars to support the assault to the crossing site. 1-41 Field Artillery Battalion moved with and fired in direct support of TF 3-69 AR. Marcone also had a company of *Apaches* flying in support of his assault. Marcone and his staff coupled their mortars and artillery with CAS to suppress the defenders as his troops approached the bridge. The task force also fired artillery where it estimated the enemy would position troops to fire demolitions to drop the bridge. TF 3-69 AR had learned from defending the bridge at JENKINS just how the Iraqis prepared bridges for demolition. At JENKINS, the Iraqis employed demolition-firing mechanisms apparently made in Germany to German army specifications. The task force analyzed the gear and reached some general conclusions about how far from the bridge the enemy engineers could, or would be. By map analysis, Marcone and his engineers reached some conclusions about where the trigger teams might be positioned, and so the redlegs from 1-41 FA leveled that ground with deadly accurate artillery fires.[110]

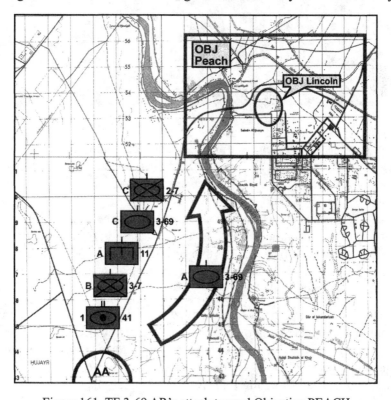

Figure 161. TF 3-69 AR's attack toward Objective PEACH

Electronic attacks against enemy command nets sought to degrade the Iraqis' ability to offer a coordinated defense. By 1500, TF 3-69 AR had secured the west shore of the bridges and A/11 Engineers began to check them for demolitions. The *Apaches* and CAS continued to engage targets on the far shore in support of the operation.[111] As TF 3-69 AR approached the bridge, the supporting artillery executed a fire plan, mixing smoke and high explosives to suppress the enemy and obscure their view of the task force as it closed on the near side. Marcone's Alpha Company "scraped" the enemy off the northwest bank while Captain Todd Kelly's troopers of Team C/2-7 IN secured the near side of the bridge and swept the eastern bank of enemy forces. Team C/3-69 AR and Team B/3-7 IN staged and prepared to assault the far side of the crossing site when called upon.

Figure 162. Aerial photograph of Objective PEACH

Just before 1600, the engineers of A/11 EN BN under the command of Captain Dan Hibner, having identified wires on the bridge abutments, conducted an assault river crossing with soldiers in RB-15 inflatable boats. They intended to disarm the explosives from both sides of the river. However, at 1615, before they could clear the bridges, the Iraqis fired the charges designed to drop the bridge. The explosion damaged the northern span, but perhaps because of the preparation fires, the southern span remained useable with three lanes. The engineers cut the remainder of the wires to prevent further destruction. Marcone sent infantry across the bridge to secure the far side. Three company teams raced across the bridge on the heels of the infantry, crossing in less than a half-hour.[112]

The Iraqis still had one card to play. As the assault force went in, the Iraqis fired perhaps as many as 200 152mm howitzers rounds on the near side support-by-fire position from which Team A/3-69 AR supported the assault. The barrage fell in minutes, suggesting that the Iraqis had massed one or more battalions and fired a time-on-target mission of several volleys. The tank company/team moved out without injury, but all of its tanks and Bradleys had scars. During the enemy's barrage, Marcone's smokers, 5/92 Chemical Company, courageously remained in position near the river to provide critical smoke cover for the soldiers working on the bridge and displaced only after their mission was completed. Because the brigade had its counterfire radar oriented elsewhere, it obtained no acquisitions, so the task force had no means of exacting revenge.[113]

Figure 163. Engineers surveying bridge at Operation PEACH

Figure 164. In anticipation of Operation Iraqi Freedom, the Iraqi army built bunkers like this one along the bridges and highways

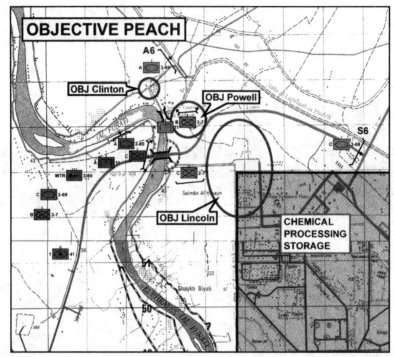

Figure 165. TF 3-69 AR attacks to seize Objective PEACH and expand the bridgehead

To expand the bridgehead, the task force had to control the road net that brought traffic to the bridge. This was a daunting task for four maneuver companies. Essentially two roads formed two sides of an equilateral triangle with the tip at the main bridge. One of the roads came into the bridgehead generally from the northeast and the other from the southeast. Accordingly, the task force continued the attack until it seized both bridges and defensible terrain encompassing the two major roads. Marcone identified an intersection about 5 kilometers east of the main bridge as key terrain. As he put it, "Charlie Company comes across and he has to get this piece of ground. If he owns this nobody can get to us quickly."[114] Accordingly, Marcone ordered Captain Jared Robbins and his tank company team east to secure a blocking position they named S6.

Once Robbins headed east, Captain Dave Benton's mechanized company team crossed and turned north, rolling up from the flank what turned out to be a reconnaissance company of the *Medina* Division's reconnaissance battalion. The *Medina's* reconnaissance troops had oriented to the west so Benton's Bradleys and tanks quickly destroyed the Iraqi BMDs and seized Objective POWELL and the near side of the canal bridge

TeleEngineering and Bridge Expansion

The combat engineers consulted with bridging experts by "TeleEngineering"[115] and began effecting repairs to the bridges at Objective PEACH immediately. By noon the next day, the 299 Medium Ribbon Bridge Company attached to the 54th Engineer Battalion was well on the way to putting a float bridge across the river. Eventually a medium girder bridge was also placed over the damaged portion of the existing bridge. Subsequently the 54th's B Company also emplaced an assault float bridge across as well.[116] It was very clear that this route would become the lifeline of the V Corps during the fight for Baghdad.

south of Objective CLINTON. With the canal bridge now under his control, Marcone sent Hibner's engineers to determine whether the bridge could be used. It could, so Captain Chuck O'Brian's tank company team moved from its support-by-fire position and assaulted over the canal bridge and through Objective CLINTON to support-by-fire position A6, north of the canal. Marcone retained a force composed of dismounted infantry and engineers to defend the Euphrates bridge.[117]

Troops rummaging around the battlefield made several discoveries. First, they confirmed that a light infantry battalion and elements of a reconnaissance battalion had indeed defended the area around the Euphrates bridge. Next, among the destroyed combat vehicles, Marcone's troops recovered the operational map discussed earlier. The map showed that reconnaissance battalion had been employed in an economy of force mission (insert pg C-10). More important, the map illustrated the coalition main effort as coming from the south on the east bank of the Euphrates. This was tangible evidence that the feints of the five simultaneous attacks had some effect on the enemy dispositions and assessment of coalition intentions. Reflecting on the map and the Iraqi perception of likely coalition actions, Colonel Will Grimsley observed, "we actually out thought him."[118]

To the south, 3rd BCT continued to root out enemy forces in and around Karbala—primarily dismounted soldiers armed with small arms and mortars. Clearing the zone permitted the division to move logistics traffic freely through the Gap. Simultaneously, 2nd BCT continued to work its way through and around restrictive terrain to get to its attack position southwest of PEACH. From there it would mount the subsequent attack to Objective SAINTS. Seizing PEACH enabled the division to cross the Euphrates where it chose. Seizing SAINTS had greater implications. SAINTS would cut off Baghdad from the south and cut off forces in the south from the regime in Baghdad. It also established the first part of the cordon around the city.

Stephen Hicks, US Army

Figure 166. Floating bridge emplaced to support additional crossings just north of Objective PEACH

The Smoke Mission at Objective PEACH

After the 1st BCT passed through the Karbala Gap on 1 April, 5/92 Chemical Company, the division's organic smoke platoon, was task organized with C/2-7 IN. The smoke platoon's task and purpose were to provide smoke haze at Objective PEACH to screen the task force's movement over the Euphrates River. This would be the platoon's first smoke mission during the war.

At approximately 1500, as the platoon approached its primary smoke position northwest of the bridge, the artillery battalion fired smoke rounds but to no effect due to unstable weather conditions. Without this concealment, the smoke platoon occupied a position along a narrow unimproved road with steep slopes on either side. The road resembled a levee and did not permit lateral movement.

Regardless of the lack of concealment, at 1515, the platoon began pumping smoke. As the smoke screen built it drifted steadily toward the smoke objective, the bridge over the Euphrates. Bradleys and tanks began crossing the bridge while engaging the enemy, using their thermal sights to see through the thickening smoke.

One hundred meters to the north of the platoon's position, the soldiers detected several Iraqi soldiers dressed in civilian clothes along with several technical vehicles (pickup trucks). The platoon leader called in a spot report and several minutes later, an *Apache* helicopter arrived and engaged the enemy from directly above the platoon's position. At approximately the same time, the wind direction shifted so the platoon leader terminated the mission. Suddenly, the platoon began to receive indirect fire. The platoon moved out and rallied at the base of the bridge. Fortunately, no one was hurt.

Staff Sergeant Wells,
platoon sergeant, smoke platoon, 92nd Chemical Company,
interview 13 May 2003.

Sealing the South: Objective SAINTS (3-4 April)

Because of all of the trafficability difficulties encountered in attempting to move around Karbala to the east, 2nd BCT did not arrive at its attack position all at once. TF 1-15 closed at around 1900 on 2 April, but it was almost 6 hours before the next units arrived.[119] Finally at 0112 on 3 April, 2nd BCT reported moving to its assault position, with an anticipated start time of 0700 that morning.[120]

As Lieutenant Colonel Marcone waited on 2nd BCT, he prepared for the worst, having received intelligence that an Iraqi Republican Guard commando battalion would attack that night. Marcone prepared to defend the bridgehead as he had at Objective JENKINS in Al Kifl, "I did the same thing I did at Kifl (Objective JENKINS). I have defensive positions, I have an FPF and I have a CAS kill box."[121] In the end the Iraqis attempted a coordinated counterattack with a commando battalion and perhaps two brigades of Republican Guard troops. The attack began about 0300 on 3 April. Throughout the night Iraqis shelled the bridgehead, intermittently firing a round or two every 15 minutes. When the Iraqis attacked, the commandos came on foot from the north while the 10th Armored Brigade of the *Medina* Division attacked mounted from the south. Although the commandos did not attack with great energy, the 10th Armored Brigade did.

The Iraqi armored brigade advanced with a tank company forward, followed by approximately 50 M113 armored personnel carriers organized in two company formations advancing in staggered columns. Marcone's troops dispatched the lead three T-72s and the brigade withdrew. The *Medina*'s armored troops lost their Brigade commander KIA in one of the three T-72s but did not give up. Instead, over the next hour, they maneuvered to the east and, between 0430 and 0500, attacked the road junction Marcone had identified as key terrain. The task force fired the linear target originally planned as an FPF and opened the CAS kill box, destroying 15 tanks and 30 M113s by combining tank and Bradley fires, artillery and CAS across a depth of 15 kilometers. As Marcone put it, "By 0530 we were done."[122]

> ## Waiting at PEACH
>
> Two things stand out about the overnight halt at Objective PEACH. The first was the sudden appearance of a battery of MLRS from 1-39 FA [firing] a battery six at approximately 0200; the real surprise was that the battery was only about 300 meters from our positions when it fired.
>
> The second was the surrender of some 400 Iraqi soldiers at around 0600. It turns out that these individuals watched the better part of a brigade combat team pass through, spent the night holed up only 600 meters from the brigade TOC, and decided to surrender first thing in the morning to a passing element from TF 2-69.
>
> "No Shit, There We Were: The Official History of A/103rd MI BN Participation in Operation IRAQI FREEDOM"

Still on the move as Grimsley's troops destroyed the Iraqi counterattack, 2nd BCT reported its lead approaching the bridge on PEACH at 0841 on 3 April. Lieutenant Colonel Charlton's TF 1-15 IN led the way. Colonel Perkins moved with Charlton and his troops.[123] The brigade traveled in column with TF 1-64 AR and TF 4-64 AR trailing. The division now had the majority of 2nd BCT's combat power

> ## A Classic Commander's Dilemma
>
> At 3 in the morning, there was only one battalion ready to attack. [I] made the decision to go without the entire brigade consolidated. The intelligence we had received said the Hammurabi [Division] was repositioning south to take SAINTS and the airport ahead of us so we didn't have the freedom to wait. It was a classic commander's dilemma.
>
> Colonel David Perkins, commander, 2nd BCT, 3rd ID, command briefing, 18 May 2003.

across the Euphrates River. TF 3-15 IN, rather than following the rest of the brigade, conducted a relief in place of 1st BCT at Objective PEACH. There they secured the bridgehead, reporting to 54th Engineers, who acted as the crossing area headquarters. This freed 1st BCT to execute its on-order attack to Objective LIONS.[124]

Essentially, SAINTS was a rectangle that encompassed the intersections of Highways 1 and 8 south of Baghdad. Perkins intended to attack and clear SAINTS with TF 1-15 IN against an estimated Iraqi infantry brigade supported by tanks and BMPs. As Charlton's mechanized infantry task force cleared SAINTS from west to east, Perkins planned to peel off his two armored task forces to attack south along Highways 1 and 8. He intended for the armor task forces to sweep through and destroy the remnants of the *Medina* by rolling them up from the rear and to clear the seam between the V Corps and I MEF zones. Once the division released TF 3-15 IN from securing the bridge, he planned to have Lieutenant Colonel Stephen Twitty's troops attack south along the Euphrates to clean up any survivors from the *Medina*. The brigade had rehearsed and drilled all of these tasks weeks earlier in Kuwait.[125] It was good they had,

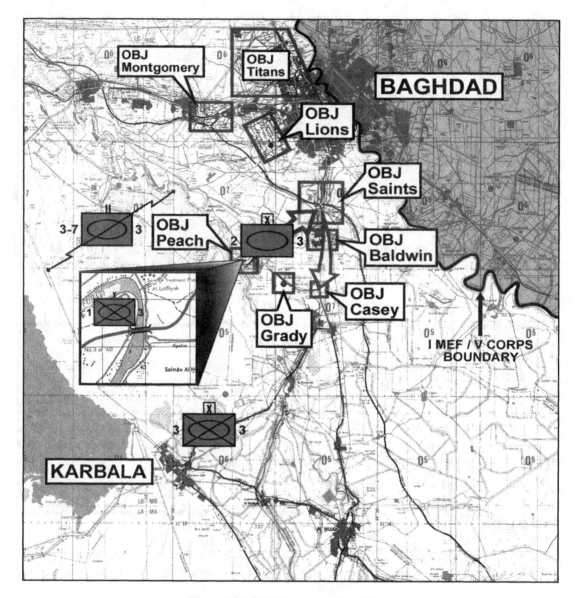

Figure 167. 2BCT attacks to SAINTS

since the brigade remained strung out from the march the night before. In fact, the brigade attacked to SAINTS straight from the march through Objective PEACH. The troops arrived at SAINTS, as one unit history put it, "smoked," but they knew what to do.

Within 20 minutes of crossing the Euphrates, Charlton's TF 1-15 IN reported contact with a platoon of T-72s and paramilitary forces in civilian vehicles.[126] After dispatching the tanks and paramilitary troops, the task force continued to advance against relatively light, but determined resistance, nearing SAINTS by 1017. On the approach to SAINTS, Charlton's troops overcame several RPG ambushes staged by irregular forces and small units of the *Nebuchadnezzar* Division. Fixed-wing air supported the attack by striking Iraqi forces defending within SAINTS itself.[127]

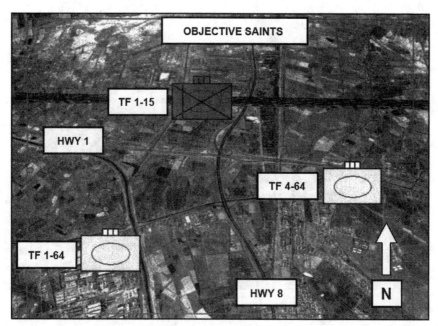

Figure 168. The 2nd BCT disposition on Objective SAINTS, displayed on an overhead photograph

TF 1-64 AR, *Rogue*, was fast approaching from the west, followed by 1-9 FA. Once across the river, the artillery occupied its preplanned position area to support the brigade's attack on Objective SAINTS. Because the position area was primarily heavily irrigated farmland, 1-9 FA deployed its howitzers in nonstandard firing positions along the road. As the artillery battalion cleared the position area for occupation, it captured 11 enemy soldiers and found a dump truck filled with small-arms, mortar, and RPG ammunition. Once in place, 1-9 FA fired 15 fire missions in direct support of the brigade's attack on Objective SAINTS, including six counterfire missions against enemy artillery firing on the brigade detected by counterbattery radar.[128]

TF 1-15 IN reached the center of Objective SAINTS about 1300, encountering heavy resistance from infantry, tanks, and other combat vehicles defending along the roads and the major highway interchange nearly in the center of the objective.[129] The task force established five blocking positions to secure SAINTS. A tank platoon from the task force moved into a blocking position on Highway 8 at the southern end of SAINTS, and at 1330 destroyed three T-72s on Highway 8. The brigade also received reports of more tanks coming south out of Baghdad. An hour later, TF 1-15 IN made contact with tanks in the palm groves on the northeast side of SAINTS and brought artillery fires and CAS in on them, as well as engaging them with TOW missiles. Many of the tanks and enemy fighting vehicles were well dug in, but there were others along Highway 8. Charlton's troops remained in contact throughout the day, destroying the defenders and defeating small-unit counterattacks.[130]

At 1245, just prior to TF 1-15 IN attacking into SAINTS, Major General Blount ordered Colonel Perkins to attack south to Objective BALDWIN and then CASEY as planned, but rather than remain, to return to SAINTS for the night. Blount's purpose was to destroy Iraqi forces south of SAINTS that may have repositioned in response to the V Corps' deceptive feints.

Mason Lowery, US Army

Figure 169. Iraqi tank burning in tree line at Objective SAINTS

Although intelligence reports indicated that most enemy forces oriented south on the east side of the river had either been destroyed or severely degraded by air strikes, Blount wanted to be sure.[131] Perkins separated from TF 1-15 to travel with the *Rogues* of TF 1-64, who would attack south on Highway 8 toward Objectives BALDWIN and CASEY. *Rogue* effected a forward passage in contact through the TF 1-15 tank platoon at the blocking position on Highway 8 and started south. *Rogue* reported very little contact until arriving at the village of Al Mahmudiya (Objective BALDWIN), where they surprised and destroyed seven T-72s, four BMPs, and a number of other vehicles literally in the streets of the town. The task force continued south, destroying numerous but mostly abandoned Iraqi combat vehicles dug into prepared fighting positions that were oriented to defend against a coalition attack from the south. Apparently, the Iraqis had repositioned at least some forces in response to the feints of the five simultaneous attacks. As *Rogue* returned north, it encountered and destroyed two more T-72s.[132]

The *Tuskers* of TF 4-64 AR followed 1-9 FA across the Euphrates at PEACH and then continued toward SAINTS. They found plenty of work on the way, destroying a menagerie of tanks, trucks, technical vehicles, and an old US Army Jeep. Even the task force's tactical operations center got into the action, destroying a T-55 in self-defense. Lieutenant Colonel DeCamp's task force traveled with its logistics units intermingled with the combat troops for protection, so everyone fought. They reached SAINTS after 1300, having killed about 40 enemy infantry and destroying 18 enemy vehicles, including 11 BMP s and two tanks. About 1500 the task force tactical operations center, one maneuver company, and the battalion field trains established a position in SAINTS east of Highway 8. C Company conducted the attack southeast on Highway 1 as Perkins had planned. The company established a blocking position on the eastern edge of SAINTS with one platoon and continued south with two platoons abreast. The two platoons advanced down the highway in staggered columns, with one platoon traveling on the southbound lanes and the other on the northbound lanes. The company command group and "Lightning 28," the Marine air and naval gunfire control team, followed the platoons. About 10 to 12 kilometers southeast of the Highway 1 and 8 interchange, the company made contact with an Iraqi mechanized infantry company that had assumed positions along the highway. Both lead tanks—C31 and C12—took heavy and accurate 30mm cannon fire from BMPs. Reacting to contact, both platoons maneuvered forward and destroyed 10 BMPs, 3 MTLBs, and numerous RPG teams, but not before taking "numerous" RPG and cannon fire hits themselves. Three tanks—C31, C32 and C11—took damage to their armor, but no rounds penetrated so C Company got away unscathed.[133]

At 1929, 2nd BCT reported all units moving to consolidate at SAINTS. The brigade defeated and largely destroyed what amounted to two battalions that opposed them in the north. After the fact, the brigade concluded that several different Iraqi units had defended on SAINTS. But, there did not seem to be any coherent, centralized Iraqi organization or command and control beyond the company or battalion level. By 0130 on 4 April, the brigade had closed on SAINTS, reporting very little enemy contact as the soldiers prepared for the next day.[134] During the evening's tactical commander's TACSAT update, Colonel Perkins reported a battle damage assessment summary of 33 T-72s, two T-62s, 19 T-55s, 12 MTLB armored vehicles, 50 artillery pieces, six BM-21 rocket launchers, 127 trucks destroyed, and 700 enemy soldiers killed. The 2nd BCT continued to clear the area and prepared to attack into Baghdad along Highway 8.[135]

Seizing SAINTS and completing the destruction of the *Medina* Division and other forces south of SAINTS effectively isolated Baghdad from the south. The brigade made several more sweeps to the south with the two armor task forces, and ultimately with TF 3-15. During these sweeps the brigade completed mopping up remnants of the *Medina* Division and other units that remained between SAINTS and Al Hillah from 3 to 6 April. "By crossing the Euphrates, rendering all enemy forces combat-ineffective, and seizing the key LOCs, the [2nd] BCT set the stage for the division to complete the cordon of the city and eventually assault into the capital."[136]

Sealing the West: Objective LIONS (3-5 April)

> "No! We have retaken the airport! There are no Americans there! I will take you there and show you! In one hour!"
>
> Iraqi Information Minister,
Mohammed Saeed al-Sahhaf
"Baghdad Bob"

Early on 3 April, as 2nd BCT moved through PEACH and attacked to seize SAINTS, the 1st BCT commander, Colonel Grimsley, called a meeting of his task force and battalion commanders at the brigade TAC to discuss their attack to seize Objective LIONS. Having accomplished the primary mission of seizing a crossing over the Euphrates at PEACH, it was time to consider the "on-order" task. Anticipating the possibility of continuing the attack, Lieutenant Colonel Smith, commander of the 11th Engineer Battalion, along with his operations officer, Major Garth Horne, and Captain James Lockridge from the battalion TAC, had already pulled the appropriate terrain products that they had produced before the start of the war. These products showed the multiple routes from PEACH to LIONS and the multiple water crossings involved to reach LIONS.[137]

Accelerating the Attack

During this meeting, Major General Blount and the division G3, Lieutenant Colonel Peter Bayer, arrived to consult with Grimsley. While Bayer and Grimsley anticipated attacking to LIONS the following morning, Blount wanted to move later that same day. According to Grimsley, "We thought we were going to spend a couple of days at PEACH quite frankly." but the CG advises, "We want you to go to LIONS, when can you go? Colonel Grimsley responds, "Sir 3 o'clock this afternoon, 4 o'clock at the latest."[138] Pete Bayer remembered this decision as important because it reflected General Blount's vision for the next few days. The previous day as Blount and Bayer watched Colonel Grimsley's troops attack into PEACH, the CG already had shifted his focus to considering an armored raid into Baghdad ending at LIONS. Blount wanted to turn the heat up and seize the airport in stride to sustain the initiative. This would also relieve pressure from 2nd BCT in SAINTS and give the division control of a key regime target as well as a location on the outskirts of Baghdad from which to launch further attacks into the city. Blount was thinking in the future, not in the present.[139]

The 3rd ID anticipated roughly a brigade-minus of Special Republican Guards left defending the airport, or rather Objective LIONS, as the corps named the turf that included the airport. The division also believed the 17th Brigade of the *Hammurabi* Division would

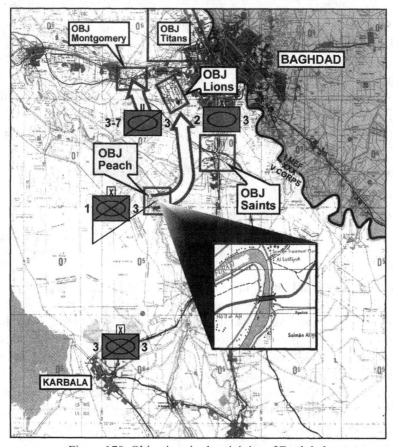

Figure 170. Objectives in the vicinity of Baghdad

relocate to defend the roads leading from the airport to the city, southwest of LIONS. The 8th Brigade of the *Hammurabi* Division remained north of Baghdad, with some elements of the *Adnan* Division cross-attached to defend the northern and northwestern approaches to the city. Additionally, the 3rd ID estimated an additional SRG battalion and two brigades of light infantry remained available to defend within Baghdad proper. Finally, they estimated an additional 15,000 paramilitary fighters would defend the city itself.[140]

In response to enemy units moving south, the 3-7 CAV had established a guard position in the vicinity of Objective MONTGOMERY, the intersection of Highways 1 and 10. Once 3-7 CAV had completed its passage through 1st BCT at PEACH and TF 3-15 IN had relieved 1st BCT of responsibility for securing the bridges, 1st BCT could begin its attack.[141]

Because the Iraqis had managed to damage part of the bridge at PEACH, Blount directed his engineers to open a second route over the Euphrates. The 54th Engineer Battalion, already controlling the crossing site, emplaced a ribbon bridge. 2nd BCT's TF 3-15 IN arrived the morning of the 3rd to relieve TF 3-69 AR of the defense of the bridgehead.[142] The conditions were now set for the 1st BCT to leave PEACH and attack to seize LIONS. TF 3-69 AR would lead the brigade, followed by TF 2-7 IN and then the remainder of the brigade.

Advancing the timetable for the attack wreaked havoc on the already congested crossing site. TF 3-15 IN was moving to relieve TF 3-69 AR from securing the bridge; TF 2-7 moved from north of HANNAH and passed over the bridge; and the medium ribbon bridge company moved forward to place the ribbon bridge in the water. All of this took place as 2nd BCT crossed the river. Consequently 1st BCT's forces arrived piecemeal at LIONS—TF 3-69 AR, TF 3-7 IN, and then finally TF 2-7. Blount understood the risk he took in not waiting to clear the traffic but felt the benefits outweighed the risk.[143]

Have a Good Fight -
The Decision to Seize the Baghdad Airport

Lieutenant Colonel Rick Carlson, as the 101st Airborne Division's liaison officer to the V Corps TAC, was in position to observe Lieutenant General Wallace's decision to have the 3rd Infantry Division seize the Baghdad International Airport.

The corps staff had been debating several options for the attack but had not yet made a firm recommendation. There were contingencies for the 101st to seize it by air assault. The staff had been considering sending the 3rd ID, but there was a concern that there might be heavy losses of vehicles and personnel in the dense urban setting.

On 3 April, Major General Blount, the commander of the 3rd Infantry Division, called Wallace on the radio (monitored in the corps TAC) and asked permission to initiate an attack on the airport immediately. Blount insisted that the 3rd ID was the right choice. He told Wallace, "Sir, we trained for this. . . We prepared for this…We're ready for this. We need to go now."

There was a pregnant pause on the radio channel and a hush in the TAC as everyone waited to hear the corps commander's decision. After several seconds, Wallace broke the suspense with his firm, confidence-building reply. . . "Have a good fight. Victory 6, OUT."

Lieutenant Colonel Rick Carlson,
101st Airborne Division liaison officer to V Corps
interview by Lieutenant Colonel (retired) Arthur Durante.

The Approach

True to his word, Grimsley had his brigade on the move shortly after 1500. At 1521 on 3 April, TF 3-69 AR's scouts, following closely behind 3-7 CAV, which continued on to MONTGOMERY, began reconnoitering the brigade's routes to LIONS.[144] The routes consisted mostly of paved two-lane roads through some small towns. The task force, traveling in a column, made its way through the towns, tight turns, and across narrow bridges that afforded ample opportunity for enemy ambush. About 10 kilometers south of Highway 1, the column received ineffective mortar fire, while the Iraqis attacked the head of the column with machine guns and RPGs. For all of these reasons, the approach march took longer than expected so the task force refueled en route to the objective.[145] At 1719, TF 3-69 AR finally moved onto Highway 1 and, at 1735, initiated preparatory fires onto LIONS.[146]

Lieutenant Colonel Marcone's troops continued their approach to a highway interchange approximately 3 kilometers to the southwest of the airfield, with the task force now in two columns, led by the *Bandits* of B/3-7 IN in the east and C/2-7 IN, *Rock*, in the west. From the interchange, the western column would launch to breach the wall around airfield. Approximately 15 feet tall, the masonry wall topped by concertina wire extended around most of the airport. Once *Rock* made a hole, the entire task force would move through it to clear the airport of the enemy.[147]

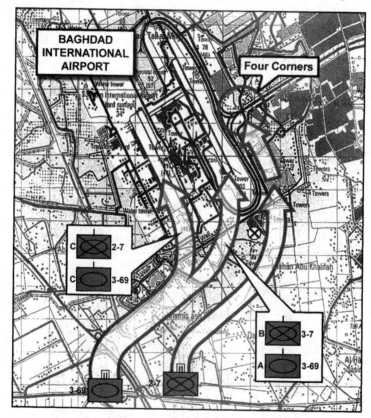

Figure 171. 1st BCT, 3rd Infantry Division's approach to BIAP

At 2115, TF 3-69 AR's combat trains turned off Highway 1 and started crossing a canal. A/3-69 maintenance team's HMMWV, carrying four people, toppled into the canal and came to rest upside down. The combat support soldiers immediately went to the aid of those in the HMMWV. Two soldiers did survive, but Alpha's team chief, Staff Sergeant Wilbur Davis, and Mr. Mike Kelly, an editor-at-large for *The Atlantic Monthly*, did not. The company trains regrouped after the rescue attempt and resumed their march to the east to support the company arriving late that night.[148]

TF 3-69's sister unit, TF 2-7 IN, had the mission to establish a blocking position along the Highway 8 intersection at the main entrance to the airport—a position defended by a Special Republican Guard battalion. This intersection inevitably became known as "Four Corners" and would be the site of intense fighting. For the moment, just driving up to the intersection proved much more difficult than anyone had imagined. Coming north from EA HANNAH (a position adjacent to the river about 20 kilometers south of PEACH), the task force had to travel more than 50 kilometers over very difficult terrain to reach the airport, arriving late that evening.[149]

Task Force 2-7 IN's unit history reports the difficulties in getting to LIONS on the dark night:

> An intricate series of irrigation canals that created a waffle-like pattern on maps and satellite imagery stood between the task force and the nearest high-speed avenue of approach. In the darkness, TF 2-7 IN pushed down small farming roads. The Bradleys actually hung over the elevated roads in some places. Under the heavy traffic, a key unsupported bridge crumbled onto the canal road. Water flooded into these areas, making them all but impassable. Turning the large tracked vehicles around was not even remotely possible; pivot steering would result in further damage to the road. Backing the vehicles down the route was the only alternative. Adding to the frustration, most task force mortar and engineer vehicles pulled trailers. Mired vehicles further blocked the route. Only a sliver of moon provided light as the rear three-quarters of the task force slowly worked its way toward LIONS, ultimately arriving too late to participate in the initial stages of the attack.
>
> The task force commander, Lieutenant Colonel Scott Rutter, and roughly a quarter of his troops, were past the crumbled bridge and continued along the original route to Highway 1. A scout section, followed by the S3, Major Coffey, B/2-7 IN, and the forward aid station, now led the element on the wrong side of the bridge collapse. Finally reaching Highway 1, the Task Force (-) sped north to the airfield.[150]

However difficult the sandstorms and desert terrain had been in the campaign's early days, this maneuver to LIONS, exacerbated by the extreme fatigue, darkness, and ever-present enemy, frustrated everyone.

Attacking Through LIONS

Approaching the airport wall on the one-lane road as planned, TF 3-69's western column encountered no enemy. Just prior to 2300 the western column punched a hole in the southwestern corner of the perimeter wall. C/2-7 IN led the way through the breach. At 0038, the rest of TF

Figure 172. Civilian aircraft destroyed on Objective LIONS, with UH-60L in foreground

3-69 AR entered the airport from the south via a gate in the wall.[151] The first company team traversed the airfield against almost no resistance, moving to the far eastern side of the end of the runway and awaiting the remainder of the task force.

Once through the wall, the task force attacked to clear its assigned sector of the airport.[152] The lead platoons of TF 3-69 broke out on the southern edge of the airfield and maneuvered to clear enemy bunker positions along the outlying service roads. At approximately 0200 the Iraqis shelled them, but Marcone's tankers and mechanized infantry buttoned up and moved on. They attacked to midway up the airfield and turned to secure their eastern flank at 0430. Reaching their assigned limit of advance, they transitioned to a hasty defense. Because the tanks were running low on fuel, the task force conserved fuel by running engines just often enough to keep their batteries charged.[153]

As the sun rose on 4 April, there was a feeling of euphoria as the embedded media from CBS, SKYNEWS, and the *New York Times* conducted interviews and beamed to the world that American forces had seized Baghdad International Airport. While US presence on the airfield was a fact and there was no chance of 1st BCT giving it up, the mission remained a work in progress.[154] It took two more days of fighting to clear the airport, including hidden tunnels, bunker systems, and outlying facilities such as the VIP terminal and the control tower.[155]

After sunrise enemy infantry in previously undetected bunkers posed a problem. Units of TF 3-69 AR spent most of the morning clearing bunkers and capturing Iraqi soldiers. For example, in one incident:

> Sergeant First Class Richard Fonder and Specialist Joseph Ramsel of A/3-69 AR dismounted their vehicle and used hand grenades to clear a bunker that was too close to fire the main gun at and too well built to destroy with machine gun fire. Twenty enemy soldiers surrendered out of the bunker. While they were processing the EPWs, Fonder and Ramsel discovered an alternate enemy fighting position where other Iraqi soldiers were about to open fire. Ten more enemy soldiers surrendered after a volley of fire.[156]

Similar incidents occurred all over the airport as the 1st BCT continued to clear it.

The lead vehicles of TF 2-7 IN finally arrived at the airport at 0500 on 4 April.[157] Moving onto LIONS, the task force received scattered small-arms fire and two RPG rounds. Lieutenant Colonel Rutter and the troops he had in tow moved rapidly to establish a blocking position at "Four Corners," the main entrance, on the eastern side of the airport. The main entrance featured a four-lane highway with a median to separate incoming and outgoing traffic. Large masonry walls with towers approximately 100 meters apart bounded the highway. Rutter's troops hastily cleared the remainder of their section of the airport. The remainder of the task force was still more than an hour away.[158]

Shortly after 0730 on the 4th, the trailing units of TF 2-7 IN entered the airport from the south. Flanked by trees on the right and an enormous wall on the left, the road they arrived on took on a gauntlet-like appearance. Sporadic small-arms fire rang out in the distance, and some rounds were fired near the convoy lead vehicle. Although the plan called for establishing the main blocking position at Four Corners, there was no "rear," and the enemy was all around.[159] Setting up a blocking position in this environment proved problematic, since the enemy might come from any direction.

The TOC vehicles moved through Four Corners and established themselves adjacent to an overpass. With most of the task force now closed on the airfield, Lieutenant Colonel Rutter began moving units into their proper locations.[160] All seemed to be quiet at first.

Rutter positioned the task force mortars, the forward aid station, PSYOP team, and combat trains around the large intersection. Exhausted soldiers cleared their immediate areas and moved into their assigned positions. After traveling through the night and essentially in contact for the past three days, everyone was relieved to finally reach the airport.[161]

Figure 173. A 3rd ID HMMWV on Objective LIONS

First Lieutenant Mark Schenck, writing in the Task Force 2-7 IN's unit history details what happened after a bombardment of several air-burst mortar rounds:

> At this point (about 1030) a Fox chemical reconnaissance vehicle drove up the overpass to conduct chemical reconnaissance. A hidden tank fired and the Fox sped off the overpass, reporting a near miss from a tank main gun round. The frantic report from the FOX and realizing an enemy tank was within range of the task force shocked everyone. It became increasingly evident that moving in at dark the task force was now virtually intermingled with the enemy.
>
> First Lieutenant (Paul) Milosovich moved a Bradley onto the bridge to scan for tanks. As soon as the Bradley reached the top of the overpass, a main gun round from a T-72 slammed into the side of the unsuspecting Bradley from behind the large wall to the south. Strapped to the outside of the Bradley, the rucksacks exploded on impact, sending burning boots, t-shirts, and TA 50 (Army equipment) into the air.
>
> The Bradley commander was thrown forward, out of the turret and onto the front deck of the Bradley. Acting without guidance and with no internal communication Private Class Gee re-aligned his Bradley on the road, pulling forward and then backing down the steep incline on the overpass. His actions prevented the T-72 from being able to fire at the vehicle again and saved the lives of his fellow crew members.
>
> The nearest unit with Javelin antitank weapons was Bushmaster, west of the overpass, protecting the task force northern flank. A four-man team armed with Javelins climbed onto the overpass to engage the tank. Less than 1 kilometer south of the battalion's TOC, three Iraqi T-72 tanks sat on a road inside a compound wall. Unknown at the time, these tanks were not the ones firing at the overpass.[162]
>
> Private First Class Davis engaged the lead tank, parked within feet of the second tank. The *Javelin* screamed off the overpass, buzzing over the battalion TOC, and slammed directly into the top of the unknowing T-72 with deafening thunder. The blast consumed the tank in a fireball and sent the heavy turret end over end more than 50 feet into the air. Secondary explosions complemented the initial blast as the internal

Figure 174. A 3rd ID Bradley on Objective LIONS

ammunition storage compartment ignited. The fire reached out from the burning tank, engulfing its neighbor and causing more explosions.[163] Davis fired a second *Javelin*, causing even more explosions on the second tank. The third T-72 began to frantically try to determine the source and direction of incoming fire. Private First Class Jefferson Jimenez engaged it. His round missed, but damaged the tank, which limped away.[164]

Rutter described the effectiveness of the Javelin this way, "...it worked great! Right down on top of them...Boom!"[165] Despite this success TF 2-7 IN's troubles were not over yet. Apparently, the T-72s were part of a larger counterattack. Iraqi observers adjusted mortar fires on the task force TOC. Captain Sam Donnelly, the assistant operations officer, detected the mortars firing from a bunker, which he pointed out to Major Coffey, the task force operations officer who was fighting from his Bradley. Coffey's gunner destroyed the mortars with his Bradley's Bushmaster 25mm chain gun. Meanwhile, hearing the ruckus, an M1 tank towing a disabled tank arrived, looking to help and did so by destroying two more T-72s coming from the south. The fight continued for 2 hours as TF 2-7 IN fought off counterattacking Special Republican Guard and paramilitary forces.[166] Although it may not have been intentionally coordinated, a second, more dangerous counterattack occurred while B/11 Engineers were clearing a compound for an EPW cage adjacent to the Four Corners position. This counterattack involved as many as 100 SRG troops, who penetrated nearly to TF 2-7 IN's TOC. Lieutenant Colonel Rutter believed the Iraqis may have been attempting to break out from what they accurately perceived to be an encircled position.[167]

> ## Soldiers Led the Way
>
> The soldiers of TF 2-7 IN rose to the occasion. All of the values their mothers and fathers and grandparents taught them, they learned. They stepped up to the plate. They did not just follow their leaders, they ACCOMPANIED their leaders. Sometimes, they LED the way! They said, "Sir, the enemy's over there. . . don't worry, we'll get you there!"
>
> Lieutenant Colonel Scott Rutter
> commander, TF 2-7 IN
> interview 15 May 2003.

Sergeant First Class Paul Smith played a critical role in foiling the enemy's counterattack. His efforts caused the failure of a deliberate enemy attack hours after 1st BCT seized the Baghdad International Airport. He and other defending troops killed an estimated 20-50 enemy soldiers. Sergeant First Class Smith prevented a penetration in the TF 2-7 IN sector, defended the aid station, mortars, and scouts, and as a final act, enabled the evacuation of wounded soldiers.[168]

While the action raged at Four Corners, Lieutenant Colonel Rutter attacked another Special Republican Guard compound to the east with his Bravo Company, commanded by Captain Stephen Szymanski. As his soldiers moved forward, the Iraqi troops began firing RPGs, machine guns and automatic rifles at them. Enemy fire from windows in the buildings and dismounts on the ground forced Szymanski to break contact.[169] Pulling back out of the compound, he called artillery on his tormentors. Artillery, mortars and A-10s all pummeled the compound. The Bravo Company soldiers followed the last mortar round back into the compound. The troops met very little resistance when they first re-entered the compound. But surviving enemy troops engaged them with small-arms fire from the second floor window of a partially destroyed building. Again calling in mortar fires, Bravo Company withdrew just out of contact.[170] Immediately effective, the battalion mortars, firing time-delayed fuses, penetrated the roof and destroyed the building and, with it, the defending enemy.[171]

Essayons: Sergeant First Class Paul Smith

On 4 April 2003, TF 2-7 IN ordered B/11th Engineers to build an enclosure to hold enemy prisoners of war. Bravo Company moved into an Iraqi military compound and began to emplace wire to connect with the walls of the compound to serve as an initial cage to hold prisoners the task force had taken.

DESERT STORM veteran Sergeant First Class Paul R. Smith, platoon sergeant of the 2nd Platoon, was directing the efforts of his soldiers. At one end of the compound, a 1st Platoon armored personnel carrier pushed in a gate to gain access to the compound—revealing some 50 to 100 SRG troops. Simultaneously, the SRG soldiers reoccupied a tower in the compound and began firing RPGs, small arms, and directing mortar fire on to the engineers. The enemy wounded three soldiers in the APC that knocked down the gate.

Smith immediately ran to the wall near the gate and lobbed a grenade over the wall, momentarily driving the enemy back. Smith dragged the wounded out of harm's way and then jumped in the APC and backed it into the center of the compound. He then moved to the vehicle commander's position to fire the .50-caliber machine gun. Using the .50, Smith engaged the enemy in the tower and those attempting to rush the gate. Private Seaman came to his assistance and supported him by passing ammunition cans up to Smith. By suppressing the enemy and killing a great many of them, Smith enabled the company first sergeant to organize a counterattack that ultimately stopped the enemy.

Sometime during that fight, enemy fire mortally wounded Smith. The action at the compound was part of a large enemy counterattack that, if it had succeeded, may well have reached the tactical operations center of the task force. Sergeant First Class Smith's courageous action saved the wounded and permitted Bravo Company to withdraw from the compound, thus enabling CAS and artillery to destroy the remaining defenders.

11th Engineer Battalion

Figure 175. Sergeant First Class Paul Smith

With the compound cleared, units moved in and occupied designated positions along what the task force called "Able Avenue." On 5 April, TF 2-7 IN soldiers also cleared the Special Republican Guard training compound on the airfield. Amenities there included running water, a weight room, and most important, no enemy contact. This served as the task force's home as they prepared for future operations.[172]

Clearing the Airport and Surrounding Areas

In the absence of working counterfire radar, Rutter's operations officer, Major Coffey, and his fire support officer, Captain Tim Swart, fired counterbattery fires on suspected enemy positions, with little effect. Task force patrols also reported sniper fires coming from a group of construction cranes at the nearby presidential palace. The task force called in both CAS and artillery. A-10 *Warthogs* and artillery destroyed the cranes and, presumably, the snipers. Sniper fires stopped and enemy shelling tapered off, allowing TF 2-7 IN and 1st BCT to focus on improving their positions at the airfield. They intended to stay.[173]

U.S. Army

Figure 176. V Corps Soldiers moving onto Objective LIONS

Shortly after reporting the US presence on the airfield to the world, the 11th Engineer Battalion commander, Lieutenant Colonel Smith, and Colonel Grimsley conducted a reconnaissance of the airfield itself. Not surprisingly, the Iraqis had built obstacles across the runways that would have to be cleared to get them back in operation. Grimsley and Smith also found that several roads cratered by coalition air strikes were of limited use. Members of the media interviewed Smith next

Airport Ministry

One of the proactive unit ministry teams was that of Chaplain (Captain) Michael Rightmyer and Sergeant Rose, assigned to 3-187 IN (101st), decided to go with the soldiers to clear the Iraqi bodies at Baghdad International Airport. It took over a week to clear all bodies. This was a vital ministry in keeping the fighting strength of the force emotionally and mentally healthy. Their support helped to give the soldiers the strength and presence of God in the horrific situation. They were the right people at the right place and at the right time. Rightmyer helped the soldiers keep their sanity and resolve during this horrific situation of sights and smells.

Chaplain (Lieutenant Colonel) Ken Brown,
101st Airborne Division chaplain

to one of the road craters at approximately 1000, asking the difficult question of "when would it be usable?" Smith projected he would finish cleaning up the mess within 24 hours. The 11th Engineer Battalion came through, clearing the runway the next day.[174]

The 11th Engineers had more to do than repair runways. As the brigade and battalion TOCs moved to occupy a hangar in the center of the airfield, it became apparent the infrastructure—water, sewers, and power—was not functioning. The engineers identified and coordinated numerous engineering requirements to jump-start a master plan for facilities management, including the supervision and control of all field sanitation projects, a cemetery for enemy remains, initial land management, and initial ordnance control.[175]

On 6 April at 0800, TF 3-69 AR held a memorial service for Sergeant First Class Wilbur Davis, who had died in the overturned HMMWV as the fight at LIONS started (promoted posthumously). On 7 April, Colonel Grimsley pulled TF 2-7 IN from the blocking position at Four Corners for a 24-hour period to provide the opportunity for some rest, maintenance, and preparation for future operations. The task force conducted Sergeant First Class Smith's memorial ceremony at 0600 that morning in a small field near the airfield, concluding with "Amazing Grace."[176] Following the service, the soldiers continued to refit and recover from the combat operations and prepared for follow-on missions.[177]

3-7 CAV Blocking at Objective MONTGOMERY

On 3 April as the 1st BCT moved to start its seizure of LIONS, 3-7 CAV moved northwest to Objective MONTGOMERY, the intersection of Highways 1 and 10, to protect the division's northern and western flanks. The cavalrymen initially reported minimal contact at the intersections around the objective where they had established checkpoints. Enemy activity increased in the early evening but then grew quiet for several hours.[178]

The checkpoints attracted the Iraqi defenders. Enemy activity picked up steadily through the early morning hours, with 3-7 CAV destroying six T-72s and one armored fighting vehicle by 0435. During the morning, Captain H. Clay Lyle's A/3-7 CAV, *Apache*, destroyed a steady stream of Iraqis attacking his Bradleys and tanks in buses, pickup trucks, and civilian vehicles. Captured Iraqis included several from the *Hammurabi* Division, which the corps had tracked moving south toward LIONS. *Apache* troop and 3-7 CAV protected the main effort at LIONS, using direct fire, CAS, and artillery to engage Iraqis—presumably from the *Hammurabi* Division—counterattacking toward the airport.[179]

Later that day, after the fighting calmed down, the Air Force reported a battalion-size tank formation on the northern side of Highway 10, only 3 kilometers from the checkpoints. The squadron commander, Lieutenant Colonel Terry Ferrell, brought half of *Apache* Troop and his tactical command post up to plan an attack. First they watched from a kilometer away as F-16s, A-10s, and British *Tornadoes* dropped munitions on the area. Then A/1-9 FA fired the target area. The air was damp and humid that evening, and it held the smoke and dust at ground level, with the wind blowing the dense smoke toward Ferrell and disrupting his view. Unable to see the target area after the CAS and indirect fires ceased, Ferrell ordered cavalrymen from *Apache* troop forward to assess the battle damage.[180]

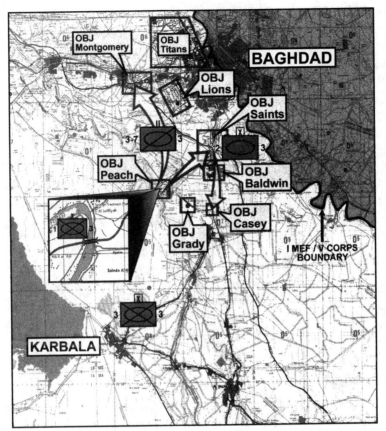

Figure 177. 3-7 CAV attacks to Objective MONTGOMERY

First Lieutenant Matthew Garrett led his platoon and the troop as it advanced in a staggered column. As Garrett led the troop forward, he noticed a high berm directly behind a small canal on the south side of the highway. While continuing to look for the enemy to the north—where the aircraft bombed—Garrett started scanning the overpass he was about to drive under. His gunner reported a possible vehicle behind the berm to their right front. Garrett had just reported possible vehicles on the south side of the highway when several of his tankers fired their main guns in the direction he had indicated. They had detected T-72s positioned every 50 meters behind the berm—on the side opposite from where the aircraft had engaged.

Altogether, 16 T-72s occupied prepared positions along the berm. Because Lyle had approached in a staggered column, each of his vehicles had a clear shot at the Iraqis. The tankers engaged so quickly that as soon as a gunner could get a lock on a target, someone else destroyed it. The Iraqis fought back and brought mortars, artillery, and air defense artillery guns used as direct-fire weapons into the fight. Lyle contacted the battalion fire support officer for suppressive fires. *Apache* broke contact as 52 rounds of high-explosive artillery smashed down directly on the remaining Iraqis. Captain Lyle's *Apaches,* along with the supporting artillery, destroyed a battalion of the Republican Guard in 15 minutes. In the end, Lieutenant Colonel Ferrell reported destroying 20 T-72s.[181]

3-7th Cavalry Squadron

Figure 178. Platoon leaders of *Apache* Troop, 3-7 CAV.(From left-to-right: Second Lieutenant Fritz, First Lieutenant Wade, Second Lieutenant Devlin, First Lieutenant Linthwaite, and First Lieutenant Garrett)

Sealing the North: Seizing Objective TITANS (6-7 April)

Up to this point, the corps was well ahead of schedule. In accordance with the original plan, Colonel Grimsley's 1st BCT occupied LIONS in the west and Colonel Perkins' 2nd BCT had secure positions to the south in Objective SAINTS. The corps needed only to seize Objective BEARS, on Baghdad Military Installation in Taji, 6 miles north of Baghdad along Highway 1, to complete V Corps' part of isolating Baghdad. Taking BEARS required destroying remaining forces concentrated around Taji. Achieving that and securing the ground would provide V Corps with a second airfield near Baghdad and cut the lines of reinforcement from and egress to the north. Originally, V Corps intended to use 101st Airborne Division to take BEARS. However, to get the airborne troops in required an air assault via routes over heavily defended urban terrain. In the end, V Corps determined that the risks of overflying the urban areas were too great. The corps assigned 3rd ID the mission and they assigned it to 3rd BCT. Ultimately the objective was refined. In the end, Allyn's brigade attacked to seize Objective TITANS, located just south of the original objective, BEARS.

The *Hammer* Brigade had been very busy around Karbala since the first day of April. TF 2-69 AR led the 3rd ID attack in zero illumination, driving north to isolate the eastern side of the city, where it confronted both sophisticated RPG ambushes and suicide bombers, leading the commander to fear that he was facing "professional terrorists."[182] After the initial attack into Karbala, both TF 1-30 IN and TF 2-69 AR fought a frustrating and wearying battle to keep Iraqi irregulars penned up in the city while the rest of *Hammer* protected division and corps units as they passed through the Karbala Gap. On 5 April, 2nd BCT of the 101st assumed responsibility for the Karbala area. 3rd BCT of 3rd ID moved north to prepare for the attack on TITANS.[183]

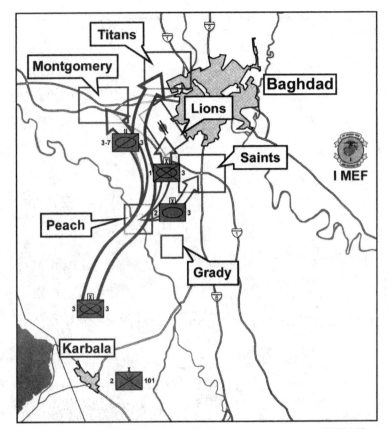

Figure 179. 3rd BCT's move from Karbala to Objective TITANS

With the attack looming, the 3rd BCT made several changes in its task organization. Earlier on 4 April, Colonel Allyn sent the 1-10 FA and TF 1-15 IN to reinforce 2nd BCT's attack on SAINTS. The 1-10 FA's 155mm howitzers were arrayed in firing positions in the southern portion of Objective SAINTS to support the effort to isolate Baghdad from any remaining Iraqi forces that might be lurking along Highway 8. The infantry helped to secure the ground. With SAINTS secured, the division reassigned both battalions back to Allyn late in the afternoon on 5 April. For the first time since the early fighting around An Nasiriyah, Allyn's entire BCT would be back together again—ready for its attack into Baghdad.[184]

Receiving the Order

Just after dawn on the morning of 6 April, Lieutenant Colonel John Harding (commander, 1-10 FA) and Lieutenant Colonel John Charlton (commander, TF 1-15 IN) met with Colonel Allyn at a road junction on Highway 1 in SAINTS.[185] They were there to get the final order for the brigade's attack to seize Objective TITANS. Harding and his battalion had come from supporting Perkins' brigade. Just gathering the brigade proved problematic because they were so spread out. In the end, Allyn got in touch with Harding via FBCB2. As Allyn put it, FBCB2 "saved them."[186] There was electricity in the air. According to Harding, "It was a great feeling for us to be together again. We were as pumped up as we could be! There was no apprehension at all about attacking Baghdad. It was all clicking like clockwork by then."[187] Standing in a

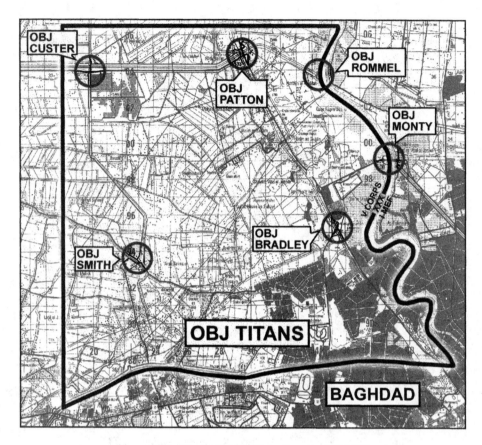

Figure 180. The 3rd BCT Objectives in TITANS

small group next to the road, the officers quickly copied the maneuver graphics onto their maps and completed their final coordination. To facilitate controlling the battle, Allyn's staff divided TITANS into numerous smaller objectives.

In garrison, *Hammer* is not stationed at Fort Stewart with the rest of the 3rd ID. Its home is 200 miles away at Fort Benning, Georgia. Fort Benning is the home of the Infantry School, and *Hammer* is the only tactical brigade on post. The brigade was exceptionally close-knit, in part because of its geographic isolation from the remainder of the 3rd ID, but also because of what its soldiers had gone through together over the past year.

In 2002, the 3rd BCT completed a grueling train-up and then a six-month deployment to Kuwait. It returned home for less than three months and then, in January 2003, deployed again to confront Iraq in this war. The soldiers had trained at the NTC together, deployed together, trained in Kuwait for six months, came home for awhile, and then returned for another round of rigorous training in the desert of Kuwait. Emotionally taut, desert-hardened, and cohesive, 3rd BCT crossed the border ready and willing. However, since crossing the border and seizing Tallil Air Base in the opening days of the war, the brigade had not fought as a single integrated unit. One or more of the maneuver task forces or supporting battalions had always been detached and fighting under the command of other combat teams.

Lieutenant Colonel Sanderson's TF 2-69 AR had been detached from the 3rd BCT immediately after the fight at Tallil Air Base and sent to the 1st BCT. They fought a ferocious battle at Al Kifl with the *Raiders*.[188] Even *Hammer*'s direct-support artillery battalion had been sent away several times, eventually supporting all of 3rd ID's maneuver brigades. But now, this vital mission provided the impetus to reunite the men and women of the *Hammer* Brigade. They were elated with the prospect; it was their turn to step up to the plate.

Moving Out

At 0508 on 6 April, TF 2-69 AR crossed the line of departure at Objective PEACH to begin a 110-kilometer attack to the northwest and north. The last 60 kilometers of that attack would be conducted under heavy fire from defending Iraqi forces.[189] The 3rd BCT moved from its assembly area west of the Euphrates, crossed the river, and continued east into Objective SAINTS, where it picked up the soldiers of TF 1-15 IN. The BCT, whole again, then turned northwest toward Objective MONTGOMERY, held by *Apache* Troop, 3-7 CAV. Delta Troop, 10th Cavalry, the BCT's organic reconnaissance troop, led the brigade toward MONTGOMERY, the farthest point north under V Corps' control.[190] As Lieutenant Colonel Harding described it, "Past that point, it was all Indian country."[191]

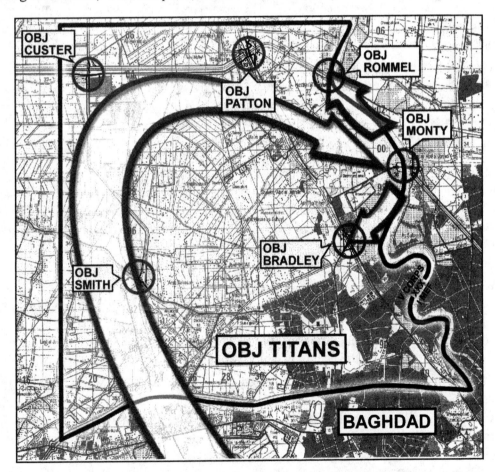

Figure 181. The 3rd BCT scheme of maneuver through Objective TITANS

TF 2-69 Armor, the brigade's main effort, followed on the heels of Delta Troop. Team *Assassin*, A/2-69 AR, led the task force, followed by Team *Hard Rock,* C/1-15 IN. The task force's combat trains followed, nestled closely behind the combat vehicles for protection. Then came Colonel Allyn's assault command post, in an M113 and three Bradleys, trailed by elements of B/317th Engineers, and the tank-pure C/2-69 AR.[192] Harding's howitzers came next, followed by TF 1-30 IN. TF 1-15 IN's combat-scarred vehicles joined the rear of the massive column as it passed.[193] Colonel Allyn rode in his HMMWV rather than the armored vehicle he normally used because his M113 had broken down and could not be fixed because of a lack of repair parts. Rather than take a replacement vehicle from one of his subordinates, the BCT commander chose to risk the ride in the light, unarmored HMMWV—a decision that nearly cost him his life.

First Contact

As TF 2-69 AR passed through the checkpoint manned by *Apache* Troop, 3-7 CAV at Objective MONTGOMERY, Captain Lyle advised Colonel Allyn that there had been firefights around the checkpoint all night and that he should expect enemy contact as soon as he cleared the checkpoint.[194] Several officers remembered Lyle saying, "Once you get 300 meters up that road, you're going to make contact."[195] The cavalryman knew what he was talking about. By that time in the war, the troopers almost always did. The HMMWVs of the brigade's reconnaissance troop pulled over and let Sanderson's tanks take the lead.

Objective SMITH, the first of many road junctions 3rd BCT had to seize, encompassed a small cluster of buildings and homes where the highway made an "S" turn to the east and then back north. At 0850, TF 2-69 AR's vanguard came under small-arms and RPG fire upon entering the objective. They returned fire and the engagement rapidly escalated, with the Iraqis responding with mortars and artillery. The task force also engaged and destroyed at least one T-72 tank and several other armored vehicles firing from reveted positions within the objective. The engagement settled into what became a familiar pattern. As each company team approached the objective, it encountered heavy small-arms and RPG fire from multiple directions. A 10-hour, nonstop running fight ensued. Allyn, still traveling close behind TF 2-69 AR, called for artillery fires from the 1-10 FA. At the same time, he targeted the Iraqi armor with CAS provided by A-10 *Warthogs*.[196]

Although it continued to fire in support of TF 2-69 AR, Lieutenant Colonel Harding's 1-10 FA came under heavy attack also. Soon after the artillerymen fired their first mission, the Iraqis fired on them with small arms and RPGs. Some of the Iraqi gunners launched their RPGs from behind buildings. The enemy gunners aimed high in the air so as to arc up and over before coming down into the artillery firing positions. Despite incoming fire, the 1-10's howitzers continued to pound away at the enemy in Objective SMITH.[197]

The 3rd BCT fought through SMITH, not stopping to clear it, so they could maintain their momentum. Subsequently, as each unit passed through, there was intermittent contact with individual Iraqi military vehicles, 'technicals', and small groups of Iraqis fighting on foot. Objective SMITH remained troublesome for several hours. The fire from the area around the overpass waxed and waned, but it didn't cease completely until TF 1-30 IN cleared the Iraqis out of the adjacent areas.

TF 2-69 AR continued north to Objective CUSTER, a sharp right turn at a canal that marked the brigade's northern boundary. The task force commander, Lieutenant Colonel J.R. Sanderson, described the 40-kilometer route from SMITH to CUSTER as "a constant gauntlet of fire."[198] It had already been a rough day. As the Task Force passed through objective SAINTS that morning, an RPG struck a 317 EN M113, killing Private Gregory Huxley and wounding two other soldiers, the first casualties of the day.[199] Later, Huxley's comrades would create an informal memorial to their fallen friend, but for now, the attack continued without pause.

At 1136 on the 6th, Captain Stu James' company team destroyed a company-size unit of Iraqi mechanized combat vehicles and a battalion of artillery along the canal. James' troops cleared the canal of several BMPs, T-62 tanks, and 18 BM-21 rocket launchers.[200] They then observed a bizarre sight as they made the turn on the canal road. Standing almost in the middle of the road, several Iraqi officers were busy stripping off their uniforms to reveal civilian clothes underneath. In full uniform or not, they were armed combatants who made no offer of surrender. The company shot and killed the Iraqis before they could complete their change of clothing.[201]

Lieutenant Colonel Sanderson determined that he would not allow his attack to bog down by fighting every single Iraqi he encountered. His mission required him to move rapidly to the north of the city and to seal it off, not to have a long, drawn-out fight in the built-up area. Accordingly, he pushed the task force to keep moving. If he received fire from a sniper on a roof, he used artillery fire or CAS and moved on.

"V Corps Battle Damage Assessment Briefing," 29 April 2003

Figure 182. Informal memorial to Private Gregory Huxley
(note hole under "I" where the round penetrated the vehicle)

Sanderson led from the front near the head of the lengthy column. In fact, Sanderson followed Captain James' tank, and James followed the lead tank platoon. Sanderson, along with his battalion fire support officer, Captain Andy MacLean, and his air liaison officer, were in place to coordinate supporting fires for James. Sanderson's fire support team called for artillery on the left side of the road and used low-flying CAS aircraft to engage Iraqi forces directly to the front. Sanderson's air liaison officer passed him in flight reports from the CAS aircraft describing the enemy resistance along the road. Reports from A-10, F-15 and F-16 pilots kept him informed on what to expect next. Sanderson said, "It was always comforting to see the A-10s coming in. The field artillery support was spot-on. You couldn't have asked for a better artillery barrage."[202] This approach was in accordance with Colonel Allyn's mantra. According to Lieutenant Colonel Harding, that was "Prep with steel, lead with lead, count the dead."[203]

At 1308, the 3rd Infantry Division's ADC-M, Brigadier General Austin, discussed the 3rd BCT's progress with Colonel Allyn. Clearly, Saddam had turned Baghdad into an "armed camp." Iraqi troops fought the brigade at every bend or corner in the road with air defense artillery, artillery, tanks, BMPs, and anything else of military value. There were so many huge secondary explosions from the destroyed Iraqi vehicles, and they were so close to the road, that Sanderson wondered whether the brigade's wheeled vehicles would get through. Large chunks of debris from exploding Iraqi tanks and BMPs rained down and often blocked the road. Many

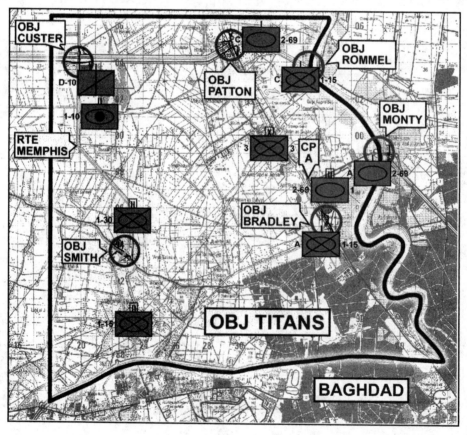

Figure 183. The 3rd BCT disposition on Objective TITANS, 6 April 2003

HMMWVs were driving with flat tires because of all the sharp metal fragments.[204] Balancing the risk, Allyn pressed on.

By 1530, the 3rd BCT seized Objective PATTON, the north/south intersection of Highway 1 where it crossed over the canal. Sanderson assigned Captain Carter Price and his company team responsibility for PATTON. Most of the task force field trains stopped within Price's protective perimeter until they were summoned to refuel and resupply the task force later in the day.

With Captain Price established on PATTON, TF 2-69 AR moved far to the south, seizing Objective MONTY—the main highway bridge over the Tigris River in Objective TITANS—and began to clear the areas around it. This was their most critical objective. Captain James' Team *Assassin* secured the bridge and several buildings around the approaches. Soon afterward, another company team attacked north from PATTON and seized Objective ROMMEL, a bridge where a canal intersected the Tigris River. For the moment, this completed the TF 2-69 AR's plan for seizing crossing sites on the Tigris.[205]

Things were fairly quiet until about 1830, when dismounted Iraqi infantry attacked the TF 2-69 AR combat trains near Objective MONTY. Colonel Allyn was in his HMMWV parked on the grounds of the Iraqi Petroleum Institute near three 2,500-gallon fuel tankers and one heavily loaded ammunition truck. The attackers poured fire into these tempting targets and at Allyn's vulnerable HMMWV. Quick return fire from Lieutenant Colonel Harding's Bradley and TF 2-69 AR eliminated the threat but not before they hit the ammunition truck. The truck

---

A Task Force Commander on Battle Command

Lieutenant Colonel JR Sanderson, a task force commander in OIF, reached several conclusions about battle command. According to Sanderson, who commanded TF 2-69 AR (*Panthers*), OIF was "a straight-up war of momentum." V Corps, including Sanderson and his troops, kept the pressure on the Iraqis day and night for 21 straight days, with difficult fights from Tallil Air Base, to Al Kifl during the sandstorm, and finally to seize and hold key points in Baghdad during 3rd BCT's attack to seize Objective TITANS.

To Sanderson, the keys to success included using doctrine both in how his task force fought and how it planned operations. To him, effectively using the military decision making process proved important. Specifically, Sanderson tried to issue clear guidance and then demanded that his subordinates first gave him a "confirmation brief" that read back to him "task and purpose" for missions he assigned. Moreover, he required company commanders to "back brief" how they intended to fight their units, including fire distribution and maneuver. This approach supported what Sanderson called the *Panthers'* rules of combat: "One, see the enemy before he sees you. Two (accounting for what happens if rule one is broken), make contact with the smallest amount of combat power forward. Three, fire distribution and control." Sanderson's task force applied these rules in preparation and execution.

Emphatic about how he led his task force, Sanderson also had strong views on leadership from above. TF 2-69 AR worked for two brigade commanders who had "completely different styles," but both were "crystal clear and articulate" in issuing their guidance and orders. As he put it, "this war was run on commander's intent." Further, he found, as did other soldiers, that the presence of two- and three-star generals forward on the battlefield was a "strong plus."

Lieutenant Colonel J.R. Sanderson, interview by Lieutenant Colonel David Manning

319

caught fire and ammunition began to cook off. Despite the drivers' and other soldiers' best efforts, the fire quickly spread from the ammunition truck to a fuel tanker. Both vehicles were completely destroyed and several soldiers were wounded, along with a member of the support platoon, who received mortal injuries while defending his vehicle. Despite the best efforts of the battalion medics, the support platoon soldier died while being evacuated.

At about this time at Objective PATTON, Captain Price came under attack by dismounted Iraqi forces moving through buildings near the crossing site on the canal. Knowing that the tank-pure Charlie Company lacked supporting infantry, Sanderson and a small group,

---

Mortars Under Attack:
Enemy Action on Objective LIONS

While conducting a hasty dismounted reconnaissance patrol and seeking a better position from which to set up the mortars, Captain Matthew Paul and Sergeant Jose Adorno, Task Force 2-7 IN mortar platoon, walked down the road the unit had used earlier to enter the airport. There they met one M1 tank from the battalion that was towing a disabled tank into the maintenance collection point. The tankers asked them where the maintenance collection point was located. Captain Paul directed them to Four Corners and continued on his search for a good firing position.

Less than 10 seconds later, the ground rumbled with the sound of approaching armor once again, and Captain Paul and Sergeant Adorno turned to move out of the way, both instinctively raising their hands to wave as they turned. Shock and horror gripped the two as they realized they were waving at a pair of Iraqi T-72 tanks. Luckily, surprise and confusion also slowed the Iraqi tankers' reactions as they too waved initially. Captain Paul yelled "T-72!" and without another word the two split, knowing they would be shot in the back if they ran straight up the road. Captain Paul darted left, off the road; Sergeant Adorno sprinted off to the right. Winding through the trees and bushes screening Four Corners, he was back with the mortar platoon in minutes.

Deciding between the two, the tanks chased Captain Paul off the road. Running for his life, the mortar platoon leader dove into a water-filled ditch beside the road, hiding in some tall reeds. The tanks rumbled forward, stopping just 40 meters from him, and began firing machine guns over his head into the wall behind him. With his face pressed into the dirt and lying perfectly still, all Captain Paul could do was wait. Just then, another enemy tank section farther east began firing on the battalion TOC and the vehicles driving across the overpass at Four Corners.

Organizing a rescue for their platoon leader, Sergeant First Class Robert Broadwater, Jr. and the mortar squads prepared to move. As the mortar crews mounted their vehicles, the US tank that had driven by earlier stopped and asked where the T-72s were. Broadwater indicated the targets to them. The tank pulled around, quickly occupying a hasty attack by fire position.

At this point, Captain Paul could hear frantic screams in Arabic from the Iraqi tank crews as they identified the M1. But it was too late for them. Both enemy tanks exploded, spraying burning debris in all directions and tossing the turrets in the air. Seconds later, a mortar track pulled up, rescuing Captain Paul and returning to the mortar platoon command post.

In the middle of all the fighting at the mortar location, the platoon began receiving calls for mortar support. Although distracted by direct fire from the Iraqi dismounts, the mortars provided the much-needed fire support. With the gun tubes already laid in, the mission was fired and repeated.

TF 2-7 IN unit history

including Captain Rapaport with infantry from *Hard Rock,* moved quickly to the north to assist the tankers.[206] At nearly the same time, the Iraqis counterattacked against US positions at both ends of the Tigris River bridge at Objective MONTY. The attackers initially consisted of dismounted infantry, but they were quickly joined by several T-72 tanks and BMPs. Captain James' *Assassins* defended vigorously as the fight for MONTY built in intensity. Thus began a 60-hour ordeal for Stu James and his soldiers. Throughout the fight at MONTY Sanderson applied every means he had to destroy persistent counterattacks, including 40 or 50 CAS missions during that first night.[207]

The *Assassins* defeated this first counterattack, and at 1912, the brigade reported to 3rd ID headquarters that the situation was under control at all locations, at least for the moment.[208] Sanderson conferred with Allyn and requested another maneuver company to secure Objective BRADLEY, the southernmost objective in TITANS. Colonel Allyn agreed and reassigned A/1-15 IN to TF 2-69 AR.

At sunset on 6 April, Allyn's BCT had forces arrayed across the breadth of TITANS. TF 1-15 IN, which had rejoined the brigade that day, oriented to the south and controlled the route into the objective area. TF 1-30 IN was clearing the last Iraqi die-hards out of the urban area around SMITH, while D/10 CAV occupied Objective CUSTER in the northwest. TF 2-69 AR had company teams on Objectives PATTON, ROMMEL, MONTY, and BRADLEY.[209]

The first day's fight to isolate the city in the 3rd ID's zone was complete. The 3rd BCT had fought through elements of the SRG, the *Hammurabi* Republican Guard Division, and possibly the corps artillery belonging to the Republican Guard. Taking TITANS set the stage for further American attacks into the city, but the Iraqis had not given up. In the coming days the division mounted attacks into the center of the city from the south. Two days after Colonel Allyn's troops seized TITANS, the 1st Marine Division entered Baghdad from the east. On 9 April marines and soldiers linked up in downtown Baghdad.

NOTES

1.   Anthony H. Cordesman, *The Iraq War: Strategy, Tactics, and Military Lessons* (Washington DC: The Center for Strategic and International Studies, 2003), 85-104. Re: declaration of air supremacy see 104.

2.   Lieutenant General David McKiernan, commander, CFLCC, interview by Colonel Gregory Fontenot, US Army, Retired, 8 December 2003.

3.   Major E. J. Degen, Major Kevin Marcus, and Major Lou Rago, notes taken when they accompanied Lieutenant General Wallace to Jalibah.

4.   McKiernan, 8 December 2003.

5.   Colonel William Grimsley, commander, 1st Brigade, 3rd ID, interview by Lieutenant Colonel David Manning, undated.

6.   Lieutenant General William Wallace, commander, V Corps, summary transcription of interview by Colonel French Maclean, US Army, 15 April 2003.

7.   Memorandum for Record, TF 2-70 AR, Operation IRAQI FREEDOM Timeline, 22 May 2003.

8.   Ibid.

9.   "V Corps Commander's Operations Assessment," 7 April 2003.

10.   "Operation IRAQI FREEDOM—By the Numbers," CENTAF-PSAB, KSA, Commander's Action Group, 9th Air Force, Shaw Air Force Base, SC, 30 April 2003.

11.   Lieutenant Colonel J.R. Sanderson, commander, TF 2-69 AR, interview by Lieutenant Colonel David Manning, 12 May 2003. "A2C2, [Army] Airspace Command and Control, is broke across the American Army. It is especially critical when you are firing artillery, MLRS. Those are things most people will catch. If you are doing a MLRS strike on something, okay, somebody will clear the A2C2. If you are down to cannon artillery and you are doing call for fire for fire support, nobody will catch that and they won't clear the airspace. And God help you if you are firing mortars because the mortar is obviously going to go above the hard deck and it really is "big sky, little bullet" theory and you could knock something out of the way."

12.   "Battle of Debecka Ridge Summary Brief," Colonel Michael Beasock, TRADOC Systems Manager for Close Combat Missiles, US Army Infantry School, Fort Benning, GA, undated.

13.   Sergeant First Class Frank R. Antenori, US Army Special Forces, email to Lieutenant Colonel Arthur Durante, US Army, Retired, 22 August 2003.

14.   "Battle of Debecka Ridge Summary Brief."

15.   Antenori.

16.   Captain Shane Celeen, commander, C/2-70 AR, interview by Captain Michael Mathews, 22 July 2003.

17.   Ibid.

18.   Ibid.

19.   Iraqi actions took place in such a convoluted command and control environment that it is hard to discern patterns of operation. The Republican Guard, regular army, and militias were controlled separately. Understanding Iraqi actions also is complicated by their efforts to shield and deceive coalition forces. Sometimes forces on the scene reacted to an attack and were joined almost serendipitously by militias. When coalition intelligence detected a unit or detected movement, they attempted to determine what the enemy intended. Sometimes intelligence estimated intentions correctly. The point is that merely detecting movement or the presence of a unit does not offer information as to intent. Finally, as of the time *On Point* went to press, very little actual information on Iraqi intentions and actions was available. The Joint Center for Operational Analysis at Joint Forces Command is doing some work on this matter, which ultimately may help clarify what the Iraqis believed was happening and what they were doing about it.

20.   Field Manual 100-5-1/Marine Corps Reference Publication 5-2A, *Organizational Terms and Symbols*, HQ Department of the Army/United States Marine Corps, Washington, DC, 30 September 1997, 1-66.

21.   V CORPS FRAGO 149M, "Limited Attacks," to OPORD 0303-343 (Cobra II), Headquarters, V Corps, Camp VIRGINIA, Kuwait, 300700ZMAR03.

22.   2nd BCT, 3rd ID, "History of Operation IRAQI FREEDOM or How to Own a Country in 30 days or Less." The unit history states that Objective MURRAY was in Habbaniyah, but it is actually in the town of Al Hidiyah about halfway between Karbala and Al Hillah on the main route between the cities.

23.   Ibid. See also "3-7 CAV Unit "History; and "3-7 CAV Command Briefing" by Lieutenant Colonel Terry Ferrell, 25 May 2003.

24.   "Historical Account," 1-9 FA, Operation IRAQI FREEDOM, undated, 5.

25.   "Battle summary, 6th Squadron, 6th Cavalry, Operation IRAQI FREEDOM," 9 June 2003.

26.   "Unit history, 10th Engineer Battalion," 1 May 2003.

27.   Perkins confirmed this via telephone with Colonel Gregory Fontenot US Army, Retired, 6 February 2004.

28.   10th Engineer Battalion. Memorandum for Record, Subject: Historical Record Keeping, 1 May 2003, 4.

29.   3rd ID Consolidated Division History, 37.

30.   1-9 FA, 5.

31.   TF 4-64 AR, "Tusker History, Operation Iraqi Freedom (19 Mar 03 – 12 April 03)," undated, 22-23. Interestingly the 3rd ID assessment report for the 31st reports the capture of a brigadier general. This report made its way to CFLCC. It is possible someone else, possibly SOF, might have captured a brigadier general commanding the 23rd Brigade, but the *Tuskers* don't appear to have made that claim. Whether a brigadier was captured or not, the *Tuskers* did capture soldiers assigned to the 23rd Brigade of the *Nebuchadnezzar* Division, and that is the notable intelligence garnered here.

32.   "3rd ID OIF Historical Document," undated, 8.

33.   TF 4-64 AR, 22-23.

34.   2nd BCT, 3rd ID. See also TF 4-64 AR and 3rd ID "OIF Historical Document, 27 April 2003," 8.

35.   "3rd ID Comments on OIF and its Role in that War ," 8.

36.   Ibid.

37.   2nd BCT, 3rd ID, 8.

38.   3rd ID "OIF Historical Document."

39.   Lieutenant General William Wallace, commander, V Corps, interview by Colonel Timothy Cherry, 14 May 2003.

40.   "OPORD 0303-343 (Cobra II Base Plan), Headquarters, V Corps, Camp VIRGINIA, Kuwait," 13 January 2003.

41.   Colonel Ben Hodges, commander, 1st Brigade, 101st Airborne Division, interview by Lieutenant Colonel William Connor, US Army, Retired, 23 May 2003.

42.   Captain James A. Page, "The Battle for An Najaf: 30 March – 02 April 2003," undated, 5.

43.   Hodges.

44.   Lieutenant General William Wallace, commander, V Corps (during OIF, interview by Colonel Gregory Fontenot, US Army, Retired, Lieutenant Colonel E. J. Degen, and Major David Tohn, 7 August 2003.

45.   Major General Dave Petraeus, commander, 101st Airborne Division, interview by Colonel Timothy Cherry, 21 May 2003.

46.   Captain James A. Page, 6. See also 101st Airborne Division decision brief on concept for isolation of An Najaf, undated, and information briefing titled "Aviation Operations in Operation IRAQI FREEDOM," undated.

47.   Lieutenant Colonel Marcus DeOliveira, commander, 1 –327 IN, "1-327 IN command briefing," 24 May 2003. During urban operations training, the BCTP's Operations Group F demonstrated or discussed various mapping tools and recommended providing the means to print maps at the lowest level possible. All deployed Army divisions fielded one or more of these software tools and most bought "plotter printers" for at least their brigades. The 101st purchased plotters for every maneuver battalion.

48.   Petraeus.

49.   Lieutenant Colonel Christopher P. Hughes, commander, 2-327 IN, interview by Lieutenant Colonel William Connor, US Army, Retired, 23 May 2003.

50.   Ibid. See also email from Lieutenant Colonel Hughes to Gregory Fontenot 20 October 2003 and interview with Captain Thomas Ehrhart, commander, D 2-327 and Captain Alberto Garnica, commander, HHC 2-327 by Major Pete Kilner, 22 May 2003.

51.   Hughes. See also email Hughes to Fontenot.

52.   Ibid.

53.   Ibid.

54.   Hodges.

55.   "101st Airborne Division After-Action Report," 30 April 2003.

56.   Captain James A. Page, 12; Hughes.

57.   "101st Airborne Division After-Action Report," 30 April 2003, Chapter 1, Brigade Combat Teams.

58.   Ibid.

59.   Lieutenant Colonel Jeffrey Ingram, commander, 2-70 AR, interview by Lieutenant Colonel David Manning, 22 May 2003. Colleagues report that Ingram is absolutely calm.

60.   Ingram.

61.   Ibid. 2-70 AR; and Lieutenant Colonel Henry "Bill" Bennett, commander, 1-320 FA, interview by Lieutenant Colonel William Pitts, 22 May 2003.

62.   Bennett.

63.   Ibid.

64.   Major John White, S3, 3 –101 AV, interview by Major Jonathan Gass, 23 May 2003. White, who did not fly that mission, believes the reported battle damage assessment almost certainly includes some double counting. Lieutenant Colonel Jeff Ingram, commander of 2-70 AR, does not necessarily doubt the number of BDA but does believe that Lieutenant Colonel Bennett and his redlegs of 1-320 FA BN inflicted much of the damage.

65.   Ibid.

66.   2-70 AR. That same day C/1-41 IN arrived and joined the task force at 1500.

67.   There is currently no way to verify the accuracy of this assertion. Evidence available is entirely circumstantial. Specifically, subsequent attacks south from Objective SAINTS revealed that the enemy had oriented their defenses to the south toward Al Hillah. A map captured at Objective PEACH also suggests that the enemy believed the corps would attack north on the eastern bank of the Euphrates. There is no documentary evidence beyond the map and the orientation of the defenses upon which to make the case that the feint at Al Hillah produced the desired outcome.

68.   Personal notes of Lieutenant Colonel Steven Smith, commander, 2-101 AV, collected by Major Jonathan Gass.

69.   Ibid.

70.   Ibid.

71.   Ibid.

72.   Lieutenant Colonel Scott Rutter, commander, TF 2-7 IN, interview by Lieutenant Colonel Arthur Durante, US Army, Retired, 15 May 2003.

73.   Major Michael A. Marti, S2, 2nd BCT, 82nd Airborne and Major Thomas J. Kardos, S3, 2nd BCT, 82nd Airborne, interviews by Major David Tohn, 17 May 2003.

74.   Colonel Arnold Bray, commander, 2nd BCT, 82nd Airborne Division, interview by Colonel Gregory Fontenot, US Army, Retired 5 November 2003. The OIF Study Group did not have the opportunity to interview as many of the 2nd BCT troops and leaders as we would have liked. Colonel Bray spent an afternoon with the authors with his records and journals and so is cited here often. Colonel Bray's patience and his copious records proved invaluable.

75.   Ibid.

76.   Ibid.

77.   Ibid.

78.   Ibid.

79.   Ibid.

80.   Ibid.

81.   Lieutenant Colonel Ed Rowe, executive officer, 2nd BCT, 82nd Airborne Division, interview by Lieutenant Colonel Arthur Durante, US Army, Retired, 17 May 2003.

82.   Marti and Kardos

83.   Ibid.

84.   Ibid.

85.   Kardos.

86.   Bray.

87.   Specialist John Hutto, HHC, 1-325 AIR, interview by Lieutenant Colonel Arthur Durante, US Army, Retired, 17 May 2003.

88.   Ibid.

89.   Mark Johnson, et. al: "In Southern Iraq, Low-Level Fighting Continues," *Knight Ridder Newspapers*, 2 April 2003, 2.

90.   Bray.

91.   Rowe.

92.   Ibid.

93.   Aamer Madhani, "Soldiers Cross Euphrates, Take Control of Bridges Around Samawah," *Chicago Tribune*, 4 April 2003.

94.   Tom Lasseter and Mark Johnson, "Soldiers in Southern Iraq Fighting to Secure Bridges, Towns," *Knight Ridder Newspapers*, 4 April 2003.

95.   Rowe.

96.   Tom Lasseter and Mark Johnson.

97.   Ibid.

98.   Rowe.

99.   Major John Altman, S2, 1st BCT, 3rd ID, interview by Major Daniel Corey, 16 May 2003.

100.   3rd ID Consolidated Division History.

101.   Ibid.

102.   Ibid.

103.   Ibid.

104.   Ibid.

105.   2nd BCT, 3rd ID, 4-5.

106.   3rd ID Consolidated Division History, 39. Colonel David Perkins, commander, 2nd BCT 3rd ID, interview by Lieutenant Colonel Edrick Kirkman, 19 May 2003.

107.   2nd BCT, 3rd ID, 3.

108.   3rd ID Consolidated Division History, 38.

109.   Lieutenant Colonel "Rock" Marcone, commander, 3-69 AR, interview by Colonel Gregory Fontenot, US Army, Retired and Lieutenant Colonel E. J. Degen 22 October 2003.

110.   Ibid.

111.   Ibid. See also 3rd ID Consolidated Division History, 39.

112.   Marcone.

113.   Ibid.

114.   Ibid.

115.   Teleengineering is the practice of sending "real-time" images via portable cameras and satellites of structural damage from the battlefield directly to structural experts operating from a sanctuary or safe location. This allows the combat engineer on the battlefield to obtain the advice of experts from many different engineering specialties.

116.   3rd ID Consolidated Division History , 40. See also 54th Engineer Battalion Daily Summary and Unit History for Task Force 3-69 AR—Operation ENDURING FREEDOM and Operation IRAQI FREEDOM.

117.   Ibid.

118.   Grimsley. See also Marcone.

119.   3rd ID Consolidated Division History. These timelines are best estimates from unit histories. TF 1-64 AR reports arriving at 0100, TF 4-64 AR reports arriving at 0600, and TF 3-15 IN merely notes an all-night movement. It is not particularly clear whether the times that are cited were Zulu or local. Colonel David Perkins opined that these times seemed right in a phone call with Colonel Gregory Fontenot, US Army, Retired on 6 February 2004.

120.   3rd ID Consolidated Division History, 38-39.

121.   Marcone.

122.   Ibid. See also unit history TF 3-69 AR. The dismounted attack from the north cannot be authoritatively identified as the commando battalion, nor can the northern attack be reported as particularly threatening. None of the unit after-action summaries report the contacts in the north as particularly serious. The task force did, however identify the corpse of the Iraqi armored brigade commander and positively identified the 10th Armored Brigade. Marcone's troops captured an Iraqi order that suggested the Iraqis planned a two-brigade attack. It is therefore possible that what Marcone perceived as a second attempt from the east by 10th Armored Brigade in fact was an attack by a brigade of the *Nebuchadnezzar* that was in the area and previously identified. Marcone believed that the troops in the two mounted attacks came from the same brigade because he saw M113s captured from the Kuwaitis in both attacks. In the end, it did not matter to the Marcone's troops since they defeated all comers that morning.

123.   Colonel David Perkins, commander, 2nd BCT, 3rd ID, interview by Lieutenant Colonel E. J. Degen and Colonel Gregory Fontenot, US Army, Retired 22 October 2003.

124.   Ibid. See also 54th Engineers.

125.   Perkins.

126.   Interview with Colonel David Perkins, commander, 2nd BCT, 3rd ID, and the 2nd BCT subordinate task force commanders' command briefing, 18 May 2003; "3rd ID Comments on OIF and its Role in that War," 12 May 2003. This interview was generated by recording the brigade command briefing and interaction of 2nd BCT officers on 18 May 2003.

127.   2nd BCT, 3rd ID, 3.

128.   1-9 FA, 5-7.

129.   2nd BCT, 3rd ID, 3.

130.   TF 4-64 AR, 34-36.

131.   2nd BCT, 3rd ID, 3. See also Lieutenant Colonel Pete Bayer G3 3rd ID, interview by Colonel Timothy Cherry, 20 May 2003, and Colonel David Perkins, commander, 2nd BCT, 3rd ID, interview by Lieutenant Colonel

Rick Perkins, 24 April 2003.

132. 2nd BCT, 3rd ID, 3. See also TF 1-64 AR, 36-39.

133. "Tusker History, Operation IRAQI FREEDOM (19 March-12 April 2003)," see 3 April 2003.

134. 2nd BCT, 3rd ID.

135. 3rd ID Consolidated Division History, 40.

136. 2nd BCT, 3rd ID, 3.

137. 11th Engineer Battalion, "Jungle Cats History," 24-28.

138. Colonel William Grimsley, commander, 1st BCT, 3rd ID, interview by Lieutenant Colonel Dave Manning, May 2003 (day not specified). See also Lieutenant Colonel Pete Bayer, G-3, 3rd ID, interview by Colonel Timothy Cherry, 20 May 2003.

139. Ibid.

140. 3rd ID Consolidated Division History, 41.

141. Ibid., 42.

142. 11th Engineer Battalion, 24-28.

143. 3rd ID Consolidated Division History, 41-42. See also 11th Engineer Battalion, 24-28.

144. 3-7 CAV reported one troop set in Objective MONTGOMERY by 1703, thus protecting 1st BCT's northern and western flanks.

145. "Unit History, TF 3-69 AR, as of mid-April 2003," undated, 74.

146. 3rd ID Consolidated Division History, 42.

147. TF 3-69 AR, 32.

148. Ibid., 42.

149. "Unit History, TF 2-7 IN, Operation IRAQI FREEDOM," undated, 24.

150. Ibid.

151. TF 3-69 AR, 43-44.

152. TF 3-69 AR, 43-44.

153. Ibid.

154. 11th Engineer Battalion, 24-28; "OIF-SG Operational Summary: Engineer," Lieutenant Colonel James Knowlton, 15 July 2003.

155. 3rd ID Consolidated Division History, 41-42. Two days of operations included subsequent counterattacks by the Iraqis and is inferred from unit histories.

156. TF 3-69 AR, 74.

157. 11th Engineer Battalion, 24-28; "OIF-SG Operational Summary: Engineer."

158. TF 2-7 IN, 25.

159. Ibid.

160. Ibid.

161. TF 2-7 IN, 25.

162. TF 2-7 IN, 26. Milosovich's name is actually spelled Mysliwiec. This bit of information emerged from an internet search revealing a web page citing First Lieutenant Paul Mysliwiec. A phone call to Colonel Will Grimsley confirmed that First Lieutenant Paul Mysliwiec commanded the Bradley hit by the T-72. Although in the unit history Gee's first name is not given, another document electronically appended by TF 2-7 IN to an electronic file it provided to OIF-SG lists Gee's first name as Wendell. That document is a far better written account of the events cited here, but since it reads like the work of a professional and was not attributed, it is not used here.

163. TF 2-7 IN, 26.

164. Ibid., 26.

165. Rutter.

166. Ibid.

167. Ibid.

168. 11th Engineer Battalion, 24-28.

169. TF 2-7 IN, 29.

170. Ibid.

171. Ibid., 30.

172. Ibid., 31.

173. Ibid.

174. 11th Engineer Battalion, 24-28; "OIF-SG Operational Summary: Engineer."

175. Ibid.

176. Ibid.

177. TF 3-69 AR, 74.

178. 3rd ID Consolidated Division History, 42.

179. 3-7 CAV unit history; and 3-7 CAV command briefing.

180. Ibid.

181. 3rd ID Consolidated Division History, 41-42; 3-7 CAV Unit History; and 3-7 CAV command briefing.

182. Lieutenant Colonel Jeffrey R. Sanderson, commander, TF 2-69 AR, interview by Lieutenant Colonel Arthur Durante, US Army, Retired, 18 August 2003.

183. "Operational History of the 3rd BCT during Operation Iraqi Freedom." This is the unit history of 3rd BCT 3rd ID.

184. Lieutenant Colonel John Harding, Commander, 1-10 FA, interview by Lieutenant Colonel Arthur Durante, US Army, Retired, 4 August 2003.

185. Ibid.

186. Colonel Daniel Allyn, Commander, 3rd BCT 3rd ID, interview by Lieutenant Colonel James Knowlton, 12 May 2003. See also Harding.

187. Harding.

188. Sanderson. See also Lieutenant Colonel J.R. Sanderson email to Colonel Gregory Fontenot, US Army, Retired, 23 November 2003. Sanderson use the word "ferocious" to describe Al Kifl in an email to Lieutenant Colonel E. J. Degen on 18 November 2003.

189. Harding.

190. 3rd BCT, 3rd ID.

191. Harding.

192. Sanderson. See also Sanderson by Manning and Sanderson email to Degen. Developing the order of March requires interpolation and interpretation of all three of these sources.

193. 3rd BCT, 3rd ID.

194. Harding.

195. Ibid.

196. 3rd BCT, 3rd ID. See also Sanderson interviews and Harding by Durante.

197. 1-10 FA Unit History: Operation IRAQI FREEDOM, 45.

198. Sanderson.

199. 317th Engineer Battalion: Operation IRAQI FREEDOM. Huxley was assigned to B/317 EN supporting TF 3-69 AR. The unit history is unclear on when Huxley was killed, but it occurred in the area of Objective SAINTS as TF 2-69 AR moved en route to the line of departure for the attack on TITANS.

200. 3rd BCT, 3rd ID.

201. Sanderson interviews and emails.

202. Ibid.

203. Lieutenant Colonel John Harding, Commander, 1-10 FA, interview by Lieutenant Colonel William Pitts, 12 May 2003.

204. Sanderson by Durante.

205. 3rd BCT, 3rd ID.

206. Lieutenant Colonel Jeffery R. Sanderson, Commander, 2-69 AR, email follow-up to interview by Lieutenant Colonel Arthur Durante, US Army, Retired, 18 August 2003.

207. Sanderson by Manning. See also Sanderson emails.

208. 3rd BCT, 3rd ID.

209. 3rd BCT 3rd ID and unit histories TF 1-15 IN, TF 1-30 IN and TF 2-69 AR.

Chapter 6

Regime Collapse

"There are no American infidels in Baghdad. Never!"

Iraqi Information Minister
Mohammed Saeed al Sahhaf,
"Baghdad Bob"

"I got on Fox News and said, *"I know where he is, tell him to stay there for 15 minutes and I will come get him"* because we were right outside the Ministry of Information."

Lieutenant Colonel Eric Schwartz,
commander, TF 1-64, 2nd BCT,
presidential palace, Baghdad

Summary of Events

As CFLCC prepared for the assault on Baghdad, the air component focused on close air support in and around Baghdad, Mosul, and Tikrit and supporting SOF units operating in the west. CFACC continued to attack strategic targets as well. CFACC also struck a number of time-sensitive targets of opportunity developed from a number of intelligence sources. Close air support in heavily defended urban environments continued whenever and wherever coalition ground forces were in contact with the enemy. Coalition airmen delivered responsive and highly accurate close air support turning the tide of battle in ground tactical engagements on more than one occasion in the final assault on Baghdad.[1]

Maritime operations continued to facilitate the safe arrival of ships carrying large volumes of humanitarian supplies from the United Kingdom, Australia, the United States, and Spain. The coalition completed clearing mines from the southern waterways leading to Umm Qasr, allowing UK and Australian Navy clearance teams to start clearing northern waterways leading to Basra. By mid-April these efforts were well under way. The scale of the problem included not only clearing mines, but coalition maritime units also had to clear 36 derelict vessels between Um Qasr and Az Zuabyr.[2]

Elements of the I MEF and V Corps completed closing the cordon around Baghdad, cutting the major routes in and out of the city. In the south, the 1st (UK) Armoured Division secured all of the southern oil fields and soon moved north to link up with elements of the 1st Marine Division in the vicinity of Al-Amara. By 10 April, coalition forces had defeated organized resistance in Baghdad. As the fighting in Baghdad tapered off, Marine and Army units headed north toward Tikrit and Mosul. JSOFT-North troops entered Kirkuk and other towns in northern Iraq.

On 4 April, both Lieutenant General Wallace and Lieutenant General Conway, commanding I MEF, could view their situation with satisfaction. V Corps and I MEF had successfully kept at bay the paramilitary that had attacked their supply convoys and threatened the LOCs. Moreover, they had nearly encircled Baghdad. The marines in I MEF crossed the Euphrates at An Nasiriyah and fought their way up the valley between the Euphrates and Tigris Rivers, then

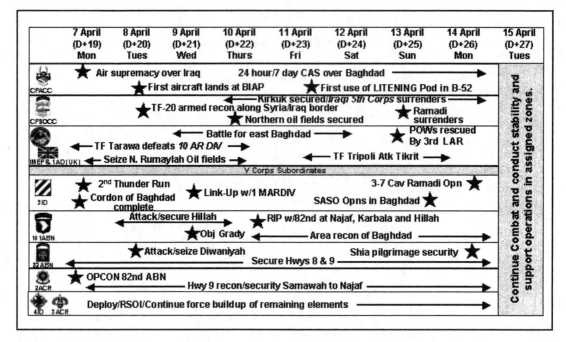

Figure 184. Regime collapse sequence of events

approached the city from the southeast. V Corps' five simultaneous attacks had taken the corps through the Karbala Gap and Al Hillah to Objectives SAINTS and LIONS—isolating Baghdad from the south and west.

With V Corps holding an arc around Baghdad from the south around to the west and northwest and the marines approaching from the southeast, only the northern half of the circle remained open. Although JSOTF-West, composed of SOF and rangers, did not close in on Baghdad, they denied any Iraqi maneuver in the desert to the west. In the north, 4th ID's absence precluded closing the circle. 3rd ID's 3rd BCT, attacking into Objective TITANS, denied Highway 1. Simply put, only Highway 2 coming south from Kirkuk remained open. Farther to the north, JSOTF-North and its 173rd Airborne Brigade fixed the bulk of Iraqi divisions on the Green Line and raised the ante by supporting *Peshmerga* attacks to the south. The Americans and *Peshmerga* threatened the two major northern cities, Irbil and Kirkuk, and the Iraqi conventional forces began to melt away under the pressure.

Equally important, from V Corps' vantage point, the "five simultaneous attacks" had flushed the Republican Guard from their hiding sites. On the move, elements of the *Adnan*, *Hammurabi*, and *Nebuchadnezzar* divisions, mixed with some regular units, proved to be juicy targets for coalition airmen and artillerymen. Moreover, the Iraqis appear to have misread the five simultaneous attacks—they were apparently unsure of the coalition's true direction of attack and when the main assault would actually start. As a result, they assumed a more southerly defensive posture. Thus, the Iraqi reaction, while vigorous, ultimately came too late to stiffen the *Medina* Division when V Corps struck. Additionally, expecting the main effort from between the two rivers, they oriented in the wrong direction. Over the next few days, V Corps and 3rd ID tested the Iraqis, conducting a series of attacks to tighten the isolation of

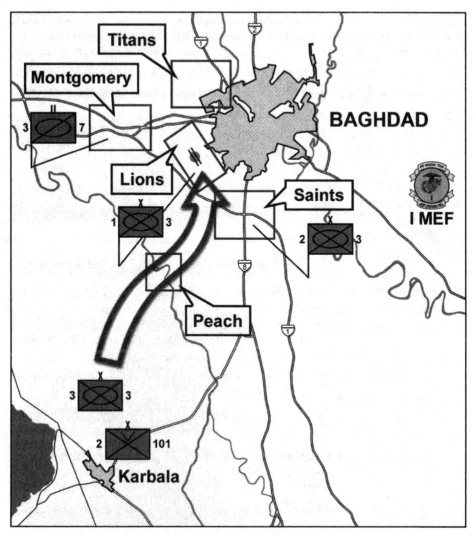

Figure 185. Attack to Baghdad

Baghdad, link up with the marines, and enter the heart of the governmental district with its lavish palaces and other sites that marked Saddam's seat of power.

The Plan for Baghdad

The CFLCC plan for reducing Baghdad was necessarily vague. As late as D-day, Lieutenant General McKiernan could not predict what the battlefield would look like when V Corps and I MEF reached the city. Planners, from CENTCOM down to the maneuver divisions, struggled to paint a picture of the city after an unknown period of fighting during the approach from Kuwait. Because of this uncertainty, V Corps planners, led by Major E.J. Degen, built flexibility into their plan. Establishing a cordon postured the soldiers and marines to react in any one of a number of ways, depending on how events unfolded. Never intended as a hermetic seal, the ring of forward operating bases would isolate the city from relieving forces and contain the defenders inside. From these operating bases, the soldiers and marines could attack into Baghdad to seize critical targets, destroy Iraqi forces, and eventually clear the city, if required.

Cordoning the city would reduce the regime's options and allow the coalition to develop the situation. Moreover, it would allow the corps and MEF to build combat power by closing their units up to the cordon, moving logistics forward, refitting after the expected fight with the Republican Guard divisions, and finish clearing the LOCs and rear area. All of these actions would set the stage for the final phase of the campaign—seizing Baghdad and removing the regime.

Of course, none of the senior commanders—Lieutenant Generals McKiernan, Wallace, or Conway—wanted to slacken the pressure on Saddam Hussein, the Ba'athist regime, or the defending forces. While the corps and MEF consolidated around the city, both planned to execute a steady stream of limited-objective raids, air strikes, psychological and information operations, and ground attacks on key targets in the city. These targets were chosen with great care to degrade the regime's actual—and perceived—control over the capital city and the country of Iraq, based on Major Rago's analysis and planning. By the time V Corps entered to the heart of Baghdad on 5 April, all major systems within the city had been dissected, studied, and targeted. Every building and section of the city were mapped and numbered. Everyone working in and around the city, on the ground or in the air, used the common graphics and systems data for targeting, thus maximizing lethality while minimizing collateral damage and fratricide. What started as an internal V Corps' planning concept for urban warfare permeated across joint, coalition, and interagency realms to make the total force more efficient and lethal.

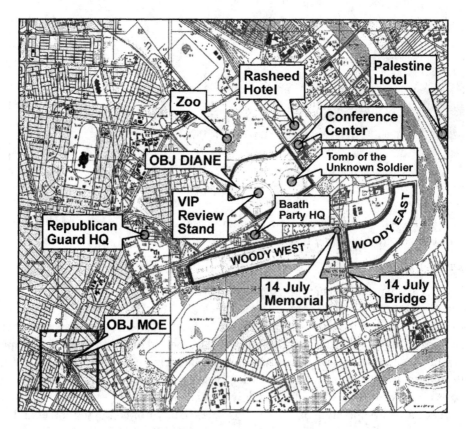

Figure 186. Key locations and objectives in downtown Baghdad

Actions Elsewhere

As the corps' and the world's eyes focused on Baghdad, the campaign continued elsewhere in Iraq. The 82nd Airborne Division concluded its fight in As Samawah and looked north to Ad Diwaniyah. The 101st Airborne Division cleared An Najaf and Al Kifl, destroying the *Fedayeen* defenders while protecting the sensitive Shiite religious and cultural sites in the town. Additionally, the 101st prepared for what would be a "hornets' nest" in Al Hillah. Farther south, the British continued their efforts to subdue Basra, and in Kuwait, the 4th ID arrived and began to receive its well-traveled equipment. The first squadron of the 2nd ACR (L) was fully integrated into the theater and under the command and control of the 82nd Airborne Division to assist in securing the LOCs. With forces in contact from Baghdad to Basra, across both river valleys, and from the borders of Iran and Turkey to the Green Line and beyond, CFLCC waged the nonlinear fight presaged in the Army's FM 3-0 and replicated in the contemporary operating environment.

Seeing the Elephant—The Human Dimension of Combat

"Seeing the Elephant" was a Civil War expression for the trauma of a soldier's first combat experience. As the soldiers and marines approached Baghdad, they too had "seen the elephant."

The fight moving north had been radically different from the force-on-force armored battle the soldiers had expected. The march north was to have been relatively easy, with some fighting against the bound-to-capitulate regular army units, but mostly cheering Shiite Iraqis in welcome parties.

But close combat with Iraqi and foreign fighters closing in from all sides in fanatical—and suicidal—waves had given the soldiers pause. Any veteran understands that combat is living on the edge and, in some ways, living to the utmost. Pumped full of adrenaline, soldiers experience time distortion and live in an almost surreal condition of alertness, with senses heightened to the point nearly of exaggeration. Accordingly, any joy is felt with hypersensitivity, as is any sad event. Wild jubilation morphs to incredible despair from one moment to the next.

In the fall of Baghdad, soldiers and marines would experience both extremes. The fight to the city left the soldiers and leaders at every level wondering about the carnage they could expect in the Iraqi capital. Not only could they expect the same ferocious paramilitary attacks in Baghdad; those forces would be stiffened by the highly trained SRG fighting on its own turf and for its very survival. With almost 15,000 of these elite soldiers, chosen for their loyalty to Saddam and favored with personal privilege, the best equipment, and the best training, Baghdad could be a truly ugly and painful fight.

Logistics and Communications Status

As combat troops fought their way into Baghdad, combat service support soldiers were busier than ever. At this point, the LOC supporting V Corps extended across a greater distance than the historic Red Ball Express, and fuel demands exceeded the highest requirement the Red Ball Express had to meet. Ammunition, food, and water also had to be brought all the way from the heart of Kuwait. The logisticians managed to keep up with the demand for critical supplies of war, but just barely. While no unit ever ran completely out of these supplies, several came close.

Yet even with this monumental success in fuel, ammunition, water, and food, the system failed to provide repair parts. Parts often made their way from the United States across a massive air and sea bridge to the supply depots in Kuwait—where they sat due to ground transportation shortages and the lack of an effective distribution system. Warehouses filled up with requisitioned repair parts, only to stay on shelves and in bins, while exhausted truckers hauled higher-priority supplies forward.

Despite the dearth of parts, the combat units sustained the drive north on the skill, experience, planning, preparation, sweat, and energy of their maintenance soldiers. Literally every brigade and battalion commander in the corps proudly bragged that he had "the best mechanics in the Army." They beamed with tales of soldiers performing miracles in repairing broken equipment, recovering abandoned and damaged vehicles, and in some cases fabricating parts out of almost nothing.[3] Yet however creative and successful the soldiers were, literally every maneuver battalion commander in 3rd ID asserted that he could not have continued offensive operations for another two weeks without some spare parts. For example, as late as 14 May, almost 45 days after combat started, one unit had only received 19 spare parts through the formal supply system. Others still had not received any.[4] The 1-10 FA kept its Paladin howitzers on the move by cannibalizing a Kuwaiti M109 howitzer the Iraqis had captured years prior and that 3rd ID subsequently took back.[5] No one had anything good to say about parts delivery, from the privates at the front to the generals at CFLCC.

While the repair parts system struggled to catch up, the signal community fared marginally better. During the march up-country, the units almost immediately outpaced the signalers' ability to provide widespread coverage. Even within brigades and battalions, the operating distances thwarted the ground-based line-of-sight radios. The Mobile Subscriber Equipment (MSE) that is the Army's primary means of providing high-bandwidth support to tactical units never had a chance of keeping up with the fast-paced advance. For the most part, the corps executed the advance on to Baghdad with a few tactical satellite radios and the widely distributed satellite-based BFT system. Indeed, Colonel Terry Wolff, the commander of 2nd ACR (L), was nonchalant about spreading one squadron across 200 kilometers of roads without any direct radio communications because the BFT provided him excellent situation awareness. If worse came to worse, Wolff knew he could always launch a helicopter to serve as a radio relay if he needed to talk to his troops directly.[6]

The pause at RAMS and the slower pace of advance from there north enabled the communicators to catch up. Once on site, they quickly built the networks and coverage the forces needed to conduct operations in and around the city. Although the communication systems were not mature in any sense, few commanders complained of communications problems in and around Baghdad in those final days of the fight.

Rolling Transition and Sensitive Site Exploitation

The coalition was doing far more than just slashing through the countryside. In areas already under control, a combination of special operations and regular forces rapidly transitioned to stability operations and support operations. In the myriad of towns and villages along the Euphrates River Valley, the local population experienced its first taste of relative freedom in almost 30 years. Rebuilding a functioning, representative local government and providing basic life support services—water, food, and power—was a hard task, made more difficult by instability in the north and the remnants of the fanatical *Saddam Fedayeen* spread throughout the region. Earning the wary Iraqis' trust and cooperation remains a slow, painstaking effort.

While some soldiers worked to help get the Iraqis back on their feet, others searched for weapons of mass destruction at sites identified throughout the region. The 75th Exploitation Task Force (XTF), built on the 75th Artillery Regiment, eventually searched more than 600 sites. Each site had an assigned priority based on the possible threat it posed to coalition forces and the surrounding civilians. The list was long and the work was slow and demanding. Although there were several reports of possible banned weapons, by the end of major combat operations, the 75th had not discovered any weapons of mass destruction.

Actions at Baghdad

Intelligence officers at all echelons continued to have great difficulty accurately describing the threat in the city. In the months leading up to the war, V Corps, CFLCC, and CENTCOM intelligence leaders and analysts spent the bulk of their energy trying to characterize what the Baghdad fight might look like. In October 2002, intelligence officers from the national level, CENTCOM, CFLCC, I MEF, and V Corps met and developed a common estimate of the enemy situation that they had separately continued to update.

Prior to D-day, intelligence officers estimated that no more that 9-12 company equivalents of the Republican Guard would successfully retreat into the city. They expected these units to be disorganized. According to the estimates, these remnants would report to the SRG, who were expected to stand and fight in the city. There was some reason to believe the Iraqis had developed a sophisticated and potentially effective city-defense strategy that would leverage all of the advantages of a prepared defense in an urban environment. Captured documents revealed a detailed plan to divide Baghdad into sectors and defend it in a manner reminiscent of the First Battle of Grozny. The international airport and the palace complex area in the heart of the city would be the most heavily defended sites in Baghdad. All intelligence reporting supported these assessments, indicating that the defense would crystallize around these two critical facilities. Prewar intelligence estimates noted the presence of paramilitary forces in large numbers but were vague on how these forces might operate. The march up-country effectively answered that question, painting the picture of the potentially dangerous and difficult fight to come.[7]

As the battle progressed, the coalition defeated but did not destroy the Republican Guard. The slew of vehicles and equipment left abandoned sparked a variety of theories about the Republican Guard's actual condition. These ranged from the view that the Iraqis would conduct a stalwart infantry-based defense of the city with the missing Republican Guard soldiers as the bedrock to the notion of a defense by disorganized remnants. Imagery and other reports inexplicably showed almost no preparations within the city. There were numerous small fighting positions but none of the deliberate defenses that common sense and Iraqi doctrine indicated. Intelligence and field reports painted a picture of mixed units thrown haphazardly into the fray with little command and control. Intelligence officers could no longer speak with assurance about which unit was where, let alone in what strength. Some units fought, some died in place under the rain of coalition fires, and some abandoned their equipment and just walked away. But were they going home or going to ground to add to the unconventional defense of the city? It was unclear whether Baghdad was a trap, a clever ruse, or a hollow shell. When 3rd ID seized and cleared the airport, one of the two sites everyone agreed would be heavily defended, the troops answered part of the question. Baghdad looked difficult, but it did not look like Grozny. Taking the airport made the armored raids—the "Thunder Runs"—feasible in the mind of the senior commanders and their staffs.[8]

Although Major General Blount and the 3rd ID settled into Objectives SAINTS and LIONS, they had not entirely reduced Objective TITANS. In accordance with the original plan, the division continued to set its part of the cordon. Although the rest of V Corps and I MEF continued to advance rapidly, they would not be players in the immediate actions at Baghdad. But neither Wallace nor Blount believed they needed to wait on securing TITANS or for the rest of the corps to get started. The 3rd ID would conduct raids and attacks to maintain the heat on the regime and to retain the initiative against the defending Iraqis and foreign fighters.

Thunder Runs

Given the ambiguity surrounding Baghdad, the division's first order of business was to probe, or raid, the city, just to see what would happen. Literally sticking his hand into what everyone expected to be a "hornets' nest," Blount ordered Colonel Perkins' 2nd BCT to conduct a thunder run into the city. While the thunder run on 5 April turned into a stiff fight for the *Rogues* of TF 1-64 AR, their success suggested that Baghdad would be defended energetically, but that the enemy no longer could mount effective resistance. Interestingly, the *Hunter* UAV showed the Iraqis setting obstacles behind the *Rogues*, apparently trying to set up kill zones if the Americans departed along the same route. The obstacles proved irrelevant since the *Rogues* continued on to the airport rather than retrace their route.[9]

Taking less than a day to assess the reaction, Wallace and Blount struck again. This time, rather than a simple one-battalion raid, the division ordered a full brigade into the heart of Baghdad. On 7 April, Colonel Perkins' 2nd Brigade *Spartans* launched a second thunder run, ending up in downtown Baghdad—the absolute heart of Saddam's regime—to demonstrate to the Iraqis and the world the Americans' freedom to move about the city. On that day Perkins made the single decision that arguably shortened the siege by weeks, if not months—he chose to stay downtown. Equally important, McKiernan, Wallace, and Blount trusted his judgment and underwrote the risks that he took. While the fighting continued in earnest for another few days and insurgents fight on today, the second thunder run broke the regime's back, and any remaining political or military leaders of rank disappeared in a flash of self-preservation.

Toppling the Statue—Army PSYOP Supports I MEF

We woke up that morning [of 9 April] in the Iraqi Special Forces training compound on the outskirts of southern Baghdad. Attached to 3rd Battalion, 4th Marine Regiment (of I MEF), who were conducting a clearing operation on the southern approach to Baghdad, [we were] moving with their TAC at the time. We were kept in a centralized location while moving so that we could be flexed to where we might be needed.

We were not sure what we were going to hit, but we were expecting a lot of resistance. The infantry unit was to be clearing door to door, while we would be broadcasting civilian noninterference messages and occasional surrender appeals when pockets of enemy forces were located. The infantry unit started its operation but was encountering no resistance at all. After a few hours of going door to door, kicking doors and entering, looking for enemy concentrations and weapons caches but finding none, they modified their plan and formed up into a column and started a general movement toward Al-Firdos (paradise) Square in [eastern] Baghdad, where the Palestine Hotel and statue [of Saddam Hussein] were located. The entire movement went a lot faster than anyone had anticipated....

Crowds of Iraqi citizens started coming out and cheering the American convoy. We started to do some PSYOP broadcasts about bringing about a free Iraq, but knowing that we were to continue some clearing operations; we were telling them to stay away from our military vehicles for their own safety. We eventually dismounted from our vehicle and continued to inform the civilians to stay back from the military vehicles. The Iraqi civilians were very receptive to us, and [we] continued to engage them with our interpreter.

As we approached the street leading into the Al-Firdos Square, we could tell that there was a very large crowd of civilians starting to form up. It looked like the infantry unit up there could use some support, so we moved our [tactical PSYOP team] TPT vehicle forward and started to run around seeing what they needed us to do to facilitate their mission.... There was a large media circus at this location (I guess the Palestine Hotel was a media center at the time), almost as many reporters as there were Iraqis, as the hotel was right adjacent to the Al-Firdos Square.

The Marine Corps colonel in the area saw the Saddam statue as a target of opportunity and decided that the statue must come down. Since we were right there, we chimed in with some loudspeaker support to let the Iraqis know what it was we were attempting to do. The reporters were completely surrounding the vehicle, and we started having to ask the reporters to move out of the way, but they would not move. We were getting frustrated, but we were also laughing about it. We dismounted the vehicle again and just started pushing the people out of the way. They were starting to really inhibit our ability to conduct our mission. The tanks . . . formed up into a perimeter around the square, with the statue in the middle.

An M88 recovery vehicle approached the statue and continued to drive up the steps right next to the statue in an attempt to bring it down. The people had already tied a noose around the neck of the statue with some rope. They were trying to just tug on it and bring it down and were hitting it with sledgehammers; it was clearly getting crazy in the square. We were no longer in crowd control, as there was just no controlling this crowd at this time. We decided to just ride along with the crowd, and we started just kind of celebrating with the Iraqi people. We actually had to have our interpreter record an ad-hoc broadcast message, informing the Iraqi people that if they did not stand back from the statue, American forces would not bring the statue down. We were afraid that some civilians would get hurt if they were too close or in the wrong spot.

All of this activity was going on within just a few blocks of where other marines were battling with snipers in a building across from the Palestine Hotel. The local Iraqi people just did not care for their well being at this point; they just wanted to see the statue come down...We looked over and now there was an American flag draped over the face of the statue. God bless them, but we were thinking from PSYOP school that this was just bad news. We didn't want to look like an occupation force, and some of the Iraqis were saying, 'No, we want an Iraqi flag!' So I said 'No problem, somebody get me an Iraqi flag.' I am not sure where it came from, but one of the Iraqis brought us the old Iraqi flag without the writing on it (added by Saddam). We got that as fast as we could and started running that up to the statue. At this time, the marines had put a chain from the boom of the recovery vehicle around the neck of the statue, and they just ran the [Iraqi] flag up the statue. It was real quick thinking on Staff Sergeant

U.S. Army

Figure 187. A sense of humor in troubled times: An unknown artist has poked fun at (and poked holes in) iconography of Saddam Hussein in Baghdad, May 2003

Plesich's part to get that Iraqi flag up there quick. But by the time the Iraqi flag got put on the statue, there had already been a lot of photos taken with the marine covering the statue with the American flag.

Somehow along the way, somebody had gotten the idea to put a bunch of Iraqi kids onto the wrecker that was to pull the statue down. While the wrecker was pulling the statue down, there were Iraqi children crawling all over it. Finally they brought the statue down, but we expected this big statue to come crashing down, to shatter or whatever, but it just slowly bent over and slid off the mounting pipes. Once the statue was on the ground, it was attacked by Iraqis with the sledgehammers and broken apart. The head of the statue was dragged through the streets, with people hitting the face with their shoes and spitting on it. After the statue was down, we started to receive a lot of intelligence on where Ba'ath Party personnel were staying and just generally got a lot of real good intelligence for use in later direct-action missions. All this information was developed with and through the human exploitation teams, which had assigned interpreters.[10]

Caring for the Fallen

Support soldiers seldom receive accolades for what they do. They made OIF possible and they deserve better. Of all the difficult and thankless jobs the Army asks support troops to do, none is more difficult or less visible than the task of the 54th QM Company. The only active-duty mortuary affairs company in the Army, the 54th deployed 176 soldiers to Kuwait to care for the remains of America's fallen.

54th Quartermaster Company

Figure 188. 54th Quartermaster Company caring for a fallen soldier's remains

These soldiers collect and process the remains of their colleagues for return to the United States. The 54th's troops approach their task with the knowledge that they are the last people who will ever see the person whose remains they are preparing for return to their families. The mission is difficult. According to their commander, "You can't see what we have [seen] and not hurt." But the 54th's view is exemplified in a painting done by one of their soldiers. The painting portrays a fallen soldier lying adjacent to his M-16, with an angel gazing down on him. The artist inscribed the painting, "Think not only upon their passing; remember the glory of their spirit."[11]

Transition to Peace Operations (10 April-1 May 2003)

"The game is over...I hope for a peaceful life for all Iraqis."

Mohammed al-Douri,
Iraq's Ambassador to the United Nations

"When it really comes down to it, [information operations] is really about changing a person's mind set."

Colonel Patrick Simon,
CFLCC C3,
chief of Information Operations

The collapse of the regime made it necessary for V Corps to shift from combat operations to stability operations and support operations. Accordingly, the information operations (IO) effort shifted from supporting combat operations and undermining the regime to restoring order and helping to reestablish civil control. It now became important to ensure stability in Baghdad by restoring public order and assisting in the "return to normalcy." With organized, conventional resistance effectively crushed, V Corps transitioned to patrolling the streets to provide presence; assisting other government agencies and special forces in their missions; and assessing, securing, and repairing the public utilities and infrastructure.[12] V Corps moved rapidly to restore internal security. Looters, opportunists, and regime die-hards all threatened to gain control of the cities in the power vacuum left in the aftermath of the Ba'ath regime's collapse. To counter this, V Corps seized the radio station at Abu Ghurayb to provide a means to disseminate messages to the people of Baghdad. Unfortunately, the station was too damaged to broadcast, so PSYOP teams resorted to mobile transmitting equipment instead.[13]

V Corps' information operations planners, under the direction of Lieutenant Colonel Chuck Eassa, moved an advance party to the corps TAC in Baghdad on 22 April to establish a forward presence in the city. The rest of the IO cell closed on Baghdad on 28 April. In conjunction with national and international agencies, V Corps and the entire CFLCC began the hard work of transitioning from combat operations to nation building, reconstruction, and restoration of a functioning, independent Iraqi civil government. This shift marked the start of the long process of rebuilding Iraq and restoring civil government to the country and continues as of this writing.[14]

Conclusion

The sound of the proverbial door slamming as the Iraqi regime fled Baghdad or went into hiding was also the sound of victory: the soldiers of V Corps, in conjunction with the

Michael Bracken, US Army

Figure 189. Bomb-damaged bridge, Baghdad

sister services and allies, achieved the first half of the coalition's strategic objective—regime removal. The second half, building a stable, democratic, prosperous, nonthreatening Iraq, is part of ongoing operations as *On Point* went to publication, and is properly the subject of a different study.

Thunder Run of 5 April

The generals called them raids or armed reconnaissance. The media described them either as attacks or raids. The troops called them "thunder runs," from Army Vietnam-era jargon used to describe the daily combat missions designed to assure the security of supply routes. Mounted combined arms units from company to brigade size executed thunder runs. The name proved to be entirely appropriate as the troops breached minefields and obstacles and fought through ambushes almost every foot of the way. More important, 3rd ID's thunder runs ultimately proved decisive in bringing down the regime.

As the situation developed during the last week of March, Major General Blount confirmed his belief in "piling on" to keep the pressure on the Iraqis. Arguably, Blount inspired Lieutenant General Wallace to mount the five simultaneous attacks that set the conditions for the corps to reach Baghdad's suburbs. Now set in Objectives LIONS and SAINTS, Blount, always aggressive, wanted to learn the nature of the defenses in Baghdad and to develop the situation in accordance with his corps commander's intent. Just as important, he had troops available.

Accordingly, with Wallace's approval, he ordered an armed reconnaissance into Baghdad. Blount assigned the mission to Colonel David Perkins of the 2nd BCT, who subsequently ordered Lieutenant Colonel "Rick" Schwartz and the troops of TF 1-64 AR to conduct what the task force's history described as "a show of force"—driving up Highway 8 into central Baghdad and then looping back southwest to Baghdad International Airport.

Lieutenant Colonel Schwartz assumed command of 1-64 AR, *Rogue*, at Fort Stewart, Georgia, on 17 July 2002. Schwartz, who commanded a company in 1-64 AR during DESERT STORM, was no stranger to the battalion or to the desert. Immediately upon assuming command, he and his unit task-organized in preparation for a deployment to Kuwait as part of Operation DESERT SPRING. Schwartz gave up his B Company, receiving in return C/3-15 IN, D/10th Engineers, an Air Force tactical control party, a counterintelligence team, and a liaison party from a marine air and naval gunfire liaison company. He and his task force deployed in September, with his lead party arriving on 11 September 2002. The soldiers of

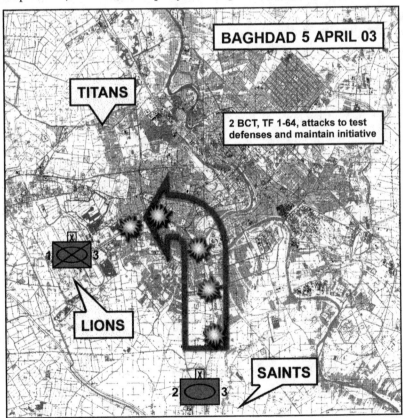

Figure 190. The 5 April thunder run route

Courtesy of 2nd BCT, 3rd ID

Figure 191. Colonel David Perkins, commander, 2nd BCT, 3rd ID

Rogue immediately began hard training. The tempo increased throughout the period leading to Operation IRAQI FREEDOM.[15]

When Colonel Perkins ordered Schwartz and his outfit into Baghdad, they had been at war for two weeks and in the field for more than six months. The task force soldiers knew each other and could organize rapidly. The task force comprised nearly 100 tracked vehicles and as many wheeled vehicles, was practiced, and had developed drills for nearly every contingency.

Scheme of Maneuver—Armor, Only Armor

In doing his mission analysis, Lieutenant Colonel Schwartz elected to leave all his wheeled support vehicles behind because of their lack of armament. The mission required a raid, by definition a short-duration operation done for explicit purposes. In this case, Perkins aimed to demonstrate the Americans' freedom of action and to gauge enemy reaction. Accordingly Schwartz concluded that the mission did not require his vulnerable combat trains. Specifically, the mission required TF 1-64 AR to "conduct a movement to contact north along Highway 8 to determine the enemy's disposition, strength, and will to fight."[16] The raid required *Rogue* to conduct a mounted attack north into Baghdad and then continue on Highway 8 as it looped to the southwest toward the airport. Then they would link up with 1st Brigade at the airport.[17] The axis of the attack was just about 20 kilometers long and required going under several overpasses and through the city. The task force's main combat power consisted of several hundred soldiers aboard 29 tanks, 14 Bradleys, and other combat vehicles, including M113s.[18]

TF 1-64 AR was not new to thunder runs; it had already conducted two smaller runs on its advance on Baghdad. However, both of those had essentially been short-duration attacks to destroy mostly unoccupied combat vehicles that had been bypassed. *Rogue* conducted what they called thunder runs I and II after crossing the Euphrates River at Objective PEACH to clear up resistance and enemy equipment on Highways 1 and 8, well south of Baghdad. During each of those missions, they encountered limited enemy resistance from dismounted infantry and paramilitary forces, some of whom used civilians to shield themselves.

Despite the relative ease of their earlier thunder runs, no one expected a thunder run into Baghdad to be easy. Captain Dave Hibner, commanding D/10th Engineers, recalled that he was called to receive a fragmentary order at 2200 on 4 April. According, Hibner and the other officers of the task force were surprised, and some were shocked, to hear that they were going to Baghdad that soon and all alone. Lieutenant Colonel Schwartz reassured them, noting that "somebody at headquarters has done the analysis, they are not going to send us in to fail, and tomorrow we are going to attack into Baghdad."[19] Reassured or not, Schwartz and his officers had their orders and they prepared accordingly. Colonel Perkins elected to accompany the task force to assure support and to provide on-scene command and control. This would enable Schwartz to concentrate on his tasks of running the direct firefight and leading his task force.

Mission Execution—Penetrating the City

With some uncertainty about how things might go, the task force staged at 0600 on 5 April for the first American incursion into Baghdad. The soldier who wrote the unit history for A Company (*Wild Bunch*) put it this way, "Truthfully, everyone's nerves were on edge for this mission."[20] Since Schwartz ordered the *Wild Bunch* to lead, they could be forgiven for having a case of nerves that morning. Team C/1-64 AR (*Rock*) followed *Wild Bunch*, and Team C/3-15 IN (*Cobra*) assumed the trail position. Captain Hibner left his mine-clearing line charge (MCLIC) and one engineer platoon behind but moved with his 1st Platoon tucked in with the *Wild Bunch*. Reflecting on Hibner's choice of his platoon, First Lieutenant Eric Canaday, 1st Platoon, D Company, 10th Engineers, recalled, "I think the reason [Hibner] did that was because I was a three-track platoon [1st Platoon lost a track to maintenance]....I had to pack my whole platoon into three vehicles. This gave me four or five shooters in the back of each track in addition to the .50-caliber machine gun and Mk-19 [40 mm automatic grenade launcher].... We had gotten extra SAWs [Squad Automatic Weapons] and 240s [7.62mm machine guns] from the other platoon and actually were able to put down a surprising amount of firepower."[21] Although he apparently had not shared his reasons with Canaday, Hibner intended exactly that. At Najaf Hibner discovered that all those 240 machine guns and .50-caliber machine guns on the tracks gave the platoon a lot of firepower and the ability to fire on the second and third stories, something that the tanks and Bradleys could not do. According to Hibner, each track could engage six targets at once—better than the tanks and Bradleys could do.[22]

Festooned with weapons, the engineers provided the task force with welcome additional firepower. Everyone had learned at An Najaf that the engineer squads provided an impressive addition to the task force's firepower, particularly when focused on the second and third floors of buildings that the tanks and Bradleys had trouble reaching from close in. Scouts and mortars remained in the task force blocking positions to maintain secure positions to which the task force could return.[23]

The task force crossed the line of departure at 0630, moving in a staggered column along Highway 8. What followed proved to be riveting television, as much of America and the world accompanied *Rogue*, TF 1-64 AR, as they fought their way downtown. As seen over Colonel Perkins' shoulder or from behind his track commander, Captain John Ives, the brigade assistant S2, the fight was prolonged and often very intense. Perkins' young captain alternately fired his M2 .50-caliber machine gun and his M-16. At one point, in the midst of reloading his .50-caliber machine gun, the young captain turned in his hatch and saw an Iraqi defender a few meters away, raising his AK-47 to fire. Acting without thinking, Ives threw the empty ammunition can he had in his hands at the Iraqi, knocking him down. Perkins then grabbed his 9mm pistol and killed the man. These types of engagements punctuated the narrative from Greg Kelly of FOX News, aboard the brigade commander's M113 APC.[24]

Only minutes into the operation, *Rogue* began taking sporadic small-arms and RPG fire. Soon they encountered both paramilitary forces and beret-wearing uniformed SRG soldiers. As the task force proceeded into town, the intensity of the fight ratcheted up. Moreover, junctions with ramps on and off of Highway 8 complicated matters, as did civilians who continued to use the highway, sharing it with the *Rogue* and occasionally with the enemy. Determining which traffic was hostile and which was not required patience and courage throughout the run. Generally, if traffic was joining the highway, the troops fired warning shots, causing drivers to turn around abruptly. But traffic passing on the opposite side of the highway had to be assessed and trail units advised. Avoiding harm to civilians who had no idea that the Americans had arrived in Baghdad proved impossible. Captain Hibner recalls that one family suffered due to secondary explosions caused when the task force destroyed a technical vehicle. The explosions injured several children and their father. At one point, a Bradley blocked a ramp and an Iraqi vehicle promptly struck it. This forced a trailing car to a halt. In this second car, the soldiers found the Iraqi colonel who served as the chief of logistics for the Baghdad district.[25] The troops brought him along for the rest of the ride.[26]

Only 20 minutes into the thunder run, *Rogue* fought hard against Iraqi regulars and paramilitary forces firing from every "niche and cranny."[27] To add to their difficulties, Staff Sergeant Diaz's tank, C12, took either an RPG or recoilless rifle hit in the right rear. Diaz, his crew, and others fought the resulting fire, hoping to save the tank.

> ## Close Contact on Thunder Run I
>
> [TF 1-64 AR] had moved 6 kilometers when a recoilless rifle disabled one of the tanks.... It hit into the tank's engine compartment and it started it on fire....The dismounted enemy converged on the disabled tank...Two members of the tank crew got on board the First Sergeant's M113 and were shot while boarding. One was shot through his eye and the other soldier was shot in the shoulder.... At one point, Wild Bunch reported over 250 dismounts attacking them.
>
> Captain David Hibner,
> commander, D/10th EN

According to Lieutenant Colonel Eric "Rick" Schwartz, "*Cobra* got hit hard and in an area that made the whole task force vulnerable at a key overpass, where we had taken a lot of fire. I had to decide if we should go to ground and provide security and give *Cobra* the opportunity to recover that tank or do we abandon the tank and keep going." [28] Schwartz halted the task force. During the halt, paramilitary and military forces began to arrive in trucks and buses, in no particular order and in no formation. The task force chewed them up with "a steady stream of coax, main gun, and 25 'mike-mike'(Bradley cannon)."[29]

Those fighting the fire and attempting to recover C12 became prime targets for the now-aroused opposition. At one point, the team commander reported that he was in contact with 250 Iraqi dismounts. Paramilitary forces descended on the burning tank. Schwartz recalled that this enemy "knew every dirty trick in the book and used it."[30] Despite the intensity of the Iraqi attack, soldiers fought the fire with some success. It appeared several times that they had the fire under control. The crew even managed to hook a tow bar to C12 to recover it, but the

Figure 192. TF 1-64 AR conducting casualty air MEDEVAC, 5 April 2003

fire flared up again. Finally, after 20 minutes of fighting the fire and the enemy, Diaz and his soldiers had to abandon the tank. But even this choice caused difficulty as the crew scrambled to recover sensitive items from the doomed tank under enemy fire. The Iraqis wounded two of Diaz's crewmen as they departed the scene as passengers in the company first sergeant's M113.[31]

One hour into the 2 hour and 20-minute operation, the thunder run became an exercise in running a gauntlet. Moving slowly and fighting in several directions, the task force suffered another blow when the Iraqis fatally wounded Staff Sergeant Stevon Booker. Booker, a tank commander, was up high in his cupola firing on Iraqi dismounted infantry and *Fedayeen* with his M-4 carbine when he was hit. Nearly simultaneously, the Iraqis hit a Bradley attached to *Wild Bunch* with an RPG, disabling it and blowing the driver out of his hatch. *Wild Bunch* halted to deal with the disabled Bradley and to evacuate Booker and the injured Bradley driver. A tank platoon maneuvered to protect the evacuation of the wounded and of the disabled Bradley. Within minutes, the *Wild Bunch* had loaded the wounded and moved on.[32]

Mission Completion—Linking Up at LIONS

As *Rogue* closed on the airport, the Iraqis tried once more to trap the task force on the road. They emplaced several slabs of concrete that produced a barrier across the highway some 3 feet tall and 2 feet thick. Covered by suppressive fire, the lead platoon leader rammed the barrier with his 70-ton M1 tank, went airborne, and broke it up enough for the rest of the task force to drive through. Surmounting this last hurdle, *Rogue* made contact with friendly troops at Baghdad International Airport. Even this happy moment was not without incident. As it approached the airport, the lead platoon reported tanks to its front. When the company commander asked the tank commander to amplify the report by passing range data, he reported 2,000 meters. The commander looked at his BFT and noted a blue icon at 2,000 meters. Scanning, the lead platoon confirmed that it had friendly forces in sight. The task force made radio contact and began passing through friendly lines.[33]

At the airport, MEDEVAC awaited those who required it. The task force passed through the perimeter and took some time to rest and refit. Refit included repairing damage, sweeping away hundreds of brass cartridges and links, and putting out fires on one Bradley and one tank. One soldier recalled that the brass casings in his track from expended rounds were ankle high. The task force evacuated the wounded and Staff Sergeant Booker's body. Lieutenant Colonel Schwartz described the scene at the airport, "[TF 2-7 IN] did a fantastic job receiving us. . . . There was a very different tone in the air. There was a tremendous feeling of loss; there was a feeling of mission success, which was a great feeling. There was everyone looking at their vehicles and wondering how we were able to survive. Bradleys had gotten hit with multiple RPGs and kept rolling...I don't think any of us had a dry eye."[34]

Are You Okay?

We linked up with 1st Brigade on the airfield [following Thunder Run I]. We went for a 4-hour break.... You would have thought there would have been a lot of high-fives, but there were a lot of soldiers in shock. There were a lot of soldiers crying; they were just emotionally spent.

"I was emotionally spent. One of my tank commanders had been killed. I had a soldier shot in the eye, shot in the forehead, shot in the shoulder, shot in the back, shot in the face.... I just needed time for myself, and one of the other battalion commanders from 1st Brigade came over and didn't say a single word. He asked me, "Are you okay?" And I said, "I don't know." He looked at me and then turned around and walked away, and that was the best thing he could have done.

"We regrouped after about 4 hours and left the airfield and went back to business. I was okay; everyone was okay. Let me take that back—we were better, but we weren't okay. We were never okay. I talked to the company commanders; I talked with the [doctors]...I had to be with everyone I could be with for my own personal well being and for theirs, to let them know what they did was right and it was justifiable and everything I asked them to do.... We regrouped and refocused and attacked two days later into Baghdad.

Lieutenant Colonel Eric "Rick" Schwartz
commander, 1-64 AR
interview, 18 May 2003.

Emotionally spent, TF 1-64 AR moved to the south of the city, reoccupying the blocking position it left that morning. The following morning, A Company held a memorial service for Staff Sergeant Booker, noting in its unit summary that he died "helping his crew, his platoon, helping his company team. He saw the need to be up there, exposed to fire, engaging the enemy to protect his crew. He didn't need to be asked, he just did it."[35]

Thunder Run of 7 April

Task: Attack to Seize Objective DIANE (Baghdad City Center)

Purpose: To demonstrate American resolve and facilitate the fall of the Iraqi regime.

Fragmentary Order to A/1-64 AR
6 April, 2003.

"They fled. The American louts fled. Indeed, concerning the fighting waged by the heroes of the Arab Socialist Ba'ath Party yesterday, one amazing thing really is the cowardice of the American soldiers. We had not anticipated this."

Iraqi Information Minister
Mohammed Saeed al-Sahhaf,
"Baghdad Bob"

Colonel David Perkins, commander of the 2nd BCT, 3rd ID returned dissatisfied with the overall results of his 5 April thunder run through downtown Baghdad. The attack proved that it could be done—that Baghdad's defenses could be penetrated at will. The soldiers fought magnificently and were a credit to their training and leadership. Although Perkins was satisfied with the tactical performance of his troops, he was not sure the message they were sending was the right one. He was disturbed with the information and perception implications of the raid. Perkins was also provoked by the Iraqi information minister, Mohammed Saeed al-Sahhaf, "Baghdad Bob's" barefaced lies to the world, declaring that not only were there no American forces in Baghdad, but that the Iraqis had repulsed the attack and inflicted massive casualties. Aside from the insult to the fighting spirit and abilities of his soldiers, Perkins appreciated the power of the information battle. Baghdad Bob's lies had an effect on the Iraqis' defensive effort—their morale and fighting zeal. More than just pandering to the Iraqi civilian population, the Iraqi military leadership actually believed that the Americans were dying in droves far south of Baghdad. Even the captured Iraqi colonel, arguably someone who should have known the true military situation, expressed shock at finding Abrams tanks and Bradley Fighting Vehicles in his capital. Not understanding how far and how fast the coalition had moved only emboldened the defenders in the city. Allowing these lies to stand would only worsen the eventual fight for Baghdad.[36]

Perkins' chain of command, Major General Blount, Lieutenant General Wallace, and Lieutenant General McKiernan, on the other hand, were pleased with the first thunder run's success. While it was a significant and ferocious engagement, the Iraqi response to the 2nd BCT *Spartans* was not the sophisticated, integrated urban defense that they feared. Moreover, the attack had clearly taken the Iraqis by surprise, confirming that the coalition firmly held the initiative.

Going Downtown: A Study in Battle Command

On the night of 5 April, wanting to maintain the pressure, Wallace and Blount decided to conduct a second attack. "Blount and I talked that night and decided we would do another thunder run. 'Buff' and I agreed they would go two intersections [major highway interchanges—this one eventually designated as Objective MOE] into town and turn and come back out. So I went to bed thinking that is what they would do."[37] With the success and experience from their first thunder run, there was no question that Colonel Perkins' *Spartans* would conduct the attack.

On 6 April, Blount directed Perkins to conduct a limited-objective attack back into Baghdad on 7 April.[38] Both officers fully understood Wallace 's intent—his purpose, in ordering the raid. The core of any Army order is the purpose and commander's intent. Since no plan ever goes as written, if the subordinate commander understands *why* he is conducting a mission, he can adapt to the inevitable fog and friction of battle or take advantage of opportunity. In this case, Wallace's, as well as McKiernan's, ultimate purpose was to render the regime "irrelevant," causing it to collapse and thus free Iraq from the dictatorship.[39] In understanding this, the 3rd ID and 2nd BCT commanders knew they had the freedom and authority to adjust the mission as the situation developed.

Colonel Perkins had in mind the possibility of going even farther into Baghdad than his orders specified. He wanted a plan that gave his commanders options should the conditions

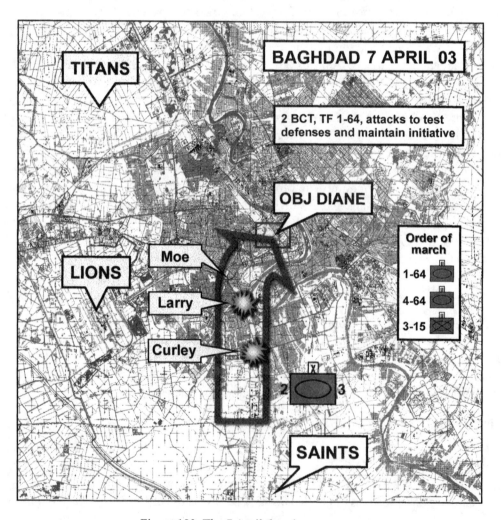

Figure 193. The 7 April thunder run route

warrant.[40] If conditions were just right, Perkins wanted to go downtown, possibly remain overnight, or even permanently. Although provoked by the Iraqi propaganda, Perkins did not become reckless. Also with the first thunder run still fresh in his memory, he did not want to have to keep repeating these missions. In his mind, it would be easier to stay downtown than to conduct these thunder runs over and over again.[4]

> ### Going Downtown
>
> I first knew they were going all the way in when I watched the blue icons turn and head downtown. [Major General] Blount and I talked and he told me that [Colonel] Perkins was going downtown. Later I was watching Dave Perkins walking around in the palace on CNN. He called Blount to ask what kind of calling card we should leave downtown. We decided on a HEAT [tank] round through the front door.
>
> Lieutenant General William Wallace,
> commander, V Corps,
> interview, 7 August 2003

Perkins had another clear rationale for going—and possibly even staying—downtown. It would hasten the regime's collapse and meet Wallace's intent by demonstrating unequivocally that the Americans were there to stay, revealing the regime's utter inability to defend its capital, and unmasking "Baghdad Bob's" blatant propaganda. Moreover, such a bold strike at the regime would boost the American morale. He had seen the Iraqis' tactics and felt that 2nd BCT could handle them. Finally, after thinking through the coming fight, Perkins worked out four conditions that he believed would make it possible to go downtown and stay:

- The 2nd BCT successfully fighting its way into Baghdad
- Seizing defensible, important, and symbolic terrain in Baghdad
- Opening and maintaining a LOC into Baghdad
- Resupplying sufficiently to remain overnight[42]

Intelligence reports indicated that after 2nd BCT's initial attack into the city, enemy forces had begun to establish roadblocks at major intersections, reseed minefields, and build other obstacles to block movement into the city. In fact, the division watched with the *Hunter* UAV as the Iraqi defenders laid a hasty minefield across Highway 8 behind the task force, attempting to seal them in during the first thunder run.[43]

This sparked a discussion in the *Spartans'* command post because of the minefield's potential impact on the mission. The discussion served to give Perkins a sense of the magnitude of risk he would assume if and when he sensed the opportunity to go into Baghdad—getting out might be harder than getting in.[44]

As events unfolded, Perkins assessed the fight and decided to turn east into the center of the city. While the reporting is not fully clear on the sequence of events for this decision, Lieutenant General Wallace noted that the first time he was aware of the change in plan was when he watched the blue icons on his BFT turn right off Highway 8. Major General Blount called Wallace and reported that Perkins had assessed the level of resistance and thought he could make it to the center of the city. Rather than question the deviation, Wallace had no thought other than to underwrite the decision. Having already weighted the 3rd ID with every asset the corps had available, to include the corps' only UAV, he was confident the *Spartans* could accomplish his mission and intent.[45]

U.S. Army

Figure 194. Soldiers destroy two AK-47s by rolling over them
with an armored personnel carrier

Once the *Spartans* made it downtown, Wallace and Blount spoke on the radio again. Blount told him that Perkins believed he had defensible terrain and he could hold his positions and stay downtown. Wallace asked Blount a series of questions focusing on if and how the division could keep the LOC open. Casualty evacuation and resupply were key issues. In a classic example of commanders at each echelon understanding intent and purpose, his questions paralleled Perkins' original criteria for staying. The three commanders all intuitively understood the opportunities—and risks—and reached similar conclusions. The exchanges between Colonel Perkins, Major General Blount, and Lieutenant General Wallace illustrate the delicate balance between executing orders as given versus following intent and exercising initiative.[46]

Scheme of Maneuver

> "Our armed forces, according to their tactics, are leaving the way open [to]…the capital, especially the commandos, are getting ready to wipe them out."
>
> Iraqi Information Minister
> Mohammed Saeed al-Sahhaf,
> "Baghdad Bob"

The scheme of maneuver called for Task Force 1-64 AR to lead the brigade from Objective SAINTS. Once downtown Perkins planned for TF 1-64 AR, *Rogue*, to seize the Tomb of the Unknowns and the adjoining park and zoo, designated Objective DIANE. TF 4-64 AR, *Tuskers*, would follow to seize two of Saddam Hussein's palaces along the Tigris River, designated Objectives WOODY WEST and WOODY EAST. Task force 3-15 IN, *China*, would take trail with the dual tasks of securing Objective SAINTS and the LOC, Highway 8. TF 3-15 IN designated the three major cloverleaf intersections along the highway from south to north as Objectives CURLEY, LARRY, and MOE.[47]

Maintaining momentum was critical. Colonel Perkins and the soldiers of the brigade had already learned that the Iraqis would swarm and mass fires on any stationary force. Given this, he intended to keep the brigade moving. The lead units would identify and engage targets as they came upon them, passing them off to trailing units as the column moved past. TF 3-15 IN would drop companies at objectives CURLY, LARRY, and MOE to secure them as the brigade moved on. Perkins' troops also planned to prepare obstacles to reduce their vulnerability to attacks from side streets and ramps.[48]

Going Downtown

> "They are sick in their minds. They say they brought 65 tanks into [the] center of [the] city. I say to you this talk is not true. This is part of their sick mind."
>
> Iraqi Information Minister
> Mohammed Saeed al-Sahhaf,
> "Baghdad Bob"

> We were told we needed to download all of our bags, all fuel, all ammo [off the bustle racks and outside of the vehicles]—everything—because we were going into Baghdad. TF 1-64 AR had learned that you need to take all that stuff off in a MOUT fight. They would shoot RPGs and catch the bustle racks on fire.
>
> Comment by unspecified company commander
> TF 4-64 AR,
> Interview, 31 May 2003.

Once again Alpha Company, 1-64 AR, *Wild Bunch*, led the attack as the brigade started north on Highway 8 at 0538.[49] *Wild Bunch* covered the task force's attached engineer company, Delta Company, 10th EN, along with the task force scouts, as they breached the hastily laid minefield about a kilometer north of the brigade's starting position at Objective SAINTS. In approximately 15 minutes, the engineers created a breach lane. The brigade started to roll through at 0600.[50]

Wild Bunch made contact 11 minutes later as the Iraqis opened fire with the familiar combination of small arms, RPGs, and mortars. A two-RPG volley struck one tank, C12,

U.S. Army

Figure 195. A soldier moves ordnance to a safe location to be destroyed

disabling it. Not wanting to stop the column and unable to restart the tank due to an additional hydraulic leak, *Wild Bunch* passed the tank off to TF 4-64 AR and the crew to TF 3-15 IN for recovery back to Objective SAINTS. The tank was evacuated back to CURLEY, where the brigade disabled the tank to prevent is use or exploitation by the enemy.[51]

At 0641, the brigade reported bypassing several hasty obstacles constructed out of overturned 18-wheel trucks and construction equipment, covered by defenders in bunkers and spider holes. The Iraqis conducted uncoordinated local fights that did not take advantage of the urban terrain. Their failure to build complex obstacles despite months of preparation time, lack of integrated combined arms tactics, and absence of integrated artillery—all indicated that the *Spartans,* despite contrary evidence in the form of the minefield, had surprised the defenders. Another possible explanation is that the regime hoped to wage an entirely unconventional defense. In any case, their efforts proved unsuccessful in defending Baghdad. That day the brigade did not concern itself with theory on why the Iraqis did what they did— it fought on. As it moved forward, the brigade came across and killed a number of Iraqis trying to recover the M1 tank disabled during the 5 April attack.[52]

The fight up Highway 8 was intense, with the column of tanks and Bradleys firing a continuous stream of machine gun, 25mm chain gun, and 120mm main tank rounds at the defenders who swarmed from the surrounding buildings and ubiquitous spider holes and bunkers along the road. The fighting developed into a 1- meter to 100-meter fight as gunners engaged technicals and bunkers at a hundred meters or so, while other crewmen fired down over the sides of their vehicles as the enemy rushed up close. Never stopping, the brigade fought through the enemy defenses that included BMPs hiding in alleyways attempting to get keyhole shots on the passing column.[53]

Figure 196. "Thunder Run," 7 April 2003

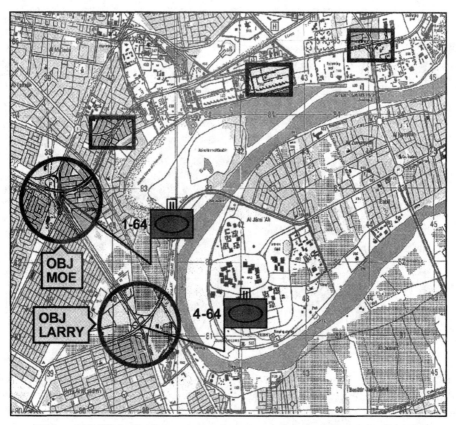

Figure 197. TF 1-64 AR movement into downtown Baghdad, 7 April 2003

Small-arms and RPG fire slowly decreased in intensity and finally stopped, for the moment at least, as TF 1-64 AR made the turn east at Objective MOE and headed toward the heart of Baghdad. Troops attacking toward Objective DIANE marveled as they passed under the notorious crossed swords they had seen on television so many times.[54]

> The mission was to bypass and not get into a pitched battle.
>
> Lieutenant Colonel Phillip DeCamp
> commander, TF 4-64 AR,
> commenting on Thunder Run II

Wild Bunch crossed to the eastern side of the park and monument complex that constituted DIANE. They established a blocking position at a key intersection adjacent to the Al Rasheed Hotel and across from the Tomb of the Unknowns, sealing the center from the north and northeast. C/1-64 AR moved into a blocking position at the western edge of the parade complex and VIP stand, sealing the center from the west and northwest. The remainder of *Rogue* followed, setting up mortars, command posts, aid stations, and a resupply point in the fields and open areas of the park.[55]

The lull did not last. Once in position, *Rogue* fought a continuous defense against poorly coordinated but persistent Iraqi counterattacks by groups of 10-20 soldiers and paramilitaries. Iraqis on foot attacked from within the zoo perimeter to the immediate north, using ammunition and weapons cached all through the area. Other fighters pressed *Rogue* from the surrounding

Mason Lowery, US Army

Figure 198. The 2nd Brigade, 3rd ID at VIP parade field, Baghdad, 7 April 2003

buildings and side streets, leading to numerous close-quarter fights in and around the buildings surrounding the park. The soldiers employed their superior armor, artillery, and mortar teams to defeat the attackers, frequently calling the indirect fires in "danger-close."[56]

Following directly behind *Rogue*, the *Tuskers* of TF 4-64 AR made first contact on Highway 8 at 0636. Facing a similar, if slightly less intense, fight as *Rogue*, the *Tuskers* made the turn at Objective MOE at 0700. Despite slackened resistance, the task force reported killing 20 Iraqi dismounted troops, a BRDM reconnaissance vehicle, and a BMP. A/4-64 AR, *Assassin*, reached Objective WOODY WEST at 0720, clearing the palace complex by 0756. While *Assassin* cleared its objective, C/4-64 AR, *Cyclone*, established a blocking position

Tanks at the Mall

Within 4 hours, Colonel Perkins' 2nd BCT penetrated the Baghdad defenses a second time and planted its flag in downtown Baghdad.

To give a sense of perspective, the 21-kilometer attack into Baghdad was equivalent to an attack on Washington, DC from the intersection of I-495 and I-95 in Springfield, Virginia, to the Mall in downtown Washington, DC; seizing the area from the Capitol to the White House to the Lincoln Memorial to the Jefferson Memorial. The 2nd Brigade parked tanks on the Iraqi equivalent of the Lincoln Memorial, aiming down the Memorial Bridge toward Arlington Cemetery.

The Americans were in downtown Baghdad, and they planned to stay.

at the July 14th Monument, a key intersection overlooking the July 14th Bridge across the Tigris River. The bridge connected to the university district, where there was an expected nest of Iraqi defenders. Although the *Tuskers* described opposition as sporadic and less than expected, they captured 25 prisoners and killed 47 dismounted troops. They also destroyed 2 BMPs, 1 BRDM, 12 artillery pieces, 19 antitank weapons, 29 technical vehicles, and 19 air defense weapons.[57]

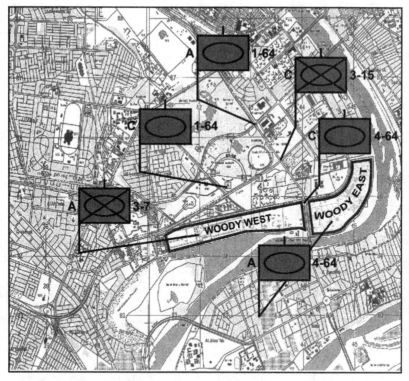

Figure 199. The 2nd BCT disposition in downtown Baghdad, 7 April 2003

TOC Strike

During the thunder run the Iraqis struck back hard at perhaps the best target they could have selected. At 0700 on 7 April, as the task forces penetrated the center of Baghdad, the Iraqis scored a direct hit with either a rocket or missile on the 2nd Brigade's tactical operations center (TOC). The devastating strike killed three soldiers and two embedded reporters, wounded 17 others, and destroyed or damaged 22 vehicles. The TOC had been coordinating and integrating the field artillery and CAS support for Colonel Perkins, enabling him to focus these efforts. The attack knocked the TOC off the air.[58]

The TOC was located in an abandoned Iraqi military compound surrounded by 10-foot-high walls. All of the support vehicles were on line approximately 15-20 feet from the tent that housed the operations center. Just before 0700 witnesses heard the whine of what sounded like a low-flying jet aircraft. What they heard was actually an incoming projectile, not an aircraft.[59]

The rocket or missile struck within a few feet of the tent and even closer to the lined-up vehicles, producing a crater 10 feet deep and 8 feet in diameter. The explosion rocked the area, knocked all the power out, and sent a fireball through the TOC. The explosion knocked several soldiers off their feet, including Sergeant First Class Stanley Griffin, who was inside the TOC monitoring the radio nets. The blast also set vehicles and tents ablaze.

After the initial shock, the officers and soldiers immediately began recovery operations—both to rescue injured soldiers and to get back into operation. Accountability of soldiers proved difficult as the troops aided the wounded or looked for friends, fought fires, or wandered about

Figure 200. The 2nd Brigade, 3rd ID TOC burning after Iraqi strike, with empty red rice bags strewn around the impact area

William Glaser, US Army

Figure 201. The 2nd Brigade, 3rd ID TOC on fire from strike

Mason Lowery, US Army

dazed. The explosion and fires produced strange and disconcerting effects among the survivors. According to First Sergeant Rodric Dalton, the brigade's Headquarters and Headquarters Company first sergeant, "It seemed as if we were in slow-motion."[60] Despite moving slowly, the company soldiers accounted for everyone within 17 minutes. Sergeant First Class Griffin recounted his own search for one of his troops, "I couldn't find [name omitted]. I walked the entire perimeter at least three times. The heat was unbearable, and there were a lot of secondary explosions coming from the burning vehicles. Then we found his remains in the front seat of his vehicle."[61] Griffin went on to say, "The soldiers were the bravest I had ever seen. They would just run in and out of the fire looking for buddies and equipment. We didn't have time to grieve; we had to get the radios back up and running, get the casualties MEDEVACed out of the area, and set up a secure perimeter. Sergeant Scott set up the casualty collection point. I thought that was very professional of him to do so."[62]

Figure 202. Destroyed HMMWV and brigade plans truck, 2nd Brigade, 3rd ID TOC

As the soldiers triaged the wounded, Captain William Glaser, the Headquarters and Headquarters Company commander, identified still-serviceable equipment. Meanwhile, the brigade executive officer, Lieutenant Colonel Eric Wesley, reestablished the command post approximately 300 meters to the south. In a battle drill never practiced before, soldiers cannibalized the remaining equipment in and around the destroyed headquarters and carried it to Wesley, who got it back into the fight.[63] Despite the carnage, the survivors managed to get into operation within 1 hour, albeit at a reduced capacity.[64]

The Decision to Stay

The strike couldn't have happened at a worse time. By the time the TOC resumed operations, it was approaching time for Colonel Perkins to decide whether his forces would stay

2nd BCT Recovering from the Strike

Captain William Glaser, commander of HHC/2 BCT, 3rd ID, was working in the brigade TOC outside Baghdad on 7 April when all hell broke loose. An Iraqi rocket or missile landed dead center on the TOC. It couldn't have happened at a worse time. The BCT had launched the Battle for Baghdad that morning, and it was approaching time for Colonel Perkins, the BCT commander, to decide whether his forces would stay in Baghdad or withdraw.

A few seconds earlier, Glaser had been working on the TOC battle board when he heard what sounded like a low-flying jet airplane. Then there was a huge explosion, and the next thing he knew he was crawling out from under the collapsed tent. Getting on his feet, Glaser saw that his soldiers had already established a casualty collection point and were performing buddy aid on casualties. He then set out to see where his first sergeant was setting up the ambulance exchange point.

As he moved to the front of the building that housed the TOC, Glaser saw Lieutenant Colonel Wesley, the brigade executive officer. Wesley's calm demeanor had an enormously calming effect on Glaser. "I don't even know what he said. It probably doesn't matter. All I remember is that he was calm and clearly in control of himself and the situation, and that infected me and bled down to everyone...He was the senior guy there, and he was creating control out of chaos. . . I knew then that we'd get through this."

As he continued around the building, Captain Glaser saw one of his soldiers, generator mechanic Private First Class Camp, a poster-quality example of a soldier—large, strong, and very tough, who volunteered for the Army immediately following the attacks on the World Trade Center on 9/11—walking toward the back of the building, wearing only one boot and his uniform pants, with shrapnel in his back and covered in blood. A female soldier was trying to get him to go to the ambulance exchange point. Camp refused her pleas, repeating, "I have to go pull security" as he trudged to the perimeter. He didn't have a weapon. Like his boot and uniform top, it had been blown away by the blast. Glaser then told Camp to go to the casualty collection point, but Camp repeated, in a daze, "Sir, I have to pull security." So Glaser asked, "Private First Class Camp, do you know who I am?"

"Of course," said Camp, "you're the CO," responding as if that were a ridiculous question. "Good," said Glaser. "As your commander, I order you to listen to this lady and do what she says." At that, Camp moved out to the ambulance point. He was evacuated to the hospital and returned to duty three days later.

Continuing around to the front of the building, Glaser saw his first sergeant, steady as a rock, directing soldiers. "The [ambulance point] is right over there," said Dalton, and Glaser saw that a sergeant was already guiding in medic personnel carriers that had responded as soon as they'd heard the impact. Glaser then noticed that fires were everywhere. The warehouse they'd occupied had held hundreds of thousands of small red rice bags, and the explosion had blasted and ignited thousands of them. They were on vehicles everywhere.

Since casualty evacuation was taken care of, Glaser took charge of the firefighting effort. He saw two vehicles with burning bags all over them. Specialist Hamlin, the driver for the operations sergeant major's vehicle, struggled unsuccessfully to put out the blaze on his HMMWV. Since they were only 20 meters from the main blaze, Glaser told Hamlin to drive the vehicle out to a safer location to put the fires out. Seeing no other soldiers around, Glaser jumped into the other vehicle. "I'll never forget," he says, "sitting in a burning vehicle, with burning plastic dripping on my arms, and staring at the yellow glow-plug light that read 'Wait.'"

Captain Glaser moved the vehicle, put out the fires on it, and then returned to the building to retrieve the stretcher that was on his HMMWV. He ran the stretcher to the casualty collection point, where

Specialist Gates took it and ran into the burning building to look for any additional casualties. Once he saw that the combat lifesavers had done everything that could be done, and the only activity was the legal officer getting cots to use as additional stretchers, Glaser stood up on a stack of pallets and issued instructions for casualty evacuation.

He told everyone where the ambulance exchange point was located and how to get there, and within minutes the soldiers evacuated the casualties and the burning building was clear of personnel. As soldiers were leaving, the fires set off secondary explosions from ammunition stored on burning vehicles. Then three soldiers from the TF 4-64 AR's unit maintenance collection point arrived on an M88, asking how they could help. Captain Glaser told them that he had the personnel issues under control, but he needed help to save the undamaged vehicles trapped inside the flames. A couple of minutes later, Glaser saw an M88 crash though the building's wall, creating an exit. The 2nd BCT soldiers then rushed in and saved their remaining vehicles. Soon after, Lieutenant Colonel Wesley came up on the net, reported what had happened, and reestablished TOC operations to support the battle.

Compiled from an interview with Captain William Glaser,
18 May 2003

or withdraw. He had three alternatives: pull out of Baghdad; run a resupply convoy into the city while TF 3-15 IN continued the fight to clear the LOC; or withdraw the leading task forces. Perkins believed that TF 3-15 IN only needed a couple of more hours to succeed in its mission. So, ignoring those three choices, he decided on a fourth option: he pushed the decision point back—bought time—by ordering the task forces in Baghdad to turn their tank engines off for the next 2 hours, only starting them to charge their batteries. This bought the TF 3-15 IN more time to clear up the LOC.[65]

Figure 203. Impact point, 2nd Brigade, 3rd ID TOC

Mason Lowery, US Army

Figure 204. The 2nd Brigade, 3rd ID reestablishing the TOC

Securing the LOC

Despite the strike on the TOC, Perkins had achieved two of his three criteria for staying. However, reaching criterion 3—opening Highway 8 into Baghdad—would be not be easy. When the TOC returned to the air sometime around 0900, TF 3-15 had not yet opened the LOC. Moreover, the tanks downtown burned fuel—whether moving or standing still—at a rate of 56 gallons per hour. They had been burning fuel for more than 3 hours. Perkins reckoned that he had 4 hours from crossing the line of departure before he would be "bingo" on fuel, the point where he had to turn around or risk not being able to make it all the way back if he was not refueled. Even with shutting down the tank engines, the clock was still ticking. With downtown reasonably well in hand, Perkins focused on supporting TF 3-15's fight on the critical LOC.[66]

> ### Field-expedient Surgery
>
> When Sergeant Scott returned from the forward surgical team, I asked "Is Corporal Brown [Colonel Perkins' driver injured in the strike on the 2nd BCT TOC] going to make it?"
>
> He responded, "Sir, I don't know but they are still working on him. When we got there, nobody could give him an IV because of his burns. I tried, the medics tried, and even the doctors could not find a vein. Then this special forces medic laying on a stretcher with an AK-47 round though his leg and waiting for a MEDEVAC, started screaming at us to bring Brown over to him. We carried Brown to the wounded medic, who pulled out a knife, cut down into Brown's leg, pulled out a vein, stuck the catheter into his vein, and then tied it off."
>
> As soon as he was done with the vein, the field surgeons carried Brown into the operating room and the special forces medic was MEDEVACed to the rear. Corporal Brown was eventually evacuated to the USS Mercy hospital ship, where he died 36 hours later.
>
> Captain William Glaser,
> commander, HHC, 2nd Brigade, 3rd ID

Task Organization

On the evening before the attack, the 2nd BCT ordered TF 3-15 IN to detach all but one platoon of B/3-15 IN. The brigade assigned Captain Ronny Johnson's resulting understrength company the mission to secure Objective SAINTS while the rest of the BCT attacked into Baghdad. Protecting the brigade's operating base at SAINTS was critical to its ability to continue the fight downtown. Moreover, a secure SAINTS would serve as a safe haven to which it could return if things went badly.

Losing B/3-15 IN left Lieutenant Colonel Twitty short of combat power. He retained only four mechanized infantry rifle platoons and three tank platoons from his cross-attached tank company. But with three objectives to secure, he needed three company-size forces. Using available resources, Twitty created three company teams. He built Team *Gator*, one tank and two infantry platoons, around A/3-15 IN, commanded by Captain Joshua Wright. Team *Rage*, built around the headquarters of Twitty's attached tank company, B/4-64 AR, consisted of one infantry and two tank platoons commanded by Captain Dan Hubbard.[67]

Twitty conjured up a third team— Team *Zan* specifically for this mission. The battalion had three battle captains in the S3 Operations section. Captain Harry "Zan" Hornbuckle, the senior captain, assumed command of the ad hoc team. Hornbuckle, a graduate of the Infantry School's Captains' Career Course, also served as an instructor in the Ranger Training Brigade (RTB) for two years. Lieutenant Colonel Twitty had confidence in Hornbuckle.[68] Twitty formed Team *Zan* with the remaining infantry platoon (four Bradleys) from B/3-15 IN, the battalion's heavy mortar platoon led by First Lieutenant Josh Woodruff, with its four mortar tracks and an M557 fire direction center track, and a reinforced engineer platoon with four M113 APCs and two M9 ACEs. Twitty also assigned the battalion fire support officer, Captain William Brodany, to the team. This not only gave Hornbuckle a fire support coordinator, it added another Bradley, with its deadly 25mm cannon, to the team's firepower. Hornbuckle also brought with him the "extra" Bradley that Twitty had drawn back in Kuwait.[69]

In addition to these units, Captain Hornbuckle had the medics of the battalion's main aid station and the command sergeant major with him, along with several members of the maintenance section, including Staff Sergeant Joe Todd, who would man a heavy machine gun to great effect during the battle. Command Sergeant Major Robert Gallagher routinely traveled in one of the battalion's M88 recovery vehicles and positioned himself at what he perceived would be the most critical point during any operation. Gallagher believed that *Zan* would be at this fight's critical point.[70] Along with Gallagher, two M577 command and control vehicles from the task force TOC joined the team.[71] The battalion's embedded journalists, one fewer after reporter David Bloom's untimely death, rounded out the team.[72] Dennis Steele, a photographer from *ARMY* Magazine, along with an ABC cameraman, took dramatic photographs and video of the fighting at CURLEY. These images would bring home to America the fierceness of this battle. Hornbuckle and the other company commanders had only 6 short hours, in the dark, to organize their teams, issue orders, refuel and rearm for the attack. Only their experience with the battalion and the hard realistic training they had gone through together made this possible. Lieutenant Colonel Twitty retained one squad of the scout platoon, the engineer company headquarters, an air liaison team from the Air Force with an enlisted tactical air controller, a PSYOP team, and a human intelligence team under his control. The rest of the scout platoon stayed back with Bravo Company at SAINTS.[73]

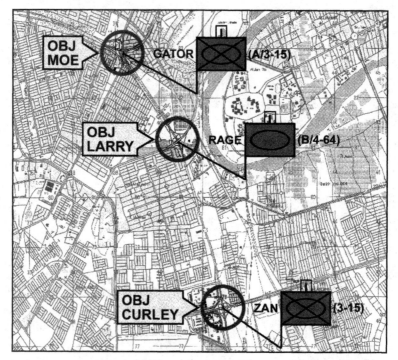

Figure 205. TF 3-15 IN disposition along the LOC, 7 April 2003

Receiving the Order

Portions of TF 3-15 IN arrived at SAINTS late on the afternoon of 6 April, after being relieved from the mission to secure the east side of the Euphrates River crossing at PEACH. That afternoon the rest of the task force attacked south on the east bank of the Euphrates to destroy remaining enemy forces south of the crossing. Lieutenant Colonel Twitty had not yet reached SAINTS when Colonel Perkins called a huddle to issue the operations order for the next morning's attack into Baghdad. Twitty sent his operations officer, Major Roger Shuck, in his place. Once he reached SAINTS and met with Shuck, Lieutenant Colonel Twitty developed his concept for the operation including organizing *Zan*. Twitty then used an empty, bombed-out building without a roof to plan and issue the attack order. Soldiers pulled a tarp over the top of a room in the building and used ponchos to prevent light from leaking out of the smashed windows. At midnight, Twitty issued the order for an attack at 0600. He then had his commanders talk through a simple rehearsal, moving yellow "sticky" notes around on a rough sketch of the objectives to show they understood his scheme of maneuver and intent. Lieutenant Colonel Twitty described issuing the order as a very dramatic and tense moment for all those present. They were exhausted and they expected a hard fight. Twitty commented, "I looked into the eyes of everyone in that bombed-out building, and for the first time, I saw real fear. After the battles in the city on 5 April by our sister task force, we knew this would be bad."[74]

Twitty developed a concept of operation similar to Perkins' scheme. He planned to secure his objectives from south to north in order. *Gator,* his mechanized infantry company team, led the task force, followed by *Rage*, his tank company team, and *Zan*. *Zan* would secure Objective CURLEY as the remainder of the task force continued on. *Rage* would secure Objective

LARRY, and *Gator* would secure the northernmost objective, MOE. Twitty intended to position himself on Objective LARRY to ensure he remained in radio range with all of his units. At 0620 on 7 April, Twitty's task force crossed the line of departure following the *Tuskers*.[75]

Execution

As 2nd BCT moved north, the enemy called up reinforcements. Enemy resistance seemed to slacken for a bit as the *Tuskers* moved north but intensified as TF 3-15 IN approached, apparently as word spread that the Americans had returned. Lieutenant Colonel Twitty sensed conditions had changed from those the task force had encountered earlier in the campaign. Twitty felt that up to this point in the campaign the enemy had shown a "certain softness" or unwillingness to fight to the death. On 7 April he sensed a grim determination in the opposition.[76]

Although the enemy's attitude may have changed, the pattern of resistance remained similar to the way the enemy fought at As Samawah and north. As they had done previously, the enemy used small fighting positions along the highway. They also used ramps and overpasses to their advantage, both for cover and to attain the advantage of high ground. Side streets and ramps afforded them access to the flanks of advancing US units as well. Finally, the enemy reinforced the fighting without apparent close coordination, but in greater and growing numbers. After the first thunder run, the brigade knew very well that the enemy would use the overpasses; accordingly, the artillery fire plan included firing airbursts over the overpasses. Twitty found that the fighting against opposition literally on the edge of the road made using artillery and CAS difficult. Nearly all of the missions called were danger-close—that is, so close to the friendly troops that they were likely to produce both friendly and enemy casualties. That did not stop the 3rd ID troops from calling danger close missions. They called plenty of them.[77]

One of the principles of military operations in urban terrain is that an attacking force requires significant engineer support, both to assure mobility by clearing obstacles and also to develop obstacles to protect the flanks of the advancing forces. TF 3-15 IN applied the principle with success during the fighting at all three objectives. Twitty's troops used armored combat earthmovers (ACEs) to knock down light poles and move wrecks to generate obstacles across streets and roads coming into the three intersections at LARRY, MOE, and CURLEY. The task force's engineering efforts paid off as the enemy continued to use a combination of dismounted and mounted attacks by both combat vehicles and "technical" trucks and attacks by suicide bombers attempting to detonate vehicles inside the Americans' perimeters.[78] The obstacles stymied the Iraqis and their foreign fighters and proved critical during the decisive fight at Objective CURLEY.

Objective CURLEY

As soon as Team *Zan* arrived at Objective CURLEY, Captain Hornbuckle organized a hasty defense around the complex road intersection and overpass. Oriented north on Highway 8, he placed the Mortar platoon with two tracks facing north and two facing south back down the highway. Hornbuckle assigned the engineer platoon responsibility for the east side of the cloverleaf intersection and the mechanized infantry platoon responsibility for the west side. The infantry platoon first had to attack to clear enemy troops from trenches and fighting positions they had built in the area Hornbuckle assigned them to defend. From the outset, Hornbuckle and Gallagher had to use everyone who had accompanied Team *Zan* to clear the perimeter and defend it. Staff troops and communicators assigned to the task force headquarters company ably pitched in.[79]

After the fact, Lieutenant Colonel Twitty described Team *Zan*'s opponents at CURLEY as "Syrian Jihadists" who came to Iraq to fight against Americans. According to Twitty, they showed no evidence of thorough or professional training, but they fought with determination. Many of the Syrian fighters occupied a large building on the northwest corner of the interchange. According to Twitty, the troops at CURLEY claimed the intensity of fire from the building made the whole structure look as if it were "twinkling and blinking."[81]

Although *Zan* troopers cleared the Iraqi and Syrian defenders out several times, the enemy reoccupied the shallow trenches around the periphery of the cloverleaf because *Zan* had two few troops to defend the entire perimeter against the onslaught of dismounted attacks. Team *Zan* literally fought a 360-degree fight. Growing bolder, small groups of attackers edged closer and closer to the position from all directions, and although the direct-lay missions

> ### Shimmering in the Sun
>
> Two days after the fighting, Private First Class David Turner, a mechanic in Headquarters and Headquarters Company, 3-15 IN, passed CURLEY. He described the streets and ground as "shimmering in the sun like gold from all the expended brass lying on the ground."
>
> TF 3-15 IN Unit History

against the large building helped, heavy fire continued to come from there.[82] The Syrians and Iraqis fought with a fierce, even fanatical, determination, pressing home their attacks. One of the mechanized infantry troops killed a woman who attacked his part of the perimeter.[83]

Figure 206. Mortar platoon vehicles of TF 3-15 IN on Objective CURLEY, 7 April 2003

The Pros from Dover—
Special Forces on CURLEY

As *Zan* prepared to depart Objective SAINTS, a small SF detachment arrived and approached the sergeant major about joining the unit as it moved north. Two SF vehicles, modified pickup trucks mounting machine guns on pedestals, merged into the convoy. The SF troops asked that they be allowed to make first contact with the local Iraqis on Objective CURLEY. They argued that if they could talk to the older men in the area, "the men with beards," perhaps *Zan* could avoid a confrontation.

Captain Hornbuckle and Command Sergeant Major Gallagher could hardly believe what they were hearing. The SF soldiers obviously had a different idea of what the situation on CURLEY would be when *Zan* got there than everyone in TF 3-15 IN had. All along, this had been planned as a high-intensity combat operation. By the time *Zan* arrived at the crossroads, TF 1-64 AR, TF 4-64 AR, and two company teams of TF 3-15 IN had all passed through, and each of them had traded heavy fire with the Iraqi and Syrian defenders. There definitely would not be an opportunity for peaceful negotiations this day, regardless of what the SF sergeant thought.

As expected, *Zan* met heavy enemy fire as it occupied CURLEY. The SF soldiers saw right away that there was not going to be an opportunity for discussions. The SF troopers, who were prepared to speak with the Iraqis showing only a minimum of arms and ammunition, quickly donned their full battle gear and prepared for the fight. Gallagher said that he watched them as they calmly put on their equipment and gathered their ammunition and weapons. He described them as being "Like the pros from Dover, come to settle this thing and get in a round of golf later."

The SF troopers gathered up a couple of infantrymen and charged into a building near the intersection. Command Sergeant Major Gallagher heard a flurry of shots and later saw the infantry soldiers dragging two of the Special Forces guys out of the building with wounds to their legs. The remainder of the SF team fought with *Zan* throughout the day.

Command Sergeant Major Robert Gallagher,
command sergeant major, TF 3-15 IN,
19 May 2003[80]

As the battle entered its fourth hour, Lieutenant Colonel Twitty radioed Hornbuckle to ask, "Zan, just tell me. Do you need extra help?"[84] Hornbuckle said no, but after months of working together, Twitty could hear the stress in his voice. Twitty sensed that Hornbuckle needed help so he sought a second opinion from Command Sergeant Major Gallagher. Gallagher, tagged as "Black Hawk Bob" by the embedded media team because he had fought and been seriously wounded in the fighting in Mogadishu in 1993, got wounded again at CURLEY. When the task force commander contacted him, Gallagher was standing next to his M88 recovery vehicle with his leg bandaged, firing his M-4 carbine at Iraqi and Syrian attackers. Gallagher answered without hesitation "We need help, and we need it now."[85]

Lieutenant Colonel Twitty accepted Gallagher's view and asked Colonel Perkins for the release of one mechanized infantry platoon from his Bravo Company, still occupying the blocking position near Objective SAINTS. Captain Johnson, commanding B/3-15 IN, joined the discussion with a counterproposal. He recommended that he come forward with his entire company.[86] Within moments, Perkins considered and accepted that plan. Apparently, Perkins sought help from the division, and Major General Blount assigned 3-7 CAV to secure Objective SAINTS, freeing Johnson to concentrate on repelling the counterattacks on the LOC.[87]

Dennis Steele, *ARMY Magazine*

Figure 207. Command Sergeant Major Robert Gallagher, 3rd Battalion, 15th Infantry, engaging Iraqis while being treated for a leg wound.

Although a captain, Johnson was a more experienced soldier than most captains. He served nine years as an enlisted soldier and NCO, reaching staff sergeant before going to Officer Candidate School. Johnson understood the situation since he had been listening to the radio and to the torrent of fire to his north. Doing his own contingency planning, Johnson had moved one of his two platoons from the southern part of SAINTS up to a position closer to him on the northern perimeter. After settling it with Perkins, Twitty told Johnson to "Get to CURLEY ASAP."[88]

Johnson wasted no time. He issued a quick order and moved out in 15 minutes. B/3-15 IN roared into CURLEY with every weapon firing, arriving just in time. As one man put it, "There was not a soldier on CURLEY that did not think he was going to die that day."[89] According to one of the embedded reporters present at the fight, by the time Johnson's company arrived, the medics had armed themselves to defend their patients; those wounded still able to fire a weapon had picked up arms; the chaplain considered picking up a weapon to help defend the wounded. "It was the most amazing thing. Captain Johnson got to Objective CURLEY within 15 minutes. The first squad leader out of his track was shot."[90] Although Johnson initially arrived with two rifle platoons, brigade ordered him to send one back south to help sort out the mess at the brigade TOC.[91]

About the same time as Johnson moved north, Lieutenant Colonel Twitty ordered Captain Aaron Polsgrove to come forward with the rearm-refuel convoy. Although originally lined up near 2nd Brigade's TOC, Polsgrove moved away after the strike and joined the combat trains command post and three "gun trucks" from the scout platoon at the northern edge of SAINTS. Polsgrove asked for an escort, but the task force had none to give so Polsgrove moved out with the three armed scout vehicles and a .50-caliber on the battalion maintenance sergeant's M113. Along the way, the defenders ambushed the supply column, killing the scout platoon sergeant and blowing his body completely from his vehicle. The column returned fire and moved on, losing one more soldier, the battalion motor sergeant, to the enemy.[92] Reaching CURLEY did not end their agony. Polsgrove "coiled" the supply trucks up in a tight circle like a wagon train in a western movie and immediately began issuing ammunition to the troops at CURLEY. The mortar platoon literally ran back and forth between the trucks and mortars with three rounds per load and fired them as soon as they got back to their guns. In the middle of this, one of the Iraqis or Syrians hit an ammunition truck with an RPG. The resulting fire spread rapidly, engulfing four more trucks.[93]

Blount reinforced the fight, reassigning TF 2-7 IN from 1st BCT to 2nd BCT at 1016 to help keep Highway 8 open.[94] TF 2-7 IN, the *Cottonbailers*, led by Lieutenant Colonel Scott Rutter, moved quickly but did not arrive with their main body until 1600. Rutter sent his operations officer, Major Rod Coffey, ahead of the main force to coordinate the relief in place at Objective CURLEY. Coffey moved out with just his Bradley and a communications HMMWV. Coffey and his party arrived at CURLEY and were immediately welcomed by enemy small-arms and RPG fire from all directions. Coffey rapidly coordinated the relief with the TF 3-15 IN executive officer, Major Denton Knapp, and returned to his Bradley so he could add it to the fight. En route to his Bradley, Coffey was severely injured when an RPG struck his communications HMMWV. Coffey refused medical care and manned his Bradley, getting the crew and dismounts into the fight on CURLEY. Coffey's crew supported Team *Zan* by laying heavy suppressive fire on enemy positions to the north of CURLEY. During the ensuing fight, a member of Coffey's crew, Specialist Nicholas Cochrane, killed three enemy fighters with four well-aimed shots from his M-16 while they were attempting to close on the position by way of an overpass. Rutter, having received numerous reports from Coffey and his gunner, Sergeant Kenneth Stephens, knew what the situation was like on CURLEY and moved his task force up as quickly as he could. Their arrival at CURLEY tipped the scales.[95]

Rutter's troops relieved Team *Zan* and, with the advantage of greater numbers, carried the fight to the Iraqis. Eventually assuming responsibility for the road, Rutter sent units attacking south and east, with tremendous success over the next two days.[96] He expanded the perimeter to gain more defensible terrain and improved the fields of fire by knocking down walls. Rutter did this to prevent enemy from gaining any positional advantage on his forces. While expanding the perimeter and clearing enemy fortifications, TF 2-7 IN tragically lost Staff Sergeant Lincoln Hollinsaid of Bravo Company, 11th Engineer Battalion, to RPG fire. Just three days earlier Hollinsaid replaced Sergeant First Class Paul R. Smith as the platoon sergeant when Smith was killed at Baghdad International Airport. With the perimeter expanded and secured, the LOC into downtown Baghdad would remain tenable. On 9 April, after the battle, some locals asked permission to give the Iraqi dead a proper burial. The Iraqis took away the bodies of the few dead fighters who were wearing army uniforms, but refused to have anything to do with the masses of dead Syrians, expressing their disgust and hatred of them to anyone who would listen.[97]

Command Sergeant Major Robert Gallagher

In 1993, Command Sergeant Major Gallagher was part of Task Force *Ranger* (75th Ranger Regiment), which attempted to capture Somali warlords in Mogadishu. During the fierce fighting on 3-4 October, he was severely wounded. Ten years later, in Iraq, the reporters traveling with his unit, TF 3-15 IN, jokingly nicknamed him "Black Hawk Bob." The name stuck. The sergeant major cultivated a hearty, gruff, and profane persona with his troops, and they affectionately called him by his nickname, although never to his face.

Gallagher stated that his philosophy and method of operation was to "go as far forward as I can and not undermine the command authority of the unit. If there's something I can do to help the companies, I'll do it." He decided that he was not happy with the traditional role of a command sergeant major—staying in the rear to assist coordinating logistics and support—the traditional "beans and bullets" approach. He felt that the officers and sergeants assigned that mission could make it work; he could be of more help elsewhere.

If he was going to circulate around the battlefield, he needed more protection than the HMMWV authorized by the unit's table of organization. He adopted an M88 heavy recovery vehicle, soon his signature vehicle. He also kept the main aid station (MAST) close to him whenever he moved. This ensured that the MAST was near the fighting but had security. The MAST guided on the M88, which, in turn, protected the medics with its heavy machine gun.

Gallagher's years of experience with 75th Ranger Regiment served TF 3-15 IN well. He brought that elite force's training and combat techniques to his new unit. He instituted focused training when the soldiers reached Kuwait. In this, he and Lieutenant Colonel Twitty saw things eye-to-eye. In Kuwait, the unit had the resources and opportunity for this type of training. The soldiers completed an exhausting but confidence-building regimen. The support soldiers trained alongside the infantrymen, learning to clear trenches, destroy bunkers, and engage targets from any position. Drivers and assistant drivers went through ambush training using live ammunition. Even the fuel handlers attached to the task force completed a live-fire exercise. This paid huge dividends later. Gallagher extended his focus to the junior officers and mid-grade sergeants, training them out of the junior soldiers' sight to preserve their authority. "It was my assessment that the sergeants and officers in mechanized infantry units tend to want to centralize training. I wanted to de-centralize it, to push it down lower in the chain, make the junior leaders more responsible, and get them to buy into the training." The team came together; Gallagher's efforts paid off on CURLEY on 7 April.

Derived from interview with Command Sergeant Major Robert Gallagher,
19 May 2003.

Objective LARRY

As Captain Johnson and Bravo Company arrived to reinforce Team *Zan* at Objective CURLEY, the fighting reached high intensity at Objective LARRY, where Twitty positioned himself. Captain Dan Hubbard, commanding Team *Rage*, composed of two tank platoons and a mechanized infantry platoon, led the fight at LARRY. Hubbard had 19 armored vehicles, including his own tank and Lieutenant Colonel Twitty's Bradley.[98] At LARRY, one tank platoon covered the northeast quadrant while another took the southeast quadrant. Hubbard's mechanized infantry platoon covered the entire west side of the objective. Enemy attacks began immediately, mainly from the south, but also from buildings to the northwest, from the crossover road to the west, and from a jumble of buildings to the southwest.[99]

Rage faced dismounted Republican Guard troops as well as some SRG, but suicide bombers and fighters in pickup trucks mounting heavy machine guns posed the main threat. The paramilitary troops attacked just as they did at As Samawah, Objectives JENKINS, FLOYD, and MURRAY. They attacked in waves using the ubiquitous Iraqi white and orange taxis, city buses, dump trucks, and in one case even a lumbering recreational vehicle. Lieutenant Colonel Twitty reported that it appeared that the defenders had loaded many of their vehicles with explosives. Often when a Bradley's 25mm cannon or a tank round struck them, they ignited with a tremendous secondary explosion.[100] The Iraqi main effort, at least for the first several hours, came from the south. Generally the attacks took the form of vehicles filled with armed men that raced toward the intersection. The vehicles' occupants fired their weapons out the windows or from the beds of pickup trucks. The enemy literally raced to their deaths against the heavy weapons of Hubbard's tanks and Bradleys, apparently with no thought other than overwhelming the Americans with numbers.[101]

At one point, Lieutenant Colonel Twitty realized that, although he was able to block the main highway with fires, the small front-age road running along the west of the elevated portion of Highway 8 would allow an attacking

> I owe my life to that ACE driver!
>
> Lieutenant Colonel Stephen Twitty, commander, 3-15 IN

vehicle to approach without being engaged until the last moment. He ordered the engineers to push up a berm of earth to block the frontage road. One ACE driver quickly accomplished this task.[102]

Just 15 minutes later, an Iraqi car, full of explosives and driving at exceptionally high speed, approached the intersection from the south. Instead of continuing straight ahead to its destruction as most of the others had done, this vehicle suddenly veered off the main road, crossed through a gap in the guardrail, and jumped the on-ramp to the frontage road, landing within 100 meters of the battalion TOC. Unfortunately for the driver, he ran directly into the newly created berm, striking it at high speed about 75 meters from Twitty's command post. The force of the impact ejected the driver through the windshield, with his body landing approximately 50 meters from the command post. When a Bradley fired at the wrecked car with its 25mm cannon, it blew up with a huge explosion that rocked the heavily armored vehicles at the overpass.[103]

Lieutenant Colonel Twitty, positioned on top of the overpass in the center of the intersection, fought alongside his troops. Within 2 hours of his arrival at LARRY, he had to reload the 25mm ammunition he carried in his Bradley fighting vehicle. After burning through the 300 rounds in the ready-rack, the reload procedure for the gun can take up to 3 minutes, requiring both the gunner and track commander to drop into the turret, and typically results in skinned hands, torn nails, and more than a bit of blood in a peacetime environment. Although Twitty and his gunner probably tried to set a speed record for the task, it must have felt like hours. Reloaded, the gunner continued to engage targets on his own, while Twitty maintained contact with his company teams, cleared supporting fires, and kept Colonel Perkins updated. Twitty estimated that Hubbard's troops killed 50 to 80 enemy troops.[104]

Objective MOE

The enemy at Objective MOE proved different from those at CURLEY and LARRY. At Objective MOE, closer to downtown Baghdad, the opposition included a combination of mounted and dismounted regular army and Republican Guard forces. These troops attacked using T-72 tanks, BMP-1 armored personnel carriers, and large-caliber antiaircraft weapons employed in the direct-fire mode. Several hundred enemy troops lurked along the road in a trench and bunker complex built among the palms and brush. Others occupied prepared positions in adjacent buildings dominating the interchange.[105]

A/3-15 IN, *Gator,* commanded by Captain Josh Wright, led the task force's attack up Highway 8. Following the *Tuskers* of TF 4-64 AR through CURLEY and LARRY, the company killed an estimated 30 Iraqis firing from trenches and buildings on the way to Objective MOE. The objective proved a veritable hornets' nest of resistance, constantly reinforced by the enemy streaming in from the east and west. As soon as *Gator* arrived, Iraqis driving armed civilian vehicles and suicidal attackers driving trucks packed with explosives also attacked toward the cloverleaf. Iraqi infantry swarmed into the area and occupied positions behind some low walls near the objective and in the buildings dominating the cloverleaf. *Gator* came under intense 360-degree direct and indirect fire.[106]

Captain Wright concluded he needed to clear the objective before he tried to defend it. First the company swept the enemy from the immediate objective area. Then Wright sent First Lieutenant Daniel Van Kirk's tank platoon deeper into the city, north of MOE, where it destroyed several Iraqi strong points established in buildings, some air defense guns firing in the direct-fire mode, and multiple Iraqi armored vehicles.[107]

After Van Kirk returned, the company consolidated on Objective MOE. The engineer platoon, led by First Lieutenant Adam Hess and his platoon sergeant, Sergeant First Class Jerod Palmer, blocked approaches to MOE by cutting down light poles to form a modern version of the ancient abatis. They also used an ACE to push debris and burning cars into defensive berms. These efforts proved worthwhile when the obstacles helped break up a savage last-light attack that climaxed with the destruction of a car bomb just 60 meters from the perimeter.[108]

In 8 hours of sustained combat using direct fire and six "danger-close" mortar missions and 20 "danger-close" artillery missions, the *Gators* destroyed more than 60 Iraqi vehicles and killed as many as 200 enemy infantrymen. Like the rest of the task force and brigade, the company team was desperately short of ammunition. During the day's fight, *Gators* fired twice its basic load of ammunition and nearly ran out of fuel.[109]

Resupplying the Brigade

As TF 2-7 IN arrived at CURLEY, Captain Johnson raced north with the supply column. Lieutenant Colonel Twitty radioed Johnson not to stop at LARRY but to keep going to MOE so the northernmost task forces could be resupplied. Accordingly, Johnson and the precious trucks raced right through LARRY. From his vantage point on the overpass, Twitty saw them go through. "Drivers were hunched down low in the cabs, driving with their left hand and firing their M-16s out the window with their right."[110] According to Twitty they were making good time. "I watched Ronny Johnson and the convoy roar past us on the way to Objective MOE. It was an incredible sight! Drivers and [track commanders] were firing as fast as they could, and they were *flying*! They must have been going 50 miles an hour when they passed me. I just cheered them on."[111]

Firing on all Cylinders—
Engineers at Objective MOE

On 7 April, as *Spartan* Brigade's Task Forces 1-64 AR and 4-64 AR sliced into Baghdad, TF 3-15 IN had the mission to secure their LOC. To do so, it developed three objectives—LARRY, CURLEY, and MOE—interchanges along Highway 8. By holding these objectives, TF 3-15 could keep the LOC open, which was critical because the *Spartan* Brigade attacked into the city without their logistics trains.

TF 3-15 IN's *Gator* would secure Objective MOE. To do so, Captain Josh Wright had two M2 platoons, an M1 platoon, and an engineer platoon led by First Lieutenant Adam Hess. Wright knew that his unit would be fighting a 360-degree battle against numerically superior forces. He gave his engineers a simple yet critical mission: delay enemy mounted and dismounted access to the objective to enable direct-fire systems to engage them, while leaving open one north-south lane for the LOC.

Hess considered the situation. He knew that speed would be critical. As soon as the enemy forces realized where *Gator* was establishing its position, they would mass forces and attack. They would come fast and furious: tanks and BMPs, RPGs, suicide cars, buses, and trucks—all attacking in droves. Hess had 2nd Platoon, B/11th Engineers' ACE, dismounted sappers, and an M113 with a mounted .50-caliber machine gun. He couldn't carry barrier material, so he would have to use existing terrain.

After surviving "RPG Alley" along Highway 8, *Gator* arrived at MOE. The engineers went straight into action. Hess sent the ACE to the most dangerous avenue of approach to dig ditches and berms in roads, push down palm trees to create obstacles and clear fields of fire, and move destroyed vehicles to make more obstacles.

Meanwhile, the sappers, under Sergeant First Class Jerod Palmer, used cutting charges to fell light posts and create an aluminum abatis. Sergeant First Class Ford, a tank commander on the scene, recalling the sappers' actions, noted, "I saw these dismounts running out in front of us, into the firefight, and I said 'Whoa, let's pull up and cover them.'" Blowing anything that would impede mobility—light posts, road signs—the sappers made demolition calculations on the fly. They set charges, dove behind tanks or their APC, waited for the blast, and then moved to their next target.

"Everyone was clicking on the same cylinder," said Hess. "They knew that they were fighting a flesh-to-steel battle when they were out there, so they were jumping. The .50-caliber machine gunner knew he had to lay great fire, and he did. The driver put the track in a place to protect the guys on the ground. The sappers had one guy doing calculations, another measuring the charge, another placing it, another doing the MDI [detonator]. Everyone did what needed to be done."

To the north, Sergeant Jason Millett drove his ACE out into the fray, pushing palm trees as he went. Soon, the Bradleys and tanks had destroyed enough attacking cars and trucks for Millett to use the wrecks to create obstacles. On two occasions, surviving attackers emerged from destroyed vehicles. Sergeant Millett engaged them with his 9mm, shooting out from his ACE's clamshell. At one point in the battle, *Gator* soldiers destroyed a bus packed with explosives when it was only 60 meters away from their perimeter. "Without the obstacles, it would have gotten us," said one *Gator* sergeant.

After 17 hours of continuous fighting, the enemy had seen enough. *Gator* had prevailed. But the fight was intense; at one point they were "black" on .50-caliber, 7.62mm coax, and small-arms ammunition. The tank platoon fired 12,000 rounds of 7.62mm in the first 10 hours of the fight. *Gator* suffered 11 wounded soldiers, but fortunately no soldiers died. After the fighting ended, Sergeant Millet used his ACE to dig a trench and bury the enemy dead that filled the fields around MOE.

Extracted from 2nd Platoon, A Company, 10th EN Unit History

The convoy reached Objective MOE, resupplied *Gator*, and continued on to the parade field at Objective DIANE to resupply the rest of the brigade. TF 1-64 AR and TF 4-64 AR rotated vehicles to the resupply point to refuel and rearm. The logistics crisis had passed. Perkins' troops met the criteria for staying downtown. Although two more days of sometimes heavy fighting in Baghdad remained, Perkins' second thunder run broke the back of conventional resistance and arguably of the regime.[112]

The Counterattack

I do believe this city is freakin' ours!

Captain Chris Carter,
commander, A/3-7 IN
Al Sijood Palace, Baghdad.

Sunrise on 8 April brought renewed counterattacks from east of the Tigris River. After intermittent probing throughout the night, the Iraqis moved small groups of soldiers and paramilitary fighters across the two Tigris River bridges to the northeast of the *Spartans'* position. TF 4-64 AR *Tuskers* took the brunt of the counterattack. The troops confronted their tormentors freshly supplied.

At approximately 0415, the enemy launched a dismounted counterattack on Objective WOODY EAST. Crossing via two bridges, they moved south along the river road near the palace that Captain Phillip Wolford's *Assassins* of A/4-64 AR occupied. At 0527 the task force fired mortars against a combination of troops and armed men in civilian clothes moving south. The *Assassins* then swept north to complete the destruction of the dismounts. Wolford, fighting in his stocking feet, having transitioned from dead asleep to attacking in short order, ordered his troops to "give both sides of the road an equal amount of love."[113] The company reached the western side of the southernmost bridge at 0619 and engaged several RPG teams. Shortly thereafter, *Assassin* observed the Iraqis using buses and trucks to reinforce their position on the eastern shore of the bridge. Wolford's troops fought as many as a hundred paramilitaries. The fighting grew intense and close. The enemy attack built in intensity rather than diminished, and the *Assassins* took two casualties. After calling in artillery and mortar missions within 200 meters of his tank, Wolford recalled, "I had to move out of here cause I was getting my ass kicked."[114] Pulling back a short distance from the bridge, Wolford brought in CAS that used JDAMS to destroy two buildings from which snipers had engaged the company. A-10s swept the riverbank of enemy infantry.[115]

While *Assassin* carried the fight at the southern bridge, the *Cyclones* of C/4-64 AR attacked north to seize the second, northern bridge. Killing numerous Iraqis, the soldiers seized control of the bridge with relative ease. *Cyclone* used plow tanks to position destroyed and wrecked technical vehicles astride the northern bridge and its approaches. With both bridges under control, the *Spartans* effectively sealed the downtown and blocked any further counterattacks from across the Tigris River.[116]

Later the troops discovered the attack had been made by a combination of uniformed Iraqis and a large group of men clad in jeans and polo shirts and wearing sunglasses, which seemed odd since the night had been dark, or as one of them put it, "dark as shit."[117] The uniformed Iraqis wore green fatigues sporting Republican Guard red triangles. Some of the Republican Guard troops attacked in BMPs. The troops even sank boats in the Tigris that night that fired on them.[118]

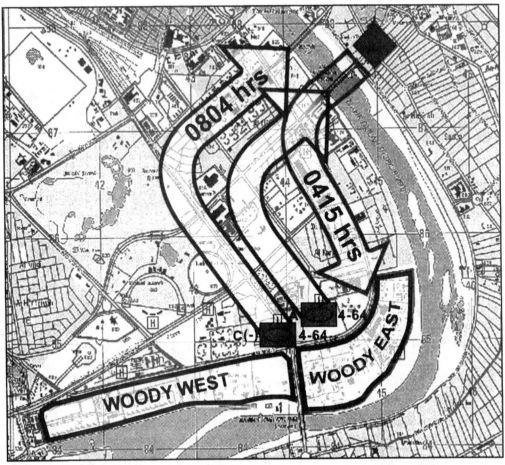

Figure 208. The Iraqi counterattack into downtown Baghdad, 8 April 2003

The 8 April Counterattack

On the morning of the 8th…we are just fighting guys on the banks of the river. There were shit-loads of guys firing from bunkers. As a matter of fact, some of these guys were waking up and stretching and yawning and were just getting hosed as they came out of their bunkers by Mk-19s [grenade launchers]. . . . The bridges had to be controlled.

Lieutenant Colonel Phillip DeCamp,
commander, TF 4-64 AR,
interview 31 May 2003

So, we backed up to the last spot where we had the small contact and we had enemy firing at us from atop the arches. My infantry fired at them with TOWs. The A-10s came in and I focused all their fires at this park [across the Tigris River]. When we moved back in, the enemy had reinforced with more guys. Two weeks after the fight, we pulled 24 dead bodies out of the bunkers. The bombs and the 30mm just caved in the bunkers.

Captain Phillip Wolford
commander, A/4-64 AR,
interview 31 May 2003

After a relatively quiet night, TF 3-15 IN fought hard the next day to defend its two remaining objectives along Highway 8. Although the Iraqis attacked with nearly the same ferocity as the day before, the task force had improved its defensive positions so the enemy achieved nothing. After the battle on the 8th, TF 3-15 IN repositioned around a   large

> ## The Power of Tanks
>
> The decision to leave an armored brigade in the center of Baghdad overnight seemed unthinkable one day and obvious the next. We must never underestimate the psychological impact of an American armored force holding the ground it takes…
>
> V Corps after-action review briefing,
> 15 July 2003

Ba'ath Party complex near as the Objective MOE, known locally as the "Aflak Building." TF 2-7 IN assumed the mission of protecting the LOC and continued to defend against sporadic attacks for the next two days.[119]

With the LOC secured and the *Spartans* entrenched downtown, it remained for 3rd ID to link up the three brigades and complete the seizure of west Baghdad. On 9 April, 3rd BCT attacked south on Highway 1 and linked up with 2nd BCT downtown. The next day, 1st BCT completed clearing Highway 8 east from the airport to downtown and linked up with 2nd BCT. The 3rd ID divided the city into zones for its subordinates to occupy and continued to destroy symbols of the regime's power.[120] On the eastern side of the Tigris River, the marines of the 1st Marine Division entered the city on 9 April and toppled the now famous statue of Saddam Hussein. With the marines now entering the city in force, the enemy threat to the V Corps' flank along the Tigris River was effectively eliminated. Along with 3rd BCT's attack south from TITANS, these were the last major combat actions to secure Baghdad.

Rather than the Grozny-like carnage and destruction predicted—and feared—Baghdad fell and the regime evaporated after only three days of hard fighting. Colonel Perkins' bold decision to stay downtown clearly drove the final nail into the regime's coffin. With soldiers and marines able to move at will throughout the city, the regime evaporated.

The Final Fighting in Baghdad—3rd BCT In TITANS

While the media focused on Colonel Perkins' *Spartan* Brigade as it conducted its thunder runs, Colonel Allyn's *Hammer* Brigade fought perhaps the most intense urban battle in the entire campaign. Although the 3rd BCT's area of operations on the northern outskirts of the city seemed calm in the early evening of 7 April, the Iraqis mounted a major counterattack just after dark. Colonel Allyn later thought the Iraqis were attempting to break out of Baghdad—or at least to open Highway 1 as an escape route for other forces still within the city.[121]

When the Iraqis began shelling soldiers on Objectives ROMMEL and MONTY, 1-10 FA lashed back with counterfires. The competing explosions reverberated back and forth across the river. The objectives were close enough to each other that soldiers on one objective could see and hear the rounds landing on the other.[122] The Iraqis followed up their barrage with a combined-arms attack at Objective MONTY, using tanks, BMPs, and dismounted Infantry.

Unfortunately for the Iraqis, C/1-15 IN, *Hard Rock*, at ROMMEL observed them as they moved southeastward along the opposite riverbank. *Hard Rock*'s fire support team engaged with indirect fires and sent reports that alerted the men of A/2-69 AR on the bridge at Objective

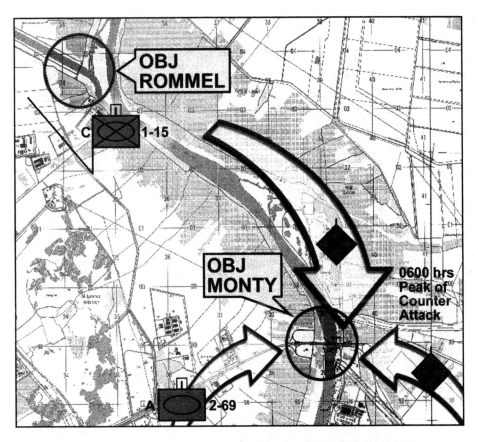

Figure 209. The Iraqi counterattack against 3rd BCT, 7-8 April 2003

MONTY to the impending attack. Lieutenant Colonel Sanderson used both artillery and CAS effectively, due he believed, in large measure to the Army's fielding of the Bradley Fire Support Vehicle. The fire support team used an integrated laser to target the enemy precisely. Sanderson believed that greatly increased the artillery's lethality.[123]

Nonetheless, the Iraqis made a concerted effort to seize the bridge at MONTY, attacking throughout the night and into the early morning of 7 April. Several times during the night, airmen struck armored vehicles firing on the friendly positions from across the Tigris. As the pressure against the bridge mounted, 3rd BCT brought concentrated fires from CAS, field artillery, and TF 2-69 AR's heavy mortars to bear. Tankers and mechanized infantry added their efforts as well. But despite the damage they took, the Iraqis persisted in drawing closer and closer to the bridge. At one point the Iraqis moved a heavy construction crane into position, apparently to remove some of the destroyed vehicles blocking the bridge approaches. *Hard Rock* spotted the crane as it crawled past Objective ROMMEL on the far side of the river. Again, the fire support team called in artillery and destroyed it.[124] At approximately 0600 on 7 April, the Iraqi attack reached its peak. According to observers, the enemy had "tons of stuff on the other side of the river."[125] The soldiers identified an entire engineer bridge company with all its vehicles and equipment, in addition to the large Iraqi infantry force armed with RPGs, heavy machine guns, and mortars.

As a company-size enemy force closed in on his position at MONTY, Captain James sent a radio message that had not been heard in this war until then. He called for the supporting artillery to fire his final protective fires (FPF).[126] Commanders in a defense designate a line just outside of their positions along which, if the defense gets desperate, all guns and other weapon systems available fire, theoretically creating an impenetrable wall of fire. Calling for an FPF is, in Army parlance, "a significant emotional event."

Captain James' fire support team had prepared for this eventuality. They had not only plotted their FPF but also adjusted live rounds until they were hitting precisely where James wanted the rounds placed. The 1-10 FA entered the firing data for James' FPF and other planned missions into the computers of their Paladin howitzers and waited for the call. When the order came to fire the final protective fires, 1-10 FA unleashed 30 minutes of continuous rapid fire, pounding the attacking Iraqis and placing a protective wall in front of the hard-pressed *Assassins*. In addition to the artillery FPF, the 3rd BCT also called in more CAS, smashing the final Iraqi assault just short of the bridge.[127] Lieutenant Colonel Sanderson recalled that "the enemy was in a caldron there. The A-10s were at treetop level doing strafing runs against enemy columns."[128] Artillery, air-delivered strikes and direct fires in combination stopped the enemy cold.

But the infantrymen and tankers were not the only soldiers in close combat. While repositioning to better support the brigade, A/1-10 FA did something few artillerymen ever do—they engaged and destroyed two T-72 tanks using direct fire from their howitzers. While moving, the artillerymen detected the tanks hidden under the trees across a canal. The artillerymen fired what they call a direct lay fire mission over "open sights." The huge 155mm projectiles smashed the tanks, and the battery moved on.[129]

Undeterred, despite the slaughter at MONTY, the Iraqis continued their efforts to recapture the bridges over the Tigris. Concerned that they might succeed, Colonel Allyn requested permission to blow the bridges to deny them to the Iraqis. This would free his forces from static defensive positions and allow them to continue to clear Objective TITANS on the west side of the river. Initially the division denied his request, but a strange situation developed. At the same time that Allyn requested permission to destroy the bridge, Iraqis strove to reach the bridge to do the same thing. In fact Iraqi sappers managed to place explosives on the eastern abutment and actually dropped part of it, but the bridge remained useable. Later, Allyn received permission to destroy the bridge. Airmen dropped the span neatly on the second try with a pair of precision-guided bombs.

U.S. Army

Figure 210. Iraqi children signal to U.S. soldiers

Silver Star Recommendation
Specialist Dwayne Turner
HHC/3-502nd, 101st Airborne Division (Air Assault)

On 13 April 2003, during limited visibility hours, Specialist Dwayne Turner distinguished himself above the call of duty through gallantry in action during combat. Elements of Alpha Company and Specialist Turner's medical platoon moved south from Baghdad, Iraq, to clear the town of *Al Mahmudiyah*. During this operation, over 200 citizens gathered around US forces, cheering the fall of the Iraqi regime under Saddam Hussein.

Iraqi paramilitary forces used the celebration to hastily prepare an ambush against Specialist Turner and his fellow soldiers. The Iraqi enemy forces opened fire on members of Alpha Company, 3-502nd Infantry Regiment, 101st Airborne Division in a compound with fragmentary grenades and a volley of a half-dozen AK-47 rifles. The initial grenade burst in the air caused multiple casualties and signaled the Iraqi enemy forces to fire with their AK-47 automatic rifles from various buildings.

After being shot multiple times from AK-47 direct fire to his arms and legs, Specialist Turner exposed himself to intense automatic fire to treat twenty-three wounded soldiers. Despite being critically wounded with a heavy loss of blood, Specialist Turner continued to provide lifesaving medical care under direct fire to two critically injured soldiers. Even with an increasing loss of his own blood, Specialist Turner remained vigilant and spirited in caring for one soldier who received multiple bullet wounds in the chest and legs. Undoubtedly, his spirited and conspicuous action and physical courage under heavy automatic fire saved the lives of at least three soldiers.

Without regard for his own welfare, Specialist Turner continued to stabilize many others for medical evacuation until he collapsed from loss of blood. His selflessness and willingness to place other soldiers' lives above his is in the greatest keeping of past and present soldiers of the 101st Airborne Division (Air Assault) and the United States Army.

Fighting raged around the perimeter of Objective TITANS for the next two days. Colonel Allyn expected to link up with marines from the 1st Marine Division within 12 to 15 hours, but the marines had to do an assault crossing of a river to enter Baghdad and thus did not arrive until 9 April. This allowed the Iraqis east of the Tigris River to concentrate their attacks against the *Hammer* Brigade in Objective TITANS.[130]

On 8 April, the third day of the fight in TITANS, the 3rd BCT sent TF 1-15 IN attacking south toward Objective LIONS, still held by 1st BCT. During this attack, Iraqi air defense artillery severely damaged an A-10 *Warthog*. The pilot managed to guide his craft toward friendly forces and ejected near Objective PEACH, where US troops recovered him.[131] V Corps spent the day consolidating positions and repelling minor counterattacks by disorganized Iraqi forces.

Early in the morning of 10 April, 3rd BCT made its last major attack. TF 2-69 AR attacked down the west side of the Tigris River along Highway 1 all the way to downtown Baghdad, linking up with Colonel Perkins' *Spartans*. Sanderson's attack, supported by an elaborate set of preparatory fires, rolled over weak and disorganized resistance.[132] TF 1-30 IN followed in support of TF 2-69 AR and cleared out the last pockets of Iraqi resistance. With this attack V Corps completed its part of the attack to seize and control Baghdad.

The 3rd BCT forces occupied the area around what is known as the "mother of all mosques," a massive structure deep in the center of Baghdad. They discovered that the apartment complex across the street from the mosque was, in reality, an elaborate deception. Instead of real buildings, it was a false front that hid a large Iraqi ammunition dump. Apparently the Iraqis hoped to shield the ammunition by hiding it and further hoped that if the coalition found it, they would hesitate to attack the dump to avoid damaging the Mosque.[133] It was not the only time the Americans discovered such a ruse, but it was one of the most elaborate. The corps spent much of the next two weeks policing up the large quantity of abandoned tanks, BMPs, and artillery pieces found on the outskirts of the city and looking for ammunition dumps.[134]

Disheartened Republican Guard and Special Republican Guard soldiers and officers returned to their homes, defeated. The paramilitaries and international mercenaries melted into the city, waiting to assess how the Americans would proceed. Even more astounding than the rapid collapse of resistance, Baghdad remained standing. Most of the infrastructure—utilities, water, power, and sewage—remained in the condition left by the failed Ba'athist regime.

"Soldiers are our Credentials"
Taking Care of Soldiers: Sergeant First Class Susan A. Pasarcik

Sergeant First Class Susan Pasarcik, finance NCO and dispersing agent of Alpha Company, 101st Soldier Support Battalion, leads 12 soldiers who are responsible for seeing to it that troops are paid in the field. As a rule soldiers' pay is done electronically, but in the field soldiers may be paid "casual pay" that gives them pocket money to buy things at field "Post Exchange" facilities. Also, the Army needs money to pay its field contractors.

Pasarcik, a mother of a toddler and married to another soldier, operated throughout OIF taking care of her troops. She and her team arrived in Baghdad with money on 14 April and began paying troops practically upon arrival. Accountable for up to $5 million, she took her team wherever it was needed.

Her efforts extended beyond paying troops and solving vendor problems. On a trip to Baghdad, a young Iraqi boy was wounded in a firefight. His father brought the boy to the Americans for help. A doctor on the scene asked Pasarcik if she could comfort the boy. She removed her helmet and flak vest because she believed they might be frightening to an injured 3-year-old. She held his hand tightly and gave him cookies from her ration packet and water.

Taking care of soldiers extends to every soldier. According to Pasarcik, "If there is a way to help you, we are going to help you—soldier, airman, marine, reservist, guardsman, we help them all."

Figure 211. Sergeant First Class Susan Pasarcik (front left) with finance team members, leading a study session for an upcoming promotion board.

Arthur Durante, US Army

NOTES

1. Anthony H. Cordesman, *The Iraq War: Strategy, Tactics, and Military Lessons* (Washington DC: The Center for Strategic and International Studies, 2003), 101-139.

2. Cordesman, 133.

3. Multiple interviews with 3rd ID brigade and battalion commanders, 8-25 May 2003. This note refers to impressions reached by the authors during the course of interviews and upon reviewing interviews of intelligence officers and maneuver commanders.

4. Ibid.

5. Lieutenant Colonel John Harding, commander, 1-10 FA, interview by Lieutenant Colonel William Pitts, 12 May 2003.

6. Colonel Terry Wolff, commander, 2nd ACR (Light), interview by Major David Tohn, 14 May 2003.

7. Colonel Steven Rotkoff, US Army, Retired, deputy C2, CFLCC (during OIF), email to Major David Tohn, 6 August 2003.

8. Ibid.

9. Lieutenant General William Wallace, commander, V Corps (during OIF, interview by Colonel Gregory Fontenot, US Army, Retired, Lieutenant Colonel EJ Degen, and Major David Tohn, 7 August 2003.

10. Staff Sergeant Brian Plesich, team leader, Tactical Psychological Operations Team 1153, 305th Psychological Operations Company, interview by Lieutenant Colonel Dennis Cahill, 31 May 2003.

11. Captain Brooks Brenkus, commander, 54th QM Co (Mortuary Affairs), interview by Chief Warrant Officer 3 Estell Watson, 2 June 2003.

12. Major Robert Foley, OIF-SG, "OIF Study Group Operational Summary: Information Operations," 15 July 2003.

13. Ibid.

14. Ibid.

15. Lieutenant Colonel Eric "Rick" Schwartz, commander, TF 1-64 AR, interview by Lieutenant Colonel Dave Manning, 18 May 2003.

16. "Task Force 1-64 AR, Summary of Unit Actions from 20 March-11 April 2003, Operation IRAQI FREEDOM," 42.

17. Thunder run is not an operational term. A raid is the proper term for the mission assigned to TF 1-64 AR, although to the troops in the task force the distinctions between a raid, a reconnaissance in force (also an acceptable term to describe the planned operation), and the term used in the unit order, "movement to contact," amount to splitting hairs. What is important is they were going downtown to test the Iraqi reaction. See FM 101-5-1/MCRP 5-2A, *Operational Terms and Graphics*.

18. TF 1-64 AR.

19. Captain Dave Hibner, commander, D Company, 10th Engineers, interview by Lieutenant Colonel James Knowlton, 14 May 2003; TF 1-64 officers, interview by Lieutenant Colonel Dave Manning, 18 May 2003.

20. TF 1-64 AR.

21. TF 1-64 AR officers interview.

22. Hibner. Captain Dave Hibner and his twin brother, Captain Dan Hibner, both fought with 3rd ID in OIF as engineer company commanders.

23. TF 1-64 AR officers interview, Hibner.

24. Captain John Ives, assistant S2, 2nd Brigade, 3rd ID, interview by Major Daniel Corey, 18 May 2003.

25. Hibner.

26. Ibid. See also TF 1-64 AR, 43.

27. TF 1-64 AR, 44.

28. TF 1-64 AR officers interview.

29. TF1-64 AR, 43.

30. TF 1-64 AR officers interview.

31. TF1-64 AR, 45; Hibner.

32. Ibid.

33. TF 1-64 AR officers interview.

34. Ibid.

35. TF1-64 AR, 45; Hibner.

36. Colonel David Perkins, 2nd BCT, 3rd ID, "Command Briefing," 18 May 2003; and Colonel David

Perkins, interview by Lieutenant Colonel Edric Kirkman, 18 May 2003. Colonel David Perkins, commander, 2nd BCT, 3rd ID; Colonel David Teeples, commander, 3rd ACR; and Colonel Arnie Bray, commander, 2nd Brigade, 82nd Airborne Division, interviews by General Frederick Franks, US Army, Retired, and Colonel Gregory Fontenot, US Army, Retired, 20 May 2003.

37. Wallace.

38. Perkins by Kirkman. See also Connor and Durante notes from the same briefing.

39. Wallace. McKiernan believed that Baghdad constituted the center of gravity largely because this was the place from which the regime exercised control.

40. Perkins, Teeples, and Bray.

41. Ibid.

42. Perkins.

43. The landmines were surface-laid on the paved road, easily identifiable and breached with the engineer equipment

44. Perkins.

45. Wallace.

46. Ibid.

47. 2nd BCT, 3rd ID Command Briefing. There are a number of interviews that illuminate these events including Perkins, those of the TF commanders and several group interviews of officers and soldiers. The second thunder run is one of the few events the OIF-SG knew enough about on arrival in theater to focus questions. More important, Perkins' troops wanted.very much to tell this story. See also 3-15 IN Operations 20 March-9 April 2003.

48. Perkins. See also Perkins, Teeples, and Bray.

49. Hibner.

50. The unit histories and chronologies do not provide an exact timeline for the breach, but an analysis of multiple unit reports suggests the breach took approximately 15 minutes.

51. TF 1-64 AR.

52. 3rd ID Consolidated History.

53. Ibid.

54. TF 1-64 AR.

55. Ibid.

56. Ibid.

57. "Tusker History: Operation IRAQI FREEDOM (19 March 03-12 April 03)."

58. Lieutenant Colonel Eric Wesley, executive officer, 2nd BCT, 3rd Infantry Division, interview by Lieutenant Colonel William Connor, US Army, Retired, 18 May 2003. See also Captain William Glaser, commander, HHC/2nd BDE, 3rd ID, interview by Lieutenant Colonel David Tohn, 10 September 2003.

59. Sergeant First Class Stanley Griffin, action operations sergeant major, 2nd BCT, 3rd ID, interview by Master Sergeant Matthew West, 19 May 2003. Captain Aaron S. Polsgrove, support platoon leader, "Support Platoon, Headquarters and Headquarters Company, TF 3-15 IN, Unit History," 16 April 2003.

60. Ibid.

61. Ibid.

62. Ibid.

63. Wesley.

64. Captain William Glaser, commander, HHC, 2nd BCT, 3rd ID, interview by Major Peter Kilner, 18 May 2003.

65. Perkins.

66. Ibid.

67. Twitty.

68. Twitty. See also "Task Force 3-15 Infantry 'Task Force China' Task Force History, Operation IRAQI FREEDOM, 20 March-1 May 2003," 5 May 2003.

69. Twitty.

70. Command Sergeant Major Robert Gallagher, command sergeant major, TF 3-15 IN, interview by Lieutenant Colonel Arthur Durante, US Army, Retired, 18 May 2003.

71. Twitty.

72. Embedded reporters were Craig White (NBC), Bob Lapp (NBC), Jake Kooser (NBC), Bernie Plunkett (NBC), Dennis Steele (*ARMY* Magazine), Adam Lusher (*London Sunday Telegraph*), and Bill Branigin (*Washington*

Post). This information comes from TF 3-15 IN unit history, which lists the reporters on a chart showing units, key leaders, and staff. TF 3-15 IN accounted for everyone.

73. Ibid. See also TF 3-15 IN.
74. Twitty.
75. Twitty. See also TF 3-15 IN, 15-21.
76. Twitty.
77. Twitty. For example, B/4-64 AR, attached to TF 3-15, fired five danger-close missions, including two 155 missions within 350 meters of his positions on LARRY. See TF 3-15 History, 17-18. See also Gallagher, re: direct lay fire missions by the battalion mortar platoon.
78. TF 3-15 IN. See also Twitty.
79. Ibid.,18. See also Twitty.
80. Gallagher.
81. Twitty.
82. TF 3-15 IN.
83. TF 3-15 IN. See also Captain Ronny Johnson, commander, B/3-15 IN, interview by Lieutenant Colonel Arthur Durante, US Army, Retired, 18 May 2003.
84. TF 3-15 IN. Twitty. See also officers of 3-15 IN, interviews by Major Pete Kilner, 18 May 2003. The group interview contributes to understanding the conditions of the fight.
85. Ibid.
86. Twitty. See also Johnson.
87. TF 3-15 IN. See also Johnson. According to Johnson, Twitty asked for a single rifle platoon, but Johnson recommended that Perkins release the whole company—that is to say, Johnson and his remaining two platoons. Perkins concurred.
88. Twitty.
89. Corporal Warren Hall, force protection detail, Medical Platoon, HHC, 3-15 IN, interview by Lieutenant Colonel Arthur Durante, US Army, Retired, 24 May 2003. See also Johnson.
90. Twitty.
91. Johnson.
92. TF3-15 IN Support Platoon History.
93. TF 3-15 IN. TF 3-15 Support Platoon History.
94. 3rd ID Consolidated History.
95. TF 2-7 IN, "Unit History of Operation IRAQI FREEDOM."
96. Lieutenant Colonel Scott Rutter, commander, 2-7 IN, interview by Lieutenant Colonel Arthur Durante, US Army, Retired, 16 May 2003.
97. Twitty.
98. Ibid.
99. Ibid.
100. Ibid.
101. Ibid.
102. TF 3-15 IN.
103. Twitty.
104. Ibid.
105. Ibid.
106. Ibid. TF 3-15 IN, 16. See also Captain Josh Wright, A/3-15 IN, interview by Major Peter Kilner, undated. Wright reported efforts of his engineer platoon leader, First Lieutenant Adam Hess, to create countermobility barriers to prevent suicide attackers from reaching his positions.
107. TF 3-15, 16.
108. Ibid.
109. Twitty. See also Wright. Captain Wright's company went "black" on ammo—Army jargon for almost out. Wright's tank platoon, for example, fired 12,000 7.62mm rounds in the 17 hours of the fight.
110. Ibid.
111. Ibid.
112. Perkins.
113. Tusker History.
114. Ibid. See also 4-64 AR commanders, interview by Colonel Tim Cherry, 31 May 2003.

115. Tusker History.

116. Tusker History. See also 4-64 AR commanders interview.

117. 4-64 AR commanders interview.

118. Ibid.

119. Rutter.

120. From the "3rd ID Consolidated Division History and After Action Review."

121. From the 3rd BCT, 3rd ID, Unit History, Power Point presentation, undated.

122. Lieutenant Colonel John Harding, commander, 1-10 FA, interview by Lieutenant Colonel Arthur Durante, US Army, Retired, 4 August 2003.

123. Lieutenant Colonel Jeffery R. Sanderson, commander, 2-69 AR, email to Lieutenant Colonel Arthur Durante, US Army, Retired, 18 August 2003. Durante also spoke by telephone with Sanderson.

124. Harding.

125. Sanderson.

126. Harding.

127. Ibid.

128. Sanderson.

129. "Unit History, 3rd BCT, 3rd Infantry Division," Power Point presentation, undated.

130. Sanderson.

131. Harding.

132. Ibid.

133. Ibid.

134. "Unit history, 11th Engineer Battalion," undated, 24-28; See also Lieutenant Colonel James Knowlton, OIF-SG, "OIFSG Operational Summary: Engineer," 15 July 2003.

Chapter 7

Implications

Soldiers, sailors, airmen and marines study history not to glorify past campaigns (well, maybe a little), but rather to prepare for future campaigns. In that vein, *On Point* also examines what the implications of the events of spring of 2003 might be. The central question is what do the events of spring 2003 tell us about the conduct of warfare in the 21st century. In suggesting what that might be, there are several cautions—the war in Iraq to remove the regime is over, but the coalition has not achieved the strategic goal of the campaign. Furthermore, individual anecdotes from OIF do not necessarily equate to trends. Still, there are implications for the way the Army and the joint team operate. This chapter suggests what some of the implications may be and what may be done about them. Some implications carry with them "lessons" that can be applied; others are only suggestive of directions that may be explored. Still others are discernible, but with insufficient clarity to suggest solutions or means of application.

The Army has a good system for collecting and then applying lessons at the tactical level. The Army is very good about developing tactics, techniques, and procedures that may be applied in similar conditions. But there are lessons or at least implications that may reasonably be discerned from OIF that transcend tactics, techniques, and procedures. These broader lessons are really only learned when they are applied in training, force structure, and combat developments. This takes time and study to determine whether what works in the short term really has application over time and in other environments. Chapter 1 and Chapter 2 reviewed the application of many lessons learned as the Army and the armed forces emerged from the Cold War era, as well as lessons learned from the post-Cold War military operations, at the Combat Training Centers, and from Army and joint experimentation. The success of combat operations in OIF suggests that many of the lessons garnered in the early post-Cold War era were learned and, more important, applied. The unique circumstances of OIF major combat operations also suggest some lessons that must still be learned and some possible implications for how the Army considers the nature of future conflict and how it structures, equips, and mans the force.

Some observers have argued that Army and Marine ground units demonstrated absolute tactical dominance based on Iraqi ineptitude. That argument assumes the difference in demonstrated capability stemmed exclusively from what the Iraqis did or did not do and on their equipment. The evidence suggests that this explanation is inadequate. The Iraqis showed considerable competence in shielding forces, in reaching similar conclusions as their opponents on what constituted defensible terrain, and in demonstrating the ability to maneuver forces despite coalition control of the air and tremendous advantages in technical means of gathering intelligence. The Iraqis successfully shielded some of their equipment and managed to mount coordinated counterattacks such as the one TF 3-69 AR repelled at objective PEACH. The Iraqis also executed ambushes and, in some cases, attained tactical surprise. They found ways to close the range and, in more than one case, fought effectively enough to compel reaction, as they did when the counterattacked the 3-7 CAV on the east bank of the Euphrates during the "mother of all sandstorms" and again at objectives ROMMEL and MONTY in Baghdad. Certainly, their ability to defeat the efforts of the 11th AHR does not suggest uniform ineptitude.

But in intense close combat, they simply could not match the US forces in marksmanship, tactical technique, and the ability to adapt rapidly. The US should not apologize for fielding better-equipped units, but neither should it concede the point on training and the qualitative superiority of US units. Nor should US forces assume a qualitative edge in all domains. The venerable rocket-propelled grenade (a lineal descendant of the World War II *Panzerfaust*) remains elegantly simple, ubiquitous, and effective.

The sections that follow discuss implications for the future that may apply to the Army and, in some cases, to joint forces collectively. First there are some observations that apply to the peculiar environment of OIF that deserve consideration under the broad heading of the Contemporary Operating Environment. The remainder of the chapter considers implications that fall within the five broad areas or themes suggested in the introduction. These areas tend to overlap in terms of implications for how the Army structures, trains, and equips forces but serve well for organizing general groupings of implications from the campaign. The areas address:

- Command and Control
- Combined Arms Operations
- Joint Integration and Support
- Deployment and Sustainment
- Information and Knowledge

The Contemporary Operating Environment (COE)—Embedded or Not

"While it is impossible to predict the exact nature of future conflict, it is possible to determine those factors which will have the greatest effects on military forces and thus form the critical variables in future military operational environments."

TRADOC COE White Paper

Chapter 1 introduced the development and publication of the Army white paper that delineated the variable in the COE and attempted to describe that environment. Several years in development, the white paper reflected the Army's assessment of fundamental change in the operational environment following the end of the Cold War. This assessment stemmed from an ongoing internal debate over what the end of the Cold War meant. Specifically, those implications suggested the conditions for which the Army should be prepared and how the Army should train and equip forces. In fact the COE, as articulated in the white paper, followed and codified perceived changes in the environment, many of which had been applied in training, leader development, and acquisition before TRADOC published the white paper. The central argument in the COE white paper is that the variables are dynamic, and thus the COE is continuously changing and requires continuous adaptation by the Army and joint forces.

The OIF experience largely validated the COE white paper and the efforts the Army made to incorporate it in training and as a means to inform force design and combat development. Arguably, OIF also demonstrated that the Army still had not fully internalized and accounted for the implications of COE. The tragic tactical defeat of the 507th Maintenance Company is an eloquent argument for this point of view. Similarly, the 11th AHR experience is very much a reflection of change in the environment not discerned or at least not fully accommodated by the Army.

OIF demonstrated that the COE is not just the enemy, but truly an environment consisting of the enemy, friendly forces, noncombatants, governmental and nongovernmental organizations, neutrals, terrain, weather, and other factors. More important, the Army's experience in—and ability to cope with—the COE as it existed in Iraq in March and April of 2003 suggests some areas worthy of consideration as the Army determines how to prepare for future combat operations or operations other than war. OIF also lends the Army a direction that transformation could take to maintain current demonstrated battlefield dominance into the middle of the 21st century.

OIF, Operation ENDURING FREEDOM, and the many other operations conducted since the end of the Cold War also demonstrate that the COE is dynamic. Friends and foes will make adjustments based on what they observed in OIF. Adaptation is therefore the rule for the Army and the other services. Specifically, adaptation in anticipation of change should characterize the way the Army designs, equips, mans, and trains units.

If the COE is valid for the Army, it has utility for joint forces as well. In the absence of easily defined threats, the COE has some acceptance in the joint community. As a conceptual framework, it has utility for the other services as well. Continuing to study the COE and attempting to anticipate the future operational environment is essential to the joint team. To support developing and encouraging study focused on understanding the implications of the operational environment, TRADOC, along with Joint Forces Command (JFCOM), hosted a joint operational environment conference in June of 2003. JFCOM will also publish the Army opposing forces strategic doctrine as a Joint Opposing Forces strategic doctrine and will begin the work of developing opposing forces doctrine to enable consistent replication of the operational environment in joint training and experimentation. JFCOM and TRADOC understand that the dynamic nature of the COE must preclude "doctrinaire" application of the COE or the development of a fixed "threat" for use in joint training and experimentation. The joint community will profit from developing a joint operational environment (JOE) not only as a means of focusing experimentation and transformation, but also to sharpen the debate on the conduct of warfare and operations in the 21st century.[1]

A cautionary note on training and readiness is necessary. The US armed forces have often been justly accused of preparing to fight the last war. In considering how to prepare for the next war, the COE and its likely successor, the JOE, is a concept, or context for considering the problem. It is not a specific threat. The COE affirms that each mission, enemy, and scenario is unique and that all of these components are dynamic. The Army should not adopt the Iraqi model as the basis for determining the operating environment. Instead, the OIF experience can inform the design of threats and scenarios. Replicating the operational environment must be so dynamic that operating in conditions of uncertainty and ambiguity becomes second nature to soldiers and their units. What can be imported from the Iraqi model is the range of threats (Special Republican Guard, regular army, *Fedayeen*, terrorists, etc.); the combination of enemy conventional, unconventional, and information operations; and the variety of conditions. These conditions range from terrain and weather combinations, simultaneous combat and humanitarian assistance, and changing political/social factors.

Considering implications for US forces is fine, but it does not address the implications of OIF from the point of view of potential adversaries. Clearly, the Iraqis learned and applied some lessons from their experiences in DESERT STORM. There is some evidence that suggests they sought to learn from others, including the Serbs and perhaps the Russians, or at least from the Russian experience in Chechnya. Saddam's posturing about killing Americans in Iraqi cities was not without basis in fact. Indeed, the Iraqis did bring US forces to battle in their cities. Friends and adversaries alike watched OIF with keen interest. What did they learn?

There are web pages on the Internet that ran commentary during the campaign and continue to draw conclusions about what worked well for the coalition and what did not. Some of these sites are interested in discovering vulnerabilities. To understand fully the implications of OIF, examining what outside observers concluded from DESERT STORM has utility. Writing in 1991 for publication in the occasional papers of a defense think tank in India, Brigadier V. K. Nair reached some interesting conclusions. Of the United States, Nair observed, "With the technological giant—the United States having "willy nilly" and progressively conducted offensive military operations against Libya, Grenada, Panama and Iraq, developing countries, especially the threshold powers, need to review their threat perceptions."[2] During and after DESERT STORM, US operations were not viewed necessarily as benevolent. Nair notes, "While fully appreciating the inadvisability of coming into conflict with a superpower, what are the courses open to third world countries to ensure survival if a confrontation is thrust upon them."[3] In short, a thoughtful observer from a country with whom the United States has no quarrel concluded from observing the US that this superpower "willy nilly" attacks countries who are at a disadvantage vis-à-vis the US. More important, he suggests that countries may have such a confrontation "thrust on them" by the US.

Nair and his colleagues writing in *War in the Gulf: Lessons for the 3rd World* suggested possible solutions to this problem of American aggression. Among other things they recommended acquisition of electronic technology, consolidation of research and development, covert acquisition of technology, establishing priority thrust lines, and developing dual-use technologies, to name a few means to close the technological gap with the US. To this technological approach, they suggested practical additions, including deception, increasing automation, developing both passive and active means to protect critical sites, and developing integrated command, control, communications, and intelligence. Of particular interest, they suggested research and development efforts in lasers, electronic countermeasures, UAVs, thermal imaging, and missile guidance technology.[4]

It is possible, and some of the evidence suggests, that the running start surprised the Iraqis because it broke the pattern of operation inherent in the concept of overwhelming force. Avoiding discernible patterns is sound policy and one that others will respect. What might contemporary observers learn from OIF? They might conclude that apparent US dependence on technical intelligence, surveillance, and reconnaissance may afford opportunity to shield, hide, or deceive. They may conclude that RPGs with more powerful warheads, including perhaps tandem warheads, may offset US armor. For that matter, they may conclude that the Iraqis did not make the best use of urban terrain, and they may confront the next US operation rather differently. They may conclude that the US forces in the field transition too slowly and are vulnerable to classic insurgency operations. They may even believe that US forces are vulnerable in nonlinear, noncontiguous operations.

In June of 2003, members of the Russian Academy of Military Sciences Scientific Council met and presented a number of essays at a conference devoted to "Lessons and Conclusions from the War in Iraq." The Russians found much to learn from and, perhaps more important, much to fear. The academics and soldiers present, like V. K. Nair before them, did not perceive that Operation IRAQI FREEDOM was a benevolent activity. One of them, Major General G. A. Berezkin, asserted that OIF represented "the first steps on the path toward the establishment of Washington's absolute hegemony in the world."[5] Beyond noting the clear and present danger that the US constituted to the rest of the world, Berezkin asserted that the United States had developed a new form of operations. To Berezkin the integration of joint forces, coupled with precision munitions, had reached a new plain requiring the "invention" of a term to describe them adequately. According to Berezkin, that new form of warfare is "joint operations."[6]

The Russians found much to applaud from a military point of view in what they perceived to be innovation, adaptation, and effective use of information and an integration among the services that is new. On the other hand, they were critical of Iraq's performance and believed that the Iraqis had the means to defeat US forces in the field. General of the Army M. L. Gareyev argued that the Iraqis did not effectively defend the approaches to Baghdad. He argued that "With thorough camouflage, combined with a large number of decoy targets and minefields, they (troops defending the approaches to Baghdad) could have played an important role in repulsing the invasion of the Anglo-American troops."[7] Gareyev also argued that Russia could learn from the US experience in combating guerilla warfare. For example, US operations in Iraq suggested to him that Russia should train and organize units to operate in "maneuver-intensive raids" and that greater attention must be paid to "reliable protection for lines of communication, command and control posts and logistics."[8] For the most part, these Russian observers did not believe the coalition handled urban warfare well and felt that a well-executed urban fight would give the US pause. The Russians also noted with satisfaction that the US did not achieve the "contactless" battle that it sought. More important, some argued that the US has a weakness stemming from the effort to fight contactless battles—they perceive that the US may be vulnerable to close combat.[9]

There are still other possible lessons for outsiders that US forces need to anticipate. The point is, as the Defense Department moves on transformation, the operational environment remains dynamic and so must the transformation effort. Equally important, friends, adversaries, and even some who are neither will seek ways to cope with perceived US strengths and exploit perceived US weakness. Adapting to stay ahead promotes adapting to keep up or get ahead. For example, what might outside observers conclude from the CFLCC's effort to build infrastructure to support the arrival and staging of units? Perhaps they will determine that denying or limiting access is the key to surviving—or at least extending—a conflict to attain a favorable diplomatic solution. US transformation must occur in the context of considering what potential US adversaries might have learned from OIF. This is the essence of understanding the implications of the contemporary operating environment and the future operating environment.

Preparation

The preparation of the theater and ongoing operations since DESERT STORM proved essential to rapid tactical and operational success in Operation IRAQI FREEDOM. The US staged ground forces primarily in a comparatively robust theater infrastructure. Despite the fact that coalition forces could not stage in either Saudi Arabia or Turkey, they enjoyed the benefits of continued presence in the theater that their predecessors in the Gulf War did not. It is hard to overstate the importance of this fact. The caveat for US armed forces is clear—a decade's preparation adjacent to the territory on which ground combat operations are anticipated may not precede the next operation.

On the other hand, the work the services did to assemble and maintain pre-positioned equipment and improve lift capabilities clearly paid dividends and are independent of the theater. Similarly, the effort the Army made to improve deployment infrastructure at Army posts in CONUS and in Europe also are important preparation tasks independent of the theater. Bases and forces stationed in Europe played a central role in OIF. European bases played important roles as power-projection platforms. NATO partnership for peace and the EUCOM "in the spirit of partnership for peace" initiatives assisted in developing the relationships that afforded overflight, staging, and basing that supported the effort in Iraq. Some nations that joined the coalition arguably did so as a means of clearly stating their commitment to their new relationships with the US. The work NATO and EUCOM did helped assure interoperability with coalition units that participated in the decade following DESERT STORM.

The proximity of Europe and efforts in the US notwithstanding, the fact is that the US forces in Iraq directly benefited from more than decade on the ground in Kuwait. This kind of situation may not apply in other contingencies. For that reason alone, there is much work to be done to assure adequate lift is available and pre-positioned equipment—whether afloat or ashore—is prepared and can be used. Marine and Army gear in those stocks has been used and used hard. Restoring that equipment and perhaps modernizing it are clearly priorities. It is not difficult to imagine contingencies that will require this equipment and contingencies where the US does not have a long-term presence.

Finally, Iraq made no direct effort to impede the buildup in the theater. Planners should consider what might have happened if Iraq had attempted a strategy based on denying access to the region. Planners might also wonder what the outcome would have been if Iraq had attacked US forces in Kuwait before they were ready for the running start. The point is that the conditions in CENTCOM in 2003 are unlikely to be replicated elsewhere.

Urban Operations

As the US armed forces prepared for operations in Iraq, the specter of large-scale urban operations haunted commanders, planners, and soldiers. There was no doubt that removing the Saddam Hussein regime from power required fighting in Baghdad, and possibly in some or all of the numerous cities along the Tigris and Euphrates Rivers en route. It was not unreasonable to suppose that large-scale urban operations would produce high casualties (coalition, Iraqi, and civilian), significant expenditure of resources, and major destruction of the infrastructure necessary for postcombat restoration of normalcy. None of this was far from the minds of those expecting to deploy to Iraq.

In the fall of 2002, when planning started in earnest, the Army's knowledge and understanding of urban operations stemmed from three sources. First, recent Army experience, including urban operations in the 1990s in Mogadishu, Somalia; Panama City, Panama; Brcko, Bosnia; and Port-au-Prince, Haiti.[10] Of course, none of these operations rivaled the scope, scale, or potential lethality of major combat in Baghdad. The Army drew also on the recent experience of others. The Russian experience in Grozny and Israeli experience in the West

Bank and Gaza provided grist for Army planners.[11] The third source was historical experience, including Hue in the Vietnam War, and Manila, Berlin, Stalingrad, and Aachen in World War II. These examples did not encourage complacency among planners or units. Not surprisingly, the Army and the joint team sought solutions that could enable the removal of the Saddam Hussein regime without the casualties and destruction historically associated with urban operations.

Eventually that search produced results. Rather than simply viewing urban areas as complex terrain occupied by an enemy force, Army planners took the approach that a city is a system of systems. Political, civil, social, religious, military, power generation and distribution, transportation, water distribution, and a host of other systems combined, interacted, and adapted constantly. Understanding these systems and how they interacted seemed key to understanding how to conduct military operations there. Accordingly, intelligence officers and planners joined traditional intelligence analysis with the system-of-systems approach in an attempt to truly understand Iraqi cities—starting with Baghdad. This drove the development of courses of action intended to defeat Iraqi forces and remove Saddam's regime from power while avoiding killing large numbers of noncombatants and destroying critical infrastructure. This approach held out the possibility of restoring basic services quickly after the end of major combat operations. Further, this analysis aided subordinate, higher, and joint headquarters in their own preparations.

Armed with recently published doctrine and provided with a reasonable understanding of his opponent and urban systems, Lieutenant General Wallace and his staff developed the scheme that would eventually be executed in Baghdad. As in any fight, the details in execution varied from the plan, but V Corps and I MEF applied what they learned—and the results of their own analysis—with great success. Paraphrasing Major General Dave Petraeus, the CFLCC rapidly adapted and fought the enemy they found rather than the one they planned on. When Petraeus said this, he meant that he fought in An Najaf first rather than in Karbala, as he had anticipated, but he would likely also agree that no one anticipated the paramilitary threat that confronted the coalition. Although the concept of isolating Baghdad and reducing the regime by means of attacks from forward operating bases seemed sound and may have worked, it was modified in execution.

Colonel Perkins and his superiors concluded that while raids into the city's core were feasible, seemed effective, and might produce the intended outcome, they also produced unintended outcomes such as "Baghdad Bob" portraying the withdrawal of Perkins' troops after his first raid as a defeat. Equally important, "Baghdad Bob" and people in Baghdad may actually have believed that Perkins' withdrawal meant that his brigade had been defeated. Thus, Perkins planned the second thunder run intending to stay if he could create the tactical conditions that would support remaining. Wallace, having thought through the same problem, underwrote Blount and Perkins on the basis of a few probing questions. The "plan" evolved in execution—as it should have, given the conditions obtained and the implications of not going downtown and staying.

New doctrine, a new way of looking at the problem, and alert leaders went a long way toward resolving the problems posed in the urban venue. But technology also contributed. For example, before they reached Baghdad, Army leaders had learned to trust BFT. Being able to track friendly units in urban terrain eased a classic problem in urban fighting—controlling the fight. Additionally, air- and ground-delivered precision munitions permitted artillery and close air support while minimizing collateral damage and noncombatant deaths. The 101st, for example, developed and executed a technique of attacking point targets with infantry following on the heels of JDAMS. To a large extent, precision munitions offset the advantage that urban terrain accorded to the defenders. Abrams tanks and Bradleys proved themselves nearly impervious to Iraqi weapons and allowed US forces to penetrate the heart of the urban areas.

Rapid fielding of the equipment necessary for urban combat also proved vital. Body armor, elbow and knee pads, and laser pointers seem trivial in comparison to the D9 Bulldozer and improved precision munitions, but body armor, pads, pointers, and similar relatively inexpensive devices protected infantrymen and made them deadly in urban terrain. The Army's decision in the fall of 2002 to procure and issue specialized equipment directly contributed to a quick victory with relatively few casualties. Fielding equipment early enabled units to train with their new equipment—better still, the stuff worked.

Army leaders and units anticipated that urban combat would be characterized by a series of transitions: battles and engagements followed by security operations and humanitarian assistance. They realized that a successful engagement in a city or town had to be followed by successful transition to postcombat operations. In preparation, major Army formations (brigades and higher) received civil affairs and psychological operations units to assist in those transitions. Few anticipated the frequent transitions from major combat to support operations and back again. For example, the 3rd Infantry, 101st Airborne, and 82nd Airborne Divisions each fought successive engagements in As Samawah, with periods of low intensity or no conflict in between.

As the Army fields Stryker Brigades and continues transformation, the OIF experience will influence combat development. Tanks and Bradleys performed brilliantly in OIF, but they did not meet all of the operational requirements. Despite their advantages in armor, tanks and Bradleys evinced a number of disadvantages —they could not elevate their weapons far enough to fire at the upper floors of buildings from close range. But as 3rd ID discovered, the lowly M113, full of engineers armed to the teeth, *could* engage the second and third stories. Clearly no weapon system is perfect for all environments, and even the superbly equipped forces that fought OIF have vulnerabilities. Adaptation, flexibility, and a mix of capabilities seem vital.

Preparation for the urban operations anticipated in OIF revealed a significant deficiency in Army training capabilities. The Army's premier urban operations training sites—Fort Polk, Fort Knox, and Hohenfels—are really just small villages. The computer simulation that drives the Battle Command Training Program's *WARFIGHTER* exercises poorly replicates urban operations. Joint and other service capabilities are no better. Fortunately, the "joint" way ahead to improve the nation's capability to conduct urban operations includes efforts to upgrade and enlarge urban operations training capabilities. Just since the buildup for OIF, the National Training Center has built a number of small "towns" in which both the opposing forces and "civilians" confront training units. At Fort Polk's JRTC, the Army has built an Iraqi village, complete with Iraqi mayor. In the fall of 2002, the Department of Defense established a cell in JFCOM to develop and experiment with concepts for urban operations that will also produce benefits. What must be done next is to build a simulation that affords joint commanders the opportunity to plan and execute realistic training in large urban areas that replicate both the urban core and urban sprawl. This task, while daunting, is not out of reach.

Although urban operations in OIF proved intense to the soldiers and marines who executed them, the coalition avoided the high rate of casualties and destruction historically associated with them. Speed, well-trained and adaptable troops, and luck all played roles in delivering this outcome. Coalition troops adapted during execution, task-organizing on the fly when required, overcoming every problem they confronted. However, it is plain that the Iraqis could have made the fight far more difficult had they not committed their relatively fragile forces to successive, suicidal attacks against armored formations. Finally, although outside the bounds of this study, prosecuting a counterinsurgency campaign in the urban venue remains difficult. Urban terrain continues to offer defenders and/or insurgents opportunity.

The initiative to assign JFCOM the responsibility for joint urban operations experimentation will have far-reaching effects because the OIF campaign appears to confirm what most soldiers understand instinctively:

- Urbanization is a trend that is unlikely to be reversed.
- Most potential opponents know they cannot confront American forces symmetrically, so they must consider, among other things, using complex and urban terrain to their advantage.
- US forces must be able to win the "close fight" inherent in urban terrain.
- US forces must be able to integrate fires with minimal collateral damage.

Operation IRAQI FREEDOM affords ample opportunity to consider the ramifications of how the armed forces have organized and prepared for combat operations in the COE. Iraq, however, is not the COE, but instead a subset of that larger context and must be understood as such.

Command and Control

Command and control is a particularly broad area of consideration. It affords the opportunity as a domain in which to consider decision making, organizations, the separate functions of command and control, and leadership, to name a just a few of the possible areas of discussion. Here the focus is narrowed to three separate areas of discussion which, while still broad, sharpen the focus and reflect those areas that could be observed with sufficient clarity and frequency as to warrant suggesting implications. Those are leadership and decision making, battle command, and how forces are echeloned.

Leadership and Decision Making

The quality of leadership and decision making in OIF—from the highest to lowest levels—is striking. Soldiers and their leaders demonstrated courage, compassion, initiative, and sacrifice. The troops and their leaders took care of each other and illustrated the ephemeral concept of unit cohesion. Leaders led from the front and made decisions based not only on enhanced command and control tools afforded by comparatively high levels of digital linkage, but also by seeing for themselves the conditions on the battlefield. Even in the 21st century, warfare is a human endeavor that requires the human touch. In OIF, the leaders and the led both demonstrated they understood this salient fact.

So why did Army leaders from Tommy Franks down perform so well? Several possibilities emerge. The body of work to produce effective leaders includes getting the right folks to join the service and continues through career-long training and education. It is difficult this early after the end of major combat operations to say with certainty what "right" looks like and what developmental assignments, training, and education should be reinforced. What is clear is that the present system of schools for troops, officers, and noncommissioned officers, and training—particularly collective training at the Army's training centers—paid dividends. As Lieutenant General Dave McKiernan put it, "I think in the Army our training, our doctrine, our leader development programs are pretty damned sound and produced soldiers and leaders who made great decisions out there and who are pretty aggressive."[12] Obviously, these institutions should remain dynamic to stay abreast of a dynamic operating environment, but they seem sound at their center. Although McKiernan asserted that Army training and education worked, in the same interview he identified the need to ramp up joint education at lower levels and go into "overdrive" at the war college level.[13]

Leading From the Front

Combat is arguably the most stressful human endeavor. It is, as Whitman described it, an "incommunicable experience." Effective leaders share that experience with their troops and inspire or steady by their presence. For this reason, the very best combat leaders lead from as far forward as possible and often farther forward than prudent, realizing their physical presence is more important than preserving themselves from harm. In OIF, soldiers felt the presence of commanders and appreciated the moral support commanders provided by their example and by their desire to help. In remarking on the effectiveness of leading from the front, Major Gerard Cribb, operations officer, TF 2-70 AR, offered the following while describing the feint to Al Hillah:

I will remember Colonel Anderson (commander, 2nd BCT, 101st Airborne Division) and Brigadier General (Ben) Freakley (assistant division commander, Operations, 101st Airborne Division) the rest of my life. Right after the artillery—we received artillery—I hear this "tink," "tink" on the TC (tank commander's) hatch and I open up (the hatch) and look over and there is Colonel Anderson. He said, "What do you need?" I'm like, "What, sir?" He goes, "I got the call, I got the read and everything, I see you're in contact here. I can have Apaches right here to try to loosen up those dismounted infantry positions. I've got three battalions of FA (field artillery) and it's all yours, Gerard."

Later Ben Freakley arrived and Cribb described him as cool among "sporadic machine gun fire" and wanted to know "Is everything ok?"

This is unbelievable. Here we are in contact and both of these guys are asking us what do we need to make our situation better. That was great—definitely made us feel good going into the fight.

After the conclusion of major combat operations, Colonel Will Grimsley wrote to the commanding general of the National Training Center to thank him and his key leaders for the work they did in preparing Grimsley's 1st Brigade, 3rd ID. According to Grimsley, "I told them I could draw a straight line correlation from how we fought in OIF successfully directly back to my National Training Center rotation."[14] In anticipation of fighting on the escarpment, the NTC replicated the conditions Grimsley expected to see in the central corridor of the training area and tailored other fights during the rotation against possible OIF scenarios. Although at the training center they trained against an enemy replicating dismounted Special Republican Guard troops, the fact that they confronted paramilitary forces did not matter since the enemy fought generally the way intelligence estimated they would. More important, the opposing forces at

Fort Irwin "replicated" the enemy in accordance with that estimate. In a manner of speaking, Grimsley's troops fought the escarpment fight before ever reaching Iraq. Major Mike Oliver, TF 3-69 AR's operations officer, noted that his task force performed much better against the actual enemy they confronted on the escarpment than they had against the "opposing forces" provided by the 11th Armored Cavalry Regiment at Fort Irwin in the fall of 2002.[15]

But this anecdote simply does not tell the whole story. No one anticipated that the paramilitary forces would fight with the fanaticism they showed or that the "mother of all sandstorms" would strike. Training, even in anticipation of highly specific conditions such as the escarpment, cannot alone produce the agility, innovation, and adaptation that the Army's troops and leaders showed. Soldiers from private to general demonstrated "values" the Army has sought to inculcate, including loyalty to each other, integrity, and courage. These must be taught and learned. Similarly, the tolerance for ambiguity that unit commanders showed—that ability to understand that even with great technology there are some things you cannot know, is also, at least in part, learned.

Toleration for ambiguity, innovation, and technical competence all contribute to effective decision making. But while sound decision making is necessary in effective leaders, it is not sufficient. The ability to lead and motivate stems from many factors, including talent. But even talented leaders can be taught how to become more effective. The Army's leaders in OIF showed they understood their business, could motivate troops, respected troops, and handled themselves with the courage, candor, and competence their troops expected. Examining how the training and education system in the Army and in the joint community contributed both to effective leadership and decision making will be an important component of helping US forces maintain the edge.

Battle Command—Enabling Commanders to Lead from the Front

The ability to describe what is to be done, to visualize the end state, and to direct execution are components of the art and science of battle command. Art implies, among other things, intuition and a feel for the battlefield. Because combat operations remain, even in the early 21st century, human endeavors, commanders must also be able to assess the battlefield for themselves and inspire and direct important actions. The best commanders, therefore, also are good leaders who lead from the front. The science of command lends itself more to the technical competence soldiers expect in their commanders, but also to the means of effecting control in execution. Lieutenant General Wallace developed and executed a battlefield circulation scheme to visit each of his divisions daily to see his commanders and look them in the eye. When Lieutenant General McKiernan needed to make critical decisions, he went forward, as he did on his visit to Jalibah on 28 March, to see and hear from his commanders personally. To lead from the front and to command effectively, commanders need support. They need the tools to communicate their vision and aids to command that enable or support control and direction. They need the means to communicate and they need the support staff to assist in assessing enemy intentions, planning operations, and directing execution. The following sections discuss aids to command, battle command on the move, and the way in which staffs operate and organize to facilitate battle command.

Aids to Command

Force XXI initiatives aimed to enable commanders to "see" their units and the perceived or actual positions of enemy units. The Army Battle Command System (ABCS) provided the core capability commanders needed to see their own forces, describe what they wanted done and, with adequate communications, talk with subordinates and their superiors. In the fall of 2002, the Army rushed to field key components of ABCS and other tools to support battle command. Many units that fought in OIF had not received the entire ABCS suite. These units bought and fielded workable solutions of their own. Most damning for the ABCS, the V Corps/US Army Europe off-the-shelf solution, Command and Control for Personal Computers (C2PC), worked better than the Maneuver Control System, the cornerstone of ABCS, and became the preferred means of tracking units and effecting command. Arguably, BFT, or as it is technically know, Force 21 Battle Command Brigade and Below (FBCB2), delivered over L-Band satellite, proved the most critical of all the various tools available.

Coupled with BFT, commanders using C2PC, ABCS, and one or two other aids—including the Automated Deep Operational Coordination System—could see their forces, plan and execute fires digitally, track the air space, and achieve high-resolution situational awareness of "blue" activities. Commanders also had access to digital map products that enabled them to produce high-resolution maps for their units and their own use. Using software such as *FalconView* and *Topscene,* they could visualize terrain with high fidelity as well. Their confidence in these systems and, as a consequence, their confidence that they understood the "blue" picture, enabled them to view fights in which their units were widely dispersed. This confidence in BFT, in particular, encouraged aggressiveness.

There are three major variables in controlling a combat engagement: "Where are my troops?" "Where is the enemy?" and "Where are we in relation to each other?" BFT enabled commanders to understand one of these three key variables. High-resolution maps on screens that showed their units helped them understand part of the third variable. For the second variable, the enemy, although few felt they had the fidelity they desired, they had sufficient grasp to fight with confidence.

All of this is fine and a plus for the Army and joint forces, but more remains to be done. No commander expressed complete satisfaction with MCS. C2PC received, by comparison, rave reviews, but what is required is a "joint" interoperable system in the hands of every unit. What remains missing is "red force tracking," some means of discerning red activities in relation to blue and identifying or at least estimating red intentions. Obviously, red is unlikely to collaborate by providing that information, so red force tracking is not going to happen, but the means to update perceived and actual red positions inherent in ABCS proved inadequate. For the most part, commander aids the Army fielded proved useful, but there is more to be done and these systems need to be proliferated.

Battle Command on the Move and Dispersed

The Army developed and fielded purpose-built command and control vehicles with broad-band satellite suites that provided the means for commanders to command from well forward and while on the move. But there were very few of these systems, none were fielded below division level, and not all of the divisions had them. Maneuver commanders down to brigade level did have satellite communications, and most combat and combat support (CS) units down to company level had BFT that enabled at least limited email via satellite. Voice communication provided by single-channel wide band (25 kHz) tactical satellite assured communications over long ranges so that brigades could talk to each other and their division. Below that level, units relied on short-range FM radios. Some units remained tied to mobile subscriber equipment (MSE), which meant, in effect, that they had no means to effect battle command on the move enhanced by ABCS until the MSE nodes caught up—which is to say, too late to support them in the advance on Baghdad. Even maneuver units depended on MSE to some extent. Thus, if the nodes were not "in" and able to communicate, maneuver brigades lacked the means to receive updated imagery. Units below brigade level rarely were able to tie into MSE. Thus, while the CFLCC C2, Major General Marks, expressed satisfaction with his ability to provide intelligence products, he noted with resignation that he had no means to "refresh" the picture provided to lower tactical units because of the digital divide stemming from the fact that the Army still relied heavily on MSE in OIF.[16]

Many of the CS and most of the combat service support (CSS) units depended exclusively on MSE to access ABCS. Similarly, these units often lacked BFT. If the Army is serious about fighting dispersed in nonlinear fights, this issue will need to be addressed.

Operation and Organization of Command Posts

Quite apart from communications and software issues to which Major General Marks alluded, the Army might profit from examining how it organizes, mans, and equips command posts. Although the Army went to war largely "networked," the structure and general concept for establishing command posts that were echeloned from front to rear—with a tactical command post (TAC), a main command post, and a rear command post—is one that World War II commanders would have recognized. These three command posts had discrete functions more or less associated with their proximity to the forward line of troops. Given a nonlinear and noncontiguous fight, reorganizing command posts to associate them by "time" rather than space may be appropriate. Thus, a corps might have an assault command post that would fight the current fight with the capability to direct and coordinate immediate effects *throughout* the corps battlespace. The corps main, possibly operating many miles away in relative sanctuary, would focus on longer-term planning and sustaining the current and near-term fights. Echeloning command posts may no longer be the best approach if and when the Army is able to solve the problem of generating reliable broadband communications on the move and dispersed.

The way staffs organized also evolved before OIF. Lieutenant General McKiernan reorganized the CFLCC staff around operational functions rather than the traditional vertical staff stovepipes. Thus, although Major General Marks, the CFLCC intelligence officer, developed and distributed operational intelligence, intelligence officers could be found in the other staff sections devoted to supporting intelligence requirements extant in operational protection, for example. McKiernan also rejected the traditional staff update and substituted a staff assessment instead—seeking to learn the "so what" of events rather than a history of events. Other units also organized multidiscipline functional cells, such as fires and effects coordination cells, that sought to apply the concept of effects-based operations. The implications of digital means to visualize, describe, and direct—along with concepts such as effects-based operations—suggest the Army needs to revisit how it organizes staffs and command posts.

The headquarters employed in OIF are larger than most commanders would prefer. During the development of ABCS and various commanders' aids, some have argued that these tools would produce smaller staffs. That goal proved illusive. Automation has not tended to reduce the size of staffs. There is energy and opportunity to examine how to organize command posts now within the present echelons and formations and, as a consequence, consider how to organize and structure echelons and formations. It is possible that developing more effective command posts may not necessarily make them more efficient in terms of size.

There is much more work to be done to fully understand or identify the implications of OIF on the general domain of command and control. BFT, for example, clearly paid dividends—enabling commanders to "see" their units to coordinate tactical decisions rapidly. Continued effort to proliferate these systems seems warranted but must be accompanied by developing the means that ensure communications pathways to enable units to enjoy the benefits of both digital communications and networks.

Echelonment

How units are structured and how they are grouped to effect command and control and the functions they perform are key components \of command and control. Structure and functions define echelons of command. In OIF, the Army employed echelons with names Napoleon would have found familiar. But to argue that echelons in the Army are the same as in Napoleon's day is as inaccurate as arguing that because we call them *ships*, the USS *Reagan*, the newest carrier in the US Navy, and USS *Constitution,* the oldest commissioned US Navy vessel, are the same and that, therefore, ships have not changed since the 18th century. Echelons are the means by which the ground forces exercise command and control and execute critical functions. Critical functions have remained fairly stable—logistics, fires, and the development of intelligence, for example, are functions that armies have had to perform and will continue to perform in combat operations. Echelons as a means to execute functions are not new either. The term "corps" to describe an echelon of ground forces dates back to Napoleon, but the functions performed by that echelon have varied historically. For example, in World War II, the corps had almost no logistics functions, but in OIF, V Corps had a great many logistics functions. In World War II, the field army had a pool of combat units that it could send to corps and divisions to weight the effort or execute particular functions. Although CFLCC is not an analogue to the field army, it performed many of the same functions but had no pool of "army-level" units. Digital means of communication, coupled with enhanced aids for commanders and emerging operations concepts, will also affect Army echelons.

The Operation IRAQI FREEDOM Study Group did not set out to examine the contribution of echelons or whether they should be restructured to eliminate one or more of them. However, in considering the Army story in OIF, echelons emerged as part of the tale. Because V Corps, as did I MEF, fought decentralized operations, some will argue that division echelon did not prove necessary. Obviously, CENTCOM could have mounted this campaign without the CFLCC as it did in the first Gulf War. Perhaps it is less obvious, but whether CFLCC could have operated without corps-level subordinates is a question that warrants consideration as well. The functions each echelon performed should drive further study and consideration of the utility of combining some functions so that an echelon could be eliminated.

The evidence of OIF does not compel conclusions on this matter except to suggest that there was more than enough work to go around for the echelons and formations fielded. The evidence suggests that all of the echelons played useful roles. For example, the CFLCC performed functions at the theater level that both I MEF and V Corps would have found difficult if they had also retained responsibility for fighting their organic units. In an interview with officers from Joint Forces Command, the OIF Study Group, the Center of Military History, and the Army War College Strategic Studies Institute, Lieutenant General Dave McKiernan articulated as clear an argument for the current echelons as can be found by describing their functions. In response to a direct question on whether the CFLCC could have controlled divisions without V Corps and I MEF, McKiernan responded, "I don't think so. I don't think you could because I am spending a lot of energy working strategic, theater-wide, operational components, cross-components and tactical (issues)."[17]

CFLCC also managed the battlespace; oversaw joint intelligence surveillance and reconnaissance; assigned priorities for resources; and dealt with theater logistics and joint reception, staging, onward movement, and integration. It is hard to see how either I MEF or V Corps could have managed these functions and its internal tactical operations. Although they often fought with their brigade and regimental combat teams widely separated, the higher headquarters—division, corps, or MEF—integrated and synchronized the air, ground, and logistics efforts that won those fights. Finally, brigades organized as tactical headquarters and not as fixed organizations. They task-organized and integrated units with whom they had never trained and took them into a fight within hours. The actions of 2nd BCT, 101st Airborne, and TF 2-70 AR in the feint on Al Hillah on 31 March epitomize the flexibility of the brigade as an echelon of command. Most important, brigades managed widely dispersed fights and showed great flexibility and initiative in execution.

Still, the Army should examine how it echelons and how it assigns functions and organizes to execute them. For example, there may be ways to leverage digital technology to reduce the number of echelons. But examining formations within echelons may prove even more useful—the Army and joint community may find ways in which joint interdependence can reduce the number of certain kinds of formations. For example, if the air component will commit to attacking deep targets that support tasks assigned to the land component, the land component may require less artillery. As another example, how the Army organizes to deliver theater logistics and how logistics are managed certainly should be examined in great detail.

Combined Arms Operations

The discussion of this broad thematic area is bounded by how units are organized now, but it is not intended to underwrite either the current organization or alternatives presently under consideration. Rather, the focus is on how the Army conducted combined arms operations in a joint context. Joint concepts and joint doctrine both reflect and affect how the Army organizes and operates now and are essential to how the Army transforms. What is clear from OIF is that combined arms and tailoring or task-organizing to create combined arms worked in OIF. Combining the battlefield effects of engineers, maneuver units, and fires clearly produced synergy. The Army proved able to task-organize on the move to create combined arms teams tailored to mission requirements and could do so on little or no notice. This stemmed from training, education, doctrine, and practice that produced a culture which supported flexible organizations on the basis of the analysis of the mission, enemy, terrain and weather, troops and support available, time available, and the proximity of civilians or critical infrastructure that might affect execution. In OIF, this produced lethal and flexible task-organized formations stemming from the complementary effects of effective battle command, intelligence, maneuver, indirect fire support, close air support, Army aviation, engineers, tactical logistics, and integration with special forces. All of this, coupled with world-class training received both in theater and prior to arriving, made for a dominant force.

As the Army considers what conclusions may be drawn from OIF, reflecting on just how these lethal, flexible, and adaptive combat teams came to be seems appropriate. Task-organizing for specific missions is possible because of inherent flexibility in the way Army units are organized. Army doctrine and concepts for the design of units provide the foundation for flexibility. Specifically, units are built on the basis of not only what they will be asked to do, but also how they will do it. Design principles include concepts of "pooling" some resources, while making others organic. Some of those principles stem from doctrine. For example, the notion that artillery is never in reserve is a doctrinal concept that leads to pooling artillery at the division echelon and higher so that artillery can be moved rapidly to support operations wherever it is required. Thus, each division has divisional artillery, and the Army fields artillery brigades that can be assigned to support corps and divisions as needed.

That design decision produces advantages in training artillery and making the maximum use of a limited resource. It is not the only way to do business, though. Artillery could be assigned as units organic to a brigade. Following World War II, the Army moved away from fixed regiments toward brigades that were assigned units as required. In practice, and to accommodate reductions to end strength, Army brigades have gradually evolved toward fixed organizations with tables of organization and equipment (TOE) and modified tables of equipment (MTOE) to accommodate a "semi" fixed structure. For example, a forward support battalion in an "armor" brigade of two tank battalions and one infantry battalion has an MTOE assigning tank automotive and turret mechanics that reflect the routine "semi" fixed status of the brigade it is assigned to support. In fact, the BCT really is an aphorism that reflects the increasingly fixed nature of brigades and stems from the regimental combat team usage current 50 years ago. Fortunately, commanders did not allow this quiet evolution to prevent them from task-organizing as required.

Choosing a concept for structuring forces based on efficiency is not inherently wrong, but neither is it inherently right. Structuring units for tactical effectiveness rather than efficiency is appealing. Many of the arguments for fielding an Army based on the fixed brigade as the basic module stem from this notion. Fixed organizations at brigade level produce both benefits and risks. The benefits in training combined arms are fairly obvious; but fixed structures may produce reluctance to task-organize and may not be affordable in the long term. Lieutenant Colonel "Rock" Marcone developed and trained "combat patrols" in TF 3-69 AR composed of tanks, Bradleys, and engineers. Whatever structure is developed should not constrain commanders from reorganizing to accommodate their analysis of mission requirements that may be discrete.

Of course, building a doctrine and concept of operations reliant on frequent task reorganization to match combat team capabilities to the specific mission requirements came at a price. The most obvious is that members of these transient combat teams rarely had the opportunity to train together before joining the fight. The initial friction between the 173rd Airborne Brigade and JSOTF-North stemmed from the fact that conventional units and SOF generally do not train together. Training and rehearsing together is clearly a key element for building effective combat teams that can adapt to the ever-changing battlefield. The second difficulty was the overuse of the low-density/high-demand units, such as military intelligence, special forces, psychological operations, and civil affairs units. As priorities shifted, these units often moved around the battlefield to meet demand.

How the Army organizes to facilitate combined arms and take advantage of joint integration and interdependence also affects modularity and therefore deployment. Weight and volume are key components of determining lift requirements, but determining what needs to go is also important. Army units, as they are organized now, often require "plugs," some of which are quite small detachments. Fixed organizations that include these plugs could simplify deployment planning and execution. Equally important, developing a fixed module at some level will enable the Army to communicate deployment requirements more quickly and clearly. Thinking through the matter of both echelons and formations within them is a key part of developing "modules" that support contingency deployment.

Generating SOF-like Qualities

Recently, the services have been asked how they could generate SOF-like qualities in their conventional forces; meaning, how can conventional forces reach the superior level of performance demonstrated by the hand-picked, specially trained and equipped special operations forces. In its preparation for OIF, the 3rd ID provides some insights into the challenges of generating SOF-like qualities. 3rd ID demonstrated lethality and adaptability and developed a tempo of operations rarely seen in conventional forces. Several factors contributed to their success. First, deploying and stop-loss generated stable, cohesive teams and leadership. Second, deploying the division early provided an uninterrupted focused training. Superb ranges at the UDAIRI Complex, supported by contract personnel, meant unlimited firing and maneuver opportunities. 3rd ID fired more than two years' worth of ammunition of all types and drove two years' worth of training miles in four months. Plus, 3rd ID fielded several key systems earlier than planned. These included the *Javelin* antitank system, Long-Range Acquisition and Scout Surveillance System (LRASSS) for scouts, satellite-based Blue Force Tracking system to provide situational awareness, and wideband satellite communications to pass voice and digital traffic across the theater. Last, contract-supported materiel innovation provided solutions to several mission-specific problems. Investing in 3rd ID paid dividends and should be examined to determine how to achieve similar excellence at less cost.

Examining formations within the current echelons may prove fruitful. Fixed organizations offer advantages on the battlefield logistically, and if they include civil affairs, psychological operations units, and other low-density plugs, they provide part of the solution to assuring the Army can deploy and field tactical "modules" rapidly. These studies and experiments obviously should also consider just how these "new" formations should be equipped to assure that the Army's tactical formations retain the edge they have now.

Joint Integration and Support: Effectiveness, not Efficiency

Perhaps the biggest accolade on the relative success of joint integration is offered by the Russian observer cited earlier, who argues that in OIF the US armed forces executed a new form of warfare, "joint operations." Obviously, that is the result of serious effort to improve joint integration since the passage of the Goldwater-Nichols legislation. Much remains to be done, but OIF shows how much has been achieved. The term "integration" used here differs from another term used to describe joint operations—interdependence. Integration is about combining resources in such a way as to produce synergy or results greater than the sum of the parts. Integration does not suggest efficiency so much as it suggests effectiveness. Interdependence, on the other hand, does suggest efficiency and therefore the elimination of capabilities in one service that may be redundant if they can be provided by another service. There are instances where interdependence makes absolute sense, and one instance was suggested in a preceding paragraph in the discussion on whether air power might enable the Army to reduce the amount of artillery that it fields. However, it is not appropriate in this effort to mandate solutions, but rather to suggest what implications might be drawn. Accordingly, integration is the term used in this discussion rather than interdependence.

Army Support to the Joint Team

By law, the Department of the Army is not a warfighting organization. Instead, the Army provides trained and ready forces to combatant commanders. The Army also provides forces to other services that enable economies across the Department of Defense. For example, the Army provides special forces, psychological operations, and civil affairs units to the Marines or elsewhere as required by the combatant commander. Similarly, theater air and missile defense units extend land-based air and missile defense wherever the combatant commander requires it. The same is true for certain kinds of support, including processing and securing enemy prisoners of war. The Army also provides port-opening, terminal management, and logistics over the shore services and thus is a major contributor to JLOTS operations. Finally, the Army provides certain common user commodities to all of the services. For example, the Army is responsible for providing fuel and bulk water to all forces ashore.

The Army did all of this and more in OIF. It provided both mandated support and support that it volunteered to provide. More than 40,000 soldiers either supported the joint team or were assigned directly in support of other services. Some 6,200 soldiers served in or supported the Coalition Force Special Operations Component Commander. More than 2,700 soldiers served with I MEF, doing everything from chemical reconnaissance to manning rocket artillery units.[18] The Army and the Marine Corps also collaborated to solve serious logistics problems. The Marine hose and reel system, the Army pipeline, and "bag farms" provided the means to assure adequate fuel reached Army and Marine ground units. Similarly, the Marine Corps provided air and naval gunfire liaison teams to the Army to assist the Army in requesting and employing Naval and Marine air.

This campaign not only illustrated the power of the US armed forces, but also showed how much more powerful the parts are when integrated rather than merely deconflicted. The campaign also suggests that the missions of the Army and Marine Corps may be converging. These two services should find more ways to collaborate and train with each other. They may also find ways to achieve interdependence that could result in efficiencies that make them more effective as well. In some ways, this might prove painful for the Army. For example, to provide marines and the joint team the ability to sustain joint land campaigns and to do so quickly may force reallocation of force structure to provide active units to theater support and CS operations in lieu of Reserve Component units that are not able to respond as quickly. That structure is not extant in the current force.

There are various solutions, but none are easy. Determining the right end strength, mix of units, and mix between Active and Reserve Component units are interrelated and not without political implications. More important, the "right" mix will be dynamic as long as the JOE remains dynamic.

Theater Air and Missile Defense

The development of theater air and missile defense (TAMD) following DESERT STORM proved successful for a number of reasons. First, the services developed joint solutions to the problem. The USS *Higgins*, an AEGIS destroyer, provided the fastest means of early warning and effectively linked the Navy's missile defense capability to the Patriot defense umbrella. Second, the Army designed and organized a formation to fight TAMD. The 32nd Army Air and Missile Defense Command afforded the means to exercise battle command over the many units that provided TAMD and supported the commander of Coalition Force Air Component Command, serving as his deputy for TAMD. The Kuwaitis added their own Patriot defenses to the fight, freeing the US Patriots to defend other friendly nations in the theater. Equally important, the 32nd afforded the CFLCC the means to maneuver Patriot units to protect the V Corps and I MEF as they advanced. Finally, the Army invested a great deal of time, money, and effort to improve the Patriot. The performance of joint TAMD in OIF validates these efforts. The resulting improvement in operational protection afforded the ground forces the ability to operate and, when required, the freedom to concentrate virtually free from the specter of enemy missile attack.

The work is not necessarily complete however. Missiles are a relatively inexpensive means both to challenge US access and to threaten US interests in a theater. The enemy adapts just as surely as the US does. In OIF, planners assumed that, as in 1991, Iraqi Scuds would be the main threat. As one Patriot battalion commander put it, "We spent four months doing a defense based on three absolutes—the primary threat to Kuwait would be the Al Hussein [Scud] missile, coming out of Baghdad, and fired at night. So, of course every one of our engagements was the Ababail or Al Samoud, out of Basra, during the day."[19] Moreover, land-attack cruise missiles emerged as a dangerous threat. Patriot and short-range air defense units can protect against the cruise missile threat, but work needs to be done to integrate these efforts into airspace management.

Other problems with TAMD warrant mention as well. Using the term "maneuver" in association with the movement of Patriot battalions to support offensive operations in OIF is kind to the point of exaggeration. Patriot is mobile, but not designed for cross-country maneuver in support of offensive operations. Examining solutions to this problem will absorb some energy in the coming years. Shooting down two friendly aircraft marred an otherwise brilliant performance. Sorting out friend from foe is unlikely ever to become foolproof, but "zero defects" is the right goal when lives are at stake.

Patriot battalions identified an implication of operating in the "rear" area in a noncontiguous fight. Lieutenant Colonel Joe De Antonna put it this way:

> There is no rear area anymore. And I think we have to adjust our training to reflect that, but we also have to adjust our resources to reflect that. I do not have hard-top HMMWVs with ring mounts. I have only a couple of crew-served weapons per unit. We only get to fire our weapons once per year. But, at the same time, I saw the expectation for us to be able to do the same thing the infantryman does. We've got to figure out how we are going to do that, and it's not going to be cheap, but if that is the expectation—and I see it as being a legitimate expectation—then we need to address that.

Special Forces and Conventional Forces Integration

The successful integration of SOF and conventional forces is one of the great stories of OIF. Effective integration took place at every echelon, from A-teams (ODAs) to the joint special operations task forces (JSOTFs). Integration occurred throughout the length and breadth of the Iraqi Theater of Operations—on land, in the air, and at sea. As a result, both SOF and conventional forces were more effective and presented the Iraqis with significantly more and different challenges. In the V Corps area, the ODAs of 5th and 19th Special Forces Groups and conventional brigades from the 3rd, 82nd, 101st, and 4th Divisions shared intelligence, fire support, medical treatment, and other support as the corps advanced toward Baghdad. For example, when the lead elements of 3rd ID approached the bridge across the Euphrates at An Nasiriyah, SOF already had "eyes on" and passed valuable intelligence that enabled a rapid and successful operation.

In the north, the JSOTF organized around 10th Special Forces Group served as the controlling headquarters for both the 173rd Airborne Brigade and a battalion of the 10th Mountain Division. A National Guard infantry battalion also supported the effort by providing security for forward operating bases. JSOTF-North performed the operational preparation of the battlespace necessary for the 173rd to conduct its operational maneuver from Europe into Bashur Airfield in northern Iraq. Units from the 10th Mountain Division's 2-14 IN provided the conventional punch and staying power for JSOTF-North to defend against Iraqi divisions counterattacking along the Green Line. The failure of those counterattacks so demoralized the Iraqis that the Iraqi V Corps surrendered to JSOTF-North. Special forces from JSOTF-North and 2-14 IN also combined to attack and destroy the terrorist camps of *Ansar Al Islam*.

CENTCOM assigned JSOTF-West the key mission of denying western Iraq to the Iraqi forces so that Scud missiles could not be launched against Jordan, Turkey, or Israel. To accomplish that mission, they were assigned National Guard conventional light infantry. A SOF task force employed tanks of C/2-70 AR(-), flown in by C-17s—demonstrating SOF, Army, and Air Force flexibility and integration executed in the middle of the campaign. After attacking into As Samawah one day, the troops of C/2-70 AR found themselves en route to operate with SOF forces more than 270 miles away the next. The combination of Abrams tanks and SOF proved extremely powerful and mobile in controlling the vast expanse of western Iraq and interdicting LOCs as Iraqi leaders and forces attempted to flee to Syria. And of course one of the first operations of the war took place offshore, where Army watercraft supported SOF troops in seizing oil platforms in the gulf.

Special Forces in Action

On 20 April 2003, a National Guard special forces ODA, was patrolling through villages and secondary roads east-southeast of Najaf. A local man volunteered the location of a senior Ba'ath Party official in the nearby town of Ghamas. He did not provide an exact location, but rather an approximate location and the name of a family dwelling. The ODA coordinated with (the special forces company to which it was attached) and the 101st to conduct a raid on the dwelling at dawn the next day. The ODA was joined by forces from the 101st Airborne and spent the night planning, preparing, and rehearsing.

At 0430, the raid convoy departed its base en route to Ghamas. The task force consisted of an assault team, a security team, a command and control element, and three blocking forces composed of troops from a scout platoon and antiarmor company of the 101st Airborne Division.

At 0515, the convoy hit the release point outside Ghamas. The 101st vehicles moved to their blocking positions at three bridges surrounding the town. The rest of the task force moved into the town. An interpreter quickly found a local guide who knew where the house was. He took the SF team to a walled two-story dwelling with a courtyard. The security team isolated the objective and provided overwatch while the assault team forcibly seized the dwelling and apprehended three adult males. Among them was Abd Hamden, the target of the raid and a senior Ba'ath Party official from Baghdad. After a tactical interrogation, one of the men provided the location of a *Fedayeen* major nearby in Ghamas. The SF and conventional force raided this house minutes later but only found his relatives. As the Americans left the town with their captives, they were cheered by locals throughout the town. A thorough interrogation of the prisoners was conducted and documented, and the prisoners were handed over to higher authorities.

The success of SOF-conventional integration was not assured by any means. After the failure at Desert One of the aborted attempt to rescue the hostages in 1979, the Special Operations Command (SOCOM) was formed, and Army Special Forces soon became a separate branch. The services resisted losing their unique, special operations-capable units to a separate command. Similarly, the regional combatant commanders resisted losing control of special operations in their respective areas of operations. Despite lukewarm reception and sometimes outright opposition, the creation of SOCOM, with its dedicated resources and mission focus, significantly improved the conduct of special operations missions but with unintended consequences. Through the 1980s and early 1990s, a physical and cultural gap grew between Army conventional and special operations forces. Once NCOs and officers joined Army Special Forces, they were separated from their conventional counterparts for the remainder of their careers. They followed different career paths, attended different schools, served in compounds or remote corners of Army posts, and deployed on separate missions around the globe. More important, they seldom operated together. In the end, special operations and conventional forces grew apart to the point that they did not always work well together.

The shift toward integration of SOF and conventional operations began with US involvement in the Balkans, and Haiti in particular. SOF units supported operations effectively, and conventional units learned to work with SOF. In Afghanistan, the momentum drawing the two types of forces closer together continued to build. By Operation ANACONDA, special forces, conventional, and interagency leaders were sitting side-by-side planning, coordinating, and executing operations. It was not always smooth or elegant, but soldiers on both sides worked to tear down the barriers between SOF and conventional soldiers.

Integration continued to improve during the planning for OIF. Collaborative planning between Third Army and USSOCOM units began early in 2002 and continued right through the campaign. The Special Operations Command and Control Element (SOCCE) embedded in V Corps served as an active participant in all V Corps planning, preparation, and deployment. Throughout 2002 and the spring of 2003, 3rd ID brigades and special forces units executing Operation DESERT SPRING worked and trained closely together. When the time came for execution, 3rd ID and its SOF colleagues were ready. As other conventional units arrived, the pattern of integration continued.

In the 1990s the mark of success for an Army unit was to conduct a successful training rotation at a Combat Training Center, combining heavy and light forces (called a heavy-light rotation). Conventional units believed that heavy-light rotations were the most complicated, but critical combination of forces because the capabilities and requirements of the two are so different. Eventually, though, training and employing diverse units, most of which had no chance to train together at home, became second nature. In OIF, the Army illustrated the benefits of heavy-light training.

Operations in Afghanistan and Iraq raised the bar for integration. In the future, effective integration must be the standard. This will require cultural, doctrinal, organizational, and training changes across the Army. In that regard, there is much to be learned from the execution of OIF in terms of SOF and conventional force integration and interoperability. Some lessons are subtle, some are easily discerned; all must be resourced and translated into action if true integration is to be achieved.

The effective conduct of SOF-conventional operations requires trained leaders and units. For example, battalion and brigade pre-command courses are already effective at teaching how to integrate combined arms and contributed significantly to the lethality of Army brigade combat teams in OIF. Adding instruction on integrating SOF and conventional forces would build on that success. OIF experience suggests that captains' education also ought to address the tactics, techniques, and procedures necessary to integrate these operations.

Effective joint SOF and Army conventional operations are dependent on common doctrine and training, understood and practiced by all. Currently, Army doctrine does not provide for integrated operations. For example, FM 3-90, *Tactics*, fails to address joint SOF and conventional operations for offensive or defensive operations. This lack of common doctrine can have disastrous effects. In OIF the SOF and conventional units' approaches to planning and execution varied, requiring adjustments on the way. As joint and Army doctrine development moves forward, it must draw SOF and conventional forces toward a common language and integrated operations. Training together at the CTCs can further the cause of integrating SOF and conventional operations. Presently, conventional and SOF elements rarely train together. Although Army SF units regularly train at the CTCs, their training rotations are usually not linked directly with conventional units. Training together will produce the trust and confidence required to assure that successful integration is the rule rather than the exception.

Liaison between Army special forces and conventional forces assured effective integration. Special forces paid a greater price than conventional forces since relatively small special forces units must liaise with conventional force units that are both more numerous and larger. In the past, when the two forces rarely worked together, liaison generally occurred at the corps level. In OIF, the number of special forces and conventional forces working together was so large that special forces units were hard-pressed to provide sufficient liaison to Army and Marine Corps formations. In fact, some entire ODAs (normally combat units) served as liaison teams. For example, ODA 916 divided into three sections, simultaneously serving as Special Forces Liaison Element (SFLE) for 3rd ID Headquarters, 3rd Brigade of 3rd ID, and 3-7 CAV. Lacking digital battle command systems that could "talk" to each other further exacerbated liaison. For example, ODA 915, providing the SFLE to the 101st, did not have C2PC, BFT, ADOCS, or other command and control systems used by the 101st.

If the trend toward greater SOF and conventional force integration continues, generating, training, and equipping liaison teams will require effort and investment. Across the area of operations and throughout the OIF campaign, the integration of SOF and conventional forces was a tremendous success. In the south, north, and west, missions were accomplished more effectively and with fewer lives lost as a result. The Army has the opportunity to build on this success.

Air Power: Flexible, Responsive, and Central to Decisive Joint Operations

Coalition air forces and ground component attack aviation drove home the qualities of flexibility and decisiveness that air power brings to the battlefield. The Coalition Forces Air Component Command demonstrated flexibility right from the outset when, for sound reasons, A and G days merged. Everyone, including the Iraqis and coalition ground troops, anticipated that a lengthy air campaign would precede any ground operations. When it did not, the air component commander still had important tasks to execute in support of his campaign to meet CENTCOM objectives. The proliferation of precision guided munitions and the fact that the coalition enjoyed air superiority enabled the airmen to undertake five separate tasks at once, some of which they may have preferred to do sequentially.

The airmen still needed to defeat or at least suppress Iraqi air defenses, attack strategic targets, attack theater ballistic missile sites, execute deep shaping operations, and provide close air support. To their credit, air component troops managed all of that and provided what the ground units acclaimed was first-class support to them. On more than one occasion, responsive, accurate close air support turned the tide for Army ground troops or, as a minimum, reduced their vulnerability to enemy combat systems. All four air forces (USAF, USN, USMC and RAF) flew for Grimsley's 1st BCT, destroying artillery that Grimsley could not defeat with his organic artillery. Instead, his artillery dealt with targets immediately to his front. Again at objective JENKINS, airmen attacked columns of paramilitary troops on the east side of the Euphrates, interdicting them before they could close with ground troops. In the fight at TITANS, airmen supported Lieutenant Colonel J.R. Sanderson's TF 2-69 AR, attacking targets at the head of the column while artillery struck targets on the left side of the road the TF was traveling. Time and again during OIF, airmen intervened at critical points on the battlefield.

Although some of the sources remain classified and therefore cannot be discussed here, the evidence suggests that the high rate of desertion among Iraqi units can be directly attributed to strikes by fixed- and rotary-winged aircraft. The Iraqi military learned to fear attack from the air in 1991. Airmen striking without warning in 2003 reprised the lesson. Air power demonstrated its efficacy once again.

Effecting Joint Integration

Joint integration in OIF stemmed from the effort to secure a commitment to joint warfare across the services, from improved joint doctrine and education, but also from investing in personal relationships. At CFLCC, Lieutenant General McKiernan believed that joint warfighting stemmed not only "from the doctrine and technical interoperability, but it is also the personal relationships."[20] Joint training and education support developing personal relationships, as does training together in service training, including the Army's Battle Command Training Program, the Army's training centers, and at the counterpart institutions of the other services.

Deployment and Sustainment

Deploying Troops: Issues and Possible Solutions Across the Department of Defense

The commitment of the services to improve deployment following DESERT STORM was sustained and effective over the last decade. Developing and fielding fast sealift, USMC Maritime Pre-position Squadrons, Army Pre-positioned Stocks, the C-17, and single port management all paid dividends during Operation IRAQI FREEDOM. Much remains to be done. The Request For Forces initiative, intended to afford greater flexibility to the regional combatant commander, did not work. Yet there is no question that the system in place did not meet the needs of commanders in contingency environments.

According to McKiernan, that system is "a peacetime efficiencies based system. So every airplane and every ship is validated and loads are validated and efficiencies gained so no space goes unvalidated. To me, it doesn't work worth a damn in contingency operations."[21] Few could be found in the theater who would defend either the Request for Forces process or the more traditional means of moving troops. Contingency operations require more flexibility. Organizing the Army in more modular fashion may also enhance deployment planning and execution.

Designing a deployment system and determining lift requirements are not for the Army alone. This is a joint matter of compelling importance to national security. The Army will play a role, but this matter will be driven by joint requirements. Arguably, the issue is so important that it will require Department of Defense leadership to determine lift requirements and develop a system that meets the needs of regional commanders.

Operational Maneuver from Strategic Distances

Operational maneuver from strategic distances is an important concept for Army transformation and relates both to how the Army organizes formations and to the general topic of deployment. Both the insertion of the 173rd Airborne BCT into northern Iraq and the accelerated deployment of the 2nd Armored Cavalry illustrate the promise inherent in this concept. While executed largely using today's doctrine, organizations, and equipment, this operation provides several insights that can be used to refine and make the concept a practical tool for joint commanders.

Simply stated, operational maneuver from strategic distances seeks to introduce new forces into the fight from outside the theater, upsetting the opponent's correlation of forces and forcing him to deal with an unexpected threat. The concept assumes that an operationally significant force, a brigade as minimum, can be delivered by air to an unimproved airfield or airfields, and "fight off the ramp." This early-entry capability complements the forcible-entry capability provided by airborne forces and the Marine Corps. Fighting off the ramp means that rather than going through deliberate buildup of combat power, staging, and preparation, the force is configured, trained, equipped, and prepared to engage in combat operations almost as soon as personnel, vehicles, and weapon systems exit aircraft.

Employment of the 173rd Airborne, although successful, was not without difficulties. "Fighting off the ramp" and supporting the force logistically proved problematic. The Army, together with the Air Force, planned, prepared, and executed the airborne assault superbly. They also executed follow-on air landing of heavy equipment and reinforcing troops professionally and effectively. But the United States has a limited number of transport aircraft with the strategic range and cargo capacity required. The 173rd jumped from the same C-17 aircraft that supported all other missions in the Iraqi theater of operations. Making operational maneuver from strategic distances routine will require difficult decisions and/or more aircraft.

One way to address the lift problem is for the Army to develop formations that provide greater lethality, survivability, and mobility than current units while reducing lift requirements. The Army's ongoing efforts with the Stryker BCTs and Future Force Units of Action are designed to do exactly that. The 173rd BCT, including TF 1-63 Armor, required 89 C-17 sorties to deploy two infantry battalions, five M1 tanks, four M2 Bradleys, a battery of 105mm howitzers, three platoons of 120mm mortars, and two *Dragoneye* UAVs.[22] In contrast, for the same number of sorties, a Stryker BCT can deliver one Stryker battalion of 700 troops, 65 Stryker variants, along with an artillery battery, organic CS, supporting CSS units, and seven days of supply. Finally, a brigade assault command post would provide command and control. Once landed, the Stryker package would enjoy greater lethality and mobility than its counterparts in the 173rd.[23] On the other hand, the 173rd has a forcible-entry capability by virtue of its ability to do an airborne assault that the Stryker does not have.

The 173rd did not fight directly off the ramp. Since the end of the Cold War, campaigns have been relatively short, high-tempo affairs. Major combat operations in 1989 in Panama were over within 24 hours; the Kosovo air campaign took 78 days; and major combat operations in DESERT STORM and OIF each lasted about six weeks. In OIF, the 173rd BCT closed the combat elements of its airborne infantry battalions within 96 hours of deployment and could have conducted light infantry offensive operations at that time. It was another 10 days before the full BCT and sufficient supplies for brigade-size operations were available. Fighting off the ramp is a doctrinal, as well as a physical and materiel, challenge. Both the 173rd and Stryker Brigades can be configured to fight off the ramp. Of course, this requires more lift since combat loading is never as efficient as cargo loading. Fighting off the ramp requires tailoring lift based on the scheme of maneuver. Doctrine and techniques to achieve this end do not currently exist, although amphibious, air assault, and airborne doctrine and techniques can provide the inspiration and starting points. Similarly, these techniques can also stimulate developing intelligence and logistics systems to support fighting off the ramp.

Last, learning from the 173rd BCT should not stop with operational maneuver. With some HMMWV motorized infantry and TF 1-63 Armor, the 173rd BCT represents an embryonic middleweight force, the forerunner of the Stryker BCT. As such, the Army can learn from this experience and refine its concepts for such forces. For example, Army transformation set a standard of 96 hours to deploy a brigade-size force anywhere in the world, and the Stryker BCTs are designed with that requirement in mind. The 173rd BCT deployment to northern Iraq demonstrates that 96 hours may not be just a "mark on the wall," but legitimate and feasible as well. The mission-scenario set that the 173rd faced was similar to the high-end small-scale contingency (SSC) missions envisioned for the Stryker BCTs, suggesting that is the appropriate focus for the design of those brigades.

Sustainment Operations

Logistics Issues

Logistically, OIF tested the Army. The size of the theater, tempo of operations, complexity, distribution of forces, nature of the threat, terrain, strategic constraints, paucity of logistics forces, and requirements to support other services proved daunting. Despite these difficulties, Army CSS troops turned in a heroic performance by providing "just enough" to sustain the fight. Significant lessons can be drawn from the OIF campaign that will enable future campaigns to be supported more effectively across the full range of logistics functions, no matter how challenging the circumstances.

From an Army logistic standpoint, the theater of operations encompassed Kuwait, Iraq, and parts of other countries in the region. The pace of operations was high, with whole brigades moving more than 100 kilometers in a single day. Customers included Army, joint, special operations, and coalition units across a vast expanse, and the pace of operations only amplified the burden on the logistics systems. Additionally, strategic and policy constraints limited which countries could be used for basing, transit, or host nation support. These same constraints had the effect of distributing the joint force across the length and breadth of the Persian Gulf. As a consequence, nearly all of the supplies and equipment required to support combat operations had to come through the relatively small Kuwaiti ports. Mobilization and deployment decisions slowed arrival of many logistics units or resulted in their elimination from the troop list altogether. As a result, the major theater logistics command, 377th Theater Support Command, was not fully operational with its required units until after the conclusion of major combat operations.

For these reasons and others, logistics in OIF were less than an unqualified success. Most logistic functions and classes of supply during the campaign functioned just barely above subsistence level. For example:

- For most of the major combat operations and into the summer of 2003, the theater stocks of food barely met demand. During major combat operations, there were times when the supply system was incapable of providing sufficient MREs for the soldiers fighting Iraqi forces.
- Early in the mission analysis and planning process, and as a result of their DESERT STORM experience, leaders at every level focused on the necessity to provide fuel to the force during the long march up-country. While there are no recorded instances of units running out of fuel during offensive operations, success was achieved by nondoctrinal

petroleum, oil, and lubricants (POL) resupply efforts. Some of these included combat arms commanders retaining control of POL tankers rather than returning them to support units.

- Package POL products such as grease and lubricants rarely reached units after they crossed the berm. Requisitions for replacement stocks went unfilled long after major combat operations ended. Units resorted to using Iraqi lubricants acquired by foraging parties and draining oil from non mission-capable equipment.

- The logistic system failed to resupply engineer explosives and barrier material to units in Iraq. Once initial supplies were depleted, units used what they captured from Iraqi forces or improvised. For example, some units disassembled explosive Mine Clearing Line Charges (MICLIC) and used the charges to destroy captured Iraqi equipment.[24]

- Ammunition resupply was also problematic. At one point in the fight, 3rd ID was forced to ask the 101st Airborne Division for an emergency resupply. After coordination, the 101st fired the missions with its own artillery as a more efficient means of accomplishing the fire support missions.[25]

- Resupply of major items of equipment was extremely limited. The one positive example of effective resupply was provision of six *Apache* attack helicopters, flown in from Fort Hood, Texas, to replace those severely damaged or destroyed.

- The medical supply system failed to work. Units were forced to resupply their unit medical platoons from the stocks held by the combat surgical hospitals.[26]

- Repair parts for vehicles and equipment simply didn't make it forward to attacking units. Brigades that attacked north from Kuwait and defeated the Iraqi forces in Baghdad did so without receiving any repair parts whatsoever.[27]

- To meet transportation requirements, the V Corps deputy commander personally approved the allocation of trucks daily.

- Soldiers across the theater did not receive mail from the time they crossed the berm until well after the fall of Baghdad.

The difficulties outlined above are not the result of any single deficiency in the logistic system. On the contrary, a number of converging factors degraded the support provided to units in combat. Despite a decade of transitioning from a Cold War defensive system, current logistics doctrine and systems do not support offensive operations across distributed battlespace. Many classes of supply are still managed as independent systems. All classes were supposed to be transported from the port as far forward as possible, ideally to the forward brigades. Medical supplies have traditionally been handled in a separate supply chain, so that the life-saving supplies could move faster. In OIF, that approach complicated supply management and distribution. In a high-tempo, long-distance operation, handling supplies at each echelon made it practically impossible for logistics leaders to streamline their efforts across the theater.

Combat developers spent the dozen years after DESERT STORM attempting to establish digital and automated logistics processes to improve logistics by establishing distribution management practices, installing in-transit visibility and upgrading automated information systems. Among other things, the intent was to reduce the infamous "iron mountains" of supplies that were pre-positioned in Saudi Arabia before DESERT STORM, by shipping supplies straight from the United States and Germany when required during the campaign. For the most part, these initiatives did not work in this complex and high-tempo campaign. As in other campaigns, logistics in OIF succeeded as a consequence of sheer hard work.

The physics of combat theaters complicate all operations, and perhaps logistics most of all. Requisitions for supplies had to make their way from the requesting unit back to the source; in some cases this meant all the way to the overseas depots. Inadequate communications and the chaos of the battlefield conspired against even getting requests through the system. Assuming all went well, critical parts, supplies, and equipment moved by air into the aerial port at Kuwait City and then to the Theater Distribution Center (TDC). Ideally the part or supply item was then placed on a truck to bring it forward. However, because attacking units continued to move away from Kuwait throughout the process, supplies did not catch up to the units that requested them. Requirements for fuel, ammunition, food, and water are easier to predict than requirements for parts, but moving the large quantities required remained difficult.

This physical problem grew worse due to cybernetic disconnects across the logistics system. Investments in "in-transit visibility" during the 1990s failed to pay off. Visibility of supplies was particularly problematic at transload points, including the TDC. Repair parts and other supply items simply disappeared from view. The automated management system lost track of whole units, as the codes designating each individual company or battalion changed as units deployed into the theater. Frustrated unit commanders compounded the problem by sending foraging parties to camps in Kuwait to try and find items they had requested. Automated systems designed to pass requisitions and track status of requests simply failed to work under the extreme stress imposed in this large and difficult theater of operations. Finally, there were not enough trucks to move supplies forward. In-transit visibility and the other initiatives of the past decade have promise, but they had not matured adequately by March of 2003 to deliver on their perceived potential.

Perhaps the most important issue contributing to the myriad problems that confounded delivering parts and supplies, from paper clips to tank engines, stems from the lack of a means to assign responsibility clearly. In the current logistics system, there is no single cargo distribution manager. Quite apart from the confusion generated by the separate management of classes of supply, there is currently no one person or unit that is directly responsible for delivery of all things large and small. Just as the Military Traffic Management Command had to organize units to provide a single port manager capability to TRANSCOM, so must the Army at least consider developing functional cargo distribution capability with the means to track and assure that supplies are distributed.

There is still another distribution issue that should be examined. Brigadier General Stultz, who worked literally around the clock attempting to get supplies forward, complained with some bitterness that hauling water consumed an inordinate amount of line haul because units preferred bottled water to water they produced in their own reverse osmosis water purification units. That is partly true—soldiers will swear that water produced from purifying river water has a chemical taste. But the truth is, even if purified river water tasted as good as boutique bottled water, there is currently no effective means to distribute water at the tactical level. Water is delivered to tactical units by 450-gallon water trailers, generally apportioned one to a company whether the company has fewer than 100 soldiers or as many as 200 soldiers. Every tank company, infantry company, and artillery battery is authorized a single water trailer. There are simply too few means to haul bulk water to the fighting troops. Bottled water, on the other hand, while bulky to the point of waste, can be hauled by everything that moves. That is why units in the field want bottled water. Water distribution is emblematic of the overall distribution problem.

Logistics Successes

There are some good news logistics stories. Under incredibly difficult conditions, logistics troops made sure that food, fuel, and ammunition got forward. Logistics troops and their leaders literally fought their way forward to get the vital supplies in the hands of the combat soldiers. The scope and scale of their effort are hard to grasp, but it was truly monumental. Joint logistics functioned across 8,000 miles and met the theater's needs without a long buildup of stocks. As one logistician put it, there were still some "iron hills," but there were no "iron mountains."

The Army Theater Support Vessel moved supplies or units from one end of the Persian Gulf to the other. The TSV and the Navy equivalent, the HSV, were responsive and capable, achieving great success in their combat debut. Army watercraft performed brilliantly, supporting everything from clearing debris from the channel into Um Qasr to supporting SOF operations. Army logistics over the shore (LOTS) capabilities also proved particularly effective, supporting Army, Marine, and UK forces and relieving pressure on the few, crowded Kuwaiti ports.[28]

The "air bridge" supporting the 173rd JSOTF-North demonstrated the tremendous utility of both strategic and tactical airlift and the enormous flexibility they provide the joint commander. Although the Turkish government ultimately allowed fuel to be supplied from Turkey, airlift met all of the 173rd's requirements initially. Other supplies, parts in particular, were requisitioned electronically through the brigade's home station in Vicenza, Italy, and its servicing logistics centers in Germany. The Army brought the required supply items and repair parts to Ramstein Air Base, where Air Force transport troops assembled and packaged them for daily delivery by air.

Setting the Conditions for Early Deployment of Logistics Units

Finally, sufficient Army logistics capabilities must be deployed early enough to meet theater requirements for joint, coalition, and Army units. Some of the tension in deciding when to deploy CSS units stemmed from a shortage of theater-opening units in the Active Component. Accordingly, the Army may need to examine whether a theater-opening organization equivalent to the 7th Transportation Group's port-opening capability is required in the Active Component. In fact, the Army has guidance that will take it in this direction. On 9 July 2003, the secretary of defense sent a memorandum to the secretaries of the military departments, the chairman of the Joint Chiefs of Staff, and the undersecretaries of defense. In this document, Secretary Donald Rumsfeld observed, "the balance of capabilities in the Active and Reserve components today is not the best for the future." He further ordered the services to "eliminate the need for involuntary mobilization during the first 15 days of a rapid response operation (or for any alerts to mobilize prior to the operation)."[29] Secretary Rumsfeld's guidance is clear and cuts to the heart of the matter where theater logistics are concerned.

Learning From the 507th Maintenance Company Experience: Implications of the Noncontiguous Battlefield

The home at 301 Sherman Avenue on Fort Leavenworth, Kansas, is the quarters designated by the Army for the director of the School of Advanced Military Studies (SAMS). This 3-story, red brick Federal, built in 1888, is situated on a historic site on the bluff overlooking the Missouri River. From the front door, one sees the very spot where ferries carried settlers and their wagons across the Missouri, leaving behind them the security of the East. From the back door, one sees the plain where those same settlers assembled into "trains" of wagons to begin the march west along the Oregon, Santa Fe, or California Trails.

Why the brief historical lesson? Because those wagon trains were heading into a dangerous operating environment. The 19th-century "battlespace" in the West was noncontiguous, nonlinear, and of varied terrain and weather. This was an environment in which a mobile, lethal, and determined enemy, prone to acts of "terrorism," could attack at any time and from any direction. This environment consisted of long lines of communication, along which there were relatively few friendly forces available to provide security. Every wagon master and every family knew that the wagon train must be organized and prepared to conduct its own defense. In the same manner, every Army supply column knew it also must be prepared to defend itself.

The ambush of the 507th Maintenance Company and subsequent rescue of some of its soldiers was one of the more dramatic events in OIF, but not the most lethal and certainly not the most decisive. Still, if it serves as a catalyst for real change, the 507th could have a positive and lasting effect that saves lives in future conflicts. Changing a culture is difficult, and in a large organization such as Army, with very definite collective opinions about serious issues, it is even more difficult. Often it takes a cathartic event to initiate such a change. The 507th ambush may be such an event, causing the Army to pause, seriously examine the provisions for security of its CS and CSS units, and initiate changes that enable logistics and support units to make contact with the enemy, survive, and continue their mission.

A Short Discussion of the 507th

Lasting perhaps an hour and a half, the agony of the 507th was not a turning point in the war. In fact, the tragedy of the 507th had no significant effect on the outcome of the war at all. What happened to the 507th merits attention for what it conveys about the nature of battles since time immemorial. Supply columns have been ambushed since they first existed.

Anytime armies are able to cut their way through a country rapidly in a "blitzkrieg"-like offensive, the result is noncontiguous warfare and nonlinear fights. But what briefs well at a war college or in a think tank is fraught with practical problems on the ground. Belton Cooper, a World War II maintenance officer, writing in his memoir, *Death Traps: The Survival of an American Armored Division in World War II,* described the area between the advancing legions of 3rd Armored Division tanks and the "rear" as the "void." According to Cooper, then a lieutenant, in the fast-paced attacks of the fall of 1944, the gap between the "front" and the "rear" often contained no friendly troops, as the infantry could not keep up.

Going to the rear with his maintenance reports required what Cooper called "running the gauntlet." As he put it, "It was logical to assume any units that we met on the road at night would probably be German." Cooper also found Germans in his way during the day. Nonlinear warfare is neither good nor bad, but it brings a special set of conditions soldiers cannot ignore, and one of them is that there is no safe place on a nonlinear battlefield.[30]

What happened to the 507th reminds those who wear the uniform and those who send them in harm's way that any defeat, however small, is catastrophic for those in the fight. More important, no one thing doomed the 507th. Instead, there was a series of events and missteps that led to this tactical defeat of a small unit— a defeat that somehow, from the safety of television studios in America, seemed incomprehensible. But this does not take account of the conditions of combat. Combat operations, even at their best, are confusing, frightening, and exhausting.

Following the incident, the Army launched a series of investigations and studies to determine the cause of the tragedy. Determining why Captain King did not understand that he was to transition from Route BLUE to Route JACKSON is one aspect. One possible cause is that he joined the 600-vehicle convoy under the control of the 3rd Forward Support Battalion, 3rd ID, after its rehearsals. It is unclear if there was any requirement or time for him to back-brief the plan to demonstrate that he understood what his unit was required to do.

A second contributing factor is the ad hoc nature of the convoy and a lack of realistic tactical road march training. The 3rd FSB is a tactical support battalion that trains at the NTC. There, logistic troops "fight" to defend their support areas and even their convoys. However, the 507th belongs to a Patriot unit that gets no opportunities to undergo the same highly realistic combat training. The 507th never trained at any of the Army's combat training centers: the NTC, the JRTC, or the CMTC.

A third contributing factor may be the distances, routes, and the duration of operations. Out of radio range with the 3rd FSB and eager to catch up, Captain King and the 507th took the shortest, most direct route to get to Highway 8 on 22 March. This shortcut, only 15 km cross-country, took 5 long hours to travel with trucks designed for paved roads. However, the entire convoy had already traveled cross-country to reach the point from which he departed, so what seems like a bad decision now may have looked prudent to King on the evening of the 22nd. Farther behind, the 507th finally reached the traffic control point at the crossover of Routes BLUE and JACKSON, but no one was directing traffic. Soldiers were present at the traffic control point, but they made no effort to turn the 507th and so, King, believing he was to continue on Route BLUE, drove past the turn and headed into An Nasiriyah.

Some commentators have wondered why the 507th did not fire on the armed Iraqis they passed on the way into An Nasiriyah. One reason may have been that the soldiers were expecting to be greeted as liberators. Moreover, the rules of engagement (ROE) were not as clear as they might have been. With some 13 sections detailing when one could fire, the ROE card concluded with guidance to "attack enemy forces and military targets." These ROE are clear enough when soldiers are well rested and when one is certain he is in hostile territory, but if the situation is ambiguous and soldiers become tired and lost, then they might, as those in the 507th did, choose not to fire. Even if they had fired on first contact, the outcome is not certain. What is clear is that once Captain King and First Sergeant Dowdy recognized they were in a hostile environment, they locked and loaded and assumed the worst.

Once the 507th entered the firefight, several other challenges hindered its defense. Several of its weapons jammed repeatedly. The sole .50-caliber machine gun did not function at all. Nonetheless, they never stopped fighting. Soldiers who might have escaped went to the aid of those who were injured or whose vehicles had been disabled by enemy fire. Surrounded, they attempted to resist until resistance seemed futile.

Carl von Clausewitz would find none of this surprising. Nearly 200 years ago, he described exactly the phenomenon that dogged the 507th. He would have described this chain of mistakes, confusion on the route, inadequate weapons maintenance, potentially confusing ROE, difficult terrain, and a traffic control point that no longer operated, as "friction." Friction produced by humans, physical conditions, and ambiguity, remain constants in warfare regardless of how sophisticated the technology of war has become. The CSA understands this, as he demonstrated in his first message to the Army. On 1 August 2003, General Peter Schoomaker observed, "War is ambiguous, uncertain, and unfair."[31]

The last point to recall about the 507th soldiers concerns the way they and the marines of Task Force *Tarawa* comported themselves. The marines did not pause to ponder why the 507th had been in An Nasiriyah or wonder whether they should take responsibility for rescuing them. Rather, they honored their predecessors' exploits at Tarawa and launched north to rescue their fellow Americans. Perhaps the lesson of the 507th soldiers stopping to help one another and the marines rescuing the survivors are the best things to remember about this darkest day of OIF.

Some have argued that what happened to the 507th is easily explained. They assert that the 507th was poorly led, poorly trained, and poorly disciplined. Others said that the 507th reflected a CSS culture of lackadaisical approach to security and that this never could have happened to a combat unit or to *their* CS or CSS unit. These are possible explanations. Another possibility is that the 507th is indicative of an Armywide problem. This view holds that the some CS and most CSS units are generally not equipped, manned, or trained to defend themselves while stationary, let alone when on the march. CSS units are generally the last units to field night vision, armor plating for "flak" vests, and other combat gear. They also have fewer radios, crew-served weapons and far less armor protection than their colleagues in combat and CS units. Finally, they do not get either the focus or resources to conduct tactical simulations or live-fire training that their colleagues in combat and CS units receive.

None of this is a problem if the 507th is a singular example of a poorly equipped, poorly trained and poorly led unit. Nor is it a problem if the Army expects to operate with clear demarcation between "front" and "rear." If, however, the 507th is indicative of an Armywide problem in training, equipping, and manning CS and CSS units, and if the Army expects to operate in a nonlinear, noncontiguous operational environment, Army leaders may need to examine everything from culture to equipment in CS and CSS units. Equally important, the Army should examine any concept that envisions operations in nonlinear and noncontiguous battlespace to determine how forces should be manned and equipped to operate in the so-called white spaces and on LOCs. Assuming that technical means of surveillance will protect those units may not be justified. The culture and expectation in the Army should be, to borrow a phrase from the Marines, that every soldier is a rifleman first, and every unit fights.

Despite these criticisms, Army CSS soldiers, noncommissioned officers, and officers overcame one of the most challenging campaign situations possible to meet the needs of the warfighting units that defeated the Iraqi armed forces and removed the Hussein regime. They did so through dedication, courage, and innovation that overcame any obstacle in their path. General Dave McKiernan offered the best testimony to the logistics troops when he noted on 1 May 2003, "the truth of the matter is we did not stop operational tempo because of any class of supply, and what was accomplished was never impeded by logistics, and I think that is a remarkable story."[32]

Information and Knowledge

This broad domain cuts across every other area discussed. Developing and communicating information and generating knowledge from information are at the heart of what the Army and other services tried to achieve in the years since DESERT STORM. Attempting to leverage information to maneuver out of contact with the enemy and to apply overmatching combat power at a time and place that US forces choose is at the heart of emerging joint and Army concepts. Communications technology, information technology, and how units are structured and equipped are all part and parcel of implications on information and knowledge. Effects-based operations and joint integration also stem from the ability to share information and knowledge. Effects-based operations, including the ephemeral domain of information operations and subsets such as perception management and electronic attack, are concerned with information and knowledge as well.

Grouping so many capabilities in the realm of information operations and the more general theme of information and knowledge complicates discussing them, but seems essential to preserve the essence of their interdependence. So while no attempt is made to separate the various components that merit discussion for purposes of organization, they include the following general areas.

- Toward Netcentric Warfare
- Information Operations
- Intelligence, Surveillance, and Reconnaissance

Toward Netcentric Warfare

Information has always enabled warfare, and the fight to protect information and to gain information has always been critical to success in battle. DESERT STORM and subsequent operations vividly demonstrate the power of information. The Global Positioning System (GPS) enabled coalition forces in DESERT STORM to maneuver with confidence across the trackless expanse of the Iraqi desert. Simultaneously, *Tomahawk* cruise missiles and laser-guided bombs struck targets with seemingly unerring accuracy. Leveraging the power of information became one of the central tenets of the 1990s' Revolution in Military Affairs (RMA), the defense establishment's campaign to continue US dominance in warfare.

Theorists, pundits, and decision makers, both within and outside the military, began to examine the opportunities to transform America's military forces into an information-age force. What evolved was a concept known as Network Centric Warfare (NCW). The proponents of netcentric warfare perceived revolutionary change in how warfare would be conducted. To netcentric warfare theorists, warfare would no longer be about fighting for terrain or to destroy forces, but would instead be a fight for information. Whoever won the fight for information would win all conflicts. For traditional theories of warfare, such as that of Clausewitz, they substituted new constructs such as systems theory, chaos and complexity theory, and nodal warfare. Each of the services also saw the net as a means to empower commanders and units with information. Service initiatives, including Army digitization and *Force XXI*, the Air Force's Effects-Based Operations, the Navy's Cooperative Engagement, and Marine Corps Sea Dragon, all sought to move from Industrial-Age warfare toward what Alvin and Heidi Toffler termed "Third Wave Warfare."

But what does this mean? Is the net really only about information and the amount of it that can be made available to commanders? There is at the heart of netcentric warfare an important concept—that anyone on the network has the information, the means to act on it, and the authority to do so. Netcentric warfare, then, is not about moving digits and ever-larger communications pipes, but rather a self-adapting system of thinking participants who are able to act rapidly on the basis of understanding both the commander's intent and the situation around them. The focus then is on waging war and not on the net as an end in itself. It is possible to lose this distinction in the pursuit of the means to move the digits.[33]

The Army's evolution toward a digitally net-enabled force actually began long before the emergence of the concept of NCW. In the 1980s, the Field Artillery branch led the Army into the information age with the adoption of TACFIRE as the means to coordinate and execute fire missions in a digital network. TACFIRE provided the Army both a proving ground for digitization and an opportunity to understand the DOTMLPF implications of net-enabled warfare. Following the lead of the artillery, each battlefield operating system (BOS) developed a digital command and control system. These disparate BOS communications tools were then loosely integrated into a broader Army Tactical Command and Control System (ATCCS).

After DESERT STORM, the Army embarked on a deliberate effort to leverage the power of information in warfare. In *Force XXI,* the Army sought to field nothing less than a digital, net-enabled force. Comparing a DESERT STORM tank battalion to a *Force XXI* tank battalion illustrates the magnitude of change the Army sought. A DESERT STORM tank battalion employed four Fire Support Teams (FISTs) that were digitally connected through TACFIRE to supporting artillery batteries. In contrast, a *Force XXI* digitized task force has 74 entities digitally connected to supporting artillery batteries, including: FISTs, scouts, Abrams tanks, Bradley fighting vehicles, and dismounted infantry and engineers.

The Army's investment in digitization paid off in OIF, or rather showed promise. Army units fought enabled by a digital network that allowed them to see their units and their activities, which let to situational understanding. Confident that they knew the location of their units, commanders could decide rapidly where, when, and how they would be employed. Additionally, because of joint initiatives in communications and networking and the provision of selected Army systems to other services, coalition ground forces could fight joint net-enabled operations.

In OIF, a combination of command and control aids provided Army commanders timely and accurate situational awareness of their units and their activities, which led to situational understanding. BFT allowed them to pass to their subordinates orders and graphics necessary to describe how they intended to fight. BFT supported joint operational commanders by providing current positions of Army forces via the Global Command and Control System (GCCS). Similarly, other components of ABCS, when combined with join systems, enabled integration of the "friendly" air picture.

A typical artillery engagement in OIF illustrates the power of the network. When an Iraqi target appeared, Army tactical forces in contact sent a digital call for fire through the AFATDS. The call for fire, including target description and desired effects, stimulated two simultaneous digital processes at the controlling headquarters. The first involved clearing fires. Using BFT, the operations staff verified that no friendly unit occupied the targeted space. This capability varied by unit depending on the how far down they had BFT. As a minimum, fire supporters could usually verify clearance with a single radio call. Using accurate mapping systems, the effects cell verified that indirect fires could be safely employed without endangering civilians or creating collateral damage to protected sites such as mosques or schools. Using the AMDWS, representatives of Army aviation, air defense, and the Air Force ensured the artillery would not adversely affect air operations. While the effects staff cleared fires, the artillery used AFATDS to execute the fire mission. AFATDS determined the optimal firing unit for the commander to approve or override. AFATDS also computed firing data for each howitzer, including ammunition type, range, direction, and number of rounds necessary to achieve the desired effect. Using these digital means, units routinely were ready to fire in less than a minute. Army net-enabled tube artillery fires generally could be cleared and delivered in less than 2 minutes.

The efficacy of net-enabled means to clear artillery fires did not apply to clearing CAS. CAS was available, responsive, and effective during OIF; but generally speaking, clearing CAS was not net enabled. Developing the systems to clear CAS digitally rather than only by voice may be an avenue worthy of exploration as part of joint transformation. If the means to provide the "blue" picture to pilots, the tactical control parties, and airborne command and control nodes existed, presumably CAS could be cleared more quickly and made even more responsive than it was in OIF. More important, shared situational understanding between air and ground forces may enable more effective combination of fires than currently possible. Finally, shared situational understanding may well further reduce the possibility of fratricide.

On the other hand, limited functionality of some of the core ABCS elements inhibited netcentric warfare. The Maneuver Control System (MCS) was the core system of the overall ABCS, but V Corps' C2PC proved more effective. As a result, only those units that had no alternative routinely used MCS. Similarly, few units used ASAS-RWS, the core intelligence system of ABCS. Due to ASAS limitations, Army units resorted to processing intelligence over secure networks using other systems. CSSCS, the core logistics system, also proved too difficult to use in a complex, overburdened network. Simpler systems, such as the Movement Tracking System, were employed instead, and CSS units accepted loss of function as the cost of utility.

Interoperability remained a problem as well. Major General "Spider" Marks recalled that at one point, he and Major General "Tamer" Amos, commanding the 3rd Marine Air Wing, became action officers to pass images Amos and the marines required because Marks could not do so digitally. Similarly, at one point the marines generated great data from one of their unmanned aerial vehicles, which V Corps needed but could not access since it had no means to link to the data stream. Interoperability proved even more difficult for coalition members, partly for technical reasons and partly for security reasons.[34] For all of these of reasons, joint and coalition forces did not fight a netcentric campaign in Iraq. It is accurate to say they fought a net-enabled campaign.

The Army employed its only digitized division, the 4th ID, in OIF. Although the 4th ID did not undertake major tactical engagements prior to the end of major combat operations, its experience tends to validate the idea of digitally networking maneuver divisions. Designated as the Army's experimental force for digitization in 1994, 4th ID has spent most of the last decade experimenting and training with a full suite of digital, networked capabilities. Largely reliant on terrestrial-based communications, the vast distances and rapid pace of operations reduced most of the functionality of the 4th ID's core ABCS components. However, as the war transitioned from mobile warfare to stability operations, 4th ID largely regained full use of its networks and their advantages. The 4th ID operations demonstrated the power of organic net-enabled surveillance and reconnaissance at the brigade level. Only 4th ID brigades employed networked UAVs, Long-Range Acquisition and Scout Surveillance Systems (LRASSS), and *Kiowa Warriors*. The 4th ID's BCTs often could see the enemy, develop the situation, and make contact on their terms.

Several implications are implicit as the services look toward a networked future. First, the forces must be able to maneuver the net, and like the Stryker Brigades, they must train to do so. Although today there is some network coverage nearly everywhere, there will probably never be enough resources to establish a complete and functioning network of communications, sensors, and systems everywhere in the world. As OIF demonstrates, the network must be built, shaped, and then maneuvered to ensure necessary connectivity and capability.

Along with maneuvering the net, OIF suggests that for fast-paced offensive operations, ground forces need to break free of terrestrial-based, line of sight (LOS) communications. The pace of operations, global reach, and noncontiguous battlespace of 21st-century military operations demand that all except the lowest-level tactical voice communications be space based. This will require significant joint investment in military satellite capabilities to ensure the entire joint force has access with sufficient bandwidth to support networked systems.

The OIF experience also suggests that networks do not have to provide a vast array of functions to be effective. Clausewitz observed, "War is a very simple thing, yet in war the simplest things are very difficult." In OIF, networks eliminated some of the difficulty of doing simple things. Commanders need to know where their forces are, where the enemy is, and how to coordinate the actions of their subordinates through passing messages, orders, and graphics. The most useful systems in OIF (C2PC, BFT, ADOCS, AFATDS, AMDWS, and MTS) provided the basic capabilities the force required.

OIF's TMD network and joint use of BFT and AMDWS reinforce the value of joint digitization initiatives. Such initiatives, and those designed to standardize networks, are vital to achieving a true NCW capability. The Army's Future Force research and development is already headed in the direction of full and complete joint connectivity.

Meanwhile, the challenges of integrating US armed forces with allies and coalition partners continue to grow. The provision of BFT and robust LNO teams to the 1st UK Armoured Division assisted in bridging the digital gap in OIF, but the growing post-Cold War disparity in technology between the US armed forces and allied forces is a fact. As the Army moves toward the Future Force and joint transformation proceeds, the gap is likely to grow wider. This is particularly likely in the area of networked battle command, where the US is investing heavily. Some likely coalition partners are unlikely to catch up, and others are investing in battle command systems of their own that are not interoperable with US systems. Solutions that facilitate integrating coalition operations will have to be found.

OIF also suggests that simply winning the fight for information will not be enough to ensure victory. Early in OIF, the US employed operational fires (air, Tomahawks, ATACMS) to destroy much of Iraq's strategic and operational communications infrastructure and to neutralize Iraq's integrated air defense system. Yet, the defending Iraqi forces continued to fight fiercely. Primarily using simple instructions, they continued to maneuver and continued to fight. The lesson is that although the Iraqis lost nearly every engagement, they did not give up simply because they had lost the war for the networks.

While not yet a truly netcentric force, the Army in OIF was clearly a net-enabled force, one that was significantly more effective because of digitization efforts since DESERT STORM. Additionally, the Army's efforts toward joint battle command enhanced the joint forces' capabilities for net-enabled operational maneuver, fires, and protection. These investments in technology should be continued. They must include education in doctrine, organization, and leader development to assure that joint forces are truly able to wage netcentric warfare.

Information Operations

Operation OIF is another step, but neither the first nor the last step, along the path of US armed forces from Industrial-Age to information-age operations. While DESERT STORM is generally considered the first information-age campaign, virtually every aspect of Army and joint information operations (IO) was more mature and robust in OIF. But much remains to be done.

Information Operations in the Campaign

Throughout the era following DESERT STORM, CENTCOM continued to conduct IO against Saddam's regime. Operation SOUTHERN WATCH had IO components inherent in maintaining the no-fly zone. Similarly, operations in the north included IO. Identifying and refining targets and building an audience for IO messages continued virtually without respite over the decade preceding OIF. However, the tempo of operations accelerated in the fall of 2002, characterized by increasingly bold efforts such as a large leaflet drop in December.

IO planning supported tactical and operational objectives, including encouraging Iraqi units to surrender, keeping civilians off the roads and out of harm's way, and preventing the destruction of the oil infrastructure. Kinetic and electronic warfare attacks focused on disrupting command and control discretely while minimizing collateral damage. Generally, CENTCOM, CFLCC, and the tactical forces fully integrated IO planning and execution during OIF. Assessing success in IO remained difficult, and it is still too early to draw many conclusions with confidence. Frankly, with a few exceptions in electronic warfare and intelligence, it is hard to make the case that US efforts in the broad category of IO produced any dramatic results. US IO may have been more successful than suggested here since success in most of the domains of IO is difficult to measure. "Battle damage assessment" is, to say the least, difficult in this arena.

Psychological Operations (PSYOP) achieved important success but experienced some disappointments as well. PSYOP units can point with satisfaction to success in minimizing damage to the oil fields and keeping civilians off roads. However, they do so with risk since there is very little evidence available yet to support that contention. It is entirely possible that the Iraqis chose not to fire their oil wells for their own reasons. Moreover, the PSYOP effort enjoyed far less success in encouraging Iraqi units to surrender. Clearly the regime respected the effort since Iraqi security forces worked hard to collect leaflets as quickly as they fell. Nonetheless, it is clear that on the whole, PSYOP produced much less than expected and perhaps less than claimed.

Kinetic and electronic attacks to disrupt or destroy critical command and control infrastructure proved more effective. The continued dramatic improvement in the accuracy of precision-guided munitions afforded planners a scalpel that US forces applied throughout the campaign. "Surgical strike" was a useful and accurate term in the conduct of IO in OIF. The means to conduct electronic attack also proved useful during the campaign. Even so, the Iraqis managed to move some units and, on the whole, retained control over the country until ground forces physically took control of the centers of power. Following the end of major combat operations, the regime's survivors and perhaps others have shown resiliency and have been able to mount a serious insurgency effort against the coalition. To do this they retained or built at least some ability to communicate, both to coordinate operations and to affect perceptions in Iraq and around the world.

Although not planned as a component of IO, the Department of Defense decision to embrace the media's desire to accompany the troops paid dividends. Embedded media showed the American public the quality of American troops and often counteracted Iraqi propaganda. Journalists embedded in Army units were given unprecedented access to information and plans. Access allowed the media to apply context to what they were reporting. Stories filed by embedded reporters tended to be better balanced than those by reporters covering the Pentagon, Central Command (CENTCOM), or Coalition Land Forces Component Command (CFLCC). Reporting during the now-infamous sandstorm is a perfect example. Reports coming from outside of Iraq often claimed that US forces had become bogged down and that the campaign was in trouble. However, journalists embedded with 3rd ID units in the field generally filed less pessimistic stories than their stateside colleagues. Journalists in the field reported the "pause" in context, thus balancing reports suggesting the campaign was coming unhinged.

Near-term Implications of Army Information Operations in OIF

Even after a decade of emphasis, IO planning, coordination, and execution remain ad hoc. The formation of 1st Information Operations Command and an IO career field are promising steps toward improving Army IO. As the Army and joint forces consider OIF and the future of IO as a discipline, the Army should examine how it organizes and resources IO planning and execution in tactical formations.

IO doctrine remains mostly unwritten. The Army's FM 3-13, *Information Operations*, begins to fill the void but was published months after major combat operations. The doctrinal void hampered planning and the education of combined-arms officers and senior formation commanders in the planning and conduct of IO. The resulting IO effort was often disjointed and not well integrated with maneuver, fires, and other combat activities. Most important, there is no joint consensus on IO, which hampered planning and execution of the joint campaign. For example, in preparing for operations in Baghdad, there was significant disagreement between Air Force and Army planners on how to approach information operations. Army planners tended to favor "soft kills," while the Air Force favored "hard kills."[35] A joint experimentation aimed at developing and testing joint concepts will prove helpful. The Air Force may well be right, at least in the effect hard kills had on fielded units.

The one clear point in IO doctrine, at least as it applies to psychological operations, is that top-down development of themes and messages often inhibits opportunity for tactical success. In OIF, as in the Balkans, centralized themes and messages sometimes proved irrelevant to local populations and situations, and centralized control of active IO was not responsive to rapidly changing situations. For example, Tactical PSYOP Teams (TPTs) were provided capitulation leaflets for the first 48 hours of the conflict. After that, the centralized message approval process proved unable to provide leaflet texts appropriate to the situations V Corps confronted.[36] TPTs were reduced to using their loudspeaker capability. The Army and the joint team should revisit PSYOP doctrine and organization to find ways to provide commanders PSYOP support that is as agile as their combat units.

There are some obvious OIF implications for Army public affairs. First and foremost, the bar has been raised with regard to media access to Army operations. The media and the American public now see embedding as the standard for reporting combat operations. Embedding provided unprecedented access to leaders and soldiers, and the American public got to see their Army accomplishing great things. From the perspective of the services, the embed program was an enormous success. Neither mission accomplishment nor the integrity of the media was compromised. The big winners were the soldiers, who fought bravely, and the American public, who got to see it first-hand. After the fact, some of the media believe they were manipulated effectively by the services or that because they could see only their part of the story, they failed to report on the context. This demonstrates more than anything else that a free press will always be wary of government and the instruments of government. The Army and the services should not expect a free ride and, for good reason, will be as wary of the media as the media are of them. The key now is to put into practice systems that will enable smooth embed operations in future contingencies and major operations. Leaders and soldiers alike must be educated in embedded media and how to assist them in the performance of their mission, while recognizing that the media's mission is not the same as their own.

Two observations about IO as a whole seem important. First, because IO as a domain is so broad and cuts across so many other domains, it is conceivable that the ability to develop a coherent IO campaign as the concept is presently conceived is illusory. Second, if IO objectives need to be developed at the top and driven downward, then execution of IO as presently conceived may mean that netcentric warfare is not desirable after all, since that form of warfare presumes anyone on the net with the means to act may do so.

The Future of Army Information Operations

IO must support reducing the uncertainty about enemy and friendly conditions on the battlefield. IO, in conjunction with intelligence, may enable deliberate attack—that is the vision for the Future Force. IO in the Future Force may enable future commanders to develop the situation before making contact, maneuver to positions of advantage largely out of contact, and, when ready, initiate decisive action with initiative, speed, and agility. To support tactical and operational requirements, IO must bring full-spectrum capabilities and effects to the fight. Future Force IO organizations must be able to operate with greater competencies in multiple disciplines and develop unique effectiveness and purpose to perform the full spectrum of IO missions and tasks. More important, the joint force must provide the tools to execute these operations and the means to measure effectiveness.

Intelligence, Surveillance, and Reconnaissance

Much has been made during the campaign and since about the "failure" of intelligence to estimate accurately the intentions of the Iraqis and the location of—or even whether—the Iraqis genuinely had the means to employ weapons of mass destruction. It is too early to assess fully whether the Iraqis had weapons of mass destruction, but it is clear they had the means to deliver them in the form of artillery and various short-range ballistic missiles. That issue is not within the province of this study, beyond reporting that the 75th Exploitation Task Force apparently did not turn up weapons of mass destruction. Generating intelligence, and whether or not CENTCOM, CENTCOM components, and ground units generated useful intelligence, is within the province of this study.

Clearly the various intelligence means within the theater produced effective and actionable intelligence that enabled planning and execution, including successful attacks on fleeting targets. CFLCC's soldiers and marines went to war with a fairly accurate idea of the location of the enemy's conventional units, Special Republican Guard, and many of the paramilitaries. Estimating intentions and tracking discrete Iraqi military units proved difficult, and paramilitary units proved nearly impossible to track and even harder to assess in terms of intentions. Even so, both technical and tactical means of generating intelligence proved effective. For example, at Objective JENKINS and again at PEACH, TF 3-69 AR benefited from warnings of enemy activity and profited from those warnings. At PEACH, the task force, thanks to intelligence, anticipated an attack from commandos. Prepared for that attack, it also defeated an unanticipated attack from conventional units.

Assessing intelligence success proved more difficult than arguing that the estimates proved inaccurate. As debriefs of captured Iraqi generals and their soldiers become available, a more accurate assessment will be possible. After seizing SAINTS, 3rd ID attacked south against suspected enemy units, and they found them, or rather, found enemy equipment oriented south and mostly unmanned. The intelligence system had detected these positions, some of which were well hidden. But that same system lacked the ability to assess their readiness and intentions with high resolution. On the other hand, 3rd ID attacked with small units, based on high confidence that the Iraqi units' lack of activity indicated they were destroyed or combat-ineffective. These attacks intended to verify assumptions based on intelligence estimates.

Major General Marks, the CFLCC C2, notes that CFLCC could generate and pass intelligence with great success within the limitations of communications technology and the systems units had to manage information. For example, the links that enabled V Corps to receive and process national and joint intelligence were in many cases not available in I MEF. Marks recalled that to solve that dilemma, "we stripped away XVIII Airborne Corps capabilities," and provided them to the MEF.[37] As noted in a preceding paragraph, the problem cut both ways. A second difficulty stemmed from what the Marine Corps' lessons learned team called the digital divide. Often units below division level simply lacked the communications means to receive updated images and other kinds of intelligence that could be shared at higher echelons. Nonetheless, units generally found ways to work around the problem via telephone or secure email. Still, there are seams based on communications, interoperability, and the structure or architecture within the CFLCC and its subordinates.

No one anticipated or estimated the intentions of the paramilitaries accurately. As Marks put it, " We did not predict that (the paramilitaries) were going to come out of the cities and expose themselves to armored vehicles and armored formations without similar protection."[38] Finally, no one believed that US forces could remotely identify and continuously track Iraqi units that chose to move by infiltration and to shield themselves where and when possible. The ability of the Iraqis to hide, with some success, from the incredible array of technical intelligence available to the coalition may give pause to those advocating that US forces will be able to develop the situation out of contact and attack from standoff distances.

Most tactical unit commanders claimed that they made every assault as a movement to contact. There is no reason to dispute that claim, other than to argue that most of these same commanders generally anticipated when contact was likely, whether they knew precise locations of the enemy or not. They knew or could anticipate where to expect contact for two reasons. First, the intelligence system identified with a fair degree of accuracy starting locations of the uniformed forces and tracked them with some success. The intelligence system also identified many of the paramilitary formations and where they might be expected, with several notable exceptions. The second reason commanders were able to anticipate contact stemmed from their own analysis of what constituted danger areas. Concealment and cover afforded in complex terrain is unlikely, at least in the near term, to become transparent to technical means of surveillance and reconnaissance. Technical means to shield tactical units are affordable, as are passive means, including camouflage, decoys, and emissions control. It is likely that the final assault in close combat will continue to feel like a movement to contact to soldiers in the lead unit for years to come, just as it did to tactical units in OIF.

The problem of locating accurately the enemy in the close battle is the justification, indeed the requirement, for the means to generate tactical intelligence and to field tactical reconnaissance units. But here too, seams exist. For example, scout platoons and brigade reconnaissance troops exist to provide the means for tactical commanders to "see" the enemy. Mounted in lightly armored HMMWVs, battalion and brigade scouts are vulnerable to RPG and cannon fires. This design is intentional and reflects a widely held view in the late Cold War era that armored and armed scouts would fight rather than conduct reconnaissance. As a consequence of this, if contact seemed imminent, commanders often chose not to use their scouts and brigade reconnaissance troops. In short, they elected to give up their "eyes" rather than risk losing them. Put another way, commanders chose not to employ scouts and brigade reconnaissance troops in the role for which they were intended. This phenomenon warrants study and arguably action to correct problems commanders perceived. Heavier scout vehicles may not be the answer; perhaps the answer is how reconnaissance units are trained and supported.

The Army should also assess long-range surveillance units. Lightly equipped helicopter-inserted long-range surveillance units organic to conventional maneuver divisions and the corps military intelligence brigade did not produce great effect for the investment of talent and the risk to those involved. There may be nothing inherently unsound in the structure of long-range surveillance units. Perhaps the issue is whether the Army is prepared to risk these relatively fragile units in fast-moving, ambiguous situations. These same units might prove useful in some other environment, but in any case, assessing the utility and the means of employing these units makes sense based on their apparent lack of utility in OIF.

On balance, military intelligence and national intelligence, surveillance, and reconnaissance means worked well. For the most part, CFLCC knew where the Iraq uniformed forces were, could target them, and could provide data on their whereabouts to tactical units. Tracking the paramilitary forces and estimating Iraqi intentions proved more difficult. Units in contact generally acquired information that, coupled with reports from higher echelons, enabled them to develop useful intelligence. Colonel Arnie Bray's paratroopers at As Samawah and the operations of the 101st at An Najaf demonstrate the efficacy of analysis of enemy patterns developed over time. Discerning patterns and developing intelligence from combat information still takes time and is likely to require time in the future as well. Structuring units to be able to do so and enabling them to receive information and intelligence generated from higher echelons seems indicated. Finally, the experience of OIF seems a reminder that the enemy gets a vote. Ambiguity is likely to remain a factor in combat operations indefinitely.

The Way Ahead for Considering Implications

It is just not possible to reach fully supported conclusions this early. For this reason, observations based on the data available do not result in conclusions, but instead are suggested as implications. Without the benefit of fully understanding enemy actions and enemy intentions, it is not possible to proceed with confidence in several areas for which implications are suggested. To some extent then, the implications suggested here are areas that may require further study. Nonetheless, taken as a body, the implications of operations for the Army in OIF are important, particularly for concepts fundamental to the way the Army and the joint team consider the execution of future combat operations. For example, what does the running start suggest about the utility of shaping and decisive operations? Are effects-based operations really feasible if the services are unable to develop and apply metrics to enemy actions that are sufficiently accurate to gauge whether the effects intended have been obtained? Is the Army notion of developing the fight out of contact feasible? Can the Army expect to develop and field forces on the basis of see first, know first, understand first, or should the Army expect the kind of ambiguity in the future that characterized the location, capability and intentions of Iraqi units in OIF? Moreover, how do forces in the field assess enemy actions as reactions to friendly actions and do so with certainty? In OIF accounting for why the enemy did some of the things they did proved difficult, if not impossible. More important, it is potentially dangerous to impute motivation for enemy actions on the basis of the intent of friendly operations. Recognizing this, Lieutenant General Wallace eventually stopped trying to make sense of discrete enemy movements and operations and focused on what the needed to do, regardless of what enemy reactions might be.

NOTES

1. JFCOM and TRADOC are moving on converging axes in developing a common approach to understanding the COE. J7 will republish TRADOC's strategic-level Opposing Forces Doctrine as a joint publication, setting the stage to a common approach to replicating the COE, at least in the context of opposing forces. In June 2003, JFCOM and TRADOC sponsored a conference on the COE to develop some ideas on how to proceed and to consider early implications of OIF on the COE.

2. Brigadier V. K. Nair, *War in the Gulf: Lessons for the 3rd World* (New Delhi: Lancer International, 1991), 97.

3. Ibid., 13.

4. Ibid., 100, 101-111, and 121.

5. Compilation of essays presented at the Russian Academy of Military Sciences Scientific Council in Moscow on 6 June 2003.

6. Ibid.

7. Ibid.

8. Ibid.

9. Ibid.

10. An important benefit of low-intensity and stability operations in urban areas in the 1990s was to raise a crop of noncommissioned and company to field-grade officers in the US Army with a firsthand appreciation of the challenges of urban operations.

11. Study of Chechyan urban defenses in Grozny and Palestinian actions in the West Bank and Gaza indicated the new directions irregular forces were taking in the defense of modern cities. In contrast, Russian and Israeli forces took decidedly different approaches to defeating those threats. In their successful offensive into Grozny, Russian forces essentially leveled the city with artillery and air power, largely ignoring destruction and civilian casualties. Far more responsive to world and Arab opinion, Israeli offensives in Palestine were extremely surgical in nature.

12. Lieutenant General Dave McKiernan, commander, CFLCC, interview by Colonel James Embrey, Colonel James Greer, Colonel Neil Rogers, and Colonel Steve Mains, 1 May 2003.

13. Ibid.

14. Colonel Will Grimsley, commander, 1st BCT 3rd ID, interview by Colonel Gregory Fontenot, US Army, Retired, 19 November 2003.

15. Major Mike Oliver, S3, TF 3-69 AR, discussion with Colonel Gregory Fontenot, US Army, Retired, 11 December 2003 at the OIF Lessons Learned Conference, Fort Leavenworth, Kansas.

16. Major General "Spider" Marks, C2, CFLCC, interview by Colonel Gregory Fontenot, US Army, Retired, 14 June 2003. Marks goes on to remark; "We can get oven-fresh imagery–as the young analysts call it–into the hands of the users but we cannot refresh it…Intel on the move is a challenge, so battle command on the move remains a problem…Static, we can provide anything; on the move is a challenge."

17. McKiernan.

18. "US Army Contributions to the Iraqi Theater of Operations," Department of the Army briefing to the Secretary of Defense, 4 June 2003.

19. Lieutenant Colonel Joseph De Antonna, commander, 2-1 ADA, interview by Major Jim Houlahan, 12 June 2003.

20. Lieutenant General Dave McKiernan, commander, CFLCC, interview by Colonel Gregory Fontenot, US Army, Retired, 8 December 2003.

21. McKiernan, 1 May 2003.

22. Deployment data for 173rd and TF 1-63 AR provided by USAREUR Movement Operations Center, Lieutenant Colonel Brad Wakefield, 16 September 2003.

23. SBCT Ready Force Movement Data (undated), provided by TRADOC Integration Cell, Fort Lewis, Washington. Sixty-five C-17 sorties deliver the Stryker Ready Force (one battalion task force); the other sorties could deliver addition brigade-level command and control, as well as combat, CS, or CSS capabilities.

24. Colonel Robert W. Nicholson, division engineer, 4th ID, interview by Colonel James Greer, 16 May 2003.

25. Colonel William L. Greer, commander, 101st Airborne Division Artillery, interview by Colonel James Greer, 15 May 2003. This confirms similar comments in interview conducted by Colonel James Greer with the 3rd ID DIVARTY commander, Colonel Thomas G. Torrance, on 12 May 2003.

26. Lieutenant Colonel Erin Edgar, division surgeon, 82nd Airborne Division, interview by Colonel James Greer, 4 May 2003. After exhausting critical medical supplies treating Army and Marine Corps wounded, and unable to obtain resupply through Army Class VIII (Medical) resupply, the 82nd medical units scrounged needed supplies from the 28th CSH. Another unit, the 212th MASH, resorted to foraging for supplies. See also interview with Colonel Canestrini, commander, 212 MASH, 30 MED BDE conducted by Lieutenant Colonel Robinson at FOB DOGWOOD on 24 May 2003.

27. Confirmed by Colonel James Greer during interviews held separately with all the brigade commanders in both the 3rd ID and 101st Airborne Division (total of 13 brigades) during 9-16 May 2003. Most brigade commanders reported receiving no repair parts at all. In an interview on 15 May 2003, Colonel Ben Hodges, commander of 1st Brigade, 101st Airborne Division, stated that in the month and a half since his brigade was committed to combat, it had received a total of five repair parts. That was the most repair parts reported received by any of the brigade commanders who had fought the major combat operations.

28. Although Army watercraft did perform many operations well, port operators believe they could have performed the mission without them. While this assertion may be so, Army watercraft won the acclaim of theater logisticians because they provided flexibility and eased the logistics burden. See MTMC feedback re: *On Point* and Colonel Victoria Leignadier interview.

29. Donald H. Rumsfeld, *Rebalancing Forces,* memorandum dated 9 July 2003.

30. Belton Y. Cooper, *Death Traps: The Survival of an American Armored Division in World War II* (New York: Random House Ballantine Books, 1998), xix.

31. General Peter J. Schoomaker, chief of staff, US Army, *Arrival Message,* 1 August 2003.

32. McKiernan.

33. There are a number of possible definitions for netcentric warfare. This one is derived from several sources with the help and advice of Dr. James Ellsworth, US Naval War College.

34. Major General James A. "Spider" Marks, C2, CFLCC, interview by Colonel Gregory Fontenot, US Army, Retired, 17 November 2003.

35. Discussions taken from Baghdad City Planning Conference held by Third Army/CFLCC at Fort McPherson, Georgia, in October 2002.

36. Master Sergeant Courtney Mabus, noncommissioned officer in charge, V Corps IO Planning Cell, discussion with Colonel James Greer, 26 April 03.

37. Marks, 17 November 2003.

38. Ibid.

Chapter 8

Transition

Peace enforcement is wearing everybody out.... This is much harder [than combat].

Lieutenant Colonel Jeff Ingram, TF 2-70 AR

It is not uncommon to conclude this kind of effort with an epilogue, a postscript that attempts to bring closure to the threads that did not fit in the main work or to take note of developments between the conclusion of the work and its publication. An epilogue is neither possible nor appropriate to *On Point* since the story is not over. The chief of staff of the Army established the study group to examine combat operations as soon after their conclusion as possible and to publish the results quickly. The president of the United States declared major combat operations over on 1 May 2003, thus this study is limited to those operations occurring on or before 1 May 2003. On 15 August, when the first draft of this manuscript was completed, the Army was planning the next phase of study of OIF and how lessons might be gleaned from the effort to transition from combat operations to those activities that FM 3-0, *Operations,* attributes to conflict termination. Accordingly, this postscript to *On Point* is properly titled *Transition.*

In his short remarks on swearing in as the 35th chief of staff of the Army, General Peter Schoomaker homed in on the single most important feature of the Army that enabled superb performance in OIF—soldiers. Schoomaker's remarks left no doubt about his view for the way ahead must assure the Army's essence—soldiers—remain on point for the nation. The chief made it clear that he will examine the Army's methods in training and leader development, how it organizes to include the mix between the Active and Reserve components, how the force is manned, and what the Army must do to remain flexible and adaptable. As he put it, "The American soldier remains indispensable. Our soldiers are paramount and will remain the centerpiece of our thinking, our systems and our combat formations."[1]

There were a number of reasons why combat operations in OIF succeeded with a minimum of loss of life on both sides and damage to Iraq's aging and fragile infrastructure. First-rate, innovative, adaptive soldiers lead that list. Schoomaker has announced his intention to focus on the heart of the Army—people. Effective leaders and sound training and leader development are the next two major reasons for success. The two are directly related and require joint involvement. Developing leaders who are able to function comfortably in the "three-block war," under the stress and ambiguity of close combat, is essential to the success of the Army and the joint team. Selecting the right soldiers and developing them as leaders requires intense effort in joint environments. *On Point* suggests the operational environment in OIF is more, not less, complex than that in which the services have traditionally assumed they would operate.

Although all of the services accept that the operational environment is more complex, none of them—and certainly not the Army—has entirely embraced the implications of those changes. Nor have they altered their systems and training to accommodate, and even anticipate, the dynamic conditions in which the services will continue to operate. Development of a joint national training capability led by the Joint Forces Command will form a key capability to enable the services to continue to produce the kind of leaders who performed superbly in OIF.

The services have important roles to play in assuring they provide leaders from private to general who are able to function in this environment. For the Army, that means examining and altering schools and training centers as appropriate. The Army's excellent training centers: the Battle Command Training Program at Fort Leavenworth, the National Training Center at Fort Irwin, the Joint Readiness Training Center at Fort Polk, and the Combat Maneuver Training Center at Hohenfels, Germany, will continue to provide the venues for collective unit training for the Army, but they too will undergo examination and alteration.

Leader development is more than training. Although expensive and time consuming, the education of soldiers and leaders who are capable of critical thinking and perspective is absolutely indispensable if the Army is to develop what General Schoomaker calls "the George C. Marshalls for the new era."[2] Leader education should seek to produce officers and senior noncommissioned officers who are able to solve complicated problems in joint and interagency contexts during operations from combat to conflict termination.

Combined arms and joint operations, the higher form of combined arms, were among the top five reasons for success in major combat operations. Combined arms organizations able to task-organize efficiently and rapidly proved essential to meeting the challenges posed in OIF. The inherent agility and flexibility disparate forces bring to the fight seem obvious now, but in recent years there have been bitter debates over exactly how to organize forces and whether units with differing mobility and combat power should even be combined. At the extreme end, one group argues for fixed units, organized at the brigade level. However, these would be difficult to "mix and match" to meet the explicit and transitory requirements of the contemporary environment. On the other extreme, there are those who argue not to change anything. Maintaining unit purity and task-organizing as required appeals to this group. This approach does not afford the "plug and play" modules that future expeditionary operations are likely to require.

At the tactical level in the JSOTFs and at the operational level in the conventional forces, *joint* operations were the rule, not the exception. I MEF and V Corps demonstrated the closest tactical cooperation between the Army and the Marine Corps since the Pacific campaigns of World War II. The air component's units moved and fought at the strategic, operational, and tactical levels and performed brilliantly at all levels. Rapid and precise attacks on time-sensitive targets at all three levels demonstrated the inherent flexibility of the air arm. Air interdiction and CAS had been a bone of contention between the Army and the Air Force, in particular. In this campaign, thanks in part to personal efforts on the part of senior leaders, but also as a consequence of the maturation of joint doctrine and joint operations, that seam practically disappeared. As Lieutenant General Wallace put it, "We've gotten more close air support and more availability of CAS and more access to CAS than I can ever remember. I go back to Vietnam, and we didn't have that kind of CAS in Vietnam."[3] CAS proved decisive in assuring tactical victory and, on more than one occasion, decisive in preventing tactical defeat. Perhaps just as important, CAS provided a strong boost to troops on the ground, who were profoundly grateful to the airmen who flew those missions. What had been a source of irritation has become a source of satisfaction and admiration.

On Point has not been able to deliver authoritatively on the importance of special operations forces (SOF) and the effectiveness of integrating SOF with conventional operations. Due mostly to continued classification of these operations, that story remains to be told. Anecdotes abound among the conventional units that attribute the best intelligence and combat information to that developed by SOF units. JSOTF-North operations appear to have fixed some of Iraqi units that manned the Green Line. JSTOF-West denied sanctuary to Iraqi units, particularly to Iraqi missile units. The heroic actions of the special operations troopers in the south stood out every day because of their close integration into V Corps and I MEF operations.

The contributions of the civil affairs and PSYOP components of SOF, while included, are difficult to assess this early. Civil affairs troops absolutely reduced human suffering and enabled the delivery of humanitarian assistance, and they are at the center of the continuing operations in Iraq. PSYOP, as part of information operations (IO), achieved some success as alluded to in *On Point*, but telling the whole story must wait because assessment of IO is perhaps the most difficult of tasks and requires details not yet available.

After World War II, the Army debriefed enemy field commanders in considerable detail to determine what they had intended, to learn how they fought and what they perceived about Allied actions. The documents and studies that emerged obviously are essential to understanding both what happened and why. Sixty years later, historians and soldiers continue to learn from that effort. As *On Point* went to the publisher, some early results of a similar effort emerged. *On Point* does not have the benefit of those early results for a number of good reasons, including sensitivity and the fact that the analysis of that data is ongoing. When that data becomes available, the relationship of enemy and coalition actions will be better understood. That understanding is essential to writing the authoritative history of Operation IRAQI FREEDOM.

In title and in themes, this study unabashedly claims the Army served *On Point* for the joint team and the nation in OIF. OIF was essentially a land campaign brought to decision in ground combat by the Army, Marine Corps, coalition ground forces and SOF. That does not mean that the ground forces achieved decision alone—they did not. The Army also provided essential services to the other members of the joint team and contributed essential C2 systems, including BFT. However mundane, both supporting theater logistics and providing C2 components are essential to sustaining joint campaigns.

In other campaigns, the Army will not be on point. Ground operations may sometimes be merely precursors to set conditions for decisive operations from the air. In Kosovo, the air campaign proved sufficient to bring Slobodan Milosevic to the table. The Army entered Kosovo as part of a coalition force to enforce the agreement won by coalition airmen. At Iwo Jima, marines paid for a B-29 base with their blood. These facts neither diminish the role of the Army in Kosovo nor that of the Marine Corps at Iwo Jima. They do emphasize the importance of joint operations in the past and their continued relevance in the future. They also suggest that each of the services must be able to lead as well as support operations. Equally important, each of the services is liable to provide the "core" of joint force headquarters. The implications of this possibility are far reaching.

In staking out the position that the Army was on point in OIF, the study group also felt bound to suggest that the Army should also be on point in supporting and leading joint transformation.

If the Army is, as asserted here, essential and on point for the joint team, it must embrace the journey to transformation. Of all the services, the Army is most dependent on the others and therefore must assume the risks inherent in working within the joint team to lead change. This may require painful choices and risks, but it is consistent with going o*n point*. It is consistent also with General Schoomaker's assertion that "the Army must remain relevant and ready."[4]

On Point accepts the risks inherent in working rapidly and with a narrow focus. These risks are many and may include errors in fact, in interpretation, and that the whole story is not told. The risks assumed in *On Point* seem worthwhile for one overarching reason—the study of war is essential to the profession of soldiering. This study aimed primarily at soldiers who perhaps experienced the war only through what they read, saw on television, or heard. It also sought to illuminate for soldiers who were there how their efforts contributed to the outcome. The story of OIF is dramatic, ongoing, and provocative. Others will complete the record; the goal here is to provoke recollection and discussion of the events of the spring of 2003 and how they fit in the context of events since Operation DESERT STORM. Perhaps the most lasting contribution of this effort is the archive containing interviews, records, and photographs. Ultimately, the archive will reside both in the Combined Arms Research Library and in the Center of Army Lessons Learned at Fort Leavenworth, Kansas. The intent is to provide the data required to complete the record.

On Point has sought to highlight, when possible, the excellence of American soldiers. They revealed themselves as courageous, adaptable, and compassionate. Most of the soldiers named in this publication are heroes—thousands of other heroes are not named. Soldiers retained their sense of humor during the darkest hours and attempted to treat even their enemies with dignity and respect. They behaved as American soldiers have traditionally toward children and civilians—to them they were generous, courteous, and sensitive. To one another, they demonstrated fidelity and often gave the ultimate gift—their lives.

American soldiers are not without their flaws, but taken as a whole, they demonstrate the best in all of us. All were touched in some way by their experiences. As Lieutenant Colonel Rick Schwartz put it after Thunder Run 1, "…we were better, but never okay."[5] American soldiers for the most part became "hardened" but never gave up their humanity. That quality, combined with their adaptability, will sustain them—as it did the 100 soldiers who reenlisted in one of Saddam's palaces in Baghdad on the 4th of July 2003. In the often-maligned "Army of One" recruiting campaign, the Army ran a television commercial that is done in sepia tones. Antique photography juxtaposes old photos of young men with their current photos as old veterans. The narrator intones that each generation has its heroes. Then the advertisement cuts to serving soldiers, concluding this one has its heroes too. The troops in OIF and those who remain on point in Afghanistan, in Kuwait, and in Iraq illustrate the fundamental truth in that advertisement—this generation has its heroes.

The story of OIF is not over. Just how it will turn out is difficult to predict. But, soldiers *on point* are prepared to carry on as required. Having won the battle to remove Saddam, they are embarked on winning the peace with no idea how long that will take. They continue to get hurt or killed, but so far they retain their compassion for each other and for the Iraqi people. They believe in what they are doing and they clearly believe that they are making a difference. This study justly concludes with a story from one of those citizen-soldiers willing to sacrifice all for the nation.

I Guess I Made an Impression

This final story came from a National Guardsman. He tells his story with candor and in a manner that clearly conveys the human aspect of battle. Moreover, he exemplifies the new reality about America's Reserve and National Guard soldiers—he is not a "weekend warrior," but rather an experienced soldier who received his *first* Purple Heart in Beirut, Lebanon, and has served in Saudi Arabia and Germany since. He offers his story but insists that his name be withheld because he does not feel his experience is exceptional—or even noteworthy.

He was wounded while performing convoy duty as a .50-caliber machine gunner on a gun truck (a truck with a .50-caliber machine gun on a swiveling ring-mount). His vehicle was the last in a convoy that was ambushed south of Baghdad on 11 July 2003. The Iraqis' target was a fuel truck, two vehicles ahead of his truck. The first RPG skidded under the tanker. A second RPG hit a concrete bridge support just as his gun truck approached. A jagged softball-size piece of concrete struck him in the lower right abdominal area, just below the edge of his flak jacket. The concrete penetrated and stuck. He begins his story just after being struck:

> While it is fresh on my mind, I would like to see if I can put this down before it slips away and I start to forget. Pain is accompanied by and met with a very wide spectrum of senses and feelings condensed into a very compact space of time:

> The physical injury manifested itself between a solid hit and a stabbing/burning sensation. Then I couldn't catch my breath. I brushed off whatever it was with the back of my right hand. Then a numbness covered me like a cloud. The truck swerved slightly, the shadow of the [highway] overpass flicked past. I started breathing again. I located the dust trail and opened up [with my machine gun]. Back to business for about 2 minutes. Then the ache started to grow. The wrecker was pulling away. We pulled up hard left, facing the dust trail.

> When the [.50-caliber machine] gun was empty, I looked down for the extra ammo. My feet were covered in brass casings, links, and broken glass. There was a large chunk of concrete lying up against the door. I said something to the driver or he said something to me. I don't remember. I started to bend down to get the extra can and that was the wrong answer. I was very aware that I was going to start hurting in a very big way. My M-16 was clipped to my LBV with a D-ring by the sling and was hanging straight down. I pulled it up and emptied it. [Firing] all seven magazines.

> The MPs had crossed the median and came up the other side of the highway. I emptied out [my M-16] as [the MPs] came into my sight picture. The MP gunner took over. It was awesome. The sand people started running. The [MPs'] Hummer hit the berm they were behind and leaped up and into them like a cat pouncing. The dust trail from the Hummer then floated up and I lost sight of what was going on. The truck [ours] had died and the shooting stopped. I could hear the MPs yelling something in Arabic.

> I started checking myself to see where and how bad [I had been injured]. The hand was a scratch. The boot was torn, but not a very big cut in the leather. I opened the door with my foot and slid out of the ring and onto the ground. Out from under the LBV, then the vest. Not much blood yet. Open the blouse. Pull up the T-shirt and uh-oh. A hole about the size of a half-dollar. The skin was

kind of torn back in shreds. A nice glimpse of internal organs, and a dusting of concrete fragments and small bits of gravel. Then the sinking feeling. Sitting down and a real sense of ache. Nausea. Then the usual way of solving that. The urge to lie down was overwhelming. Then the urge to sit up. The pavement was too hot. Somebody helped me limp over to the shade of the overpass, where I laid down. Then I rolled over on my side and the need to pull my legs up and curl in a ball took over. Then slightly rocking back and forth. I started to get angry. This pain was nothing I couldn't just gut my way through. I was joking with the guy trying to help me.

Then things didn't seem funny anymore. I met something very ugly in the way of pain in my side. I put my hand over it and pushed down on the dressing. Wrong answer. I could feel my upper lip starting to sweat that cool moist sweat like a fever. My mouth got dry. I start clinching my teeth. It was like I was getting a good grip of something to hang on to. And down this dark tunnel. I started seeing zigzag lines in my peripheral vision and kind of a dark circle around everything. I wasn't mad anymore. Everything seemed to be way off. I was scared of where this pain was going to go. I was bleeding pretty good. The pressure dressing hurt, but I covered it up and slowed down the [blood] flow. I was holding my breath, more and more, and pressuring up to ride out the pangs. I would pant between them. People were talking to me and I have no idea what they said.

The aircrew was there in 17 minutes. It felt like 17 days. I saw them fly as they cleared the bridge coming in. I could see the bottom of the chopper. They landed right on the road just past the truck. Dark green with a Red Cross. The door was open. What a sight. I was way beyond being able to fight it off and I knew I was hurt. My eyes leaked a few tears just before I started trembling. Then I wanted, really wanted it all to stop. I knew I was safe. I saw them running up, but didn't hear them. Everything was muffled. [It] took two sticks to get the IV in. I saw him fill the needle and watched the little stream of fluid fly out of it against the clear blue sky. I could feel the hands all around holding me down. The last words I heard were "You're going to sleep now, you'll be OK. . . 3, 2, . . ."

And then I don't remember much of anything for two days. When I woke up, they had laid the Battle Flag across my feet. And nobody said a word about it. The pictures of my boys were on the stand next to my bed, and somebody had given me three little desert Beanie Bears. I still didn't know what day it was. I was down for almost five days.

When I finally stood up, they told me that I could go down and see the prisoners if I wanted. They even gave me a camera to borrow and a roll of film. The interpreter told me that they had been asking about me. Apparently, our convoy was the first one they had seen that had two gun trucks, and mine was a complete surprise. They had tried to shoot the fueler and missed. Then I showed up. I guess I made an impression.[6]

On a more positive note, on Sunday, 14 December 2003, Lieutenant General Rick Sanchez and Ambassador Paul Bremer announced that SOF troops and soldiers from the 4th Infantry Division had captured Saddam Hussein. The troops captured Hussein without a fight, denying him the opportunity to honor his claim that he would be a martyr, but never a captive. Hussein, without his retinue and sporting nearly six months of beard, emerged from a hole in the ground just large enough for him to lie in. Appearing haggard and disheveled, the dictator had only two retainers and a drug dealer's horde of $100 bills. No one believes that capturing Hussein means the end is in sight. But it was surely good news. One of the great truths of this campaign is that combat operations alone will not attain the desired end state. Operations ongoing now will be decisive, not those that the troops concluded in downtown Baghdad.

On Point has attempted to deliver on the mission assigned the OIF Study Group in April of 2003. All that remains is to suggest work that others might do to develop a more complete study of the Army in OIF than we have been able to achieve. There are a number of areas *On Point* has not covered that deserve further study, or areas that were addressed but could not fully examine with the evidence at hand or were discussed without access to all of the evidence.

US Transportation Command's *So Many, So Much, So Far, So Fast* is arguably one of the best official histories of DESERT STORM. This little book has not been read by many of those who wrote about DESERT STORM or disparaged the deployment to Saudi Arabia in 1990 as ponderous. TRANSCOM's history argues rightly that the deployment to DESERT STORM in 1990 was a tremendous achievement. On the other hand, it is meticulous in noting problems. TRANSCOM and the service components of that specified command worked hard to solve the problems identified in DESERT STORM. Hopefully, TRANSCOM will produce as careful and thoughtful a history of the deployment to Kuwait and elsewhere in support of OIF. The record of this most recent effort is essential to determining the right course for the future and affects all of the armed forces.

Colonel Rick Swain's *Lucky War: Third Army in Desert Storm* is another first-class official history that illuminated important issues from the perspective of the Army service component command in that war. Third Army morphed from a service component command to a functional component command in OIF. A similar history is urgently needed now since it may help shape how the Army and the Marine Corps approach the problem of fielding a coalition and joint functional land component command. How the CFLCC organized, how it functioned, and how it operated and collaborated with the other components needs to be assessed and reported.

On Point provided only an overview of operational and tactical logistics. The story of getting fuel forward and the heroic efforts of logisticians from the depots to Logistics Support Area Adder is a rich and interesting tale that needs to be told. The story of the Army's Materiel Command (AMC) also needs to be told. In this tale, the role of civilians, both civil service and contractors will be illuminated. AMC civilians and contractors served in tactical units in combat and kept things running long after parts ran out. AMC's civilian workforce produced everything from bombs to bullets, without which OIF could not have been fought. There are a host of compelling soldier stories that need to be told which ran the gamut from the harrowing convoys hauling supplies forward during the mother of all sandstorms to the misery of repairing engines under tarpaulins, using flashlights and fluorescent chemical lights.

Army hospital units saved coalition and Iraqi lives under dangerous and difficult conditions. They did so under difficult and dangerous conditions. At one point during operations at Objective RAMS, the 212th MASH had every trooper that could not wield a scalpel on the perimeter wielding a rifle. At Objective CURLY, the medics hunkered down, prepared to fight to protect the wounded. Medics and medical evacuation crews performed what some might describe as miracles and did it with precision and compassion. Medical support troops foraged for supplies, kept generators running, and did a host of other mundane but daunting tasks under severe conditions. They too deserve to have their story told.

Although *On Point* has been able to survey the tactical-level fighting in narrative form, it has not accounted for all of the tactical fights. For example, *On Point* reviewed the 82nd Airborne's operations at As Samawah but did not discuss their subsequent operations. The 82nd fought important engagements aimed at securing the lines of communication and reducing Ad Diwaniyah after As Samawah that are not covered here but warrant examination. Similarly, there are numerous tactical engagements that deserve further investigation and more thorough accounting than possible in *On Point*. To complete the story, junior officers, noncommissioned officers, and soldiers need to tell their stories. Junior officers and noncommissioned officers and their troops carried the tactical fights that produced success. They have a contribution to make to the body of knowledge regarding combat operations—their accounts will inform the way we train and educate soldiers and their leaders.

On Point tantalizes, but does not deliver on the many and varied tactical actions of special operations forces. Their story clearly needs telling. The sheer diversity of special operations forces will make their story complex, but to understand really what happened in OIF their account is absolutely essential. Similarly, joint and Army intelligence efforts could not be examined fully here—that effort must come later. As it becomes possible to do so, assessing the success of intelligence efforts needs to be done.

At some point it will be possible to develop a reasonably clear sense of what the Ba'athist regime's leadership intended and how it directed execution. That accounting and the thinking and efforts of the Iraqi military leadership will enrich understanding of US vulnerabilities and successes. Determining the composition and intent of the paramilitary forces that operated in OIF will probably be more difficult. The effort to understand their motivation and operations will be essential to understanding the campaign from the perspective of the Iraqi military and paramilitary alike. More important, such an effort will help the services consider implications of the campaign that may apply elsewhere.

Finally, there are two important general accounts that should be undertaken from the Army point of view. *On Point* will need to be revised once Iraq operations are better understood, when units that fought major combat operations return from Iraq and are able to update their own histories, and when participants are more readily available for follow-up interviews. The second effort is more important—that is the history of operations since 1 May. Collection of data for that effort is under way by the Center of Military History, but that work cannot be completed and the story cannot be written until operations against the insurgency are concluded.

NOTES

1.   General Peter J. Schoomaker, chief of staff, US Army, 1 August 2003.
2.   Ibid.
3.   Lieutenant General William Wallace, commander, V Corps, summary transcription of interview with Colonel French Maclean, US Army, Retired, 15 April 2003.
4.   Schoomaker.
5.   Lieutenant Colonel Eric "Rick" Schwartz, commander, TF 1-64 AR, 2nd BCT, 3rd ID, interview by Lieutenant Colonel Dave Manning, undated.
6.   Personal account of [name withheld], "The full range of emotion," 23 July 2003.

About the OIF-SG Team

The team formed under the leadership of Brigadier General Mark O'Neill, assisted by Colonel James Greer, Colonel Charles Taylor, and Colonel (retired) Gregory Fontenot. As study group director, Brigadier General O'Neill developed baseline guidance and the terms of reference. Colonels Greer and Fontenot and Lieutenant Colonel David Tohn served as the lead writers and de facto team leadership for collectors in the field. Major Ike Wilson played a key role in the development of this effort, prior to reporting to the 101st Airborne Division in Mosul, Iraq. Colonel Taylor provided linkage with the Army Staff and supported the team in its near-term efforts to ensure that short-term observations and lessons gathered would have an immediate impact on the Army and deploying formations.

Lieutenant Colonel E.J. Degen joined the team in July, straight from his assignment as the V Corps chief of plans, to assist with the writing and editing of the book.

The study group's advance party formed at Fort Leavenworth, Kansas, and departed for Continental United States Replacement Center (CRC) training and processing at Fort Benning, Georgia, on 17 April 2003. They established facilities for the main body in the Combined Forces Land Component Command headquarters at Camp DOHA, Kuwait, and began the initial collection effort. The main body, drawn primarily from the Army branch proponents within the Training and Doctrine Command, assembled and led training in gathering data, conducting historical interviews, and archive procedures at Fort Leavenworth 15–20 April 2003. The Center for Army Lessons Learned, the 44th Military History Detachment, and the US Army Forces Command historian, Mr. Bill Stacey, supported that training.

Following this training, the study group deployed to Fort Bliss, Texas, for CRC training conducted by the 334th CRC Battalion, US Army Reserve, and returned to complete issue of equipment and training to support research in the field. They returned to Fort Bliss and deployed on 5 May. After initial in-processing in Kuwait, the main body deployed into Iraq to begin collection on 7 May. They completed formal data collection in-theater by 15 June, to include input from several collectors who canvassed the US European Command and key locations within the United States to trace the story back to the source.

The writing effort began on 18 June and delivered the first draft on 15 August 2003. Subsequent drafts followed over the next few months. Concurrently, a data management and archiving team began cataloging and processing the 330 gigabytes of data and transcribing 3,750 interviews. This data forms the basis for continued research.

Retired General Frederick M. Franks, Jr. formed the final component of the study group as mentor and senior adviser to the team. The Army chose him on the basis of his experience in

DESERT STORM as commander of VII Corps and because of his role in assimilating lessons learned from that war. Finally, he had also supported V Corps when it faced the possibility of deploying in the late summer of 2002.

Members

COL (R) CORY C. AYLOR
CHAPLAIN (MAJ) PETER A. BAKTIS
MAJ CRAIG C. BORCHELT
SFC (R) TIMOTHY BOYD
MAJ JAMES B. BRASHEAR
LTC (R) JACK BURKETT
MAJ WILLIAM W. BURNHAM
LTC TIMOTHY BURNS
LTC DENNIS J. CAHILL
CW3 (R) J.D. CALL
CW4 MICHAEL R. CAMPBELL
MR. ROBERT A. CASSELLA
COL TIMOTHY D. CHERRY
LTC (R) WILLIAM M. CONNOR
MAJ DAVID A. CONVERSE
MAJ DANIEL R. COREY
LTC MICHAEL J. CURRY
MR. PHILLIP R. DAVIS
MRS. ROSE DAWSON
LTC EDMUND J. 'EJ' DEGEN
MAJ ROBERT J. DIETRICH
MAJ CYNTHIA A. DILLARD
MAJ GERALD O. DORROH, JR.
LTC (R) ARTHUR A. DURANTE, JR.
MR. AL FEHLAUER
LTC(R) FREDRICH LEE FINCH
MAJ BRIAN K.FLOOD
MAJ ROBERT F. FOLEY
COL (R) GREGORY FONTENOT
GEN (R) FRED FRANKS
MAJ JONATHAN O. GASS
LTC SCOTT GEDLING
MAJ DANIEL B. GEORGE
MR. JOHN GOODLOE
MAJ JONATHAN GRAFF
COL (R) CHARLES JOSEPH GREEN

MAJ ROBERT GREENWAY
COL JAMES K. GREER
LTC (R) RICHARD A. GRIMES
LTC (R) JOHN M. HAMMELL
MAJ JAMES M. HOULAHAN
MAJ AUDREY HUDGINS
MR. ED IRICK
MAJ DEMETRIUS L. JACKSON
SGT JERIMIAH JOHNSON
MAJ KENNETH KELLEY
MS. ROBIN KERN
MAJ JEFFREY W. KILGO
MAJ PETER G. KILNER
LTC EDRIC A. KIRKMAN
MAJ LAURA KLEIN
MAJ (R) GEORGE KNAPP
COL JAMES A. KNOWLTON
LTC DAVID J. KOLLEDA
SGM VICTOR A. LeGLOAHEC
LTC DAVID R. MANNING
MAJ MICHAEL L. MATHEWS
MRS. SANDRA J. MILES
MAJ ANDREW MORTENSEN
MR. SCOTT A. MYERS
BG MARK E. O'NEILL
MR. MARK E. OSTERHOLM
LTC JACK J. PAGANO
MSG HARRY L. PARRISH, JR.
LTC CHARLES P. PIERETT
LTC WILLIAM PITTS
CW4 JAMES M. PRUITT
MR. ROBIN D. QUINTRELL
MAJ DAVID RAUGH
MAJ ANTHONY G. REED
SSG WARREN W. REEVES
LTC JUDITH D. ROBINSON

MAJ TRAVIS E. ROOMS

LTC (R) JAMES RUTH

MAJ CHAD SKAGGS

LTC (R) QUENTIN W. SCHILLARE

COL (R) JAMES L. SPEICHER

COL WILLIAM S. SPRAITZAR

LTC FRANK D. STEARNS

MAJ RICHARD STROYAN

MAJ ADAM A. SUCH

MAJ ROBERT H. TALLMAN

COL CHUCK TAYLOR

CSM (R) J.C. TERLAJE

LTC DAVID W. TOHN

MAJ JOHN A. TOWNSEND

LTC ALEXANDER H. VONPLINSKY, III

LTC ROBERT S. WALSH

MAJ CHRISTOPHER P. WATKINS

CW3 ESTELL WATSON

MSG MATTHEW J. WEST

LTC DARRELL WILLIAMS

MAJ PAUL V. WILLIAMS

MAJ ISAIAH WILSON, III

Combined Forces Land Component Command (CFLCC) Order of Battle
1 May 2003[1]

CFLCC Headquarters

CFLCC Early Entry Command Post (EECP)
        1 x TSC-93C TACSAT Terminal (TACON)
        1 x TSC-143 TACSAT Terminal (TACON)
        1 x Data Package (TACON)
CFLCC Forward Command Post
        1 x TSC-85 (TACON)
        1 x Deployable KU-Band Earth Terminal (TACON)
        1 x Single Shelter Switch (TACON)
        1 x Data Package (TACON)
CFLCC HQ Support Battalion
        HHC/CFLCC
        3rd Army Liaison Team
        244th Army Liaison Team
        930th Army Liaison Team
        Personal Security Det/1/410th Military Police Co (-) (TACON)
        228th Signal Det (Mobile Communication)
        1st Chemical Det (JA Team, 12-hour augmentation)
        Planning and Control Team/132nd Engineer Battalion (-) (Attached)
        Civil Affairs Tactical Planning Team/A/352nd Civil Affairs Command (TACON)
        318th Press Camp HQ (OPCON)
        19th Public Affairs Detachment (OPCON)
        22nd Mobile Public Affairs Detachment (OPCON)
        372nd Mobile Public Affairs Detachment (OPCON)
        Army Space Support Team 3/1st Space Battalion (DS) (USA)
        Army Space Support Team 13/1st Space Battalion (DS) (USA)
3rd Military Police Group (Criminal Investigation) (-) (OPCON)
        10th Military Police Battalion (-) (Criminal Investigation Division) (OPCON)
        375th Military Police Detachment (Criminal Investigation HQ Cell)
Office of Reconstruction and Humanitarian Assistance (ORHA)
142nd Military Intelligence Battalion (Linguist) (OPCON)
82nd Airborne Division Quick Reaction Force
75th Exploitation Task Force (75th Field Artillery Brigade, XTF) (-)[2]
        HHB, 75th Field Artillery Bde
        Combined/Joint Command and Control Exploitation (C2X)
        Technical Escort Unit Joint Response Team (OPCON)
        Toxic Material Escort Team/Technical Escort Unit Chemical-Biological Intelligence Support Team (OPCON)
        Bio Research Program Lab/Naval Medical Research Center
        Mobile Chemical Lab/Edgewood Chemical and Biological Command

Sensitive Site Team 1 (with 75th XTF Forward)
Sensitive Site Team 2 (with 75th XTF Forward)
Sensitive Site Team 3 (with 75th XTF Forward)
Sensitive Site Team 4 (In Tikrit collocated with 4th ID)
Mobile Exploitation Team – A (with 75th XTF Forward)
Mobile Exploitation Team – B (Baghdad International Airport)
Mobile Exploitation Team – C (Returning to Baghdad International Airport)
Mobile Exploitation Team – D (In Tikrit collocated with 4th ID)
Media Exploitation Team
87th Chemical Co (Recon/Decon) (OPCON)
787th Ordnance Co (-) (Explosive Ordnance Disposal)
Direct Support Team/Defense Threat Reduction Agency
JWICS Mobile Intelligence Communications System
1 x TSC-93C TACSAT Terminal (TACON)
1 x TSC-143 TACSAT Terminal (TACON)
1 x TTC-48 Small Extension Switch (TACON)

ARCENT KUWAIT
HHC ARCENT—KUWAIT
Elements/1-179th Infantry (-) Task Force Patriot Defender (OPCON)[3]
C/1-152nd Infantry (Attached)
L/3/2nd Armored Cavalry Regiment (Quick Reaction Force) (OPCON)
D/3-43rd Air Defense Artillery (OPCON)
249th Engineer Battalion (Prime Power) (-) (OPCON)
       HHD/249th Engineer Bn (Prime Power)
       A/249th Engineer Bn (Prime Power)
180th Engineer Detachment (Utility) (OPCON)
Team/155th Engineer Detachment (Utility) (-) (OPCON)
Facilities Engineer Detachment A (-) (OPCON)
5/3rd Military Police Co (OPCON)
63rd Ordnance Co (Modular Ammo) (-) (OPCON)
1244th Transportation Co (Medium Truck 20-foot Container)
872nd Maintenance Detachment (OPCON)
110th Chaplain Detachment

ARCENT QATAR
HHC ARCENT—Qatar
B/1-124th Infantry (Attached)
Elements/TF 3-43rd Air Defense Artillery
       C/3-2nd Air Defense Artillery (ADCON)
       E/3-43rd Air Defense Artillery (ADCON)
       C/2-124th Infantry (ADCON)[4]
       Element/516th Maintenance Co (Patriot DS) (ADCON)
3/101st Chemical Co (Smoke/Decon) (OPCON)
Facilities Engineer Detachment F (TACON)

Facilities Engineer Team
410th Military Police Co (Combat Support) (-) (OPCON)
438th Military Police Detachment (Law and Order) (OPCON)
69th Signal Co (Cable and Wire) (OPCON)
550th Signal Co (Theater Strategic)
Joint Tactical Air-Ground Station Det 1/1st Space Battalion (ADCON)
755th Adjutant General Co (Postal) (-) (ADCON)
766th Ordnance Co (Explosive Ordnance Disposal) (TACON)
831st Transportation Co (ADCON)
Elements/6th Medical Logistics Management Center AMC FWD - SWA (ADCON)
HSC/205th Medical Battalion (Area Support)
719th Medical Detachment (Veterinary Services) (ADCON)
983rd Medical Det (Preventative Medicine) (ADCON)
9th Finance Battalion
119th Chaplain Detachment (OPCON)

ARCENT SAUDI ARABIA
HHC ARCENT—SA
TF 3-43rd Air Defense Artillery (+) (Attached) (TACON to JTF-SWA (CFACC) for Firing Authority)
 HHB/3-43rd Air Defense Artillery
 A/3-43rd Air Defense Artillery
 B/3-43rd Air Defense Artillery
 C/3-43rd Air Defense Artillery
 A/1-1st Air Defense Artillery (Attached) Bahrain
 B/1-1st Air Defense Artillery (Attached) Bahrain
 A/1-124th Infantry (Attached) Bahrain
 A/1-179th Infantry (Attached) Saudi Arabia
 B/1-179th Infantry (Attached) Saudi Arabia
 580th Signal Co (Theater Strategic)
 153rd Military Police Co (Combat Support) (Attached)
 516th Maintenance Co (Patriot DS)
 1/1042nd Medical Co (-) (Air Ambulance) (Attached)

MARCENT—DJIBOUTI

MARCENT—DJ CFLCC Liaison Element (OPCON)
226th Quartermaster Detachment (Water Purification) (OPCON) (USA)
CENTCOM MIL Working Dog Detachment (OPCON) (USA)
Platoon/40th Signal Battalion (Corps Mobile Subscriber Equipment) (TACON) (USA)
Navy Emergency Medical Surgical Team (OPCON)
520th Medical Detachment (Theater Army Medical Lab)(OPCON) (USA)
Civil Affairs Tactical Planning Team/A/354th Civil Affairs Brigade (OPCON)
Detachment 1/23rd Adjutant General Co (Postal) (OPCON)
Defense Contracting Management Agency Detachment (OPCON)

Det/87th Expeditionary Security Force Squadron (OPCON) (USAF)
Marine Air Control Squadron 2, Air Traffic Control (OPCON)
Blood Team (OPCON)
Veterinary Tech Detachment (OPCON)
Logistics Civilian Augmentation Program LNO (OPCON)

ETHIOPIA

Team/201st Military Intelligence Battalion (Signal Intelligence) (TACON to CFSOCC)

Logistics Task Force 787th (CAMP SNOOPY, ETHIOPIA) (OPCON) CJTF HORN OF AFRICA
HHD/787th Corps Support Battalion
      21st Transportation Co (Cargo Transfer)
      297th Transportation Co (Cargo Transfer) (-)
      758th Maintenance Co (Non-Divisional DS)
      Team/887th Quartermaster Co (Petroleum Oil Lubricants)
      511th Movement Control Team (Cargo Documentation)
      330th Movement Control Team (Cargo Documentation) (-)
      Section/436th Movement Control Battalion (-) (ADCON)
      978th Quartermaster Detachment (Supply)
      388th Medical Battalion (Logistics) (-)

OMAN

Team/142nd Movement Control Team (Port)
Team/151st Adjutant General Co (Postal) (-) (USA)
Team/109th Medical Detachment (Veterinary) (USA)
440th Medical Det (Blood Support Unit) (USA)

CFACC- Prince Sultan Air Base, SAUDI ARABIA

1st Battlefield Coordination Detachment (USA)
      HQ Element
      Operations Section
      Plans Section
      Intelligence Section
      Air Defense Section
      Airspace Management Section
      Airlift Section
      410th Support Detachment (Ground Liaison) (OPCON) (USA)
      411th Support Detachment (Ground Liaison) (OPCON) (USA)
      412th Support Detachment (Ground Liaison) (OPCON) (USA)
      413th Support Detachment (Ground Liaison) (OPCON) (USA)
      434th Support Detachment (Ground Liaison) (OPCON) (USA)

244th Theater Aviation Brigade (OPCON)
HHC/244th Theater Aviation Bde (ADVON)
1-147th Aviation (Echelon Above Corps Command Aviation) (UH-60) (OPCON)
G/149th Aviation (CH-47)
UH-60 Det/A/1-159th Aviation (OPCON)
1/A/5-159th Aviation (CH-47)
B/5-159th Aviation (CH-47D) (Attached)
UC-35 Det/A/1-214th Aviation (OPCON)
UH-60 Det/C/1-214th Aviation (OPCON)
E/111th Aviation (Air Traffic Service) (-)
C-12 Flight Detachment /Operational Support Airlift Command (Kuwait) (OPCON)

204th Air Traffic Services Group (OPCON)
Tactical Airspace Integration System Contractors (Attached)
B/1-58th Aviation (Air Traffic Service) (-)
E/131st Aviation (AVIM) (-)
F/58th Aviation (Air Traffic Service Support Maintenance)

32nd Army Air and Missile Defense Command (OPCON) - Kuwait
HHB/32nd AAMDC
11th Air Defense Artillery Brigade (-) (OPCON)
    TF 2-1st Air Defense Artillery (Patriot) (OPCON)
        C/5-52nd Air Defense Artillery (-) (Attached)
        D/5-52nd Air Defense Artillery (-) (Attached)
        A/3-2nd Air Defense Artillery (Pax Only) (Attached)
        178th Maintenance Co (Patriot DS)
    TF VIPER (OPCON) (Jordan) ARCENT—SA (TACON for ADA)
        1-7th Air Defense Artillery (Patriot)
        1-1st Air Defense Artillery (Patriot) (-)
            HHC/1-1st Air Defense Artillery
            C/1-1st Air Defense Artillery
            D/1-1st Air Defense Artillery
        B/3-124th Infantry (Attached)
        16th Signal Battalion (ADA Mobile Subscriber Equipment Area Support) (-)
(OPCON)
            HHC/16th Signal Bn
            B/16th Signal Bn
        51st Maintenance Co (Patriot DS)
        518th Maintenance Co (Patriot DS)
JTF COBRA (Israel) (TACON to 32nd AAMDC)[5]
        HHB/69th Air Defense Artillery Bde (Corps)
        5-7th Air Defense Artillery (Patriot) (-)
            HHB/5-7th Air Defense Artillery
            A/5-7th Air Defense Artillery
            E/5-7th Air Defense Artillery

        Deployable Intel Support Element/66th Military Intelligence Group (-)
        92nd Military Police Co (Combat Support)
        A/72nd Signal Battalion (Theater Tactical)
        19th Maintenance Co (Patriot DS)(-)
TF ADA—NORTH - Turkey (OPCON CENTCOM)[6]
    Extended Air Defense Task Force (EADTF)
        Det/HHB/5-7th Air Defense Artillery
        B/5-7th Air Defense Artillery
        D/5-7th Air Defense Artillery
        3 x Royal Netherlands Air Force Patriot Batteries
        Det/19th Maintenance Co (Patriot DS)(-)

416th Engineer Command (ENCOM) (-) (OPCON)
HHC/416th ENCOM (-) Arifjan
36th Engineer GP (Construction) (-) (OPCON) Tallil
    46th Engineer Battalion (Combat Heavy) (-) (OPCON) Umm Qasr
        HSC/46th Engineer (Combat Heavy)
        B/46th Engineer Co (Combat Heavy)
        C/46th Engineer Co (Combat Heavy)
    62nd Engineer Battalion (Combat Heavy) (OPCON) Iraq
        808th Engineer Co (Pipeline)
    92nd Engineer Battalion (Combat Heavy) (OPCON)
    109th Engineer Battalion (OPCON) Tallil
        HHD/109th Engineer (OPCON)
        A/46th Engineer Bn (Combat Heavy)
        63rd Engineer Co (Combat Support Equip)
        68th Engineer Co (Combat Support Equip)
        95th Engineer Detachment (Fire Fighting) (OPCON)
        520th Engineer Detachment (Fire Fighting) (OPCON)
        562nd Engineer Detachment (Fire Fighting) (OPCON
    368th Engineer Battalion (Combat Heavy)
        379th Engineer Co (Combat Support Equip)
    30th Engineer Battalion (Topographic) (-) (OPCON)
        Det/100th Engineer Co (Topographic) (Echelon Above Corps) (OPCON)
        Sqd/175th Engineer Co (Topographic) (Echelon Above Corps)
    B/249th Engineer Battalion (Prime Power)
        Team/2/B/249th Engineer Bn
        Team/4/B/249th Engineer Bn (OPCON)
        Team/4/B/249th Engineer Bn
        2 x Teams/4/B/249th Engineer Bn
        Team/4/B/249th Engineer Bn
        3/B/249th Engineer Bn
        6/B/249th Engineer Bn
        308th Engineer Detachment (Real Estate)
    Facilities Engineer Team 21

Facilities Engineer Detachment B
Forward Engineer Support Team M (OPCON)
1457th Engineer Battalion (Combat Wheeled) (ADVON)
HHC/926th Engineer Battalion (Combat)
323rd Engineer Team (Fire fighting)

513th Military Intelligence Brigade (-) (OPCON)
HHC/513th Military Intelligence Brigade (-)
202nd Military Intelligence Battalion (+)
 HHC/202nd Military Intelligence Bn
 A/202nd Military Intelligence Bn (-)
 B/202nd Military Intelligence Bn (-)
 Company Operating Base-S (TACON)
 Joint Interagency Control Group (TACON)
203rd Military Intelligence Battalion (Operations) (OPCON)
 HHC/203rd Military Intelligence Bn
 A/203rd Military Intelligence Bn (-) (OPCON)
 Joint Captured Material Exploitation Center/Defense Intelligence Agency (TACON)
221st Military Intelligence Battalion (Tactical Exploitation) (Attached)
 HHC/221st Military Intelligence Bn
 B/221st Military Intelligence Bn
 H/121st Military Intelligence Bn (Long Range Surveillance)
 D/202nd Military Intelligence Bn
 Detachment 1/Southwest Asia Field Office
141st Military Intelligence Battalion (Linguist) (-) (OPCON)
 A/221st Military Intelligence Bn (OPCON)
 HHC/306th Military Intelligence Bn (Internment and Resettlement)
 COMTECH/323rd Military Intelligence Bn (OPCON)
201st Military Intelligence Battalion (Echelon Above Corps Signal Intelligence) (-)
 A/201st Military Intelligence Bn (-)
 HOC/201st Military Intelligence Bn (-)
 A/323rd Military Intelligence Bn (OPCON)
 306th Military Intelligence Co (-) (Linguists)
297th Military Intelligence Battalion (Operations) (-)
 HSC/297th Military Intelligence Bn
 A/297th Military Intelligence Bn
 Army Element/Joint Surveillance Targeting Attack Radar System (JSTARS)
 B/224th Military Intelligence Bn (Unmanned Aerial Vehicle) (OPCON)
323rd Military Intelligence Battalion (Operations) (-)
 HSC/323rd Military Intelligence Bn
 B/323rd Military Intelligence Bn

335th Theater Signal Command (-) (OPCON)
11th Signal Brigade (-) (OPCON)
 HHC/11th Signal Bde

40th Signal Battalion (Theater Tactical) (Attached) (- Detachment with MARCENT Djibuti))

> 286th Signal Co (ADA Mobile Subscriber Equipment Area Support)

63rd Signal Battalion (-) (OPCON)

504th Signal Battalion (Composite) (-) (Attached)

313th Signal Co (Range Extension) (-)

54th Composite Signal Battalion (Theater) (-)

> 235th Signal Co (TACSAT)
>
> 385th Signal Co (Theater Strategic)
>
> Directorate of Information Management-KUWAIT

151st Signal Battalion (Telecommunications Area Support) (-)

114th Signal Co (TROPO Light) (-)

352nd Civil Affairs Command (-) (OPCON)

402nd Civil Affairs Battalion (-) (OPCON)

407th Civil Affairs Battalion

Free Iraqi Forces

Military History Group (Provisional) (OPCON)

30th Military History Detachment (DS 75th XTF)

35th Military History Detachment (DS 377th TSC)

48th Military History Detachment (Attached 101st Abn Div)

50th Military History Detachment (DS CFLCC)

51st Military History Detachment (DS 4th ID)

102nd Military History Detachment (DS 3rd ID)

126th Military History Detachment (DS 352nd CACOM)

135th Military History Detachment (DS 3rd COSCOM)

305th Military History Detachment (DS V Corps)

322nd Military History Detachment (DS CFLCC)

I Marine Expeditionary Force (Reinforced) (TACON)[7]

Marine Expeditionary Force HQ Group

> Command Element/11th Marine Expeditionary Unit (TF Yankee)
>
> > 2nd Battalion, 6th Marines (CP Security)
>
> 15th Marine Expeditionary Unit (Special Operations Capable) (MEUSOC)
>
> > Battalion Landing Team 2/1
> >
> > > S/5-11th Marines (155T)
> >
> > Marine Medium Helicopter Squadron 161 (Reinforced)
> >
> > Detachment/Marine Heavy Helicopter Squadron 361 (-)
> >
> > MEU Service Support Group 15
>
> 24th Marine Expeditionary Unit
>
> > Battalion Landing Team 2/2
> >
> > > F/2-10th Marines (155T)
> >
> > Detachment/Marine Attack Squadron 231 (-)
> >
> > Marine Medium Helicopter Squadron 263 (Reinforced)

Detachment/Marine Light Attack Helicopter Squadron 269
Detachment/Marine Heavy Helicopter Squadron 772 (-)
Detachment/Marine Heavy Helicopter Squadron 461
MEU Service Support Group 24
1st Intelligence Battalion (-) (Reinforced)
1st Force Recon Co (-) (Reinforced)
I MEF Force Liaison Element
6th Communications Battalion (-)
9th Communications Battalion (-)
1st Radio Battalion (Signals Intelligence) (-) (Reinforced)
3rd Air and Naval Gunfire Liaison Co
4th Air and Naval Gunfire Liaison Co
3rd Civil Affairs Group
Elements/358th Civil Affairs Brigade (USA)
402nd Civil Affair Battalion (-) (TACON) (USA)
        Displaced Civilian Team (USA)
Detachment/9th Psychological Operations Battalion (Tactical) (-) (USA)
19th Public Affairs Detachment (ADCON) (USA)
354th Mobile Public Affairs Detachment (OPCON) (USA)
367th Mobile Public Affairs Detachment (OPCON) (USA)
HHD/468th Chemical Battalion (-) (USA)
D/86th Signal Battalion (Major Unit Support) (OPCON) (USA)
C/40th Signal Battalion (TROPO) (OPCON) (USA)
Interrogation/Debriefing Team/513th Military Intelligence Brigade (USA)
Army Space Support Team 5, 1st Space Battalion (DS) (USA)
108th Air Defense Artillery Brigade (-) (DS) (USA)
        2-43rd Air Defense Artillery (Patriot) (-) (USA)
                HHC/2-43rd Air Defense Artillery
                A/2-43rd Air Defense Artillery
                B/2-43rd Air Defense Artillery
                C/2-43rd Air Defense Artillery
                D/3-2nd Air Defense Artillery (TACON)
        Platoon/7th Chemical Co (Bio Identification and Detection System)
        (OPCON) (USA)
        431st Chemical Det (JB, Augmentation for 24-hour operations) (OPCON)
        (USA)
        208th Signal Co (Mobile Subscriber Equip Area Support) (-) (OPCON)
        (USA)
        Elements/3-124th Infantry (Patriot Security) (USA)
        C/1-124th Infantry (Attached) (USA)
1st Marine Division (-) (Reinforced)
    Headquarters Bn/1st MARDIV
    1st Marine Regiment (-) (Reinforced), (Regimental Combat Team 1)
        HQ Co, 1st Marine Regiment
        3rd Battalion, 1st Marine Regiment

> 1st Battalion, 4th Marine Regiment
> 2nd Battalion, 23rd Marine Regiment
> 2nd Light Armored Recon Battalion (-)
> 5th Marine Regiment (-) (Reinforced), (Regimental Combat Team 5)
> > HQ Co, 5th Marine Regiment
> > 1st Battalion, 5th Marine Regiment
> > 2nd Battalion, 5th Marine Regiment
> > 3rd Battalion, 5th Marine Regiment
> > 2nd Tank Battalion (-) (Reinforced)
> > 1st Light Armored Recon Battalion (-)
> > C Co, 4th Combat Engineer Battalion, 4th MARDIV
> 7th Marine Regiment (-) (Reinforced), (Regimental Combat Team 7)
> > HQ Co, 7th Marine Regiment
> > 1st Battalion, 7th Marine Regiment
> > 3rd Battalion, 7th Marine Regiment
> > 3rd Battalion, 4th Marine Regiment
> > 1st Tank Battalion (-) (Reinforced)
> > 3rd Light Armored Recon Battalion (-)
> 11th Marine Regiment (-) (Reinforced)
> > HHB (-)/11th Marines
> > Det/HHB 10th Marine Regiment (Radar/Maintenance)
> > 1st Battalion, 11th Marine Regiment (155T) (+)
> > > I/3-10th Marines (155T)
> > 2nd Battalion, 11th Marine Regiment (155T)
> > 3rd Battalion, 11th Marine Regiment (155T)
> > 5th Battalion, 11th Marine Regiment (155T) (+)
> > > R/5-10th Marines (155T)
> > 3-27th Field Artillery (MLRS) (USA)
> > 1st Field Artillery Detachment (2 x Q37), 18th Field Artillery Brigade (USA)
> 1st Recon Battalion (-) (Reinforced)
> 2nd Assault Amphibian Battalion (-) (Reinforced)
> 3rd Assault Amphibian Battalion (Reinforced)
> 1st Combat Engineer Battalion (-) (Reinforced)
> 2nd Combat Engineer Battalion (-) (Reinforced)
> 2 x Platoons/323rd Chemical Co (-) (Smoke/Decon) (Attached) (USA)
> 1/101st Chemical Co (Smoke/Decon) (OPCON) (USA)

3rd Marine Air Wing (-) (Reinforced)
> Marine Wing HQ Squadron 3
> > Detachment/Marine Wing HQ Squadron 2
> Marine Air Group 11 (-) (Reinforced)
> > > Marine Aircraft Logistics Squadron 11 (-) (Reinforced)
> > > Marine Aircraft Logistics Squadron 14 (-)
> > > Detachment/Marine Aircraft Logistics Squadron 31
> > > Marine Aerial Refueler/Transport Squadron 352 (-) (Reinforced)
> > Detachment/Marine Aerial Refueler/Transport Squadron 234 (6 x A/C)

Detachment/Marine Aerial Refueler/Transport Squadron 452 (6 x A/C)
Marine Fighter/Attack Squadron 232
Marine Fighter/Attack Squadron 251
Marine Fighter/Attack Squadron (All Weather) 121
Marine Fighter/Attack Squadron (All Weather) 225
Marine Fighter/Attack Squadron (All Weather) 533
Marine Tactical Electronic Warfare Squadron 1
Marine Tactical Electronic Warfare Squadron 2
Marine Air Group 13 (-) (Reinforced)
    Marine Aircraft Logistics Squadron 13 (-)
    Marine Attack Squadron 211 (-)
    Marine Attack Squadron 214
    Marine Attack Squadron 223 (-)
    Marine Attack Squadron 311
    Marine Attack Squadron 542
Marine Air Group 16 (-) (Reinforced)
    Marine Aircraft Logistics Squadron 16 (-)
    Detachment/Marine Aircraft Logistics Squadron 26
    Marine Medium Helicopter Squadron 263
    Marine Heavy Helicopter Squadron 462
    Marine Heavy Helicopter Squadron 465
Marine Air Group 29 (-) (Reinforced)
    Marine Aircraft Logistics Squadron 29 (-)
    Marine Medium Helicopter Squadron 162
    Marine Medium Helicopter Squadron 365 (-)
    Marine Heavy Helicopter Squadron 464
    Marine Light Attack Helicopter Squadron 269 (-)
Marine Air Control Group 38 (-) (Reinforced)
    Air Traffic Control Detachment B/Marine Tactical Air Command Squadron
    Marine Air Control Squadron 1 (Reinforced)
    Marine Air Wing Communications Squadron 38 (Reinforced)
    Marine Tactical Air Command Squadron 38
    Marine Air Support Squadron 1
    Marine Air Support Squadron 3 (Reinforced)
    2nd Low Altitude Air Defense Battalion (-)
    3rd Low Altitude Air Defense Battalion
    Marine Unmanned Aerial Vehicle Squadron 1
    Marine Unmanned Aerial Vehicle Squadron 2
Marine Wing Support Group 37 (-) (Reinforced)
    Marine Wing Support Squadron 271 (Fixed Wing)
    Marine Wing Support Squadron 272 (Rotary Wing)
    Marine Wing Support Squadron 371 (Fixed Wing)
    Marine Wing Support Squadron 372 (Rotary Wing)
Marine Air Group 39 (-) (Reinforced)
    Marine Aircraft Logistics Squadron 39 (-)

Marine Light Attack Helicopter Squadron 169
Marine Light Attack Helicopter Squadron 267
Marine Medium Helicopter Squadron 268
Marine Medium Helicopter Squadron 364
Marine Light Attack Helicopter Squadron 369
498th Medical Co (Air Ambulance) (TACON) (USA)
I MEF Engineer Group
30th Naval Construction Regiment
Naval Mobile Construction Battalion 5
Naval Mobile Construction Battalion 74
Naval Mobile Construction Battalion 133
Naval Mobile Construction Battalion 4
Naval Construction Force Support Unit 2 (-)
Underwater Construction Team 2 Air Detachment
22nd Naval Construction Regiment
HHC/265th Engineer Group (USA)
130th Engineer Battalion (Corps Wheeled) (USA)
168th Engineer Co (Panel Bridge) (Attached) (USA)
299th Engineer Co (Medium Ribbon Bridge) (Attached) (USA)
459th Engineer Co (Medium Ribbon Bridge) (Attached) (USA)
478th Engineer Battalion (Combat Mechanized) (USA)
SPO/Facilities Engineer Support Team-M (Return of Services) (DS) (USA)
2nd Marine Expeditionary Brigade (TF *Tarawa*)
2nd Marine Expeditionary Brigade Command Element
Detachment, II Marine Helicopter Group
II MEF Liaison Element
Co C, 4th Recon Battalion, 4th MARDIV
Det/4th Civil Affairs Group
1 x Co Free Iraqi Forces
2nd Marine Regiment (-) (Reinforced) (OPCON) (Regimental Combat Team 2)
HQ Co
1st Battalion, 2nd Marine Regiment
3rd Battalion, 2nd Marine Regiment
2nd Battalion, 8th Marine Regiment
1st Battalion, 10th Marine Regiment (155T)
Co A, 2nd Combat Engineer Battalion
Co A, 8th Tank Battalion
Co C, 2nd Light Armored Recon Battalion
Co A, 2nd Assault Amphibian Battalion
Co A, 2nd Recon Battalion (Reinforced)
Combat Service Support Battalion 22 (AMPHIB EAST)
2 x Platoons/413th Chemical Co (Smoke/Decon) (USA)
Follow On Forces
3rd Battalion, 23rd Marine Regiment
4th Combat Engineer Battalion (-)

4th Light Armored Recon Battalion (-)
2nd Battalion, 25th Marine Regiment
Truck Co, 4th MARDIV
1st (United Kingdom) Armoured Division (-) (Reinforced)[8]
    7th Armoured Brigade (OPCON)
        HQ and Signals Squadron
        1st Battalion, The Black Watch
        1st Battalion, The Royal Regiment of Fusiliers
        The Royal Scots Dragoon Guards
        2nd Royal Tank Regiment
        3rd Regiment, Royal Horse Artillery
        32nd Armoured Engineer Regiment
    16th Air Assault Brigade (Army/Royal Air Force) (OPCON)
        HQ and Signals Squadron
        1st Battalion, The Parachute Regiment
        3rd Battalion, The Parachute Regiment
        1st Battalion, The Royal Irish Regiment
        7th Parachute Regiment, Royal Horse Artillery
    3rd Commando Brigade (-) (OPCON)
        HQ and Signals Squadron
        40 Commando Group
        42 Commando Group
        29 Commando Regiment, Royal Artillery
    Direct Support Team/402nd Civil Affairs Battalion (USA)
    Elements/358th Civil Affairs Brigade (USA)
1st Force Service Support Group (FSSG) (-) (Reinforced)
    Detachment /HQSVC Battalion
    1st Dental Battalion
    4th FSSG Forward (West)
    Combat Service Support Group 11
        HQ/Combat Service Support Group 11
        Combat Service Support Battalion 10
            Combat Service Support Company 111
            Combat Service Support Company 115
            Combat Service Support Company 117
    Combat Service Support Group 13
        HQ/4th Landing Support Battalion
        Combat Service Support Company 133
        Combat Service Support Company 134
        Combat Service Support Company 135
    Combat Service Support Group 14
        4th Supply Battalion (-)
    Combat Service Support Group 15
        1st Supply Battalion (-)
        Combat Service Support Battalion 12

        Combat Service Support Battalion 18
        Health Services Battalion
        Combat Service Support Battalion 22
        Combat Service Support Company 151
    555th Maintenance Co (Patriot DS) (USA)
    Transportation Support Group
        1st Transportation Support Battalion (-)
        6th Motor Transport Battalion, 4th FSSG
        7th Engineer Support Battalion (-) (Reinforced)
        6th Engineer Support Battalion (-) (Reinforced), 4th FSSG
        8th Engineer Support Battalion (-) (Reinforced), 2nd FSSG
    716th Military Police Battalion (USA)
        HHD/716th Military Police Bn
        194th Military Police Co (Combat Support) (USA)
        977th Military Police Co (Combat Support) (USA)
        988th Military Police Co (Combat Support) (USA)
    101st Chemical Co (-) (Smoke/Decon) (OPCON) (USA)
    1/51st Chemical Co (Smoke/Decon) (OPCON) (USA)
    378th Corps Support Battalion (USA)
        HHD/378th Corps Support Bn (USA)
        727th Transportation Co (Medium Truck Palletized Load System) (USA)
        777th Maintenance Co (DS) (USA)
        319th Transportation Co (-) (Petroleum) (Attached) (USA)
        Det 1/757th Transportation Battalion (Rail) (Attached) (USA)
    Preventative Med-Mobile Medical Augmentation Readiness Team 2 (TACON) (USA)
    Forward Support MEDEVAC Team (USA)

V Corps (OPCON)

Main CP
    86th Signal Battalion (Theater Tactical Support)
        HHC/86th Signal Bn
        B/86th Signal Bn (Command Support)
        C/86th Signal Bn (Minor Unit Support)
    1 x TSC-85 TACSAT Terminal (OPCON)
    2 x TSC-93C TACSAT Terminal (OPCON)
    59th Military Police Co (for duty as Joint Visitors Bureau)
    Army Space Support Team 1/1st Space Battalion (DS) (USA)
    4th Air Support Operations Group (+) (USAF)
        2nd Air Support Operations Squadron (-) (USAF)
        74th Air Support Operations Squadron (-) (USAF)
    7th Joint Task Force (-) (7th Army Reserve Command)
Rear CP
    A/86th Signal Battalion (Command Support)
    280th Rear Operation Center (Attached)

10th Logistics Planning Augmentation Team
V Corps Special Troops Battalion (Provisional)
    HHC/V Corps
        2-325th Infantry (-) (OPCON)
        C/2-6th Infantry, 3rd Brigade, 1st Armored Div (CP Security)
        Staff Engineer Section/V Corps
        308th Civil Affairs Brigade (-) (OPCON)
            432nd Civil Affairs Battalion (-)
            490th Civil Affairs Battalion (-) (OPCON)
        319th Mobile Public Affairs Detachment (OPCON)
        22nd Mobile Public Affairs Detachment (-) (ADCON)
        350th Mobile Public Affairs Detachment
        114th Chaplain Team (Attached)
        115th Chaplain Detachment (Attached)
    450th Chemical Battalion
        59th Chemical Co (Smoke/Decon) (Attached) (-), 10th Mtn Div (Light
Infantry)
            1/59th Chemical (Smoke/Decon)
            2/59th Chemical (Smoke/Decon)
        7th Chemical Co (Bio Detection and Identification System) (-)
            3/7th Chemical Co (Bio Detection and Identification System)
            5/7th Chemical Co (Bio Detection and Identification System)
        371st Chemical Co (Smoke/Decon)
            3/51st Chemical Co (Recon)
            3/59th Chemical (Smoke/Decon)
            4/59th Chemical (Smoke/Decon)
            6/68th Chemical Co (Smoke) (Attached), 1st Cavalry Division
        51st Chemical Co (Recon) (- 1st and 3rd Platoons) (Attached)
        314th Chemical Co (Smoke/Decon)
    Terrain Squad/320th Engineer Co (Topographic) (-)/130th Engineer Brigade
    Tactical Interrogation Team (GS) (OPCON)
    Interrogation/Debriefing Team/513th Military Intelligence Brigade (TACON)
    Battle Damage Assessment Team (Attached)
    707th Ordnance Co (Explosive Ordnance Disposal)
    9th Psychological Operations Battalion (OPCON) (-)
        346th Tactical Psychological Operations Co (-)
        Special Operations Media Support Team B/3rd Psychological Operations
Battalion
    76th Adjutant General Band
    396th Adjutant General Co (Postal)
    2 x Co/Area Teams (Free Iraqi Forces)
3rd Infantry Division (Attached)
    HHC/3rd ID
    3rd Rear Operations Center (Division)
    2nd Marine Liaison Element (Note: On 13 July 2003, the 2nd Marine Liaison

Element was redesignated the 2nd Air and Naval Gunfire Liaison Company, its former designation)

3-7th Cavalry

    A/1-9th Field Artillery (155SP) (DS)

3rd Division Artillery (DIVARTY)

    1-39th Field Artillery (MLRS/TA) (GS) (+)

        C/3-13th Field Artillery (MLRS), 214th Field Artillery Brigade (Attached)

    Small Extension Node G53/C/123rd Signal Battalion

    Small Extension Node G75/C/123rd Signal Battalion

    Tactical Air Control Party/15th Air Support Operations Squadron

1-3rd Air Defense Artillery (OPCON)

3rd Engineer Brigade

    937th Engineer Group (Combat) (DS)

        94th Engineer Battalion (Combat Heavy) (DS) (-)

        C/54th Engineer Battalion (Corps Mech) (DS)

        535th Engineer Co (Combat Support Equip) (DS)

        652nd Engineer Co (Multirole Bridge Co) (DS)

        671st Engineer Co (Medium ribbon Bridge) (DS)

        814th Engineer Co (Multirole Bridge Co)

        336th Engineer Det (Fire Fighting)

        4 x D9 Bulldozers

103rd Military Intelligence Battalion (-)

    HHOC/103rd Military Intelligence Bn

    Analysis & Control Elmt/HHOC/103rd Military Intelligence Bn (OPCON to G2)

    Tactical HUMINT Team 48/325th Military Intelligence Bn (OPCON to G2)

    D/103rd Military Intelligence Bn (-)

        3/D/103rd Military Intelligence Bn

    Tactical HUMINT Team 7/165th Military Intelligence Bn (TACON) (GS)

    Tactical HUMINT Team 9/165th Military Intelligence Bn (TACON) (GS)

E/51st Infantry/165th Military Intelligence Battalion (Long Range Surveillance-Corps) (Attached)

    Long Range Surveillance Det/311th Military Intelligence Battalion (Attached)

123rd Signal Battalion (-)

    55th Signal Visual Information Co (Combat Camera) (-)

        1st Combat Camera Team

3rd Military Police Company

3rd Military Police Company

50th Public Affairs Detachment (Attached)

C/9th Psychological Operations Battalion

    Deployable Print Production Center Team/3rd Psychological Operations Co

    Tactical PSYOP Detachment 1550/346th Tactical Psychological Operations Co

    Tactical PSYOP Detachment 1560/361st Tactical Psychological Operations Co

315th Tactical PSYOP Co
    Tactical PSYOP Detachment 1270 (-)
    Deployable Print Production Center 3/3rd Tactical Psychological Operations Co (OPCON)
    Tactical PSYOP Detachment/318th Tactical Psychological Operations Co
422nd Civil Affairs Battalion (-) (OPCON)
    B/411th Civil Affairs Bn
1st Brigade, 3rd Infantry Division
    HHC/1st Bde, 3rd ID
    TF 2-7th Infantry
    TF 3-7th Infantry
    3-69th Armor
    C/1st Cavalry (Brigade Recon Troop)
    1-41st Field Artillery (155SP)
    11th Engineer Battalion
    A/103rd Military Intelligence Battalion
        HQ/A/103rd Military Intelligence Bn
        OPS/A/103rd Military Intelligence Bn
        1/D/103rd Military Intelligence (TACON)
        Tactical HUMINT Team 47/325th Military Intelligence (TACON)
    Small Extension Node G21/A/123rd Signal Battalion
    Small Extension Node G22/A/123rd Signal Battalion
    3rd Forward Support Battalion (Attached)
2nd Brigade, 3rd Infantry Division
    HHC/2nd Bde, 3rd ID
    TF 3-15th Infantry
    TF 1-64th Armor
    TF 4-64th Armor
    E/9th Cavalry (Brigade Recon Troop)
    1-9th Field Artillery (155SP) (-)
    10th Engineer Battalion (-)
        148th Engineer Detachment (Topographic)
    2/3rd Military Police Co
    92nd Chemical Co
    B/103rd Military Intelligence Battalion (-)
        HQ/B/103rd Military Intelligence Bn
        OPS/B/103rd Military Intelligence Bn
        2/D/103rd Military Intelligence Bn (TACON)
        Tactical HUMINT Team 46/325th Military Intelligence Bn (TACON)
    B/51st Signal Battalion (Contingency Area Support)
    26th Forward Support Battalion
    15th Air Support Operations Squadron (USAF)
3rd Brigade, 3rd Infantry Division
    HHC/3rd Bde, 3rd ID

TF 1-15th Infantry
TF 1-30th Infantry
TF 2-69th Armor
1-10th Field Artillery (155SP)
     D/10th Cavalry (Brigade Recon Troop) (OPCON)
121st Engineer Battalion (Combat Heavy)
317th Engineer Battalion (Combat Heavy)
C/103rd Military Intelligence Battalion
C/123rd Signal Battalion
203rd Forward Support Battalion
17th Air Support Operations Squadron

4th Brigade, 3rd Infantry Division (-)
1-3rd Aviation (AH-64D) (-)
Team A/2-3rd Aviation (UH-60) (OPCON)
D/1-58th Aviation (Air Traffic Service) (OPCON)
603rd Aviation Support Battalion

TF IRON (OPCON from 101st Abn Div)
HHC/3-187th Infantry
A/3-187th Infantry
B/3-187th Infantry
C/3-187th Infantry
D/2-187th Infantry
3/Combat Observation and Lasing Team/3-320th Field Artillery
3/C/2-44th Air Defense Artillery
3/C/326th Engineer Battalion (+)
     Squad/1/C/326th Engineer Bn
Ground Surveillance Radar Team/311th Military Intelligence Battalion
Team/Tactical Air Control Party/19th Air Support Operations Squadron (USAF)
Tactical PSYOP Team 1093/9th Psychological Operations Battalion
Team/55th Signal Visual Information Co (Combat Camera)
431st Civil Affairs Battalion (-) (OPCON)

3rd Division Support Command (DISCOM) (-)
HHC/3rd ID DISCOM
703rd Main Support Battalion
566th Medical Co (Area Support) (Attached) (DS)
126th Medical Detachment (Forward Surgical Team)
555th Medical Detachment (Forward Surgical Team)
745th Medical Detachment (Forward Surgical Team)

ADVON/1-13th Armor/3rd Brigade, 1st Armored Division

4th Infantry Division (OPCON)
HHC/4th ID
Division Assault/Tactical Command Post
Intel Support Element/ACE/104th Military Intelligence Battalion

Shadow Tactical Unmanned Aerial Vehicle/B/104th Military Intelligence Battalion

Tactical UAV Logistics Support Team Contractors

4/4th Military Police Co

Terrain Team /610th Engineer Detachment

Element/C/1-8th Infantry (Force Protection)

Division Main CP

11th Air Support Operations Squadron (-) (USAF)

3rd Weather Squadron (-) (USAF)

4th Adjutant General Band

610th Engineer Detachment (Terrain) (-)

1308th Engineer Detachment (Topographic) (-)

Vertical Construction Squad/223rd Engineer Battalion (Combat Heavy)

362nd Tactical Psychological Operations Co (-)

HQ/362nd Tactical Psychological Operations Co

Product Development Detachment/362nd Tactical PSYOP Co

Tactical PSYOP Team 1671/Tac PSYOP Detachment 1670/362nd Tactical Psychological Operations Co

JWICS Mobile Intelligence Communications System 5

5/4th Military Police Co

Army Space Support Team 14, 1st Space Battalion (DS) (USA)

Division Support Element

4th Rear Operations Center

978th Military Police Co (Combat Support)

6 x Contractors

4th ID Division Artillery

HHB/4th ID DIVARTY

A/3-16th Field Artillery (TF LOG)

2-20th Field Artillery (MLRS/TA) (-)

HSB/2-20th Field Artillery

A/2-20th Field Artillery (MLRS)

B/2-20th Field Artillery (MLRS)

C/2-20th Field Artillery (Target Acquisition, 2 x Q37) (-)

6-27th Field Artillery Battalion (MLRS), 75th Field Artillery Brigade (Attached)

2/231st Field Artillery Detachment (Target Acquisition)

Tactical HUMINT Team 37/D/104th Military Intelligence Battalion

Tactical PSYOP Team 1681/Tac PSYOP Detachment 1680/362nd Tactical Psychological Operations Co

Team 10/418th Civil Affairs Battalion

1-44th Air Defense Artillery (-)

HHB/1-44th Air Defense Artillery

Assault CP Sentinel Radar/1-44th Air Defense Artillery

D/1-44th Air Defense Artillery (-)
3/C/1-44th Air Defense Artillery (-)
2nd Chemical Battalion (Attached)
HHD/2nd Chemical Bn
11th Chemical Co (Smoke/Decon)
46th Chemical Co (Mech Smoke) (-)
1/3/44th Chemical Co (NBC Recon)
555th Engineer Group (Combat) (Attached)
HHC/555th Engineer Group
14th Engineer Battalion (Combat Wheeled) (-)
HHC/14th Engineer Bn
B/14th Engineer Bn
223rd Engineer Battalion (Combat Heavy) (-)
167th Engineer Co (Assault Float Bridge)
200th Engineer Co (Multirole Bridge Co)
285th Engineer Co (Combat Support Equip) (-)
HQ and Maintenance Platoons/285th Engineer Co
957th Engineer Co (Assault Float Bridge)
1041st Engineer Co (Assault Float Bridge)
938th Engineer Team (Fire Fighting) (DS)
Facilities Engineer Detachment A (-) (OPCON)
104th Military Intelligence Battalion (-)
HHOC/104th Military Intelligence Bn
4 x Tactical HUMINT Team/205th Military Intelligence Brigade
A/15th Military Intelligence Bn (Hunter Unmanned Aerial Vehicle)
4th Military Police Co (-)
2/4th Military Police Co
3/4th Military Police Co
43rd Military Police Detachment (Division Support Criminal Investigation)
124th Signal Battalion (Mobile Subscriber Equipment) (-)
HHC/124th Signal Bn
A/124th Signal Bn
B/124th Signal Bn (-)
C/124th Signal Bn (-)
A/16th Signal Bn
534th Signal Co (-) (Area)
230th Finance Battalion (- element with 336th Theater Finance Command))
350th Mobile Public Affairs Det
502nd Personnel Service Battalion
2/449th Adjutant General Co (Postal)
1/795th Adjutant General Co (Postal)
1/834th Adjutant General Co (Postal)
418th Civil Affairs Battalion (-)
HHC/418th Civil Affairs Bn
General Support Co/418th Civil Affairs Bn

1st Brigade, 4th Infantry Division
 HHC/1st Bde/4th ID
 Element/11th ASOC (USAF)
 G/10th Cavalry (FOX)
 TF 1-8th Infantry (Attached from 3rd Brigade)
  B/4th Engineer Battalion (-)
  Maintenance Support Team/1-8th Infantry
 TF 1-22nd Infantry
 TF 1-66th Armor (- BALAD Force Protection)
 3-66th AR
 4-42nd Field Artillery (155 SP)
  1/C/2-20th Field Artillery (Target Acquisition) (Q36)
  5/C/2-20th Field Artillery (Target Acquisition) (Q37) (TACON)
 A/1-44th Air Defense Artillery (-)
  3/A/1-44th Air Defense Artillery (DS)
  2/1/Sentinal Radar/HHB/1-44th Air Defense Artillery (DS)
 44th Chemical Co (Recon/Decon) (-)
  2/G/1-10th Cavalry (NBC Recon)
  1/44th Chemical Co (Decon)
  2/46th Chemical Co (Mech Smoke)
  4/46th Chemical Co (Mech Smoke)
 5th Engineer Battalion (Combat Mech) (-) (Attached)
  HHC/5th Engineer Bn
  B/5th Engineer Bn
  C/5th Engineer Bn
 299th Engineer Battalion (-)
  HHC/299th Engineer Bn
  B/299th Engineer Bn
  C/299th Engineer Bn
  A/14th Engineer Bn (Combat Wheeled) (DS)
  1/285th Engineer Co (Combat Support Equip)
  Vertical Construction Capability/223rd Engineer Bn (Combat Heavy)
 A/104th Military Intelligence Battalion (+)
  Tactical HUMINT Team 24/D/104th Military Intelligence Bn
  Tactical HUMINT Team 32/D/104th Military Intelligence Bn
  4/D/104th Military Intelligence Bn (TACON)
 1/4th Military Police Co
 1670th Tactical PSYOP Det/362nd Tactical Psychological Operations Co (-)
  Tactical PSYOP Team 1671/1670th Tactical Psychological
 Operations Det
  Tactical PSYOP Team 1672/1670th Tactical Psychological
 Operations Det
 Teams 1, 5, 7/418th Civil Affairs Bn
 4th Forward Support Battalion
  HHC/4th Forward Support Bn

    D/4th Forward Support Bn
    240th Forward Surgical Team (DS)
    1 x Forward Support MEDEVAC Team/571st Medical Co (Air Ambulance)
   Terrain Team/610th Engineer Detachment
  2nd Brigade, 4th Infantry Division
   HHC/2nd Bde/4th ID
   Element/11th Air Support Operations Squadron (USAF)
   H/10th Cavalry (Brigade Recon Troop)
   2-8th Infantry
   1-67th Armor
   3-67th Armor
   3-16th Field Artillery (155 SP)
    1/231st Field Artillery Detachment (Target Acquisition) (Q37)
    2/C/2-20th Field Artillery (Target Acquisition) (Q36)
   B/1-44th Air Defense Artillery
    1/B/1-44th Air Defense Artillery
    2/B/1-44th Air Defense Artillery
    1/A/1-44th Air Defense Artillery
    2/A/1-44th Air Defense Artillery
    2/3/Sentinel Radar/1-44th Air Defense Artillery
   588th Engineer Battalion
    2/285th Engineer Co (Combat Support Equip)
   B/104th Military Intelligence Battalion (+)
    Tactical Unmanned Aerial Vehicle/B/104th Military Intelligence Bn
    Tactical Unmanned Aerial Vehicle Contract Log Support Team
    3/D/104th Military Intelligence Bn
    Tactical HUMINT Team 33/D/104th Military Intelligence Bn
    Tactical HUMINT Team 27/205th Military Intelligence Brigade
   1/G/1-10th Cavalry (NBC Recon)
   1/46th Chemical Co (Mech Smoke)
   Team 2/55th Signal Visual Information Co (Combat Camera)
   Terrain Team/610th Engineer Detachment (Terrain)
   1690th Tactical PSYOP Det/362nd Tactical Psychological Operations Co
   Teams 2, 6, 8/418th Civil Affairs Battalion
   204th Forward Support Battalion
    1982nd Medical Detachment (Forward Surgical Team) (DS)
    1 x Forward Support MEDEVAC Team/571st Medical Co (Air Ambulance)
  3rd Brigade, 4th Infantry Division
   HHC/3rd Bde/4th ID
   Element/13th Air Support Operations Squadron (USAF)
   B/9th Cavalry (Brigade Recon Troop)
   TF 1-12th Infantry
    C/4th Engineer Battalion

Tactical PSYOP Team 221/362nd Tactical Psychological Operations Co (-) (TACON)

Team A/418th Civil Affairs Battalion (TACON)

TF 1-68th AR

A/4th Engineer Battalion (-)

1/A/4th Engineer Bn (+)

1 x M113A2/2/A/4th Engineer Bn

C/3-29th Field Artillery (155SP) (TACON)

3-29th Field Artillery (155 SP) (-)

HSB/3-29th Field Artillery

A/3-29th Field Artillery

B/3-29th Field Artillery

3/C/2-20th Field Artillery (Target Acquisition) (Q36)

2/3/C/1-44th Air Defense Artillery

4th Engineer Battalion (-)

HHC/4th Engineer Bn

A/4th Engineer Bn (-)

B/14th Engineer Bn (-)

3/285th Engineer Co (Combat Support Equip)

Vertical Construction Capability/223rd Engineer Bn (Combat Heavy)

C/1-44th Air Defense Artillery (-)

1/Sentinel Radar/HHB/1-44th Air Defense Artillery (TACON)

3/46th Chemical Co (Mech Smoke)

2/4/44th Chemical Co (Recon)

C/104th Military Intelligence Battalion (+)

2/D/104th Military Intelligence Bn

Tactical HUMINT Team 33/D/104th Military Intelligence Bn

Tactical HUMINT Team 34/D/104th Military Intelligence Bn

6 x Contractors

Teams 3 & 9/418th Civil Affairs Battalion

Tactical PSYOP Detachment 1680/362nd Tactical Psychological Operations Co (-)

Team 3/55th Signal Visual Information Co (Combat Camera)

64th Forward Support Battalion

2/A/4th Engineer Battalion (+)

915th Medical Detachment (Forward Surgical Team)

1 x Forward Support MEDEVAC Team/571st Medical Co (Air Ambulance)

Terrain Team/610th Engineer Detachment

4th Brigade, 4th Infantry Division

HHC/4th Bde

F/1-58th Aviation (Air Traffic Service)

Element/11th Air Support Operations Squadron (USAF)

Element/3rd Weather Squadron (-)

1-4th Aviation (AH-64D) (-)

HHC/1-4th Aviation
A/1-4th Aviation (- Elements for Tactical Combat Force and Reserve)
B/1-4th Aviation
C/1-4th Aviation
D/1- 4th Aviation (Aviation Unit Maintenance)
2-4th Aviation (UH-60) (General Support Aviation) (-)
1-10th Cavalry (OH-58D, M3A2)
Element/11th Air Support Operations Squadron (USAF)
3/G/1-10th Cavalry (NBC Recon)
A/5th Engineer Battalion
Remote Vehicle Team/TUAV/B/104th Military Intelligence Battalion
Tactical HUMINT Team 36/D/104th Military Intelligence Battalion
Team 4/418th Civil Affairs Battalion
1-17th Field Artillery (155 SP)
2/C/2-20th Field Artillery (Target Acquisition) (Q36)
Tactical PSYOP Team 623/362nd Tac Psychological Operations Co (-)

E/704th Div Support Element (-)
Tactical Maintenance Team/E/704th Main Support Battalion
3/D/1-44th Air Defense Artillery
3/44th Chemical Co (Recon/Decon)
Terrain Team/610th Engineer Detachment (Terrain)
Tactical HUMINT Team 5/D/104th Military Intelligence Battalion
Control Ground Station 3/ACE/104th Military Intelligence Battalion
Secure Mobile Anti-jam Reliable Tactical Terminal/C/124th Signal Battalion
3 x Small Extension Node Teams/B/124th Signal Battalion
Liaison Team/418th Civil Affairs Battalion
404th Aviation Support Battalion
9 x Contractors
4th Division Support Command (DISCOM)
HHC/4th ID DISCOM
704th Main Support Battalion (-)
HHD/704th Main Support Bn
A/704th Main Support Bn
B/704th Main Support Bn
C/704th Main Support Bn
68th Quartermaster Co (Water)
95th Maintenance Co (Test, Measurement, Diagnostic Equip)
Logistics Support Element (USMC Forward)
Logistics Support Element (Army Materiel Command)
101st Airborne Division (Air Assault) (-) (OPCON)
Assault Command Post/101st Abn Div
Force Entry Switch Team/B/501st Signal Battalion
Multichannel TACSAT/C/501st Signal Battalion
Direct Intelligence Support Element/ACE/HSC/311th MI

Control Ground Station Team 5/5/D/311th MI
DMAIN/101st Abn Div
 101st Adjutant General Band
 63rd Chemical Co (Smoke) (- line platoons to maneuver brigades)
  HQ Platoon/63rd Chemical Co
 326th Engineer Battalion (Combat) (-)
  HHC/326th Engineer Bn
   938th Engineer Team (Fire Fighting)
   275th Ordnance Detachment (Explosive Ordnance Disposal) (-)
  887th Engineer Co (Light Equipment) (-)
 37th Engineer Battalion (Combat) (Attached)
 2 x D9 Bulldozers
 311th Military Intelligence Battalion (-) (Combat Electronic Warfare Intelligence)
  Analysis and Control Element/HHSC/311th Military Intelligence Bn (-)
  HHSC/311th Military Intelligence Bn (-)
  D/311th Military Intelligence Bn (-)
  Long Range Surveillance Det/311th Military Intelligence Bn
  2 x Counterintelligence/HUMINT Team A/311th Military Intelligence Bn
 Special Forces Liaison Element/1 Special Forces Group (Airborne) (Attached)
 318th Tactical Psychological Operations Co (-)
 501st Signal Battalion (-)
  HHC/501st Signal Bn (-)
  Force Entry Switch/A/501st Signal Bn (-)
  Small Extension Node/A/501st Signal Bn
  Multichannel TACSAT/C/501st Signal Bn
  C/501st Signal Bn (-)
 19th Air Support Operations Squadron (-) (USAF)
 2 x CAT-A Teams/431st Civil Affairs Battalion
DREAR/101st Abn Div
 C/3-101st Aviation (AH-64D)
 Light Airfield Repair Package/887th Engineer Battalion (-)
 Det/D/311th Military Intelligence Battalion (+)
  Tactical HUMINT Team/1/205th Military Intelligence Bn
  Tactical HUMINT Team/2/205th Military Intelligence Bn
 System Hardware Avail & Reliability Calculator/C/501st Signal Battalion
 101st Military Police Co
  31st Military Police Det (CID Division Support Element)
 101st Soldier Support Battalion
 27th Support Center (Rear Area Operations Center)
 1st Rear Operations Center (Division)

> 51st Support Center (Rear Area Operations Center)
> 101st Rear Operations Center (Division)
> 610th Movement Control Team (Division Support)
> 613th Movement Control Team (Division Support)
> 632nd Movement Control Team (Regulating)
> B/431st Civil Affairs Battalion (-) (OPCON)

F/51st Infantry (Long Range Surveillance)/519th Military Intelligence Battalion
2-44th Air Defense Artillery (-)

> HHB/2-44th Air Defense Artillery (-)
>> 1/1/HHB/2-44th Air Defense Artillery
>> 3/D/2-44th Air Defense Artillery
> C/2-320th Field Artillery (105T)

101st Finance Battalion (-)
101st Personnel Services Battalion (DS)

> HHC Platoon/351st Adjutant General Co (Postal)
> 2/834th Postal Services Platoon
> 1/841st Postal Services Platoon

40th Public Affairs Detachment (OPCON)
354th Civil Affairs Brigade (-) (OPCON)
2nd Brigade, 101st Abn Div

> HHC/2nd Bde (-) 101st Abn Div
> 1-502nd Infantry (-)
>> HHC/1-502nd Infantry
>> A/1-502nd Infantry
>> C/1-502nd Infantry
>> D/1-502nd Infantry
> 2-502nd Infantry
> 3-502nd Infantry
> 2-17th Cavalry (OH-58D) (-) (OPCON)
> TF 2-70th Armor (-), 3d Brigade, 1st Armored Div (OPCON)
>> HHC/2-70th Armor
>> A/2-70th Armor
>> B/2-70th Armor
>> C/1-41st Infantry
>> B/1-502nd Infantry
> 2-101st Aviation (AH-64D) (OPCON)
> 1-320th Field Artillery (105T) (DS)
> B/326th Engineer Battalion (+)
>> 3/A/326th Engineer Bn
>> Team 2/275th Ordnance Detachment (Explosive Ordnance Disposal)
>> Team 3/275th Ordnance Detachment (Explosive Ordnance Disposal)
>> 1 x D9 Dozer
> B/2-44th Air Defense Artillery
>> 3/1/Sentinal Radar/HHB/2-44th Air Defense Artillery
> B/311th Military Intelligence Battalion (+)

Ground Surveillance Systems Platoon/B/311th Military Intelligence Bn (+)

Ground Surveillance Radar Team 2/6/D/311th Military Intelligence Bn

Tactical HUMINT Team 1/B/311th Military Intelligence Bn

Tactical HUMINT Team 2/B/311th Military Intelligence Bn

Tactical HUMINT Team 3/4/D/311th Military Intelligence Bn

Collection and Jamming/D/311th Military Intelligence Bn

Analysis and Control Team /B/311th Military Intelligence Bn

Retransmission Team 3/D/311th Military Intelligence Bn

Teams 1, 2, 3, 5/Long Range Surveillance/311th Military Intelligence Bn

2/63rd Chemical Co (Smoke)

526th Forward Support Battalion

160th Forward Support Team

B/801st Main Support Battalion (-)

Water Team/A/801st Main Support Battalion

Tactical Air Control Party/19th Air Support Operations Squadron (-) (USAF)

Force Entry Switch/B/501st Signal Battalion

Small Extension Node/B/501st Signal Battalion

Multichannel TACSAT/C/501st Signal Battalion

B/431 Civil Affairs Battalion

HQ Team/B/431st Civil Affairs Bn

GS Team 3/B/431st Civil Affairs Bn

Free Iraqi Forces/3/B/431st Civil Affairs Bn

GS Team 4/B/431st Civil Affairs Bn

Free Iraqi Forces/3/B/431st Civil Affairs Bn

GS Team 7/B/431st Civil Affairs Bn

GS Team 8/B/431st Civil Affairs Bn

3rd Brigade, 101st Abn Div (TF IRON)

2-327th Infantry

3/63rd Chemical Co (Smoke)

3-320th Field Artillery (105T) (DS)

C/1-377th Field Artillery (-) (155T) (DS)

3/C/2-44th Air Defense Artillery

3/Sentinel Radar/HHB/2-44th Air Defense Artillery

3/C/326th Engineer Battalion

3/3/887th Engineer Bn

C/311th Military Intelligence Battalion

1/C/311th Military Intelligence Bn

Ground Surveillance Systems Team 4/6/D/311th Military Intelligence Bn

Ground Surveillance Systems Team 5/6/D/311th Military Intelligence Bn

Tactical HUMINT Team 1/D/311th Military Intelligence Bn

3/Team/B/431st Civil Affairs Bn
Free Iraqi Forces/3/ Team/B/431st Civil Affairs Bn
626th Forward Support Battalion
    Water Team/A/801st Main Support Bn
    Elements/801st Main Support Bn (-)
    E/801st Main Support Bn
    Team/1/50th Medical Co (Air Ambulance)
TF RAKKASAN
    HHC/3rd Brigade (-)
    C/326th Engineer Battalion (-)
    Force Entry Switch/C/501st Signal Battalion
    Small Extension Node/C/501st Signal Battalion
    6/Team/B/431st Civil Affairs Battalion
    Free Iraqi Forces/6/B/431st Civil Affairs Battalion
    TF RAIDER 2-187th Infantry (-)
        HHC/2-187th Infantry
        A/2-187th Infantry
        D/2-187th Infantry
        2/C/2-44th Air Defense Artillery (-)
        2/C/326th Engineer Bn (+)
        1/3/877th Engineer Bn (-)
        102nd Quartermaster Co (Petroleum Supply)
    TF LEADER 1-187th Infantry (-)
        HHC/1-187th Infantry
        A/1-187th Infantry
        D/1-187th Infantry
        1/C/2-44th Air Defense Artillery (-)
        1/C/326th Engineer Bn
        1/C/2-44th Air Defense Artillery (-)
        2/1/Sentinel Radar/HHB/2-44th
2/C/326th Engineer Battalion
    1/3/877th Engineer Bn (-)
Team/2-3 Det/318th Public Affairs Det
101st Movement Control Team
Team/801st Main Support Battalion (-)
101st Aviation Brigade
    HHC/101st Aviation Bde
    Tactical Air Control Party/19th Air Support Operations Squadron (-) (USAF)
    Weather Team/19th Air Support Operations Squadron (USAF)
    1-101st Aviation (AH-64D)
    3-101st Aviation (AH-64D)
    6-101st Aviation (UH-60)
        Pathfinder Det
    C/8-101st Aviation (AVIM)
    Small Extension Node/A/501st Signal Battalion

Eagle-Intel/Analysis and Control Element/HHSC/311th Military Intelligence Battalion
      Common Ground Station Team 3
   1/D/2-44th Air Defense Artillery
   4/D/2-187th Infantry (Attached)
159th Aviation Brigade
   HHC/159th Aviation Bde
   Tactical Air Control Party/19th Air Support Operations Squadron (-) (USAF)
   4-101st Aviation (UH-60)
   5-101st Aviation (UH-60)
   7-101st Aviation (CH-47) (-)
      A/7-101st Aviation
      B/7-101st Aviation
   9-101st Aviation (UH-60)
   50th Medical Co (Air Ambulance) (-) (DS)
   D/2-44th Air Defense Artillery (-)
      1/2/Sentinel Radar/HHB/2-44th Air Defense Artillery
   B/8-101st AVIM
   Small Extension Node/A/501st Signal Battalion
   Weather Det/19th Air Support Operations Squadron (USAF)
TF DESTINY (Forward Arming and Refueling Point SHELL)
   HHC/101st Aviation Bde (-)
   Tactical CP/1-101st AV
      Class III and V Platoon/1-101st Aviation (+)
      D/1-101st Aviation (Aviation Unit Maintenance)
   Tactical CP /2-101st Aviation
      Class III and V Platoon/1-101st Aviation (+)
      D/2-101st Aviation (Aviation Unit Maintenance)
   Tactical CP /3-101st Aviation
      Class III and V Platoon/1-101st Aviation (+)
      D/3-101st Aviation (Aviation Unit Maintenance)
   Tactical CP /2-17th Cavalry
      Class III and V Platoon/2-17th Cavalry
      D/2-17th Cavalry (Aviation Unit Maintenance)
   Small Extension Node/C/501st Signal Battalion
101st Airborne Division Artillery (-)
   HHB/101st DIVARTY
   1-377th Field Artillery (155T) (- C Battery with 3rd Brigade)
101st Division Support Command (DISCOM)
   HHC/Materiel Management Center DISCOM (-)
   801st Main Support Battalion (-)
      HSC/801st Main Support Bn
      A/801st Main Support Bn (-)
      C/801st Main Support Bn
      591st Medical Log Team

8-101st Aviation (AVIM) (-)

HHC/8-101st Aviation

A/8-101st Aviation

Small Extension Node/B/501st Signal Battalion

129th Adjutant General Co (Postal) (-)

3/129th Postal Services Platoon

4/129th Postal Services Platoon

Tactical PSYOP Detachment 1080/318th Psychological Operations Co

Free Iraqi Forces Company

Elements/1st Armored Division (-) (OPCON)

HHC/3rd Brigade

4-1st Field Artillery Battalion (155SP)

HHB/4-1st Field Artillery

82nd Airborne Division (-)

HHC/82nd Airborne Div (-)

82nd Airborne Division Assault CP

2nd Brigade/82nd Abn Div

HHC/2nd Bde

1-325th Infantry

3-325th Infantry

TF 1-41st Infantry (-), 3d Brigade, 1st Armored Division

A/1-41st Infantry

B/1-41st Infantry

C/2-70th AR

2-319th Field Artillery (105T) (-)

407th Forward Support Battalion (-)

B/307th Engineer Battalion

B/313th Military Intelligence Battalion

B/82nd Signal Battalion

B/3-4th Air Defense Artillery (-)

2/21st Chemical Co (Smoke/Decon)

2/82nd Military Police Co (+)

2/618th Engineer Co

96th Civil Affairs Battalion (Tactical)

Element/301st Psychological Operations Battalion

Team/49th Public Affairs Det

2 x Companies/Area Teams (Free Iraqi Forces)

TF 1-82nd Aviation (-)

A/1-82nd Aviation (+) (OH-58D)

A/1-17th Cavalry (OH-58D)

1st Brigade, 101st Abn Div (OPCON)

HHC/1st Brigade (-), 101st Abn Div

1-327th Infantry

3-327th Infantry (Attached)

2-320th Field Artillery (155T) (DS)

A/326th Engineer Battalion

    Team 1/275th Ordnance Detachment (Explosive Ordnance Disposal)

A/2-44th Air Defense Artillery

    2/2/SENT/HHB/2-44th Air Defense Artillery

A/311th Military Intelligence Battalion (Combat Electronic Warfare and Intelligence) (-)

    Analysis and Control Team-E/A/311th Military Intelligence Bn

    Ground Surveillance Systems Platoon/A/311th Military Intelligence Bn (+)

        Team 1/6/D/311th Military Intelligence Bn (PPS-5D)

        Team 6/6/D/311th Military Intelligence Bn (IREMBASS)

    3/Collection and Jamming/D/311th Military Intelligence Bn

    Ground Surveillance Systems Team 1/D/311th Military Intelligence Bn

    Ground Surveillance Systems Team 6/D/311th Military Intelligence Bn

    Tactical HUMINT Team 1/4/D/311th Military Intelligence Bn

    Tactical HUMINT Team 1/A/311th Military Intelligence Bn

    Tactical HUMINT Team 2/A/311th Military Intelligence Bn

    Retransmission Team 1/D/311th Military Intelligence Bn

426th Forward Support Battalion

    274th Forward Support Team

    Team/1/50th Medical Co (Air Ambulance)

    Water Team/801st Main Support Bn

    1/63rd Chemical Co (Smoke)

Tactical Air Control Party/19th Air Support Operations Squadron (-) (USAF)

Force Entry Switch/A/501st Signal Battalion

Small Extension Node/A/501st Signal Battalion

Tactical PSYOP Detachment 1070/318th Psychological Operations Co

Team 4/B/431st Civil Affairs Battalion

    Free Iraqi Forces/4/Team/B/431st Civil Affairs Bn

82nd Division Support Command (DISCOM)

    HHC/82nd Division Support Command (-)

    782nd Main Support Battalion (-)

    1/1/108th Military Police Co (Combat Support)

    Platoon/8th Ordnance Co (Palletized Load System Ammo)

    330th Movement Control Battalion

        592nd Movement Control Team (Division Support)

    Materiel Management Section/2nd Support Center

    82nd Personnel Services Battalion (DS)

    C/82nd Soldier Support Battalion

313th Military Intelligence Battalion (-)

    D/313th Military Intelligence Bn

    E/313th Military Intelligence Bn (Long Range Surveillance Detachment) (-)

307th Engineer Battalion (-)

618th Engineer Co (Light Equipment) (-)
82nd Signal Battalion (-)
    HHC/82nd Signal Bn (-)
HHB/319th Field Artillery (-)
HHB/3-4th Air Defense Artillery (-)
D/21st Chemical Co (Smoke/Decon)
82nd Military Police Co (-)
301st Psychological Operations Battalion (-)
49th Public Affairs Detachment (-) (OPCON)
82nd Finance Det (DS)
102nd Military History Det (TACON)
14th Air Support Operations Squadron (-) (USAF)
Staff Weather Officer/18th Weather Squadron (USAF)
Operating Location-S/621st Air Mobility Operations Group (USAF)

11th Attack Helicopter Regiment (OPCON)
HHT/11th AHR
2-6th Cavalry (AH-64D)
6-6th Cavalry (AH-64D)
1-227th Aviation (AH-64D), 1st Cavalry Division (Attached)
5-158th Aviation (-) (UH-60)
A/7-159th Aviation (+) (AVIM) (DS)
B/864th Engineer Battalion (Combat Heavy)
Team/55th Signal Visual Information Co (Combat Camera)
Small Extension Node B32/Element/22nd Signal Brigade
Detachment 3/4th Air Support Operations Group (USAF)
633rd Movement Control Team (DS)
Team A/1-66th Armor (BALAD Force Protection) (From 4th ID)
    HQ/A/1-66th Armor
    2/B/1-8th Infantry
    2/A/1-66th Armor
    2/B/4th Engineer Battalion

12th Aviation Brigade (OPCON)
HHC/12th Aviation Bde
TF 5-158th Aviation (Command Aviation) (-)
    B/158th Aviation (UH-60)
    B/159th Aviation (CH-47)
    F/159th Aviation (CH-47)
    A/5-159th Aviation (CH-47) (-)
3-58th Aviation (Air Traffic Service) (-)
    HHC/3-58th Aviation
    D/3-58th Aviation
    F/3-58th Aviation
2 x Aircraft/1-214th Aviation (CH-47) (-) (Attached)
F/106th Aviation (CH-47)
B/7-159th Aviation (-) (AVIM) (DS)

Elements/4th Air Support Operations Group (-) (USAF)
Small Extension Node B61/Element/22nd Signal Brigade
Small Extension Node B76/Element/22nd Signal Brigade
2nd Armored Cavalry Regiment (Light) (-)
    HHT/2nd Armored Cavalry Regiment
    1st Squadron, 2nd Armored Cavalry Regiment (-) (Reception, Staging, Onward Movement, and Integration in Kuwait)
    2nd Squadron, 2nd Armored Cavalry Regiment
        84th Engineer Co
        D/51st Signal Battalion (Contingency Support)
        DS Det/B/411th Civil Affairs Battalion
        Tactical PSYOP Det/361 Psychological Operations Co
        Personnel Det/A/18th Personnel Services Battalion
        1/449th Adjutant General Co (Postal)
    3rd Squadron, 2nd Armored Cavalry Regiment (-) (Reception, Staging, Onward Movement, and Integration in Kuwait)
    Support Squadron, 2nd Armored Cavalry Regiment (-) (Reception, Staging, Onward Movement, and Integration in Kuwait)
3rd Armored Cavalry Regiment
    2-5th Field Artillery (155 SP), 212th Field Artillery Brigade (Attached) (Force Field Artillery Headquarters)
    89th Chemical Co (Smoke/Decon/Recon)
    C/16th Signal Battalion (-)
        Element/313th Signal Co
    54th Engineer Battalion (Corps Mech) (- Company C with 3rd Infantry Division Engineers)
        43rd Engineer Co (Combat)
        248th Engineer Co (Combat Heavy)
    66th Military Intelligence Co (Combat Electronic Warfare and Intelligence)
        Tactical PSYOP Detachment (Loud Speaker)/361st Tac Psychological Operations Co
    A/411th Civil Affairs Battalion
    DS Det/490th Civil Affairs Battalion
    Support Squadron/3rd Armored Cavalry Regiment
        Medical Troop/Support Squadron /3rd Armored Cavalry Regiment
        Maintenance Troop/Support Squadron/3rd Armored Cavalry Regiment
        Supply and Transport Troop/Support Squadron/3rd Armored Cavalry Regiment
        4/502nd Personnel Service Detachment
        3/912th Adjutant General Co (Postal)
    4 x CH-47/12th Aviation Brigade
    6 x UH-60 Medical Evacuation Aircraft/30th Medical Brigade
    1 x TSC-85 TACSAT Terminal (OPCON)
    1 x TSC-93C TACSAT Terminal (OPCON)
    Element/13th Air Support Operations Squadron (-) (USAF)

V Corps Artillery
> HHB (-)/V Corps Artillery
> Small Extension Node/C/501st Signal Battalion
> 17th Field Artillery Brigade (GS to V Corps) (Force Field Artillery HQ for 3 ACR)
>> HHB/17th Field Artillery Bde
>> 1-12th Field Artillery (MLRS)
>> 3-18th Field Artillery (155SP)
>> 5-3rd Field Artillery (MLRS)
> 41st Field Artillery Brigade (GS to V Corps) (GSR 101 DIVARTY)
>> HHB/41st Field Artillery Bde
>> 2-18th Field Artillery (MLRS), 212th Field Artillery Brigade (Attached)
>> 1-27th Field Artillery (MLRS)
>> 234th Field Artillery Detachment (Target Acquisition) (2 x Q37)
>> 214th Field Artillery Brigade (GSR 3rd ID DIVARTY)
>> HHB/214th Field Artillery
>> 2-4th Field Artillery (MLRS) (Attached)
>> 2nd Field Artillery Detachment (Target Acquisition) (2 x Q37)
> L/3/2nd Armored Cavalry Regiment (Light)
> Rapid Equipping Force

31st Air Defense Artillery Brigade (-) (OPCON)
> HHB/31st Air Defense Artillery Bde
> 5-52nd Air Defense Artillery (Patriot) (-)
>> HHB/5-52nd Air Defense Artillery
>> A/5-52nd Air Defense Artillery
>> B/5-52nd Air Defense Artillery
>> E/5-52nd Air Defense Artillery
>> 507th Maintenance Co (Missile)
> 6-52nd Air Defense Artillery (Patriot) (-)
>> HHB/6-52nd Air Defense Artillery
>> A/6-52nd Air Defense Artillery
>> B/6-52nd Air Defense Artillery
>> D/6-52nd Air Defense Artillery
>> E/6-52nd Air Defense Artillery
>> 549th Maintenance Co (Missile)
> C/3-124th Infantry (Attached)
> 578th Signal Co (Range Extension) (Attached)
> C/17th Signal Battalion (Mobile Subscriber Equipment) (-) (Attached)

130th Engineer Brigade
> HHC/130th Engineer Bde
>> Small Extension Node A62/C/32nd Signal Battalion
>> Small Extension Node A76/C/32nd Signal Battalion
> A/94th Engineer Battalion (Combat Heavy) (-)
> 52nd Engineer Battalion (Combat Heavy) (-)
> 122nd Engineer Battalion (Corps Wheeled) (-)
> 168th Engineer Group (Construction)

864th Engineer Battalion (-) (Combat Heavy)
    HSC/864th Engineer Bn
    A/864th Engineer Bn (Combat Heavy)
    C/890th Engineer Bn (Combat Heavy)
    38th Engineer Co (Medium Girder Bridge) (Attached)
    320th Engineer Co (Topographic) (-) (Attached)
    642nd Engineer Co (Combat Support Equip) (Attached)
    475th Engineer Team (Fire Fighting)
565th Engineer Battalion (Provisional)
    HHD/565th Engineer Bn
    74th Engineer Co (Multirole Bridge Co) (Attached)
    502nd Engineer Co (Assault Float Bridge) (Attached)
    814th Engineer Co (Medium Ribbon Bridge) (Attached)
    C/70th Engineer Bn (Combat Mech), 3rd Brigade, 1st Armored Division
    317th Maintenance Support Team
    544th Engineer Team (Light Weight Diving) (Attached)
        77th Maintenance Support Team
    74th Engineer Team (Light Weight Diving) (Attached)
142nd Engineer Battalion (Combat Heavy) (-)
489th Engineer Battalion (Corps Mech)
HHD/439th Engineer Battalion (Engineer Headquarters)
Facilities Engineer Detachment B (-) (OPCON)
2 x D9 Bulldozers
205th Military Intelligence Brigade (-)
HHC/205th Military Intelligence Bde
302nd Military Intelligence Battalion (Operations) (+)
    A/325th Military Intelligence Bn (Counterintelligence/Interrogation/Exploitation)
15th Military Intelligence Battalion (Aerial Exploitation) (-)
    HHC/15th Military Intelligence Bn
165th Military Intelligence Battalion (Tactical Exploitation) (-)
    B/15th Military Intelligence Bn (-) (Ground Control Station) (OPCON)
    B/141st Military Intelligence Bn (Linguist) (-) (Attached)
223rd Military Intelligence Battalion (Linguist) (C2 and HUMINT) (CA National Guard) (-)
    2 x Sensitive Site Exploitation/Sensitive Site Teams (Attached)
    224th Military Intelligence Battalion (Unmanned Aerial Vehicle) (- Company B with 513th Military Intelligence Brigade (OPCON)
325th Military Intelligence Battalion (-) (Rear CI/HUMINT Ops)
    HHC/325th Military Intelligence Bn
    B/325th Military Intelligence Bn (CI/HUMINT)
519th Military Intelligence Battalion (Tactical Exploitation) (-)
    HHSC/519th Military Intelligence Bn
    A/519th Military Intelligence Bn (Attached)

F/519th Military Intelligence Bn

A/223rd Military Intelligence Bn (Linguist)

356th Military Intelligence Co (Linguist)

2/D/165th Military Intelligence Bn (Counterintelligence)

18th Military Police Brigade

HHC/18th Military Police Bde

211th Military Police Battalion (Guard)

HHD/211th Military Police Bn

135th Military Police Co (Combat Support)

143rd Military Police Co (Combat Support)

307th Military Police Co (Combat Support)

323rd Military Police Co (Combat Support)

855th Military Police Co (Combat Support)

1139th Military Police Co (Combat Support)

503rd Military Police Battalion (Attached)

HHD/503rd Military Police Bn

65th Military Police Co (Combat Support)

94th Military Police Co (Combat Support)

108th Military Police Co (Combat Support) (- one squad from 1st Platoon with 82nd DISCOM)

519th Military Police Battalion (Attached)

HHD/519th Military Police Co

204th Military Police Co (Combat Support)

233rd Military Police Co (Combat Support)

549th Military Police Co (Combat Support)

51st Military Police Detachment (Law and Order)

30th Military Police Detachment (Criminal Investigation)

709th Military Police Battalion (OPCON)

HHD/709th Military Police Bn

527th Military Police Co (Combat Support) (Attached)

551st Military Police Co (Combat Support) (OPCON)

1166th Military Police Co (Combat Support)

720th Military Police Battalion

HHD/720th Military Police Bn

64th Military Police Co (Combat Support) (Attached)

401st Military Police Co (Combat Support) (Attached)

411th Military Police Co (Combat Support) (Attached)

511th Military Police Co (Combat Support) (Attached)

615th Military Police Co (Combat Support) (Attached)

855th Military Police Co (Combat Support)

Det/178th Military Police Co (Narcotics Dog Team)

Det/178th Military Police Co (Bomb Dog Team)

156th Military Police Detachment (Law and Order)

Tactical PSYOP Det/362nd Tactical Psychological Operations Co (TACON)

22nd Signal Brigade (OPCON)

HHC (-)/22nd Signal Bde

17th Signal Battalion (Corps Mobile Subscriber Equipment Area Support) (-Company C with 31st Air Defense Artillery Brigade)

32nd Signal Battalion (-) (Corps Mobile Subscriber Equipment Area Support)

440th Signal Battalion (Corps Mobile Subscriber Equipment Area Support)

982nd Signal Visual Information Co (Combat Camera) (-)

B/63rd Signal Battalion (-) (OPCON)

44th Signal Battalion (Theater Tactical) (-)

    HHC/44th Signal Bn

    A/44th Signal Bn (Command Support)

    C/44th Signal Bn (Minor Unit Support)

51st Signal Battalion (Contingency Support) (-)

    HHC(-)/51st Signal Bn

    A (-)/51st Signal Bn

    C/50th Signal Bn

    514th Signal Co (TACSAT/TROPO) (-)

V Corps Rear Detachment (Kuwait)

    82nd Support Detachment (Corps Rear Area Operations Center)

        A/2-124th Infantry

        B/2-124th Infantry

    Corps Liaison Teams

    V Corps RSOI Cell (with LNOs)

    19th Area Support Group (Provisional) (Camp C2)

    3rd ID Rear Detachment (Camp NEW YORK)

    4th ID Rear Detachment (Camp PENNSYLVANIA)

    1st Cavalry Div Rear Detachment

    101st Airborne Div Rear Detachment (Camp PENNSYLVANIA)

    1st Armored Div Rear Detachment

    11th Attack Helicopter Regiment Rear Detachment (Camp UDARI)

    12th Aviation Brigade Rear Detachment (Camps UDARI/VICTORY)

    3rd Armored Cavalry Regiment Rear Detachment (Camp UDARI)

    V Corps Artillery Rear Detachment

    31st Air Defense Artillery Brigade Rear Detachment (Camp VIRGINIA)

    2nd Chemical Battalion Rear Detachment

    450th Chemical Battalion Rear Detachment (Camp VIRGINIA)

    130th Engineer Brigade Rear Detachment

    205th Military Intelligence Brigade (Camp VIRGINIA)

    18th Military Police Brigade Rear Detachment (Camp VIRGINIA)

    22nd Signal Brigade Rear Detachment (Camp VIRGINIA)

    308th Civil Affairs Brigade Rear Detachment (Camp VIRGINIA)

    9th Psychological Operations Battalion Rear Detachment (Camp VIRGINIA)

    3rd Corps Support Command Rear Detachment (Camps VIRGINIA/VICTORY)

    18th Soldier Support Group Rear Detachment

    30th Medical Brigade Rear Detachment (Camp VIRGINIA)

    19th Support Center Rear Detachment

205th Finance Battalion (Camp VIRGINIA)
18th Soldier Support Group
    HHD/18th Soldier Support Group
    90th Personnel Support Battalion
        90th Adjutant General Co (Postal HQ) (-)
            2/342nd Postal Service Platoon
            3/342nd Postal Service Platoon
            3/312th Postal Operations Platoon
            4/23rd Postal Operations Platoon
            4/129th Postal Operations Platoon
    24th Personnel Support Battalion
        129th Adjutant General Co (Postal) (-)
    546th Personnel Support Battalion (Attached)
        341st Adjutant General Co (Postal HQ)
            1/341st Postal Service Platoon
            2/341st Postal Service Platoon
            4/90th Postal Service Platoon
        454th Replacement Co (Attached)
    208th Finance Battalion
    76th Adjutant General Band
3rd Ordnance Battalion (Explosive Ordnance Disposal) (DS from 52nd Ordnance Group)
    HHD/3rd Ordnance Bn
    18th Ordnance Co (Explosive Ordnance Disposal)
    759th Ordnance Co (Explosive Ordnance Disposal) (OPCON)
    761st Ordnance Co (Explosive Ordnance Disposal)
    787th Ordnance Co (Explosive Ordnance Disposal) (OPCON)
3rd Corps Support Command (COSCOM) (OPCON)
    HHC/Special Troops Battalion/3rd Corps Support Command
    Civil Affairs Tactical Planning Team/308th Civil Affairs Battalion
    Det/308th Civil Affairs Battalion
    19th Support Center (Materiel Management)
    44th Support Center (Rear Area Operations Center)
    27th Movement Control Battalion
        HHC/27th MCB
        2nd Transportation Co (Heavy Equipment Transporter)
        27th Transportation Co (Attached)
        383rd Movement Control Team (Attached)
        619th Movement Control Team (Airfield Opening)
        635th Movement Control Team (Regulating)
        1032nd Transportation Co (Medium Truck 20-foot Container)
    801st Corps Support Battalion
    24th Corps Support Group (DS to 3rd Infantry Division)
        HHC/24th Corps Support Group
        258th Rear Area Operations Center (Corps)
        258th Movement Control Team (Area)

51st Movement Control Detachment (Division Support)
Det/129th Adjutant General Co (Postal)
3rd Solider Support Battalion (-) (DS)
87th Corps Support Battalion
    HHD/87th Corps Support Bn
    24th Ordnance Co (Modular Ammo Palletized Load System) (-)
    59th Quartermaster Co (Petroleum Supply) (OPCON)
    102nd Quartermaster Co (Petroleum Supply)
    226th Quartermaster Co (-) (Supply)
    348th Transportation Co (-) (Petroleum Oil Lubricants) (OPCON)
    529th Ordnance Co (Modular Ammo Palletized Load System)
    632nd Maintenance Co (Non-divisional DS)
    1207th Transportation Co (Medium Truck)
    Team 2/54th Quartermaster Co (Mortuary Affairs)
16th Corps Support Group (Initially Rear CSG) (O/O DS to 1st Armored Division)
    HHC/16th Corps Support Group
    317th Support Center (Rear Area Operations Center)
    Materiel Management Team 2/19th Support Center
    626th Movement Control Team (Area Support)
    26th Quartermaster Co (Supply)
    685th Transportation Co (Medium Truck)
    316th Quartermaster Co (Water Supply)
  13th Corps Support Battalion
    HHD/13th Corps Support Bn
    317th Maintenance Co (Non-divisional DS)
    512th Quartermaster Co (Water Supply) (Attached)
        205th Quartermaster Team (Water Purification)
    547th Transportation Co (Light/Medium Truck)
    730th Quartermaster Co (Supply)
    205th Quartermaster Team (Water Purification) (Attached)
    274th Movement Control Team (Regulating)
  181st Transportation Battalion
    HHD/181st Transportation Bn
    40th Transportation Co (Medium Truck 5K)
    212th Transportation Co (Palletized Load System)
    296th Transportation Co (Petroleum Oil Lubricants) (OPCON)
    377th Transportation Co (Heavy Equipment Transporter)
    418th Transportation Co (Medium Truck 5K)
    515th Transportation Co (Medium Truck 5K POL)
  485th Corps Support Battalion
    HHD/Corps Support Bn
    26th Quartermaster Co (Supply)
101st Corps Support Group (DS to 101st Airborne Division)
    HHC/101st Corps Support Group
    Materiel Management Team 2/2nd Support Center

41st Support Center (Rear Area Operations Center)
561st Corps Support Battalion
    HHC/561st Corps Support Bn
    102nd Quartermaster Co (Petroleum Oil Lubricants Supply)
    196th Transportation Co (Palletized Load System)
    253rd Transportation Co (Light/Medium Truck)
    372nd Transportation Co (Light/Medium Truck)
    548th Transportation Co (Light/Medium Truck)
    851st Quartermaster Co (Supply)
    Team/196th Quartermaster Det (ROWPU) (-)
548th Corps Support Battalion
    HHD/548th Corps Support Bn
    137th Quartermaster Co (Field Service)
    349th Quartermaster Co (Supply)
    546th Transportation Co (Light/Medium Truck)
    581st Quartermaster Co (Supply) (DS)
    584th Maintenance Co (Non-divisional DS)
    588th Maintenance Co (DS)
    811th Transportation Co (MOADS Palletized Load System)
    494th Transportation Co (Light/Medium Truck) (-)
142nd Corps Support Battalion (DS to 3rd Armored Cavalry Regiment)
    HHD/142nd Corps Support Bn
    251st Support Center (Rear Area Operations Center)
    209th Quartermaster Co (Supply) (DS)
    602nd Maintenance Co (Non-divisional DS)
    603rd Transportation Co (Palletized Load System)
    733rd Transportation Co (Palletized Load System)
    812th Quartermaster Co (Supply)
    2632nd Transportation Co (Light/Medium Truck)
1 x TSC-85 TACSAT Terminal (OPCON)
1 x TSC-93C TACSAT Terminal (OPCON)
7th Corps Support Group (Rear CSG)
    HHC/7th Corps Support Group
    309th Support Center (Rear Area Operations Center)
    71st Corps Support Battalion
        HHD/71st Corps Support Bn
        147th Maintenance Co (Non-divisional DS)
        227th Quartermaster Co (Supply)
        240th Quartermaster Co (Supply) (Attached)
        634th Movement Control Team (Division Support)
    19th Ordnance Battalion (Maintenance) (Attached)
        HHC/19th Ordnance Bn (Maintenance)
        58th Maintenance Co (GS)
        71st Maintenance Co (Missile)
    418th Quartermaster Battalion (Petroleum Oil Lubricants Supply)

HHC/418th Quartermaster Bn
59th Quartermaster Co (Petroleum Oil Lubricants Supply)
233rd Quartermaster Co (Petroleum Oil Lubricants Supply)
277th Quartermaster Co (Petroleum Oil Lubricants Supply)
528th Quartermaster Co (Petroleum Oil Lubricants Supply)
371st Corps Support Group
HHC/371st Corps Support Group
HHD/37th TRANSCOM (Transportation Control Element)
Forward Support Co Logistics Assistance Office
157th Quartermaster Co (Field Service)
811th Ordnance Co (Modular Ammo)
321st Ordnance Battalion (DS/GS Ammo)
HHD/321st Ordnance Bn
24th Transportation Co (Ammo Palletized Load System) (Attached)
77th Maintenance Co (Attached)
163rd Ordnance Co (Modular Ammo)
345th Corps Support Battalion (Attached)
HHD/345th Corps Support Bn
217th Transportation Co (Heavy Equipment Transporter) (Attached)
377th Transportation Co (Heavy Equipment Transporter)
428th Quartermaster Co (DS Supply)
1058th Transportation Co (Light/Medium Truck)
1086th Transportation Co (Palletized Load System)
1087th Transportation Co (Light/Medium Truck)
1123rd Transportation Co (Light/Medium Truck)
1245th Transportation Co (Palletized Load System) (Attached)
22nd Transportation Det (Trailer Transfer)
548th Corps Support Battalion (Attached)
HHD/548th Corps Support Bn
51st Transportation Co (Medium Truck Palletized Load System) (Attached)
396th Transportation Co (Medium Truck Palletized Load System) (-) (Attached)
627th Movement Control Team (Area) (Attached)
692nd Corps Support Battalion (Water) (Attached)
HHC/692nd Corps Support Bn
288th Quartermaster Co (GS Water Supply)
196TH Quartermaster Detachment (Water Purification) (-)
326th Quartermaster Detachment (Water Purification)
406th Transportation Detachment (Trailer Transfer) (Attached)
64th Corps Support Group (DS to 4th Infantry Division)
HHD/64th Corps Support Group
130th Support Center (Rear Area Operations Center)
345th Support Center (Rear Area Operations Center)
458th Movement Control Team (Port Opening)

535th Movement Control Team (Area)
588th Movement Control Team (Area)
28th Personnel Services Battalion
544th Corps Support Battalion
    HHC/544th Corps Support Bn
    263rd Maintenance Co (Non-Divisional DS)
    289th Quartermaster Co (GS Supply) (-)
    300th Quartermaster Co (Supply) (DS)
    541st Transportation Co (Petroleum Oil Lubricants 5K)
    664th Ordnance Co (MOADS)
    1460th Transportation Co (Palletized Load System)
    62nd Quartermaster Co (-) (Water Teams)
    Team/54th Quartermaster Co (Mortuary Affairs)
553rd Corps Support Battalion
    HHC/553rd Corps Support Bn
    282nd Quartermaster Co (Supply) (DS)
    442nd Quartermaster Co (Field Services)
    991st Transportation Co (Palletized Load System)
    705th Transportation Co (Medium Truck 7.5K)
    743rd Maintenance Co (Non-divisional DS)
    1404th Transportation Co (Palletized Load System)
180th Transportation Battalion
    HHD/180th Transportation Bn
    2nd Transportation Co (Heavy Equipment Transporter)
    11th Transportation Co (Heavy Equipment Transporter)
    287th Transportation Co (Heavy Equipment Transporter)
    401st Transportation Co (Medium Truck Palletized Load System)
    430th Quartermaster Co (Field Service)
    475th Quartermaster Co (Petroleum Oil Lubricants Supply)
    596th Maintenance Co (Non-divisional DS)
    600th Transportation Det (Trailer Transfer Point)
    656th Transportation Co (Petroleum Oil Lubricants 5K)
    751st Quartermaster Company (DS/GS Supply)
    1229th Transportation Co (Light/Medium Truck)
    2133rd Transportation Co (Medium Truck)
30th Medical Brigade
    HHC/30th Medical Bde
    28th Combat Support Hospital (Attached)
        160th Medical Detachment (Forward Surgical Team)
        274th Medical Detachment (Forward Surgical Team)
        934th Medical Detachment (Forward Surgical Team)
    36th Medical Battalion (Evacuation) (Attached)
        HHD/36th Medical Battalion
        82nd Medical Co (Air Ambulance) (Attached)
        159th Medical Co (Air Ambulance)

507th Medical Co (Air Ambulance) (Attached) (OPCON)
565th Medical Co (Ground Ambulance) (Attached)
61st Medical Battalion (Area Support) (-)
    HHD/61st Area Support Medical Bn (-)
    546th Medical Co (Area Support) (Attached)
    581st Medical Co (Attached)
    549th Medical Co (Area Support) (Attached)
    591st Medical Logistics Co (Attached)
93rd Medical Battalion (Dental) (-)
    HHD/93rd Medical Bn (Dental) (-)
    113th Medical Co (Combat Stress Control)
    257th Medical Co (Area Support Dental Services)
    502nd Medical Co (Area Support Dental Services)
    561st Medical Co (Area Support Dental Services)
    673rd Medical Co (Area Support Dental Services)
    21st Medical Detachment (Veterinary Services)
    43rd Medical Detachment (Veterinary Services) (OPCON)
    72nd Medical Detachment (Veterinary Services)
    218th Medical Detachment (Veterinary Services) (Attached)
    248th Medical Detachment (Veterinary Services)
    255th Medical Detachment (Preventative Medicine Entomology) (Attached)
    2 x Teams/787th Medical Detachment (Preventative Medicine Sanitation) (OPCON)
212th Mobile Army Surgical Hospital
    1st Medical Detachment (Forward Surgical Team)
    254th Medical Detachment (Combat Stress Control)
    624th Medical Detachment (Forward Surgical Team)
    628th Medical Detachment (Forward Surgical Team)
    912th Medical Detachment (Forward Surgical Team)
    936th Medical Detachment (Forward Surgical Team)
1st Medical Brigade (Attached)
    HHD/1st Medical Bde
    21st Combat Support Hospital (Corps) (Attached)
    56th Medical Battalion (Evacuation)
        HHD/57th Medical Bn
        57th Medical Co (Air Ambulance)
        296th Medical Co (Ground Ambulance)
        484th Medical Co (Logistics)
        571st Medical Co (Air Ambulance) (- Forward Support MEDEVAC Teams)
        690th Medical Co (Ground Ambulance) (DS)
        708th Medical Co (Ground Ambulance)
        883rd Medical Co (Combat Stress Control) (Attached)
        14th Medical Detachment (Preventative Medicine Sanitation)
        85th Medical Detachment (Combat Stress Control) (Attached)
        223rd Medical Detachment (Preventative Medicine) (OPCON)

        528th Medical Detachment (Combat Stress Control)
        714th Medical Detachment (Preventative Medicine Entomology) (OPCON)
        2 x Combat Stress Fitness (Restoration) Team (OPCON)
    111th Medical Battalion (Area Support)
        546th Medical Co (Area Support)
        549th Medical Co (Area Support)
        581st Medical Co (Area Support)
62nd Medical Brigade
    HHC/62nd Medical Bde
    10th Combat Support Hospital (Corps)
        240th Medical Detachment (Forward Surgical Team)
        915th Medical Detachment (Forward Surgical Team)
    109th Medical Battalion (Area Support)
    421st Medical Battalion (Evacuation)
        HHD/421st Medical Bn
        54th Medical Co (Air Ambulance)
        514th Medical Co (Ground Ambulance)
        61st Medical Detachment (Preventative Medicine)
        98th Medical Detachment (Combat Stress Control)
        200th Medical Detachment (Preventative Medicine Sanitation)
        792nd Medical Detachment (Preventative Medicine Sanitation)
        945th Medical Detachment (Forward Surgical Team)
    172nd Medical Battalion (Logistics Forward) (-) (OPCON)
        482nd Medical Co (Logistics)
        551st Medical Det (Logistics) (-)
    320th Expeditionary Aeromedical Evacuation Squadron Aeromedical Evacuation
    Liaison Team (DS) (USAF)
    320th EAES Mobile Aeromedical Staging Facility (DS) (USAF)

377th Theater Support Command (-) (OPCON)
HHC/377th Theater Support Command
321st Materiel Management Center (-) (OPCON)
Civil Affairs Tactical Planning Team/A/354th Civil Affairs Brigade (OPCON)
Civil Affairs Tactical Planning Team/414th Civil Affairs Battalion (General Purpose)
105th Chaplain Detachment
Army Materiel Command Logistics Support Element (AMC LSE) Southwest Asia (OPCON)
    AMC LSE SWA HHC (-)
    AMC Combat Equipment Battalion - QATAR
    AMC Combat Equipment Battalion - KUWAIT
    AMC Combat Equipment Battalion (Provisional) - ARIFJAN
    AMC Logistics Support Element FWD - UZ / KZ
    AMC Logistics Support Element FWD - BAGRAM
    AMC Logistics Support Element FWD - QANDAHAR
    AMC Logistics Support Element FWD - KABAL
    AMC Logistics Support Element FWD - SHAMSI

AMC Logistics Support Element FWD - DJIBOUTI
AMC Logistics Support Element FWD 2/6th Cavalry – AL AS SALEM
AMC Logistics Assistance Office - SAUDI ARABIA
AMC Logistics Assistance Office - KUWAIT
1109th Aviation Certification Repair Activity Depot (AVCRAD)
Element/Defense Logistics Agency (-) (OPCON)
1 x Forward Support MEDEVAC Team (3 x UH-60) (Attached)
3rd Personnel Command (PERSCOM) (OPCON)
    105th Personnel Services Battalion (Jordan)
        721st Postal Company HQs
            4/721st Adjutant General Co (Postal)
       806th Postal Co (-)
          1/806th Postal Co
          2/806th Postal Co
    149th Personnel Services Battalion
        349th Personnel Services Detachment
    444th Personnel Services Battalion (OPCON)
    678th Personnel Services Battalion (-)
        1/413th Adjutant General Co (Postal)
        1/554th Adjutant General Co (Postal)
        2/678th Adjutant General Co (Postal)
        3/834th Adjutant General Co (Postal)
    461st Personnel Services Battalion (-)
    324th Personnel Replacement Battalion
        B/18th Adjutant General Co (Postal)
        813th Personnel Replacement Co
        814th Personnel Replacement Co
    755th Adjutant General Co (Postal)
83rd Chemical Battalion
    7th Chemical Co (Biological Detection and Identification System) (- 1st and 5th Platoons with 450th Chemical Battalion)
    68th Chemical Co (Heavy), 1st Cavalry Division (OPCON) (- 6th Platoon with 371st Chemical Battalion)
    172nd Chemical Co (Smoke)
    181st Chemical Co (Attached)
    310th Chemical Co (Biological Detection and Identification System) (-)
220th Military Police Brigade (-) (OPCON)
    1-124th Infantry (-)[9]
        HHC/1-124th Infantry
    1-152nd Infantry (+ FIST teams from 76th Separate Infantry Brigade)
    1-162nd Infantry (-)[10]
    1-293rd Infantry (- D Company TACON to 143rd TRANSCOM)
        HHC/1-293rd Infantry
        A/1-293rd Infantry (- 3rd Platoon attached to 11th ADA Brigade)
        B/1-293rd Infantry

C/1-293rd Infantry
3-124th Infantry (-)[11]
    HHC/3-124th Infantry
    A/3-124th Infantry
118th Military Police Battalion
    HHD/118th Military Police Bn
    115th Military Police Co (Combat Support)
    119th Military Police Co (Combat Support)
    363rd Military Police Co (Combat Support)
    933rd Military Police Co (Combat Support)
    1166th Military Police Co (Combat Support)
    438th Military Police Detachment (Law & Order)
        40th Military Police Detachment (Criminal Investigation)
        34th Military Police Detachment (Law Enforcement)
        500th Military Police Detachment (Law Enforcement)
        Law Enforcement Activity
    Tactical Psychological Operations Detachment 1540
304th Military Police Battalion (Internment and Resettlement)
    HHD/304th Military Police Bn
    229th Military Police Co (Combat Support)
    1138th Military Police Co (Guard)
504th Military Police Battalion
    HHD/504th Military Police Bn
    170th Military Police Co (Combat Support)
        2/410th Military Police Co (Combat Support)
    300th Military Police Co (Combat Support) (-)
    302nd Military Police Co (Combat Support)
607th Military Police Battalion
    HHD/607th Military Police Bn
    220th Military Police Co (Combat Support)
    340th Military Police Co (Combat Support) (Attached)
800th Military Police Brigade (Internment and Resettlement) (OPCON)
    HHC/800th Military Police Brigade
    115th Military Police Battalion (Enemy Prisoner of War/Counterintelligence)
        HHD/115th Military Police Bn
        186th Military Police Co (Combat Support) (+)
        812th Military Police Co (Combat Support)
        814th Military Police Co (Guard)
    320th Military Police Battalion (Enemy Prisoner of War/Counterintelligence) (Attached)
        HHD/320th Military Police Bn
        211th Military Police Co (Guard)
        314th Military Police Co (Guard)
        447th Military Police Co (Guard)
        47th Military Police Team (Dog Team)

381st Military Police Detachment (Enemy Prisoner of War/Counterintel Liaison)

400th Military Police Battalion (Internment and Resettlement)
 HHC/400th Military Police Bn
 373rd Military Police Detachment (Internment and Resettlement Processing)
 379th Military Police Detachment (Internment and Resettlement Processing)

530th Military Police Battalion (Internment and Resettlement)
 HHD/530th Military Police Bn
 649th Military Police Co (Combat Support)
 670th Military Police Co (Combat Support)
 336th Military Police Detachment (Internment and Resettlement Processing)

724th Military Police Battalion (Internment and Resettlement) (OPCON)
 HHD/724th Military Police Bn
 267th Military Police Co (Combat Support) (OPCON)
 223rd Military Police Co (Combat Support) (OPCON)
 822nd Military Police Co (Guard) (OPCON)
 395th Military Police Detachment (Internment and Resettlement Processing)

744th Military Police Battalion (Enemy Prisoner of War/Counterintelligence) (Attached)
 HHD/744th Military Police Bn
 79th Military Police Co (Combat Support)
 320th Military Police Co (Combat Support)

377th Military Police Detachment (Internment and Resettlement Processing)
346rd JAG Det (Brigade Liaison)
381st JAG Det (Brigade Liaison)
B/13th Psychological Operations Battalion (OPCON)

304th Civil Affairs Brigade (-)
 HHC/304th Civil Affairs Bde
 414th Civil Affairs Battalion (OPCON)
 486th Civil Affairs Battalion (-) OPCON)
  Civil Affairs Tactical Planning Team/486th Civil Affairs Bn
  Displaced Civilian Team/486th Civil Affairs Bn

38th Ordnance Group (Ammunition)
 HHC/38th Ordnance Group
 802nd Ordnance Co (Medium Lift Ammo) (+)
 Platoon/60th Ordnance Co (Heavy Lift Ammo)
 Platoon/63rd Ordnance Co (Medium Lift Ammo) (OPCON)
 226th Maintenance Co (DS) (Attached)

52nd Ordnance Group (Explosive Ordnance Demolition) (-) (OPCON)
 79th Ordnance Battalion (Explosive Ordnance Disposal) (DS)
  HHD/79th Ordnance Battalion
  38th Ordnance Co (Explosive Ordnance Disposal) (GS)
  47th Ordnance Co (Explosive Ordnance Disposal)
  725th Ordnance Co (Explosive Ordnance Disposal)
  766th Ordnance Co (Explosive Ordnance Disposal) (OPCON)

143rd Transportation Command (TRANSCOM) (OPCON)
    757th Transportation Battalion (Rail) (-) (OPCON)
    D/1-293rd Infantry (TACON)
    3/A/1-293rd Infantry (OPCON)
    7th Transportation Group (Attached)
        18th Weather Detachment (OPCON) (USAF)
        6th Transportation Battalion
            HHC/6th Transportation Bn
            15th Transportation Co (Medium Truck Palletized Load System) (Attached)
            68th Transportation Co (Medium Truck) (Attached)
            551st Transportation Co (Cargo Transfer) (OPCON)
            478th Transportation Co (Medium Truck Palletized Load System)
            89th Transportation Co (-) (Medium Truck) (OPCON)
        10th Transportation Terminal Battalion[12]
            HHC/10th Transportation Bn
            97th Transportation Co (Heavy Boat)
            155th Transportation Co (Cargo Transfer)
            287th Transportation Co (Heavy Equipment Transporter)
            403rd Transportation Co (Cargo Transfer) (-) Turkey
            650th Transportation Co (Port Operations Cargo) Turkey
        11th Transportation Battalion (Terminal)
            HHD (-)/11th Transportation Bn
            119th Transportation Co (Terminal Service)
            368th Transportation Co (Cargo Transfer)
            149th Transportation Detachment (Port Operating Crane)
            159th Transportation Detachment (Port Operating Crane) (OPCON)
        24th Transportation Battalion (Terminal) (OPCON)
            HHC (-)/24th Transportation Bn (Terminal) Kuwait Naval Base
            73rd Transportation Co (Floating Craft) (OPCON)
            558th Transportation Co (Floating Crane Maintenance)
            567th Transportation Co (Cargo Transfer)
            824th Transportation Co (-) (OPCON)
            1098th Transportation Co (-) (Medium Boat) (OPCON)
            169th Transportation Detachment (Port Operations)
            492nd Transportation Detachment (Harbor Boat Master)
            411th Logistics Supply Vessel Detachment
            469th Logistics Supply Vessel Detachment
            805th Logistics Supply Vessel Detachment
            1099th Logistics Supply Vessel Detachment
        106th Transportation Battalion
            HHD (-)/106th Transportation Bn
            96th Transportation Co (Heavy Equipment Transporter)
            126th Transportation Co (Medium Truck Palletized Load System)
            233rd Transportation Co (Heavy Equipment Transporter)

513th Transportation Co (Medium Truck 40-foot Container)
594th Transportation Co (Medium Truck)
1454th Transportation Co (Medium Truck Palletized Load System)
109th Transportation Co (Medium Truck) (Attached)
483rd Transportation Detachment (Trailer Transfer)
32nd Transportation Group (Composite)
346th Transportation Battalion (Motor Transport)
HHD/346th Transportation Bn
720th Transportation Co (Medium Truck)
419th Transportation Battalion (Attached)
HHC/419th Transportation Bn
3079th Cargo Distribution Center (Provisional) (Theater Distribution Center) (OPCON)
131st Transportation Co (Medium Truck)
459th Transportation Co (Medium Truck)
719th Transportation Co (Medium Truck)
781st Transportation Co (Medium Truck)
1083rd Transportation Co (Heavy Equipment Transporter)
1128th Transportation Co (Medium Truck) (Attached)
1136th Transportation Co (Medium Truck)
1148th Transportation Co (Medium Truck)
227th Transportation Co (-) (GS)
528th Maintenance Co (-) (Watercraft Maintenance)
195th Transportation Detachment (OPCON) (Arifjan)
257th Transportation Co (Heavy Equipment Transporter)
471st Transportation Detachment (Trailer Transfer) (OPCON)
595th Transportation Detachment (Trailer Transfer)
370th Transportation Co (Medium Truck Palletized Load System) (Pax Only)
Host Nation/Logistics Civilian Augmentation Program
Naval Costal Warfare Group 1 (TACON) (OPCON NAVCENT)
TSV-USAV SPEARHEAD (USA)
LSV 4 (OPCON) (USA)
LSV 6 (OPCON) (USA)
42nd Movement Control Detachment (OPCON) (USA)
3rd Theater Army Movement Center
53rd Movement Control Battalion (Echelon Above Corps) (OPCON)
HHD/53rd Movement Control Bn
152nd Transportation Co (-) (OPCON)
70th Movement Control Team (Area)
94th Movement Control Team (Cargo Documentation)
146th Movement Control Team (Port) (OPCON)
151st Movement Control Team (Area)
152nd Movement Control Team (Area)
171st Movement Control Team (Cargo Regulating)

        199th Movement Control Team (Area)
        259th Movement Control Team (Cargo Regulating)
        319th Movement Control Team (Area Support) (USA)
        384th Movement Control Team (Regulating)
        394th Movement Control Team (Cargo Documentation) (OPCON)
        408th Movement Control Team (Cargo Documentation)
        462nd Movement Control Team (Cargo Documentation) (OPCON)
        596th Movement Control Team (Cargo Documentation)
        576th Movement Control Team (Cargo Regulating)
        609th Movement Control Team (Area)
        628th Movement Control Detachment (Cargo Documentation)
        940th Movement Control Team (Cargo Documentation)
        958th Movement Control Team (Cargo Regulating)
        80th Movement Control Team (Cargo Documentation) (-) (OPCON)
        216th Movement Control Team (Port) (-) (OPCON)
     194th Transportation Detachment (Contract Supervision)
     436th Movement Control Battalion (Echelon Above Corps) (-)
        HHD/436th Movement Control Bn
     450th Movement Control Battalion (Echelon Above Corps)
        HHD/450th Movement Control Bn
        32nd Movement Control Team (Cargo Documentation)
        62nd Movement Control Team (Area)
        142nd Movement Control Team (Port) (-) (OPCON)
        261st Movement Control Team (Cargo Regulating)
        265th Movement Control Team (Port)
        312th Movement Control Team (Area)
        329th Movement Control Team (Airport)
        339th Movement Control Team (Cargo Regulating)
        399th Movement Control Team (Cargo Regulating)
        541st Movement Control Team (Cargo Documentation)
        564th Movement Control Team (Cargo Documentation) (OPCON)
        602nd Movement Control Team (Cargo Documentation)
        650th Movement Control Team (Cargo Documentation)
        823rd Movement Control Team (Cargo Regulating)
        839th Movement Control Team (Cargo Regulating)
        961st Movement Control Team (Area)
        969th Movement Control Team (Cargo Regulating)
     455th Transportation Detachment (Contract Supervision)
43rd Area Support Group
     HHC/43rd Area Support Group
     31st Rear Operations Center (-) (OPCON)
     541st Maintenance Battalion
     18th Corps Support Battalion (DS)
        HHD/18th Corps Support Bn
        41st Transportation Co (Palletized Load System)

249th Quartermaster Co (Repair Parts) (Attached)
608th Ordnance Co (Modular Ammo) (-)
629th Transportation Co (Medium Truck)
846th Transportation Co (Medium Truck 40-foot Container)
998th Quartermaster Co (Water Purification) (OPCON)
1001st Quartermaster Co (Field Service) (DS) (Attached)
1032nd Transportation Co (Medium Truck)
68th Corps Support Battalion (-)
    HHD/68th Corps Support Bn
    18th Quartermaster Detachment (Yard Operations)
    16th Quartermaster Co (Field Service) (GS) (OPCON)
    183rd Maintenance Co (DS) (OPCON)
    311th Quartermaster Co (Mortuary Affairs)
    827th Quartermaster Co (GS)
    887th Quartermaster Co (Heavy GS)
    Detachment 4/872nd Maintenance Co (OPCON)
    417th Chemical Detachment (Augmentation for 24-hour operations)
541st Maintenance Battalion (Direct Support/General Support)
    HHD/541st Maintenance Bn
    53rd Quartermaster Co (Petroleum Oil Lubricants Supply)
    104th Transportation Co (Medium Truck)
    246th Quartermaster Battalion (Mortuary Affairs)
        246th Quartermaster Co (Mortuary Affairs)
    872nd Ordnance Det (OPCON) (DS)
    1014th Quartermaster Co Transportation Co (Medium Truck)
    1168th Transportation Co (Light/Medium Truck)
Civil Affairs Tactical Planning Team/414th Civil Affairs Battalion
171st Area Support Group (-) (OPCON)
HHC/171st Area Support Group
352nd Corps Support Battalion
    HHD/352nd Corps Support Bn
    456th Quartermaster Co (Supply)
    849th Quartermaster Co (DS Supply)
    889th Quartermaster Co (DS Supply)
    2220th Transportation Co (Medium Truck)
Det/31st Rear Operations Center (OPCON)
1208th Quartermaster Platoon (Water Supply)
Facilities Engineer Detachment C (OPCON)
Civil Affairs Tactical Planning Team/486th Civil Affairs Battalion
Displaced Civilian Team/486th Civil Affairs Battalion
Morale Welfare Recreation Team/377th Theater Support Command (-) (OPCON)
Oman
Morale Welfare Recreation Team/377th Theater Support Command (-) (OPCON)
Turkey
Direct Support Team/486th Civil Affairs Battalion (-)

226th Area Support Group
    189th Corps Support Battalion
        HHD/189th Corps Support Bn
        455th Quartermaster Co (Contract Supervision)
        855th Quartermaster Co (DS Field Service)
KUWAIT Area Support Group
    Team/31st Support Center (Corps Rear Area Operations Center)
    693rd Quartermaster Co (GS Supply) (OPCON)
    647th Movement Control Team (Port) (Attached)
49th Quartermaster Group (Petroleum and Water) (-) (OPCON)
    HHC/49th Quartermaster Group
    809th Quartermaster Detachment (Petroleum Liaison Team)
    240th Quartermaster Battalion (Pipe and Terminal Operations) (-)
        19th Quartermaster Co (Terminal/Pipeline Operating)
        109th Quartermaster Co (Terminal/Pipeline Operating) (OPCON)
        267th Quartermaster Co (Pipeline Operations) (OPCON)
        952nd Quartermaster Co (Pipeline and Terminal Operations) (Attached)
        260th Quartermaster Battalion (-) Lab
    260th Quartermaster Battalion (Petroleum Oil Lubricants Supply) (Attached)
        HHD/260th Quartermaster Bn
        79th Quartermaster Co (Water Supply) (Attached)
            267th Quartermaster Team (Water Purification)
        238th Transportation Co (Petroleum Oil Lubricants) (Medium Truck)
        281st Transportation Co (Petroleum Oil Lubricants) (Medium Truck 5K)
        325th Transportation Co (Petroleum Oil Lubricants) (Medium Truck 5K)
        773rd Transportation Co (Petroleum Oil Lubricants) (Medium Truck 5K)
        (OPCON)
        803rd Quartermaster Co (GS Supply)
        827th Quartermaster Co (GS Supply)
        1174th Transportation Co (Petroleum Oil Lubricants) (Medium Truck)
        1555th Quartermaster Co (Water Purification)
        1013th Quartermaster Co (-) (Field Service) (Attached)
        220th Quartermaster Detachment (Water Distribution) (Attached)
            186th Quartermaster Detachment (Water Purification)
        266th Quartermaster Detachment (Water Purification)
        417th Transportation Detachment (Contract Supervision) (Attached)
        Kellogg Brown and Root Trucks
    362nd Quartermaster Battalion (Petroleum Oil Lubricants Supply)
        HHD/362nd Quartermaster Bn
        110th Quartermaster Co (Petroleum Oil Lubricants Supply) (OPCON)
        353rd Transportation Co (-) (Medium Truck 7.5K)
        360th Transportation Co (Petroleum Oil Lubricants) (Medium Truck 5K)
        416th Transportation Co (Medium Truck 7.5K) (Attached)
        425th Transportation Co (Medium Truck 7.5K) (-) (OPCON)
        740th Transportation Co (Medium Truck, 40-foot Container)

946th Transportation Co (Medium Truck 7.5K)
2222nd Transportation Co (Medium Truck 7.5K)
559th Quartermaster Battalion (Water Supply)
1208th Quartermaster Co (Water Supply)
202nd Quartermaster Detachment (Water Purification)
54th Quartermaster Co (Mortuary Affairs) (-) (OPCON)
Civil Affairs Tactical Planning Team/414th Civil Affairs Battalion (-)
Direct Support Team/414th Civil Affairs Battalion
3rd Medical Command (MEDCOM) (-) (OPCON)
HHC/3rd Medical Command
520th Medical Detachment (Theater Army Medical Lab)
86th Combat Support Hospital
HHC/86th Combat Support Hospital
32nd Medical Detachment (Blood Support Unit)
Team/787th Medical Detachment
1932nd Medical Detachment (Head and Neck Surgery)
MFT 86
MFT-Center for Health Promotion and Preventative Medicine - IRAQ
3rd Medical Battalion (Area Support) (Provisional)
HHD/3rd Medical Bn (Area Support)
112th Medical Co (Air Ambulance)
520th Medical Co (Area Support)
547th Medical Co (Area Support)
205th Medical Co (Area Support) (-)
965th Medical Co (Dental Area Support) (Attached)
437th Medical Co (Ground Ambulance) (-)
109th Medical Detachment (Veterinary Services) (-)
788th Medical Detachment (Preventative Medicine) (-)
6th Medical Logistics Management Center (-)
424th Medical Battalion (Logistics Rear)
161st Medical Battalion (Area Support)
804th Medical Brigade
HHC/804th Medical Bde
47th Combat Support Hospital (Corps) (Attached)
HHD/47th Combat Support Hospital
3rd Medical Team (Infectious Disease)
4th Medical Team (Neurosurgery)
44th Medical Detachment (Pathology)
252nd Medical Detachment (Neurosurgery) (OPCON)
286th Medical Team (Eye Surgery)
1888th Medical Detachment (Head and Neck Surgery)
865th Combat Support Hospital (-)
HHC/865th Combat Support Hospital
207th Medical Team (Head and Neck Surgery)
115th Field Hospital (Attached)

110th Medical Battalion
HHD/110th Medical Bn
1042nd Medical Co (Air Ambulance) (-) (OPCON)
336th Theater Finance Command (-) (OPCON)
18th Finance Group
338th Finance Co
469th Finance Group
266th Finance Group (-)
4th Finance Battalion
15th Finance Battalion
8th Finance Battalion (ADVON)
49th Finance Battalion (ADVON)
230th Finance Battalion (ADVON)
Detachment 35/24th Finance Battalion
US Army Special Operations Command LNO

JSOTF-North
173rd Airborne Brigade (TACON)[13] (USA)
HHC/173rd Airborne Brigade
1-508th Infantry
2-503rd Infantry
B/2-14th Infantry, 10th Mountain Division (Light Infantry) (OPCON)
10th Military Police Co, 10th Mountain Division (Light Infantry) (OPCON)
TF 1-63rd Armor (-), 1st Infantry Division (OPCON)
HHC/1-63rd Armor
C/1-63rd Armor
B/2-2nd Infantry
74th Long Range Surveillance Detachment
2-15th Field Artillery (-), 10th Mountain Division (Light Infantry)
D/3-319th Field Artillery
173rd Combat Support Co
173rd Engineer Detachment
B/110th Military Intelligence Bn (-), 10th Mountain Division (Light Infantry)
3/544th Military Police Co
86th Contingency Response Group (USAF)
404th Civil Affairs Battalion (-) (TACON)
Direct Support Det/443rd Civil Affairs Bn
930th Tactical Psychological Operations Detachment (-) (TACON)
201st Forward Support Battalion, 1st Inf Div
501st Forward Support Co
250th Med Detachment (Forward Surgical Team)
US Army Europe CSS Force Entry Module
26th Marine Expeditionary Unit (Special Operations Capable) (-) (TACON) (USMC)[14]
Battalion Landing Team 1/8
Detachment/Marine Attack Squadron 223

Marine Medium Helicopter Squadron 264 (Reinforced)
Detachment/Marine Light Attack Helicopter Squadron 167
MEU Service Support Group 26

CJSOTF-West (Jordan)
Elements/TF Seminole/1-124th Infantry (Attached) (USA)
Elements/2-14th Infantry (Attached) (USA)
30th Corps Support Battalion (USA)
    HHD/30th Corps Support Bn
    269th Signal Co (Echelon Above Corps Contingency) (USA)
    778th Maintenance Co (Non-Divisional DS) (Attached) (USA)
    826th Ordnance Co (Modular Ammo) (USA)
    960th Quartermaster Co (Petroleum Oil Lubricants Supply) (USA)
    1161st Transportation Co (Medium Truck Palletized Load System) (USA)
    Heavy Rigger Det/824th Quartermaster Co (USA)

Military Traffic Management Command—Southwest Asia, Bahrain (598th Transportation Terminal Group)[15]
831st Transportation Battalion (USA)
    HHD/831st Transportation Bn
    Field Office – Kuwait
    Field Office – Saudi Arabia
    Field Office – Qatar
    1394th Deployment Support Brigade
    Deployment Support Team/599th Transportation Terminal Group
    Deployment Support Team/833rd Transportation Battalion
    76th Transportation Detachment (Contract Supervision)
    276th Movement Control Detachment (Automated Cargo Documentation)
    352nd Transportation Detachment (Contract Supervision)
    369th Transportation Detachment (Port Terminal Supervision)
    400th Movement Control Team (Cargo Documentation)
    491st Movement Control Team (Automated Cargo Documentation)
    499th Movement Control Team (Cargo Documentation)
    502nd Transportation Detachment (Contract Supervision)
    1184th Transportation Terminal Unit

NOTES

1. A snapshot compiled from unit records based on a CFLCC task organization briefing dated 010300Z May 03. OIF task organization changed frequently, and this order of battle reflects the end of major combat operations on 1 May 2003. This is an order of battle (identification and command structure of a unit), not a task organization (temporary modification of the size and composition of a unit to meet mission requirements); therefore, organic subunits of a headquarters or the cross attachment of organic subunits within battalion-level formations may not be reflected. The intent was inclusion. Late-arriving units were cross-checked against force closure reports from 15-31 April on the CENTCOM JOPES Ops 2 newsgroup. Army unit designations are based on US Army Force Management Support Agency descriptions. Abbreviations, acronyms, and other terms used are in the glossary.

2. Order of battle for 75th XTF components from CFLCC task organization and CFLCC-JTF 4 email dated 010330Z May 03, Subject: Battle Update Assessment Notables.

3. The 1st Battalion, 179th Infantry, 45th Separate Infantry Brigade, Oklahoma Army National Guard, deployed only its Alpha and Bravo Companies.

4. The 2nd Battalion, 124th Infantry, 53rd Separate Infantry Brigade, Florida Army National Guard, deployed with only its three line companies. HHC, Delta Company, mortars, and fires support teams did not deploy. Initially, the companies were used for force protection.

5. JTF *Cobra* was activated in March 2003 by US European Command and contained Army, Navy, and Air Force assets. Only the Army units are shown.

6. Operation DISPLAY DETERRENCE was a NATO Article 4 deployment commanded by the US Army Extended Air Defense Task Force (EADTF). Article 4 of the North Atlantic Treaty states in part, "The Parties will consult whenever…the territorial…security of any of the Parties is threatened." Turkey was threatened.

7. The primary sources for US Marine forces and supporting Army units were MARADMINs 507/03 and 578/03, listing Marine and Army units, respectively, eligible to participate in the Navy Presidential Unit Citation awarded to I MEF for actions from 21 March to 24 April 2003 and announced on 3 November 2003.

8. From 21 March to 24 April 2003 elements of the 1st (UK) Armoured Division were under the operational control of the I MEF.

9. The 1st Battalion, 124th Infantry, 53rd Separate Infantry Brigade, Florida Army National Guard, deployed as a unit minus its Delta Company, mortars, and fire support teams. Initially, elements were task organized for force protection.

10. The 1st Battalion, 162nd Infantry, 41st Separate Infantry Brigade, Oregon Army National Guard, deployed as a unit minus its Delta Company, mortars, and fire support teams. Initially, elements were task organized for force protection.

11. The 3rd Battalion, 124th Infantry, 53rd Separate Infantry Brigade, Florida Army National Guard, deployed as a unit minus its Delta Company, mortars, and fire support teams. Initially, elements were used for force protection.

12. Elements of the 10th Transportation Terminal Battalion (-) were located in Iskenduren and Incirlik, Turkey, and in Kuwait on 1 May 03.

13. Although a subordinate of the Combined Forces Special Operations Component Command, not the Combined Forces Land Component Command, these units are included here to provide visibility to Army units deployed in support of special operations forces during Operation IRAQI FREEDOM. This order of battle does not list SOF units assigned to either JSOTF.

14. "The United States Marine Corps in Operation Iraqi Freedom Facts and Figures" report draft of 23 December 2003 states that 26th MEU was inserted into northern Iraq during the period 11-16 April 2003, initially under the tactical control of JSOTF-North.

15. This information is contained in the slides used by the commander of the 598th Transportation Terminal Group for a briefing to the National Defense Transportation Association titled "MTMC-SWA Operation Enduring and Iraqi Freedom," dated 14 August 2003. Other supporting units included those 598th TRANS units assigned to MTMC-Europe and MTMC-Turkey.

Glossary

A

A2C2	Army Airspace Command and Control
AAA	Anti-Aircraft Artillery
AAMDC	Army Air and Missile Defense Command
AASLT	Air Assault
ABC-BL	Army Battle Command Battle Lab
ABCS	Army Battle Command System
ABN	Airborne
ACC	USAF Air Combat Command
ACE	Armored Combat Earthmover (M9)
ACE	Analysis and Control Element
ACOM	US Atlantic Command
ACP	Assault Command Post
ACR	Armored Cavalry Regiment
ACR(L)	Armored Cavalry Regiment (Light)
AD	Armored Division
ADA	Air Defense Artillery
A-DAY	Initiate Air Operations
ADC-M	Assistant Division Commander—Maneuver
ADC-O	Assistant Division Commander—Operations
ADCON	Administrative Control
ADOCS	Automated Deep Operations Coordination System
ADVON	Advanced Echelons
AEF	Air Expeditionary Forces
AEGIS	Advanced Electronic Guided Intercept System
AFAC	Airborne Forward Air Controller
AFAR	Airborne Field Artillery Regiment
AFATDS	Advanced Field Artillery Tactical Data System
AH	Attack Helicopter
AHB	Attack Helicopter Battalion
AHR	Attack Helicopter Regiment
AIR	Airborne Infantry Regiment
AMC	Army Materiel Command
AMDWS	Air and Missile Defense Warning System
AMPHIB	Amphibious
ANGLICO	Air and Naval Gunfire Control Team
AO	Area Of Operations
AP	Assault Position
APC	Armored Personnel Carrier
APOD	Aerial Port Of Debarkation
APOE	Aerial Port Of Embarkation
APS	Army Pre-Position Stocks

AR	Armor
ARCENT	Army Central Command
ARFOR	Army Forces
ARNG	Army National Guard
ASAP	As Soon As Possible
ASAS	All Source Analysis System
ASAS-RWS	All Source Analysis System-Remote Work Station (see also RWS)
ASB	Aviation Support Battalion
ASOC	Air Support Operation Center
ASPB	Army Strategic Planning Board
AT	Anti-Tank (i.e., AT-3)
ATACMS	Army Tactical Missile System
ATBM	Anti-Theater Ballistic Missile
ATCCS	Army Tactical Command and Control System
AUS	Australia
AVCRAD	Aviation Certification Repair Activity Depot
AVIM	Aviation Intermediate Maintenance
AVLB	Armored Vehicle Launched Bridge
AVN	Aviation
AWACS	Airborne Warning And Control System

B

BCE	Before Common Era
BCOTM	Battle Command On The Move
BCT	Brigade Combat Team
BCTP	Battle Command Training Program
BDA	Battle Damage Assessment
BDE	Brigade
BFT	Blue Force Tracking
BG	Brigadier General (1 star)
BIFV	Bradley Infantry Fighting Vehicle
BIAP	Baghdad International Airport
BMD	USSR Design Airborne Vehicle (IFV)
BMP	USSR Design Vehicle (IFV)
BN	Battalion
BOS	Battlefield Operating System
BRDM	USSR Design Reconnaissance Vehicle (IFV)
BRT	Brigade Reconnaissance Troop
BTR	USSR Design Armored Personnel Carrier (APC)
BTRY	Battery
BUA	Battle Update Assessment

C

C1	Personnel Department at Combined Staff
C2	Intelligence Department at Combined Staff
C2	Command and Control
C2X	Command and Control Exploitation
C2PC	Command and Control for Personal Computers
C3	Operations Department at Combined Staff
C4	Logistics Department at Combined Staff
C4ISR	Command, Control, Communications, Computers, Intelligence, Surveillance and Reconnaissance
C5	Plans Department at Combined Staff
C6	Communications Department at Combined Staff
CA	Civil Affairs
CACOM	Civil Affairs Command
CALL	Center for Army Lessons Learned
CARL	Combined Arms Research Library
CAS	Close Air Support
CAT-A	Civil Affairs Team—A
CAV	Cavalry
CBRN	Chemical, Biological, Radiological, and Nuclear
CENTCOM	US Central Command
CFACC	Combined Forces Air Component Command
CFLCC	Combined Forces Land Component Command
CFSOCC	Combined Forces Special Operations Component Command
CFZ	Critical Friendly Zone
CG	Commanding General
CGS	Common Ground Station
CGSC	Command and General Staff College
CGSOC	Command and General Staff Officers' Course
CH	Cargo Helicopter
CH	Chaplain
CI	Counter Intelligence
CID	US Army Criminal Investigation Command
CJTF	Combined and Joint Task Force
CM&D	Collection Management and Dissemination
CMH	Center of Military History
CMTC	Combat Maneuver Training Center
COE	Contemporary Operating Environment
COG	Chief, Operations Group or Center of Gravity
COL	Colonel
COLT	Combat Observation Lasing Team
COMCFLCC	Commander, Combined Forces Land Component Command
CONPLAN	Contingency Plan

CONUS	Continental United States
COSCOM	Corps Support Command
CP	Command Post
CRC	Continental United States (CONUS) Replacement Center
CS	Combat Support
CSA	Chief of Staff of the Army
CSC	Convoy Support Center
CSG	Corps Support Group
CSH	Combat Support Hospital
CSI	Combat Studies Institute
CSM	Command Sergeant Major
CSS	Combat Service Support
CSSCS	Combat Service Support Control System
CTC	Combat Training Center
CWO	Chief Warrant Officer (2 thru 5)

D

DAADC	Deputy Area Air Defense Commander
DCG	Deputy Commanding General
DCG-O	Deputy Commanding General for Operations
DCG-S	Deputy Commanding General for Support
DET	Detachment
DISCOM	Division Support Command
DIV	Division
DIVARTY	Division Artillery
DOD	Department of Defense
DOTMLPF	Doctrine, Organizations, Training, Materiel, Leader Development, Personnel and Facilities
DRE	Deployment Readiness Exercise
DS	Direct Support
DSN	Defense Switched Network
DTG	Date-Time Group
DTRA	Defense Threat Reduction Agency

E

EA	Engagement Area
EADTF	Extended Air Defense Task Force
EIS	Enhanced Information Systems
EN	Engineer
ENCOM	Engineer Command
EOD	Explosive Ordnance Disposal
EPW	Enemy Prisoner of War
ERDC	US Army Engineer Research and Development Center
ETAC	Enlisted Terminal Attack Controller

EUCOM	US European Command
EXORD	Execution Order

F

F/A	Fighter/Ground Attack Aircraft (i.e., F/A-18)
FA	Field Artillery
FAIO	Field Artillery Intelligence Officer
FARP	Forward Arming and Refueling Point
FBCB2	Force XXI Battle Command, Brigade and Below
FIF	Free Iraqi Forces
FIST	Fire Support Team
FLAGINT	Intelligence generated by "flag or general" officers
FM	Field Manual
FM	Frequency Modulation
FOB	Forward Operating Base
FORSCOM	US Army Forces Command
FOX	M-93 FOX NBC Reconnaissance System
FPF	Final Protective Fires
FRAGO	Fragmentary Order
FROG	Free Rocket Over the Ground
FSB	Forward Support Battalion
FSE	Fire Support Element
FSSG	Force Service Support Group
FSSP	Fuel System Supply Point
FST-V	Fire Support Team Vehicle
FWD	Forward

G

G1	Corps and Division Personnel Staff
G2	Corps and Division Intelligence Staff
G3	Corps and Division Operations Staff
G4	Corps and Division Logistics Staff
G5	Corps and Division Civil/Military Staff
G6	Corps and Division Communications Staff
GAC	Ground Assault Convoy
GBR	Great Britain
GCCS	Global Command and Control System
G-Day	Start of Major Ground Combat Operations
GEN	General (4 star)
GI	Government Issue
GOPLATS	Gulf Oil Platforms
GPS	Global Positioning System
GS	General Support
GSR	Ground Surveillance Radar

GSR	General Support Reinforcing
GWOT	Global War On Terrorism

H

HE	High Explosive
HEAT	High-Explosive Anti-Tank
HET	Heavy Equipment Transporter
HHB	Headquarters and Headquarters Battery
HHC	Headquarters and Headquarters Company
HHD	Headquarters and Headquarters Detachment
H-HOUR	Time of Attack
HHOC	Headquarters and Headquarters Operations Company
HHSC	Headquarters and Headquarters Service Company
HKT	Hunter Killer Team
HOW	Howitzer
HMMWV	High Mobility Multipurpose Wheeled Vehicle
HMS	Her Majesties Ship (British Warship)
HQ	Headquarters
HRC	Heavy Ready Company
HSC	Headquarters Support Company
HSV	High Speed Vessel
HUMINT	Human Intelligence
HVA	High-Value Asset

I

IBOS	Intelligence Battlefield Operating System
IBS	Integrated Broadcast Services
ID	Infantry Division
IFOR	Implementation Force
IN	Infantry
INSCOM	US Army Intelligence and Security Command
IO	Information Operations
IREMBASS	Improved Remotely Monitored Battlefield Sensor System
IRF	Immediate Ready Force
ISR	Intelligence, Surveillance and Reconnaissance
ITO	Iraqi Theater of Operations
IVIS	Inter-Vehicular Information System

J

JA	Unit Designator for Chemical Detachment (NBCE) (JA)
JAC	Joint Analysis Center
JACE	Joint Analysis and Control Element
JDAMS	Joint Direct Attack Munitions System
JDISS	Joint Deployable Intelligence Support System
JFACC	Joint Force Air Component Command
JFCOM	Joint Forces Command

JLOTS	Joint Logistics Over The Shore
JOE	Joint Operating Environment
JOPES	Joint Operation Planning and Execution System
JRAC	Joint Rear Area Coordinator /Command
JRTC	Joint Readiness Training Center
JSOTF	Joint Special Operations Task Force
JSOTF-NORTH	Joint Special Operations Task Force-North Iraq
JSOTF-WEST	Joint Special Operations Task Force-West Iraq
JSTARS	Joint Surveillance Target Attack Radar System
JTF	Joint Task Force
JTFC	Joint Term Fusion Cell

K

kHz	Kilohertz
KIA	Killed In Action
KM	Kilometer
KNB	Kuwaiti Naval Base
KSA	Kingdom of Saudi Arabia

L

(L)	Indicates a non-mechanized (light) unit
LAM-TF	Louisiana Army Maneuvers Task Force
LBV	Load Bearing Vest
LCD	Limited Conversion Division
LCU	Landing Craft Utility
LD	Line of Departure
LMSR	Large, Medium-Speed Roll on/Roll off (RORO) Ships
LOC	Line(s) of Communication
LOS	Line of Sight
LOTS	Logistics Over the Shore
LNO	Liaison Officer
LRASS	Long-Range Advanced Scout Surveillance System
LRS	Long-Range Surveillance
LRSC	Long-Range Surveillance Company
LSA	Logistics Support Area
LSE	Logistics Support Element
LSV	Logistics Support Vessel
LT	Large Tug
LTC	Lieutenant Colonel

M

MAJ	Major
MARADMINS	Marine Administrative Messages
MARDIV	Marine Division
MASH	Mobile Army Surgical Hospital
MAST	Main Aid Station

MCS	Maneuver Control System
MDI	Military Demolition Igniter
ME	Main Effort
MECH	Mechanized
MEDEVAC	Medical Evacuation
MEF	Marine Expeditionary Force
MET	Mobile Exploitation Team
MEU	Marine Expeditionary Unit
MEUSOC	Marine Expeditionary Unit Special Operations Capable
MI	Military Intelligence
MIA	Missing In Action
MICLIC	Mine-Clearing Line Charge
MIL/mm	Millimeter
MLRS	Multiple Launch Rocket System
MOADS	Maneuver Oriented Ammunition Distribution System
MOPP	Mission Oriented Protective Posture
MOUT	Military Operations in Urban Terrain
MP	Military Police
MPF	Maritime Pre-positioning Force
MPS	Maritime Pre-positioning Squadron
MRC	Medium Ready Company
MRE	Meal-Ready-To-Eat
MRLS	Multiple Rocket Launch System
MSC	Military Sealift Command
MSE	Mobile Subscriber Equipment
MSG	Master Sergeant
MSR	Main Supply Route
MTLB	USSR Design Armored Personnel Carrier (APC)
MTMC	Military Traffic Management Command
MTOE	Modification Tables of Organization and Equipment
MTS	Movement Tracking System

N

NATO	North Atlantic Treaty Organization
NAVCENT	US Naval Forces Central Command
NBC	Nuclear, Biological, Chemical
NCOIC	Non-Commissioned Officer In Charge
NCW	Network Centric Warfare
NGIC	National Ground Intelligence Center
NIMA	National Imagery and Mapping Agency (now NGA)
NMS	National Military Strategy
NSA	National Security Agency
NTC	National Training Center

O

OBJ	Objective
ODA	Operational Detachment Alpha
ODS	Operation Desert Storm
OEF	Operation Enduring Freedom
OH	Observation Helicopter
OIF	Operation Iraqi Freedom
OIF-SG	Operation Iraqi Freedom Study Group
O/O	On Order
OOTW	Operations Other Than War
OPCON	Operational Control
OPFOR	Opposing Forces
OPLAN	Operations Plan
OPORD	Operations Order
OPS B	BCTP Operations Group B
OPS C	BCTP Operations Group C
OPS F	BCTP Operations Group F
OPT	Operational Planning Team
ORCON	Originator Controlled
ORHA	Office of Reconstruction and Humanitarian Assistance

P

PA	Position Area
PAA	Position Artillery Area
PAC	Patriot Advanced Capability
PAO	Public Affairs Officer
PAX	Passenger
PEO	Program Executive Officer
PERSCOM	Personnel Command
PGM	Precision Guided Munitions
PIR	Priority Intelligence Requirements
PL	Phase Line
PLEX	Plans and Exercises
PM	Preventive Medicine
POL	Petroleum, Oil and Lubricants
POMCUS	Pre-positioned Equipment Configured in Unit Sets
PROPHET	AN/MLQ-40V Voice Collection System
PSAB	Prince Sultan Air Base
PSYOP	Psychological Operations
PTDO	Prepare To Deploy Order

Q

QM	Quartermaster

R

(R)	Retired
RA	Regular Army
RAF	Royal Air Force
RAP	Rocket Assisted Projectile
RB	Rubber Boat (RB-15, Inflatable Boat)
RC	Reconnaissance Transport Aircraft (i.e., RC-135)
RCC	Regional Combatant Commands (formerly unified commands)
RCT	Regimental Combat Team
R&D	Research and Development
RECON	Reconnaissance
REL	Releasable
RFF	Request For Forces
RG	Republican Guard
RIO	Task Force Restore Iraqi Oil
RMA	Revolution in Military Affairs
ROE	Rules of Engagement
ROWPU	Reverse Osmosis Water Purification Unit
RPG	Rocket Propelled Grenade
RRP	Rapid Refueling Point
RSOI	Reception, Staging, Onward Movement and Integration
RTB	Ranger Training Brigade
RTE	Route
RWS	Remote Work Station (See also ASAS-RWS)

S

S1	Brigade and Battalion Personnel Staff
S2	Brigade and Battalion Intelligence Staff
S3	Brigade and Battalion Operations Staff
S4	Brigade and Battalion Logistics Staff
S5	Brigade and Battalion Civil/Military Staff
S6	Brigade and Battalion Communications Staff
SADARM	Sense and Destroy Armor
SAMS	School of Advance Military Studies
SAW	Squad Automatic Weapon
SBCT	Stryker Brigade Combat Team
SE	Supporting Effort
SEAD	Suppression of Enemy Air Defense
SEN	Small Extension Node
SETAF	Southern European Task Force
SF	Special Forces
SFLE	Special Forces Liaison Element
SG	Study Group
SGT	Sergeant
SIPRNET	Secure Internet Protocol Router Network

SOCCE	Special Operations Command and Control Element
SOCCENT	Special Operations Command for CENTCOM
SOCOM	Special Operations Command
SOF	Special Operations Forces
SOP	Standing Operating Procedure
SP	Self Propelled
SPACECOM	United States Space Command
SPG	Special Republican Guard
SPOD	Sea Port Of Debarkation
SRG	Special Republican Guard
SSC	Small-Scale Contingency
SSE	Sensitive Site Exploitation
SSG	Staff Sergeant
SST	Site Survey Team
SWA	Southwest Asia

T

TA	Table of Allowance (i.e., TA-50)
TA	Target Acquisition (i.e., MLRS/TA)
TAA	Tactical Assembly Area
TAAMCOORD	Theater Army Air and Missile Defense Coordinator
TAC	Tactical Command Post (TAC CP)
TACFIRE	Tactical Fire Control System
TACON	Tactical Control
TACP	Tactical Air Control Party
TACSAT	Tactical Satellite
TAMD	Theater Air and Missile Defense
TBM	Tactical (or Theater) Ballistic Missile
TC	Tank (or Track) Commander
TCP	Traffic Control Point
TDC	Theater Distribution Center
TEK	TeleEngineering Kit
TF	Task Force
TOC	Tactical Operations Center
TOE	Tables of Organization and Equipment
TOPSCENE	Tactical Operational Scene
TOW	Tube-launched, Optically-tracked, Wire-guided Missile
TPFDD	Time-Phased Force and Deployment Data
TPFDL	Time-Phased Force and Deployment List
TPIO-ABCS	TRADOC Program Integration Office for ABCS
TPT	Tactical PSYOP Team
TRADOC	US Army Training and Doctrine Command
TRANS	Transportation
TRANSCOM	US Transportation Command
TROPO	Troposphere

TSC	Theater Support Command
TSV	Theater Support Vessel
TTP	Tactics, Techniques, and Procedures

U

UAV	Unmanned Aerial Vehicle
UH	Utility Helicopter
UK	United Kingdom
UN	United Nations
USA	United States Army
USAID	US Agency for International Development
USAF	United States Air Force
USAFE	United States Air Forces in Europe
USAR	United States Army Reserve
USAREUR	US Army Europe
USAV	United States Army Vessel
USCENTCOM	US Central Command
USCG	United States Coast Guard
USMC	United States Marine Corps
USN	United States Navy
USS	United States Ship
USSOCOM	United States Special Operations Command

V

W

WFX	Warfighter Exercise
WMD	Weapon(s) of Mass Destruction
WO	Warrant Officer (WO-1)

X

XTF	Exploitation Task Force

Y

Z

ZULU	Greenwich Mean Time

Bibliography

Interviews, Discussions, Notes, and E-mail Correspondence

(Persons listed here are those who were cited in *On Point)*

General (Retired) Frederick M. Franks, Jr.
General (Retired) Dennis Reimer
General (Retired) Gordon Sullivan
Lieutenant General David McKiernan
Lieutenant General (Retired) Dan Petrosky
Lieutenant General William Wallace
Major General Keith Alexander
Major General Robert Blackman
Major General Claude "Chris" Christianson
Major General Bobby Dail
Major General Ann Dunwoody
Major General David Kratzer
Major General James A. "Spider" Marks
Major General Dave Petraeus
Major General Henry Stratman
Major General J.D. Thurman
Brigadier General Jack Stultz
Colonel Daniel Allyn
Colonel Charles A. Anderson
Colonel Kevin Benson
Colonel Steve Boltz
Colonel Arnold Bray
Colonel Kenneth Canestrini
Colonel Melvin R. Frazier
Colonel Michael Gearty
Colonel William L. Greer
Colonel William Grimsley
Colonel Clyde Harthcock
Colonel Marc Hildenbrand
Colonel Ben Hodges
Colonel Carl Horst
Colonel Victoria Leignadier
Colonel Rodney Mallette
Colonel Gregg Martin
Colonel Robert W. Nicholson
Colonel Gary L. Parrish
Colonel David Perkins
Colonel Steven W. Rotkoff
Colonel Patrick Simon

Colonel Jeff Smith
Colonel Teddy Spain
Colonel David Teeples
Colonel Thomas G. Torrance
Colonel Bill Wolf
Colonel Terry Wolff
Lieutenant Colonel Joseph De Antonna
Lieutenant Colonel Carl Ayers
Lieutenant Colonel Daniel Ball
Lieutenant Colonel Mike Barbee
Lieutenant Colonel Pete Bayer
Lieutenant Colonel Henry "Bill" Bennett
Lieutenant Colonel Ken Brown (chaplain)
Lieutenant Colonel Rick Carlson
Lieutenant Colonel John Charlton
Lieutenant Colonel Trent Cuthbert
Lieutenant Colonel Phillip DeCamp
Lieutenant Colonel E.J. Degen
Lieutenant Colonel Ivan Denton
Lieutenant Colonel Chuck Eassa
Lieutenant Colonel Erin Edgar
Lieutenant Colonel Scott Fehnel
Lieutenant Colonel Terry Ferrell
Lieutenant Colonel Wesley Gillman
Lieutenant Colonel John Harding
Lieutenant Colonel John Huey
Lieutenant Colonel Christopher P. Hughes
Lieutenant Colonel Jeffrey Ingram
Lieutenant Colonel "Rock" Marcone
Lieutenant Colonel John McPherson
Lieutenant Colonel Jerry Pearman
Lieutenant Colonel Edward Rowe
Lieutenant Colonel Scott Rutter
Lieutenant Colonel Jeffrey R. Sanderson
Lieutenant Colonel Eric "Rick" Schwartz
Lieutenant Colonel Steven Smith
Lieutenant Colonel Stephen Twitty
Lieutenant Colonel Bradley Wakefield
Lieutenant Colonel Robert P. Walters, Jr.

Lieutenant Colonel Eric Wesley
Major William Abb
Major John Altman
Major Prentiss Baker
Major David Carstens
Major Anthony Cavallaro
Major Phillip Chambers
Major Kevin Christensen
Major Gerard Cribb
Major Michael Gabel
Major Brad Gavle
Major Matthew Glunz
Major Thomas J. Kardos
Major John Lindsay
Major Matthew R. Littlejohn
Major Kevin Marcus
Major Michael A. Marti
Major Michael Millen
Major Robert Mooney
Major Mike Oliver
Major Chris Parker
Major Laura A. Potter
Major Lou Rago
Major Robert Sanchez
Major Kyle Warren
Major Julius Washington
Major John White
Captain Brett Bair
Captain Brooks Brenkus
Captain Chris Carter
Captain Shane Celeen
Captain John Cochran
Captain Sean Connely
Captain Ron Cooper (chaplain)
Captain Thomas P. Ehrhart
Captain Brett T. Funck
Captain Alberto Garnica
Captain William Glaser
Captain Dave Hibner
Captain Karen E. Hobart
Captain John Ives
Captain Travis Jacobs
Captain Ronny Johnson
Captain Jeffrey McCoy
Captain Chris Medhurst-Cocksworth

Captain Mike Melito
Captain Gary Morea
Captain Henry Perry
Captain Robert L. Smith
Captain Phillip Wolford
First Lieutenant Aaron H. Anderson
First Lieutenant Matthew Garrett
First Lieutenant Jason King
First Lieutenant Christian Wade
Second Lieutenant Ryan Booth
Second Lieutenant Luke Devlin
Second Lieutenant Jason Fritz
Second Lieutenant Bradley Koerner
Second Lieutenant Jon Linthwaite
Chief Warrant Officer 4 Henry Crowder
Chief Warrant Officer 4 Rocky Yahn
Chief Warrant Officer 2 Jay Dehart
Chief Warrant Officer 2 John Tomblin
Command Sergeant Major Robert Gallagher
Command Sergeant Major Brian Stall
Master Sergeant Courtney Mabus
First Sergeant Michael Moore
Sergeant First Class Curtis Anderson
Sergeant First Class Frank R. Antenori
Sergeant First Class Javier Camacho
Sergeant First Class Jason Christner
Sergeant First Class Stanley L. Griffin
Sergeant First Class Susan A. Pasarcik
Sergeant First Class Kevin Ricks
Staff Sergeant Michael Brouillard
Staff Sergeant Dillard Johnson
Staff Sergeant Brian Plesich
Staff Sergeant Joe Todd
Staff Sergeant Antonio Wells
Sergeant Daniel Voss
Specialist Manuel Avila
Corporal Richard Bergquist
Corporal Warren Hall
Specialist Ryan Horner
Corporal Brian Hubbard
Specialist Eric Huth
Specialist John N. Hutto
Private First Class Anthony Jackson
Dr. James Ellsworth, US Naval War College

Group Interviews

Interview with CFLCC planning staff

Members of SOCCE-Kuwait and 19th SF Group

Multiple interviews with 3rd ID brigade and battalion commanders

Brigade S2s, 3rd ID and 101st Abn Division

Interviews with V Corps planners

3rd BCT, 3rd ID officers

1-327 Infantry RTOs and drivers

1-227 AHB pilot interviews

3-15 Infantry officers

Interview with members of B/2-6 CAV

Interview with members of C/3-7 CAV

4-64 AR commanders interview.

TF 1-64 AR officers interview.

Interviews with several Iraqi brigadiers and staff colonels

Interview with Iraq Team, Forces Directorate National Ground Intelligence Center (NGIC)

Books/Articles

Arnold, Steven L. "Somalia: An Operation Other Than War." *Military Review.* December 1993.

Arnoldy, Ben. "Syrian Volunteers Fought US Troops In Southern Iraq." *Christian Science Monitor,* 11 April 2003.

Battle Labs, Maintaining the Edge. TRADOC Pamphlet. Fort Monroe, Virginia, 1994.

"Battle of Debecka Ridge Summary Brief." Colonel Michael Beasock. TRADOC Systems Manager for Close Combat Missiles. US Army Infantry School. Fort Benning, GA, undated.

Biddle, Stephen. *Afghanistan and the Future of Warfare: Implications for Army and Defense Policy.* Strategic Studies Institute: November 2002.

Bowden, Mark. *Black Hawk Down: A Story of Modern War.* Boston: Atlantic Monthly Press, 1999.

Buchanan, Allen. "Self-Determination, Secession, and the Rule of Law" in Robert McKim and Jeff McMahan, eds. *The Morality of Nationalism.* New York: Oxford University Press, 1997.

Bykosfsky, Joseph, and Harold Larson. *The Transportation Corps: Operations Overseas.* Washington, DC: Office of the Chief of Military History, 1957.

Castillo, Victor. "Why An Army? Full Dimensional Operations and Digitization" (Power-Point presentation), <http://www.army.mil/vision/Documents/overview.ppt>, accessed on 11 October 2003. Since October 2003 the Army has updated this website and deleted Castillo's chart.

Collins, Lieutenant Colonel Tom. *Forward Deployed Army Force in Italy Proved its Worth During Iraq War* (Draft), unpublished.

Connel, Rich and Robert J. Lopez. "A Deadly Day for Charlie Company." *Los Angles Times,* 26 August 2003.

Cooper, Belton Y. *Death Traps: The Survival of an American Armored Division in World War II.* New York: Random House Ballantine Books, 1998.

Cordesman, Anthony H. *The Iraq War: Strategy, Tactics, and Military Lessons.* The CSIS Press. Center for Strategic and International Studies. Washington, DC. September 2003.

Cox, Mathew. "Stretched Thin." *Army Times,* 23 June 2003.

Czerwinski, Tom. *Coping with Bounds: Speculations on Non-Linearity in Military Affairs.* Washington, DC: NDU Press, 1998.

Damrosch, Lori F. *Enforcing Restraint: Collective Intervention in Internal Conflicts. New York: Council on Foreign Relations Press,* 1993.

Department of the Army, *The Way Ahead, Our Army at War.* <http://www.army.mil/thewayahead/quality6.html>, accessed 17 December 2003.

Dilanian, Ken. "Airborne Jumps Into Northern Iraq." *Philadelphia Inquirer.* Knight Ridder Newspapers, 26 March 2003.

Durch, William J. and James A. Schear. "Faultlines: UN Operations in the Former Yugoslavia." Ed. William J. Durch. *UN Peacekeeping, American Policy, and the Uncivil Wars of the 1990s,* 1990-2000.

Forward . . .From the Sea. United States Navy, Washington DC, Dept of the Navy, 1994.

Franks, General Frederick M. Jr. "TRADOC at 20: Where Tomorrow's Victories Begin." *ARMY,* October 1993

Glenn, Dr. Russ. *Heavy Matter: Urban Operations Density of Challenges.* Santa Monica, California, RAND, 2001.

Grahm, Bradley, and Vernon Loeb. "An Air War of Might, Coordination, and Risks." *Washington Post,* 27 April 2003.

Hargrove-Simon, Elaine, "Journalists Who Lost Their Lives in the War with Iraq." *Silha Bulletin,* University of Minnesota. Silha Center for the Study of Media Ethics and Law. Spring 2003- Special Issue, Volume 8, Number 3.

Johnson, Mark, et. al. "In Southern Iraq, Low-Level Fighting Continues." *Knight Ridder Newspapers,* 2 April 2003.

Lasseter, Tom and Mark Johnson. "Soldiers in Southern Iraq Fighting to Secure Bridges, Towns.*" Knight Ridder Newspapers,* 4 April 2003.

Madhani, Aamer. "Soldiers Cross Euphrates, Take Control of Bridges Around Samawah." *Chicago Tribune,* 4 April 2003.

Manwaring, Max G. "Peace and Stability Lessons from Bosnia." *Parameters,* Winter 1998.

Matthews, James K. and Cora J. Holt. *So Many, So Far, So Fast:* United States Transportation Command and Strategic Deployment for Operation Desert Shield/Desert Storm. Washington, DC, 1992.

Merritt, General Jack N. US Army, Retired. *"A Talk With the Chief,"* *ARMY,* June 1995.

Murray, Williamson, and Major General Robert H. Scales, Jr. *The Iraq War, A Military History.* Cambridge, MA: The Belknap Press of Harvard University Press, 2003.

Nair, Brigadier V.K. *War in the Gulf: Lessons for the 3rd World.* New Delhi: Lancer International, 1991.

Peacekeeping and the Challenge of Civil Conflict Resolution. ed. David A. Charters. Center for Conflict Studies, University of New Brunswick, 1994.

President George W. Bush. public radio address. 2030, 11 September 2001. Capitol, Washington, DC. Transcript from, <http://www.whitehouse.gov/news/releases/2001/09/20010911-16.html>, accessed 15 July 2003.

President George W. Bush. Address to Congress. 20 September 2001. Capitol, Washington, DC. Transcript from <http://www.whitehouse.gov/news/releases/2001/09/20010920-8.html>, accessed 15 July 2003.

Reimer, General Dennis J. US Army, Retired, and James Jay Carafano, ed. *Soldiers Are Our Credentials* Washington, DC: Center of Military History, 2000.

Romjue, John L. *American Army Doctrine for the Post-Cold War.* Fort Monroe, VA: TRADOC, 1990.

Ross, Colonel Blair. Public Affairs Officer. US Army Europe, "A Transformed Force in Legacy Clothing." (Unpublished).

Russian Academy of Military Sciences Scientific Council. Compilation of Essays presented in Moscow, June 6, 2003.

Shinseki, General Eric K. USA, Chief of Staff. (Prepared remarks at the Association of the United States Army Association Army Seminar) Washington, DC, 8 November 2001.

Spiller, Dr. Roger J. *Sharp Corners: Urban Operations at Century's End.* Fort Leavenworth, Kansas: Combat Studies Institute, 2001.

Strange, Dr. Joe. *Centers of Gravity and Critical Vulnerabilities.* Marine Corps University Perspectives on Warfighting No. 4, 1997.

Sullivan, General (Retired) Gordon R. and Michael V. Harper. *Hope is Not a Method.* New York: Times Business, Random House, 1996.

Swain, Richard M. *Lucky War: Third Army in Desert Storm.* Fort Leavenworth, Kansas: CGSC Press, 1997.

Toffler, Alvin and Heidi. *War and Antiwar: Survival at the Dawn of the 21st Century.* Boston: Little, Brown, and Company: 1993.

US Army Peacekeeping Institute, Bosnia-Herzegovina After-Action Review Conference Report. Carlisle Barracks, PA: US Army War College.

Woodward, Susan L., *Balkan Tragedy.* Washington, DC: The Brookings Institution Press, 1995.

Army, Joint, and US Government Documents/Publications

Field Manual 3-06. *Urban Operations.* Headquarters, Department of the Army. Washington, DC. June 2003.

Field Manual 6-0. *Mission Command: Command and Control of Army Forces.* Headquarters, Department of the Army, Washington, DC. 11 August 2003.

Field Manual 100-5. *Operations.* Headquarters, Department of the Army, Washington, DC. June 1993.

Field Manual 100-17-3. *Reception, Staging, Onward Movement and Integration.* Headquarters, Department of the Army. Washington, DC. 17 March 1999.

Field Manual 101-5-1/Marine Corps Reference Publication 5-2A. *Organizational Terms and Symbols.* HQ Department of the Army/United States Marine Corps. Washington, DC. 30 September 1997.

Joint Publication 4-01.8. *Joint Tactics, Techniques and Procedures for Joint Reception, Staging, Onward Movement and Integration.* Joint Chiefs of Staff, Washington, DC, 13 June 2000.

FORSCOM Regulation 500-3-3. *FORSCOM Mobilization and Deployment Planning System* (FORMDEPS). Volume III, Reserve Component Unit Commander's Handbook. Fort McPherson, GA. 15 July 1999.

FORSCOM Regulation 500-3-5. *FORSCOM Mobilization and Deployment Planning System* (FORMDEPS). Volume V, FORSCOM Demobilization Plan. Fort McPherson, GA. 31 December 1998.

Battle Lab . . . Force XXI. Defining the Future. Headquarters, US Army Training and Doctrine Command, Fort Monroe, VA. May 1995.

Battle Lab . . . Maintaining the Edge. Headquarters, US Army Training and Doctrine Command, Fort Monroe, VA. May 1994.

GAO-02-96. *Major Challenges for Army Transformation Plan.* US General Accounting Office. November 2001.

ST 3-90.15 *Tactics, Techniques and Procedures for Tactical Operations Involving Sensitive Sites.* Futures Development and Learning Center, US Army Combined Arms Center. Fort Leavenworth, KS. December 2002.

TRADOC. *Support to the Warfighter. Title X Integration Futures Development and Learning Center,* US Combined Arms Center. Fort Leavenworth, KS (PowerPoint briefing).

TRADOC. *Title X Support Catalogue.* 13 Feb 2003.

Documents

Rather than list each document discretely, this bibliography will list records groups by unit or command. The bibliography is limited to those records groups that the writing team used. The OIF archive includes some 119, 000 documents and 68,000 photographs, many of which were not used because of classification or because they were not pertinent to the terms of reference for *On Point* records. Groups include briefings, plans and orders, reports and unit histories, and after-action reviews.

United States Central Command.

United States European Command.

United States Army Europe—This records group primarily pertains to training and deployment of United States Army Europe units.

United States Forces Command—This records group is fairly small and focused on Forces Command updates and deployment records.

United States Transportation Command—This records group includes records from all three service component commands. The Military Traffic Management Command records group includes data provided by 598th Transportation Terminal Group that provided single port management in theater.

Training and Doctrine Command—This records group is fairly small and devoted to tactics, techniques and procedures for military operations. It contains some after-action reviews, including example Battle Command Training Program after-action reviews.

Coalition Forces Air Component Command—This records group is not large, but research focused on air tasking order execution, related special instructions and commander's intent for each air tasking order cycle, thus enabling an understanding of the air effort. These records include the CFACC Campaign Briefing.

Coalition Forces Special Operations Component Command—Due to classification, *On Point* cites very few documents from this group, but the OIF archive has a fairly broad collection of SOF documents. This records group includes records for JSOTF-West, North, and 173rd Airborne Brigade

Coalition Joint Psychological Operations Task Force.

Coalition Forces Land Component Command—For obvious reasons this is the most complete of the CENTCOM component command records groups. CFLCC echelon above corps units are cited as separate records groups. This group of records includes the staff and the general body of records associated with the CFLCC headquarters. The records of the CFLCC headquarters provided the basis for understanding the land component campaign. This records group also includes records from Office of Reconstruction and Humanitarian Assistance (ORHA), the organization that preceded the Coalition Provisional Authority (CPA).

- 75th Exploitation Task Force
- 32nd Army Air and Missile Defense Command
- 416th Engineer Command

- 335th Theater Signal Command
- 513th Military Intelligence Brigade
- 352nd Civil Affairs Command
- 377th Theater Support Command—The 377th records group is quite large as it includes everything from military police prisoner of war processing units to Army Materiel Command support activities located in the theater from Kuwait to Qatar.
- Task Force RIO (Restore Iraqi Oil).

I Marine Expeditionary Force—This records group is by no means as complete as similar records groups for V Corps and its subordinates, but it contains graphics and orders that enabled a general understanding of I MEF operations in the context of the CFLCC campaign. It also contains the records of US Army enabler units in support of Marine operations, such as chemical defense, signal, engineers, and military police.

V Corps—This records group and those of the units assigned to V Corps are cited more than any other group in the collection.

- 3rd Infantry Division—The 3rd ID records group includes subordinate unit records, reports and histories down to the battalion and separate company echelon.
- 4th Infantry Division—Not as complete as the other division records groups since *On Point* focused on major combat operations.
- 82nd Airborne Division—Not as complete as other division records groups and focused on the 2nd BCT.
- 101st Airborne Division—The 101st records group includes subordinate unit records, reports, and histories down to the battalion and separate company echelon.
- 1st Infantry Division (-)—A small collection of records from the 1st Brigade units deployed, primarily 1st Battalion, 63rd Armor Regiment.
- 1st Armored Division (-)—A small collection of records from the 3rd Brigade units deployed, primarily Task Force 1-41 Infantry and Task Force 2-70 Armor.
- 2nd Armored Cavalry Regiment (Light).
- 3rd Armored Cavalry Regiment.
- 11th Attack Helicopter Regiment.
- 12th Aviation Brigade.
- V Corps Artillery.
- 31st Air Defense Artillery Brigade.
- 130th Engineer Brigade.
- 205th Military Intelligence Brigade.
- 18th Military Police Brigade.
- 22nd Signal Brigade.
- 18th Soldier Support Group.
- 3rd Ordnance Battalion (explosive ordnance disposal).
- 3rd Corps Support Command.
- 1st Medical Brigade.
- 30th Medical Brigade.
- 62nd Medical Brigade.

Army Documents/Publications

"*US Army Contributions to the Iraqi Theater of Operations*," Department of the Army briefing to the Secretary of Defense, 4 June 2003.

Department of the Army (DAMO-SS) Information Paper, "*Army Strategic Planning Board Functions and Organizations,*" 28 August 2003.

Gordon R. Sullivan, General, CSA, *SUBJECT: "Reshaping Army Doctrine,"* Memorandum for Lieutenant General Frederick M. Franks, Jr., 29 July 1991.

General Gordon R. Sullivan's letter to the field titled "*Force XXI,*" 12 March 1994.

General Gordon R. Sullivan's memorandum titled "*Force XXI Experimental Force Prime Directive,*" 14 February 1995.

Personal Message for General Galvin, et al. (senior Army commanders), "*Louisiana Maneuvers, 1994,*" DTG 091415MAR92.

United States Army Intelligence Center "*Operation IRAQI FREEDOM Consolidated Lessons Learned (DRAFT),*" 22 August 2003, 34.

"Mission Overview, Free Iraqi Forces," produced by Task Force *Warrior*, Colonel James D. Doyle, 26 April 2003.

"Operation IRAQI FREEDOM—By the Numbers," CENTAF-PSAB, KSA, Commander's Action Group, 9th Air Force, Shaw Air Force Base, SC, 30 April 2003.

Letter from Major General Thomas R. Turner, commanding general, Southern European Task Force, to Brigadier General Timothy D. Livsey, Deputy Commanding General for Training, Combined Arms Center. Fort Leavenworth, KS, 23 October 2003.

Donald H. Rumsfeld. *Rebalancing Forces.* Memorandum dated 9 July 2003.

General Peter J. Schoomaker, Chief of Staff, US Army. *Arrival Message*, 1 August 2003.

Briefing prepared by SAMS Deployment OPT, undated, held in Combined Arms Research Library, Fort Leavenworth, KS.

Operations in Iraq, First Reflections. United Kingdom, Ministry of Defence. July 2003.

Operation Iraqi Freedom-Study Group Operational Summaries

Major Robert Tallman. "OIFSG Operational Summary: PSYOP," 15 July 2003.

Lieutenant Colonel Scott Gedling. "OIFSG Operational Summary: Army National Guard,"15 July 2003.

Major Daniel Corey. "OIFSG Operational Summary: Intelligence," 15 July 2003.

Major David Converse. "OIFSG Operational Summary: Psychological Operations"

Major Robert Foley. "OIFSG Operational Summary: Information Operations"

Lieutenant Colonel David Kolleda. "OIFSG Operational Summary: Transportation"

Captain Michael Mathews. "OIFSG Operational Summary: EPW Operations in OIF"

Index